W9-DIU-092

MIELZINER

MIELZINER

MASTER OF MODERN STAGE DESIGN

MARY C. HENDERSON

FOREWORD BY FRANK RICH

PUBLISHED IN ASSOCIATION WITH THE NEW YORK PUBLIC LIBRARY FOR THE PERFORMING ARTS

BACK STAGE BOOKS

AN IMPRINT OF WATSON-GUPTILL PUBLICATIONS/NEW YORK

THIS BOOK IS DEDICATED TO JEAN PORTER.

The theatre is not an exclusively literary form.
Although the playscript is the essentially important element, after that is finished,
actors, designers, directors, technicians "write" the play together.

——Elia Kazan, *A Life* (1988)

FRONTISPIECE: COSTUME DESIGN FOR *THE MADWOMAN OF CHAILLOT,* 1964.

(COURTESY OF THE ESTATE OF HILDA AND EDWARD KOOK)

TITLE PAGE: SCENE DESIGN FOR *JOURNEY TO JERUSALEM,* 1940. (COURTESY OF BUD H. GIBBS)

ACQUIRING EDITOR: DALE RAMSEY

DESIGNER: ARETA BUK

PRODUCTION MANAGER: ELLEN GREENE

TEXT SET IN WEISS, DESIGNED BY EMIL RUDOLF WEISS, 1926; CAPTIONS SET IN OPTIMA, DESIGNED BY HERMANN ZAPF, 1958.

COPYRIGHT © 2001 MARY C. HENDERSON

FOREWORD © FRANK RICH

FIRST PUBLISHED IN THE UNITED STATES IN 2001 BY WATSON-GUPTILL PUBLICATIONS,

A DIVISION OF VNU BUSINESS MEDIA, INC., 770 BROADWAY, NEW YORK, N.Y. 10003

WWW.WATSONGUPTILL.COM

LIBRARY OF CONGRESS CATALOG CARD NUMBER: 00-101808

ISBN 0-8230-8823-5

MANUFACTURED IN CHINA

SECOND PRINTING, 2002

2 3 4 5 / 05 04 03 02

CONTENTS

FOREWORD

Of all the artists who play crucial roles in theatrical productions, few are less celebrated, less understood, and less well known to audiences than designers. Stage designers are not architects. They are not decorators. They are not technicians. The greatest designers are all these things, but also far more; they serve as full-fledged collaborators in the creation of plays and musicals. And of the many fine designers who came of age with the modern theatre in the twentieth century, few, if any, were greater than Jo Mielziner.

Mielziner's list of credits—some nearly 300 shows stretching from the 1920s until his death in the mid-seventies—is synonymous with the history of the American theatre of his time. He worked with the most important writers—Tennessee Williams, Arthur Miller, Richard Rodgers, and Oscar Hammerstein II, among countless others—as well as with the most influential directors, such as Elia Kazan, Joshua Logan, and George Abbott, and choreographers, including George Balanchine, Jerome Robbins, and Agnes de Mille. Mielziner's job as designer was not mainly, as is generally thought, to devise floor plans or engineer the logistics of set changes or create pretty, idle "atmosphere." That was the easy part. "Literalism has no place in the theatre," Mielziner once wrote, and in his best work he was in on the production from an early stage, struggling with playwright and director as a team to find a poetic visual metaphor that would both express and enhance the deepest meaning of a text.

Williams said that Mielziner's design for the original, 1947 Kazan production of *A Streetcar Named Desire* with Marlon Brando and Jessica Tandy helped inspire his script revisions. No wonder: That classic Mielziner evocation of a decaying, shabby-genteel New Orleans is at one with the dark foreboding of Williams's tragedy. So central was Mielziner's translucent design for the original production of Miller's *Death of a Salesman* two years later—with its hallucinatory evocation of memory and loss—that it influenced every major production of the play for the next half-century.

But if you put those sets side by side and next to other Mielziner designs of the period, such as those for *Annie Get Your Gun* and *South Pacific*, you would not necessarily recognize them as being the work of the same man. That's because a set designer, while very much an artist, does not have a definitive style; he must selflessly serve the style set by a play's author even as he boldly augments it. Were a designer to stamp his own aesthetic ideas on every production, he would smother plays rather than serve them; conversely, were he to be too timid, he would stand in the way of a play's ability to realize its full potential. In other words, no designer can "save" a poor script, but a designer can all too easily diminish or sabotage a good one. Remarkably, Mielziner was able to maintain the tricky balance between artistic integrity and selfless theatrical collaboration throughout a prolific career that, like the commercial theatre itself, spanned a spectrum ranging from high drama to pure fluff, from extravagant musicals to low-budget theatrical stunts.

One reason the role of stage designers is so little understood is that too often the evidence of their artistry is thrown away when a play closes. It's posterity's good fortune that Mielziner conserved his papers and gave them to the Billy Rose Theatre Collection of The New York Public Library—an example one can only hope more designers will emulate. In creating this authoritative account of Mielziner's life and work, Mary Henderson was able to draw on this extraordinary archive as well as on her own many gifts as one of the American theatre's wisest and most knowledgeable historians. The story she tells is not just an account of one brilliant theatrical practitioner, but of the creation of much of what constitutes the classic canon of Broadway at its peak.

———Frank Rich

It all began with a phone call. In 1987, critic and writer Henry Hewes called to ask if I would be interested in writing a biography of Jo Mielziner. After meeting with the executors of the Mielziner estate, Edward Kook and his son-in-law Bud Gibbs, I agreed. Unfortunately, Eddie Kook, who died in 1990, is not here to see the culmination of his dream, a book about his closest friend. Along the way to its completion, several other Mielziner contemporaries whom I had the privilege to interview also passed away.

In my preliminary research, I was pleased to discover that I had seen sixteen Mielziner-designed productions, and was about to be exposed to all of his design files, bequeathed along with his preserved papers to the Billy Rose Theatre Collection of The New York Public Library for the Performing Arts. It took me a year to go through the myriad preliminary sketches, working drawings, blueprints, color specifications, painters' elevations, floor plans, and exquisitely rendered final scene paintings, and two years to read through the files, all of which I examined and organized.

I wish I could say that a definitive psychological profile of Jo Mielziner emerged from his papers, but it did not. Only after speaking to more than a hundred people who knew him did I get closer to the real Jo. Theatrical design took precedence over everything else in his life and kept him at a distance from his wives and children; his deepest friendships were with his colleagues in the theatre, most notably Eddie Kook and Joshua Logan. Without fail, everyone with whom I spoke eventually described him as a "gentleman": soft-spoken, fastidious in dress, remarkably even-tempered, good-humored, and courteous to all.

Creators are revealed through their art, and it is to Mielziner's art that we must look for the man. Fortuitous events turned the talented Jo to the theatre, and he reveled in it throughout his life. During his more than fifty-year career, he had the rare opportunity to design many of the landmark productions of the American stage, and he also left his imprint on the architecture of a number of theatres around the country. Sadly, not quite twenty-five years after his death, in 1976, he is all but unknown. Once a show closes and the scenery is taken from the stage, nothing remains as evidence of the creative imagination that gave the production its special environment. In surveying the 1994–95 season on Broadway, *New York Times* drama critic Vincent Canby lamented, "The awful truth: Broadway depends more on inventive scenic design than it does on inventive, original new work." The awful truth: The fame of a theatrical artist is limited to his or her own time. Maybe books such as this will help rekindle interest in the unsung work of the designers who collectively "wrote" the plays (to paraphrase Elia Kazan) of the greatest period in American theatre.

—— Mary Henderson
October 2000

ACKNOWLEDGMENTS

My list of thanks begins with Henry Hewes for suggesting that I write this biography in the first place. Without the confidence of Bud Gibbs and the late Eddie Kook, I could not have commenced the journey. Once they gave me the job, they never interfered with my work, and Bud Gibbs, despite his busy law practice, was always ready to help remove obstacles from my path. To all three, I extend my greatest thanks.

The sponsorship of The New York Public Library enabled the publication of the Mielziner biography to go forward. The NYPL's director of publications, Karen Van Westering, and Bob Taylor, curator of the library's Billy Rose Theatre Collection, recognized the value of a book created from the library's holdings. As a result of their endorsement, Gerald Schoenfeld of the Shubert Organization, the Mary P. Oenslager Fund of the New York Community Trust, and the Tobin Foundation of San Antonio generously provided the financial support to make what otherwise would have been an expensive publication accessible to everyone interested in the theatre. I am deeply indebted for their assistance. Without the enthusiastic support of Dale Ramsey, formerly of Watson-Guptill, I am not sure this book would have been published at all. To Marian Appellof, who had to step in at the last minute to complete the editing, I give thanks for her skills, patience, and good humor.

During 1991, a National Endowment for the Humanities Fellowship enabled my full-time devotion to the project. I was also greatly helped by a grant from the Graham Foundation for Advanced Studies in the Fine Arts to gather reproductions of Mielziner designs.

My daily plodding through the papers at The New York Public Library for the Performing Arts was made possible through the kindness and cooperation of Dorothy Swerdlove and Bob Taylor, past and current curators of the Theatre Collection, respectively. The staff was helpful and respectful of my work at all times, and I am enormously grateful to them: David Bartholomew, Dr. Roderick Bladel, Donald Fowle, Christopher Frith, Christine Karatnytsky, Susan MacArthur, Brian O'Connell, Daniel Patri, Louis Paul, Mary Ellen Rogan, the late Edward Sager, Betty Travitsky, Maxine Trost, Kevin Winkler, and the squadron of pages. To Richard Buck, I owe special appreciation for the many favors, large and small, and to Julius Crockwell, gratitude for easing my almost daily commute. Thanks also go to Earl Christian, Edmund Koeppel, and Heidi Stock at the library's copy services.

Librarians and curators of various collections around the country provided assistance: the late Dr. William H. Crain, Melissa Miller, and Cathy Henderson at the Harry Ransom Humanities Research Center, University of Texas at Austin; Linda Hardberger and Cristina E. Martínez at the McNay Art Museum, San Antonio; the late Robert L. B. Tobin and his staff at the Tobin Foundation, San Antonio; Dr. Howard B. Gotlieb and his staff at the Mugar Memorial Library, Boston University; the staff at the New Hampshire State Library; B. J. Allen and Linda Maloney of the Truro Historical Museum, Cape Cod; James Carr and the late Margaret Adams of the Margaret Adams Archives, Cape Playhouse and Cinema, Cape Cod; Marty Jacobs and the late Dorothea Hecht, Museum of the City of New York; Barbara Michaels at the archives of the Ethical Culture School, New York; Sarah Woodcock of London's Theatre Museum; Jean Ashton, head of Special Collections of Columbia University's libraries; and James Ryan and Elmon Webb of United Scenic Artists, Local 829. I was also helped by Marietta P. Boyer, Pennsylvania Academy of the Fine Arts; Lois Woodyatt, National Academy School of Fine Arts; Janet Lorenz of the Margaret Herrick Library of the Academy of Motion Picture Arts and Sciences; David LeVine of the Dramatists Guild; Paul P. Novosal, S.M., of the Marianist Archives, St. Louis; the staff of the Wisconsin Center for Film and Theatre Research, Madison; David Burgevin and the staff at the National Museum of American Art, Smithsonian Institution, Washington, D.C.; Margaret Norton of the San Francisco Performing Arts Library and Museum; Brigitte Kueppers and the staff of the University of California at Los Angeles; Pamela C. Jordan and Susan Brady of the Yale University libraries; Geraldine Duclow of the Theatre Collection at the Philadelphia Free Library; Cindy Cathcart of the Vogue/Condé Nast Archive; Sally Pavetti and Lois MacDonald of the Eugene O'Neill Center; Nena Couch of the Lawrence and Lee Theatre Research Institute, Ohio State University; Howell W. Perkins of the Virginia Museum of Fine Arts; the staff of the Morgan Library, New York; and Marice Wolfe of the Vanderbilt University Library.

My interviews with Mielziner's associates spanned three years. I begin with those who have since died: playwrights Mildred Harris and Robert E. Lee; costume designers Lucinda Ballard, Irene Sharaff, Robert Mackintosh, Elizabeth Montgomery, Percy Harris, Patricia Zipprodt, and Miles White; directors Joseph Anthony, John Fearnley, and Peter Glenville; choreographer-director Jerome Robbins; composer Morton Gould; choreographer Agnes de Mille; lighting designer Richard Nelson; actors Burgess Meredith and Morris Carnovsky; theatre administrator Warren Caro; general managers Max Allentuck and Irving Schneider; master stage technicians Leo Herbert and Ted Van Bemmel; Victor Samrock, general manager of the Playwrights Company; Mielziner's office manager, Word Baker, and one of his secretaries, Sally Haring; critic Walter Kerr; and Mielziner's friend and colleague Sam Leve. Actress and writer Edith Meiser brought firsthand observation of Jo's marriage to Marya Mannes and provided information that I could not have found in any other way. Helen Hayes, who played in five Mielziner sets, provided insightful details about Jo and his brother, Kenneth MacKenna. The most recent losses have been Mielziner's longtime associate John Harvey and his protégé, friend, and colleague Peter Feller. To both of them, I owe a special debt.

Mielziner's living contemporaries and collaborators with whom I talked are directors and choreographers Elia Kazan, Gilbert Cates, and Joseph Hardy; playwrights Arthur Miller, Jerome Lawrence, Dan Taradash, Robert Anderson, Arthur Laurents, Frank Gilroy, and Peter Stone; composer Hugh Martin; designers Theoni V. Aldredge, Alvin Colt, Patton Campbell, Carrie F. Robbins, Jennifer Tipton, David Hays, and Lester Polakov; producers and general managers Robert Whitehead, Stuart Ostrow, Cy Feuer, Doris Cole Abraham, Arthur Cantor, Joseph Harris, and Samuel Liff; and actors Julie Harris, Karl Malden, Haila Stoddard, and Phoebe Brand.

Without the help of technicians to realize his effects in paint, canvas, and light, Mielziner could not have achieved his onstage magic. I interviewed Robert McDonald, former business manager of International Alliance of Theatrical Stage Employees and, incidentally, a descendant of the founders of T. B. McDonald, the early scene shop; and IATSE members Arthur Siccardi, the late Mitch Miller, and Arnold Abramson.

While Mielziner was wearing his hat as a designer of theatre buildings, he collaborated with another group: architects Kevin Roche and Edward Larabee Barnes; technical advisor Robert Brannigan at Lincoln Center; Donald Seawell, chairman of the board of the Denver Center for the Performing Arts; Harold Tedford, director of theatre at Wake Forest University; and Alan Billings and Robert Schnitzer, formerly of the University of Michigan. My understanding of the subject of lighting in the theatre was considerably enhanced by George Izenour, to whom modern-day designers owe an incalculable debt.

Locating Mielziner's office staff was not easy, but I was well rewarded when I found them: Mary Beatty, May Boehlert (Katz), Florence Brown, Paul Libin, and Elizabeth Schauffler (Garfield), as well as Sandra Hance and Phyllis Malinow, Mielziner's last two secretaries, provided me with essential information.

No designer can function without hard-working assistants. During his long career, Mielziner hired more than fifty, and I was lucky enough to interview over thirty of them. Many went on to their own successful design careers in theatre, opera, ballet, television, or movies.

My gratitude goes to George Jenkins, one of Jo's earliest assistants, who later built a distinguished career as a designer for Broadway and Hollywood. I met with Paul Trautvetter, who ran Jo's studio for four years in the 1960s, the last important era in Jo's life. Ming Cho Lee came to Jo's studio as a rough beginner and left it as a designer who went on to realize his great potential. Together these men represent nearly twenty years of Jo's active design life, and I owe them an immense debt of thanks. I must also include Betsy Lee, Ming's wife.

Other Mielziner assistants or associates provided various pieces of his artistic life: Lloyd Burlingame, Carole Lee Carroll, Warren Clymer,

Mitchell Dana, Jeff Davis, Lowell Detweiler, Kathleen Dilkes, the late John Doëpp, Ben Edwards, Beverly Emmons, Aristides Gazetas, Edward Gilbert, Hugh Hardy, Stephen Hendrickson, Lisa Jalowetz Aronson, John T. Jensen, Harry Kardeman, Jack Lindsay, Lawrence Miller, Robert Mitchell, John Moore, Roger Morgan, Lynn Pecktal, Leigh Rand, Steven Rubin, Patricia Stuart, Christopher Thee, Furth Ullman, Fred Voelpel, Leor C. Warner, Gilbert Wechsler, and Stuart Wurtzel. One of Mielziner's chief assistants was the late Richard Casler, whose wife, Sami, graciously agreed to talk to me about her husband. I interviewed Mielziner's four University of Utah interns: Gary Daines, Greg Geilman, J. Robin Modereger, and Byron Olson. I also heard from seven of his Bennington College interns: Priscilla Alexander, Regina Klein Charvat, Margradel Lesch Hicks, Carol Friedman Kardon, Carol Levin, Nancy Steinmetz Murray, and Katherine Spoerl Rose. Van Phillips and Bridget Beier, Jo's assistant on the Purdue University production of *Marathon 33*, filled in the blanks on that special experience in his career.

For Jo's architectural and commercial work, I talked with David Beer, Francis Booth, and Alexander Anderson. Patricia Messore of the Trinity Repertory Theatre related the saga of the last days of the ANTA–Washington Square Theatre. Hugh Hardy, who began as a design assistant in Jo's studio, views his work on the Lincoln Center project as the turning point that took him back to architecture. For important information on Mielziner's contributions to the United Nations inaugural conference in San Francisco, I am indebted to Oliver Lundquist, who also supplied me with visual material.

Among the others who provided information are Mrs. Mary Tyler Cheek McLenahan, the late Viggo Rambusch, Dr. Joel Rubin, Shirley Rich, Yvonne West, Perry Silvey, Charlotte Chase and the late Joseph Chase, Alan Anderson, Denny Beach, Andreas Brown, Ted Chapin, Eileen Darby, Bert Fink, James Frasher, Bury Fredrik, Bernard Gersten, Patrick Horrigan, Steve Karmen, Jerome Kilty, Miles Kreuger, Stephanie McCormick, Eleanor Mayer, Ronald Naversen, Bruce Newman, and the late Dorothy Rodgers, as well as Ian Dow, Cyril Griffiths, and the late Sir John Gielgud in England.

I move next to the people who informed me of Jo's personal life. Before her death, in 1993, I had a long conversation with Jean Macintyre Mielziner, Jo's third wife. Her sisters, Cornelia Foley and Margery Ferguson, contributed to my knowledge of that relationship. David Blow, the son of Marya Mannes, Jo's first wife, gave me helpful information about his mother. For information about Annie Laurie Witzel, Jo's second wife, I relied on her nephew George Schreiber, her stepdaughter Elizabeth Nimick, and her friends Laszlo Kepessy, Bill Johns, and Sylvia Alloway. Angie Moccia supplied me with important information about Gloria Dickson, Mielziner's final companion. Via my friend Esther Enzer, I interviewed Jo's first cousin Orla Mielziner; I also spoke with Walter Mielziner, a more distant cousin. Peter Stearns, a grandson of Ella Mielziner's sister, Ethelyn Friend Middleton, provided me with family history about the Friends, as did Perry Wilson Anthony, whose father, Edward, was a friend of Leo and Ella Mielziner in Truro. I also interviewed Dr. Thomas Bellezza, Jo's physician.

My gratitude to friends and colleagues is boundless. Richard Stoddard took my many pleas for information with grace and fortitude. Fellow biographers were also delighted to help; I name them with pleasure along with the subjects of their books: Steven Aronson (Leland Hayward), Russell Flinchum (Henry Dreyfuss), the late Lyle Leverich (Tennessee Williams), the late Louis Sheaffer (Eugene O'Neill), Helen Sheehy (Eva Le Gallienne), and Dan Sullivan (William Inge). My friends Clark Marlor, Faith Sangster, Haila Stoddard, and Anna Crouse also provided me with information. Kent Paul led me to Ron Hull of Nebraska Educational Television, which has a filmed interview with Mielziner. Van Phillips provided me with an audio-tape of a Mielziner lecture at Purdue University, and Pamela Jordan of the Yale School of Drama discovered another taped lecture in the school's files. I am indebted to Paul Segal for the tour of the Dakota apartment building, where Jo lived and worked. I found a treasure trove of family history in the care of Joanna Schlesinger Caproni, whose parents had bought Kenneth MacKenna's house in Truro. Robert Bolton, one of Jo's contemporaries from their days at the New York School of Design, provided me with rich material about Jo's life and the milieu in which they both began their careers.

The owners of the many Mielziner drawings and scene designs were eager to share for the purposes of this book what they have come to regard as treasures. From the designs in their possession, I was able to study, then choose from them the works to be published here. At the top of the list are Mielziner's children, Michael, Neil, and Jennifer, and Bud Gibbs, Paul Stiga, and Jules Fisher. Others include Elia Kazan, Betsy and Ming Cho Lee, Douglas Colby, Brenda Vaccaro, Florence Henderson, Karen Chapman Bond, Alice Carey, Bridget Beier, Matt Conley, Sandra Hance, Thomas Logan, Henry Hewes, the estate of Hilda and Edward Kook, George White, Mary Tyler Cheek McLenahan, Amy and Martha Curtis, Roxanna and Michael Devlin, Robert Anderson, William Appleton, the late John Doëpp, Greg Kayne, John Ross, Ron Hull, James Ryan and Robert Gilroy, Ian Dow, Harold Tedford, and Kathleen Dilkes. Because many Mielziner designs were sold after his death, I was unable to locate the owners of some of the examples reproduced here after making a good faith effort to find them. Eileen Darby and Martha Swope supplied information about designs in photographic form when I could not find originals. John Crowley at Harry N. Abrams generously checked his files for reproductions of Jo's designs, and Michelle Metcalfe searched the Theatre Collection at the University of Texas for the last elusive photos. Marc Bryan-Brown and a cadre of photographers across the country provided me with excellent reproductions of Mielziner designs.

I cannot close without acknowledging the contributions to scene design research by the late Orville K. Larson, whose writings and conversations with me over the years encouraged me to press on with a difficult subject. I regret that he did not live to see the completion of this biography, in which he was keenly interested.

To all those unnamed by me because of a faulty memory, but who provided me with tidbits of information, or aimed me at people who could add more substantial memories of Mielziner's career or life, I give my thanks.

Finally, I could not have written this book without the cooperation of Jo's children, Michael, Neil, and Jennifer. I hope they will forgive me for having forced them to dredge their memories. I was deeply saddened by the loss of Michael Mielziner, who died in 1998 without seeing his father's life and work in print.

—— Mary Henderson
    October 2000

ABOUT THE BILLY ROSE THEATRE COLLECTION

The Billy Rose Theatre Collection of The New York Public Library for the Performing Arts has served researchers throughout the world since 1931 and is generally recognized as the premier repository for the documents of theatre, film, radio, and television. In addition to countless photographs, playbills, posters, manuscripts, and personal archives, the Library has amassed an impressive array of original set and costume designs by such renowned stage artists as Boris Aronson, Howard Bay, Donald Oenslager, Oliver Smith, and Patricia Zipprodt, among scores of others. It was with tremendous pride that in 1963, The New York Public Library accepted the designs and papers of Jo Mielziner, who for forty years was the dominant figure in American set design. The Mielziner Collection has, over the years, served the research needs of innumerable working designers, students of design, directors, writers, and theatre historians. It has twice been the core of major exhibitions at Lincoln Center. That the Library has joined in the publication of *Mielziner: Master of Modern Stage Design* is not only eminently appropriate, but also demonstrates its continuing commitment to preserving and disseminating the legacies of those artists who have helped define the quality of theatre around the world.

—— Bob Taylor, Curator
    Billy Rose Theatre Collection

INTRODUCTION

When Jo Mielziner died in a taxicab on the way home from an afternoon appointment with his doctor, the news of his passing spread quickly throughout New York's theatrical community. It proved (once again) how small and interwoven the Broadway world can be despite opposite perceptions. As the set designer of producer David Merrick's upcoming production of a musicalized version of *The Baker's Wife*, a French movie that had made a stir in America in 1940, he had met with Merrick's technical team only that morning and was returning to the Dakota apartment building, where he lived and worked, to meet with Jennifer Tipton, a young lighting designer. She was taking over his usual chore of lighting the show. After the morning meeting, Leo Herbert, the prop man for Merrick, flew immediately to Boston to another of the producer's shows and was met with the news of Jo's death immediately on passing through the stage door.

OPPOSITE: JUST PRIOR TO HIS DEATH, JO MIELZINER HAD COMPLETED THE RENDERING (SCENE PAINTING; SHOWN HER IS A DETAIL) FOR DAVID MERRICK'S PRODUCTION OF ***THE BAKER'S WIFE*** **(1976),** BUT HE HAD NOT FINISHED THE PLANNING AND CONSTRUC-TION OF THE ACTUAL SET. HE HAD SPECIFIED RIGHT AND LEFT TURNTABLES FOR INTE-RIOR AND EXTERIOR SCENES, A BACKDROP, A STAIRWAY, AND ELEMENTS TO GIVE IT THE LUSH FRENCH LOOK THAT HE ENVISIONED. HIS ONETIME PROTÉGÉ AND FRIEND MING CHO LEE COMPLETED THE WORK. UNFORTUNATELY FOR JO'S REPUTATION, THE SHOW FLOPPED OUT OF TOWN. (COURTESY OF JULES FISHER)

The date was March 15, 1976. Mielziner's closest friend Eddie Kook had jokingly warned him that morning of the Ides of March, the fateful day when Julius Caesar fell under the knives of his assassins. For Jo, the end was less dramatic. Dr. Thomas Bellezza, who had just examined him at one o'clock, insisted that he check himself into a hospital for tests. It had not been good news for Jo, who could not have looked forward to relaying this information to Merrick's office. Although Jo had never in his life spent time as a patient in a hospital, he had lived with constant reminders of the infirmities of his advancing years. He had fought hard not to surrender to old age. When he went, he told Eddie Kook, he wanted to die with his shoes on, preferably at his drawing board in the middle of a brush stroke. He almost got his wish, when his heart gave out just four days short of his seventy-fifth birthday in the middle of designing a show.

The following morning the death of Jo Mielziner was announced on the front page of *The New York Times* with the full account of his life and career (and a tribute by the *Times* drama critic Clive Barnes) on page 38 in the regular obituary section. The news spread to other major newspapers throughout the nation and was placed on the wire services to everyone else. The *Times* obituary, although somewhat inaccurate, hit all the high spots. It avoided a "staggering recitation of examples of [his] creative talent in a highly specialized field," but noted that he had designed such musical triumphs as *Guys and Dolls, South Pacific, Carousel, Pal Joey, Street Scene, Gypsy, The Most Happy Fella, Annie Get Your Gun,* and *The King and I,* as well as such vastly divergent plays as *Death of a Salesman, A Streetcar Named Desire, Winterset, Mister Roberts, Picnic, Tea and Sympathy, Look Homeward, Angel,* and *Child's Play.* His work in designing theatres was not slighted nor were his books and other activities. Not really a fan of Mielziner's style, Clive Barnes in his accompanying tribute nonetheless recognized Jo's contributions to scene design. It was Mielziner, he wrote, who first understood "that almost cinematic mystery of place" that he brought to plays like Tennessee Williams's *The Glass Menagerie* and Arthur Miller's *Death of a Salesman.* Concluding his appreciation, Barnes quoted a British critic who attested to the superiority of American stage design over the rest of the world. "And that superiority,"

stated Barnes, "owes an enormous amount to the scenic imagination and theatrical gestures of Jo Mielziner."

The New York season that Jo Mielziner had entered in 1924 was at high tide, almost at its crest. Two-hundred-and-one new productions and twenty-nine revivals moved into the standing theatres, some fifty-odd in number, most of them built since 1900 with a few leftovers from the previous generation.

Jo Mielziner was twenty-three years old and had designed four of those 230 productions. The professional scene designers had yet to prove their indispensable worth to the collaboration. True, the names of designers began popping up on the title page in the program credits rather than in the space in the back usually reserved for "Gowns by Saks Fifth Avenue," "Piano courtesy of Mason Hamlin," and "Victrola by Victor Talking Machine Company." But if the producers could recycle bits and pieces of previous sets when assembling a current show or buy "center door fancy-middle class," "center door fancy-millionaire" stock scenery from one of the manufactories in and around Times Square, they did—with or without the services of a scene designer. When the Theatre Guild began sending out touring companies of their New York successes in 1927, they asked Jo Mielziner to redo *The Guardsman,* his and their success of 1924. He agreed to "make all working drawings, subject to approval, supervise the construction of the sets, and the dressing and lighting of the production" and to make use of his *Pygmalion* units and "whatever parts of the original production are necessary." (This meant that he had to cannibalize two of his own sets to produce one for the road to save money for the Guild.) All of this he contracted to do for five hundred bucks.

For ten years, scene designers had been making strides in forcing recognition of what they could do for productions. No seasoned playgoer of the time could forget the starkly simple geometrics of Robert Edmond Jones's design for *The Man Who Married a Dumb Wife* at the old Wallack's Theatre in 1915, or Lee Simonson's brilliant salmon pink and purple curtain for *The Farce of Pierre Patelin* (1916), which he did for the Washington Square Players in 1916 at the tiny Bandbox Theatre. Both sets were done on the slimmest of budgets but with the greatest originality and with sensitivity to the text.

IN 1915, ROBERT EDMOND JONES (1887–1954) WAS COMMISSIONED TO PROVIDE THE SCENERY FOR **THE MAN WHO MARRIED A DUMB WIFE.** THE ENGLISH DIRECTOR HARLEY GRANVILLE-BARKER THOUGHT IT RIGHT FOR THE COMEDY, USED IT, AND LAUNCHED THE CAREER OF JONES AND THE MOVEMENT THAT BECAME "THE NEW STAGECRAFT" IN AMERICAN THEATRE. (COURTESY OF PAUL STIGA)

Although Broadway producers resisted hiring these new specialists, the small and unconventional play-producing organizations like the Theatre Guild, the Provincetown Playhouse, of which Robert Edmond Jones was one-third of the artistic management, and the Neighborhood Playhouse knew full well that the scene designer could plumb the play's inner depths and provide a depth of meaning and nuance to the production that perhaps neither the playwright nor anyone else had even divined.

Most of the experiments in scene design were happening away from Times Square and in the Little Theatres of the hinterlands, but there were signs and portents in that season of 1924–25 that the new concepts would not go away and were steadily encroaching on

Urban introduced new methods of building, painting, and lighting scenery to the American theatre, and audiences responded enthusiastically to the improvements. As in other years, the *Follies* of 1924–25 was the most popular presentation on Broadway that season.

Meanwhile, American designers like Jones were making steady inroads on the establishment theatre during that season. His best work was inspired by Eugene O'Neill's *Desire Under the Elms*, a mordant melodrama of New England life, which was originally staged at the Greenwich Village Theatre but was moved to Broadway to complete its run.

His colleague at the Provincetown, Cleon Throckmorton, designed an unforgettable setting for a group of Eugene O'Neill's one-act sea plays grouped under the name SS *Glencairn*, for their new season, as well as a roster of other plays. He also became the designer for another experimental group, The Stagers, which had a brief life uptown. Another Provincetowner, Donald Oenslager, who had appeared only as a bit actor, not as a designer, at the Provincetown, had commenced his real vocation in the theatre at the Neighborhood Playhouse and was now making his professional debut as a designer with a production of John Galsworthy's *Bit o' Love* on Broadway.

Another auspicious Broadway debut that season was made by Mordecai Gorelik, who had talked playwright John Howard Lawson into allowing him to design *Processional*, a production planned by the Theatre Guild. It was the beginning of a career that ultimately led to his association with the leftist Group Theatre in the 1930s. Lee Simonson, a member of the Theatre Guild's governing board and the principal designer for the organization, was inactive during the entire season (either because of a nervous breakdown, according to Gorelik, or because he was writing a book, according to Mielziner) and was replaced by a number of other designers, among them Mielziner and Gorelik.

The new generation also included Woodman Thompson, a former instructor of scene and costume design in the first drama curriculum in the country at the Carnegie Institute of Technology in Pittsburgh. Thompson landed what turned out to be the plum assignment of the season, designing Arthur Hopkins's production of

Broadway. After all, Livingston Platt, whose experiments in scene design and lighting predated those of Jones and his successors, had already moved into the mainstream of Broadway. He designed three shows that season and his stylish sets still merited attention by the critics. A decade earlier, Flo Ziegfeld had taken a chance when he hired the Viennese designer Joseph Urban to oversee the sets for his annual revues, but it turned out to be a brilliant stroke. Urban's settings were as much a part of the entertainment as Ziegfeld's show-girls and comedians. With his European background and training,

What Price Glory? He went on to design three other productions that season, all on Broadway. Although a Broadway career still lay ahead of her, Aline Bernstein designed both sets and costumes for the Neighborhood Playhouse production of *The Little Clay Cart*, an exotic Hindu drama, with her memory of her apprenticeship with Norman Bel Geddes still fresh in her mind. Geddes, in a class by himself, continued to enlarge his reputation on Broadway, designing not only the Gershwin musical *Lady, Be Good* but also a spun-sugar comedy titled *Quarantine* for veteran producer Edgar Selwyn, and Philip Barry's *The Youngest*.

Thus, in that season of 1924–25, the past, present, and future, met and merged. The past was represented by Ziegfeld and his rapidly increasing imitators among revue producers, plus A. H. Woods, William A. Brady Sr., and David Belasco, and their imitators with their mostly meretricious comedies and melodramas; the present, by producers Winthrop Ames, Arthur Hopkins, and Ray Comstock in a range of cautious experiments, and by the brothers Shubert with their diet of crowd-pleasers; and the future, by the Theatre Guild and the avant-gardist groups downtown at the Provincetown and the Neighborhood playhouses and elsewhere in the city. Nowhere were the divisions more striking than in what critics and reviewers of the time persisted in labeling "stage decor." It was the one element in theatrical production which was still in rebellion against the past, dissatisfied with its present status and whose future was still ahead.

The rebellion was nearly a decade old in 1924 and was focused on the kind of stage settings that were concocted by David Belasco. From the 1890s to the early 1920s, the Belasco set was subjected to the sincerest form of flattery: it was imitated by every producer and manager but was never really bested. It was both ideal and benchmark. In his early years in California, Belasco considered himself a rebel as he stripped away the old-fashioned painted wings and borders and put "life" on the stage in all its cluttered detail. The theatre of his youth was a theatre of benign conspiracy between audience and performers to pretend that the artifice seen as presented bore some semblance to real life. It was a *trompe-l'oeil* picture that the audience saw, which the performers played against and not with.

It was the end result of a long evolution that had started in the Italian Renaissance several hundred years before.

Prior to Belasco, producer Henry Abbey brought over Sir Henry Irving and his company for an American tour in 1883. The Star Theatre on 13th Street in New York became the home for Irving's totally realized productions down to the lowliest acting role and minutest scenic detail. He had taken all the scenery, lighting effects, props, and costumes from his famous Lyceum Theatre in London to re-create his productions in New York. Audiences were impressed, the critics were impressed, and the theatrical profession was not only impressed but also astounded by what could be achieved onstage.

The men responsible for Irving's scenery, Hawes Craven and Joseph Harker, could no longer be considered scene painters but had slipped over the line into the realm of designer-artists. They provided a visual *mise-en-scène* that was fully integrated into the action of the play; they bathed it in soft, colored atmospheric lighting to heighten the three-dimensionality of the scenery; and they constructed the props of *papier mâché* to look more real than the actual objects. Only one producer in America at this time, Augustin Daly, took almost as much care with his presentations, but even his artist was no match for Irving's. The engagement of Irving's company proved very lucrative for the English star and his American sponsor alike, a lesson not lost on New York's major producers.

Belasco, who was residing in New York in 1883 and probably saw both the Irving and Daly productions, added his own embellishments to scenery and lighting. He made further improvements when he took over a Broadway theatre (the Republic) in 1901 and could function as his own producer, director, designer, and theatre owner.

Working independently in his own theatre, Belasco probably created the most perfectly realized naturalistic stage settings, often to the point of overload. The canvas never flapped on a Belasco set, the windows moved up and down at the touch, the doors were solid wood, the rocks were made of plaster, live birds chirped in their cages, fresh tulips grew in the window boxes, and real flapjacks were flipped on an actual grill. Obsessive attention to inconsequential detail was lavished on dramatic junk, most of which he wrote or co-wrote with other playwrights. (With the exception of two Belasco plays which Puccini turned into the operas *Madame Butterfly* and *The Girl of the Golden West*, nothing else that he produced has survived his time.) Belasco's two assistants, Ernest Gros and Louis Hartman, remained with him for years as his specialists in scenery and lighting and displayed a loyalty to the "Master" that was unmatched on Broadway.

In the season of 1924–25, Belasco was still going strong. He produced four shows, two of which had better than respectable runs. The Ossa of superfluous detail piled upon the Pelion of melodramatic claptrap obviously continued to sell tickets, much to the chagrin of the young Turks, who were rebelling against his kind of theatre and struggling in small or antiquated playhouses on tiny budgets. What many of the upstarts envied was Belasco's total control of his productions and his extraordinary use of lighting, concepts that he had apparently arrived at without ever having heard the names of Edward Gordon Craig or Adolphe Appia.

Although Appia, the Swiss standard bearer of the new theatrical thinking, was the first to promulgate and put into practice the theories that were later to sweep Europe, he was largely unknown in America until the 1920s. But to the young designers of the early years of the century and the avant-garde critics and writers who had read his works in French or German, he was a demigod and great emancipator. At first, Appia wanted nothing less than a clean sweep of all scenery and conventional lighting equipment from the stage. The emphasis, he wrote, was to be on the performer, whom he regarded as the prime agent of expression of the dramatic event, whether opera or play. He wanted to see the actors freed from set poses and tricks and from the nineteenth century's obsession with authentic period costumes. Since the performers were to be the central focus, every element on stage would be subordinate or in relationship to them. The painted stage and all manner of artifice, which included the *illusion* of reality, should be banished. In their place, elemental pieces—cubes, pillars, ramps, steps, and simple curtains—should be artfully arranged to suggest locale or objects to the audience, with a stretch of the collective imagination. Above all, lighting was to be the life-giver of the event. He believed that it could be used as scenery to unite the actor and the scenic elements,

to have motion and plasticity, to create atmosphere through color and focus, and to define the scenic environment. Every element, actors, scenery, lighting, should come under the control of a single mentality so that the synthesis of all elements would be complete and interwoven.

These concepts were powerful and heady stuff to budding designers like Jones, Simonson, and later Mielziner, who took the boat to Europe to see for themselves. What they saw thrilled and inspired them, but they had already been introduced to the possibilities of a new and different stagecraft through the work and writings of Edward Gordon Craig, the son of the great English actress Ellen Terry and the protégé of Henry Irving himself, who had begun as a child actor in Irving's famous company in London.

In 1897, at the age of twenty-five, Craig began formulating his ideas for a new experimental theatre. Beginning in 1900, he designed a series of productions in London, which displayed an eerie similarity in imagination to the work of Appia on the continent. (Neither Craig nor Appia knew of each other or each other's theories until 1914.) For a production of Ibsen's *The Vikings*, in which Ellen Terry starred, Craig had stripped the stage of all scenery except for background curtains and the most rudimentary props. For *Much Ado about Nothing*, he suggested the church interior by training a strong shaft of light through an invisible stained-glass window, which spilled a profusion of colors on the stage floor.

While he was applying his ideas to actual productions, he was also setting his ideas down on paper. In 1905, he published a small book, *The Art of the Theatre*, which appeared first in German, then in English. He wrote it in the form of a dialogue between a Director and a Playgoer and in it he pleaded for the unity of production under one person, for the theatre to be recognized as an art, and also for a school in which the art of the theatre could be studied in all of its aspects. Echoing Appia, he put the performers at the center of theatrical production *within* a three-dimensional environment and not *against* flat painted backgrounds. He, too, wanted to cleanse the stage of all artificiality, and urged a reliance on simple structural units, which could be moved and rearranged and colored by light to suggest all manner of scenes.

In 1903, at about the same time that Craig was busy expounding his theories in London, a young artist named Livingston Platt was experimenting with scenery and lighting in a small theatre in Bruges, Belgium. Born in Plattsburgh, New York, in 1874, Platt had traveled to Paris in the 1890s to study art, but became sidetracked by an overriding interest in the theatre. His work in Bruges caught the eye of the Belgian Minister of Fine Arts, who prevailed upon him to design sets for several opera productions. Whether or not Platt was acquainted with the seminal ideas of Appia and Craig is not known. It is entirely possible that he independently arrived at similar conclusions himself. Whatever the case, his early theatrical experiments occupied the same spiritual plane as Appia and Craig.

In 1911, Platt returned to the United States and was invited by a prominent Boston socialite to be the artistic director of a small theatre that she had created on her estate in Newton, just outside Boston. For several years, Platt created impressionistic scenery, using diffused and minimal lighting on a neutral background to give the impression of depth on a tiny 12-by-20-foot stage. He also designed scenery for the Castle Square Theatre in Boston. He described one of his sets for *The Comedy of Errors* at the Castle Square as consisting of a "cyclorama [curved backdrop in a neutral color] lit with hot yellow, a single sail showing above a low wall of yellow." The actress Margaret Anglin liked it and asked him to design her classical productions in the same manner. For them, he lengthened the stage apron into a forestage to allow interchangeable units to be slipped into place for rapidly changing Shakespearean scenes. He enunciated his own theory when he said: "We have carried the photographic method to its farthest development, and it seems to me that the next step in theatrical art is toward a more imaginative stage. All superfluous details should be eliminated and the settings should stimulate the audience to create in their own imaginations the dominant features of the play."

Platt's unique sense of design led him inevitably to New York, where he worked for the younger generation of producers, who gave him a degree of latitude to explore different styles. In the season of 1924–25, Platt designed at least three productions. (In the cast of one of them was a young actor named Kenneth MacKenna,

Jo Mielziner's brother.) It is not easy to explain why Platt never received his due as an authentically American voice in the development of the new national style. He has remained in the shadows of theatrical history perhaps because the young Turks thought of him as belonging to an earlier generation, or perhaps, too, because his open homosexuality displeased the not so tolerant world of his time, despite his obvious talents.

Another push into the modern world came from Joseph Urban, a Viennese designer, who came to America in 1911 with three complete opera productions for the Boston Opera Company along with his crew of Austrian scene painters. Born in 1872, which put him in an older European tradition, he was a trained architect but his talents extended into book illustration and interior decoration. Once Urban took over the Boston Opera as general stage director a year later, he began making changes that reverberated a few hundred miles south to New York. Replacing the dark and ponderous overwrought settings that were traditional for grand opera, he introduced lighter structures, impressionistic scene painting in vivid and varied color, and exquisite lighting. He treated the stage as an architectural environment with many invisible planes rather than a flat stage floor surmounted by an expanse of space. He designed platforms and ramps and broke up space within the opening with narrow walls, sometimes altering the dimensions of the stage proscenium opening itself. Over it all, he cast an aura of fairy-tale unreality, as if exhorting the audience to remember that the theatre is a special place.

In 1914, he designed *The Garden of Paradise* in New York, which led to a complete turnabout in his career. The production was not a success, but Urban's sets aroused a great deal of comment. An associate of Florenz Ziegfeld's urged him to catch a performance of the show just to see the scenery. So impressed was Ziegfeld that he immediately engaged Urban to work on the annual editions of his now famous but predictable revues, the *Follies*. Urban reluctantly agreed on the condition that Ziegfeld would not interfere in any way with his creativity.

Ziegfeld did not regret his promise. Urban's sets were second only to the pulling power of some of Ziegfeld's stars in keeping the *Follies* alive and popular for many more years.

Urban did not confine his activities to providing extravagant effects for the *Follies*. He also designed Ziegfeld's musicals and shows for other producers and from 1917 to his death in 1933, he functioned as Artistic Director of the Metropolitan Opera. Perhaps his most important contribution was setting up a scenery shop in 1919, first in Yonkers, then in New York on 24th Street and Eleventh Avenue, closer to his activities. It was at this studio that he introduced his continental stagecraft to American theatre craftsmen. Aided by the Austrian artisans he had brought with him, Urban used methods that eventually became established practice in America. Many young designers received their practical training in the techniques of scene construction and painting at the Urban Studio, Norman Bel Geddes and Jo Mielziner among them. After Urban's death, his studio continued in a downtown Manhattan location under the leadership of his two principal assistants, Rudolph Adler and Gus Wimazal. It was renamed the Triangle Scenic Studio.

Urban's technique of painting scenery consisted of using strong colors as a base coat, then covering it with specks of different colored paint in built-up layers. Called "pointillage," it was a technique derived from the French Impressionists. When light was applied to it, the surface took on a textured feeling; when colored light was directed onto it, the color picked up one of the flecked layers to make it appear dominant. By playing different colored lights on the same surface, it was possible to make the scene change colors as if by magic. Urban's painters blocked out the design on expanses of canvas placed on the floor, not hung on frames on the back walls of the theatres or high-ceilinged paint shops. Using long-handled brushes, they could paint from a standing position rather than on precarious scaffolds (or "bridges") in mid-air. To alter the size and shape of the proscenium opening, Urban employed what came to be known as "portals," pieces of scenery on either side of the stage designed to create an inner proscenium. Using this structure, designers could exercise control over the size and shape of the stage picture.

Although Urban softened the edges of the photographic realism that was the hallmark of scenery both in America and Europe in the early decades of the century, he did not entirely abandon it. He blended it with the colors and curves and the ethereal light of the romantic tradition. Rather than strip the stage to its bare essentials, he more often than not overfilled it with beautifully built and executed scenery. The sets could become so complex to shift for scene changes that it often resulted in long stage waits and intermissions. Urban's scenery retained its European, even more particularly, its Viennese, painterly style, strongly reminiscent of Gustav Klimt and Egon Schiele, under whose influence he had grown up. Urban created sets that were marvels but did not significantly contribute to the development of a distinctly American style. What was important was his stagecraft, which gave the native American designers the techniques necessary to launch their new movement. He led them into the twentieth century.

By 1924, the American designer had its leader in the person of Robert Edmond Jones. (A small alteration in his middle name had changed Edmund to Edmond in his post-Harvard years.)

He was graduated in 1910, remaining at Harvard for the next two years as an art instructor. Then he abruptly left for New York, where he was slowly beginning to discover his vocation. Among his former Harvard classmates and friends were the future critic, writer, and teacher Kenneth Macgowan, and the then and future political radical John Reed. They encouraged him in his theatrical ambitions to the point of taking up a collection from his friends ("The Robert Edmond Jones Transportation and Development Company") to send him to study the contemporary currents in European theatre. Another friend promised to get him an audience with Gordon Craig in Florence, where Craig had set up an atelier. For inexplicable reasons, Craig refused to see him and Jones, disappointed, went instead to Berlin to observe the theatrical experiments of Max Reinhardt, at that time head of the Deutsches Theater and one of Craig's principal German disciples. While there, he designed scenery as a project for Shelley's *The Cenci*. After the outbreak of war in Europe, he returned to the United States in the late fall of 1914.

Back in New York, he was hired almost immediately by the Stage Society of New York to conduct a demonstration of a model stage and lighting as an accompaniment to an exhibition of photographs of European avant-garde productions, prints, plans, three-dimensional scale models, and some original drawings, including a few of his own. The Society commissioned Jones to design sets and costumes for a one-act play, Anatole France's *The Man Who Married a Dumb Wife*. They rented the old and decrepit Wallack's Theatre on Broadway and 30th Street, presumably for a next-to-nothing sum, and hoped to shake the jaded New York audiences out of their complacency. They succeeded.

The little play was a curtain raiser to Shaw's *Androcles and the Lion*. New Yorkers reacted with enthusiasm after the opening on January 17, 1915.

The set for *The Man Who Married a Dumb Wife*, which launched the "New Stagecraft," was all right angles forming an outsized door and window cut into a flat background that was painted in black, white, and tones of gray. Bursts of bright and bold colors came from the costumes, which Jones also designed. At the first matinee performance, two young brothers, accompanied by their mother, sat in the balcony and marveled at what they saw. The younger brother was Joseph Mielziner, who would one day serve in Jones's studio as an apprentice.

Jones's set was the star of the production but not in the way that David Belasco's sets usually were. Although its freshness and simplicity were a tonic from the relentless realism of the Belasco-like set, what put it apart was its appropriateness to Harley Granville-Barker's direction of a sprightly but slight comedy about a man whose dumb wife regains her power of speech and drives him to the brink with her incessant chatter. The setting went to the heart of the script, suited the style of the director, and, above all, complemented, even enhanced, the performances of the actors. Although Jones and other New Stagecraft designers were not always on the mark, what Jones demonstrated in that first stroke was the value of including the designer as a vital participant *from the moment of inception* of a theatrical production. In America, it was a new concept, but in Europe it had been allowed to flower to maturity in the state-subsidized continental theatres. With commerce driving the engine of creativity in American theatre, fresh ideas took a long time to germinate from European seeds, and when they

did, they were almost always mingled with Yankee variations after landing on American soil.

The war in Europe slowed the importation of continental trends, turning America inward culturally to permit its theatre (as well as its other arts) to develop freely and without foreign seductions. In 1915, Jones had set the stage, literally and figuratively, for the coming of age of American theatre, but he became impatient. "What is the future of designers of scenery who have caught the spirit of the new theatre?" he asked. "Must we quit for a while? Sit back and wait for the playwrights, producers [directors], and actors to catch up with us?" Luckily for him and for designers of like mind and their spiritual godchildren, all three were waiting in the wings.

Joining Jones in his quest for scenic integrity on the stage were Lee Simonson and Norman Bel Geddes, two men who were a study in contrasts. Simonson, the son of German-Jewish immigrants who prospered in America, was sent to the innovative Ethical Culture School in New York, graduating in 1905. He went off to Harvard, where he found Jones and Macgowan. He went to Paris to study at the Académie Julian, which was coincidentally where Leo Mielziner, Jo's father, received his training during the 1890s. In the summer of 1909, Simonson was witness to the first season of the Ballets Russes in Paris and a week of Max Reinhardt's repertory in Munich at the Künstlertheater. The scenery and costumes of Léon Bakst and Alexandre Benois exposed him to raw and bold colors and forms that he had not seen on the stage before, and Reinhardt's productions demonstrated what could be achieved when one mind and vision conceived the total theatrical work.

A few years after he returned from Europe, still intending to be an artist, Simonson received a call from Philip Moeller, a young director with an experimental theatre group, the Washington Square Players. Would Simonson design some stage settings for the Players at the little Bandbox Theatre on 57th Street? Thus occurred a casual beginning to an association with a group of people who were to be his friends, enemies, and artistic compeers for more than twenty years, as the Theatre Guild metamorphosed from the Washington Square Players and Simonson emerged as one of its six leaders. For the first few years after taking Moeller's assignment to design Andreyev's *Love of One's Neighbor* in 1915, Simonson learned on the job about setting a script to a stage, but his training as an artist and the ideas he had assimilated from Reinhardt and the Russian designers in Europe, plus his prodigious talents, became more than adequate preparation for his new-found vocation. In 1916, his design for *The Farce of Pierre Patelin* mixed pink, purple, yellow, and turquoise in a set that sent the trend-conscious Broadway audiences running to the shabby little Bandbox.

Norman Geddes was a few years younger than Jones and Simonson, and was born to a working-class family in Adrian, Michigan. Unlike them, he went no further than the ninth grade in formal education. He studied at the Cleveland School of Art and later at the Chicago Art Institute for brief periods, until his disaffection with what and how he was being taught drove him away. For him, there was no *Wanderjahr* in Europe. (When he did go abroad, he was nearly thirty and unimpressed by what he saw.) Geddes began to make his way as an art director in the commercial art world and advertising. By night, he wrote plays and built model theatres and dreamed of a different life. He married and added part of his wife's name (Belle) to his, becoming forever after Norman-Bel Geddes. (The hyphen was later dropped.)

One of his plays together with the sets he designed for it built into a model theatre came to the attention of Aline Barnsdall, who was about to found a small experimental theatre in Los Angeles, which, in those days, was hardly fertile ground for things theatrical. On the strength of what she saw and read, she hired Geddes as designer and technical director. In 1916, the Little Theatre of Los Angeles, launched under her leadership and with her money, joined the burgeoning little theatre movement in the United States. Before it went the way of most of the little theatres of the time, Geddes was able to spend two seasons designing experimental plays for her and her group.

Geddes found himself in Los Angeles without a job and without prospects. Down to his last dollars, he managed to receive from philanthropist Otto Kahn enough money to take himself and his family to New York in search of a fresh career. There, Bobby Jones hired him almost immediately as lighting director for a summer stock stint in Milwaukee in 1918. By the end of 1919, he had begun to receive note as an innovative scene designer. His recognized gifts as a lighting designer were responsible for making changes in the arrangement and control of lighting instruments in Broadway theatres.

Geddes designed musical comedies and revues, drawing-room comedies, and an opera for the Metropolitan during the next years. (Later, he designed movies for D. W. Griffith and Cecil B. DeMille.) Nor did he bother himself with a theory of the theatre or a reworked modern European philosophy. He was probably the most American in his natural ingenuity and independence. What Geddes added to Jones and Simonson was a sense of the total physical space of the theatre, not just what was behind the proscenium arch. When Max Reinhardt looked for an American designer for his gargantuan 1924 production of *The Miracle*, he took it to Norman Bel Geddes on the strength of Geddes's designs for a theoretical production of Dante's *Divine Comedy*.

Working with Reinhardt in Vienna over several months, they planned the conversion of the Century Theatre on Central Park West into a medieval Gothic cathedral, which spilled into the auditorium. Within a vast space, 200 feet long by 120 feet wide by 110 feet high, he created "a primeval forest, a banquet hall, a wedding chapel, a setting for a black mass, a great throne room for the coronation of an empress, a public square, a stable interior, a roadway through a wintry forest and a cathedral," so that each scene could segue into the next like motion picture dissolves, a theatrical spectacle that few were able to forget.

In 1919 the New Stagecraft designers received an exhibition devoted to their preliminary paper-and-paste visions at a gallery in New York. The sketches, photographs, plans, and models in reduced scale were the precedents for their onstage art, as Simonson labeled them, the "records of intention." If Craig and Appia and the Russians could trumpet their wares in exhibitions throughout the world, why not the Americans in America? With the cooperation of Stephan Bourgeois, the show opened at the Bourgeois Galleries in April. Jones was represented in it, as were Geddes, Simonson, and Urban, among the more famous names. The exhibition was a critical and popular success and paved the way for other shows, even some solo exhibitions, in the future. The exhibition was its own message: the day of the American designer had arrived.

Jones, Simonson, and Geddes at first had trouble finding artisans to build and paint their scenery. The painting was especially crucial because they were using colors to create textures and spreading them in expanses of subtle shades in techniques that the painters at the established scene studios found confusing. Joseph Urban kept his own studio busy with Ziegfeld's shows and Metropolitan operas. A vacuum continued to exist for the Broadway productions until Jones discovered Robert W. Bergman, a young artist then working for the Lee Lash Studio, the largest scene-by-number supplier in the country. Far from being intimidated by the kind of scenery demanded by the New Stagecraft designers, Bergman, or "Berg," reveled in it. With promises of work from Jones, Geddes, and producer Margaret Hewes, and financial backing from friends and business associates, the Bergman Studio was created and developed into the finest scenery shop in the country.

Located on West 39th Street between Broadway and Eighth Avenue, it was within a stone's throw of the Metropolitan Opera House and all of the Broadway playhouses. Jones and another designer, Raymond Sovey, took office space in the narrow five-story building, where three floors were knocked out to provide a forty-foot vertical working area. An eyewitness described its ordered chaos: "huge iron frames sliding up and down bare brick wall; splotches of paint most anywhere on the floors; buckets of colored powder; men in overalls reminiscent of Joseph's coat strolling about in search of something; men kneeling and painting canvas with a huge paintbrush; men on scaffoldings slapping and daubing; men with three inch brushes painting 'detail' as big as your fist." Many years after its passing, Jo Mielziner remembered it as a combination of two buildings, each with a counterweighted paint frame capable of holding fifty-foot drops. There was also floor space for painting on the ground. He also remembered that there was always a plentiful supply of poor-grade whiskey "which almost ruined the studio."

In 1952, with the help of Lucille Ashworth, Oenslager edited the notes of her late husband, Bradford Ashworth, one of the studio's master painters, and published them as "Notes on Scene

Painting." It remains the only source of information on the techniques used principally by the Bergman studio painters, many of which are lost to today's craftsmen.

Other studios eventually arose to follow the dictates of the New Stagecraft designers, but while it was in business, the Bergman Scenic Studios remained the favorite of all of them. According to Mielziner, it was also a hangout for the designers, "a stimulating place to gossip and exchange ideas even if you were not there on business." Before the unions came down heavily against the practice, it was not inconceivable that designers would climb into a pair of overalls and wield a paintbrush on their own sets in order to get the color or effect that they wanted. Jones often watched the progress of the painting. Often he would gently chide the painters, "Got a little tired there?" It would then be redone.

Another problem for the young designers of the early twenties was achieving the lighting effects that were an integral part of their scenery. Inspired by the lighting aesthetics of Appia and Craig but without an exact vocabulary of communication, they had to rely on the skills of stage electricians for their effects. It was often a difficult working relationship and only rarely a union between kindred spirits. David Belasco's lighting, which had always seemed to be the benchmark for everyone else's productions, was not for them. Admired for his wizardry in lighting, which was frequently achieved by overloading every nook and cranny above and around the stage with men manipulating special spotlights, Belasco was aided by the awesome technical abilities of Louis Hartmann, who could create to order the effects that the Master wanted. The rebels considered it self-conscious gimmickry rather than a perfect marriage between set and lights, but they were unfailingly impressed by Hartmann's technical know-how. While in a real sense the young designers had to make up the lighting vocabulary for the effects they needed as they went along, several became proficient enough to be their own "lighting designers" long before it had begun to be thought of as a specialty.

As they had found Bergman for painting their sets, they now encouraged a young entrepreneur named Edward Frankel Kook, who was ready to seize the main chance in lighting. Although Jones and company did not directly put him in business, as they did with Bergman, they provided Eddie Kook with the fertile ground to lay the framework of a future business. In March of 1923, Kook, trained as an accountant, moved over to the Display Stage Lighting Company as chief bookkeeper and through his work became involved with the Provincetown Playhouse, one of Display's clients. There he met Cleon Throckmorton and the two young men started the New York Stage Equipment Company to handle all aspects of technical theatrical production, using Throckmorton's abilities in design and lighting sets and Kook's business acumen. The business, however, fizzled and Kook returned to Display Stage Lighting after some eighteen months.

Recognizing the need for some kind of middleman between the designer and stage electrician, Kook filled the void by immersing himself in knowledge about lighting equipment and the stage so that he could suggest to the designers ways to effect their special demands. He soon became the person all the designers called with their problems. What he could not answer himself, he put to Display's shop manager, Joseph Levy, the man who could field the technical questions. And he never stopped courting the designers, whom he sensed were exerting more and more control over all aspects of the physical production. At the Theatre Guild, he met the fledging designer Mielziner.

By the early twenties, the New Stagecraft designers had begun to swell, which gave producers a choice of a number of talents to call upon for their shows. One of the practices of the time—probably the most odious to all the young designers—was to ask them to submit sketches for a show with the vague promise that the job would be theirs if the producers liked what they saw. What was even worse was to get the job and do the work on the basis of a small advance. If the show succeeded, they usually received the rest of their fee. If it failed, the producers would turn their empty pockets inside out to signal to them that no more money would be forthcoming.

The designers *en masse* resented this treatment and discussed several times a course of action to prevent these and other abuses, but without any consensus. Should they set up an independent protective guild or join with the shop scene painters in their union? The stagehands and the actors had already unionized, and the old-time scene painters had formed a protective association as early as 1892. In 1912, the shop painters and muralists set up the Scenic Artists Association, an independent labor organization, which allied itself in 1918 with the Brotherhood of Painters, Decorators, and Paperhangers to become Local 829 of the American Federation of Labor.

The designers hired Morris L. Ernst, a distinguished labor lawyer of the time, who urged them to form a collective and even offered to write a charter to establish their own organization. After prolonged thrashing about, Jones, Urban, Simonson, Throckmorton, Geddes, and a few others, acting for the rest of their colleagues, decided on something that fell between a protective guild and a union. Artists first and businessmen second, they elected to form a guild *within* the protective embrace of Local 829, but it later proved to be not the happiest of marriages. Unlike their brethren who labored in shops for employers, worked in their shirt sleeves, and received hourly wages under a collective agreement, the designers always considered themselves independent, self-employed artist-contractors. In August of 1923 (not 1922 as Mielziner later insisted), the designers reluctantly lined up to join, each paying fifty dollars, and were issued union cards. On September 1, Jo Mielziner received his card, Number 22.

With their union in place and with their status as collaborators in production growing with each new scenic triumph, the young designers looked to Robert Edmond Jones to provide spiritual leadership. Although he is barely remembered today, every American designer in whatever theatrical workplace, whether live, filmed, or electronic, owes him a debt. Through his own transcendent art and the sheer magnetic force of his personality, he brought status to scene designing that it never had before, he made sure that studios and lighting companies were set up to answer the special needs of the designers, he saw to it that the stage artists were organized for their own protection, and most important, as stated by Lee Simonson, he "was the first to win recognition in this century for the scenic designer as an indispensable collaborator in the interpretation of a script." With Jones, theatrical production finally became a true collaboration in America. But, surprisingly, his work did not dominate in the same way that the work of Appia and Craig prevailed in Europe. Jones's colleague, Dutch-born Hermann Rosse, summed it up best when he stated that the total oeuvre of the New Stagecraft became a "communal creation, one man adding to what another man has already done." Although no one could have been conscious of it then, American theatre was ascending both in the quality and the quantity of its creations, all emanating from New York. Europe was still recovering from the long winter of World War I and was in the throes of its political fallout. Culturally, Americans had always lagged a generation behind the Europeans, but in the theatre, Eugene O'Neill, Robert Edmond Jones, and the others, including Jo Mielziner, were beginning to catch up.

1
THE MISCHLING

Ella Lane McKenna Friend, born on March 18, 1873, in Manchester, New Hampshire, was the direct descendant of John Friend, who came to the Massachusetts Bay Colony probably from Bristol, England, in the early 1630s. He was a master carpenter by trade and lived and died in Salem. In 1638, he was entrusted with building the first permanent structure for Harvard College, which had been founded just two years earlier. He worked sporadically on the building for two years, supervising the workers and donating some of his own labor, while Henry Dunster, the first president of Harvard, raised the funds to complete each stage. John left a large family, which insured the continuation of the line.

He was succeeded in future generations by Friends with Christian names, repeated again and again, such as John, James, Richard, and Josiah. Josiah Ober Friend, Jo's great grandfather, founded a business with his brothers as ship chandlers for the deep-sea fishermen of Gloucester. They all became important and prosperous citizens. Josiah married Caroline Sayward, who came from a "good" Gloucester family, and together they produced ten children. One of their sons, Albert, born in 1843, served in the Civil War as a private and was wounded in battle. When he returned to Gloucester, he probably joined the family business. Much to his family's chagrin, the woman he chose as his wife was well below their station. She was the descendant of Irish Catholic immigrants and her name was Margaret Alice McKenna.

OPPOSITE: THE YOUNG JOSEPH MIELZINER DISPLAYED SUCH ARTISTIC PRECOCITY THAT HE RECEIVED A SCHOLARSHIP TO THE PENNSYLVANIA ACADEMY OF THE FINE ARTS AT AGE 16, WON PRIZES WHILE THERE, AND RECEIVED TWO TRAVEL GRANTS TO EUROPE. SOMEONE (HIS FATHER, PERHAPS) FOUND THIS EXAMPLE OF HIS WORK SO GOOD THAT HE HAD IT LITHOGRAPHED. (COURTESY OF THE ESTATE OF HILDA AND EDWARD KOOK)

Margaret McKenna was born in 1847, in Mason Village (now Greenville), New Hampshire, very close to the Massachusetts border, but when she met Albert Friend, she was living in Lynn, Massachusetts, with her parents, Michael Henry and Ann (Keenan) McKenna. She was only fourteen when she fell in love with Albert Friend and sixteen when he asked her to marry him. Under the watchful eye of Michael Henry, who accompanied them to Boston, Margaret and Albert were married in 1866, when she was nineteen and he was almost twenty-three. They settled at first in Gloucester, where Albert worked as a bookkeeper in the family business, then in Manchester, New Hampshire.

For five years, the marriage appeared to be an idyll. Three daughters were born to them: the first, Ethelyn, fifteen months after their marriage; their second, Alice, followed two years later, and the third, Ella, in 1873. Then something happened to shatter the marriage, which Margaret divulged only to her divorce lawyer when she and Albert finally separated. With three young daughters to support, she decided (in her own words) to use "her positive passion to put [her] impressions into words" to find work as a writer, which she did. Years later, one of the Boston newspapers that she worked for sent her to Paris as a reporter and for most of her career, she lived and worked in France.

In 1892, her daughter Ella, living with her in Paris, happened to meet a charming young art student named Leo Mielziner. Ella was nineteen and Leo was not quite twenty-three. Leo fell madly in love with the beautiful New Englander at first sight and he did something that he continued to do for the rest of his life: He wrote poetry to her to mark the occasion, which Ella carefully preserved.

When he met Ella, Leo had been in Paris studying art at the Académie Julian for about two years. He was the descendant of many generations of rabbis and learned men on both the paternal and maternal sides of his family. The name Mielziner was created by Leo's grandfather, Rabbi Benjamin Leib ben Meir, born about 1797 in the province of Posen in Poland, probably in a small village near Gnessen (Gniezno). When the authorities made Jews choose Occidental surnames, Rabbi Benjamin took his from Mielcyzn, a baronial estate in the government of Bromberg, Posen, where he

led a Jewish community. Over the years, it had various spellings: *Mielczynski, Mielczyner, Mielziener,* and *Mielzijner.* By about 1820, the spelling had settled as Mielziner.

Barely twenty years of age, Rabbi Benjamin had taken as his bride Rosa Rachel Caro, a descendant of the revered scholar and rabbi Joseph Caro. The Caro strain was blonde, which accounts for the mixture of light- and dark-haired children in successive generations. (Leo and Ella's children reflected the combined strains in Leo Jr.'s light brown hair and blue eyes and Jo's darker hair and green eyes.)

Leo's father, Moses, the fourth child and third son of Rabbi Benjamin and Rosa, was born in 1828 at Schubin, in northwestern Poland, where his father led the Jewish congregation. By tutoring young Jewish boys, Moses was able to pay his way through several university degrees, finally receiving a Ph.D. from the University of Gnessen. A gentle and otherworldly man, he learned to speak and write in many languages. In 1861, he took as his wife the dainty, fair-skinned Rosette Levald, the daughter of a Copenhagen silversmith. For girls of her generation, Rosette was comparatively well-educated. Sent to a Parisian "finishing school" to learn French and to be grounded in literature, music, and art, she developed into a cultivated, well-read woman, a fitting mate for Moses.

Living in Copenhagen, Moses was caught up in the Reform Judaism movement, spending a large portion of his time in combing the vast reservoir of Jewish doctrine and literature for arguments to support the loosening of strict orthodoxy. He taught, wrote, lectured, and in 1859, he published *The Institution of Slavery Among the Ancient Hebrews,* which unbeknownst to him was translated (but not immediately published) in America and much quoted in the Abolitionist movement. Its thesis, grounded in religious precedent that slavery was antithetical to the Jewish religion, gave aid and comfort to the anti-slavery factions in the North prior to the Civil War.

The Reform movement aroused condemnation not only from the Danish government but also the Orthodox rabbinate itself. Reform Jews were being forced to reconsider their positions. With a growing family to support in a period of reaction, Moses reluctantly accepted a call to go to New York to become the spiritual leader of a congregation in the Lower East Side. In August 1865, the family moved to 22 Jefferson Street, New York City. Later, Moses and Rosette moved to East 10th Street and the twins Belle and Leo were born on December 8, 1869. The Mielziners had ten children altogether, one of whom died in infancy.

The Mielziner family eventually settled in Cincinnati. The move offered promise of ready assimilation into the society of the city along with such delights as an art museum and academy, regular concerts, several newspapers, a literary publication, a number of theaters for both English and German plays and operas, and beer gardens for the large German population. Dr. Mielziner taught and flourished at the Hebrew Union College which became the center for Reform Judaism. In 1894, Moses published his *An Introduction to the Talmud,* the first work of its kind in the English language as a text for the seminarians. It has undergone revision but is still in use today.

The Mielziner children were educated in the public schools of Cincinnati and at home. When Leo was graduated from Woodward High School, he knew he wanted to be an artist and was testing his father's liberal beliefs. Moses intended his son for the rabbinate, but relented. After three years at the Cincinnati Art Museum Academy, Leo set out for Europe in the summer of 1890. Because his mother still had family in Denmark, his first stop was the Royal Academy in Copenhagen, but he had his sights set on Paris. In the fall, Leo finally reached Paris and enrolled at the École des Beaux-Arts to study painting under Jean-Léon Gérôme, one of the lesser lights of the period, but a brilliant technician of the slick romanticized pictorial school. After the École, Leo moved on to the Académie Julian on the Rue Dragon, one of the oldest and most traditional academies, to study with Adolphe Bouguereau, another arch-academician.

Although he must have been aware of the work of the avant-gardists led by Édouard Manet and the Impressionists, Leo's style appeared not to be affected by what was going on around him. Instead, he worked on perfecting his own technique, which he recognized as suitable for a portraitist and capable of providing him with a modest income. Many years later, when his son Jo assessed his father's talents, in a letter to a friend he wrote, "Dad was an

extraordinarily gifted man who used about ten percent of the ability that the good Lord blessed him with. . . . His paintings were never as free or as brilliant as the [later] charcoals or lithographs."

Whatever their reservations, the elder Mielziners accepted Ella Friend with good grace and Leo and Ella were married in Boston in 1896. In what faith to raise their future children did not seem to present a problem to the young couple. Both accepted the fact that they would be *Mischlings*, Jew and Christian, of recent immigrant and colonial ancestry, of middle European and English-Irish backgrounds, with genetic strains of reticence and ambition blended into one. A more serious and immediate problem was Leo's choice of livelihood. Artists, even those who were relatively successful, hardly ever achieved stable, secure incomes.

At first, they settled in New England, where their first two children were born. The firstborn, Levald, died in infancy, and their second son, named for his father, came into the world in 1899 at Canterbury, New Hampshire. Ever lamenting the lack of completeness to his technique, Leo wanted to return to Paris and Ella was not against the idea. Not only was her mother there, but Ella's favorite sister, Ethelyn, had settled in Paris.

Ella's return to Paris was sweetly seasoned by a major personal coup. She received a commission from *Vogue* magazine to submit a monthly article (beginning in September 1900) on fashion and cultural events in Paris under her own imaginative by-line "Aube du Siècle." She was to be paid $30 per article. What Ella seems not to have known when she and the two Leos sailed out of Boston was that she was pregnant with her third child.

In the late summer of 1900, the Mielziners settled in a tiny flat in a pension run by Madame Delarue at 15, rue Boissonade, in Montparnasse in the fourteenth arrondissement of Paris, where many artists, French and American, found cheap quarters. At the head of the tucked-away street, then a cul-de-sac, was a wrought-iron fence and gate. The ancient Luxembourg Garden was a short walk away. It was there, at number 15, that their third and final son, Joseph, was born on March 19, 1901.

Shortly after Joe was born, the family moved to slightly bigger quarters at 17, rue Boissonade, where the windows overlooked the

garden of the Franciscan order of St. Vincent de Paul. Leo Sr. soon joined the Colarossi Academy for training as a sculptor under Gustav Courtois. Leo also rented a studio at 9, rue de la Campagne Première, a warren of tiny ateliers in one building.

The Mielziners immediately plunged into the social life of their set, made up mostly of young married American couples, who were either artists or writers. The Mielziner boys, Leo Jr., usually called Junior by his parents and their friends, and Joseph or Joe or Joe-boy, spent their earliest years within this milieu. Their flat at no. 17 was cramped. There was one bedroom for Ella and Leo, a sitting

room, a kitchen, and a small ante-room, which doubled as the boys' nursery. No matter how slim were Ella's means, she always managed to find a few francs for a *bonne d'enfants* and a *femme de chambre*, who might also be prevailed upon to prepare some of the meals. Many years later, Ella wrote a brief and romanticized chronicle of Joe's early life, picturing it as a time when he was surrounded by books and French illustrated papers at home and exposed to the great art museums of Paris in his trips outside the rue Boissonade. It is probably true that both boys learned French before they learned English and both were encouraged in the love, appreciation, and practice of art. Ella reports that Joe was an early critic, pronouncing *"joli"* or *"pas joli"* when he saw something he liked or disliked, respectively. He thought elephants were *"joli"* and for his birthday and Christmas, he usually received an assortment of woolly elephants, china elephants, wooden elephants, plaster elephants, and edible chocolate elephants. What he considered *"pas joli"* was announced for all to hear and was occasionally embarrassing to his mama. It could be someone's face or hat, or a ragged beggar on the Paris streets.

Living was cheap in Paris, a place where a few francs went a long way, a place where it was possible to raise a family and establish a community. But these were not easy times financially for the Mielziners. While they were in Paris, Ella provided the principal support for the family from her *Vogue* job and occasional newspaper assignments. Leo was frequently away, spending part of each year in America. After his father's death, Leo was expected to make long periodic visits with his mother and sisters in Cincinnati, sometimes for months at a time. He was absent for several Christmases and the family burdens fell heavily on Ella. As he became more and more proficient in portrait painting, Leo was beginning to receive commissions, mostly from well-to-do Jews, in the States. One commission would lead to another and his stay would lengthen accordingly. When he did a portrait, he would send part of the money to Ella, who would pay the bills and help out her mother, who was always broke and considered an impossible spendthrift by her daughters.

As they grew older, Ella was concerned about the schooling for the boys. Ella wanted to send her boys to the École L'Alsacienne, a prestigious Protestant-run school on the rue d'Assas, favored by

English-speaking residents in Paris, but it was expensive. When Joe was ready for kindergarten, she managed to scrape together enough money to enroll them in the École L'Alsacienne, but not for a full year. All the little boys were required to wear black sateen pinafores buttoned behind and belted with a wide blue and white striped belt with a leather buckle. They also were sent to dancing class, where one of their partners was the prim and proper little Eva Le Gallienne. (Her mother, Julie Le Gallienne, was one of Ella's lunching companions.) Friends of the Mielziners began to comment on the boys' broken English. Admitting that it was a bit "picturesque," Ella began hunting for an affordable English school. In 1908, the boys were sent off to Plemstall Rectory, which was located on the outskirts of Chester in England, and run by an old Oxonian, Dr. Johns, and his wife. The school was really the Johns's home, where he and his assistant taught a half-dozen boys at a time. The nearby Plemstall Church dated from the twelfth and thirteenth centuries. Because he was so young, Joe spent a lot of time in the Johns's kitchen, learning from the cook how to drop his "h's". The following year, the boys were sent to Dagmar Home School on the grounds of Hatfield House, the ancient seat of Lord Salisbury, in Hertfordshire, run by Mr. Sheehan-Dare. Their playground was the palace grounds. The students were required to go to chapel in the Salisbury palace, dressed in striped gray trousers, black Eton jackets, white Eton collars with buttons, starched white shirtfronts with studs and a black waistcoat, with a straw hat or bowler on their heads. In the classroom, they wore short trousers and a sweater or a striped blazer, with a striped tennis cap with visor. All was very formal and very strict, and punishment was meted by the rod. The boys took tea with the Sheehan-Dares in small groups to learn proper deportment, and were given breakfast promptly at the same time every morning. Since breakfast consisted of bread fried in bacon fat, it behooved the boys to be at table on time, otherwise the bread and fat congealed into a thick white slab. In the English tradition, the boys took a cold sponge-bath daily and a warm bath on Saturday. One sport or another was on the agenda every day and so was the reading of poetry and plays.

Joe exercised his right of rebellion against the formality and strictures at one point in his stay at the Dagmar Home School, which was later described by his cousin Lamar Middleton in a column marking Joe's debut as a scene designer in 1923. One bright afternoon after school, young Master Joseph saw a clothesline full of blazers worn by the school's cricket team. Thinking the colors "pas joli," he removed them from the line and took them to his room, where he redyed them in a pail of ink and water and returned them to the line. The misdeed was discovered a few minutes before the school match the following day and there was the devil—and Joe—to pay.

Perhaps his early schoolboy experiences were responsible for Joe's lifelong loathing of the classroom. Although his English

improved considerably, he never entirely abandoned the English broad "a" and slurred "r." He never learned to spell well and always felt inhibited by what he perceived to be his inability to write. What Joe lacked in scholarship, he more than made up for in disposition. His mother declared him to be "an angel of goodness," sweet of temperament and gentle in his ways, something of a contrast to his brother, who was more highly strung. Leo Jr., however, showed precocity in writing and was a bright and apt student in the classroom. But Joe was sketching and painting at an early age and listening to his father's dictum that he must learn "eye memory," the eidetic ability to store impressions and images in the mind so that he could reproduce them from memory on paper. One of his father's artist friends was so impressed with one of Joe's handiworks, a wax sculpture of a Percheron, that he cast it in clay.

When the children were not at school or in Paris, they were usually on holiday with Ella in Leo's absences. Often they went to Clamart, just outside of Paris, where she would rent rooms during the summer months. It was at Clamart that the boys saw their first dirigible, to their great glee. To help pay for the holidays, Ella would often rent the Paris flat or Leo's studio.

To economize, Ella dressed the boys in hand-me-downs and would often revivify her own wardrobe with just a change of ribbons or ruching. If she received a gift of money from Leo's family, she would buy clothes. A five-dollar gift from Aunt Ernestine Mielziner bought three suits for Joe, kid gloves for both boys, collar buttons, studs, and cufflinks. The boys, both blondes as children, generally wore sailor suits or short tan velveteen pants and white blouses. Everything would be reported to Leo in her long, rambling, daily letters to him.

Whenever the boys were at school and she could afford it, she joined Leo for a short stay in Cincinnati or Boston or New York or wherever he was completing a portrait commission. Finally, Leo's career as a portraitist was picking up speed in the States. Ella, unable to stand the long separations from her husband, planned to return the family to America, knowing full well that she would sacrifice her job for *Vogue.* In the fall of 1908, she packed up and left Paris to join Leo after she had deposited her sons at school in Hertfordshire, entreating a friend of Leo's to keep an eye on them and bring the boys back with him when he returned to New York in the spring. The friend, E. G. W. Russell of *The Delineator*, one of the better magazines of the time, agreed, and he would often report on them to the Mielziners: "The boys are wonderful—almost too well bred. Everything I give them to eat is Joe's 'favorite dish' and everything we do, Leo assures me, is 'lovely.'" Russell took them on a whirlwind tour of London, including a stop at the zoo to see Joe's beloved elephants, before leaving with them for America.

In 1909, when the boys finally touched American soil, Leo Jr. was almost ten and Joe just eight years old. In September, the reunited family moved to an apartment in New York at 204 West 70th Street, and began their new life.

Although Joe Mielziner was a child of seven when he left Paris, he retained a sentimental attachment to it for the rest of his life. It became his spiritual home and when he was an adult there was hardly a year that he did not return to the city of his birth for a kind of psychic renewal. New York, on the other hand, was where he wanted to live and work and where he wanted to die. Whatever temptations he may have had when he was older to move out of New York for even short periods to a university campus, he shook off. From childhood, little Joe's life seemed to flow with the city. He grew up with it in the twentieth century, marched to its tempo, and became part of it

Leo Jr. and Joe were immediately enrolled at P. S. 87 on West 78th Street and were plunged headlong into the realities of New York City life. On their first day, Ella dressed them in their Eton suits and sent them off to school. When they returned home, their suits were in serious disarray, as were their faces. Ella sent them back the next day in more suitable clothes, but nothing really helped the boys, with their strange accents, British overlaid on French, and their sissy ways, which made them the target of their schoolmates. The Mielziner boys knew cricket and rugby but were not acquainted with baseball and American sports. Little Joe was once beaned by a hardball thrown by one of his teammates during a game at recess and was knocked unconscious, much to the glee of his peers.

They were also not faring well academically. The boys may have learned gentlemanly deportment at the English schools but it was

AFTER JOE AND LEO JR. ARRIVED IN AMERICA, THEY WERE WHISKED OFF TO NEW HAMPSHIRE FOR THEIR FIRST TASTE OF AMERICAN LIFE. (ESTATE OF JO MIELZINER)

JOE MIELZINER SHOWED TALENT AT AN EARLY AGE AND WAS ENCOURAGED BY HIS FATHER TO SKETCH AT EVERY OPPORTUNITY. HIS DRAWINGS AT MID-CHILDHOOD SHOW A WITTY, QUITE SOPHISTICATED CARTOON QUALITY. (BILLY ROSE THEATRE COLLECTION, NYPL-PA)

soon apparent that they had not learned arithmetic and spelling and knew next to nothing about the history of their own country. It was not a happy time for the Mielziner boys and it became obvious to their parents that something had to be done.

Through Leo's increasing clientele in the world of prosperous New York Jews, he found out about the Ethical Culture School, which also chanced to be an easy walk from West 70th Street to Central Park West. Another happy coincidence was that the founder and director of the school, Dr. Felix Adler, had been a student of Rabbi Moses Mielziner. Founded in 1878 as a Free Kindergarten, the school began to add grades yearly until it encompassed education from elementary to high school. Its avowed purpose was ethical but nonsectarian. It appeared to provide a perfect fit for the Mielziner boys.

Early in 1910, Leo applied to the school for his sons, requesting scholarship aid. Without a steady contribution from Ella, the family's income fluctuated wildly and was wholly dependent on Leo's portrait commissions, as much as $1,000 for an oil. One of the school representatives, checking into the family background, visited his studio and reported it to be a modest one. The children were placed on half tuition. (Full tuition for Joe in the third grade was $170 and for Leo Jr., in the sixth grade, $200.) For both boys, the Ethical Culture School was a vast improvement over P. S. 87 and the family breathed more easily.

After completing the eighth grade, Joe was placed in the school's newly created experimental "arts high school" program. Reminiscing years later, he wrote: "Prior to that year, I was academically a complete failure, my grades were all below freezing. My school day thoughts and attention were all turned to the joys of painting in which craft I was at that time well advanced beyond my years. The moment my science class took up the subject of color, and history became art, my whole school life changed. The grades went from 0° to temperate, if not tropical levels."

Leo Jr. left Ethical Culture in November of 1915 just after he began his third year in high school. Whether he became disaffected with the school or wanted to get out into the world—or whether the family finances were so strained that it was impossible for him

to continue—is not known. He took a course in the "theory and practice of internal combustion engines" and worked for the next two years in a machine shop while taking courses at New York University. Then he went to work in a shirt and a tie for Kuhn, Loeb, one of the pioneering Jewish investment firms on Wall Street, through the benevolence of Felix Warburg. In April of 1918, he appeared in a bill of one-act plays for the Sunday Evening Clubs of the Ethical Culture Society. He not only acted in Lord Dunsany's *The Lost Silk Hat,* but he also directed it and designed the scenery. It was possibly at one of these performances that the prominent actress Grace George saw the young actor and carried the news of him home to her husband, the even more prominent Broadway producer, William Aloysius Brady.

Leo Sr., with two children in private schools and rent to pay on a studio and an apartment, was rounding up as many commissions for portraits as he could handle. Although they were not particularly lucrative, the charcoal sketches that he made of celebrities on commission from magazines and newspapers were probably the most enjoyable for him. In 1908, a few months before his family arrived, the *New York Herald* sent him up to Mark Twain's home in Redding, Connecticut, to do a sketch to be reproduced in the newspaper. After he finished, Twain looked at the picture and was pleased. Thirty years before, he had been sketched by Abbott Thayer, a well-known portraitist of the time, who gave him a nose that looked like a banana. He thanked Leo for not giving him a banana.

During his lifetime, Leo was to paint (or draw) four presidents from life, justices of the supreme court, politicians, and contemporary celebrities such as General Pershing, Thomas Edison, Alexander Graham Bell, Wilbur Wright, John D. Rockefeller, and J. P. Morgan, signing his pictures with a soft-sided curved triangle within which he inserted his initials "L M." But the bulk of his clientele came from the well-to-do Jewish families both in New York and Cincinnati, who would open up doors for him to other commissions. Felix Warburg became Leo's New York Lorenzo de' Medici. In one of Leo's down periods, the financier sent a check for $1,000 for a portrait of his daughter, which must have been a gesture of pure philanthropy. Since Warburg's wife was a Schiff, Leo was passed on to the Schiff family and from them to other families.

Leo might have had a lucrative career as a society portrait painter, but did not have the temperament for it. When his son Joe in later years was able to stand back and assess his father, he described him as "charmingly indolent." Leo found greater satisfaction in baking a loaf of fine bread or preparing a *galantine de veau* for dinner guests than in working on a portrait for a rich client. But Leo's indolence was more a lack of any great ambition to achieve a mark in life at the sacrifice of life's simple pleasures. He secretly confided to Ella that he hoped that their sons would not be so afflicted. They were not.

No matter how poor they were, the Mielziners managed to escape New York in the summer months. They usually went to Maine or New Hampshire, and lived in makeshift quarters or "camps," which in New England terms can mean anything from a simple shack with canvas sides to a substantial house with all the amenities. During the summer of 1915, with start-up money borrowed from Leo's brother Benjamin, the Mielziners ran a boys' camp, Camp Saltspray in West Point, Maine, on the shores of Casco Bay, with Leo Jr. and Joe serving as camp assistants and Ella as camp mother. Leo mailed out a description of Camp Saltspray to names he culled from the rolls of the Ethical Culture School. He promised to provide a rugged outdoor camp life with an ethical and cultural program. For this and more, they charged $200 for a period from June 13 to September 1.

There is no indication that the Mielziners profited from this venture, but it gave them an entire summer away from New York at little cost to them. For one of their campers, a nine-year-old named James Rorimer, it was the event that helped to shape his life. Many years later, in 1955, when James Rorimer became director of the Metropolitan Museum of Art, culminating a life as one of the foremost curators in America, he traced the beginnings of his interest in the world of art to the Mielziner family camp during the summer of 1915.

The Mielziners did a great deal of moving about the city in those pre- and postwar days. Because Ella was anxious to move out of West 70th Street, Leo found a larger apartment in a "model tene-

ment" at 441 West 28th Street, where they remained until 1917, when the family moved to Greenwich Village, first to West 12th, then to West 10th Street, and finally to 47 Washington Square South, where Ella and Leo remained for many years. The Village was the happiest milieu for both of them. Ella enjoyed its bohemianism and Leo was close to his artist friends and the Salmagundi Club on lower Fifth Avenue, which became his second home.

Although neither she nor Leo Sr. had attended a college or university, Ella expected her sons to be educated. Her disappointment in Leo Jr.'s decision to leave school was compounded by Joe's withdrawal from Ethical Culture's arts high school after his first year. Joe, who had shown an astonishing precocity in drawing and painting under his father's tutelage, was now proposing to leave home and study art at the age of sixteen. Ella could not resign herself to what she thought would be a duplication of Leo's life of struggle and financial distress as an artist. If Joe had to go into art, she hoped he would land some sort of commercial context that would provide him with a decent livelihood.

Joe may have wished to study art abroad, but because the war was on in Europe, he looked to his best options in the States. Without a high school diploma, he would not have been admitted

to any of the universities with good art departments, so he submitted his best art work to the Pennsylvania Academy of the Fine Arts in Philadelphia, the oldest and probably the most prestigious art school of its day. It prided itself on giving instruction that was "fully equal from a technical standpoint to that obtainable in Europe." Joe's obvious talent earned him a scholarship to the school and he moved to Philadelphia early in December of 1917 to study art full time.

Most of his day was taken with classes in drawing and painting, decorative painting, costume sketching, and color and composition. Most, if not all, of the instructors were themselves products of the Academy and although many had studied abroad, the position of the school was distinctly traditional. Joe's favorite was Henry Bainbridge McCarter, who had spent five years studying under the nineteenth-century American painter Thomas Eakins. At the age of twenty-three, "Mac" went to Paris and fell in love with Impressionism and abandoned the Eakins academic style. His paintings exhibited a skill in manipulating light with color, and as he grew older, the colors in his landscapes became more and more brilliant.

In addition to classes, the students at the Academy were required to attend the exhibitions drawn not only from the school's art collections but also from traveling and loaned exhibitions in its galleries. They needed no encouragement to visit the other rich collections within Philadelphia's environs. Students were also taken on trips to rural areas to draw and paint the landscapes and were required to sketch city life and zoo animals. But it was not all work and no play for Joe. From time to time, he and his fellow students were invited to dances at private girls' schools in the area and Joe occasionally spent a Saturday or a Sunday as a guest at the home of one of girls he had met. In a long rambling letter home, he described the boisterous carousing of some of his schoolmates and decided that overindulgence in drink was "disgusting."

During his first term at the Pennsylvania Academy, Joe did very well in his art classes, adjusted nicely to his new surroundings and made many friends. But upon America's entry into the war, he begged his parents to allow him to contribute to the war effort in some way. Ella had taken it into her head that he should try to get into the University of Pennsylvania as an extension student, but instead Joe wanted to join several of the boys at the Academy who had gone down to Hog Island, where the American International Shipbuilding Corporation was building ships for the war effort. He told Ella and Leo that he could make $3.85 per day at Hog Island and would be able to save up enough money to pay for his tuition, room, and board for the fall term.

With his parents' permission, he landed a job at Hog Island and was put to work painting steel plates for the ships. It is doubtful that anyone took him really seriously. His boyish good looks made him appear even younger than his seventeen years. Moreover, Joe always carried a sketch pad with him. Although he had asked and received permission from one of his superiors to make sketches, he was ordered one day to report to the office immediately, where his pad was confiscated and he was questioned by the military personnel and secret service men assigned to American International. His inquisitors were polite and were probably surprised by this pink-cheeked youth, but he was nonetheless detained for several hours while they decided what to do with him. He was released and escorted to the train to go home, and was told that he was "damned lucky" not to have been put in the jailhouse for the night. The following day he returned to the yard and was warned not to sketch again. They did not return his drawings.

Letters from home that summer of 1918 brought the news that Leo Jr. was desperately trying to get into the Army Tank Corps, but could not pass the rigorous physical for that type of service. He finally enlisted in the Army in August and was sent to Fort Slocum, New York, for basic training. When it was discovered that he could type, he was quickly assigned as company clerk and his dreams of going overseas with the Tank Corps were almost dashed. Eventually, after much persistence, he received a clean bill of health from the company doctor and transferred to Camp Colt in Gettysburg, Pennsylvania, on the eve of the November 11th Armistice. A few months later, he was discharged from the Army, having received a promotion to corporal approved by his commanding officer, Lt. Colonel Dwight D. Eisenhower of the Tank Corps.

After his brother's enlistment, Joe put pressure on Leo and Ella to allow him to enlist. He would not be eighteen until March of

1919, when he was convinced the war would probably be over. Perhaps, because they were encouraged by the turn of events in Europe, they relented and signed the necessary papers to allow him to enlist. In October of 1918, within a few weeks of the signing of the Armistice, Joe was on his way to Parris Island, South Carolina, for boot training with the United States Marine Corps. His early letters home were full of enthusiasm for Marine life. Within a few days of military service, he fell victim to the pernicious flu of 1918–19 and landed in the hospital for a few weeks, followed by confinement in his barracks for recuperation for several more weeks. Life on that flat island lost its charm as he had to combat his illness, the heat, humidity, bugs, and boredom, but he never lost his enthusiasm for military training. Joe's career in the Marines lasted six months. After basic training, he was put on prison guard duty. His regiment, the Sixth Marines, was sent overseas without him, and Joe was discharged in April 1919.

He went back to New York to ponder his next move. When his brother Leo Jr. rejoined the family after his military discharge, he, too, was at loose ends until Felix Warburg came to the rescue and rehired him as a clerk at Kuhn, Loeb. Of all the Mielziners, only Leo Jr. had a head for business and probably could have prospered in a Wall Street career, but his interest in the stage fostered by his parents turned him away from a potentially lucrative career. When he had an opportunity to become an assistant to Broadway producer Winthrop Ames on a show that Ames was mounting, he left Kuhn, Loeb to take it. Unfortunately, his continued employment with Ames hinged on the fate of the show, which flopped quickly. He might have gone back to Kuhn, Loeb, had not fate and William A. Brady intervened.

Remembering Leo Jr. as an attractive young actor in amateur productions, Grace George, Brady's wife, called to ask him whether he would be interested in a part in *At 9:45*, a mystery play in production by her husband. (His answer was never in doubt.) Brady signed the young actor to a three-year contract and Leo Jr. was given a featured role. The play was written by Owen Davis, one of Broadway's most prolific playwrights of the time, and a member of Brady's stable. It tried out in Atlantic City before moving to Brady's

Playhouse Theatre on Broadway on June 28, 1919. (One of the other members in the cast was a pretty young ingenue named Nedda Harrigan.) The play, a standard murder mystery of no great importance, had a relatively successful run (for those days) of 139 performances, but more important, it launched Leo's career under the management of one of Broadway savviest producers.

Leo Sr. was inordinately pleased that his son was using his given name in his professional acting debut, but his joy was short-lived. Producer Brady told his young actor that the name Leo Mielziner Jr. was a big stretch for a marquee and to come up with something with a theatrical ring to it. After conferring with Ella, he took her

suggestion to use a matronymic. He chose her mother's maiden name McKenna and on his own added Kenneth as a first name because of its alliteration. Adding an "a" to Mc, he was transformed into Kenneth MacKenna, promising young juvenile of Broadway. His family slipped easily into the new appellation and he was "Kenneth" or "Ken" to them and to everyone else for the rest of his and their lives.

Joe, after spending part of the summer of 1919 with Ella, who was staying with friends in Maine and New Hampshire, applied for admission to the National Academy of Design School at the end of September. Founded in 1825 by a group of New York artists, the immediate purpose of the National Academy was to give young artists a place to study. For the next few months, Joe was able to live at home, taking the subway to the school while he continued his art training.

Among his classmates at the National Academy were Moses Soyer, Maxwell Simpson, and Robert Philipp. Joe seems to have been an active and well-liked member of his class, both socially and academically, and was regarded as a studious and serious art student. The ingenuity that he was later to display as Jo Mielziner, the scene designer, was in evidence at this early stage. The decorations designed by the students for the school's annual "Bal Masqué" were used as an exercise in composition class, the purpose being to enlarge the designs for actual use in the wall panels. Classmate Robert Bolton's sketch was done entirely with a five-inch French curve, a drawing instrument used by draftsmen to make irregular curves. Joe's assignment was to enlarge the drawing to six by twelve feet. His solution was to take the five-inch French curve downtown to have it made into a five-foot "solar print" enlargement. He then carefully glued the outline of the enlarged curve onto a piece of cardboard, cut it out with a razor blade, making an exact, oversized replica of the small French curve, with which he copied the original drawing to exact scale. According to Bolton, the scheme worked flawlessly.

In the 95th Annual Exhibition of the student works at the National Academy, Joe's paintings drew enthusiastic comments from art critics and several sold. But despite his success there and although he enjoyed the National Academy, he decided to resume his studies at the Pennsylvania Academy for the 1920 spring term.

Whenever he was at home in New York, he and his father had long discussions about art and artists. Leo was anxious to sharpen his son's critical faculties and was pleased with many of Joe's acute assessments. Leo's involvement with the various artists' groups in New York led to friendships with George Bellows, Edward Hopper, John Sloan, and less prominent artists, most of whom then lived or had their studios in Greenwich Village at one time or another. The Mielziners entertained their artist friends and were entertained by them, and Joe met many contemporary artists.

Early in 1921, he was invited by George Bellows to talk about art in his Greenwich Village studio. The session so stimulated him that when he returned to the Academy in the spring, he was able to complete a term's work in a few weeks. His diligence at the easel was rewarded. He won the Faculty Prize for his painting, but more important, in the spring of 1921, he was awarded one of the school's most coveted prizes, the Cresson Traveling Scholarship. The scholarships of $500 each gave students the opportunity for travel and study in Europe for four months during the fall term.

For the summer, Joe was persuaded by Kenneth to go to Detroit for a summer stock job with Jessie Bonstelle's theatrical company. The Bonstelle Stock Company played in Detroit for the summer and in Buffalo and elsewhere for the rest of the year. Whenever she was in town, Jessie used Bill Brady's offices to conduct her business, an arrangement that made it very convenient for Brady's stable of actors to find work during Broadway's summer doldrums. Kenneth was signed for the 1921 summer season as her lead juvenile. He told Miss Bonstelle about his talented brother who had designed the scenery for the Pennsylvania Academy's annual student dramatic frolic but little else. At this moment in his life, Joe still intended to be an artist, but was listening to Ella's and Kenneth's repeated urging to forsake pure art in favor of scene design. He took the job in Detroit at the usual summer stock pittance, but intended to use the opportunity to see how things worked backstage with a professional company. His duties encompassed a little bit of everything, but primarily he was to assist a man named Lou Bromberg, the scene designer, and to help build and paint the sets. He also acted a bit, assisted in stage managing, swept the stage a

JOE'S CLASS AT THE NATIONAL ACADEMY OF DESIGN IN NEW YORK, 1919. IT INCLUDED SUCH BUDDING ARTISTS AS ROBERT PHILIPP AND MOSES SOYER, AND MANY OTHERS WHO EVENTUALLY MADE NAMES FOR THEMSELVES IN FINE OR COMMERCIAL ART. THE INSTRUCTOR WAS CHARLES COURTNEY CURRAN, TOP ROW, CENTER; JO IS SEATED AT FAR RIGHT IN THE FRONT ROW. (COURTESY OF ROBERT BOLTON)

lot, and even got a chance to design one set. Above all, he learned a lot about the process of stage production from Bonstelle.

Although Bonstelle was fiftyish and slightly pot-bellied, she always played the leads in the plays produced by the company, from Mis' Nelly of N' Orleans to Peter Pan, and directed herself in quite a few of them. She assembled solid young performers, many of whom went on to much greater glory than she ever achieved. Katharine Cornell and Guthrie McClintic were Miss Bonstelle's "graduates," as were Josephine Hull, Melvyn Douglas, and William Powell. During the summer of 1921, Frank Morgan, Walter Abel,

and Edith Meiser were in the company, as was a pretty ingenue named Sylvia Field. Edith Meiser remembered that the dressing rooms for actors playing the lesser roles were located on the third floor backstage under the roof of the theatre, where, without air conditioning, the temperature would melt the greasepaint from their faces. When the young male actors were not on stage, they were in the habit of stripping down to the skin. Joe quickly put a stop to that practice with a sign he painted and put up on the walls: "No nudity in the presence of ladies." Edith Meiser also remembered how attractive were the Mielziner brothers, each in his own way. Kenneth looked Nordic with blonde hair and blue eyes, while Joe was darker haired and green-eyed, with a slight Mediterranean cast

to his features. Both were romancing Sylvia Field at the same time in brotherly competition, but no one doubted their devotion to each other. Although Joe did not complete the entire summer season, the company threw a party for him when he left to go on his Cresson travels. It was a memorable and important summer for him.

In August, Joe sailed for Europe to begin his studies in Paris and to be reintroduced to the city. What he had remembered of it, he had seen with a child's eyes. Now he could drink in all of its grace and charm with the eyes of an artist. He was enthralled. He moved into a boarding house at 14, rue Bernard-Palissy, which also housed seven of his fellow academicians. Their landlady was Madame Pons, who happily served as den mother to her American charges. Although his time was his own to do with as he pleased, he was expected to participate in parlor discussions with his schoolmates and accumulate a body of work to show his instructors in Philadelphia. His $500 scholarship had to cover not only his passage to and from Europe but all of his expenses, including art supplies. France, as indeed all of Europe, was in the grip of an exploding inflation and he had to manage his money as carefully as he could. Most of his time was taken up with exploring the museums in and around Paris. His companion around town was a fellow student and southerner, Weeks Hall, who lived, when he was not away at school, in one of the last family-owned antebellum plantations in Louisiana. By the following February, when it was time to leave, Joe was determined to try again for another Cresson, so that he could return to Europe for another tour.

During the spring term at the Pennsylvania Academy, Joe won one of the most prestigious prizes the school offered, the Thouron Prize in composition. Inspired by McCarter's evident interest in him in composition class and fired by his experiences in Paris, his work in final term had placed him on the school's honor roll. He won his second Cresson scholarship and joyfully anticipated not only his trip abroad in the fall but a summer working at Joseph Urban's scene studio, where he knew he would further immerse himself in the process of creating scenery from the ultimate professional in the business.

To get to Urban's studio, Joe had to take a train to Yonkers, where the huge facility was located. Urban had bought and converted an abandoned ice-skating rink into a scenery shop so that he had the space for his painters to work on the floor, rather than on scaffolding precariously lifted to the rafters of a building, which was the prevailing American practice. After the canvas was painted, the workmen would cut out sections to nail to frames to form flats and scenery pieces, a process in reverse order from the American custom, which was to apply the canvas to the wood frames, then paint it. Paints, lumber, netting, canvas, and other supplies were stored in the vast basement beneath the street floor, where there were also showers for the workers. To the original contingent of Viennese artisans, carpenters, and painters he had brought over with him, Urban had recruited other workers from Austria and hired students and apprentices (like Joe) to complete his staff. In an annex next to the studio, Urban installed a kitchen and dining room and fed good, hot Viennese fare, washed down with a little wine, for the entire staff every day. It was a beehive of activity that never ceased a moment during its two decades of life.

Urban and his seasoned staff had an unvarying routine. After the master had completed the designs and finished drawings, they would be translated into scale drawings, from which models would be made to exact measurements for any necessary adjustments, then the final shop drawings would be prepared for the construction crew once everything had been approved. Urban himself supervised every detail of the construction and the painting of the sets, which were then trucked to the theatre where he would oversee the setting up of the scenery and specify the lighting. He wanted no mishaps or surprises when the scenery was ready for the first technical and dress rehearsals. Urban provided Joe with a model of preparation that he absorbed for future use.

Joe's job at the studio was to assist in stretching the canvas and priming it for painting by the craftsmen. His apprenticeship was hard work that required young arms, strong muscles, and stamina. Working with the German-speaking artisans, he picked up a little German that he could use in his planned visit to Vienna in the fall. His one-on-one discussions with Urban were stimulating, and the designer was good enough to provide him not only with suggestions about study in Vienna but also with the address of his mother. With

his thoughts now seriously leaning toward a career in scene design, Joe packed and left New York in mid-September of 1922 for Europe.

His first stop was again Paris. After a week spent visiting museums and collections and a few old friends of his family, he took the train to Vienna, where his friend from the Academy, Ed Beegle, had found himself and Joe rooms at Neulinggasse 13.

Joe arrived in Vienna in early October and settled in to explore its art and to take classes at the Kunstgewerbeschule (art school) in scene design. The early modernist movement in Vienna had encompassed architecture and industrial and decorative design and spread to Germany, where its most prominent offshoot was that of the Bauhaus, the school associated with architect Walter Gropius. Viennese modernism influenced theatre art in design, production, and playwriting. It was here that Max Reinhardt had arrived in 1922 to take over the Redoutensaal, a ballroom within an eighteenth-century Viennese landmark palace, which he turned into a theatre without benefit of a proscenium arch or front curtain. With only a platform backed by a curved screen, Reinhardt and his designer Alfred Roller staged intimate dramas and chamber operas using simple screens and small props. Later Reinhardt took over the Josefstadt Theatre, where he produced a broader repertory and more elaborate scenery with another designer, Oskar Strnad, within a traditional structure.

When Joe arrived in Vienna, the theatre season had not yet begun, which allowed him to concentrate on his work with Professor Strnad at the Kunstgewerbeschule. He found his instructor interesting and technically proficient and was also impressed that Strnad believed that the focus of dramatic production should be on the actors and not on the scenic artist. Joe was assigned to create scenery for Shaw's *Androcles and the Lion* and make complete and detailed scale drawings, floor plans, and studies for lighting and cast grouping. He wrote home and asked Ella to send him art supplies, which he found hugely expensive and scarce in Vienna. (He reported that a good paint box cost one million kroners.)

An actors' strike closed the Viennese theatres and it snowed continuously for two weeks, which kept him largely housebound. Without classes and unable to move about, he used the time to fall in love

with Lillian Gaertner, a fellow student at the Kunstgewerbeschule, with whom he spent almost the entire two weeks, to the discomfort of her chaperone, a proper Viennese *Hausfrau*. His passion was not so grand that he did not bid her farewell when the propitious moment arrived to continue his travels. He assured his parents that he was able to lose his heart "without losing that equally vital organ, my head." (Gaertner later worked for Joseph Urban's studio and became a costume designer for the Metropolitan Opera Company.)

When Beegle was refused a visa to Germany, Joe went alone to Berlin. To him, Berlin was an unfriendly city where *Ausländers* were treated very badly. He was also conscious of a rampant anti-Semitism in the air. He wrote his parents that the prices of everything were instantly jumped whenever a foreigner bought anything—from an admission ticket to a museum or a meal. Even though he was paying four thousand marks (about $10) a day for his cramped and unheated room and his money was running low, he decided to stick it out for the planned ten days. He immediately got tickets to the most interesting productions in the city. Once he began attending the Berlin theatres, he decided that what he saw was worth enduring the uncomfortable atmosphere. The first production he attended was the Reinhardt production of *Hamlet* with Germany's leading actor, Alexander Moissi, in the title role. Although he appreciated Moissi's acting technique, he found fault with his interpretation of the Dane as a weak and bitter man, and with Reinhardt's staging:

> In Reinhardt's use of the podiums (platforms and steps of hollow construction) [he] defeats his purpose in constructing plastic sets which so obviously sound hollow and unreal and take away any real feel of the solid plastic set. Every movement of an actor is accompanied with the hollow sound of his footsteps. Particularly in the case of the Ghost, it irritated me. Such small problems are to my mind very essential in the general effect to be produced.

He got tickets for Reinhardt's *Orpheus in the Underworld*, Leopold Jessner's *Macbeth*, and a production of *Liliom*, and sent home tiny thumbnail sketches of the sets, using the training of his father's eye memory to reproduce them on paper after each performance. Of all that he saw, he was most impressed by Jessner's productions.

Joe returned to Paris for a few weeks back at Madame Pons's. He was again shocked at the inflation, which had further increased just a few months after his initial visit. He did a quick accounting and discovered that his stays in Vienna and Berlin had cost a good deal more than he had anticipated, but by planning carefully and staying away from bookstores (the one luxury he had permitted himself) he could probably squeeze the funds for his trip to Rapallo, Italy, to visit Gordon Craig. He read Craig's books in preparation for his trip and caught the 24-hour third-class train to Italy for a few days with Craig. After walking miles to Craig's villa, he could not rouse anyone with his door-knocking and was afraid that his trip was all in vain. Finally, a boy answered the door and asked him in English what he wanted. When he explained his mission, he was told to wait. Finally, Craig appeared and questioned him closely. Satisfied with Joe's answers, he talked to him for hours, inviting him to spend the night at the villa. When, later, it became fashionable among critics and scenic artists to belittle Craig on the grounds that his designs were "impractical, undisciplined and unrelated to the actual proportions and conditions of the theatre," Joe affirmed that Craig's soaring imagery and his poetic flights "raised the vision of our drama" beyond the realm of canvas and wood.

Returning to New York by way of Paris early in February, Joe had a brief reunion with his family and then went back to Philadelphia to finish the spring term at the Academy. After that, he rejoined his parents, who were spending the summer in a cottage in Crugers, a Hudson River resort in Westchester County that offered an escape mostly for Jewish families from the city. In the fall, Joe returned to Philadelphia to complete his education at the Pennsylvania Academy, whereupon, at the age of twenty-two, he considered himself an accomplished painter and draftsman, well-trained and well-read, but with no personal message. Meanwhile, he had a living to earn. Kenneth, with Ella's backing, was pushing him toward a career in theatrical set designing. All he needed was a little luck.

LEO SR., KENNETH (NÉ LEO JR.), AND JO, POSED BEFORE A PORTRAIT OF KENNETH THAT WAS TO BE INCLUDED IN AN EXHIBITION OF LEO'S WORK IN 1928. (ESTATE OF JO MIELZINER)

2
APPRENTICESHIP

Back in New York, Joe faced the future with the help of his family. It was his brother Kenneth who assumed the role in Joe's life that his parents, particularly his father, should have played. From the time he was a small child, Kenneth was conscious that his mother was constantly economizing on the necessities and trying to squeeze out what luxuries she could afford on Leo's erratic income. Kenneth wanted more than the necessities and his ambitions included his brother. For the rest of his life, Kenneth was a major force in directing Joe's career and there was probably no one whom Joe respected more than his brother.

Joe's total preparation for launching himself into the theatre consisted of a bit of academic training in Vienna and a bit more technical and practical experience with Joseph Urban's studio and Jessie Bonstelle's stock company, his reading of the works of Appia and Craig, and his first-hand observations of the New Stagecraft both in Europe and America. Although Strnad had put him through the paces in the mechanics of scene design in such practices as the drafting of floor plans, building and painting plans (elevations), and the rest of the drawing-board preparation, he had been, on the whole, disappointed in his experience at the Kunstgewerbeschule.

OPPOSITE: MODEL OF MIELZINER'S FIRST SET (ASSEMBLED BY MING CHO LEE), DESIGNED FOR JESSIE BONSTELLE'S DETROIT SUMMER SEASON AT THE GARRICK THEATRE, 1921. JOE GOT HIS CHANCE TO DESIGN A SHOW HALFWAY THROUGH THE SEASON, PROBABLY ***THE SIGN ON THE DOOR*** BY CHANNING POLLOCK. HE ADMITTED LATER THAT THE BOLD COLORS AND STRONG DESIGN OF THE SET OVERPOWERED THE ACTORS. THE ANCIENT SYMBOL HE USED IN THE DESIGN WAS TO BECOME THE INFAMOUS SWASTIKA OF THE THIRD REICH. (ESTATE OF JO MIELZINER)

Joe's apprentice work at the Urban studio in Yonkers had left him with no great feeling for the design work that was produced there. Although he considered Urban a brilliant technician, he did not admire his "candy-box-cover art," however skillfully achieved. But he had carefully observed enough of Urban's methods to realize how and what could be accomplished by well-trained craftsmen working from thoroughly conceived plans and on relatively generous budgets.

In sharp contrast, his exposure to Jessie Bonstelle's scene shop grinding out a different set every week on the barest of budgets with limited time and materials had shown him what could be done with imagination and ingenuity. He was also aware that his maiden effort as a scene designer had been dreadful. Called upon to design an Oriental screen denoting an atmosphere of wealth and taste onto the dingy gray walls of a typical stock company interior setting, he created a gigantic dragon in black and vermilion against a gold background in the center of the upstage wall of the set. When he first saw it from out front, he was appalled by what it did to the actors, who seemed to shrink in size before it. The local critics praised the setting as a cut above the usual at Bonstelle's, but Joe knew differently. He felt as if he had committed a crime against the theatre and all humanity.

Joe considered that his most significant preparation for a career in scene design was his own observation of theatrical productions in Europe. While he was in Paris, the Moscow Art Theatre had just arrived and Joe got a ticket in the cheapest section at the back of the house for their first performance. Unfortunately, the boxcar containing the scenery and costumes was lost in one of the Paris railroad yards, and Stanislavsky, the theatre's great artistic leader, appeared before the curtain and explained in flawless French that the company would have to perform without scenery, props, costumes, or special lights. He asked the audience to be patient. When the curtains parted, a man came out and lit a single candle on a small wooden table. Two actors followed him. They sat down on kitchen chairs and began to play a dramatized scene from *The Brothers Karamazov.* Even from his seat at the rear of the auditorium, Joe could see and hear perfectly. The experience taught him that less was sometimes

more in lighting the stage as long as the actors moved to speak within its range. He was convinced by this experience that simplicity had its own truth on the stage, an idea he would never forget but was only infrequently allowed to put into practice in his long career.

Joe's greatest enthusiasm was reserved for the work of Leopold Jessner and his designer Emil Pirchan. Jessner's *Macbeth,* one of the last productions he saw before he left Berlin, astonished him. Jessner was considered an "Expressionist" director, who assaulted his audience with unrealistic and unsentimental visual symbols. To Jessner the theatre was an unreal place that should not be used to expose mundane living. As a director, he was so passionately fond of platforms and steps on the stage that *Jessnertreppen* (Jessner's steps) became a hallmark for all of his productions. Following Craig's dictates, he was totally in charge of every production down to the last nuance of acting, refusing to allow any impromptu bits of business by the actors. He used bold colors and colored lighting, shadows and mood lighting, neutral backgrounds, and simplified, suggested scenery. There was withal a great deal of artifice in all of his productions. Although Prussian politicians thought he gave English and German classical drama a leftist interpretation, which did not sit well with them, Jessner became the head of the Berlin State Theatre and was also director of the National School of Dramatics. Pirchan, his principal designer, became the agent of his vision, supplying the means through the scenery and lighting to achieve the director's results. For Joe, it represented the perfect collaboration between director and designer. He recorded his impressions of Jessner's *Macbeth* in his 1923 travel notes:

> Jessner knows so well the emotional value of color, sound, of three-dimensional form and of rhythm. His figures are always sculpturesque and definitely expressive in movement. His actor gestures with his whole body, because this is more significant than any facial expression, which might easily be lost in the weight and depth of Jessner's tremendous scene.
>
> Realizing the suggestive power of rhythmical sound and movement combined, he introduces into the witch scene an ominous,

pulsating sound accompanied by the howl of the wind, while the witches—simply three ghostly green twisting masses of light— vaguely outline by their radiance the figure of Macbeth in the background. Throughout the play the throbbing of this note re-occurs with growing intensity, culminating in the crisis of the murder. In the banquet scene which is simply reeking with horror, the rhythmical beating grows as Macbeth's conscience troubles him. The color too of this scene emphasizes his increasing feeling of guilt, the very walls of the banquet chamber glow more blood-red, and his cloak, scene by scene, becomes in its deepening crimson an actual symbol of his crime. In Jessner's use of the most primitive symbols lies his strength.

Thus, Joe, at the brink of his career, was an amalgam of vivid impressions and powerful theories from Europe plus his own half-formed ideas and insufficient training, but he was not unlike many incipient designers entering the field at the time. The New Stagecraft and its practitioners in America did not arise from the vanished nineteenth-century stock company system, which had provided the training ground for all of the theatrical craftsmen, beginning with apprentice work. A novice progressed to master scene painter or master carpenter or master machinist and took years to go from stage to stage, but at the end, the preparation produced experienced artisans and, more rarely, artists of the theatre. With the advent of the New Stagecraft designer, who did not expect to lift a hammer or handle a brush, these master artisans were downgraded to stagehands and technicians. Still, designers needed to make themselves responsible for knowing how the entire process worked.

The first generation of New Stagecraft designers, then, was academically educated rather than experientially trained within the professional theatre. Many were products of George Pierce Baker's famed "47 Workshop" in play production at Harvard; others came from newer theatre programs at universities, such as the Carnegie Institute of Technology in 1915, and many, like Joe, had training in the fine arts. From the twenties onward, the new generation of performers and directors entered the theatrical profession with a relatively high level of education but with a minimum of experience.

And for almost everyone, the ground was level, with talent, drive, and a little luck.

It was luck, talent, and a quick mind that lifted Kenneth MacKenna from amateur theatrics into the big time. Between 1919, when he started, and 1923, he had been in seven Broadway shows and had gone on the road with two of them. When his three-year contract with Bill Brady was up in 1922, he moved on to other producers and to the Theatre Guild. Along the way, he became known as a promising leading man, good-looking, personable, with the air of a college instructor. He read prodigiously, carefully analyzed the theatrical scene about him, and was ready to pull Joe along on his coattails.

He made it known to everyone that Joe was destined for a career in scene design, and introduced him to the up-and-coming members of his own theatrical generation, one of whom was Bill Brady Jr. Bill Sr. had yanked his son into show business after he had completed prep school and sent him on the road as manager of his touring companies. By the time he was twenty-three (in 1923) and after a tutelage under Jessie Bonstelle, Bill Jr. was directing some of his father's shows. But it was not enough for him; he wanted to follow in his father's footsteps as both producer *and* director. He launched his career with a production of *The Earthquake,* by Theodore Liebler. Joe was hired to do the scenery. The play, about the moral fallout after a catastrophic earthquake, opened on June 28, 1923, in Stamford, Connecticut, where it got a rave review from the local critic, who compared it to the work of Eugene O'Neill. It then proceeded to Long Branch, New Jersey, where it was seen by a critic from *Variety* and torn to shreds: "With the makeshift scenery, poor acting by recognized artists of skill, who were not wholly at blame, the play bearing the Brady endorsement was hailed as the worst ever on the sea coast." Needless to say, *The Earthquake* never reached Broadway.

Realizing that Joe was smarting from this initiation, Kenneth took him to the Theatre Guild offices, where he was rehearsing in the Guild's production of John Galsworthy's *Windows.* Joe was hired as assistant to Lee Simonson, the Guild's chief designer, and was also expected to stage-manage and take small roles, whenever necessary.

Kenneth thought the latter would imbue in Joe the feel of the stage from the actor's point of view. Aside from the bit parts he took for Jessie Bonstelle, the only other time Joe trod the boards was the spring of 1917, when he and his brother were in their teens. Answering a call for "supers" (the euphemism for "walk-ons" or extras was supernumeraries) for actor Robert Mantell's two-week season of Shakespearean plays, the boys went down to the 44th Street Theatre and got jobs. Years later, Joe recalled the experience to the producer Edgar Lansbury, who was Mantell's nephew: "The first time I ever set foot on the professional stage, I was showered during a four-minute scene by that great actor. His dramatic and articulate verbiage was generously lubricated by sputum." He received one dollar per performance and thoroughly enjoyed the experience. His only complaint was about the lack of laundry facilities for the tights that he had inherited, unwashed, from who-knows-how-many other wearings.

The Theatre Guild was still new when Joe went to work as general technical factotum for Simonson, who supervised the scene designers for all the Guild productions. Founded in the spring of 1919 by a group of young, inexperienced, well-intentioned Ivy-leaguers, the Guild began as a kind of theatrical commune. Most of

the early members had been involved in the Washington Square Players, a prewar amateur group that had originated in a Greenwich Village bookshop. Old Broadway hands considered them a bunch of well-off dilettantes with arty ideas and gave them a brief tenure on their turf. But precisely because of these reasons—combined with a missionary zeal to do something about the state of American theatre—they were able to succeed.

The first committee consisted of nine people, two of whom (Lawrence Langner, a patent attorney, and Maurice Wertheim, a banker) contributed $1,000 to begin their season. Otto Kahn, the renowned philanthropist and arts enthusiast, offered the Garrick Theatre, a worn-out playhouse on West 35th Street, at a minuscule rental for their early productions. Using scraps of scenery found at the Garrick and working with the cheapest of materials, Rollo Peters designed and built their first production, Jacinto Benavente's *The Bonds of Interest*, which was directed by Philip Moeller, another of the Guild's founders. Their second production, St. John Ervine's *John Ferguson*, succeeded beyond the Guild's expectations because, for a while, it was the only show in town. The Actors' Strike of 1919 had closed down Broadway, but not the little Garrick, where the Guild's credo of profit-sharing was in harmony with the ideals of the nascent actors' union. No pickets appeared on West 35th Street and the show did so well that the Guild decided to move it to the Fulton Theatre on Broadway. Indeed, taking their successes from the Garrick to Broadway became established custom for the Theatre Guild, until the entire operation moved uptown and swam in the mainstream.

When Joe joined the ranks, the Theatre Guild's board had been shaken down to six people and was managed by Theresa Helburn as Executive Director. Perhaps unrecognized by everyone at the time, the Theatre Guild was fast becoming the crucible of the future American theatre, and the time would come when American playwrights, including Eugene O'Neill, entrusted their new works' premieres to them.

Joe made lifelong friends among the Guild's company and even fell in love with one them, Winifred Lenihan. Besides following Lee Simonson around, he was assistant stage manager for Bernard Shaw's *Saint Joan*, while appearing onstage in both of them early in

the 1923 season. (It was at this moment that Joe became Jo, dropping the final "e" as the single concession to "going Broadway" with his name.) Lenihan, the object of his affections, was Brooklyn-born and Irish-American and was the first Shavian Saint Joan ever. A couple of years older than Jo, she was also a graduate of Jessie Bonstelle's stock company. She had picked up training at the American Academy of Dramatic Art before getting her break in the profession. As Saint Joan, she was described as a "wisp of a girl . . . [with] that frail loveliness which seems to be a part of the spiritual Irish type. . . ." In addition to her physical attractiveness, she was as smart as a whip, the type of woman to whom Jo was eternally attracted. (She later became the first director of the Theatre Guild's School of Acting, directed radio dramas, and performed. She eventually married and retired from the theatre.)

Jo's apprenticeship with Simonson may have been rather trying, for Simonson was given to fits of temperament, functioned best in a kind of mad disorder, and certainly did not follow the book as Jo had learned it under Joseph Urban. He jotted down floor plans first, then made preliminary drawings known as elevations, and infrequently got around to doing drawings of the full set known as "renderings." Nothing was ever really fixed in Simonson's plans. He was agreeable to last-minute changes when his scenery was being built in the scene shop and would accept suggestions from the craftsmen, if he liked their ideas. But he was also opinionated, high-strung, and caustic. When Jo Mielziner delivered a eulogy for him many years later, he recalled one vivid incident that conveyed Lee's personality.

> The period was the early '20s. The place, the old Garrick Theatre. The hour was late, very late, at night after some ten hours of intensive rehearsal. The production, the Theatre Guild's Man and the Masses [by Toller].
>
> The stage designer, and in this case, also the stage director, was making an 11th hour attempt to stimulate some vitality into an exhausted cast trying to do a final scene.
>
> Lee Simonson was pale with fatigue—his large expressive black eyes dilated—his commanding voice husky but vibrant and loud.

> He stood in the first row facing the stage. Behind him, his stage manager and his young apprentice both ready to make a dash for home after a long tiring rehearsal. In those days, the status symbols of a young man were pearl gray spats and the carrying of a walking stick.
>
> The stage manager afforded both symbols—the apprentice only a slim cane.
>
> Simonson now turned toward the stage again and said, "Now for the last time, let me feel some vitality and pace from each one of you!"
>
> The worn-out actors made a brave attempt—but not enough for this man. With arms wildly beating out an emphatic tempo, suddenly Simonson turned half around, grabbed the apprentice's cane and with a renewed, almost frenetic tempo—each downbeat brought the slender walking stick crashing on to the concrete forestage.
>
> By the time the finale was over, the stick was splintered into shreds.
>
> A pause—then the director said, "That's a bit better! Everyone here at eleven in the morning."
>
> Without another word, off he went out of the theater. The stunned apprentice looked at the remnants of his cane and followed the rest of the cast out into the night.
>
> On arrival at the Garrick the next morning, the apprentice found a delivery man with a long slender, elegantly wrapped box.
>
> On opening up the package, he found almost smothered in a dozen American Beauty roses an encased walking stick—not just a cane but a magnificent piece of Malacca, pigskin-bound handle, and gold-banded.
>
> A card engraved "Lee Simonson" was written in his minute but clear hand: "Keep up the good tempo."

Simonson was probably not a good director or teacher but he was a superb designer at his height and often a brilliant writer-theoretician. He believed that stage sets began with a ground plan, the arrangement of scenery within the limitations of space on stage, which are derived from the action of the play and movements of the actors, known as "blocking." Once the ground plan is approved by the director, the designer is free to create the picture for and around it. "The function of stage scenery, " he wrote, "is to help in creating that necessary reality of every production, to induce an audience, as soon as the curtain is up, to accept the world of the play and vicariously to live in it." Simonson considered himself a pragmatist. He was also an eclectic artist and, like Jones and Mielziner, was trained as a painter and had a painter's eye. There was always a decorative quality about his set designs, an unshakable sense of balance and a feeling of fluidity as his stage pictures appeared to move in concert with the actors. Simonson also helped to develop the modern concept of stage lighting. When the Guild took over the Garrick, it had almost no lighting equipment, but Simonson with the help of his stage electrician Michael O'Connor began to install in gradual stages a flexible lighting system that could supply the effects that the designer felt necessary. Simonson was also a pioneer in formulating the "light plot," a blueprint for the placement of lighting instruments and for supplying lighting cues. When the apprentice Jo had appeared onstage in *The Failures*, one of the productions designed by Simonson, he was presumably able to judge for himself the effectiveness of the designer's theories in practice.

Despite the low salary, Jo was working full-time for the Guild and enjoying the company of its dedicated group of young professionals. During his tenure at the Guild, he met the young, energetic salesman for the Display Lighting Company, Edward Kook. Jo and Eddie became fast friends and Kook became Jo's mentor in the exploration of the possibilities of light, teaching him how and what could be done for his sets through the evolving art of stage lighting.

Kenneth, on the other hand, had outgrown the Guild's opportunities for him and was cast in a leading role in a play titled *Nerves*, by Stephen Vincent Benét and John Farrar, which was to be Bill Brady Jr.'s virgin venture on Broadway. The cast also included Winifred Lenihan, Humphrey Bogart, Mary Phillips, and Paul Kelly. When Jo was signed to design the scenery, he had to bid farewell to Simonson and his comrades at the Theatre Guild for the sake of advancing his career.

The play was scheduled to open on September 1, 1924, along with six other productions on the same night. By the time many of the critics caught up with it, it had already closed. However, it was seen by the tart-tongued reviewer of the *New York Herald*, Alexander Woollcott. The play tells of a group of Yale graduates who go off to war as pilots after a first-act mad rush to get engaged to a bevy of lovely girls. Two of the young men are untidily in love with the same girl, but one (played by Kenneth) seems to be winning out. (Woollcott was mildly amused by its "musical comedy flavor" but professed to be startled by "one perilous scene when it looked as though the two Yale men might complete the picture by becoming engaged to each other.") In the second act, Kenneth rises above his "nerves" and performs a heroic act that costs him both his legs. Back home, it looks as if Kenneth will get the girl (Winifred Lenihan), when she sees his sacrifice, but he does the right thing and gives

NERVES (1924) WAS JO'S FIRST BIG BREAK ON BROADWAY. THE CAST: FIFTH FROM LEFT AND CONTINUING TOWARD THE RIGHT ARE PAUL KELLY, KENNETH MACKENNA, AND WINIFRED LENIHAN; AT EXTREME RIGHT ARE MARY PHILLIPS AND HER FUTURE HUSBAND HUMPHREY BOGART. (FOR HIS BROADWAY DEBUT AS A DESIGNER, JOE BECAME JO.) (BILLY ROSE THEATRE COLLECTION, NYPL-PA)

her up to his rival. Humphrey Bogart played Lenihan's brother and got the best notice of the show.

Jo's name as designer appeared inauspiciously only in the final credits of the program, not on the title page. Unfortunately, Bill Brady Jr., faced with a flop, was unable to pay Jo's fee. When Jo asked him for his money, he was given the same old refrain that the stage was a risky business and he had to be able to play the game as a gambler. When his situation became known to the stagehands on the show, they grabbed the RCA Victrola, which was used in the first act, and loaded it into a taxicab for him after the last performance. He installed his "payment" in the small apartment he and Kenneth were sharing on Waverly Place in Greenwich Village. It was the first of Jo's many experiences with the cunning of producers and the ingenuity of stagehands.

Undaunted by the failure of their play, Benét and Farrar submitted another effort, this time to Bill Jr.'s father, William Brady Sr. The play, *That Awful Mrs. Eaton,* was based on an incident of history concerning President Andrew Jackson's championing of the low-class wife of one of his cabinet members. Jessie Bonstelle, who had previously presented it with her company in Detroit, directed a cast of thirty-five on the stage of the Morosco Theatre—to no avail. The notices were poor, but Jo was singled out by the critic of the *Christian Science Monitor* for portraying the White House scenes in "faultless taste [which] gave much beauty and dignity to the play." For those who were in attendance after the first night, there were changes in the play and scenery. On Brady's orders, the lovely eighteenth-century chairs that Jo had rented for one of the important scenes, the President's cabinet meeting, were returned to save money. The removal of the chairs necessitated the removal of most of the dialogue in that scene and for the rest of the brief run, many actors played their lines standing up.

A few weeks after his second failure, Jo received a call from Lee Simonson of the Theatre Guild to ask whether he would be interested in designing a production of Ferenc Molnár's *The Guardsman,* which was to star Alfred Lunt and Lynn Fontanne. The Theatre Guild board was not optimistic about the comedy's chances of succeeding—it had been a failure years before under the title

WILLIAM A. BRADY SR. PRE-EMPTED HIS SON FROM THE PRODUCTION OF ***THAT AWFUL MRS. EATON*** **(1924)** TO PRESENT IT HIMSELF. SEEN HERE: (TOP), A WHITE HOUSE RECEPTION ROOM DURING ANDREW JACKSON'S FIRST TERM; (BOTTOM), THE TER-RACE OF MRS. JOHN C. CALHOUN'S HOME. ALL SKETCHES WERE DRAWN AND PAINTED IN VERY SMALL SCALE TO SUBMIT TO BRADY FOR APPROVAL. (*TOP:* HARVARD THEATRE COLLEC-TION, HOUGHTON LIBRARY; *BOTTOM:* W. H. CRAIN COLLECTION, UNIVERSITY OF TEXAS THEATRE ARTS COLLECTION)

LEE SIMONSON (1888–1967) TURNED THE DESIGN OF ***THE GUARDSMAN*** **(1924)** OVER TO JO MIELZINER, WHO EVOKED THE DECOR OF A NINETEENTH-CENTURY VIENNESE OPERA HOUSE, COVERING THE WALLS IN RED DAMASK WITH BLACK "MAR-BLE" TRIM. (ESTATE OF JO MIELZINER)

Where Ignorance Is Bliss—and were astounded when the rave reviews poured in after the opening on October 13, 1924. The critics were enchanted by the way Lunt and Fontanne interwove their performances into an ensemble of two, and the public embraced the unbelievable plot because the skill of the two actors made it credible. For five weeks it sold out at the Garrick, and was moved to the Booth Theatre, on West 45th Street, for an extended run. When it finally closed nearly nine months later, it had filled the Guild's coffers. After that, the Guild board decided to send the Lunts on the road in 1927 with a repertory of four plays. Jo was asked to redo the sets for the show and made another $500 for his troubles. When he toted up his earnings for 1924, he found that he had made $3,000.

With six more months to go in the theatrical season, Jo was engaged to design *Mrs. Partridge Presents*, to be produced and directed by Guthrie McClintic, a man who was destined to figure large in Jo's career. From the time McClintic left Seattle for New York to be an actor, his career was a study in persistence. Diverted from acting into what would be his true vocation as a director, he launched his own career by writing an angry letter to producer-director Winthrop Ames, demanding that he pay attention to him. Written after many rebuffs and rejections by producers and their underlings, the letter expressed the kind of frustration that besets many young people trying to find a wedge into a difficult profession. McClintic described himself as one of the young Americans " who feel that they have a place in the American theatre too." Impressed by the young man's boldness, Ames reacted by offering him a job in his organization, which gave McClintic the opportunity to observe how the great man worked. The patrician Ames was an anomaly among the rough and tough fraternity of early producers, but he enjoyed great success on Broadway and the respect of the theatrical community. The nervous McClintic tried to emulate Ames's imperious style of directing, but he lacked his cool temperament and equanimity and frequently boiled over into small thunderstorms of rage, which passed quickly. His career would mesh with that of a young actress he had met while both worked for Jessie Bonstelle in the very early twenties. Her name was Katharine Cornell.

Cornell was not made in the usual ingenue mode and was having a difficult time finding her place in the theatre. She was dark, strong-featured, attractive in an exotic sort of way, and somewhat boxy in figure. But in 1921, both she and McClintic suddenly made it big—he as producer and director of A. A. Milne's *Dover Road* (which Ames backed) and she in the part of the high-strung flapper in *A Bill of Divorcement*, who believes that she has inherited the taint of her family's insanity. It was the part of a lifetime. To top off their separate successes, they married while they were basking in critical acclaim. From that point on, their individual careers not only bloomed but were inextricably combined when Cornell decided to become her own producer (with her husband directing her shows, of course) in 1931. She endured as one of the few genuine Broadway stars of the thirties and forties.

Belonging to their generation and sharing their viewpoint on most things, Jo almost became a part of their entourage as their designer. Their professional relationship endured for twenty-five years. As his design collaborator, he found McClintic to be a man of strong opinions, but possessed of one of the keenest eyes for the visual that he ever worked with, and a sense of discipline that Jo learned from him. McClintic knew what he wanted and when he wanted it, but was always open to Jo's suggestions. Some of Jo's greatest triumphs as a designer were prepared for McClintic, which helped prove his theory that working with a strong and stimulating director could result in extraordinary stage settings. Between them, they built an almost ideal working relationship. Jo also knew that if he pleased McClintic, he was also pleasing Cornell, who tended to leave most of the details of her productions to her husband, but was canny enough to know that whatever Jo did enhanced her work.

Another successful partnership for Jo was with a group of actors who had originally organized in 1922 under the name Equity Players. Inspired by their triumph in the Actors' Strike of 1919 but still smarting from the treatment they suffered at the hands of the Broadway producers, about thirty or so launched their own producing cooperative to compete with them at their own game. The board of directors resembled a short Who's Who of the theatre of the time, and included the old and the new among its stars. George Arliss, Ethel Barrymore, Josephine Hull, Laurette Taylor, Roland Young, Blanche Yurka, John Drew, Jane Cowl, Edith Wynne Matthison, and Alfred Lunt were among its members. Dudley Digges, a "graduate" of the Theatre Guild, was artistic director, and Francis Wilson, the standard bearer of the actors in their fight to be recognized, was president.

The group changed their name to the Actors' Theatre after a few seasons, merging in 1926 with the fast-sinking Greenwich Village Theatre Company led by Kenneth Macgowan, who became artistic director of the combined groups. They managed to hang on for six seasons, producing an eclectic roster of old and new plays at the 48th Street Theatre, which they leased for their first few seasons until evicted by the landlord, William Brady Sr. Guthrie McClintic eventually replaced Macgowan as artistic director and hired Jo for three of their subsequent productions.

The Theatre Guild and the Actors' Theatre Players became a special showcase for Jo's talents and brought his apprentice years to an end. More and more, his work was catching the eye of the Broadway regulars. Yet, in the fall of 1925, Jo spent five months as assistant to Robert Edmond Jones. Although he had enjoyed working for Lee Simonson and learned much from his Theatre Guild experiences, he was slowly evolving a different creative ideology. With Jones, he forged a special bond. He had come to know him from his work on Broadway, from meeting him at Robert Bergman's studio on West 39th Street where Bobby had his office, and from his writings. In 1923, Jones, in collaboration with Macgowan, had written *Continental Stagecraft*, which detailed ten weeks of their travels in France, Sweden, Czechoslovakia, Germany, and Austria. Wherever they went, Jones would sketch the scenery they saw at the theatres. These plates, some of them in color, were reproduced to illustrate the text and they are in many ways works of art themselves.

Bobby's manner was genteel and his methods relaxed but thorough. Under a calm exterior, there was a steeliness about him that commanded respect; unlike Simonson, he would never have resorted to beating a walking stick to splinters to make a point, rather he would speak quietly but forcefully and at great length—very great length—to make sure that all of his points were understood. Jones loved to draw and paint and made intermediate sketches and experiments with color before he knew what he wanted. When he had decided what he wanted, he would usually produce a finished drawing that would show the figures of actors in the sets and the type of lighting he had in mind. In Jones's hands, ordinary scene renderings became works of art. The miracle was that the actual stage scenery always matched his original conceptions on paper.

Jones sketched all the time and from his penciled musings would emerge first the incipient design, then Jones's final ideas, which Jo had to translate into practical working plans and elevations for the carpenters and painters. When Jo was hired as his assistant, he discovered that Jones was drafting his own plans and elevations on

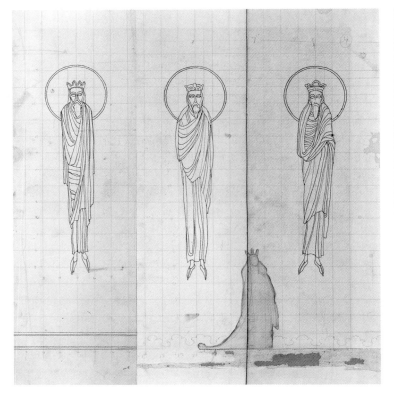

brown wrapping paper, which could not be reproduced on a blue-printing machine. Jo had expected to do the drafting himself, and in the course of his training in art and scene design he had learned to work on tracing paper from which duplicates could be made mechanically. He had to persuade Bobby to abandon opaque brown paper in favor of translucent paper so that duplicates could be blue-printed and distributed to the workmen. Many times, Jo had to sneak into Bobby's studio at night to make heads-and-tails of the pencil scratchings. Although Bobby painted his own drawings, he occasionally allowed Jo to paint his costume sketches as an indication of the confidence he felt in his young protégé.

For many years, Jones, who always knew how he wanted his sets lighted, worked with a stage electrician named George Schaff, who had the soul of an artist and the skill of a master mechanic. The son of a Swiss-born artisan, Schaff began his theatrical career by making an electric sign for the old Empire Theatre and was hired by its owner, producer Charles Frohman, to work in the theatre. Later he became house electrician for the Plymouth Theatre when producer and director Arthur Hopkins controlled it. Because Jones was working almost exclusively for Hopkins as his designer in his early career, he and Schaff quickly established a professional rapport that resulted in advances in the art and instrumentation of theatrical lighting. Many years after the fact, Jo described the communication between the two men. "For hours on end, as one would talk with a playwright or a stage director, Jones would discuss with Schaff all the subtleties of sensitive light changes from the beginning to the end of the play; and when words proved inadequate, Bobby's mood drawings would illustrate and clarify the difficult points. At these meetings there would be no reference to specific pieces of equipment or to the numbers of gelatin colors—not that Jones wasn't perfectly familiar with them, but that he was dealing with his master electrician in his own way."

Jones personally supervised every detail of every production he designed, not just the construction, painting, and lighting, but props and costumes as well. When Arthur Hopkins's business manager complained to him about the expense of eighteenth-century quills and sand-shakers on a desk far upstage in one of the sets that would not be visible to the audience, Jones replied that the actors should "feel the sense of period when working in this set!" When Jo found him dressed in a costume he had designed for one of the actresses in *The Buccaneer* in a fitting room at Eaves Costume Company, Jones told his assistant that he had to see what it felt like. Jo's amusement was ill concealed as he watched Bobby move around the room bedecked in a seventeenth-century ball gown dripping with period jewelry and an elaborate wig atop Jones's equine mustached face.

Without doubt, Jones was influenced early by the changes in the whole concept of scenery in Europe, but he rejected the notion that one column should be "made to do the duty for a cathedral." For him, good scenery was not a picture, but "something conveyed . . . a feeling, an evocation." Curiously, although his one attempt at abstract and symbolic scenery for a production of *Macbeth* directed by Arthur Hopkins failed on Broadway, the designs for it are frequently published as representative of the New Stagecraft. Jones's most memorable setting was for Shakespeare's *Richard III*, for which he employed a single sculptural mass that he altered to represent different scenes by adding props and screens and furniture, all lighted imaginatively to express changes of locale and mood.

For the first twenty years of his career, Jones was one of the most prolific, busiest, and most sought-after designers in New York, and certainly the most renowned. Jones's longest association was with the producer-director Arthur Hopkins, which spanned nineteen years. But he designed for practically every experimental group in New York in his time, including the Provincetown Players, the Neighborhood Playhouse, the Washington Square Players, the Experimental Theatre, Inc., the American Laboratory Theatre, the Equity Players, and the Group Theatre, as well as for commercial producers, the Theatre Guild, and opera companies in New York, Philadelphia, and Chicago. With but few exceptions, he designed all of the plays of Eugene O'Neill.

Through his writing as well as his designs, Jones became the prophet of the New Stagecraft and its voice. He wrote no textbooks or manuals of stagecraft but expressed a kind of religious fervor about the theatre and its mission. His most famous work, *The Dramatic Imagination*, 1941, which distills the quintessence of all of his ideas about the theatre and design, might well have become the New Stagecraft's manifesto, had it appeared in 1915. Upon its publication, Jones sent a copy of his book to Jo with this curious inscription:

> *Dear Jo—*
>
> *Don't be put off by this odd inscription! It expresses the sense of affection, paternity (slightly on the left side, I must admit) and admonishment I always feel when I think of you. I hope you like the book.*
>
> *Best wishes always,*
> *Bobby*

Ever the mentor and mystic, Bobby still regarded his friend as son and assistant. For the rest of his life, Jo reciprocated this feeling of Bobby as idol and father-figure. Jones's powerful influence resonated in many of Mielziner's sets for the next ten years. Jo's conscious integration of lighting into the design of his settings came from Bobby's obsessive attention to the subtleties of lighting and Jo never forgot his dictum that the "sole aim of the arts of scene-designing, costuming, lighting is . . .to enhance the natural powers of the actor." In all of Bobby's designs, he sketched the actors, not merely so that he could assess the scale of scenery to actor, but also to remind himself for whom he was designing. Jo followed the practice.

Although Jo assisted Jones sporadically over the new two years, his apprenticeship ended in June 1925. During the summer, he rented a house on Cape Cod for $50 and accompanied eighteen-year-old Jim Rorimer, who had been one of the paying boys at Leo's camp in 1915, on a Grand Tour in Europe as tutor in art. When he returned to New York, he prepared several productions and he also found time to begin the courtship of a strikingly beautiful young woman named Marya Mannes.

Marya Mannes, born Marie, was the only daughter of David Mannes, a concert violinist, and Clara Damrosch, a concert pianist and sister of Walter Damrosch. Clara and Walter were children of the renowned violinist and orchestra conductor Leopold Damrosch, who was born in Posen, Poland, a contemporary of Moses Mielziner. Like Moses, Leopold migrated to America in the late nineteenth century to start a new life with his family. In 1916, David and Clara, having abandoned their concert careers, founded the Mannes College of Music, in New York. Marya, who was nicknamed Ma Mie, an adaptation of the French for "my friend," was born with a spirit of rebellion in her genes. From earliest childhood, she displayed an unwillingness to do the usual and a talent for doing the outrageous. Whatever her indulgent, loving parents wanted her to do, she would opt for the opposite.

As a child, she was expected to learn to play an instrument, preferably the piano, on which her mother began her lessons. Ma Mie rebelled and music lessons were dropped. When she had finished her education at Miss Veltin's School in New York's West Side, her parents expected her to go on to college as had her brother Leopold, but Ma Mie refused. College was dropped in favor of several months in London studying sculpture and art. When she lost her interest in sculpture, she took up writing—and serious party-going.

It was at this point that she changed her first name to Marya, explaining to her parents that it was the Polish equivalent of her real name and why not? The new name and new freedom were tonic to her. She discovered men and sex and the theatre, all at about the same time.

Back in New York, she wrote *Foul Is Fair,* a three-act modern adaptation of *Macbeth,* which was produced at a summer stock theatre in Woodstock, New York. While no one thought of moving it to Broadway, its production on even so limited a scale nevertheless fed her ambition to become a playwright. In the course of her

party-going with the young theatre set, it was probably inevitable that she would meet the twenty-four-year-old Jo, whose initial scenic endeavors in the theatre of 1925 gave promise of a designer with a future on Broadway. He was also good-looking. Marya Mannes was later to write that Jo: ". . . barely older than me, . . . had all the qualities most of the contemporaries I met seemed to lack: talent, intelligence, wit, and kindness." She was only twenty-one when she fell in love, and on March 31, 1926, she married Jo Mielziner.

It was a match that most parents dream of. Linked by ties of heritage, family friendship, and mutual interests, the young pair seemed to have everything going for them: looks, talent, promises of good things to come for each of them, and the blessings of their families and friends. Marya, too, was a *Mischling,* with a Jewish grandfather and a Lutheran grandmother on her mother's side, but with no real religious background or training. Of course, Marya's was not to be the usual wedding. There was no church, no veil, no ring. The bride wore a dress (designed by her groom) of ivory satin, Empire style, with a high collar of old family lace and a square neckline, and she wore a wreath of gardenias on her head. The wedding took place in the small auditorium of the Mannes School with an Episcopal priest administering the rites. In her autobiography, Marya described the day: ". . . there was joy and gaiety and champagne afterward, and my husband and I were off on a wave of happiness first to the old Brevoort Hotel for the night, then to a boat to take us to Spain and France."

Starting with their long honeymoon, life was almost idyllic for the young couple. They moved into an apartment of their own on East 61st Street. Jo's career was zooming and Marya was writing plays. She was also meeting Jo's circle of friends and loving them. Once, when Jo and she went backstage to visit Alfred Lunt and Lynn Fontanne in their dressing room, Fontanne "made a special fuss" about Marya, asking her to sit down while she applied a line over Marya's eyelashes with a make-up pencil. "'There!' she said, You must always do that, my dear. Now you are perfect!'"

For the next few years, they spent summers in Cape Cod, and they moved again in 1928 to East 53rd Street. Cracks began to appear in the relationship. Jo was still an adoring husband but was increasingly involved in his designing. Two of Marya's plays were optioned by Broadway producers, but she was beginning to realize that breaking into show business was not an easy process. She complained to her parents that she missed her freedom and she confided to her brother Leopold that she had begun an affair with a Catalonian biologist at the Rockefeller Institute. In the summer of 1929, under some pretext as an excuse to go abroad alone, she followed her lover to Spain, where he was being treated for tuberculosis in a hospital near Barcelona. She wrote to Leopold that she had not the heart to tell Jo—yet.

One event might have saved the marriage, the success of Marya's play, *Café*. Brought to Broadway by William A. Brady Sr. and John Tuerk, it opened at the Ritz Theatre on August 28, 1930, after a tryout in Asbury Park, New Jersey. According to Marya, the play, a comedy, was about the "rootlessness and conflicting loves" of expatriates in Paris. The play lasted four performances. Although Jo consented to having his name on the poster for the out-of-town performances, he had it removed from the program when it was transferred to Broadway. The play was trounced by the critics, who described it as dull and aimless. Wilella Waldorf, writing in the *New York Post*, said: "The best part of the production was the setting, which did more to suggest Paris than all of the characters put together. The program carried no reference whatever to the designer." Its failure was a brutal shock to Marya's ego. Jo must have suffered, too. In all the lists of his production that he compiled for publication, he always omitted *Café*.

If her secret infidelity and her public failure as a playwright were not enough to place heavy strains on the marriage, her refusal to have children must have administered the *coup de grâce*. She was also unhappy that her husband was not more adventurous sexually, a fact she seemed to confess freely to everyone within earshot. She wanted out of the marriage at all costs. She took a small apartment near the Rockefeller Institute to be closer to her Spanish lover and

subsisted on what she could earn on her own and what her parents were able to provide. "I had at least the minimal decency," she later wrote, "to refuse alimony from a man whom I had deeply, if unwillingly, hurt."

Even Marya, conscious that she had spread pain in a wide swath, felt compelled to write to Ella and Leo Mielziner and explain the reasons for her actions. She took all the blame and hinted at the root causes for her unhappiness. Although she considered Jo a "perfect husband," she confessed that she did not feel a closeness to him "chemically . . . [and] physiologically." She concluded her letter:

> *I kept feeling more and more that I married in an embryonic state, before having the faintest idea of what I was and what I really wanted. And Jo's wonderful adjustment to life and success in work only accentuates my maladjustment and insufficiency.*

If she had married at twenty-eight, she admitted, "none of this would have happened." In a subsequent note, when she had definitely decided to make the separation final, she asks to remain their friend and signs it: "Affectionately, Ma Mie."

Marya left Jo in October of 1930 for the trial separation. One year later, they were divorced. There was no doubt that Marya had cut deep wounds into Jo's psyche, which took a long time to heal. It was many years before he forgave her, but he eventually did. Fulfilling the faith that her parents had in her, Marya made her mark as a writer. Her outspoken commentary on the social, cultural, and political scene in books and in essays for the *New Yorker* and *The New York Times*, among others, and her later appearances on television, were proof positive that she had channeled her immature rebellion against established custom into trenchant, if sometimes outrageous, social criticism. She married two other men and had a son by one of them. When Marya and Jo were both in mellow middle age and successful, they resumed their relationship, becoming good friends and dinner companions.

3
BROADWAY 1925–1935

In the season of 1924–25, when Jo Mielziner made his entrance as a scene designer on Broadway, Burns Mantle, yearly chronicler of the New York theatre, counted 230 productions, the first time in history that the number 200 was breached. For each of the next five theatrical seasons, until the effects of the Depression began to be felt, the number of shows to reach Broadway hovered around and even surpassed this mark. The high point was reached in the season of 1927–28, with 264 productions. The dominant fare was the straight drama, with musicals, revues, and revivals making up the rest. Occasionally, the critics could take their pick of six or seven openings on the same night. To accommodate this flood of productions, theatres were built at a record pace. Between 1925 and 1928, thirteen new theatres sprang up in the side streets radiating from Broadway to join the sixty-odd playhouses already in existence.

A hit in those days consisted of a longevity of one hundred performances, or about twelve weeks on the boards, which would insure payback of the original investment, if not a hefty profit. Escalating costs of materials and labor and a different mode of production had driven expenses upward in the early twenties, but in the late twenties it was still possible to produce a play for under $10,000, almost double what it had cost before the war. An elaborate musical or revue needed several times the amount of capitalization for a play but was usually made up at the box office. The century-old $2 top price for theatre tickets became a thing of the past as prices edged up to $6.60 (which included a federal tax of 10 percent) for a big musical or a *Ziegfeld Follies*.

OPPOSITE: THE FIRST ILLUSTRATION IN JO'S BOOK, *DESIGNING FOR THE THEATRE.* ONE OF HIS FAVORITES WAS THIS "THREE CABBIES" SCENE FROM *SWEET AND LOW* **(1930)**, PRESENTED TO HIS FRIEND EDDIE KOOK. ALTHOUGH IT APPEARS TO HAVE A MONOCHROMATIC BACKGROUND, IT IS ACTUALLY BRUSHED IN VERY SUBTLE COLORS RANGING FROM PURPLE TO GREEN IN SEAMLESS STROKES AND IS AN OUTSTANDING EXAMPLE OF JO'S RENDERING TECHNIQUE IN PRE-AIRBRUSH DAYS. (COURTESY OF THE ESTATE OF HILDA AND EDWARD KOOK)

Between 1925 and 1935, the name of Arthur Hopkins led the list of the new breed of producers, which also included William Brady, Jr., Guthrie McClintic, Brock Pemberton, Herman Shumlin, Max Gordon, Dwight Deere Wiman, Gilbert Miller, Alfred de Liagre, and John Golden. Miller, the son of Henry Miller and Bijou Heron, both stars on Broadway, received his training in management with Charles Frohman, Inc. John Golden began by building theatres in the literal sense as a bricklayer on the old Harrigan (lately Garrick) Theatre. Coming from a newspaper family in Kansas, Brock Pemberton started as a second-string theatre critic in New York before he joined the office of Arthur Hopkins to learn the business. (Hopkins himself was a former newspaper reporter and press agent who ventured into booking vaudeville acts.) Herman Shumlin was another ex-newspaperman, having begun as a reporter for the old *New York Clipper*, and later learning the ropes as a theatrical press agent. Dwight Deere Wiman, the scion of the John Deere farm equipment manufacturing company, was stagestruck from child-hood. Alfred de Liagre (Yale), not finding the banking business to his liking, turned to stage managing before joining with fellow Ivy Leaguer Richard Aldrich (Harvard) in producing ventures. By a different route Max Gordon was slipped into show business by his brother Cliff, a comedian with a German comic act in vaudeville, when such things were the rage. Max Gordon started at a tender age as an "advance man" for traveling vaudeville shows.

The new producers rapidly adapted to the changing conditions of the theatre of the time. They were better able to cope than their elders with the demands of the theatrical unions, which had multiplied rapidly since the beginning of the century and covered nearly everyone (with the exception of the audience) who set foot in a theatre. They learned to negotiate with theatre owners and to deal not only with playwrights, directors, designers, and performers but also their personal and business agents. Several of them hitched their stars to playwrights following the lead of the Theatre Guild, which had a lock for a while on the talents of Eugene O'Neill, Maxwell Anderson, and S. N. Behrman. Arthur Hopkins, for example, produced five plays by Philip Barry, but also never passed up an interesting script by an unknown, which may have helped in his undoing.

The flood of plays created a feast for the theatre critics. They wrote about everything and everybody—except themselves; critics rarely examined (in print) their job and their role. One of the best, John Mason Brown, thoughtfully considered the role of the reviewers and critics in a brief essay, "The Men on the Aisle," in 1930, in which he describes the evolution of a review:

> *His usual method is to begin with a sentence that expresses his own feelings in the color of its adjectives, even while it states the facts in its who, when, where, and what. This is followed with a detailed plot summary, for the benefit of his readers who may not be able to see the play but who still want to talk about it, or who want to know whether it is the kind of play to which they can safely take their husbands and children. Then comes a paragraph on the acting, and perhaps, a slight sentence on the directing and setting. . . .*

Directors and designers, after several decades of proving themselves important cogs in the creation of theatrical production and who may have thought the battle won, must have felt a pang on reading "a slight sentence on the direction and setting." True, it has always been difficult to assess the job of directors because critics and public alike were and are still not quite sure of what they do. Or if they consider themselves *cognoscenti* of the theatre, they will venture an adjectival comment like "expert" or "inept" or "busy" or "imaginative." Most directors, past and current, would agree that the best directing tends to be unobtrusive; so saying, they must accept their lot as the least understood and least appreciated of the theatrical collaborators and be content with the "slight sentence" from the reviewer.

On the other hand, the designer's work is always highly visible and it would seem, in the face of the revolution of the entire concept of scenery in America from 1915 onward, that critics could award them more than that "slight sentence." Victor Hugo had said that settings should be the "silent characters" of the dramatic presentation, and it was a theory that the New Stagecraft designers had heartily espoused. In 1917, at the very beginning of his career, Robert Edmond Jones wrote that the scenery "isn't there to be looked at, it's really there to be forgotten." There was, perhaps, a slight contradiction in the thinking of the early exponents of the

New Stagecraft. Yes, they wanted their work to be noticed, and no, it should not be so noticeable that the audience becomes distracted by it. Jo Mielziner was fond of saying that the scenery should "disappear" from the consciousness of the audience thirty seconds after the curtain rises, if it is well designed. However, he also ruefully admitted that "scene designers are the forgotten people on the theatrical totem pole."

What was notable about the new movement in Europe was that Appia and Craig and their disciples abroad applied its principles (with rare exceptions) not to the contemporary plays of their day but to the classics. Shakespeare was favored by all for experiments in settings and Greek dramas came in second. If they designed for contemporary playwrights, the plays were usually the nonrealistic or symbolic works of Ibsen. The new scene designers found little room in which to maneuver in providing scenery for the bulk of late nineteenth and early twentieth-century drama with its unrelenting realism.

When a few adventurous playwrights turned to themes heavy with psychology and sociology, they cast aside the illusion of reality in their treatment of contemporary problems, deconstructing the conventions of well-made drama in plot, characterization, and dialogue. Lumped under the rubric of "expressionism," their dream plays, dramas of psychological discord, plays of fantasy combined with social disruption, and propagandistic plays lent themselves neatly to the work of the experimentalists on both sides of the Atlantic. The scenic imagination soared once it was freed from the earthbound bonds of the realistic drama. Scenery that could be simplified down to a few structural nonrepresentational units, backdrops, and curtains painted in brilliant, surreal colors and patterns, and lighting that set mood with shifting colors and intensities complemented and enhanced the plays for which they were designed. American designers were extraordinarily inventive in providing settings for expressionistic and symbolic dramas, which came mostly from Germany, Czechoslovakia, and Russia. To its credit, the Theatre Guild introduced many of the works of the European modernist theatre and did not ignore the experimental work of American playwrights. Lee Simonson provided stunning scenery for many of them.

Although looked upon as interesting digressions from the normal fare on Broadway, plays of the "isms" did not sell tickets in the commercial theatre of America and so they became the property of experimental and little theatres as well as university groups throughout the country. The realistic play was the standard on Broadway for many years and hobbled the imagination of the restless scene designers who wanted to do more than create imitations of Park Avenue interiors or Southern barnyards.

It was the genius of designers like Jones, Simonson, Geddes, and, later, Mielziner who could imbue the realistic play with poetic overtones that could not have been on the printed page: for instance, Jones with *Desire under the Elms*, Simonson with *Roar China*, Geddes with *Dead End*, and Mielziner with *Street Scene.* In an interview with Norris Houghton, who was preparing a series of articles for *Theatre Arts* magazine in 1936 on how scene designers work, Mielziner told him that when he started working in the theatre, he began by creating the visual picture of the entire play, but gave it up so that he could "hunt out the most telling line that conveys the atmosphere and the background. This may give me an idea for a significant piece of furniture, a quality of light or shadow, a color combination; it may not be an entire setting at all—just something that is associated with the dramatic significance of the moment, but which may become the clue to, or indeed the cornerstone of, the whole setting."

Jo entered the year 1925 with one resounding Broadway success, *The Guardsman*. His sets for the Theatre Guild production got more than a "slight sentence" of praise from the critics, and a photograph of his rendering for the opera box scene was reproduced in black-and-white for the November issue of *Theatre Arts* magazine. Brother Kenneth continued to tout Jo's talents and when he was cast in *The American Venus*, the saga of a girl from Centerville who tries her luck in the Miss America Contest in Atlantic City, he got Jo a job designing the sets. The film featured beauty pageant scenes shot in an early version of Technicolor on Jo's sets. The picture's star was Esther Ralston, but the cast also featured—in addition to Kenneth as the heroine's wimpy boyfriend—Edna May Oliver, Louise Brooks, and a very young Douglas Fairbanks Jr.

Jo's first Broadway show for 1925, *Mrs. Partridge Presents,* opened on January 5. A comedy by Mary Kennedy and Ruth Hawthorne, it marked Jo's first association with Cornell and McClintic. It featured the veteran star of a previous Broadway era, Blanche Bates, who practically donated her services to give it a life of 146 perform-ances, which in those days constituted a comfortable and modestly profitable run. Jo's next assignment was a modern classic, Ibsen's *The Wild Duck,* which he designed for the Actors' Theatre. It was co-directed by two fine actors in the group, Dudley Digges and Clare Eames, and had a distinguished cast of seasoned actors. Because of them, Ibsen had an unusually respectable run. Although Jo's sets for both productions of necessity had to be realistic to suit the plays, they were done with a feeling for color and texture that was devel-oping as he continued to evolve as a designer.

JO'S RENDERING FOR THE FIRST SCENE OF THE ACTORS' THEATRE PRODUCTION OF THE **WILD DUCK** (1925). THE OUTSIZED DOORS, HEAVY FURNITURE, AND SUBDUED COLORS CON-VEY THE STOLIDITY OF A WELL-TO-DO NORWEGIAN HOUSEHOLD. JO'S ABILITY TO PRODUCE SCENE PICTURES WAS DEVELOPING RAPIDLY. (HARVARD THEATRE COLLECTION, HOUGHTON LIBRARY)

After a summer retreat on Cape Cod with his family, Jo began the 1925–26 season with a call from Arthur Hopkins to do a play titled *First Flight*, written by Anderson and Stallings, the team that won plaudits for *What Price Glory?* during the previous season. Unfortunately, although the man at the *Times* singled out one of Jo's sets for praise, he did not care much for the play, which closed quickly. Jo's next assignment, *Caught*, did not fare much better. In rapid succession after the opening of *Caught* (October 9) came *The Call of Life* (October 9), *The Enemy* (October 20), and *Lucky Sam McCarver* (October 21). The fact that his name appeared so frequently in the credits of the programs did not escape the eyes of the critics, who were beginning to take special note of Jo's sets. While all three of these plays did not outlive their time, two of them were instrumental in widening his circle in the theatrical community. *The Enemy* was written by Channing Pollock, one of the most prolific playwrights of the time. Although most of his plays were potboilers, more than a few of them had substantial runs, *The Enemy* among them. *Lucky Sam McCarver* was a flop, but it was written by Sidney Howard and produced by Dwight Deere Wiman and William Brady, Jr., all three of whom became commanding presences on Broadway. Howard later had his greatest success with *They Knew What They Wanted*, which has endured in the Frank Loesser musical *The Most Happy Fella* (the premiere of which Jo designed many years later).

Although Howard was one of the first playwrights to recognize Jo's unique talents, it was the co-producer of his play, Dwight Deere Wiman, who had the greatest impact on Jo's career as a result of this production. Wiman had formed a partnership with William Brady, Jr., which lasted for five years, largely, one suspects, to learn the business from the professional producer-son of the ultimate professional producer-father. Beyond the partnership, Jo became Wiman's designer of choice through his many years of producing, and the two men formed a close professional and personal friendship until the producer's death in 1951. Despite his wealth—or perhaps, because of it—Wiman was a modest and private person in the flamboyant world that he chose to inhabit, and assumed an almost paternalistic role to the people who worked for him.

THE CALL OF LIFE (1925), PRODUCED BY THE ACTORS' THEATRE, WAS A GRIM TALE ABOUT PATRICIDE IN VIENNA; IT STARRED EVA LE GALLIENNE AS THE DESPERATE DAUGHTER OF THE DYING MAN. THE FIRST ACT, IN THEIR APARTMENT, WAS LIGHTED WITH AN ICINESS THAT CONVEYED THE MOOD. THIS IMAGE COMES FROM A BOOK OF MINIATURE RENDERINGS REDRAWN FROM MEMORY BY JO AS A GIFT FOR "MY MASTER AND MOST ADORED FATHER, DECEMBER 8, 1929." (W. H. CRAIN COLLECTION, UNIVERSITY OF TEXAS THEATRE ARTS COLLECTION)

LUCKY SAM MCCARVER (1925) BROUGHT JO PRAISE FROM THE CRITICS AND A CHANCE TO WORK WITH SIDNEY HOWARD, A YOUNG PLAYWRIGHT, AND UP-AND-COMING PRODUCER DWIGHT DEERE WIMAN. THIS ROUGH DESIGN FOR A PALAZZO IN VENICE DISPLAYS JO'S EARLY PENCHANT FOR TOWERING WINDOWS IN HIS SETS. ALEXANDER WOOLLCOTT DID NOT RECALL "EVER HAVING HAD OCCASION TO APPLAUD THE SCENERY OF A PRODUCTION BY WILLIAM BRADY, BUT THE SETTINGS BY JO MIELZINER COMPEL THE BREAKING OF AN OLD TRADITION." (W. H. CRAIN COLLECTION, UNIVERSITY OF TEXAS THEATRE ARTS COLLECTION)

Jo's final design in 1925 was for *The Unseen*, a Brady–Wiman production that opened and closed in Boston, but the Boston critics liked Jo's two settings of a drawing room and a studio, describing them as properly atmospheric. For the year, he earned $7,350—a very good sum for a novice designer. Although, like his mentor Jones, Jo liked to do everything himself, his schedule became so crowded that he had to hire an occasional draftsman to help prepare the technical drawings for the scene shops. Most of the time, he had to do his own scouting for props and fabrics. On one of his forays to a decorator's shop to look for tapestries, Jo was mistaken for a messenger by the head salesman, who called the office of the producer to find out whether he should send the fabrics with him. His boyish appearance always belying his age, Jo was prompted to grow some hair on his upper lip just to make himself look older.

Early in 1926, just before his marriage to Marya Mannes and an extended European honeymoon, Jo designed two more Broadway shows. He did his second Ibsen play, *Little Eyolf*, for Brady and Wiman, which showed their unflagging zeal for presenting unusual fare on Broadway. Without the presence of a Mrs. Fiske, Ibsen's plays were generally indigestible for typical New York audiences no matter how competent the cast. Mrs. Fiske, the grande dame of serious actresses of the previous era, chewed up the scenery in her

Ibsen presentations and people came to the brooding Norwegian dramas just to watch her.

The Masque of Venice was another Brady–Wiman production (with the addition of Brock Pemberton as third producer and director), but it did not fare well either. Among the cast, along with Jo's brother Kenneth, were Antoinette Perry and Osgood Perkins. Antoinette Perry had been one of David Belasco's protégées. She had two careers, first as an actress, then as a director after an absence of many years from Broadway. (It was for her work with the American Theatre Wing that she has been immortalized in the "Tony" Awards.) Perkins later received the part of a lifetime as Walter Burns, the acid-tongued editor in the Hecht and MacArthur hit, *The Front Page* (1928).

When Jo and Marya came home from their grand tour, they returned to the good news that Kenneth finally had a hit in *What Every Woman Knows*, which starred Helen Hayes in what became one of her favorite roles. It had opened in April after their departure and played 268 performances before it went out on the road for another six months. For the balance of the year, Jo worked on *Seed of the Brute* for Brady and Wiman and *Pygmalion* for the Theatre Guild. Again, he was with old friends. His friend from Bonstelle days, Walter Abel, was in *Seed of the Brute*, and Lynn Fontanne, a Guild stalwart, was the star of *Pygmalion*. But because Jo was away so long on his wedding trip, he had few jobs and his earnings for the year dropped to $3,400.

The next year, 1927, proved to be much busier and more lucrative. For the second half of the 1926–27 season, he designed four productions, of which one was an out-and-out failure (*Mariners* by Clemence Dane), one an unsuccessful but necessary experiment (*Right You Are, If You Think You Are* by Luigi Pirandello), one a moderate success (*The Second Man* by S. N. Behrman), and one a considerable hit (*Saturday's Children* by Maxwell Anderson). *Saturday's Children*, Jo's first assignment of the year, was another production by the Actors' Theatre, now with Guthrie McClintic running the group. The assignment brought Jo in closer contact with playwright Maxwell Anderson, who had seen six of his plays mounted on Broadway in less than five years. Anderson was freed from onerous duties as a newspaperman for the *New York World* by the 1924 success of *What Price Glory?* Afterward, to the mid-fifties, there was hardly a season on Broadway that did not carry at least one play by him. If Jo had to hitch his wagon to a star playwright, Anderson was certainly the best choice. Jo had a hand in some of Anderson's greatest triumphs.

Saturday's Children tells of a young married couple beset by financial and other worries that threaten the bedrock of their relationship. When their problems drive them apart, they rekindle the early romantic flush of their marriage by treating each other as illicit lovers. (Unfortunately, Anderson and his wife, whose real-life marriage was failing, were not able to do the same; they split up a few years later.) The play was a hit, and Jo was enveloped in the general rosy glow of its success. Anderson, mindful of Jo's contribution, remained loyal to Jo for thirty years.

With *The Second Man*, Jo was introduced by the Theatre Guild to the playwright S. N. Behrman, with whom he would enjoy the same kind of warm professional relationship as he did with Anderson. Behrman's plays were highly polished comedies of literate people caught in unusual situations from which would arise a series of amusing reactions. For Jo, it was again a case of catching a playwright at the beginning of his career and establishing a strong loyalty. He was to design five more of Behrman's plays over the years, including Behrman's last.

In an exact reversal of the usual Broadway mode, Jo involved himself in another project when he heard speculation that one of the group production units, either the Theatre Guild, the Actors' Theatre, or the Provincetown Playhouse, might mount a production of *Faust*. On his own and without benefit of a contract, he created a model for the epic drama, perhaps because he had hopes of being chosen by one of these groups to design it. He constructed in scale a sculptural mass, which pivoted to denote changes of scene. After his flight into wishful thinking with *Faust*, he got down to brass tacks to design a series of British plays for the first few months of the Broadway season. Noël Coward's *The Marquise* was followed by Shaw's *The Doctor's Dilemma*, which was succeeded by another Coward play, *Fallen Angels*. Despite stellar casts, none of them did extraordinarily well at the box office.

DESIGNERS—AND JO WAS NO EXCEPTION—DELIGHT IN THE ST. PAUL'S PORTICO SCENE IN **PYGMALION** (1926), WHICH CAN GIVE FLIGHT TO THEIR IMAGINATION. THE CRITICS LOVED JO'S "ACHIEVEMENT IN ILLUSION" AND BROOKS ATKINSON OF THE *NEW YORK TIMES* THOUGHT IT "EXTRAORDINARILY IMAGINATIVE AND EFFECTIVE." (BILLY ROSE THEATRE COLLECTION, NYPL-PA)

SATURDAY'S CHILDREN (1927), THE SECOND OF THE PLAYS BY MAXWELL ANDERSON THAT JO DESIGNED, WAS A DEPARTURE FROM HIS USUAL ASSIGNMENTS TO DO ELABORATE INTERIORS. FOR IT, JO HAD TO DESIGN A MODEST KITCHEN APPROPRIATE TO A YOUNG MARRIED COUPLE IN THE TWENTIES. THE STAR OF THE SHOW WAS RUTH GORDON. (BILLY ROSE THEATRE COLLECTION, NYPL-PA)

THE SECOND MAN (1927), ANOTHER GUILD PRODUCTION, STARRED ALFRED LUNT AND LYNN FONTANNE IN A COMEDY OF MANNERS, AMERICAN STYLE, AND HAD ONLY ONE SET: THE STYLISH APARTMENT OF A HIGH-LIVING NOVELIST. IT, TOO, HAD THE LOOK OF BEING ASSEMBLED FROM THE GUILD'S WAREHOUSE. SMALL WONDER THAT JO WAS THEIR FAVORITE SCENE DESIGNER. (BILLY ROSE THEATRE COLLECTION, NYPL-PA)

JO'S SET FOR SHAW'S ***DOCTOR'S DILEMMA*** (1927) REDUCED EVERYTHING TO A LARGE WINDOW AND THE BARE ESSENTIALS OF AN ARTIST'S STUDIO. (THE SOFA AT RIGHT HAD JUST SEEN DUTY IN *RIGHT YOU ARE, IF YOU THINK YOU ARE.*) (BILLY ROSE THEATRE COLLECTION, NYPL-PA)

Jo's income of $6,400 for 1927 improved considerably over the previous year, as did his reputation as a quietly competent, often resourceful designer. The Theatre Guild, always strained for finances, appreciated his dexterity in recycling scenery from show to show. Although a member of something that called itself a union, Jo was left to negotiate his own fees. The Actors' Theatre paid him $1,000 per production, the Theatre Guild and Brady and Wiman, considerably less. He was also using assistants more, but could not afford anyone full-time. During the twenties, the income of designers was not commensurate with their contributions to the productions, nor did it keep pace with the rewards flowing to the other theatrical collaborators. Producers stood to gain most from the success of a production (so long as they did not use their own money). The playwrights were a not-so-distant second. When they set up the Dramatists' Guild in 1926, they established a contract (Minimum Basic Agreement) with producers, which could reap them large rewards from a stipulated flat percentage of the gross proceeds of the production, no matter the success or failure of the enterprise. (That has since changed, with playwrights sharing in the net profits pool *after* the deduction of production expenses.) Actors at the top also did very well, while actors at the bottom only scraped by despite their union contracts. Kenneth MacKenna thought it a good year when he could make $5,000 as an actor on Broadway in the twenties.

In January 1928, Jo added three more playwrights to his list of those to whom he had contributed his talents. Early in January, *Cock Robin*, a whodunit by Philip Barry and Elmer Rice, allowed him to design a set within a set, since the play concerned a group of amateur actors who were putting on a drama that took place in an eighteenth-century English grog shop. But the Theatre Guild's production of Eugene O'Neill's *Strange Interlude* was infinitely more challenging.

Although O'Neill's plays were largely the design province of Jones and Simonson, Jones may have thought Jo was the best designer for the show. Running for nine acts and set against six different scenes, it elicited as many different opinions as there were critics. Called the "greatest play of the century" by Benjamin De Casseres and a masterpiece by others, it was also roundly trounced as a "long-winded bark at the moon" and a "sordid mess." No matter what the critics said, it was the Theatre Guild's greatest triumph to date. *Variety's* critic marveled at the sets that could be shifted so easily, but were rich despite their simple construction. Months later, *Theatre Arts* magazine published Jo's rendering for the final act, noting that he had caught O'Neill's "aging afternoon" with his "softened twilight hues." Brooks Atkinson of the *Times* seems not to have been impressed with Jo's lighting and commented: "Limitations of space in the John Golden Theatre are said to be responsible for the indifferent lighting of Mr. Mielziner's utilitarian sets." Since it was pleasant being associated with a success of such magnitude, Jo reveled in the celebrity that rained on everyone connected with the production. Years later, he admitted that he had not been pleased with his handiwork at the time and would have designed it differently in other circumstances.

In March, Jo, Marya, and Kenneth joined Ella and Leo for the opening of an exhibition of Leo's paintings and portraits at the Cincinnati Art Museum. For the summer, everyone journeyed to Truro in Cape Cod and in September, Kenneth bought a small Cape Cod cottage and fifty surrounding acres of land on the north side of the Pamet River in Truro for a few thousand dollars. Jo rented a house nearby for a few summers.

For several years, Kenneth had been using the interludes between acting jobs on Broadway to make movies at the Paramount Studios in Astoria. Despite his talent and good looks, he had not been able to find a niche on Broadway that would ensure good roles every season. Early in 1929, largely through the good offices of playwright George Middleton, he received a tempting offer from the Twentieth Century–Fox Studios in Hollywood. Now that the movies talked, the moguls quickly realized that they needed not only trained speaking actors but directors who had experience with dialogue. Kenneth was given a three-year contract to star in and direct Fox movies for $130,000. Since, during his best years in New York, an income of $10,000 was considered almost munificent, his Fox contract meant, he told his parents, "absolute security for all of us." At Fox, he was among friends, such as Middleton and Guthrie McClintic. But he missed his family and did not adjust well to his new milieu in Hollywood.

ACT VIII OF O'NEILL'S *STRANGE INTERLUDE* (1928) TAKES PLACE ABOARD THE AFTERDECK OF A YACHT. IN IT, JO MAKES USE OF HIS DEVELOPING TECHNIQUE OF SELECTIVE REALISM, PROVIDING ONLY WHAT WAS NECESSARY (LIFE RING, DECK FURNITURE, LOW RAILING) TO DEPICT THE SCENE AND MOOD VISUALLY. ONE CAN IMAGINE THE BRIGHT BLUE OF THE SKY. (BILLY ROSE THEATRE COLLECTION, NYPL-PA)

STRANGE INTERLUDE (1928) REQUIRED SIX DIFFERENT SCENES. IN DEFERENCE TO THE THEATRE GUILD'S LIMITED BUDGET, JO KEPT THE SETS SIMPLE, EMPLOYING ATMOSPHERIC LIGHTING WHENEVER HE COULD AND PAINTED DROPS. THE LAST SCENE IN THE PLAY (SHOWN), WHICH WAS ONE OF THE MOST SYMMETRICAL SETS HE EVER DESIGNED, HAD TO CONVEY A SENSE OF DECAY AND MORTALITY. (ESTATE OF JO MIELZINER)

Jo's summer was cut short by the press of work for the upcoming season on Broadway. He and Marya had moved to the apartment on East 53rd Street, where he had more space for himself and his assistants. His first show, *The Grey Fox*, a drama about Machiavelli, opened in late October of 1928. It had been written by a university professor and tried out the previous year at Yale's School of Drama with George Pierce Baker as director. The play was produced by Brady and Wiman and starred actors Henry Hull and Chrystal Herne, but its stage life was brief.

In November, Jo had three plays open within a few days of each other—and two in the same evening. *The Jealous Moon*, another production of Brady and Wiman, opened on the 20th, and six days later both *The Lady Lies* and *A Most Immoral Lady* (Brady and Wiman again) were launched on the 26th. (Multiple openings on the same night were not rare in those days of 200-plus seasons, but for Jo to have designed two shows for the same opening night must have been hectic and soul-satisfying to him.) Since the leading lady of *The Jealous Moon* was Jane Cowl, who enjoyed a huge popularity, it probably had a longer run on Broadway than the play merited before it decamped for its road tour. The most successful of the lot was *A Most Immoral Lady*, which starred Alice Brady. Her performance, said the critics, saved the play from an early death and ended Jo's year on a happy note. Not only were his critical notices getting better, his earnings for 1928 reached $9,000. The second half of the season found him with assignments for five productions from January through April.

The first, *Street Scene*, reunited him with the elder Brady as producer and Elmer Rice as playwright. In it, Rice created a slice of New York life in the best naturalistic mode of playwriting, and for it Jo created a setting that almost every critic in New York praised as being a perfect reproduction of the facade of a city brownstone. (Many years later, Rice told an interviewer that he had chosen the

THE GREY FOX (1928) IS THE TALE OF THE EVOLUTION OF NICCOLÒ MACHIAVELLI INTO THE CUNNING AND CYNICAL HEAD OF STATE OF FLORENCE. JO DESIGNED A SEMI-PERMANENT SET FOR ALL SEVEN DIFFERENT LOCALES, USING LIGHTING TO HELP CHANGE THE SCENE AND ALTER THE MOOD. WILELLA WALDORF OF THE *NEW YORK POST* DID NOT LIKE THE PLAY BUT CALLED IT "ONE OF THE MOST STRIKING SCENE PRODUCTIONS IN TOWN." SHOWN HERE IS THE OFFICE IN THE SECOND CHANCERY OF FLORENCE. (W. H. CRAIN COLLECTION, UNIVERSITY OF TEXAS THEATRE ARTS COLLECTION)

A MOST IMMORAL LADY (1928), A LESS THAN SCINTILLATING COMEDY, WHICH STARRED ALICE BRADY AND HUMPHREY BOGART, WAS SAVED BY BRADY'S PERFORMANCE. THE *NEW YORK TIMES* CRITIC WAS PLEASED TO SEE THE RETURN OF PAINTED SCENERY IN PLACE OF THE ALL-TOO-SOLID STUFF OF A PREVIOUS ERA. IN THE FINAL SCENE, JO CREATED (MOSTLY OUT OF PAINT) THE INTERIOR OF A RUSSIAN CABARET. RAISING THE STAGE TWO FEET AT THE FOOTLIGHTS AND SLOPING IT DOWNWARD, HE MANAGED TO CONVEY THE ANTIC MOOD OF THE FINAL SCENE. (BILLY ROSE THEATRE COLLECTION, NYPL-PA)

actual building that Jo used for his design, which was not the truth.) Kenneth was incensed by the suggestion that Jo had simply used a camera to reproduce the setting for *Street Scene* and wrote to the editor of the *New York American* to defend his brother:

> The dimensions, optical illusions—sight lines—and lighting of a theater preclude the use of a replica of a house. The startlingly "real" effect achieved in this case is the result of great study and creative imagination not only as to architectural design, but in getting the texture, color, and I might almost say, smell of the grimy old tenement. Skillful and dramatic use of lighting played no little part in this.

(Rice, incidentally, received similar criticism and was accused of acting as a cameraman and not a playwright in recording the ordinary lives of ordinary people.) The play opened on January 10, 1929, played 601 performances, and won the Pulitzer Prize. Jo received what must be the supreme accolade that any designer can expect. Atkinson in the *Times* wrote: "Jo Mielziner has designed one of those illuminating settings that can never be dissociated from the performance, since they serve the play accurately in mood as well as fact." And he realized that the tenement set was no "clever imitation. It is the essence of New York. In sum, it is true."

Before the 1928–29 Broadway season drew to a close, Joe designed several more duds before his final assignment brought him his due both in acclaim and money. He kept busy, however, with a succession of here-tonight-and-gone-next-week productions and, as usual, did his level best to make them look as good as possible. With *The Little Show*, the season was redeemed for Jo. It was his first revue in an era that brought several of the genre to Broadway every season. Not only did it represent a change of pace but it also gave the producers Brady and Wiman respite from their schedule of serious plays. According to a reminiscence of Jo in his book *Designing for the Theatre*, Wiman "admired intimate revues of the English type, full of witty social and political implications, and decided to create one for Broadway." Wiman was, of course, running against the tide of usual Broadway revues that were imitations of Ziegfeld's creations, all trying to outdo each other in extravagance. Wiman not

IN 1935, SIDNEY KINGSLEY WOULD WRITE *DEAD END*, WHICH WITH NORMAN BEL GEDDES'S SETTING WOULD BE PRAISED AS THE QUINTESSENCE OF NEW YORK'S STREET LIFE. BUT PRECEDING IT WAS ELMER RICE'S **STREET SCENE (1929)**, A SLICE OF NEW YORK LIFE THAT WAS HAILED AS MORE FACT THAN FICTION. FOR THIS PLAY JO DESIGNED THE FACADE OF A NEW YORK BROWNSTONE TENEMENT (ABOVE), GIVING IT AN ODD BEAUTY BY BOTH DAY AND NIGHT. WHEN THE PLAY WAS REBORN AS A MUSICAL IN 1947, RICE INSISTED ON REVIVING THE ORIGINAL DESIGN FOR IT (BELOW), OVERRIDING JO'S OBJECTIONS. (COURTESY OF THE ESTATE OF HILDA AND EDWARD KOOK)

THE LITTLE SHOW (1929), THE
FIRST REVUE THAT JO
DESIGNED, HAD TWENTY-
SEVEN DIFFERENT SONGS AND
SKITS, EACH OF WHICH
DEMANDED ITS OWN SET-
TING. IN PLACE OF CUMBER-
SOME SETS AND LONG STAGE
WAITS, JO USED PAINT AND
CANVAS PLUS INGENIOUS
LIGHTING TO TRANSFORM
THE STAGE TWENTY-SEVEN
TIMES. HIS DESIGNS FOR
THREE SCENES ARE SHOWN
HERE. THE BIG HIT WAS THE
NEXT TO LAST NUMBER,
WHICH FEATURED LIBBY
HOLMAN SINGING "MOANIN'
LOW" (TOP). IN CHANGING
THE ANGLE FOR THE TYPICAL
THREE-SIDED BOX SET TO
MAKE THE SIDE WALLS AND
CEILING SEEM TO CONVERGE
AT A CENTER POINT RATHER
THAN INTO A STRAIGHT BACK
WALL, JO TRIED A TECHNIQUE
THAT HE WAS TO USE SEVERAL
MORE TIMES IN HIS CAREER.
("MOANIN' LOW" COURTESY
OF JULES FISHER; OTHERS
COURTESY OF PAUL STIGA)

only co-produced but also co-directed the entertainment, which contained lyrics and music "mostly by Howard Dietz and Arthur Schwartz" amid the twenty-seven sketches and song and dance numbers, mostly performed by the principals Fred Allen, Clifton Webb, and Libby Holman. Among the many contributors were George S. Kaufman and Marya Mannes. The critics were by and large delighted with most of it, but again singled out Jo's sets for special praise because they did not try to out-Ziegfeld Ziegfeld. Robert Littell of the *Evening Post* praised the simplicity of the "astonishing variety of beautiful, humorous, fantastic, imaginative settings. It was a delight to look at them, and they were always there, no matter whether the spoken material was worth listening to or not."

In the summer, with Marya in Europe on her marital "sabbatical," Jo spent most of his time on his upcoming seven scheduled productions without feeling guilty for abandoning her to his work. Out of his total assignments, two closed out of town before reaching Broadway, one never got off the drawing board, three were out-and-out flops, and only one of them, *Jenny*, a co-creation of the bedridden playwright Edward Sheldon and Mrs. Margaret Ayer Barnes, achieved a reasonable run.

Jo worked on three other shows that fall, but none got to Broadway. In late October *Dread*, by Owen Davis, moved out of Brooklyn's Majestic Theatre into oblivion. It was a psychological thriller that featured Spencer Tracy as a ladykiller with an evil eye. Brady and Wiman's *Mrs. Cook's Tour*, with Mary Boland, closed in Philadelphia in November. The scenes ranged from Mrs. Cook's house in New York to the gangway of the SS *Royalmania* to a Monte Carlo hotel to the Ritz in Paris to the United States Customs in New York, and finally back to her house.

The Red General, which was to be produced by Joseph Verner Reed and Kenneth Macgowan, never left Jo's drawing board, but it gave him an opportunity to experiment with lighting projections. Using a large scale model of the set, he trained miniature projectors onto a pair of curved half-columns of canvas stretched on hoops, which he placed upstage on either side of a permanent backdrop. He discovered that an image "projected onto the convex surface of the two columns created unusual depth" in miniature but not when expanded to full size onstage. From this exercise, he learned that the effect in miniature was not always a sure way of "solving lighting problems for the actual stage."

Jo closed the season of 1929–30 with Jed Harris's production of Chekhov's *Uncle Vanya* in April. Harris as producer and director, Lillian Gish, Osgood Perkins, and Walter Connolly in the leads, and Jo were all given lavish praise by the critics. A mixture of erratic temperament, gargantuan ego, and more than a dash of genius, Harris could sometimes create productions of great beauty and truth, particularly for nuanced Chekhovian plays. As a director, working with actors in his coaxing, quiet manner, he could elicit great performances.

All through the twenties, producers took stabs at productions of the major modern European playwrights, frequently getting insurance by the casting of stars in the leading roles. Harris's favorite hobby was to fly in the face of convention—particularly of Broadway's custom—by doing the outrageous. He asked Lillian Gish to take the role of Helena in a new translation of *Uncle Vanya* by Rose Caylor, Ben Hecht's wife. Although Gish was probably the most popular film star of the time, she had never appeared on Broadway and had not played before live audiences for many years. Unfortunately, Harris gave her very little direction in the rehearsals and she admitted to being so petrified on opening night that she refused to look at the critical notices the morning after. When she did, she read how impressed all the critics were with her performance.

To make her appearance more emphatic, Harris rearranged the scenes to have her enter at the beginning of the play. Although she had no lines, she was supposed to walk across the stage with her luggage as if she had just arrived at her husband's country estate. She was dressed in a semi-transparent dress, which under Jo's lights was rendered diaphanous, revealing her slender but shapely torso. The audience went wild when she paused midstage, surrounded by a halo of light, to look back at the struggling porter. So successful were Harris's manipulations that, to everyone's surprise but his, *Uncle Vanya* quickly repaid its investors and was sent out to play to 200,000 people on the road.

JO'S SETS FROM **_UNCLE VANYA_** (1930), JED HARRIS'S AUDACIOUS BROADWAY PRODUCTION OF THE CHEKHOV PLAY STARRING LILLIAN GISH, LENT ENCHANTMENT TO THE MEMORABLE PERFORMANCES BY GISH AND THE REST OF THE CAST, ESPECIALLY THE BACKDROP FOR THE GARDEN SCENE (TOP) WITH ITS DELICATELY PAINTED VERTICAL LINES TO LOOK LIKE TAPERED TREES AND SPLOTCHES OF COLOR TO REPRESENT FOLIAGE. THE SECOND SCENE (BOTTOM), AN INTERIOR OF THE HOUSE, IS DOMINATED BY A MASSIVE MASONRY STOVE FLANKED BY OUTSIZED WINDOWS, DELIBERATELY OUT OF SCALE WITH THE FIGURES. (COURTESY OF ALICE CAREY)

JO'S SETS FROM **MR. GILHOOLEY** (1939), A MELODRAMA SET IN DUBLIN, PRODUCED AND DIRECTED BY JED HARRIS. THE DORMERED CEILING OF THE BOARDING HOUSE ROOM (ABOVE), WHERE MR. GILHOOLEY (ARTHUR SINCLAIR) TAKES THE YOUNG GIRL (HELEN HAYES) IS PROPERLY CLAUSTROPHOBIC AND PRESAGES AN UNHAPPY RESOLUTION. THE DARK DUBLIN STREET (BELOW) WITH LIGHT COMING ONLY FROM A DOORWAY AND A FEW WINDOWS INTENSIFIES THE LONELINESS OF THE GIRL SEATED ON THE PARK BENCH. (COURTESY OF JULES FISHER)

Very early in September, on the cusp of the new season on Broadway, Wiman and Brady and their associate Tom Weatherly produced a second edition of *The Little Show*, again mostly with lyrics and music by Dietz and Schwartz. Monty Woolley, Wiman's old mentor from Yale, helped Wiman stage the show. Jo and his colleague and friend Ray Sovey designed the settings and costumes, respectively, perhaps a bit more elaborately than for the first *Little Show* but decidedly without the trappings of a *Follies* or a *Scandals*. Despite the pleasant music and the presence of Al Trahan and J. C. Flippen, both delightful clowns, the critics found it dull and it closed after a relatively short run.

The next two shows Jo designed met a similar fate. Jed Harris's *Mr. Gilhooley* brought Jo together with Helen Hayes for the first of the five shows she was to play in his sets. It opened in late September and lasted barely a month, which must have left a large dent on Harris's ego. Based on a novel by Liam O'Flaherty, it told of a loveless May–December affair that ends with the murder-suicide of the unlikely (and unlucky) couple played by Hayes and the Irish actor Arthur Sinclair. A few weeks later another dramatic dud, *Solid South*, opened and closed within the space of a few weeks. The play, labeled a satirical comedy, was set in the homestead of an old whiskey-soaked unreconstructed Southern major, played by Richard Bennett, and attempted to extract some humor from his hatred of "damnyankees." Also in the cast was a bright ingenue named Bette Davis.

Jo's final show for 1930 was *Sweet and Low*, a revue produced by Billy Rose, who was married to Fanny Brice. Jo described their meeting:

> In Corn Beef and Roses [*the early title for the revue*] . . . each time Billy Rose discussed some vaudeville act, he would say, "I don't want this to look like vaudeville." As an example, he had three very amusing dancers who were successful in vaudeville of their day. But they always wore ill-fitting full-dress suits, top hats and canes, and Rose said, "Can you do anything to make them look differently?" Well, it happened on my way to the theater that day, it was a grizzly rainy winter afternoon, I went by the Plaza Hotel, and in the rain was sitting a group of old cabbies waiting for fares that weren't appearing on that miserable day. And I had noticed the

silhouette and not only the swaybacked old horses, and the ancient carriages, but these men were all wearing battered top hats. So I said to Billy, "If they would wear old hats and coachman's coats, I'll give them umbrellas to carry instead of canes. Would they work that way?" Billy said, "I'll make them work that way," and he did.

Although it was hokey, very much like the old-time vaudeville that Rose wanted to avoid, the revue ran largely because of Fanny Brice, George Jessel, and James Barton. When it did not make a million for Rose, he was depressed by what he considered its failure.

While Jo was working on the show, a suitcase of his was stolen during the out-of-town tryout. In casual conversation, he mentioned his loss to Rose and Brice. The day after he returned to New York, the bell to his studio rang and when he opened the door, there was his suitcase. He was never able to explain its miraculous appearance but he suspected that Brice's underworld connections through her first husband, Nicky Arnstein, may have been responsible for the return of the suitcase intact. It was a story that Jo told many times with great relish.

Jo did so well financially in 1930 that he was able to hire both an assistant and an accountant and get a studio away from home at 229 East 38th Street. He had set his minimum fee at $1,000, which could be negotiated downward for the right producer. Robert Barnhart did most of his drafting, but Jo kept tight reins over the designs and the colors. He signed contracts for five more shows for the balance of the 1930–31 season, which began for him with *Anatol*, by Arthur Schnitzler. In the cast were Joseph Schildkraut, Patricia Collinge, and Miriam Hopkins. The production marked the first time that Jo received credit for designing the costumes as well as the sets. The play about the last flings of a *boulevardier* about to get married was set in and around *fin-de-siècle* Vienna and given a musical background of Viennese waltzes played by a full orchestra. The show had only a brief fling on Broadway, but the critics applauded Jo's sets.

In 1931, Katharine Cornell, urged on by husband Guthrie McClintic, formed her own production company to present plays of her choosing. For the first play under her banner, *The Barretts of*

Wimpole Street, she asked Jo to design the sets and costumes. Playing Elizabeth Barrett opposite the Robert Browning of Brian Aherne, Cornell transformed the play into her most enduring success. After playing it on Broadway for 372 performances, she took it on the road, revived it time and again, took it back on the road, and prolonged its life into the age of television, for which she did a version in 1955. Jo was overjoyed; on the day of the first full dress rehearsal, he sat in the orchestra while she and her cast reacted to the set. In his zeal to create the right atmosphere, he had gone to

THE CHRISTMAS EVE SCENE FROM ***ANATOL*** (1931), COMPLETE WITH SNOWFALL. IT IS ALMOST VIENNESE OPERETTA-LIKE IN FEELING. THE *NEW YORKER'S* ROBERT BENCHLEY WAS AMONG THE CRITICS WHO RHAPSODIZED OVER JO'S SETS. HE THOUGHT THAT THEY WERE SIX OF THE LOVELIEST STAGE SETS WITHIN PROSCENIUM FRAME (PORTALS) HE HAD EVER SEEN AND PROFESSED TO BEING REDUCED TO A SODDEN MASS OF SHIRTFRONT BY THE MUSIC. "HEARD WITH MR. MIELZINER'S SETTINGS AS A BACKGROUND, IT IS ALMOST MORE THAN THIS OLD HAPSBURG HEART CAN BEAR." (COURTESY OF WALTER MIELZINER)

BECAUSE ALL OF THE ACTION TOOK PLACE IN ELIZABETH BARRETT'S BED-SITTING ROOM IN **THE BARRETTS OF WIMPOLE STREET** (1931), JO HAD TO CREATE A BUSY VICTORIAN ROOM LOADED WITH PROPS, BUT HE REALIZED THAT ONCE THE ROOM WAS ESTABLISHED IN THE AUDIENCE'S MIND, ATTENTION WOULD BE ENTIRELY FOCUSED ON KATHARINE CORNELL AND THE ACTORS SURROUNDING HER. (VANDERBILT UNIVERSITY LIBRARY)

SIXTEEN SETS WERE USED FOR **THE HOUSE BEAUTIFUL** (1931); THE SCENES HAD TO SHOW CHANGES IN THE HOUSE OVER A PERIOD OF THIRTY YEARS THROUGH SUBSTITUTIONS OF PROPS AND BACKDROPS. JO DISPLAYED AN INGENUITY IN LIGHTING REMARKABLE FOR THE TIME: SCENERY WAS CHANGED DURING BLACKOUTS, A STAGECRAFT TECHNIQUE THAT WOULD BECOME STANDARD IN FUTURE DECADES. (BILLY ROSE THEATRE COLLECTION, NYPL-PA)

a secondhand letter collector and bought a few handwritten notes and stamped envelopes of the exact period of the play and placed them on Elizabeth Barrett's writing table. When Cornell picked them up during the inspection of the set, she suddenly turned front and exclaimed: "Why, how wonderful! Are you out there, Jo?" (The lessons of Robert Edmond Jones were not lost on his disciple.) When Dorothy Parker, pinchhitting for Robert Benchley at the *New Yorker*, saw the show, she was unrestrained in her enthusiasm for Jo's scenery: "I do not believe that there is half enough screaming about Mr. Mielziner," she wrote. "Show me, that's all I ask you, anybody better in our theatre."

Joseph Urban, not Jo, was supposedly the first choice of producer Crosby Gaige as the designer for his production of Channing Pollock's *The House Beautiful*, but illness forced him to withdraw. The title of the play describes not only a house built in "West Hills, New Jersey," by a newlywed couple but the structure of the marriage as it progresses from 1901 to 1930. Darkness and the ticking of a clock indicated the lapse of time, according to the program. One of the critics perceived what Jo was up to in this production. He described "settings of half and full stage dimensions that are changed [in darkness] with a rapidity that rivals the speed of a motion picture fade-out." The play, a flop, engendered one of Dorothy Parker's one-line critiques that has lasted longer than the memory of the play: "The House Beautiful is the Play Lousy."

On a happier note, the production brought together Jo and Worthington Miner, its director, who became lifelong friends and, for a while, neighbors in the same apartment building. It also introduced him to a pretty young actress named Annie Laurie Jaques, who would later figure in his life.

In May, Billy Rose recycled bits and pieces of *Sweet and Low*, added new numbers, retitled it *Billy Rose's Crazy Quilt*, and brought it to Broadway after three weeks of rehearsal for a short run before sending it out on the road with Fanny Brice, supported by Phil Baker and Ted Healy. Rose retrieved Jo's sets from Cain's warehouse but omitted all mention of Mielziner from the program and paid him no fees for the reuse of his scenery. Whatever Jo felt about Billy's underhandedness, he did nothing about it, moving on to Dwight

Deere Wiman's *The Third Little Show,* which opened on the first of June. The critics pronounced it better than *The Second Little Show* but not so good as *The Little Show.* The presence of Beatrice Lillie at the top of the bill and sketches by Noël Coward, Marc Connelly, and S. J. Perelman helped to keep it afloat.

Broadway in the early thirties was afflicted with several maladies, some of which would never go away. The Great Depression had settled over the country, and even some of the producers who had been regarded as unassailable fortresses were broke. The Shuberts went into receivership; many went to bankruptcy court; still others simply folded up their Broadway tents and quietly slipped away. Many "angels" who had made their cash on Wall Street and squandered it on shows uptown disappeared with their worthless paper stocks and bonds. The banks that held the mortgages on Broadway playhouses found themselves the proud owners of same. There were fewer hits and more flops, probably due to the psychology of the time, which made people demand more for their money. Producers dropped the prices on tickets to try to lure customers away from the movies. The touring road was drying up, and most of the famous downtown theatres across America were either being recycled as movie theatres, converted to nontheatrical uses, or simply torn down.

There appeared to be more opportunity in the sun- and money-drenched hills of Hollywood than on the Great White Way, and many playwrights, directors, actors, dancers, choreographers, and designers deserted New York. Some came back, chastened by their experiences, but many more remained and made new careers for themselves on the silver screen. Vaudeville was dying, so comedians such as Jack Benny, Ed Wynn, and Jimmy Durante found a haven in radio, a medium of entertainment that had been held in open disdain for many years.

More than 200 shows made it to Broadway for the season of 1931–32, but according to Burns Mantle, there were four failures for every success. Although Jo had a minuscule percentage of those productions, several of his shows were major hits. To begin the season, he designed four large, lavish sets for *I Love an Actress,* by the Hungarian playwright Laszlo Fodor. Most critics considered

THE THIRD LITTLE SHOW (1931) WAS TO BE THE LAST OF THE DWIGHT DEERE WIMAN INTIMATE REVUES. THE SHOW-STOPPING NUMBER, A DITTY BY NOËL COWARD CALLED "MAD DOGS AND ENGLISHMEN," WAS SUNG BY BEATRICE LILLIE. JO CARTOONED HIS SET FOR THE NUMBER WITH A BACKDROP THAT NOT ONLY SHOWED THE HOT SUN BUT ALSO SPOOFED THE BRITISH, PICTURING THE BANK OF ENGLAND AMID NATIVE HUTS. (BILLY ROSE THEATRE COLLECTION, NYPL-PA)

it synthetic Schnitzler, and it shut down. For his second production, Jo was reunited with playwright S. N. Behrman and the McClintics for *Brief Moment.* Its principal attractions were its classy dialogue and Alexander Woollcott in a featured role. With so much star power, the production had a respectable run and turned a modest profit.

Jo had designed revues, but he had yet to design a musical comedy; he was now to get his chance with *Of Thee I Sing,* the first of more than fifty musicals he was to design during his long career. Since it was being produced by Sam Harris and directed by its co-author (with Morrie Ryskind) George S. Kaufman, Jo was among friends, but he had not yet been introduced to the composer and lyricist, George and Ira Gershwin, who had been writing musicals

since their first success *Lady Be Good!* in 1924. *Of Thee I Sing* would prove to be something special in the development of American musicals. The Depression was slowly rendering the inane books and silly songs of the twenties' musicals into relics of a more care-free, bygone era. In a satirical turn, the authors took aim at some venerable and not so venerable American institutions: Congress, the Presidency and Vice Presidency, the Supreme Court, political conventions, beauty pageants, marriage, and motherhood. When it opened the day after Christmas, the critics ran out of superlatives in their reviews. Everyone who had a hand in its making had his or her share of the overall praise. *Of Thee I Sing* also received the Pulitzer Prize, the first musical ever to be so honored.

Largely because of his fee plus a weekly royalty for *Of Thee I Sing*, Jo ended the year 1931 with his best financial record to date. He was also elected to the Coffee House Club, which had been founded in 1914 by a group of defectors from the stuffy old Knickerbocker Club. Relaxed in style and conveniently located for lunch at 45 West 45th Street, just a few blocks from Jo's studio, it became one of his favorite haunts.

In November, after his divorce from Marya and before he would be tied up with *Of Thee I Sing*, Jo had managed to slip away to spend a few weeks with Ken in California. Instead of taking a train, he decided to fly, his first trip in an airplane. He described the experience in a letter to his parents as the "most thrilling 36 hours I have ever spent." He went from snow in Ohio to hot sun in Kansas and flew in full moonlight for the last leg of the trip. On weekends Jo and his brother went boating and sunbathing on Catalina Island. For Jo, it was rest and rehabilitation from a busy work schedule and wrenching personal adjustments. The brothers were each other's closest confidants. "Ken has saved my life in so many ways," he wrote Ella and Leo, "that I am convinced that the cat isn't the only living being with nine lives! Not only to be with him but to have the restful luxury of this place is perfect. Already I feel that I have caught up with myself." It is very likely that Jo discussed his rela-tionship with Annie Laurie Jaques, whom he had been seeing for several months. After Jo left, Kenneth felt more alone and remote from the center of things than ever.

When Marya moved out of his life, Jo was disconsolate, but in a world filled with pretty young actresses it was not possible to remain in retreat for very long. He met Annie Laurie Jaques (pronounced "Jakes") and within a few weeks, Jo was in love again. Annie Laurie was almost as tall as he, slender, stylish, with bobbed blonde hair and almond-shaped blue eyes. In her lively company his wounded ego could heal.

Annie Laurie was the younger daughter of Colonel and Mrs. Charles Everett Jaques of Chicago's Northside, both of colonial American stock and the Chicago Social Register. Colonel Jaques, a former officer in the Quartermaster Corps, was heir to the Kansas City Baking Powder Company fortune, but he spent little time in the family business. His passion was travel and he and his wife circled the globe several times, taking their daughters Hallie and Annie Laurie with them. Annie Laurie, a born rebel, would have none of the social life of her conservative parents. When she was in her very early twenties, she somehow persuaded them to let her go to school in New York. Since Colonel Jaques had settled a trust fund on each of his girls, Annie Laurie assumed control of her life very quickly. Also known as Laurie or Jaksie, she was a flapper out of the pages of an F. Scott Fitzgerald story. A free spirit, a hedonist, and a poker player of the first order, she could also figure skate, fly an airplane, ride a horse, and do just about anything she had a mind to do. Her goal was to go on the New York stage or break into the movies. For a while, she did both. She was a stand-in for Louise Brooks when movies were being made in Astoria and landed a few small parts on Broadway. She captured a decent part in a show called *Five Star Final*, which was directed by Tony Miner. He cast her again in *The House Beautiful*, which is when she met and fell in love with the designer of the show.

Jo and Laurie were married in a church in Westport, Connecticut, on January 17, 1932, soon after Jo's divorce from Marya became final. The happy couple honeymooned at Palm Beach, but only briefly; since Jo had to get back to the drawing board, a longer trip had to be deferred. Back in New York, they moved into Laurie's apartment off Sutton Place, then to another apartment on East 39th Street. After finishing his work on *Bloodstream* in late March, he and

Laurie along with Colonel and Mrs. Jaques sailed on the SS *Roma* for Palermo, Italy. Leo and Ella saw them off and left them with one of Leo's poems and a basketful of toys, containing jacks, jumping rope, and marbles, in case they got bored.

On their first anniversary, in 1933, the pair went off on a round-the-world trip on the SS *Stella Polaris*. When they stopped in Italy, they spent time visiting Ella and Leo, who were on vacation in Capri from January to March, a gift, no doubt, from Kenneth. Jo did some sketching and painting on the trip. When they returned to New York, Laurie found them a summer place about twenty-five miles north of the city on South Mountain Road in New City, New York, a Hudson Valley town that attracted an arty and show business crowd from Manhattan. Jo was delighted with her find, a remodelled red barn with a large, light studio. They could play tennis at the communal court, and swim in Maxwell Anderson's swimming hole nearby. In the fall, Jo and Laurie moved into a larger apartment, two floors of a townhouse, at 113 East 61st Street. While it was being readied for them, Mrs. Jaques put them up at the Hotel Delmonico, paying all expenses. Their rent was an outrageous $166.66 per month, but with Laurie's income and Jo's own, they were able to afford it.

Jo did not want Laurie to work, but she was not a housewife. Moreover, Jo wanted a family, but she was not eager to oblige. Somewhat accident prone and often physically sick with minor ailments, Laurie simply could not sit still. (Kenneth once described her as having a "nervous and active temperament.") She took interest in things like the Lindbergh baby kidnapping trial, for which she got up very early each morning so that she could catch a train to New Jersey to get a good seat in the courtroom. She had money to do what she pleased. What Jo wanted from a wife neither Marya nor Annie Laurie could—or should have had to—give him. The only model he had was his parents' enduring relationship, which had involved much sacrifice on Ella's part and the submersion of her own ambitions. Jo's marriage to Laurie would begin unraveling in 1936.

With the dubious exception of *Bridal Wise*, Jo's contributions at the end of the 1931–32 season enriched his coffers somewhat, burnished his reputation a lot, but were disappointing failures. Dwight

Deere Wiman and his associate producer Tom Weatherly beckoned him to design *Gay Divorce*, a musical that introduced him to Cole Porter and Howard Lindsay, and the Theatre Guild called him for another Behrman comedy, *Biography*.

Gay Divorce starred Fred Astaire, Claire Luce, and Luella Gear and was Astaire's last Broadway appearance before he departed for Hollywood. Everything meshed in it—sets by Mielziner, costumes by Ray Sovey, singing and dancing by Astaire and Luce, the direction and the choreography, the Porter score—everything but the underlying comedy, which was not very funny. But the show, which introduced one of Porter's most durable hits, "Night and Day," went on to become a successful Hollywood film, *Gay Divorcée*, starring Astaire and Ginger Rogers.

Biography, Jo's final show for the year, proved to be the Theatre Guild's only hit in their lackluster season. It starred Ina Claire as an artist who faces writing her autobiography with all the attendant complications of reviewing her past. Luckily, the scenery for the

play did not strain Jo's imagination or skills, because from November on he was designing an opera based on O'Neill's *The Emperor Jones*, with music by Louis Gruenberg, for the Metropolitan Opera. According to Jo's account, someone (name unknown to him) at the Met persuaded Gatti-Casazza, the general manager, to engage him for the job. It was a particularly challenging task because the entire play takes place in one day on an island in the West Indies. He had to transform a relatively benign jungle scene by day into a sinister and unearthly setting by night, and the only way he could think of doing it was with lighting. When he presented the preliminary sketches to Gatti-Casazza and his staff, accompanying it with a verbal explanation of everything he planned to do, the only responses were in Italian, which had to be translated for him. After a particularly long exchange between the general manager and his staff, Jo realized that they had all understood his English perfectly and that their only cavil was that "none of them had ever in their lives seen leaves of the size and shape you have shown in your jungle designs today." He was told to proceed to the final renderings, which they wanted him to finish that day!

Jo's sets were a departure for the Met—a welcome one according to some critics, who were not pleased with its usual antiquated sets and less than imaginative lighting. For all this imagination and work, Jo was paid a paltry $750, a fee much lower than what he charged Broadway producers. At this point in his career, the prestige of working for a great opera company was compensation enough. He hoped it would open the way for other opportunities.

During 1933, Jo was absent from Broadway for nearly nine months on his marriage sabbatical. With his 1932 income of more than $10,000 and Annie Laurie's trust fund income, the young couple lived very comfortably. After years of accepting almost every design assignment offered to him, it was a pleasure for Jo not to have to meet deadlines and face the demands of producers and directors for a while. When he returned to his studio he was busier than ever with new assignments. *Champagne Sec,* a new version of Johann Strauss's *Die Fledermaus* by Lawrence Langner, was tried out by Wiman at the Westport Country Playhouse, Langner's Connecticut retreat. Jo was not optimistic about its chances for success. He was unimpressed with much of the cast—they were "terribly little theatre"—but he liked the principal performers, including Peggy Wood,

JO'S SET DESIGN FOR THE METROPOLITAN OPERA PRODUCTION OF A MUSICAL VERSION OF EUGENE O'NEILL'S *THE EMPEROR JONES* (1933). THE JUNGLE THAT WOULD EVENTUALLY DESTROY JONES LOOKS APPROPRIATELY TWISTED AND MENACING, BUT IT WAS JO'S LIGHTING FOR THE OPERA THAT TOOK ONE'S BREATH AWAY. (MUSEUM OF THE CITY OF NEW YORK)

IN ACT III OF **MERRY MOUNT** (1934), AN OPERA THAT BORROWS HEAVILY FOR PLOT FROM BOTH *FAUST* AND THE SALEM WITCH TRIALS, THERE IS A DREAM SCENE IN WHICH THE YOUNG PASTOR FROM THE VILLAGE SUCCUMBS IN HIS SLEEP TO THE BRIBES OF THE DEVIL. HE ENVISIONS HIS VILLAGE ENGULFED IN FLAME, WHICH JO DEPICTED IN A SPEC-TACULAR SCENIC AND LIGHTING DISPLAY. (METROPOLITAN OPERA ARCHIVES)

Helen Ford and George Meader. (Kitty Carlisle played Prince Orlovsky.) Confounding his predictions, the critics enjoyed the production and liked his sets.

Before the end of 1933, Jo had designed four unsuccessful productions in rapid succession. Only one, Jed Harris's production of *The Lake*, starring Katharine Hepburn, has remained memorable, on the basis of Dorothy Parker's zinger about Hepburn's acting ability: "She ran the gamut of emotions from A to B." Forgotten is the praise that she, the play, and the scenery got from other critics. At year's end, Jo had earned less than $6,000, but his phone was ringing.

The Metropolitan Opera invited Jo to return to design the world premiere of *Merry Mount*, an American opera by Howard Hanson. It opened in a matinee performance on February 10, played six performances in the 1933–34 season, and then was heard no more. Critics were so pleased by Jo's sets of a colonial seventeenth-century Massachusetts village that they wondered in print why he was not hired on a regular basis at the Met, an implied wish with which he concurred. Unfortunately, neither *Merry Mount* nor *The Emperor Jones* remained in the Met's repertory, and Jo was not asked to design another set for the company until many years and several general managers later.

Jo finished the Broadway season of 1933–34 with some design challenges. For the first time in his career, he suffered some severe criticism for his work on *Dodsworth*, adapted by Sidney Howard from Sinclair Lewis's novel and produced by Max Gordon. Its many scenes shifted from Zenith (somewhere in the Midwest) to steamships plying the transatlantic route, to luxurious hotels in London, Paris, and Berlin, to Switzerland and Naples, and back to Zenith. (No wonder Jo became Howard's favorite designer and problem-solver.) Many of the critics who wrote favorably of the play, starring Walter Huston and Fay Bainter, were displeased with

FROM ***DODSWORTH*** (1934). JUMPING TO SITES ALL OVER THE WORLD, SCENES CHANGED AT A DIZZYING PACE IN SIDNEY HOWARD'S DRAMATIZATION OF SINCLAIR LEWIS'S NOVEL THE SCENE PICTURED IS OF THE OFFICE OF THE PRESIDENT (PLAYED BY WALTER HUSTON) OF THE REVELATION MOTOR COMPANY IN THE MIDWEST. BEHIND THE OUTSIZED WINDOW CENTER STAGE, JO CREATED THE IMPRESSION OF THE AUTOMOBILE FACTORY PAINTED ON A TRANSPARENT CURTAIN, A DEVICE HE WOULD USE AGAIN AND AGAIN. ALSO, ON THE WALLS, HE DESIGNED A PAIR OF LIGHT FIXTURES USING OUTSIZED GEARS TO CREATE AN ART DECO EFFECT. (BILLY ROSE THEATRE COLLECTION, NYPL-PA)

Jo's sets. Described as dreary, ugly, stuffy, and heavy, Jo's *Dodsworth* scenery was defended in an entire column by critic Richard Lockridge in the *New York Sun*. He began his lively defense by taking a swipe at "the scenery boys" who felt a few years back that plays "might as well be done away with altogether" by throwing "Appia at your head, and speak[ing] of Gordon Craig, and laugh[ing] harshly at a suggestion that scenery is made for plays

FOR *YELLOW JACK* (1934), A PLAY ABOUT YELLOW FEVER THAT WOULD BE CONSIDERED A DOCUDRAMA TODAY, JO WENT BACK TO HIS ROOTS IN THE NEW STAGECRAFT BY DESIGNING A MUTABLE "UNIT SET," WHICH BY THE ADDITION AND SUBTRACTION OF VARIOUS ELEMENTS COULD BE MADE TO REPRESENT ALL TWENTY-NINE DIFFERENT SCENES, SOME OF WHICH WERE IN FLASHBACK. HE CREATED A CENTER UNIT AND A SERIES OF LEVELS AND TRANSPARENT BACKDROPS, BUT RELIED HEAVILY ON LIGHTING EFFECTS TO ALTER SCENES AND MOODS. (ESTATE OF JO MIELZINER)

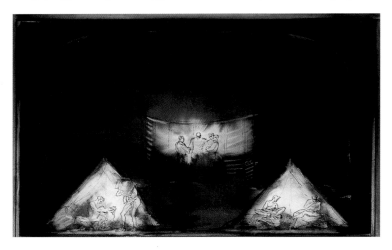

and not plays for scenery." He declared that Jo's settings "look pretty much like the places they are supposed to be."

Dodsworth had been an exercise in realism kept within the limits of existing stage technology. Jo's next job, on *Yellow Jack*, called for twenty-nine scene changes without resort to complicated and expensive solutions. What Jo and director-producer Guthrie McClintic sought in this Sidney Howard "docudrama" on Dr. Walter Reed's research into the causes of yellow fever was cinematic-style dissolves and quick changes. Jo's designs became such a triumph of scenic art that his renderings for *Yellow Jack* were later exhibited at the Museum of Modern Art. (He presented his preliminary drawings to Kenneth.) From *Yellow Jack*, Jo proceeded to another experiment in dramatic production, for *The Pure in Heart*, by John Howard Lawson. It surrealistically fused acting, movement, scenery, and music to serve Lawson's thesis that society crushes the innocent. But nobody seemed interested in this thesis, in Lawson's poetic overlay, or in Jo's "appropriate scenery"—which, as Walter Winchell noted in the *New York Mirror*, "is what play reporters say when they are not excited by the scenery."

For a summer break, Annie Laurie talked Jo into going to Eaton Ranch, a dude ranch in Wolf, Wyoming. Jo took along work: designs that were promised for the first half of the 1934–35 season. While Jo spent most of his time designing *Romeo and Juliet* (for the McClintics) in their cabin, his wife found what she wanted in the arms of a ranch employee, Curly Witzel. Jo left after a month, and Annie Laurie stayed on to become better acquainted with her cowboy. She and Witzel would be married after her divorce from Jo, in 1937. (Years later, when Jo was with his third wife, Jean McIntyre, three taxis pulled up to the front entrance at the Dakota. From the first emerged Marya Mannes and her husband, who resided there; from the second, Jo and Jean; and from the third, Annie Laurie and Witzel. For an instant, Jo's past and present met and merged on that New York sidewalk.)

The Mielziners' plan that summer was also to go to Central City, Colorado, to see Kenneth play Iago to Walter Huston's Othello in a production of the play by Robert Edmond Jones. Mishap followed mishap on the road to Colorado, and it looked as if Jo and

Annie Laurie would not make it. Finally, Jo left his exhausted wife behind, chartered an airplane, and arrived for the performance just in the nick of time. To Ella and Leo he wrote that Ken's Iago "surpassed craft in a brilliant fashion. I know of no actor today who could in my opinion give so colorful and awful and biting a performance."

Ken returned to New York in the lead of *Merrily We Roll Along*, by Kaufman and Hart, for which Jo designed the sets. The elder Mielziners must have been gratified by Robert Garland's review in the *World-Telegram*: "*Merrily We Roll Along* is brilliant, all right. And in more ways than one. Brilliant are several of the nine sets which Mr. Jo Mielziner has provided. Brilliant is the acting of Mr. Kenneth MacKenna and some others." The nine sets moved the action of the play from 1934 backward in time to 1916. The Sam Harris production occasioned one of Jo's memorable *bons mots*. Trying to be helpful to the production office by suggesting ways to cut down the physical size of the scenery and thus save money on stagehands, he went to speak to Kaufman (the director as well as co-author) about his plan. He was greeted by Kaufman's usual sarcasm: "To what do I owe this honor?" Jo replied: "I came to see you about *Merrily We Roll Along*." Then asked Kaufman: "Is it still running?" "Yes," answered Jo, "backward." From that point on, Kaufman listened.

When Samson Raphaelson's *Accent on Youth*, produced by Crosby Gaige, opened on Christmas night of 1934, it was almost lost in the shuffle amid seemingly more exciting premieres during the hectic holiday period. The Cinderella-style love story was deemed "lightly good-humored and pleasantly insane" by Atkinson of the *New York Times*. Audiences gave it a comfortable run. (Sometime during the run, Kenneth MacKenna took over the lead, which may have been a case of Jo's influence with the producer as well as a payback for all of Kenneth's early boosting of his younger brother's career.) Jo's creation of a penthouse apartment was as charming and attractive as the play. But his *pièce de résistance* was reserved for the McClintics' *Romeo and Juliet*, for which Jo also designed the costumes. It opened on the penultimate day of the year and brought the critics to their feet.

ANNIE LAURIE JAQUES, JO'S SECOND WIFE, WAS AN AVID DUDE RANCHER. SHE PERSUADED JO TO ACCOMPANY HER TO THE EATON RANCH IN WYOMING IN 1934 AND EVEN GOT HIM ON A HORSE. MOSTLY HE STAYED BEHIND IN THE CABIN TO WORK. (ESTATE OF JO MIELZINER)

FROM **MERRILY WE ROLL ALONG** (1934). APART FROM SEVERAL MORE ELABORATE INTERIOR SCENES, MOST OF JO'S SCENERY WAS AS SIMPLE AS THE ONE SHOWN, WHICH USES A STREET LAMP, A PARK BENCH, AND A MANHATTAN BACKDROP TO EVOKE MADISON SQUARE PARK. (BILLY ROSE THEATRE COLLECTION, NYPL-PA)

JO LIKED WHAT HE DID FOR KATHARINE CORNELL'S ***ROMEO AND JULIET*** (1934). BY USING STRONG COLORS AND A PRIMITIVE PERSPECTIVE IN THE BACKDROPS (ESPECIALLY IN THIS DROP OF VERONA), HE FLEW AGAINST THE ESTABLISHED TRADITION OF DRENCHING THE SCENES VISUALLY WITH DARK COLORS AND MOOD LIGHTING TO PRESAGE THE TRAGEDY. AS IF HE WERE DESIGNING A MUSICAL COMEDY, HE GAVE IT A LIGHTER, MORE YOUTHFUL AND VIGOROUS LOOK, WHICH MAY HAVE INTENSIFIED THE TRAGEDY OF THE YOUNG LOVERS (ABOVE). HE CREATED A SHALLOW CURTAINED STAGE WITH RIGHT AND LEFT ENTRANCES. BEHIND IT WAS A SLIGHTLY DEEPER STAGE WITH A SECOND CURTAIN (BELOW), AND FINALLY, FOR THE INTIMATE SCENES, AN UPSTAGE ARCH. HE COULD THEN MOVE SCENES QUICKLY WITH THE ACTION, KEEPING THE PART OF THE STAGE NOT IN USE IN SHADOW. (COURTESY OF JULES FISHER)

JO ALSO DESIGNED THE COSTUMES FOR ***ROMEO AND JULIET.*** SHOWN IS THE COSTUME DESIGN FOR LADY CAPULET. (ESTATE OF JO MIELZINER)

When McClintic and he had discussed the scenery before Jo left for his Wyoming vacation, Jo was gratified by the willingness of the director to set Shakespeare's play in the early Renaissance rather than in the usual later period. Jo liked the naïveté of the painter Giotto, whose frescoes he had seen in Assisi, Italy, the previous year, and wanted to evoke their simple style and uncomplicated colors in his scenery. Jo's costumes became the subject of an entire column in *Women's Wear Daily*. Again, Jo used platforms, curtains, and painted backdrops to set and change the play's many scenes and keep the action fluid. The lighting design, for which McClintic took credit in his autobiography, was the result of Jo's tact in dealing with an imaginative director yet at the same time maintaining control over his end of the production. Although Katharine Cornell extended the play's run to accommodate the demand for tickets, it was such an expensive production that it still lost money.

Although Jo's program credits had been sometimes listed as "Production designed by Jo Mielziner," costumes and lighting design had rarely been credited separately to him. For *Romeo and Juliet* the McClintics gave him credit for costume design as well as the sets. To help him, he hired Rose Bogdanoff, whom he called upon for assistance from 1934 to 1945, whenever he was able to get producers to allow him to take on costume design as well. For fifteen years, her talents were sought after also by Robert Edmond Jones, Norman Bel Geddes, and Donald Oenslager. She eventually achieved recognition as a costume designer in her own right. In 1948 she became head of the costume design department for NBC and continued to design for Broadway until her premature death at the age of fifty-three.

Jo's status as a designer was enhanced by the increasingly ingenious work he did in 1934. His fees were now among the highest on Broadway, and many producers paid them willingly, knowing that the Mielziner stamp had begun to have significance for their shows. They knew that Jo was always prepared, always on time, always facile in solving problems, always ready to cut costs wherever he could and to make compromises. Hiring Jo for $2,000 (or more) might have seemed expensive at the outset but it was often

balanced by not having to pay for unexpected adjustments to the scenery in the late stages of production. They also recognized that his name had begun to acquire a special cachet on the program. As for Jo, he made so much money that year that he had to hire an accountant.

Jo's first commission for 1935 was *De Luxe*, a dramatization by novelist Louis Bromfield (in collaboration with John Gearson) of a French novel by Edouard Bourdet. Producer Chester Erskin allowed Jo to spend great sums of money on lavish sets, which prompted Robert Garland of the *World-Telegram* to exclaim that Cecil B. De Mille "could ask no more." In one scene, Jo used a device that has since become standard: Melvyn Douglas (the play's star) is seen telephoning Violet Heming (its other star); when she answers, the stage lights go out and microphones pick up both ends of the conversation. When the lights come back up, the scene is in Heming's apartment.

Like Jones, Simonson, Geddes, and many others, Jo had to work through the stage electricians to get the lighting effects he wanted, even though he specified in great detail what was needed. With the production of *Panic*, his name finally appeared on the program as the designer of the sets *and* the lighting. *Panic*, a "modern tragedy" by Archibald MacLeish, was to be produced for three nights only by the Phoenix Theatre, Inc. (not to be confused with the off-Broadway company of a later time). Almost everybody associated with the production (including Martha Graham, Rose McClendon, Orson Welles, and others) either donated their services or reduced their fees to a bare minimum, as did Jo. A verse drama that deals with the crushing effects of the Depression on society, the play's unlikely hero is a banker who attempts to save the beleaguered American banking system and fails. Critic John Mason Brown called it "one of the season's most well-intentioned, but outstanding bores."

Jo's last two entries in the 1934–35 season, *Flowers of the Forest*, by John Van Druten, and *Kind Lady*, by Edward Chodorov, failed despite the presence of great Broadway stars. However, he was

FROM ***WINTERSET*** (1935). THE MOST FAMOUS SET FROM THE PLAY IS JO'S ARCHING BROOKLYN BRIDGE (THIS PAGE). LESS WELL KNOWN IS THE OTHER SCENE IN THE PLAY (OPPOSITE, TOP), THE BASEMENT FLAT OF ITS HERO, MIO. (*THIS PAGE*: ESTATE OF JO MIELZINER)

anticipating his work on a far more interesting play for the new Broadway season.

When Guthrie McClintic asked Jo to design Maxwell Anderson's *Winterset* for a September opening, he gave him the script of a verse drama based loosely on the trial and execution of Sacco and Vanzetti, which was still smoldering in the minds and hearts of many liberal-thinking people. Jo loved the play but felt compelled to speak out with strong conviction about the opening scene of Anderson's script. He thought it wrong, he told McClintic, that the audience would be looking at the river bank with its clutter and shoddy buildings underneath the Brooklyn Bridge but without seeing the bridge itself. He wanted to turn the scene around so that the bridge would be visible as it soared toward an unseen landing and its majestic architecture could represent, perhaps, a metaphor for hope and faith. Anderson resisted but agreed to visit the riverfront on the Brooklyn side to see what Jo had in mind. With McClintic on his side, Jo described to the playwright how the bridge, the river it spans, and the moonlight and mist could provide the scenic complement for the actors and the verse they were speaking. Reluctantly, Anderson agreed to allow Jo to go ahead, and *Winterset* became one of the highest achievements of Jo's entire career in the theatre. John Mason Brown was the first among the critics, all of whom were unanimous in the praise of the scenery, to recognize what Jo could bring to a production. In his review of September 26, 1935, he wrote:

> *In his visualization of the bridge, Mr. Mielziner has provided* Winterset *with one of the finest backgrounds our contemporary theater has seen. It is a setting of great majesty and beauty that is full of strength and alive with a poetry of its own. It is as simple, direct and impressive as one wishes the play were.*

Brooks Atkinson thought both the bridge scene and the set for the "cheerless, barren tenement basement [that] is a proper place for treachery and stealth" should be exhibited at the Metropolitan Museum. Sidney Howard was moved to put his own sentiments in a letter to Jo: "I thought when I saw *Jubilee* [a show that opened later] that no production could be more beautiful than that. Then I saw

LEFT: MAXWELL ANDERSON (1888–1959), IN A 1933 PHOTOGRAPH. BEGINNING IN 1925 WITH A PRODUCTION OF *FIRST FLIGHT* AND ENDING IN 1958 WITH *THE DAY THE MONEY STOPPED*, JO WAS TO DESIGN A DOZEN OF MAXWELL ANDERSON'S PLAYS. THE CLOSE GIVE-AND-TAKE OF PLAYWRIGHT AND DESIGNER, WHICH JO WAS ALSO TO ENJOY WITH OTHER WRITERS, IS ESSENTIAL TO A SUCCESSFUL PRODUCTION, BOTH THEN AND NOW. THE MOST MEMORABLE OF THEIR COLLABORATIONS WAS **WINTERSET (1935)**, WHEN ANDERSON GAVE A LITTLE MORE THAN HE HAD PLANNED. (*TOP:* MUSEUM OF THE CITY OF NEW YORK; *LEFT:* BILLY ROSE THEATRE COLLECTION, NYPL-PA)

JO DESIGNED BOTH THE COSTUMES AND SETS FOR **PRIDE AND PREJUDICE** (1935).
SHOWN IS A COSTUME FOR THE CHARACTER ELIZABETH BENNET. HE USED THE *LADIES'*
BOOKS OF THE EARLY NINETEENTH CENTURY, SELECTED CLOTHES OF THE ERA TO
SKETCH, ASSIGNED THEM TO CHARACTERS IN THE PLAY, SWATCHED THEM WITH FABRICS
OF HIS CHOICE, AND HAD THEM MADE BY EAVES COSTUME COMPANY. HIS ZEAL FOR
AUTHENTICITY LED HIM TO FIND THE CORRECT SWORDS AND SCABBARDS FOR THE
OFFICERS DOWN TO THE BUTTONS ON THEIR UNIFORMS. MUCH TO HIS SURPRISE, AN
ARMY MAJOR WAS QUOTED IN A LETTER TO THE *NEW YORK TIMES*, SAYING THAT HIS
EVENING WAS SPOILED BY THE USE OF AN INCORRECT SCABBARD. JO IMMEDIATELY DIS-
PATCHED A LETTER TO THE EDITOR IN WHICH HE DEFENDED HIS HISTORICAL ACCU-
RACY, CHALLENGING THE MAJOR TO A DUEL IN SHUBERT ALLEY, WITH SWORDS AND
SCABBARDS OF CHOICE. (COURTESY OF THE AUTHOR)

Winterset, which really is the most beautiful and right setting of a play that I have ever seen."

Whenever he received an assignment that called for something out of the ordinary, Jo was at his best. He could invent ways to shift scenes rapidly or create a special effect by his ingenuity alone. For ten years, he had borrowed heavily from his mentors. There was a lot of Jones in his *Romeo and Juliet*, a bit of Simonson in his *Yellow Jack*, and something of Craig and Appia in his *Little Eyolf* and *Faust*, but *Winterset* was pure Mielziner. By seeing poetry in the pedestrian and by investing it with three dimensions, he created not scenery but scenic art. *Winterset* triumphantly freed Jo from the past and assured him of a special place in a craft that in the hands of a Jones, Simonson, Geddes, or Mielziner could become an art, albeit ephemeral.

For Jo, *Winterset* was the point of maturation in his develop-ment—and it glorified a season that would also display Jo's fellow designers brilliantly in plays of high caliber: *Dead End* (Norman Bel Geddes), *Idiot's Delight* (Lee Simonson), *Victoria Regina* (Rex Whistler), *Porgy and Bess* (Serge Soudekine), as well as developing talents in *Awake and Sing!* (Boris Aronson), *Paths of Glory* (Henry Dreyfuss), *First Lady* (Donald Oenslager), *Cyrano de Bergerac* (Claude Bragdon), and *New Faces of 1936* (Stewart Chaney). It was a watershed year for Jo, Broadway, and the art of scene design.

After *Winterset* and before the end of the year, Jo designed *Jubilee* for Sam Harris and Max Gordon, a dramatization of Jane Austen's *Pride and Prejudice* by Helen Jerome, and *Hell Freezes Over* by John Patrick. Each further displayed the depth of his talents as a designer. The most notable event during the course of Jo's work on this last play was his reacquaintance with Joshua Logan. Jo had met Logan when he had appeared in a bit part in *I Was Waiting for You*, but it was when he directed *Hell Freezes Over* that Jo began a friendship with Logan that would endure to the end of his life. Among the many shows they collaborated on were some of the greatest suc-cesses in Broadway's history. *Hell Freezes Over*, unfortunately, was not one of them.

THE ENTIRE ACTION OF ***HELL FREEZES OVER*** (1935) TAKES PLACE IN THE WRECKED DIRIGIBLE *WHITE HOPE* AT THE SOUTH POLE. THE ALL-MALE CREW DIES ONE BY ONE IN A VARIETY OF HORRIBLE WAYS UNTIL THERE IS NO ONE LEFT ON THE STAGE, WHICH DID NOT MAKE FOR A MERRY EVENING FOR THE AUDIENCE. JO'S SET, FULL OF BUCKLED BEAMS, HANGING WIRES, AND SCATTERED DEBRIS, WAS IN THE RIGHT KEY FOR THE PLAY BUT WAS AN EFFECTIVE SET WASTED ON AN INEFFECTIVE SCRIPT. (SMITHSONIAN INSTITUTION)

JO MIELZINER

Rockwell Kent 1930

4
FAMILY MATTERS

Just before he returned to America from his wartime service with the Jewish Welfare Board in July of 1919, Leo Mielziner wrote in one of his daily letters to Ella: "I'm glad the inherent Mielziner modesty has been attenuated in our boys so that they have the necessary weapons with which to hold their own in this world."

As his sons prospered, they assumed more and more of the financial support of their parents. Relieved of the burden of making a living from his art, Leo did less and less serious portraiture and was content to dabble his days away. He spent most of his time at the Salmagundi Club, where he was known as "Doc." Dressed in a white coat (when he painted) and sporting a goatee and wire-rimmed glasses, he could have easily been taken for a Viennese psychiatrist. He was content to cook, write poetry to his wife on special occasions, and lecture whenever he was asked, all the while watching the steady rise of his sons' fame and fortunes.

OPPOSITE: THE 1930 CEILING (DETAIL) THAT JO MIELZINER AND ROCKWELL KENT DESIGNED FOR THE CAPE CINEMA AT DENNIS ON CAPE COD. IT HAS BEEN CAREFULLY PRESERVED BY THE RAYMOND MOORE FOUNDATION, WHICH OWNS AND OPERATES THE MOVIE THEATRE IN TANDEM WITH THE MORE FAMOUS CAPE PLAYHOUSE, ONE OF THE OLDEST SUMMER THEATRES IN THE COUNTRY. (MARGARET ADAMS ARCHIVES, CAPE PLAYHOUSE-CINEMA)

Leo and Ella were still living in Greenwich Village in the early thirties, but spent their summers at Kenneth's summer place in Truro, which they had named "Little Hollow Downs" and where the Mielziners were neighbors to a number of friends, most of them artists and writers. Edward and Jo Hopper had a house in South Truro, not far from the Mielziners. Kenneth had bought his parents a pony named Spot and a cart, so that they could move about the area without an automobile. The elder Mielziners thus became a

familiar sight in Truro, sailing by in their cart wearing their summer straw hats. Leo joined the local golf club, while Ella worked tirelessly at her hobby, genealogy. Jo and Marya, later Jo and Annie Laurie, came up from New York when Jo's increasingly busy life permitted.

In the summer of 1931, Leo either fell or slipped in an accident, probably involving the cart and pony, at the Truro place and tore ligaments in his leg and landed in Massachusetts General Hospital, in Boston. (The pony, not known for his sweet temperament, had previously dumped the movie actress Kay Francis, who at the time was being courted by Ken, on one of her rare trips to Cape Cod.) Perhaps sensing their father's mortality, Kenneth and Jo overreacted to the accident and telegrams and letters of concern flew from coast to coast, from sons to parents, and back again. The following winter Kenneth bought rail tickets for Leo and Ella to travel to California, and the following spring he sent them to Capri for several months. When they returned to New York, Ella and Leo gave up their apartment and moved into a more convenient residence, the Hotel Fairfax on East 56th Street.

In 1933, Leo began having "stomach" ailments and Ella's eyesight began to deteriorate. Treatments restored her sight, but Leo's problems were not resolved so satisfactorily. He was examined by physicians who must have suspected that Leo was suffering from something more serious than indigestion. Although both Ella and Leo smoked—Leo was rarely seen without a cigarette—and drank spirits in moderate quantities, doctors had few suspicions then about the links of smoking or drinking to gastrointestinal cancer. Leo's problems increased and he began having difficulty swallowing. During the summer of 1934 when both Ken and Jo visited their parents in Truro, their anxiety about Leo's condition mounted and they quickly decided to take charge of their parents' lives.

Kenneth MacKenna was the classic example of the firstborn son. On reaching manhood, he felt that it was his duty to take care of his entire family: mother, father, and sibling. Responsible, intelligent, and clear-headed, he was constantly setting up strategies for his family, as if he knew instinctively what was best—and he was usually right. He managed his money carefully, no doubt a result of

KENNETH'S HOUSE IN TRURO, CAPE COD, 1928. HE BOUGHT THE HOUSE OSTENSIBLY AS A SUMMER AND WEEKEND RETREAT FOR HIMSELF BUT TURNED IT OVER TO LEO AND ELLA AS A PERMANENT HOME DURING THE 1930S. THE HOUSE, ABOUT ONE HUNDRED YEARS OLD WHEN HE BOUGHT IT, WAS SURROUNDED BY FIFTY UNDEVELOPED ACRES. KNOWN AS THE JOSHUA SNOW HOUSE, THE MIELZINERS REFERRED TO IT AS "LITTLE HOLLOW DOWNS." THE HOUSE, SOLD BY KENNETH IN 1949 TO DOROTHY AND DONALD SCHLESINGER, HAD A CACHE OF LETTERS AND PERSONAL ITEMS ABANDONED BY THE MIELZINERS IN THE BASEMENT. THE HOUSE IS NOW OWNED BY ANSEL CHAPIN. (COURTESY OF JOANNA SCHLESINGER CAPRONI)

the lean years with his parents. Rather than have Leo and Ella
return to the Hotel Fairfax, Kenneth decided to have his little
blue-shuttered Truro house made into a winter home for them. He
installed a heating system and, with Jo's design input, added onto
the house so that Leo would not have to climb stairs. The elder
Mielziners were delighted to become full-time Cape Cod citizens.

In the winter of 1934, Leo's condition worsened and a specialist diagnosed cancer of the esophagus. He prescribed a series of
radiation treatments for Leo, but privately warned Ella, Kenneth,
and Jo that the prognosis was very grave indeed. After the treatments, Leo seemed to improve and he returned to Truro to take up
a relatively normal life. Kenneth and Jo took care of the bills and
provided almost daily encouragement. Kenneth often ended his
letters with one of Leo's famous taglines: "Courage, mon ami, le
diable est mort!"

On the morning of August 11, 1935, a few months short of his
sixty-sixth birthday, Leo died, surrounded by his wife and sons. His
passing was noted by New York and Cincinnati newspapers; the
New York Tribune accompanied his obituary with a self-portrait made
by him in 1931 and given to "Jo-boy, with love, from Dad." He was
buried in Jamaica Plains, just outside Boston.

All three Mielziners were devastated by Leo's death, but Ella,
who was at his side throughout the last months of his illness, recovered more quickly than her sons. After his father died, Kenneth
was never able to bring himself to return to Truro and he rented
out "Little Hollow Downs" the following summer. Finally, in 1949
he sold the house, its contents, and fifty-two acres surrounding it
for $15,000 to family friends, Dr. and Mrs. Donald Schlesinger of
New York, who had rented the house four previous summers. In
the basement of the house, a cache of old letters, Christmas cards,
and family photographs, carefully preserved in boxes by Ella, was
abandoned or forgotten by the family. Dating from the Mielziners'
Paris days, they constitute a rich memorial to Leo and Ella and
their sons.

By now, Kenneth, like Jo, had married and divorced. After he
had received the lucrative contract from Fox to go to Hollywood
to play in and direct movies, he entertained the idea that he could

LEO AND ELLA, TRURO, CIRCA 1932. (COURTESY OF JENNIFER MIELZINER)

WITH JO ON THE BEACH AT
CAPE COD, EARLY THIRTIES.
ELLA SMOKED THROUGHOUT
HER LIFE, FIRST CIGARETTES,
THEN CIGARS, FINALLY A PIPE.
(COURTESY OF JENNIFER
MIELZINER)

KENNETH AND HIS BRIDE KAY FRANCIS, CIRCA 1931. THE UNION DID NOT LAST LONG. (BILLY ROSE THEATRE COLLECTION, NYPL-PA)

continue doubling in both theatre and films. He played the husband of the up-and-coming star Kay Francis in the movie *The Virtuous Sin* (1931). They fell in love and were married in Avalon, on Catalina Island, shortly after the completion of the movie in January 1931. Kenneth was Kay's third and last husband. Born Katherine Gibbs in the early 1900s, Kay was slightly younger than Kenneth in years but older in experience. Endowed with a striking combination of jet black hair and ivory skin, she had a dazzling smile, beautiful eyes, and charisma. Combining her good looks with a chic wardrobe, Kay discovered early that she could open doors that women less blessed than she could not.

Kay's mother, a former actress, had left her husband, returned to the stage, and dragged Kay along with her on tours. When Kay was fourteen, her mother sent her to a boarding school in Ossining, New York, then later to the fashionable Cathedral School of St. Mary in Garden City, on Long Island, for one year. Kay then went on to secretarial school (at Katherine Gibbs, of course) and after a series of

jobs, she started working with a woman who earned her living booking social events for debutantes. Kay quickly began to move in high society. In 1922, she met and married socialite James Dwight Francis, who, unfortunately, became an alcoholic and a wastrel. She divorced him but retained his surname for the rest of her life.

Kay set her sights on the theatre next. Always plagued by a noticeable lateral lisp, in which "r" and "l" came out sounding like like "w," Kay was advised by Dwight Deere Wiman to take speech lessons, which helped a bit but never fully corrected the impediment. She understudied Katharine Cornell in *The Green Hat* because she was similar to Cornell's physical type, but her career as an actress did not advance until she was cast as a vamp in *Gentlemen of the Press* for Paramount Pictures in 1929. After acquiring and shedding two husbands, she began her ascent in Hollywood and gradually escalated her salary to several thousand dollars a week. She was well on her way to becoming a rich woman when she met and married Kenneth.

Kenneth took Kay to meet Leo and Ella, driving her up to Truro in his sleek Cadillac. (To his surprise, Leo recognized her as a model who had posed for him in the early twenties.) For the first two years of their marriage, despite their differences, Kenneth and Kay seemed to be making a go of it. But Kay's moviemaking schedule—she rose at six in the morning and was not home until eight at night—led her to seek release through alcohol. Since Kenneth was nearest at hand, she directed her drunken abuse at him. In February of 1934, citing mental cruelty, she divorced Kenneth. She made the occasion the focus of a party for which she turned a restaurant entrance into the gangway of a ship and put up a big sign in the ballroom that read: "Merrily We Roll Along Without Kenneth MacKenna," a reference to the title of the Broadway hit in which he was starring at the time.

Merrily We Roll Along, which opened late in September of 1934, with sets by Jo, was Kenneth's first hit. It lasted for 155 performances, which encouraged the producer, Sam Harris, to send it on tour. Philadelphia, the first stop on the road, was unfortunately not pleased with the show and the planned tour screeched to a halt. Luckily, Kenneth could fall back on his financial reserves to tide him over. But he was forced to face the reality that, at thirty-six, he had not become a leading man on Broadway nor a star in Hollywood and would have to reassess his goals. At the same time, he had begun seeing a lot of his female lead in *Merrily*, Mary Phillips Bogart, who, with her husband, Humphrey, was a member of Kenneth's social circle. Like Kenneth, she was trying to keep her career alive in New York. Although married to Bogart, she felt free to enjoy male company during her long separations from him—and he was evidently savoring the charms of Hollywood starlets. But this "arrangement" and the separations were putting great strains on the Bogarts, and their marriage ended in divorce in 1937. In 1938, Mary and Kenneth MacKenna married; they enjoyed near-perfect marital contentment for the rest of their lives.

Now Jo, after experiencing the death of his father, the failure of one marriage, and the rocky condition of his second, was pondering his own choices with some inner turmoil. He felt emotionally and professionally drained and wondered whether he had made the right decisions. When he had started out in the theatre, by his own admission he "entered the profession chiefly for material reasons and with the feeling that I was really a painter and theater design was just a way of putting a little butter on my bread." For years he kept telling himself that as soon as he put enough money aside, he would go back to the easel, but once he became immersed in designing scenery, he discovered that it was, in his own words, "a rich field in expression and emotionally satisfying." Most of all, he enjoyed the complexity of it. He confessed:

> Upon analyzing my feelings about my childhood ambition, I saw that the canvas on which I wanted to express myself was not necessarily limited to 30 × 40 inches but, as I believed at that time, could very easily be expanded to a stage opening of 30 × 40 feet. However, the transposition from the easel painter to the scenic designer is not a direct one. . . . The ideal background for a theater artist is a composite of many arts and crafts. . . . [A] good recipe might be: one part painter and draftsman, one part architect, one part sculptor, one part couturier, one part electrical engineer, and the final and most important part, the dramatist. This concoction has

no potency unless shaken so violently that no single part, with the possible exception of the dramatist, dominates the brew.

Jo wrote those words in "Death of a Painter," an article published in *American Artist* in 1949. He went on to say that the prime difference between the easel painter and the scene designer is that the latter practices an interpretative art, which deals not only with the three dimensions of the artist but adds time as the fourth dimension, which lifts it above the pictorial. He concluded the essay by saying that the theatre is no place for a designer who is an "egomaniac," for designers are hemmed in by the very real limitations of time, space, and money and are forced to bend their art to the will of a platoon of decision-makers (playwright, producer, director, technicians), which robs them of the independence that most artists prize.

The easel painter in him had died, he said, before reaching maturity. With almost a dozen years of experience and more than his share of critical success, he may have still felt a residue of uneasiness about abandoning painting for scenic design, but after the acclaim that he received for *Winterset*, Jo never again doubted that his career belonged in the theatre. Because the careers of both Jones and Simonson had been gradually slowing down, Jo was getting more and more assignments from the Theatre Guild, where they had reigned supreme. He remained the designer of choice for Cornell and McClintic. The best of Broadway's producers were increasingly looking to him, usually at the urging of the playwrights, who knew that a Mielziner set could make a mute but powerful difference in the acceptance of their plays. Playwright Sidney Howard's blunt dictum was "Get Mielziner" whenever a problem was anticipated with the scenery.

Jo's design schedule was now so crowded that he hired full-time assistants and a secretary for his studio-office at 1441 Broadway. As his income increased there were few demands on it, for several years at least; when Annie Laurie left Jo, like Marya, she did not ask for alimony. Jo continued to share with Kenneth the financial upkeep of Ella, who more than ever needed their help, but she was not a burden. They found a comfortable country inn for her, Hawley Manor, in Newtown, Connecticut, that served good food and where she could read, smoke her pipe, hook rugs, and otherwise keep occupied. The inn had a rose garden where she could bask in the warm weather, contented.

With his work completely engulfing his life, with steadily rising stature as a scene designer, with his existence seemingly organized and secure, Jo still felt that he lacked a center. When he had met Annie Laurie, she was in the throes of one of her periodic enthusiasms, attending the Lenten sessions at a Paulist church in New York conducted by Father Fulton J. Sheen, a golden-tongued Roman Catholic priest. She, a professed atheist, had challenged him to convert her. In what became his stock-in-trade technique, he threw back the challenge to her to give him three good arguments for atheism. When she could not, he had her on the first step of conversion. She began taking instruction from him, which lasted almost a year. Her enthusiasm began to abate when she started to see Jo; indeed, she confessed to Sheen that she was seeing a married man (Jo was technically still Marya's husband, although she was divorcing him) and her guilt because of it prevented her from continuing on her course. He predicted to her that she would not be happy until she had resolved her spiritual conflict.

After she married Jo, she asked him to accompany her to Father Sheen's sessions. He was dazzled by Sheen and wanted to know more about Catholicism. After a few months, the priest advised him that if he decided to convert, he would be eligible for the Pauline privilege, which would enable him to marry Annie Laurie in a Catholic ceremony, signifying an acceptance of the union by the Church. When Jo affirmed his serious intentions, Sheen set in motion the application for the Pauline privilege from Rome. Unfortunately, by the time it arrived in 1936, Laurie had decamped for Wyoming and was in the arms of her cowboy. But Jo went through with his conversion and was accepted into the Church in 1936, a few months after his father's death. Before Leo's death, he had discussed his interest in conversion with his parents. According to Jo's recollections in an article published many years later in *The Sign*, Leo was pleased that Jo chose a "real" religion, if he could no longer stay in the faith of his forefathers. But his father beseeched him to continue to take pride in his Jewish heritage. Ella was not

quite so enthusiastic about the conversion, although she could not offer any forceful arguments against his decision. She had made only erratic efforts to provide her boys with religious instruction beyond what she felt were the universal moral precepts. (She herself eventually became a Unitarian.)

It may have been Sheen who first gave Jo a copy of G. K. Chesterton's *Orthodoxy*, an exegesis of Chesterton's own conversion to Roman Catholicism. Jo was attracted to Chesterton's reasoning, particularly in his postulation that a man must put himself in the world, not retreat from it, as many disillusioned people did in the turbulent years before and after World War I. *Orthodoxy* became the favorite and probably most influential book in Jo's life. It came to his attention, he wrote:

> . . . *during a period in my life when I was going through an internal struggle which, in a sense, was the desire to embrace a strong faith that would make demands on my life. In opposition to this was my concern and fear and doubts that accepting the dogma of, in my case, Catholicism would restrict what I felt was freedom of thought, and the dangers of a closed mind on the social and intellectual level. In Orthodoxy, Chesterton showed me the answer. In this book he convinced me, to my complete satisfaction, that in accepting a credo, I gained a freedom rather than lost one. It was a freedom I did not enjoy previous to the time of my accepting a definite faith.*

He went on to say that, as an artist, he constantly accepted the limitations and boundaries of the materials he employed to express himself. "If I was told," he continued, "that my canvas had unlimited depth and unlimited breadth, I would feel frustrated rather than free."

A convivial man, Jo liked to be in the swirl of events and the theatre was proving to be his natural habitat. An inherently disciplined man, he was attracted to the complete system that Catholicism provided. Comprehensive, compact, and requiring discipline, Catholicism appeared to him to have all the answers.

Jo received his first communion from Father Sheen in the Church of the Blessed Sacrament, in New York, on Christmas Day of 1936. After the Mass, he approached his mentor with tears streaming down his face. He showed him a gold cross, which had been made from the wedding ring from his marriage to Annie Laurie. Jo used it as a symbol: "This was," he told Sheen, "her gift to me—the gift of Faith and the cross of Christ." By way of comfort, the priest assured Jo that he was still free to marry again. Because he had not married either of his wives in a Catholic ceremony, he could still invoke the Pauline privilege, which had already been granted. Noting his failures in choosing a wife, Sheen even tried to play matchmaker by introducing him to a woman he knew, but his choice did not take. For the rest of his life, Fulton Sheen remained not only Jo's closest spiritual adviser but a warm friend and confidant.

Never having been a practicing Jew, Jo may have been perceived by some as hiding his background so that he could reach for acceptance in a society that retained a seemingly inextinguishable anti-Semitism at most levels. But Jo's world—the world of the theatre—was dominated by Jews in high places. Lawrence Langner, Max Gordon, John Golden, Jed Harris, Sam Harris, and many other producers with whom Jo worked were Jews. His closest friend, Eddie Kook, was a Jew. And most importantly, the theatrical community—probably from the beginning of time—exhibited a tolerance for individual differences and deviations that few other professions know or even try to cultivate. In the theatre, nobody makes much of being a Jew, a Catholic, a Protestant, a homosexual,

short-statured, bald-headed, pockmarked, dark-complexioned, overweight, gravel-voiced, or anything else. Barriers fall easily among theatre people, who seem to make room for all so long as everyone performs well and steps on no one's toes.

Once he was converted, Jo's devotion was clear, simple, and lifelong. If he had been looking for a philosphical center for his life—particularly at this juncture in it—Catholicism provided it. Sheen believed that conversion starts with a crisis, "a moment or a situation involving some kind of suffering, physical, moral or spiritual; with a dialectic, a tension, a pull, a duality, or a conflict." So it had been with Jo.

Another powerful factor must have been the rich and theatrical panoply of the Roman Catholic ritual. As a man of the theatre, Jo could not have been immune to its high drama, to the brilliantly hued vestments of its priests within the dimly lighted sanctuaries. As an artist, he could enjoy the churches' stained-glass windows, through which light streamed and colored the interiors. In Europe, he reveled in the ecclesiastical art produced by the master artists that adorned the walls and altars of ancient cathedrals—to which he began making yearly pilgrimages after his conversion. Steered by a powerful mentor and predisposed by his own romantic temperament, he found in Roman Catholicism a perfect spiritual home and an intellectual center.

5
BROADWAY JO

I n 1936, with a dozen years in show business and more than his share of commercial hits and artistic successes behind him, Jo Mielziner was sitting on top of the world. Although the Depression still lay heavily on the nation, he was largely unaffected by it, as assignments, both theatrical and nontheatrical, continued to flow into his studio at 1441 Broadway and he could command fees that none of his colleagues could match. Not only was he able to afford a staff, a studio, and an office, but also he secured an agent to handle his other-than-theatrical projects. If he was making money, he was also disposing of it very rapidly through the expenses his new enterprises were generating. At first, Jo ventured enthusiastically into other avenues to make his living but, with few exceptions, he had little success and often minimal satisfaction in any of them. He inevitably returned to his drawing board and the theatre. It became a lifelong pattern.

Changing hats for an instant, Jo became a Broadway producer, probably at the instigation of his brother, Kenneth, who was at loose ends during the mid-thirties. Jo and Kenneth joined forces in producing *Co-Respondent Unknown*, a play by Mildred Harris and Howard Goldman that had been making the rounds of a number of producers. Although Kenneth decided not to act in it himself, he directed the play as well as co-produced it. (There was also a third co-producer, a man named John C. Mayer, who was usually described in the press releases as a "businessman.") The cast included Ilka Chase and James Rennie as the husband and wife and Phyllis Povah as the husband's mistress. Peggy Conklin played a fake "other woman."

The plot revolves around the difficulty (then) of getting a divorce in New York State except on the grounds of adultery. When a popular actress returns from a long road tour to find her husband in flagrante delicto with his mistress, she and her husband agree to a divorce on the grounds of adultery and hire a surrogate "co-respondent" to provide the evidence. Instead of merely posing as the co-respondent, the young woman spends the night with the husband. When the deed is discovered, the mistress angrily breaks off the afffair, but the actress forgives her husband, with whom she is reunited at the final curtain. It was considered an "adult" play and quite racy in its time. Everyone made a bit of money but not a fortune, and for a brief period the play had an afterlife on the subway circuit and at summer stock theatres, but then was heard of no more. Many years later, after another play, *The Moon Is Blue*, broke taboos on Broadway (and in Hollywood in 1953 as a movie), Jo tried to reintroduce *Co-Respondent Unknown* as a potential film, but by that time no one seemed interested.

Instead of being chastened by the experience of producing, Kenneth and Jo took options on other plays and announced impending productions, but nothing came of them. Kenneth stayed in the Broadway orbit for another year, appearing in two inconsequential and short-lived plays. He decided to take a job as the New York story editor for Metro Goldwyn Mayer. In 1938, MGM, evidently pleased with his work, summoned him to California, where he climbed the corporate ladder to become head of the story department for the studio. His talent for recognizing potential material for movies paid off handsomely, even though it meant sacrificing his ambitions for becoming a leading actor and director on both coasts. Although he continued to return to New York every year to survey the Broadway scene in his capacity as the MGM scout for movie material and to see Jo and Ella, his career was centered in Hollywood for almost the rest of his life.

Like many of his colleagues, Jo was not immune to the lure of well-paying commercial and industrial design. The man who had made the smoothest transition from stage design to industrial design and became the most renowned and successful in that field was Norman Bel Geddes. In 1927, he opened an office for industrial design and within five years had forty people working for him. Adhering to the dictum established by the architect-designer Louis Sullivan that form follows function, Geddes and his firm designed and redesigned thousands of diverse products, including master plans for cities, an early IBM typewriter, adjustable chairs, portable radios, toilets, tableware, textiles, portable hangars for the Army Air Force, and the never-to-be-forgotten "Futurama" for General Motors at the 1939 World's Fair

Another of Jo's colleagues, Henry Dreyfuss, a former Geddes assistant, began in the theatre a few years after Jo, and eventually became a good friend. His own career as a scene designer appeared to be progressing nicely until 1935, when he designed *Paths of Glory*, a play adapted by Sidney Howard from the Humphrey Cobb novel. Even though his ingenuity and innovative use of space were praised, Dreyfuss quit Broadway and opened an office with his wife, Doris Marks, to concentrate on industrial design. He was responsible for the design of thousands of products during his lifetime, many of which displayed a distinctive theatrical flavor. Whenever he could, Dreyfuss would try to involve Jo in a project that he felt would best utilize his talents.

There were some compelling reasons why Jo and his brethren in professional scene design were attracted to industrial design. First of all, it was lucrative. Many of Jo's contemporaries during the 1930s barely scratched out a living in the theatre, so they would be grateful to receive a commission to design a store window or an industrial show or consult on an architectural project. Another important reason was the dearth of theatre assignments for all but a very few each season, as the number of openings on Broadway steadily declined (prompting United Scenic Artists to suspend all membership applications for a while). Moreover, designers like to keep busy; without assignments, they could keep their pencils sharpened but their creative juices could dry up.

Jo's first nontheatrical assignment had actually occurred in 1930, when he was engaged by Raymond Moore to help design the ceiling mural, curtain, proscenium, and lobby of the Cape Cinema in Dennis, on Cape Cod. His co-designer was nominally the artist and illustrator Rockwell Kent, then at the peak of his career. Moore, as a young artist, had migrated to Provincetown, whose artistic atmosphere had been the seedbed for both Eugene O'Neill and Robert Edmond Jones, as well as scores of artists and writers. Moore tried writing plays, then decided that his true vocation lay in establishing a theatre company. In 1926, he bought an old church and had it moved and rebuilt (with the help of stage designer Cleon Throckmorton) in the middle of a three-acre meadow. Successful from the beginning in attracting stars and high-caliber talent for his ten-week summer seasons, Moore's experiment paid off, and three years later he decided to build an intimate movie theatre on his property. He commissioned Kent and Jo to supply the interior decorations, for which Jo was to receive $5,000 and Kent $500, under the terms of their contract.

The mystery of how much was Kent's contribution and how much was Jo's may be best answered by the files in the Mielziner archive. Kent seems to have contributed the lithe figures, real and fictive, that race across an expanse of some 6,400 square feet, painted in an array of colors dominated by an intense blue (later to become Jo's signature color). The mural was advertised at the time as the largest in the world. Jo's job was to integrate the figures in the overall design, provide the remainder of the design, supervise the painting and installation, and oversee the lighting. The curtain was decorated with a brilliant gold and tangerine sun against a red background and was engineered to open and close like an oriental screen. All the work on the mural and curtain was done in New York by the scene shops that Jo used in his theatre work, and when they were completed, they were trucked to Cape Cod and installed by a crew of ten Broadway stagehands.

A political radical, Kent at first wanted no part of Massachusetts, the state that had persecuted and executed Sacco and Vanzetti (the event that had inspired Maxwell Anderson's *Winterset*). But, according to his own account, after being plied with four martinis over lunch in New York, he took the commission. He even turned up for the dedication of the Cape Cinema in early July of 1930.

Another lucrative commercial job came along six years later when Jo designed a portable stage for the Johns-Manville Company. Between 1936 and 1942, he worked on a dozen nontheatrical projects, five of which were "on speculation," which he eventually did not land. For the few years that Jo was represented by agents, only one of them brought him any significant nontheatrical assignments. Most of the time, he was approached directly by the person or company requesting his services. In New York, he did window displays for John-David, a men's haberdasher, and for Steuben.

In March of 1937, he had one of the more lucrative jobs of his early career through Leland Hayward, a top agent in Hollywood who had represented Kenneth MacKenna for a few years. (Hayward's agency eventually represented such Hollywood stars as Fred Astaire, Henry Fonda, Judy Garland, Katharine Hepburn, Gregory Peck, and Ginger Rogers, and such literary figures as Edna Ferber, Dashiell Hammett, Ernest Hemingway, Hecht and MacArthur, and Lindsay and Crouse.) Through Hayward, Jo was commissioned to create the designs and lighting for the *Pan American Casino Revue*, an industrial show that was part of a celebration in Dallas of a hands-across-the-borders mini World's Fair. For the work, he received $1,200 per week for twelve weeks, which represented a large part of his income for 1937. Jo redesigned the interior of a Dallas auditorium into what must have been one of the earliest examples of a dinner theatre. At a cost of $174,000, he created twelve terraces that surrounded an 80-foot-wide stage with 25-foot runways along the sides, plus a lower stage with an opening of 40 feet. The color

FOR THE **PAN AMERICAN CASINO REVUE** (1937) IN DALLAS, JO PAINTED THE CEILING, WALLS, AND FLOOR A DEEP BLUE AND OUTLINED THE PLANES OF THE STEPPED-UP LEVELS IN SILVER. THE EFFECT WAS A STUNNING, PRE–LAS VEGAS-STYLE SETTING. (BILLY ROSE THEATRE COLLECTION, NYPL-PA)

scheme throughout was periwinkle blue and silver. Jo and Eddie brought down a crew from New York to handle the installation of the lighting equipment, which Jo used to create lighting effects that drew acclaim. Jo also created the scenery for the revue, for which he received added kudos. The entire show was done Texas-style— lavish, large, and costly.

Through his seat on the board of TWA, Hayward also exercised his influence to get Jo a commission to design an airline terminal on New York's Park Avenue. Although it was a spectacular design that incorporated a roofline like a wingspread, it was never built. When Hayward began his career as a Broadway producer, he did not forget Jo's multifaceted talents.

In 1938, Jo worked on the first of the seasonal *Esquire* men's fashion shows. (He did a total of three.) In March, he was asked to address the executives of the men's retail and wholesale industry. In his brief speech, he stressed (predictably) the importance of the setting of the product in store windows, but also emphasized the value of lighting in selling merchandise, referring to *Our Town* and *Julius Caesar*, shows then playing on Broadway that, in the absence of elaborate scenery, relied heavily on dramatic lighting.

During this period, Jo also designed a glass-brick curved wall for the famed El Morocco nightclub, a French millinery shop for the

Marshall Field department store in Chicago, and an elaborate display unit for Schenley Distillers Corporation, in tandem with Lee Simonson. Jo's responsibility included the design of attendants' uniforms as well as a mock nightclub and a package store. For the war effort, Jo designed a poster, which was included in an exhibition early in 1942 at the American–British Art Center. It was later sent to Washington, where it appeared to be lost in the official morass.

Jo's industrial designing ranked with the best of his time and that may have been the root of his problem. It was often better than the client deserved or wanted. A case in point were his sleek storefront designs for I. J. Fox, who ran a hard-sell, off-the-rack fur business on Fifth Avenue. Jo's elegant windows may well have scared off the kind of customers Fox wished to attract. Once he accepted a commission, Jo's innate good taste guided his pencil and produced excellent designs that did not necessarily fulfill the needs of his clients or descend to their level. Throughout his career as an industrial designer, he saw many of his well-wrought ideas die on the drawing board. Jo was even commissioned by Eddie Kook to design several lighting fixtures for his Century Lighting Company, but it is doubtful they were ever manufactured in any quantity.

Although fastidiously polite to everyone, and warm and often caring in his relations with his associates, outside of his family the only person to whom Jo bared his all was Kook, or Kookie, as he was often called. Why they were attracted to each other is a mystery of how any friendship begins. Psychologists liken friendship between two people to love between two people. It is often built on imponderables, explainable on some ground of common interests but defying reason on others. When they met in their very early twenties, Eddie and Jo were both on the move in their careers. As time proved, each was able to boost the other in his rise. Eddie, born on New York's Lower East Side of immigrant Orthodox Jews, and Jo, half-Jew, part-WASP, part Irish-Catholic, Parisian-born, and unconventionally educated, had seemingly clashing styles. While Eddie could sometimes be brash in speech and abrasive in manner, Jo was always gently spoken and well mannered. Yet to the end of their days, both were eager learners, acquiring knowledge by careful listening to experts in other fields, and both used this trait to listen to pool their knowledge over a wide spectrum of mutual interests. From his experience sitting at the feet of Gordon Craig during his student travels in Europe, Jo had become fascinated by the potential of light as an element of scenery. Eddie had learned about lighting through his early employment with the Display Stage Lighting Company, for which he kept the books.

Eddie had an instinct that stage lighting would someday become a special province dictated not by the technicians and stage electricians in the theatre but by the scene designers. He was shrewd enough to predict that producers would be reluctant to go along with elaborate stage lighting if it meant that they would have to foot the bill for complicated equipment. Although the principle of renting lighting equipment (rather than buying it outright) had already been established, stage electricians tended to be unimaginative and cautious in specifiying the equipment for shows to avoid the wrath of pinch-penny producers. With the arrival of early leaders of the New Stagecraft, the bare minimum was not enough; they demanded more and better lighting, sophisticated controlling systems, and special effects that could not be procured "off the rack."

In 1927, while he was still working for Display, Eddie Kook began laying plans for an independent company with Joseph Levy, the brother of Saul, who had given Eddie his first accountant job. Joe Levy, the man in charge of Display's shop, had extraordinary ingenuity in solving technical problems and was a born inventor. As they became increasingly disaffected with the day-to-day running of Display, they were convinced that the combination of Eddie's salesmanship and Joe's creative genius could be the basis of a sound business venture. On August 10, 1929, with Saul's backing, they founded Century Lighting Company and opened their offices and a small factory at 351 West 52nd Street on the fringe of the theatre district. When Display began having financial difficulties in the early years of the Depression, Century was poised to take over a large share of its business. Kook and Levy's major competition came from Kliegl Brothers Lighting Company, which had been founded by two immigrant Austrian brothers in 1896. The Kliegls had established a strong foothold in stage lighting by creating

special housings for incandescent lamps and, later, a high-intensity spotlight, the Klieglight, which became synonymous for any fixture providing bright white light.

In 1930, within months after founding their company, Kook and Levy issued their first Century catalog and distributed it to the regional, community, and school theatres throughout the country. They quickly discovered that the catalog could be a major factor in the growth of the business and the revenues from this enterprise would help finance their development of new and special lighting equipment for the New York stage, which would then become the prototypes for equipment to be sold in their next catalogs. Thanks to this simple formula, Century grew and prospered throughout the Depression, and hardship never beat on its doors.

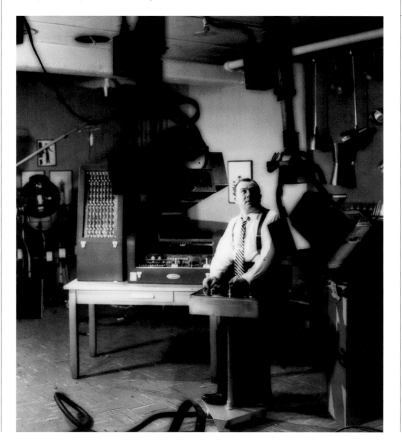

EDWARD F. KOOK, CIRCA 1945. JO MIELZINER'S FRIEND FOR ALL SEASONS, HE SPENT AS MUCH TIME BACKSTAGE IN THE THEATRES OF BROADWAY AS HE DID IN THE SHOP OF CENTURY LIGHTING, THE COMPANY THAT HE FOUNDED WITH JOSEPH LEVY. (COURTESY OF THE ESTATE OF HILDA AND EDWARD KOOK)

Eddie Kook's talent for listening paid off as designers described to him the artistic effects they wanted for their scenery. He would rush back to the shop and explain them to Joe Levy, and his partner would translate the designers' demands into equipment that would accomplish almost exactly what they had specified. Designers would confidently return again and again to Eddie with their problems and special needs, and producers were happy that Century would provide the ever more sophisticated lighting as long as they did not have to pay for the experimentation.

In the early thirties, Eddie had the good fortune to find out about the experimental work in lighting done by Stanley McCandless, who taught stage lighting at Yale University's School of Drama. Eddie hired McCandless, who inspired the company to continue to improve its products and make it prosper accordingly. In 1932, McCandless published *A Method of Lighting the Stage,* which set forth a basic system that time and technological improvement have not erased but have made simpler to achieve. In a preface to a fourth edition of his book, McCandless wrote, "Visibility, naturalism, composition, and atmosphere are the objectives for lighting no matter what the form of theatre or type of production." In the late thirties, McCandless was joined by George C. Izenour, a Yale colleague, who was immersing himself in the key element of stage lighting: control. Using layman's terms, Izenour wrote perhaps the most succinct statement to define control:

> First, each piece of equipment must be mounted someplace relative to the acting area; second, it must be directed at something; third, its rays must be modified as to color; fourth, the area which the rays strike must be determined as to size and sometimes shape; and fifth, its intensity must be controlled.

Izenour, too, became a consultant for Century Lighting. The mission of McCandless and Izenour was clear: to develop better and more versatile lighting instruments and provide greater control while evolving the overall aesthetics for their applications.

Control of lighting units in the theatre is achieved by dimmers, which can vary the intensity of illumination. The greatest revolution in stage lighting has occurred in the development of dimmers.

The earliest ones were operated by a stagehand from a cumbersome control board in the wings, which adjusted the amount of current flowing through the cables to the instruments. In its earliest manifestations, lighting was the province of the stagehand-electrician, who was guided by a set of instructions to vary the lighting according to the time, setting, and mood of the play, and to create special effects (dawn, moonlight, storms, sunsets) as needed. All these adjustments were made by shifting levers and turning dials, one at a time, everything carefully timed. Often the stagehand could not see the scenes he was lighting and had to rely on his watch or on what he heard on the stage. Of course, advancing technology has changed all that.

Eddie Kook and Joe Levy were determined to utilize each new development as it came along and often worked in tandem with the General Electric Company. Eventually, Century and its competitors developed sophisticated control systems that automatically perform all the myriad lighting adjustments that had heretofore been done manually.

Century also developed a spotlight, the Leko (the acronym combines the first two letters of the partners, Levy and Kook). It is a standard in the industry today. Jo Mielziner always credited Eddie Kook with being his mentor in lighting and relied on his expert advice. Eddie, on the other hand, credited Jo with being his mentor in matters of taste and relied on his artistic judgment. Eddie also encouraged Jo to do his own lighting design. Most of the early New Stagecraft designers of Jo's generation insisted on working out their own plans for lighting their scenery but had to learn to communicate with the stage electricians, who rigidly controlled things. It was inevitable that someone would come along to wrest the controls of lighting from the electricians. Most scene designers were often too busy or not technically equipped to do more than give general instructions to the stagehands and would wait until the technical rehearsals to fine-tune the lighting as they watched it from the auditorium. With Eddie's guidance, Jo (and many of his colleagues in the profession, but by no means all) immersed himself in the technical aspects of lighting in order to give very specific commands to the stagehands, and later, to his assistants, who prepared the "light plots" for his designs. When he produced his drawings in color, he always painted them as they would look with the lighting he wanted, including spotlights on actors' faces, dark and light areas, shadows, and so on. Jo, along with Jones, Simonson, and others came to insist in the early thirties that *they* design the lighting for all their shows. By 1935, with *Panic*, Jo was receiving program credit for lighting design, but it was not until United Scenic Artists recognized lighting design in 1962 as a separate branch of stage design that he could receive a contract and fee for his services. Prior to that the lighting fee was either built into his charges for designing the scenery or was handled in a sub-rosa contract between him and the producer, outside the official purviews of the union.

The person who actually invented the role of the lighting designer as a separate specialist was Abe Feder. Feder was entranced with stage lighting from the age of fourteen, watching the Great Thurston, a magician, as he manipulated lighting in the practice of his wizardry. He found his way to New York, picking up any work in the theatre he could. His breaks came with the Group Theatre and the Federal Theatre Project, particularly in his association with Orson Welles, who allowed him to work out his stage lighting ideas. For Welles, he created two memorable productions, *Macbeth* and *Doctor Faustus*, using light as it had never been used before, as scenery and curtains. To make lighting design more precise, Feder assigned numbers to the lighting instruments to avoid the verbal calls and finger-pointings by which designers described what they wanted. Secondly, whenever the equipment at hand was not sufficient to the effect, he adapted it or invented something to achieve it. Feder forced the recognition of the lighting designer on a reluctant theatrical industry, which felt it already had too many specialists. As noted earlier, even after gaining acceptance, his craft had to wait nearly thirty years for the union to set up a membership for lighting designers.

Feder was followed by a generation of lighting designers, none more outstanding than Jean Rosenthal, the first of many women who have taken up the specialty. Rosenthal, Feder's brilliant one-time assistant, broke new ground in the theatre, both as a woman and a pioneer in the new field. When she began her career in the

mid-thirties, women had been accepted, albeit reluctantly, as scene and costume designers, but had not made their mark backstage.

For Rosenthal, a beam of light was palpable and real and laden with emotion. She used it as a sculptor uses clay to shape and form an image. She did things with light that no one thought feasible or possible. Her innovations were readily adopted by her colleagues and became part of the palette of the lighting artist. She improved upon Feder's numbering scheme by drawing the shapes of the various instruments in their positions around the stage and showing the kinds of beams they created in the light plot. She produced precise charts for the colors and the focus of the lights so that nothing was left to chance or accident. Eventually, everyone did it her way.

Jo admired the work of Feder, Rosenthal, and other lighting colleagues, but in his mind it was the job—and the obligation—of scene designers to light their own sets. How could the lighting be entrusted to another, who did not go through the same process of step-by-step creation as the designer? Indeed, Jo would denigrate lighting designers as "scene designers who don't know how to draw." Yet his assistants carefully translated Jo's ideas for lighting his sets into precise light plots and charts, using the methods they had learned through the work of Feder and Rosenthal. Their carefully wrought instructions were then handed to the stage electricians. When Jo arrived for the technical rehearsals, he could tinker with the lighting to his heart's content, knowing that the major part of the work had been done.

Eddie and Jo's close association brought them reciprocal rewards. At various points in their careers, Eddie recommended Jo to producers and, whenever he could, Jo specified Century Lighting Company equipment. (Of course, the ultimate choice resided in the hands of the producers, who could and did overrule Eddie and Jo in favor of others countless times.)

From 1936 to 1942, Jo designed, lighted, and in some cases, costumed fifty Broadway productions and one ballet. His work for those years ranged from a high of eleven to a low of six shows. For the five years before he went into the Army in 1942, his income fluctuated between $25,000 and $35,000 per year, a munificent sum in a harsh economy. Although his competitors were men and women of extraordinary talent, he clearly dominated the field. For one thing, the contributions of pioneers Jones, Simonson, and Geddes were fitful during those years, though whenever and whatever any of them designed was usually impressive and duly noted by the critics.

As would be expected, Jo's office was deluged with applications for assistantships from aspiring young designers trying to learn the ropes from the masters. In the absence of any union apprentice system, most, if not all, of the fledglings spent time as assistants to important working designers like Jo. In Jo's studio, on the penthouse floor of 1441 Broadway, were crammed a studio area equipped with drawing boards and tools of the trade for the assistants, his own office, and space for his secretary. (A bright aerie high above the rooftops of the Garment District to the south and the Theatre District to the north, it contained 600 square feet of space, for which he paid $70 per month.) Jo kept regular business hours, usually from 9:30 A.M. to 6 P.M., but he made it known at the start that assistants were expected to stay late if a job had to be completed and to go out of town for technical rehearsals before the New York opening. There was no paid overtime at his office.

Everything was part of the assistants' job. Jo demanded meticulous draftsmanship combined with design talent, but he never delegated any design responsibility, nor did any of his assistants presume to impose on his designs. All the designing, the choosing of colors, and the painting and rendering were done by Jo. Because lighting had become such a vital element of his designs, he always hired assistants with strong lighting credentials. He would subsequently, and without fail, ask the producers for program credit for his assistants. If for any reason Jo was unable to attend a rehearsal or out-of-town tryout and the assistant went in his place, Jo would notify everyone beforehand, by letter if need be, that his assistant was due the same respect and had the same authority to make decisions as he himself.

For the help Jo needed, Eddie Kook, who had established a vast network of contacts not only in New York but in the regional and university theatres, would scout out and alert Jo to the available talent. In the early thirties, Bob Barnhart, an independent designer trying to get a foot in the door for his own Broadway career,

assisted Jo between assignments. Eventually he worked in a managerial capacity for Studio Alliance, one of the largest of the scene shops. He and Walter Jagemann were among the best of Jo's early assistants, dependable and responsible, men Jo felt free to call back for several weeks or months when he became especially pressed with work. The Viennese-born Jagemann had greasepaint in his blood; several of his ancestors had been actors in Goethe's company in Weimar and a few others had pulled ropes backstage in Viennese theatres in the time of Franz Schubert. The young Jagemann had started in the technical department at the Metropolitan Opera and later worked for Joseph Urban's studio. For a while, in 1937, when he seemed to be doing well on his own, he began working for Jo. He left after a few years and then returned in the mid-1940s. In the early fifties, to support his family, Jagemann had to take a job as a foreman with the National Scenery Studio, of which Jo was part-owner.

When Jo's assignment included designing the costumes as well as the scenery and lighting, he invariably brought Rose Bogdanoff into the studio to assist him. Unfortunately, her romantic attachment to Jo often embarrassed him, but he cherished her talents and hired and recommended her whenever he could.

Since Jo was often overwhelmed by work, he needed someone to work alongside him full-time, and occasionally it was even necessary to hire a second assistant. For a while, Barnhart was joined by a young Finnish Canadian named Sointu Syrjala, who had trained at the Boston Museum School of Fine Arts and the National Academy of Design. He landed his first job on Broadway while he was working for Jo in 1931, and thereafter had a busy few years both in New York and in summer stock. A second assistant to Walter Jagemann in the late thirties was Lemuel Ayers, fresh out of Princeton and the University of Iowa. In 1943, because of Jo's absence due to military service, Ayers was picked by the Theatre Guild to design Rodgers and Hammerstein's *Oklahoma!*

One of Eddie Kook's scouting finds was George Jenkins, who later became the first of Jo's assistants to move on to a successful career of his own, both on Broadway and in Hollywood. In the fall of 1938, when Jagemann announced that he was leaving Jo's studio,

Jo immediately sought another assistant for the rest of his busy season. Eddie told him about the young Jenkins, who, with a solid and well-rounded background, became the prototype for all the assistants to follow him. In Philadelphia, Jenkins had been an architectural draftsman, had worked in industrial design and interior decoration, and in his off-hours had designed and built scenery for theatres. He became acquainted with Kook through his designing of the lighting for a ballet company.

Jenkins considered his employment by Jo to be one of the greatest opportunities in his life. He matched Jo's pace in the office and poured out the drafting for the construction of sets, props, and special furniture. In those pre-Polaroid days, he would make the rounds of furniture and antique shops to sketch chairs and tables so that Jo could make his selection without leaving the office. He would visit fabric shops and return with swatches to select materials. He would research the period of the show and come back to the studio laden with books or magazines. He would deliver the plans to the scenery shops, notifying them of changes, checking colors, and solving any immediate problems. When Jo began designing the lighting, Jenkins would draw up the technical light plots and plans. Sometimes the colors would be tested within a large all-purpose model (built by Jo's assistants) under miniature lights so that Jo could choose the colors and see how they would appear under stage lighting. Jenkins would accompany Jo to the technical rehearsals and record the final instructions on the intensities and colors of the lights. Most of the time he, Jo, and Jo's secretary would be alone in the studio, but when Jenkins himself needed assistance, Jo would hire additional, temporary staff to help with the drafting and preparation of floor plans, "builder's elevations" and "painter's elevations," which were the blueprints of the design world. Everything was drawn to scale and in cross-section, where necessary, so that nothing was left to chance when the plans were deposited with the scenery houses.

Jenkins recalled one moment when Jo, pressed for time, asked him to color one of the drawings that was going to the paint shop. So accustomed had the painters become to the Mielziner style that when Jenkins showed it to them at the scenery shop, they looked at it, then at him, and said, "Jo Mielziner didn't do this."

Another part of the assistants' responsibility was to construct a three-dimensional model of the set to scale and expressly for the theatre in which it would appear. Since Jo believed the model was merely to show the arrangement of the stage space and the relationships of the elements of scenery to each other, he insisted that it be left unpainted or "white." He intended the model to be a tool not only for himself but also for the director, so that each could have a visualization of how the set looked onstage and how actors could move within it. Made of glue and artist's construction board, models were fragile; most disintegrated or disappeared or were deliberately destroyed. Only a few have survived.

Besides his assistants, another component of Jo's success was the quality of the painting and construction of the sets as he visualized them. In the booming twenties, there was enough work to keep almost a dozen shops humming all the time. Some were construction shops, while others painted the sets almost exclusively. A few made only props. In an industry not usually known for gentle business manners, there was an esprit de corps among the shops. When a shop got a bit frenetic it would farm out part of the building or painting to a rival shop just to get the job done. In the supercharged atmosphere of those times, the craft shops always pulled together for the sake of the shows.

Among the oldest and most established of the shops were the Triangle Scenic Studios, an offshoot of Joseph Urban's old Yonkers studio, and the T. B. McDonald Scenic Construction Company. Two of Urban's employees, Rudolph Adler and Gus Wimazal, both master craftsmen, joined forces to found Triangle, occupying a huge building at the foot of West 43rd Street, near the Hudson River. The McDonald shop had its unusual origin in a small ironworks attached to a New Jersey racetrack. During slack times, the blacksmith would fabricate iron braces and sills for scenery ordered by the Broadway producers. As lucrative orders flowed into his ironworks, McDonald decided to set up a shop to make scenery on commission. His son, Thomas Bernard—Bernie to the trade—took over and expanded the business to include carpentry, painting, and drapery for stage curtains. They opened a huge plant on West 30th Street between Eleventh and Twelfth Avenues. For nearly

fifty years, T. B. McDonald dominated the business of fabricating scenery for Broadway and Bernie and his brother Albie were founts of wisdom concerning what could or could not be done scenically on a stage.

During the twenties, other scene shops occupied warehouses on the bustling but run-down western periphery of the theatre district. A few endured for two or three decades, while others could not weather the Depression. Robert Bergman's shop specialized in painting wizardry and lasted for more than thirty years. His company painted most of the sets designed by the early New Stagecraft designers, all of whom relied on Bergman's master painters Bradford Ashworth and Kenneth Hartwell to make scenery canvas look like their designs. Bergman's chief talent lay in solving difficult problems posed by the designers. Jo called him the magician of scene painting. His most original innovation came to be known as "Bergman's bath." Thin washes of color would be trickled over a scene flat as it was tipped off the floor and the excess sponged off by the "paint boys" to form a kind of glazing. Designers liked it because it gave a patina to the scenery.

The other important shops of the time were Nolan Brothers Scenic Studios, Turner Scenic Construction Company, Vail Scenic Construction Company, and Studio Alliance. The shops' bids for work were always broken down into two departments: construction and painting. Not infrequently, one shop would be given the construction contract while another would handle the painting. When the estimates were submitted to the producers after the customary "bid sessions," they underwent close scrutiny by the designers as well as the producers. Since it was an extremely competitive business, designers had to develop sensitive antennae to detect which bids were too low to complete the job as they envisioned it. Producers, on the other hand, looked for bargains and went with the lowest bids unless the designers raised such a howl that they were forced to reconsider. Someone of Mielziner's stature was usually listened to, but most of the time producers saved money when they could. Designers had their favorite scene shops and sometimes gave them sub-rosa tips on how an economy here or a change there would help to lower the bid. Everyone knew that this undercutting was going on, but it became an acceptable conspiracy.

Once Triangle or McDonald or any other of the shops got the job, it had to be constructed and painted on a tight schedule, and there was no margin for error. The shops would take the designers' drawings and convert them into "shop drawings"—detailed blueprints for the actual construction of the set. Painter's elevations would be matched color for color, tint for tint, until the designers approved the shades, and the set could be painted. Everything was accomplished under the watchful eye of the designers or their assistants. If there were any hitches in the process, the designers were accountable as well as the shops.

Together, designers and the craftsmen in the scene shops wrought small miracles. Close up, the stretched canvas that stood for walls appeared to be daubed with layers of paint, inexpertly applied. But onstage, under the lights, it looked solid and three-dimensional and beautifully painted. Jo always took special pains to pay tribute to the scene shop artisans.

Early in 1936, Dwight Wiman's production of *A Room in Red and White* opened and died an early death, but Jo's set for it, a stylish drawing room, elicited this comment from Robert Benchley: "I have not forgotten Jo Mielziner's stupendous room in red and white. I just don't know what to say about it. I am afraid that its dazzling grandeur only accentuates the pretentiously phony quality of the whole unfortunate occurrence. I may be wrong but I don't think so." If the 1920s had been the battleground for the acceptance of the New Stagecraft, in the 1930s, with the battle won, the critics surveyed the contributions of the designers with a new and wary sophistication. Like Benchley, they had begun to weigh the scenery's relationship to the whole with increasing awareness of its function and were no longer hesitant about expressing their appraisal of its component value. When all of the elements of a production clicked, they were quick to see not only that the scenery helped but how it helped. When there was not a meshing of the production parts, they looked to see which one of the elements was at fault: script, acting, directing, scenery, or costumes.

In Jo's early days in the theatre, designers were not even given the scripts to read before working on the scenery. Jo would tell a story about his experience with the veteran tough-as-nails producer Al Woods, who threw Jo out of his office when he asked for a copy of the script to read. In the thirties, when designers did read scripts, the most conscientious among them often tried to compensate for recognizably flawed ones by providing overpowering scenery— usually with the blessing of the producer. Critics began to see through the device and, as Benchley did, struck to the heart of the problem; they could pounce on designers for any self-indulgence they perceived, whether justified or not. In Jo's long career, he was the recipient of all these types of comments.

Jo had a banner year in 1936, not simply because of the number of shows he did (eleven) but because of the quality of the productions and the diversity of the plays and musicals on which he worked. Almost all of them presented some challenge to the now-renowned Mielziner ingenuity. It was a year in which he deliberately pared down scenery in some plays to shift the emphasis from the play to the players, in which he used revolving stages, wagon stages, and sets that flew out of sight, in which he added the names of George Abbott, George Balanchine, Richard Rodgers, and Lorenz Hart to his growing list of converts to the Mielziner style. The best advertisement for Jo's increasingly minimalist approach was embodied in his work then on view on the Broadway stage. Although it was not necessarily less expensive than conventional scenery—in some cases, it was considerably more costly because of its special fabrication—it always enhanced the shows.

After the door shut on *A Room in Red and White*, Jo had better luck with his second entry, a dramatization of the grim Edith Wharton novella *Ethan Frome*, which told of pure love gone awry through unlucky circumstance. Pauline Lord, Ruth Gordon, and Raymond Massey were the leading players, and Guthrie McClintic directed. In her autobiography, Ruth Gordon remembered that everything was right about it, including the clothes that Jo designed along with the scenery. Again, McClintic went along with Jo's solution of making the scenery simple and suggestive rather than literal.

The play calls for interiors of a kitchen and bedroom of a modest New England farmhouse and exterior scenes of a snowy landscape. For Jo, it was important to maintain the tension of repressed emotions in both the interiors and exteriors. His biggest challenge was the scene in which Ethan (Massey) and Mattie (Gordon) take an ill-fated toboggan ride. Because he wanted to preserve the brilliance

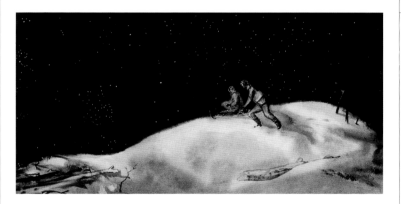

RENDERINGS FOR *ETHAN FROME* (1936). AT TOP IS THE SCENE FOR THE ATTEMPTED SUICIDE OF THE UNFORTUNATE LOVERS IN ACT III; BELOW IS THE EXTERIOR OF STARKFIELD CONGREGATIONAL CHURCH IN WINTRY EVENING LIGHT. ONE OF THE IMPORTANT LESSONS THAT JO LEARNED FROM ROBERT EDMOND JONES WAS TO PLACE THE ACTORS WITHIN THE DESIGNS SO THAT HE WOULD HAVE A SENSE OF THE SCALE OF FIGURE IN RELATION TO SET. THROUGHOUT HIS CAREER, JO NEVER FORGOT TO SKETCH AT LEAST ONE FIGURE IN HIS DESIGNS.(*TOP*: COURTESY OF JULES FISHER; *BOTTOM*: COURTESY OF PAUL TRAUTVETTER)

JO'S SETTING FOR THE "SLAUGHTER ON TENTH AVENUE" BALLET WAS NOT ONLY THE HIGHLIGHT OF **ON YOUR TOES** (1936), IT SURVIVED IN A THEN UNDREAMED-OF WAY. THE CHOREOGRAPHER GEORGE BALANCHINE REPEATED JO'S DESIGN WHEN HE REVIVED THE BALLET FOR HIS COMPANY, THE NEW YORK CITY BALLET, IN 1968. IT IS STILL IN USE TODAY. (COURTESY OF MRS. NORMA LANGWORTHY AND THE RODGERS AND HAMMERSTEIN ORGANIZATION)

of snow in moonlight and the crunchy sound that it makes when someone walks on it, he could not resort to the usual materials for creating snow and had to do a great deal of experimentation. He described the problem:

> We finally ended up using ground quartz, because it made the noise, the crunching noise that was right. The glitter was obtained by powdered mica and the third element we found absolutely necessary was to put rat poison in the whole mixture; because the quartz was too expensive and heavy to use pure, we had bought coarse meal as a bulk, and after a day's experiment we discovered we had young visitors that joined us at night and were soon going to eat away all of our snow.

On Jo's next project, *On Your Toes*, George Abbott, the theatre's great Renaissance man, was the author of the book and was involved in the staging of the musical, presumably with the blessings of Dwight

Wiman. Actor, playwright, director, producer, play doctor—whatever came his way, Abbott did it with panache and enormous authority, and Broadway regulars insisted that there was an "Abbott touch" that could turn a lackluster project into a hit. His own interpretation of his touch was that he made the actors "say their final syllables." Abbott's touch, if such there was, resided in his choice of shows: scripts with plenty of plot and action, crisp dialogue, and stories with a dollop of sentimentality. To these he added his own high standards. To Abbott the libretti or books of the twenties' musicals had been unadulterated twaddle, saved only by the music of giants like Kern and Gershwin. With *On Your Toes* he felt that he was moving in the right direction by providing a coherent plot and reinventing the dance component, which was used in most shows without much rhyme or reason. In this respect the contributions of George Balanchine, the choreographer of *On Your Toes*, added to its success; his show-stopping number "Slaughter on Tenth Avenue" was later reworked by him and added to the repertory of the New York City Ballet. (The Richard Rodgers score continues to be danced with Jo's scenery.)

Jo was assigned *On Your Toes* because, unquestionably, Wiman preferred him above all others. Abbott almost immediately enjoyed a great rapport with the designer. Although the director considered variety, not speed, the hallmark of his productions, he was grateful to Jo for providing him with fast scene changes. Because of Abbott's concentration on the performers, he relied upon his collaborators to make the right decisions. Mielziner never failed him through eight more productions.

Jo's next assignment, Shakespeare's *Hamlet*, was another challenge, one he felt he never met. In a note to Lee Simonson, dated late in 1948, Jo wrote, "Today, were I designing *Hamlet*, I would do a completely different version than that which I designed for Gielgud in 1936. I don't look upon it as one of my better jobs." When Guthrie McClintic and Katharine Cornell produced the play starring the brilliant young John Gielgud, they hired Jo but agreed that the actor would be involved in the selection of a period in which to set and costume it. Jo sensed that Gielgud did not want it done in a Gothic style and suggested the seventeenth century of Charles I of

IF THERE WAS AN INSPIRATION FOR THE SETTING THAT JO DESIGNED FOR **HAMLET (1936)**, IT OWED MORE TO LEOPOLD JESSNER (AND THE FAMED JESSNERTREPPEN) THAN TO VAN DYCK. THE SET WAS A MASSIVE STRUCTURE WITH STAIRWAYS LEADING FROM LEVELS ABOVE AND MEETING PLATFORMS BELOW TO PROVIDE A VARIETY OF ACTING AREAS, EASILY CHANGED BY ADDING DRAPES AND PROPS. PICTURED IS THE GREAT HALL, WHICH SERVED AS THE THRONE ROOM AND THE PLAYERS' SCENE. NOTE THE GIANT SHADOWS CAST BY JO'S LIGHTING. (VIRGINIA MUSEUM OF FINE ARTS)

A CHARACTER PAINTING (RATHER THAN A COSTUME SKETCH) OF JOHN GIELGUD AS HAMLET, 1936. WHEN THE ORIGINAL COSTUME DESIGN, WHICH JO PRESENTED TO GIELGUD, WAS STOLEN FROM THE ACTOR'S APARTMENT YEARS LATER, JO RE-SKETCHED IT AND SENT IT TO HIM. (COURTESY OF BUD GIBBS)

England, which placed it in the Van Dyck era. (Gielgud later confessed that he would have preferred the style of Rembrandt.)

The production was a triumph, and Gielgud was hailed as one of the best Hamlets of modern times. Jo had his misgivings about the scenery, and so did Gielgud, who later voiced an actor's complaint: "Effective as stairs always are to vary heights and grouping, they are a bit hard on actors who must spend the whole evening negotiating

them." Whatever Jo's thoughts were as he was creating the scenery, he knew enough to invest some of his own money in the show, which broke records for a Shakespearean production on Broadway (132 performances) up to that time.

Jo remained in historical periods for his next two commissions. The first, *Daughters of Atreus*, was a modern retelling of the Agamemnon-Klytemnestra-Electra-Iphigenia saga in verse and prose, all condensed into one play. The next, *Wingless Victory*, which was set in Salem, Massachusetts, in 1800, was a dark tale of miscegenation that ends in tragedy. The last of his assignments for 1936, *The Women* by Clare Booth, brought him back to the contemporary world and challenged him in many quick and varied scenes to move almost three dozen actresses on and off the stage without having them constantly bump into each other.

The "company" of Maxwell Anderson, Guthrie McClintic, and Jo Mielziner was reunited with *High Tor*, a comedy-fantasy that opened early in 1937, starring Burgess Meredith and Peggy Ashcroft in her American debut. Mixing fantasy and reality, Anderson tells a tale of grubby real-estate developers trying to flim-flam the young owner of a mountain above the Hudson River into selling them his property. The mountaintop is also apparently inhabited by the ghosts of a Dutch captain, his wife, and his crew, who have waited two centuries for the ship that will take them back to Holland. Although the play perplexed many critics, the acting earned high praise.

This was Jo's last Broadway show of the 1936–37 season. For the next few months, his studio was busy with work on his industrial commissions, which lasted to the end of the summer, but Jo was back again with the team of Anderson and McClintic to begin his new season in September with *The Star-Wagon*, which resembled *High Tor* in its combination of fantasy and realism. Set in a small town in eastern Ohio, the play moves backward and forward in time, giving Burgess Meredith, again the hero of the piece, a chance to show his versatility. The star-wagon of the title is a prototype automobile that the hero invents in his bicycle shop.

Most of the Mielziner-designed productions of these years combined elements that were much in vogue with designers to insure

FOR **HIGH TOR** (1937), JO
DESIGNED A MOUNTAINTOP
RISING AGAINST THE SKY
WITH THE HUDSON RIVER
BELOW. ALTHOUGH IT WAS A
SINGLE-SET SHOW, JO'S LIGHT-
ING, WHICH SUFFUSED THE
SUMMIT AND CHANGED AS
THE DAY PROGRESSED FROM
EARLY EVENING TO THE FOL-
LOWING MORNING, GAVE THE
SHOW A MAGICAL QUALITY.
THIS WAS PARTICULARLY
EFFECTIVE IN THE SEQUENCES
WHEN THE GHOSTS OF A
CREW OF A LONG-LOST
DUTCH TRADING VESSEL
WANDERED ACROSS THE
MOUNTAIN. (ESTATE OF JO
MIELZINER)

the smooth flow of the action during scene changes. Some of the scenes were set on platforms equipped with wheels so they could move on and off the stage, either to the wings or to the back wall of the theatre; other scenes were attached to pulleys so they could be lifted up or "flown" out of sight by a counterweight system operated by the "flymen"; still others could be put on turntables so they could rotate with one set visible to the audience while the other was being "dressed" for the next scene backstage. The single or unit set with changeable drop curtains and portable pieces was always an option for classical or epic plays for the New Stagecraft practitioners. And there was always the moving, mutable lighting, which

could, in the hands of a master, itself become scenery. Color and focus could impart the illusion of something solid and palpable. Lighting has always had a mystique among designers; it is the one element that engenders ceaseless experimentation.

It was also possible to use lighting to change scenes through the use of painted slides magnified and projected onto expanses of neutral light-reflecting surfaces. Before advances were made in the equipment to project scenery with great clarity and precision, designers had to tolerate fuzzy images, no matter how good their slides were. Projected scenery advanced slowly because of the inadequacy of the lighting source. In America, the use of projections

THE STAR-WAGON (1937) WAS SET IN A LITTLE
TOWN IN EASTERN OHIO AT THE TURN OF
THE CENTURY (ABOVE). THE MAJOR PROP IN
THE SHOW WAS, OF COURSE, THE PRIMITIVE
AUTOMOBILE, THE "STAR-WAGON," WHICH
WAS BUILT TO ACTUALLY BE DRIVEN ACROSS
THE STAGE. JO ALSO DESIGNED THE COS-
TUMES FOR THE PRODUCTION. ONE THAT
HE CREATED FOR LILLIAN GISH (RIGHT), A
GIBSON GIRL-ISH BLOOMER AND BLOUSE
COMBINATION, MADE THE GOSSIP COLUMN
OF MAN-ABOUT-TOWN LEONARD LYONS.
GISH WORE IT TO THE FIREMAN'S BALL FOR
THE STAGE RELIEF FUND AND WON A PRIZE
FOR IT—TWO BOTTLES OF PERFUME AND
A BROOCH, WHICH SHE FELT BELONGED
RIGHTLY TO JO. HE GRACIOUSLY DECLINED.
(TOP: W. H. CRAIN COLLECTION, UNIVERSITY
OF TEXAS THEATRE ARTS COLLECTION;
RIGHT: BILLY ROSE THEATRE COLLECTION,
NYPL-PA)

was further impeded by the architecture of the theatres. In Europe,
stages traditionally average 90 feet deep or more, allowing projectors to be mounted backstage and the images to be projected onto
the rear of a translucent surface. Actors performed in front of these
rear-projections. But American stages, built with much less depth,
could not accommodate sophisticated rear-projection equipment;
therefore, using front-projection, designers had to make sure that
the projections cleared the heads of the actors and nothing "spilled"
onto the acting area.

With Eddie Kook at his side, Jo began utilizing projected
scenery almost from the start of his career. Eddie would take one of
Jo's scaled drawings to Joe Levy, who would convert it into a slide
either to replace three-dimensional scenery or as a complement to
it. As Jo progressed as a designer, he relied more and more on projected scenery to handle his special effects and wished that he
could someday replace the all-too-solid stuff with projected images.
(That day would come, but not in his lifetime.)

For Jo's next show, *Susan and God*, written and directed by Rachel
Crothers and produced by John Golden, he designed three settings,
one of which he nested within another. It was hung high in the
rafters and lowered into place for the scene. The play starred
Gertrude Lawrence, dressed gorgeously in Hattie Carnegie clothes.
The production started out under a cloud. Osgood Perkins, who
played opposite Lawrence, died of a heart attack after the first performance in Washington, D.C. The understudy, Paul McGrath, took
over but the entire cast was shaken for a few weeks before the show
moved in October of 1937 for its Broadway opening. Lawrence,
coming off Noël Coward's *Tonight at 8:30*, had leaped immediately
into *Susan and God*, not only because she loved the play but also
because she needed a solid role in a solid play that had the chance
of a good run—after years of high living, she was teetering on the
brink of insolvency. Fortunately, she received brilliant reviews for
her performance from the critics in New York and in twenty-seven
other cities where the company toured.

In the play, a well-to-do woman returns from Europe full of an
exciting new religion she has found during her travels, the "religion
of love." Proselytizing to everyone, she has conveniently forgotten

her own alcoholic husband and troubled daughter—until her epiphany in the final scene. In New York, the play ran a year and a half, then continued on the road until the beginning of 1939. The production succeeded in repairing Lawrence's finances and added immeasurably to her reputation around the country. To the end of her life, the name of Gertrude Lawrence was writ large on Broadway marquees.

A Broadway production of Shakespeare's *Antony and Cleopatra* in November of 1937 occasioned one of the most famous one-line reviews in the history of Broadway. John Mason Brown, writing in the *New York Post,* began his review: "Tallulah Bankhead barged down the Nile last night as Cleopatra—and sank." Jo was not spared from his general disapproval:

> Although there is no one on the stage who can do justice to
> Shakespearean verse, the production is as heavily set by Jo
> Mielziner as if it were to be acted by some pre-Benson mummers
> who had played with Irving and Tree and were well up on the
> worst features of their scenic traditions. The text's free, burning
> spirit is no better captured in Reginald Bach's dull direction than
> it is in Mr. Mielziner's cumbersome and unimaginative settings.

The critic's colleagues were kinder, but Brown's opinion meant a great deal to Jo, and he spent the rest of his life trying to live it down. (He had also designed most of the costumes.) When Jo was displeased with anything he did, or when unfavorable reviews of his efforts caused him pain, his response was to drop the show and its records from his memory and his files. He gave a rendering of one of his designs to a Catholic school auction and disposed of the rest.

For the production of *Too Many Heroes,* author Dore Schary, producer Carly Wharton, and director Garson Kanin were all new to their roles on Broadway. Although Kanin had acted in a show (*Spring Song*) designed by Jo, this was the first professional collaboration for all of them. Unfortunately, it was not a success.

Delos Chappell, on the other hand, was coming to the end of his days as a Broadway producer with a comedy-fantasy called *Father Malachy's Miracle.* For a few weeks, he kept the readers of *Variety* titillated by his indecision over putting the play into production.

THIS IS A RENDERING FOR ONE OF THREE STYLISH SETS THAT JO DESIGNED FOR **SUSAN AND GOD** (1937). THE SECOND ACT'S BEDROOM WAS BROUGHT DOWN FROM THE FLIES TO NESTLE WITHIN THE FIRST ACT'S TERRACE ROOM. FOR REASONS UNKNOWN, JO MIELZINER'S NAME WAS OMITTED FROM THE CREDITS IN THE PROGRAM, ALTHOUGH IT WAS ACKNOWLEDGED BY THE PRESS THAT HE WAS THE DESIGNER. THERE IS ONE POSSIBLE EXPLANATION: SINCE RACHEL CROTHERS, THE PLAYWRIGHT-DIRECTOR, WAS NOT AN EASY PERSON TO DEAL WITH AND JOHN GOLDEN'S REPUTATION FOR PENURY WAS WELL KNOWN ON BROADWAY, THERE MAY HAVE BEEN A CLASH OF PERSONALITIES IN THE MOUNTING OF THE PRODUCTION. JO NEVER AGAIN WORKED FOR GOLDEN AND NEVER DESIGNED ANOTHER CROTHERS PLAY. (COURTESY OF NEIL COLLINS/RICHARD STODDARD)

Finally, he decided to go ahead with it, engaging Al Shean, of the vaudeville team of Gallagher and Shean, to play Father Malachy, with Tony Miner as director, and Jo as designer. The miracle in the play, adapted from a novel, has to do with Father Malachy's acceptance of a dare to prove that God can still perform miracles. He prays that the Garden of Eden dance hall located directly opposite his church be spirited away to an island in the sea—and he gets his wish. To perform this scenic legerdemain, Jo came up with the simplest of solutions:

> You may recall that Father Malachy's Miracle *had a big cli-
> mactic scene where during a dance somebody opens a window, looks
> out and says, "Good Lord, seagulls." The implication is that the
> entire dance hall has been lifted from its moorings and set out to sea.
> There were many discussions as to how this was going to be
> achieved. We naturally all rebelled at the idea of a set that would be
> lifted in the air or would shake and I objected to all the suggestions

FATHER MALACHY'S MIRACLE
(1937) PRESENTED ANOTHER
CHALLENGE TO JO'S INGENU-
ITY. HE RELIED ON THE AUDI-
ENCE'S IMAGINATION AND
THE ACTORS' SKILL TO TRANS-
PORT THE INFAMOUS GARDEN
OF EDEN DANCE HALL TO AN
ISLAND FAR AWAY WITHOUT
RESORTING TO ANY STAGE
TRICKS OR LIGHTING SLEIGHT-
OF-HAND. HE APPARENTLY
KNEW WHEN THE SCENE
DESIGNER SHOULD EXERCISE
RESTRAINT. (COURTESY OF
JULES FISHER)

of salt spray coming into the windows or the sight of waves beating against the back door. So I said let's leave it to the audience's imagination, and to the art of the actor, and this is what we did. And I think it worked.

After *Father Malachy's Miracle*, there were two quick failures in succession: *Barchester Towers* was adapted from the Anthony Trollope novel about the pother surrounding the appointment of a new dean for the Barchester diocese. Though a delight on the printed page, on the stage it was considered "little more than a handsomely dressed bore." Most of the critics reserved their small praise for Jo's cluttered Victorian sets. In January 1938 came *Yr. Obedient Husband*, to which Jo was steered by his agent Leland Hayward, who was coincidentally representing its leading players, the film stars Fredric March and Florence Eldridge. Both had begun promising stage careers in the early twenties and trouped through the country playing a repertory of Theatre Guild hits in any kind of available playhouse in 132 cities.

As husband and wife, they had joined a Hollywood circle that was intellectual, slightly radical in politics, sexually liberated, and disaffected by what the big studios were churning out in the early days of the talkies. By the late thirties, the Marches were ready to go back to Broadway to try to resuscitate their stage careers. Unfortunately, they did not choose the right vehicle to do the job.

Without skipping a beat after the closing of *Yr. Obedient Husband*, Jo was summoned by Dwight Wiman to work on *On Borrowed Time*, Paul Osborn's dramatization of a novel by Edward Watkins. A modern fantasy combining sentiment and humor, the play deals with how an old man and his grandson try to outwit death in the personification of Mr. Brink by trapping him in an apple tree. The production, highly praised in all aspects, competed with Thornton Wilder's *Our Town* for all the honors in the season of 1937–38 and played for nearly a year. Jo had suggested the name of Joshua Logan to Wiman as director. It was not Logan's first directing job, but it was his first real hit.

Unfortunately, Jo's next production, *Save Me the Waltz,* died quickly in February of 1938. Why, wondered Wilella Waldorf of the *New York Post,* had Max Gordon, Sam Harris, Robert Sinclair, Jo Mielziner, and a highly talented cast—veterans all—gotten mixed up in the play in the first place? (The question was asked many times along the Street of Dreams but never adequately answered.) Critics and public alike, however, were enchanted with Wiman's May production of *I Married an Angel,* which reunited Jo with Rodgers and Hart, George Balanchine, costume designer John Hambleton, and Joshua Logan. Another fantasy in a season already filled to the brim with them, *I Married an Angel* had an excellent cast that included Dennis King, Walter Slezak, Vivienne Segal, and the ballerina Vera Zorina. The plot is pure Hungarian pastry, concerning a hero who vows that he will never marry again unless she is an angel. Presto! down from heaven comes Zorina, who marries him, sheds her wings, and during the course of the musical becomes a mortal woman with human faults. Since the production involved quick scene changes in full view of the audience, Jo decided to try something new. In addition to using his device of setting scenes on movable platforms manipulated by motors and stagehands to keep up the pace, he designed a curtain with a series of horizontal transparent stripes that, when lighted, looked like a Venetian blind being opened to reveal the next scene. It was, according to one viewer who still remembers it, a spectacular and memorable effect.

Another device Jo used was called a "rear-fold traveler," his own improvement on a curtain developed by Bernie McDonald and a designer named Peter Clark. It had been used in Ziegfeld shows as a decorative curtain that gradually moved across the stage with folds gathering offstage and leaving taut the onstage, visible part of the curtain. What Jo wanted to accomplish with the rear-fold traveler was the avoidance of the "scene-in-one," a bit of show-padding performed while stagehands changed the scene behind a curtain— for Jo and many others, the bane of musical comedies because it invariably slowed the pace. Although he had used a prototype of the rear-fold traveler in the first *Little Show,* he charged his assistant George Jenkins to come up with a better version. Jenkins got in touch with a company in Ohio that made noiseless curtains on

THE APPLE TREE IN ***ON BORROWED TIME*** (1938), WHICH BECAME THE FOCAL POINT OF THE PLAY, WAS ENGINEERED AND BUILT BY HENRY GEBHARDT, ONE OF THE MASTER PROP BUILDERS IN THE BUSINESS AT THE TIME. IT HAD TO GIVE THE ILLUSION OF BEING A REAL TREE, AND AT THE SAME TIME BE STURDY ENOUGH TO HOLD THE ACTOR PLAYING MR. BRINK (FRANK CONROY) AND WITHSTAND A YEAR'S WORTH OF PERFORMANCES. (BILLY ROSE THEATRE COLLECTION, NYPL-PA)

WITH EIGHT CHANGES OF SCENERY IN ***I MARRIED AN ANGEL*** (1938), JO HAD TO LOOK FOR ECONOMY IN CHANGING THE SETS. THE FURNITURE AND PROPS WERE LIMITED IN EACH SCENE, YET THEY HAD TO EVOKE THE SCENE IMMEDIATELY, AS THEY DID FOR THIS HOTEL ROOM IN PARIS. FOR IT, JO USED FREE-STANDING WALLS AND AIRY COLORS. (ROBERT L. B. TOBIN COLLECTION, THE MCNAY ART MUSEUM)

tracks and worked with them until they came up with a light, reliable curtain. By lighting through the decoratively painted curtain as it moved across the stage, it could, according to Jo, "regain those precious seconds when the scene behind was ready to be revealed and to heighten the sense of flow." Jo used the device again and again. So did other designers.

In his lyrics for *I Married an Angel,* Lorenz Hart lightly touched Jo with immortality by including his name in one of the speak-sing sequences in the musical. The angel heroine, welcoming some of her sisters from heaven to her house, has this exchange with one of them, Clarinda:

CLARINDA: What a modern house!
     Nothing could be keener.
ROSALINA: Tell us who designed it.
ANGEL: Jo Mielziner.

Richard Rodgers, brimming with delight over the success of the musical, telegraphed Kenneth: "I still maintain that the show would only have one-quarter of its present value without [Jo's] contribution. You really ought to be proud of him. I know I am."

By August of 1938, Jo was back at his drawing board for the new season, having taken time out to marry again. After his divorce

from Annie Laurie in 1937, he wasted little time in finding consolation among the pretty actresses he met at parties, at the theatre, or through his good friends. Now in his mid-thirties, Jo looked years younger, and his fame as Broadway's leading scene designer enhanced his appeal. He began seeing Eva Langbord, an attractive young actress who had been in *Panic,* in 1935, and who had taken over Margo's role in *Winterset* the following year, but the relationship ended without marriage. Sometime in 1937, he met Jean Macintyre, an ingenue in her mid-twenties who had just completed a long stint with the Lunts in the Theatre Guild's production of *Idiot's Delight.* Jean had been making slow but steady progress in her career, but when Jo entered her life, she gave up acting.

Born on July 16, 1911, Jean was a *kamaaina,* a Hawaiian whose lineage included, on her mother's side, white Hawaiian settlers descended from a Boston printer named Edwin Oscar Hall. Her father, Malcolm Macintyre, was born in a town near Edinburgh, Scotland, and was taken to Hawaii as a young man to escape the cold, dreary Scottish weather in the hope that his frail health would improve under sunny skies. After marrying Florence Hall in 1908, he prospered with an insurance company there, but he died at fifty-five, leaving his family well fixed for life.

Jean, the second eldest of the children, did not manifest any extraordinary interest in the theatre until her college years. After she finished high school in Hawaii, she and her sister Cornelia visited London, where they took in the museums, historic places, and the theatre. Jean attended Wheaton College, in Massachusetts, and the University of Hawaii; at the latter, she became involved with a theatre group and began thinking seriously of becoming an actress. By the early thirties, she had set her sights on New York.

Armed with a letter of introduction to Theresa Helburn, of the Theatre Guild, from a friend of a friend, she arrived in New York in 1932. Helburn allowed her to attend Guild rehearsals, and eventually Jean was given a few walk-ons and understudy jobs in Guild productions. She made her "official" Broadway debut in *She Loves Me Not,* a Dwight Deere Wiman show, which opened late in 1933 and played for almost a year. When one of the actresses left the cast, she took over a featured role for the balance of the run.

JEAN MACINTYRE, 1936. WHATEVER ASPIRATIONS SHE MAY HAVE HAD FOR A CAREER, SHE SOON ABANDONED THEM AFTER MEETING JO MIELZINER. JEAN IS SEATED TO THE LEFT OF LYNN FONTANNE IN THE THEATRE GUILD'S *IDIOT'S DELIGHT.* (BILLY ROSE THEATRE COLLECTION, NYPL-PA)

Thereafter, she acted small roles, fell back on radio shows when she was not working on Broadway, and played a season with a winter-stock company on Long Island. Helburn had not forgotten her, however, and Jean landed a good role in the Theatre Guild production of *Idiot's Delight*, which had a Broadway run of 300 performances. But as an actress, Jean confided to her sister Cornelia, she seemed to be hard to cast. She was somewhere between a comedienne and a leading lady but did not fit neatly into either of those categories. Her career received an unexpected boost when the redoubtable critic George Jean Nathan included Jean's name as one of the ten most beautiful women on the New York stage in his *Esquire* column. She was also brainy, and the combination of beauty and brains was exactly what attracted Jo Mielziner. With his Pauline privilege to marry as a Catholic already in hand, he was able to pursue Jean in earnest. On May 26, 1938, after a short engagement, Jo and Jean were married at St. Matthew's Church, in Washington, D.C., by Monsignor Fulton Sheen. They honeymooned in Italy.

Reinvigorated after his honeymoon, Jo returned to find Max Gordon beckoning, this time for a revue, *Sing Out the News*, conceived and directed by Charles Friedman, with lyrics and music by Harold Rome; Kaufman and Hart took care of the sketches. It was sometimes described as the uptown, Broadway version of *Pins and Needles*, a politically left-leaning revue that became a show business phenomenon during the thirties. (The entire amateur cast had come from the ranks of the International Ladies' Garment Workers Union.) *Sing Out the News*, with a professional production team and cast and all dressed up in Mielziner scenery, opened not quite a year after *Pins and Needles* but lasted a bit over a hundred performances, compared to the nearly one thousand for its spiritual antecedent. One of the executives from *Esquire*, with whom Jo had worked on fashion shows, had seats for the opening, thanks to Jo, and found himself sitting next to Orson Welles, who (he reported) "broke two fingers applauding and dived for his program saying 'What a grand set—who did them—Mielziner?'"

In April of 1938, America's leading playwrights (save Eugene O'Neill), tiring of the foibles and eccentricities of Broadway producers, decided to band together to produce their plays. The playwrights

were Maxwell Anderson, S. N. Behrman, Sidney Howard, Elmer Rice, and Robert E. Sherwood, and the company was called simply the Playwrights Company. Stewarded by John F. Wharton, a prominent show business attorney, and managed by Victor Samrock, an expert in the ways of show business, they turned over the script for their first production, Sherwood's *Abe Lincoln in Illinois*, to Jo in May, about a month before he sailed off on his honeymoon. When Jo had heard about the scheme for the organization some months earlier, he had written to Wharton with a proposition of his own. He asked about the possibility of an arrangment between designer and producer that covered more than one production. He hinted that he would reduce his fees in such an arrangment in return for guarantees to design their shows. Although his offer was not acted upon, the Playwrights Company turned to him no less than twenty times during its history, making him the de facto rather than the official company designer.

Elmer Rice was to direct *Abe Lincoln*, and Jo hurriedly wrote him about his ideas for the scenery. The script presented a fascinating problem and a difficult one, and he regretted not being able to confer with Rice in person before his honeymoon. What he did was set down his preliminary thinking, most of which was finally incorporated but also gave Rice an almost unconscious blueprint for directing the play.

FROM **ABE LINCOLN IN ILLINOIS** (1938). WHEN THE SHOW BECAME SO POPULAR THAT IT HAD TO BE MOVED TO A LARGER THEATRE, THE PLAYWRIGHTS COMPANY ASKED JO TO RETHINK THE SCENERY IN TERMS OF THE LARGER HOUSE AND A PROJECTED ROAD TOUR. HE ELIMINATED ALMOST ALL OF THE BACKGROUNDS, SUBSTITUTED A BLACK CYCLORAMA (REAR CURTAIN), AND FOCUSED THE LIGHTING ON THE ACTORS. (COURTESY OF PAUL STIGA)

In general, the fact that the script needs an intensified realism, great speed and yet simplicity, makes me feel like describing the various scenes as vignettes of highly intensified realism stripped down to dramatic essentials. The use of complete, i.e., three walls and a ceiling, box sets, is unnecessary, unwieldy and useless expense. Turntables I have discarded for the same reason. What I see are walls of sets built on small trucks [platforms on wheels]—trucks being built in the back of flats with the wall of another set behind it. In other words, a two-faced wall, with about 18" of weighted platform on castors between them.

To get the sense of ceilings, I see simplified borders [short curtains hung above the stage], one of rough beams with a hanging oil lamp which, with slight changes, might serve for both the Tavern Scene and the first scene. Another border, with slight changes, might serve for Edwards' parlor and possibly Campaign Headquarters. The use of these borders would prevent that feeling of emptiness above, which I think would be very undesirable in these sets.

If light is to play as important a role as I feel it should, I would like very much to overcome the constant blacking-out between scene changes. No matter how short a change is, the total blacknesss acts as too strong a punctuation—in fact, a period, which accentuates the episodic element of a multi-scene play. To remedy this problem and also to give great realism to many effects which might be painted and not built, I suggest playing the production behind a very fine hair screen of gauze. Let me hasten to add that I am not referring to the heavy net gauze which makes the audience seem far away from the actors—with this sort of gauze, it is impossible to see the net when it's lit from behind, and in no way does it impair either audibility or visibility.

This would mean that at the end of a scene the picture literally melts out into light, not blackness. The following picture fades in without a jar, visually.

Another important point—I feel the need of a visual dramatic kick for Lincoln's departure from Springfield in the end. As you yourself suggested, Bob, the possibility of having the last scene actually at the Springfield depot platform would give a great opportunity. I see the end of Lincoln's railway coach and the motley crowd of his Springfield friends and soldiers lit in a dramatic light when Lincoln mounts the steps of the high and ornate Victorian parlor car and speaks to the crowd. It is a very effective trick, and fortunately a simple one technically.

For the last picture, as the crowd breaks into "Glory Hallelujah," what can happen is this: Up to now, the actual proscenium opening for the previous sets has been moderately small. At the finale a double movement is achieved, giving the effect not only of Lincoln's train moving off, but of the enlarged scope of fate in front of him [Lincoln]. The crowd itself (on a small castor platform) slowly starts to move off in one direction while the train (which is also on castors and only the end of the car is actually seen) slowly moves in the opposite direction. This, with the slowly fading light on the crowd and a pin spot [light] on Lincoln's face, will give a very dramatic sense of movement to the final picture.

The only part of Jo's preliminary plans for the scenery for *Abe Lincoln* that did not work was his idea of placing the actors behind a scrim (the gauze curtain that he described). The actors hated it, feeling that they were playing behind a blanket with a loss of all rapport with the audience. There was also enough residual light behind it to see stagehands scurrying across the stage, another miscalculation on Jo's part. It was abandoned after the first technical run-throughs.

The play and the production received praise from the critics in its out-of-town tryout and later in New York, but the public did not respond by immediately lining up at the box office. It took several weeks before it was selling out, but it succeeded in running for almost five hundred performances. More than a year later, while the show was still running, Jo wrote a piece for the *New York Times* (October 22, 1939), which for the first time, gave him an opportunity to make public his evolving philosophy concerning scenic design. In "Scenery in This Play?," he noted that after the sceneryless *Our Town*, people were questioning box office people: "Is there scenery in this play?" (Even the *New Yorker* noticed the public reaction and published a Helen Hokinson cartoon showing two matrons asking the same question at the box office. Jo had a slide of it made and used it for many years whenever he spoke or lectured.) The proper question, Jo avers in the article, is "Is there theatre in this scenery?" which he explains in terms of what he did in working out the scheme for *Abe Lincoln in Illinois*. He describes the technique as "implied scenery," by which he meant that he eliminated anything that detracted from the actors. Because the technique worked superbly in *Abe Lincoln*, it justified Robert Edmond Jones's theory about evocative scenery and further convinced Jo that he was on the right track.

The Playwrights Company called upon Jo for their second production, *Knickerbocker Holiday*, a musical with book and lyrics by Maxwell Anderson and music by Kurt Weill. It was originally conceived by Anderson as a satire on the administration of Franklin D.

Roosevelt, whom he regarded as a tyrant in the mold of the dictatorial Dutch governor Peter Stuyvesant. Anderson's pro-Roosevelt colleagues at the Playwrights Company were disconcerted by his script, and Weill, who had worshipped Roosevelt while he was in Europe, was perplexed by Anderson's stance. Finally, when Logan was brought in as director-cum–play doctor, not only were the changes substantial but the focus of the book was altered to permit Stuyvesant to become a more sympathetic character.

In the role of Stuyvesant, Walter Huston also offered advice for improving the book. He suggested giving Stuyvesant a bit of vulnerability and he asked for a special song to be written to indicate it. Anderson and Weill complied in the course of one day. Although *Knickerbocker Holiday* is rarely revived, it contains one song that appears to be evergreen: "September Song." Originally half-sung, half-spoken by Huston, it has established itself as one of the great romantic ballads of popular music.

The team of Rodgers and Hart, George Abbott, George Balanchine, Irene Sharaff, and Jo Mielziner reunited to create

THE MODEL OF **KNICKERBOCKER HOLIDAY** (1938), UNTYPICALLY CONSTRUCTED OF PAPER, PLASTER, AND WOOD, SOMEHOW SURVIVED THE TRASH HEAP TO WHICH JO USUALLY CONSIGNED HIS WORKING MODELS, WHICH HE CONSIDERED JUST TOOLS. IN 1953, JO GAVE IT TO THE MUSEUM OF THE CITY OF NEW YORK. (MUSEUM OF THE CITY OF NEW YORK)

FROM **THE BOYS FROM SYRACUSE** (1938). TO GIVE A SUGGESTION TO COSTUME DESIGNER IRENE SHARAFF OF WHAT HE HAD IN MIND FOR THE (VERY) FREE ADAPTATION OF SHAKESPEARE'S *COMEDY OF ERRORS,* JO WROTE TO HER IN HOLLYWOOD TO TELL HER THAT HE WAS PLANNING TO USE "A FEELING OF 14TH CENTURY TUSCAN PAINTING, WITH A COMPLETE DISREGARD FOR PERSPECTIVE." EVERYTHING WAS PLAYED IN FRONT OF A DECORATIVE CURTAIN AND THE LARGE SET PIECES WERE REALIGNED UP AND DOWN THE STAGE TO PROVIDE QUICK CHANGES. (BILLY ROSE THEATRE COLLECTION, NYPL-PA)

THE ONLY SET LISTED IN THE PRO-
GRAM FOR **STARS IN YOUR EYES** (1939)
IS "SOUND STAGE '7,' MONOTONE
PICTURE CORP., HOLLYWOOD." THE
LARGE, OPEN SPACE OF A MOVIE
SOUND STAGE ALLOWED JO TO WORK
WITH MANY OF THE DEVICES HE HAD
USED IN PAST MUSICALS: PLATFORM
STAGES, REAR-FOLD TRAVELER, TRANS-
PARENCIES, ETC. FOR ONE SCENE, HE
PROJECTED SOME FILM FOOTAGE
ONTO A LARGE SCREEN BEHIND JIMMY
DURANTE AND MILDRED NATWICK.
SHOWN IS THE TRANSPARENCY FOR
A BALLET SEQUENCE. (BILLY ROSE
THEATRE COLLECTION, NYPL-PA)

The Boys from Syracuse in November of 1938. The show, with its basketful of wonderful songs, proved a hit, and Jo was finally accorded credit for his lighting design in the program—the first time for a regular Broadway production. It was also the last production Jo designed that year.

Before he accepted *Mrs. O'Brien Entertains,* Jo reported to George Abbott, who was producing it, that he was swamped with offers for the fall season, and he let it be known that his services would not come cheaply. Although he had been asking for weekly royalties for years, producers usually turned him down. If they wanted him badly enough, he was able to extract from them more than the union-minimum fees in sub-rosa contracts, without the knowledge of the union. But Jo continued to explore the possibility of increasing his take on shows by establishing the principle of a weekly royalty. On occasion in the past, he had agreed to forego his usual conditions to sign on for a reduced fee with a weekly royalty to be paid until his full fee had been met, or he would agree to do a show for less than he usually asked with a weekly royalty to commence after the tenth week of the run. Unfortunately, he had been hurt by some of his decisions when the shows he designed under these arrangements folded soon after they opened. Now he was asking for his full fee *plus* a weekly royalty. Abbott balked at this new proposition, as did the other producers for whom Jo designed. Eventually, squirming under the arrangement, most producers gave Jo what he wanted. The value of a Mielziner set to a production could not be underestimated. Jo was probably thankful that *Mrs. O'Brien Entertains* was designed under the standard contract; the play was dismissed as a "cartoon of life among the immigrants."

A day after *Mrs. O'Brien* opened (February 8, 1939), Jo had a second and happier opening for the new year with *Stars in Your Eyes,* a Wiman production by J. P. McEvoy (book), Dorothy Fields (lyrics), and Arthur Schwartz (music). It starred Ethel Merman, Jimmy Durante, Mildred Natwick, and a large contingent of dancers from the ballet world led by Tamara Toumanova and including Jerome Robbins. The plot was almost nonexistent, but the presence of Merman and Durante ensured a modest run. Its competition on Broadway was a musical up the street, Cole Porter's *Leave It to Me.*

In it, a young performer named Mary Martin was stopping the show every night with "My Heart Belongs to Daddy."

Next Jo designed for the Playwrights Company again: S. N. Behrman's *No Time for Comedy*, starring Katharine Cornell; Guthrie McClintic (of course) was the director. All were Mielziner partisans. (The production became a joint production between the Playwrights Company and the McClintics.) Cornell had never had played much comedy and was frightened to death of pulling the play down because of a bad performance. Laurence Olivier, still relatively unknown to Americans at the time, was cast as Cornell's leading man and was an ideal foil. Surrounded by a perfect cast, Cornell gave one of the best performances of her career.

Too Many Girls, which opened on October 18, 1939, was Jo's first of the new Broadway season. It brought him back into the Abbott–Rodgers and Hart orbit and gave him a chance to design the campus of Pottawatomie College, at Stop Gap, New Mexico. Although the book was silly, the high level of energy generated by a young cast that included, among others, Eddie Bracken, Desi Arnaz, and Van Johnson gave it a healthy run.

Immediately following this came a complete change of pace for Jo with another production by the Playwrights Company, Maxwell Anderson's *Key Largo*, about the Spanish Civil War. Anderson wanted Paul Muni to play the lead role of the troubled hero, and Muni and his wife, Bella, wanted desperately to "go back to civilization," which to them meant New York. At first he thought he was wrong for the part, but Muni talked himself (with the help of wife and playwright) into accepting the assignment. King McCloud, the hero of *Key Largo*, who is haunted by deserting his comrades on a battlefield in Spain, was just the kind of character that Muni could sink his histrionic teeth into. The critics applauded his performance and appreciated the high purpose of Anderson's poetry, but the Playwrights Company production was not a runaway hit. However, it was successful enough to go on tour with Muni.

Morning's at Seven was the second of Paul Osborn's plays produced by Wiman, directed by Logan, and designed by Mielziner. It marked the first time any of them had worked with costume designer Lucinda Ballard, who would become not only a leading designer for four

FROM ***TOO MANY GIRLS*** (1939). AS LONG AS THERE WAS ENOUGH SPACE FOR THE LARGE CAST AND CHORUS, THE SCENERY COULD SERVE MAINLY AS A BACKGROUND FOR THE COLLEGE CAMPUS NONSENSE ON STAGE. (BILLY ROSE THEATRE COLLECTION, NYPL-PA)

FROM ***KEY LARGO*** (1939). WHEN THE SHOW OPENED IN TRYOUTS OUT OF TOWN, MAXWELL ANDERSON OBJECTED TO THE LONG WAIT NECESSITATED BY "STRIKING" (REMOVING) THIS SCENE AND SETTING UP THE SECOND, A WHARF AND COTTAGE ON KEY LARGO, FLORIDA. JO SIMPLIFIED THE SPANISH HILLTOP SCENE AND REDUCED THE WAIT, KEEPING INTACT THE FLORIDA SET. (COURTESY OF PAUL STIGA)

MORNING'S AT SEVEN (1939)
WAS A SINGLE SET, WHICH
ELICITED THIS COMMENT
FROM BROOKS ATKINSON
OF THE *NEW YORK TIMES:*
"[MIELZINER] HAS SET THE
PIECE PERFECTLY BY FILLING
THE STAGE WITH REAR
PORCHES AND FAÇADES OF
TWO MCKINLEY PERIOD
HOUSES AFTER THE PUNGENT
STYLE OF BURCHFIELD."
(MUSEUM OF THE CITY OF
NEW YORK, JOHN BENNEWITZ
COLLECTION)

FROM *TWO ON AN ISLAND* (1940). IN ONE SCENE THAT CALLED FOR TWO TAXICABS, JO SKETCHED TWO SKELETONIZED TAXIS, WHICH WERE MADE OUT OF METAL STRIPS BENT TO
FORM THE CONTOURS OF THE CABS IN A KIND OF WIRE SCULPTURE AND PRESAGED JO'S USE OF ENTIRE SKELETONIZED SETTINGS. THE PHOTO AT RIGHT SHOWS HOW THE CABS
ACTUALLY LOOKED ON STAGE. (*LEFT:* W. H. CRAIN COLLECTION, UNIVERSITY OF TEXAS THEATRE ARTS COLLECTION; *RIGHT:* BILLY ROSE THEATRE COLLECTION, NYPL-PA)

decades on Broadway but also one of Jo's favorite collaborators. (Unlike costume designer Irene Sharaff, with whom Jo had worked on many shows but never socialized, Ballard also became his friend.) The play, a comedy whose gentle small-town humor was dwarfed by its major Broadway competition, Lindsay and Crouse's *Life with Father* and Kaufman and Hart's *The Man Who Came to Dinner,* held on for just 44 performances. Years later, all Jo remembered of it was the "rich talent of the personalities involved in the production." (In 1980, the play was revived on Broadway with an all-star cast for an extraordinary run of 564 performances—with a set, reminiscent of Jo's original, designed by William Ritman.)

A month later, for Guthrie McClintic's new show, *Christmas Eve,* Jo agreed to reduce his fee by $500, with the difference to be made up by a payment of $50 per week until it was paid off. Not only did it *not* open on Christmas Eve (December 27 instead), it never made it into the new year, closing on December 30, 1939, after six performances. Fraught with Freudian overtones, the play seemed to be carrying a serious message, but no one believed in the characters.

By the frequency of Jo's assignments for the Playwrights Company, the critics could not fail to notice that Jo was becoming their house designer. Elmer Rice, one of the members, had written a charming play, *Two on an Island,* about a pair of out-of-towners who hope to conquer the Big City, she as an actress and he as a playwright. Their perambulations through the city take them to almost a dozen locations but Jo was, as usual, obligated to do the scenes as economically as possible.

Higher and Higher, the new Rodgers and Hart show, had Jo working again with Wiman and Logan. It opened in April of 1940 and proved one of the few misfires of Rodgers and Hart and the producing team. Conceived as a vehicle for the talents of Vera Zorina, when she was unable to take the role it had to be readjusted for Marta Eggert, an attractive Hungarian performer who could sing but not dance. It was the last of Jo's commitments for the season.

With the war in Europe now capturing everyone's attention, replacing the economic Depression with a psychological depression, the new theatrical season of 1940–41 opened tentatively and produced during its course very few successes. The biggest hits were such escapist fare as *Arsenic and Old Lace, My Sister Eileen, George Washington Slept Here,* and *Lady in the Dark.* Jo's first entry in early October was *Journey to Jerusalem* by Maxwell Anderson. The Playwrights Company production was a quick failure. A dramatization of the boyhood of Jesus (played by Sidney Lumet), it had a huge cast but no stars—except, perhaps, for the scene designer.

Jo was a bit luckier with *Pal Joey,* produced and directed by George Abbott, with a book by John O'Hara (adapted from his own *New Yorker* stories, with an assist from Abbott), and music and lyrics by Rodgers and Hart. The show was built around the character of Joey Evans, a down-at-the-heels entertainer working at a Chicago nightclub, where he falls in love with a pretty girl. He drops her when a wealthy middle-aged woman takes a fancy to him and builds him his own club. The cast included June Havoc, Vivienne Segal, Van Johnson (in a small role), and starred Gene Kelly in the only leading role he ever had on Broadway. Opening on Christmas in 1940, the show pleased the critics as an "adult musical," possibly because there is no pat or happy resolution to Joey's life.

SHOWN HERE FROM RODGERS AND HART'S **PAL JOEY (1940)** IS CHEZ JOEY, THE TONY NIGHTCLUB THAT THE HERO RUNS COURTESY OF HIS RICH LOVER. (ROBERT L. B. TOBIN COLLECTION, THE MCNAY ART MUSEUM)

Flight to the West, which opened at the end of December of 1940, was another play from the prolific Elmer Rice produced by the Playwrights Company. It was one of the few entries on Broadway in the days before the nation became embroiled in World War II that made audiences acknowledge that something important was going outside the theatre. Rice's device of assembling a diverse group of people in a space isolated from the rest of the world is one of the hoariest of all dramatic constructions, but he gave it a contemporary twist. On board a transatlantic clipper flying from Lisbon to the United States are refugees from the turmoil in Europe, each (aside from the crew) representing either a different ethnic or political group. It was a talky play, but the talk was absorbing and the play enjoyed a healthy run amid all the escapist fare on Broadway.

Jo's greatest disappointment for the year, which was also combined with frustration and anger, was the out-of-town closing of a Harold Rome musical produced and directed by Eddie Dowling. The show, titled *The Little Dog Laughed,* was a fantasy partially set in Brooklyn, partially set in Fairyland. When it opened in Boston, Elliot Norton of the *Globe* gave it an encouraging review and was especially enthralled by one scene in which a forest moved onto the stage. Jo, he thought, designed with the correct amount of whimsy, which was lacking in other aspects of the production.

What happened between the Boston and the New York opening is barely hinted at in Jo's correspondence. In a postmortem letter to Dowling, a disgusted Jo recalled that the producers had shown a "crudity and inefficiency of the typical amateur," but he absolved Dowling of any blame. "I just want to express to you my disappointment that my first 'Eddie Dowling Production' should have fizzled out in such an unhappy way. You had a great property there and I know you were on the right track." Their next association was not to be so troubled.

With his career in full swing and a beautiful bride by his side, the only thing missing from Jo's life was children. Neither Marya nor Annie Laurie had been willing to bear children, and now, at the age of thirty-seven, Jo felt that the time was more than ripe to begin a family. At twenty-seven, Jean—to his enormous delight—wanted children immediately. When no pregnancies occurred during the early years of their marriage, they consulted doctors, who discovered that Jo was infertile. After being treated by a leading specialist in male infertility, the Mielziners decided to explore the option to adopt.

They applied to the Catholic Home Bureau in New York, which, among its other philanthropic activities with children, had been placing babies for adoption since 1899. On the surface, Jo and Jean

THE ACTION OF **FLIGHT TO THE WEST** (1940) TAKES PLACE ABOARD A PAN AM CLIPPER. BY ENCASING THE SET IN A FALSE PROSCENIUM, JO KEPT A SENSE OF CLAUSTROPHOBIA WHILE GIVING THE TWENTY ACTORS ROOM FOR TÊTE-À-TÊTES IN EVEN TIGHTER SPACES. HE BASED HIS DESIGN ON ACTUAL AIRPLANE INTERIORS. (BILLY ROSE THEATRE COLLECTION, NYPL-PA)

looked to be ideal potential parents. Age, income, and background were all in their favor. Unfortunately, the eternally immeasurable element is temperament. Whether Jean and Jo were suited to rear children at that time could not be and probably would not have been accurately judged, but future events inevitably and unfortunately yielded an answer.

Adoption practices fifty years ago were vastly different from the kind of process in place today. The Catholic Home Bureau was perhaps representative of the way children and parents were matched. The first child who came to the Mielziners and who was named Michael (the name, coincidentally, of Jo's favorite Catholic saint, the keeper of the faith) was the product of a Catholic mother and a German-Jewish father. Born on June 22, 1938, little Michael was two and a half years old and had lived in several foster homes before the Mielziners adopted him in January of 1941. The last was an Italian home, probably in Brooklyn, because he remembers being driven over a bridge to the Mielziners' East Side apartment and retains memories of being pulled from his foster mother's arms and turned over to Jean. It was not the best way to start a new life.

Michael was a bright, strong-minded, and willful little boy. Either the chemistry was all wrong between him and Jean or she lacked the patience to see him through his painful period of adjustment. As a result he became unmanageable. With Jo either in his studio or on the road supervising technical rehearsals, Jean often had no help with the balky child and was without expert advice on how to deal with him. Jo and Jean decided that a brother might give Michael a playmate and help ease the situation. They returned to the Catholic Home Bureau a year and a half later for their second child, whom they named Neil, for Jean's brother. Neil had been born on October 10, 1939, to an Irish-American mother and was also two and a half when he joined the family. But the arrival of Neil only served to complicate matters. Neil was a frail and shy child and had rickets from a previous poor diet, requiring extra care. He did not, however, become intractable and his presence had a calming influence on Jean while giving her a little more confidence as a mother. Jo, however, had just received a commission in the Army reserves and had to depart early in June of 1942, leaving Jean to cope with the two children.

Jean had moved into Jo's duplex apartment on East 61st Street, which he had shared with Annie Laurie, but they had begun thinking about getting a place in the country. Almost everyone they knew—Joshua and Nedda Logan, Dorothy and Richard Rodgers, Lawrence and Armina Langner, and many other of Jo's professional associates—was buying weekend houses in Connecticut and the Mielziners decided to follow suit. Jo preferred a comfortable, old-fashioned New England house to anything contemporary and they appeared to find exactly what they wanted in Newtown, Connecticut, on Boggs Hill Road. The century-old house was run down, but it came with twenty acres and an ancient eighty-foot stone barn, all for the cost, in March of 1940, of $16,360. With the war clouds gathering, they had to postpone their plans for extensive renovations. After the war, they hired an architect from Danbury to make changes to the house.

When the time came for Jo to enter the military, they gave up the New York apartment and changed their address to Boggs Hill Road, Newtown. They bought a 1940 Ford station wagon, and for a few months Jo commuted into the city to his studio. He was finding the life he had always wanted.

Jo began the new year, 1941, with a murder mystery, *Mr. and Mrs. North*, adapted by the seasoned playwright Owen Davis from the whodunits by Richard and Frances Lockridge. The critics were kind to the play, but it was no competition for *Arsenic and Old Lace*, which opened a few blocks away at the Fulton Theatre. *Cream in the Well*, by Lynn Riggs, which opened a week later, recounted an unrelieved string of tragic events beginning with the incestuous love of the heroine for her brother and ending with her suicide. Another serious theme was embedded in S. N. Behrman's *The Talley Method*, which had Jo back working with the Playwrights Company. Its road to Broadway was rocked by changes in the cast, the director, and the play itself, all to no avail. Ultimately directed by Elmer Rice, it had a short run and was one of the Playwrights' notable failures.

Herman Shumlin, who had departed from directing *The Talley Method* in February, was certainly more comfortable later in the spring with Lillian Hellman's *Watch on the Rhine*. Not only had he directed all of Hellman's previous plays, but he had hired her as a play reader in his office in the early thirties. Shumlin knew how to handle her and her plays, which were finely crafted dramas in the tradition of the "well-made play," a genre that is long on plot and economical in dialogue and situation, with all the loose ends tied

up as the curtain falls. A Southerner and a Jew, Hellman was drawn to the far left politically, though she never joined the Communist Party, which had been fashionable among intellectuals in the thirties. She could just as easily ridicule fuzzy-headed left-wingers as she could attack with deep fervor the far right. And she tackled difficult subjects. In *Watch on the Rhine*, which she said was inspired by Henry James, she tested the liberal stance of a certain class of rich Americans when confronted with hard truths about the lengths to which some people will go to fight for their beliefs. In the play, an ardent anti-Nazi, the husband of the daughter of a rich First Family of Virginia, must take extreme measures to protect himself from disclosure to the wrong people. Hellman told Jo exactly what she wanted on the set of the play to create the accumulated clutter of generations of the family. Privately, Jo thought the play too literary and talky, but it enjoyed a solid run for almost a year.

In the seasons before America's entry into the war, *Watch on the Rhine* was one of several that reflected playwrights' concern with the fighting in Europe and the conflict between political ideologies. In *The Wookey*, which began Jo's designing activities for the new

LILLIAN HELLMAN WAS AS USUAL VERY DEFINITE ABOUT WHAT SHE WANTED FOR THE SET IN **WATCH ON THE RHINE** (1941) AND JO TRIED TO ACCOMMODATE HER. HE GAVE THE SETTING A KIND OF FADED ELEGANCE, MIXING ANTIQUES MIXED WITH UTILITARIAN FURNITURE TO GIVE THE IMPRESSION THAT THE FAMILY SHE CREATED CARED LITTLE FOR MATERIAL THINGS AND MUCH MORE FOR MATTERS OF THE MIND AND HEART. (COURTESY OF GREG KAYNE)

Broadway season of 1941–42, the dramatic conflict is between the individual and the state. The plot concerns a British tugboat captain (played by Edmund Gwenn) who dislikes Winston Churchill's ideas, but when the salvation of his friends and his country is at stake, he marches to his duty to defend it. Though the power of its message was diluted by sentimentality, it did achieve status as one of the better war dramas of the era.

With the frightening events of the war moving ever closer, Broadway continued to offer escapism. *Best Foot Forward*, the first musical of the season, was a strictly formula show rescued by the youth and bounce of the cast under George Abbott's lively direction, Gene Kelly's choreography, Miles White's costumes, and Jo's sets.

Both the Playwrights Company and the Theatre Guild were knee-deep in difficulties in the early forties. Both needed a hit desperately when they joined forces to take a chance on Maxwell Anderson's *Candle in the Wind*, another variation on the events in Europe. The creative team that they assembled in this co-production left nothing to chance: Helen Hayes as its star, Alfred Lunt as its director, sets and lighting by Jo Mielziner, and Miss Hayes's costumes by the renowned haute couture designer Valentina. In June of 1941, Alfred Lunt wrote to Jo:

> *Let me tell you how deeply happy I am that you are to do the sets—as a matter of fact it was one of the conditions under which I'd direct the play—and the fulfillment of a vision I've had ever since you did the scenery for* The Guardsman—*but you know all that. Now! Let me apologize at the beginning. Let me ask your forgiveness for many annoyances that are ahead for I shall be very tiresome and unreasonable and testy—because there isn't a detail in the theater that I am not interested in from the price of a scrim to the hanging of an X-ray [lighting equipment]. I shall bewilder and annoy you, but remember through it all, that way down deep inside I am a child at heart . . . so I beg your pardon, now, Dear Joe—I apologize—I'm sorry—it's all my fault—you are a great artist, etc., etc., etc. And that's that—*

Lunt was true to his word but his disarming approach and his true sense of theatre made up for any annoyances Jo may have felt. Lunt

THE WOOKEY (1941), SET IN WARTIME LONDON, WAS ACCOMPANIED BY THE ACTUAL SOUNDS OF GERMAN BOMBING (SUPPLIED, SAYS THE PROGRAM, BY THE BRITISH MINISTRY OF INFORMATION). THE TWO PHOTOGRAPHS SHOW THE WOOKEY FAMILY'S HOUSE AND BACKYARD BEFORE AND AFTER IT HAS BEEN BOMBED. (BILLY ROSE THEATRE COLLECTION, NYPL-PA)

bombarded him with sketches and suggestions, all of which Jo took with good grace. The critics loved Miss Hayes, thought Lunt's direction was brilliant, and applauded Jo's sets of a Versailles garden and a Nazi concentration camp, but the play, about a woman who attempts to rescue her lover from the clutches of the Gestapo, did not bring the hoped-for success.

Although the general perception persists that George S. Kaufman rarely produced, wrote, or directed a clinker, there were exceptions. When he and Edna Ferber had completed *The Land Is Bright*, Kaufman approached producer Max Gordon with a proposition that became a prophecy. If Gordon agreed to produce the play, he assured the producer, "It will mean a great deal of prestige for you—doing a play by Edna and me—even if it isn't a hit." The play was a kind of high-class soap opera whose bubbles burst after about ten weeks.

There is no record that Max Gordon gained in prestige because of producing it. Since the scenery was enormously elaborate and expensive, Gordon warehoused it to use bits and pieces of it for future productions. When Jo discovered that Gordon's office had neglected to pay bills for some of the furnishings, Jo sent him a gently chiding letter, in which he reminded him that he had bought them taking his designer's 33 percent discount and passing the discount on to the producer. "As you well know," Jo wrote with a bit of self-righteousness, "many designers deal with these firms on the understanding that the manager pays the retail price and the designers get the 33% commission. I will have nothing to do with this sort of business." Gordon paid.

The transplanted English playwright Charles Rann Kennedy liked to write dramas with metaphysical messages, which the public usually resisted. He had enjoyed one great success in 1908 with *The Servant in the House,* about a bishop who serves in the house of his brother disguised as a butler. Although he had written about a dozen plays in the intervening years, only half of them were ever produced. In 1941, he came out of retirement with *The Seventh Trumpet,* which he also directed. Rather than describing to Jo directly what he wanted for the scenery, he chose an oblique route by writing to the actress Carmen Mathews, who was to play one of the principal roles, and sending a copy of it to the designer. It was a detailed plan, which gave instructions down to the kind of flowers he wanted in the flower beds and what lighting effects he envisioned. "I do think the more mystically ethereal and April-day lovely and *English* we can keep it, the better," he wrote. Jo was not pushed by the playwright's manipulations into giving his best, but the script proved so crushingly bad that Kennedy's *sub rosa* machinations were all for naught.

By the turn of the new year, America had entered the war and Broadway was feeling its effects. Only sixteen productions were still playing on Broadway when the new season began in September of 1941, but eighty-three new entries arrived—with few successes. One of the new plays was *Solitaire,* adapted by John Van Druten from a novel by Edward Corle. It was produced by Dwight Wiman, directed by Dudley Digges, and designed by Jo. The critics recognized resonances in it of *On Borrowed Time* in its telling of the relationship between a young girl and an old drifter. Since the actress playing the little girl was Pat Hitchcock, the precocious child of film director Alfred Hitchcock, the production probably got more attention than it deserved. But the play closed quickly.

Although Jo had designed the settings for George Balanchine's balletic choreography in three Broadway shows, he had not, like many of his colleagues, designed the scenery for any ballets. When he was approached by the still young American Ballet Theatre to design scenery for Antony Tudor, one of its principal choreographers, he was initially delighted. Faced with an almost nonexistent budget for the sets and woefully inadequate facilities for the production, he was appalled. Tudor's choreography for *Pillar of Fire*

(based on Arnold Schoenberg's string sextet *Verklärte Nacht*), Jo's scenery, and the brilliant dancing by Tudor and his company (with Jerome Robbins and Donald Saddler in lesser roles) brought critics and balletomanes to their feet at the April 8, 1942, opening at the Metropolitan Opera House. Jo had designed the costumes as well as the scenery and lighting and was convinced after this initiation that the two most important elements for ballet were the costumes and the lighting, particularly the latter. After the premiere of *Pillar of Fire,* the lighting had to be scaled down because the company was not able to afford the elaborate controls that Jo needed for the set. Years later, he concluded that the fault was his in not "recognizing the limitations of production facilities" in designing the scenery.

Jo did not make it to the opening of *By Jupiter,* on June 3, 1942, at the Shubert Theatre in New York; by that time, he had received his Army commission. But he had the satisfaction of knowing that he left Broadway on a high note. Dwight Wiman and Richard

THIS RENDERING OF THE MAIN SET OF ***PILLAR OF FIRE*** (1942) REFLECTS THE SOMBRE TONE OF THE BALLET. THE BALLET CONTINUED TO BE DANCED FOR MANY YEARS, BUT WITHOUT JO'S LIGHTING EFFECT OF THE DARK SKY CUT THROUGH BY STREAKS OF RED, WHICH HE HAD PAINTED INTO HIS DESIGN. (COURTESY OF THE ESTATE OF HILDA AND EDWARD KOOK)

Rodgers produced *By Jupiter*, Joshua Logan directed it; Rodgers and Hart provided the book, music, and lyrics; and Robert Alton choreographed the dances. Based on *The Warrior's Husband*, by Julian Thompson—it had a long history from its first incarnation in 1921 as a one-act play and a reincarnation in 1932 as a three-act play starring Katharine Hepburn and her glamorous legs—the Rodgers and Hart musical was by far the most successful version. The last show co-written by Rodgers and Hart, it was the biggest hit of their career, in which Jo's sets and lighting and Irene Sharaff's costumes were adjudged part of its general enchantment. In a letter to Maxwell Anderson, Jo confided that he was happy that he was able to "do one more setting before I got in." Burns Mantle wrote that the scenery for *By Jupiter* was "a nice one to remember him by." Late in May, Jo closed his studio at 1441 Broadway and reported for duty.

Jo was one of a group of New York scene designers who had decided that if and when they were asked to serve, they wanted to be able to deal their own hand in their choice of military assignments. In February of 1942, twenty designers hired two putative camouflage experts to teach them the art and science of camouflage, Herbert Kniffen of the American School of Design and Baron Nicholas Cherkassoff, a former Russian Army captain. Calling themselves the Camouflage Society of Professional Stage Designers, they each paid $50 for membership in the group to offset the costs of renting an office and paying the lecturers. They prepared homework assigned by the Baron, who critiqued their projects in class. After completing their "course," they continued to work together, electing Jo as their president and meeting occasionally at Vail Scenic Studios. Finally, when they thought they were ready, they offered their services to the military. Several of the members were rejected for medical reasons, while others were accepted as enlisted men. Only two of the group, Jo and Donald Oenslager, received commissions. Both were over-aged for military service, but because of their prestige and self-guided training, the Army valued them.

Now forty-one, Jo was assigned Serial Number 0473236 and told to report to Jefferson Barracks, in St. Louis, Missouri, for training. For a while, all he and his fellow stage artists did there was decorate interiors and design landscaping, while waiting for the real training to begin. Eventually, he and the others completed the Army's course and he was sent to Fort Belvoir, in Richmond, Virginia, to join the 936th Engineer Camouflage Battalion of the Army Air Base, serving as Executive Officer. For a few months, Jean and the boys lived in a little house close to the base, but when the Mielziners began adoption proceedings for another child, a year-old girl named Jennifer, the cramped quarters became too much for her and she returned to Newtown. For the duration of the war, she kept house, took care of three children, and shoveled thirteen tons of coal during each of the Connecticut winters that Jo was away. Since the distance from Richmond to New York and from there to Newtown was not great, he was able to get frequent furloughs to visit his family and friends.

Jo's military career with the camouflage corps was fraught with frustrations, not the least of which was the drastic drop in income. As an Army captain, and later a major, his pay never topped $300 per month, as compared to about ten times that as a Broadway scene designer. Consequently, he had to go into debt to carry his house and family and was not able to repay it for several years after he left the military. Furthermore, although he made many friends while in the service, he was unhappy with the Army brass and the

military mind. Once, when he was on leave in New York, he told Sam Leve, one of his younger colleagues, that Army personnel were "geniuses in stupidity," prompting Sam to ask: "How do they manage to come out ahead in assault?" Jo answered that the enemies were probably greater geniuses in stupidity. One of his other gripes was that his feet seemed to have grown while he was in the Army. When he returned home, he could not fit into his civilian shoes.

Some of the camouflage work he found interesting. He used to say that when he designed scenery, he was no good unless he revealed a situation immediately to the audience, but in camouflage, the reverse was true. Before the development of radio-directional aids (radar) later in the war, bombing depended exclusively on what

A MUSICAL VERSION OF *THE WARRIOR'S HUSBAND,* A PLAY MADE FAMOUS BY KATHARINE HEPBURN'S LEGS, *BY JUPITER* **(1942)** WAS A WELCOME RELIEF FROM THE DESIGNER'S SUCCESSION OF MODERN INTERIORS. JO CREATED COLORFUL SETS USING PAINTED BACKDROPS OF A MYTHICAL GREEK CAMP AND A TENT INTERIOR. ALONG WITH IRENE SHARAFF'S VIVID COSTUMES, IT WAS A FEAST FOR THE EYES. (MUSEUM OF THE CITY OF NEW YORK, JOHN BENNEWITZ COLLECTION)

JO'S EAGERNESS TO PARTICIPATE IN THE WAR WAS TEMPERED BY HIS ACTUAL EXPERIENCE ONCE HE WAS IN THE MILITARY. HOWEVER, HE ENJOYED THE RANK, PRIVILEGES, AND WEARING THE UNIFORM. (ESTATE OF JO MIELZINER)

their work, made excellent *camoufleurs*. Fort Belvoir itself became a laboratory for their ideas. Many years later, it was described in *Masquerade*, a book about wartime camouflage:

> At Richmond . . . the base was designed to blend with surrounding civilian areas. The long low troop barracks were each painted in two pastel colors divided down the center, to resemble semi-detached family dwellings. False chimneys for nonexistent fireplaces, small awnings, white picket fences, and a variety of shrubs and "front lawn" treatments added to the make-believe. All military vehicles were parked under trees, carports, or raised camouflage nets called flat-tops. Civilian cars were permitted on the base, but instead of being crowded into huge parking lots they were allowed to park at random along the many streets of this fictitious "suburban community."
>
> For better protection, aircraft were dispersed and individually concealed, and hangar shapes were broken up with carefully placed nets. Mielziner had the field's runways coated with textured asphalt to reduce glare, then spray-painted them in patterns of green, brown, and yellow ocher to blend into the local countryside. By applying light and darker shades of color at certain points a three-dimensional foliate effect was also achieved.

Jo was transferred from Fort Belvoir to the headquarters of the Army Air Force Training Command in Fort Worth, Texas, at the end of October of 1943. There, Jo taught airmen what to look for on their bombing raids. He reminded them that the enemy was just as practiced in the art of camouflage as the Americans. He described one incident that clearly demonstrated German ingenuity. After several months of bombing what the British and American forces knew to be an important aircraft factory, they found that the Germans continued to retain a strong air and ground defense of the area instead of abandoning it as a useless wreck. A reconnaissance plane came back a few weeks later with photographs of the target, which confirmed that it had been destroyed. The camoufleurs studied the pictures thoroughly and recommended that the bombers return and hit it again, this time with incendiary bombs. When they did, the target exploded in fire. What had looked like a mass

the bombardier could see on the ground through his bombsights. Since the airplanes flew at such high speeds, bombing depended on split-second timing and often the bombs did not hit the targets at all. Camouflage compounded the difficulties on both the friendly and enemy sides of the war and constituted a real weapon. The problem was not only to hide Allied defenses from the enemy but also to spot the enemies' disguises. To create camouflage, the designers had to analyze colors, textures, shapes, and shadows as they would appear from the air. To penetrate camouflage, the eye had to be trained to spot any irregularities in all of these things almost instantaneously. Designers, particularly scene designers and muralists who practiced trompe-l'oeil techniques in the course of of wreckage had actually been made of stage materials. Major Mielziner described it as "light, flimsy stuff—just like the setting for a war play. It covered a big wooden framework and the Germans were rebuilding the factory underneath it."

After six months in Texas, Jo wanted to depart from the camouflage unit and pulled strings to get transferred to the Office of Strategic Services in Washington. He asked his friend Monsignor Sheen for a letter of recommendation to General "Wild Bill" Donovan, the head of OSS, whom the priest knew quite well. Sheen obliged and sent a letter. Noting that it was very seldom that he wrote such letters, he said that he was making a rare exception for "one of the finest men it has ever been my privilege to know." Despite help from Sheen and from other friends in high places, it took several months to obtain the transfer. Finally, it came through and Jo spent the last six months of his Army service in Washington with the OSS. At the beginning of November of 1944, he was placed on inactive service and went back to home, hearth, and family in Connecticut.

Although Jo may have suffered disenchantment with military life, several of the men with whom he worked became warm friends and others associates in some of his nontheatrical projects. One, Leslie Cheek, had a good deal in common with Jo, and they formed a long-lasting friendship. Cheek was descended from the wealthy family that had developed a coffee blend named Maxwell House. Educated at Harvard and then at the Yale School of Architecture, he nurtured an interest in the theatre, taking courses with Donald Oenslager in the Yale School of Drama. In 1935, because of the Depression, he could not find a job in an architectural firm, and after teaching fine arts at the College of William and Mary, he became the director of the Baltimore Museum of Art. At Fort Belvoir, Cheek rewrote the Army's camouflage training manual.

Leslie Cheek and Jo saw each other as kindred spirits. Jo's gentility, his style, his professionalism, his exuberant self-confidence coupled with his knowledge of art and scene design were all mirrored in Leslie Cheek despite their difference in social and economic background and education. Cheek showed his appreciation of Jo's talent the one way he could, by giving him a one-man exhibition of his work in 1967, at the Virginia Museum of Fine Arts, and by having the museum purchase several examples of his work.

The man who became Jo's most enduring Army friend was Stanley Kusman, a Catholic priest who was both Jo's chaplain and his roommate in the officers' quarters at Jefferson Barracks. In a few weeks' time, Father Kusman completely destroyed any stereotypical notions in Jo of the aloof Catholic priest. The "Padre" was a fun-loving, joke-cracking, ebullient, and dynamic man as well as a dedicated and caring priest, a brilliant scholar, and a master of five languages. Because of his personal charisma, he was sometimes called the "poor man's Bishop Sheen"; he had earned a master's degree in philosphy at Catholic University under Fulton Sheen. Once, serving at the front during the war, Chaplain Kusman, alone and unarmed, went out beyond the battle lines to find and carry out the bodies of fifty-seven soldiers who had died at their concealed posts. For this act, ensuring the men's proper burial, he was awarded a Purple Heart and was nominated for a Bronze Star.

Jo found in Kusman a companion unlike Eddie Kook, a confidant with whom he could share his innermost thoughts about his religion. When the Padre celebrated his golden jubilee in the Church, in 1974, Jo journeyed to San Antonio to speak in his friend's honor. If Jo got nothing more out of his military service than friendships with men he admired and respected, he returned to civilian life seasoned by his experiences and ready, in the fall of 1944, to begin another phase of his life.

6
BACK TO BROADWAY

When Jo took off his uniform and put on what his small son Michael described as his "money-making suit" in the fall of 1944, he had missed two full seasons on Broadway. About a dozen shows that had opened during his absence were still on the boards and at least two of them would set records for some time to come. They were almost all of them escapist plays and musicals. Even those that recognized that a war was going on throughout the world did so almost tangentially. No great war play is ever written while the battle rages—nor ever will be. When audiences passed through the doors of the theatres in those perilous times, they asked for surcease from the daily problems, personal and global, and Broadway did its best to satisfy them. *Life with Father*, filled with nostalgia for a more innocent era, was still going strong with its umpteenth change of cast, and *Oklahoma!*, the triumph of the new collaboration between Richard Rodgers and Oscar Hammerstein II, was being hailed as a landmark in the development of the American musical. The most audacious and controversial play of the war years was Thornton Wilder's *The Skin of Our Teeth*, which attacked humankind's propensity to wage purposeless war through the ages and has remained a play for all seasons. There were other serious plays, none of which have stood the test of time but which dealt interestingly with racism and its pernicious effects. These faint rumblings in the 1940s presaged things to come as playwrights were coming to grips with the fatal faults of American society.

OPPOSITE: JO EMPLOYED A PALETTE OF BRILLIANT COLORS IN CREATING THE WEST INDIAN SETTINGS FOR *CARIB SONG* (1945). THIS RENDERING SHOWS HIS ADAPTATION OF AIRBRUSH TECHNIQUE FROM HIS ARMY CAMOUFLAGE DAYS. THE SHOW GAVE JO A CHANCE TO DESIGN FOR AN AFRICAN-AMERICAN ENSEMBLE. WHILE EXPERIMENTING WITH COLORED GELS ON THE LIGHTS TO BRING OUT THE ACTORS' SKIN TONES, HE CONCLUDED THAT DARK-SKINNED PEOPLE "CARRY OFF COLORS SO MUCH BRIGHTER AND RICHER THAN THEIR PALE-FACED BROTHERS AND SISTERS." (COURTESY OF BUD GIBBS)

Jo saw many old familiar faces on Broadway, but there were new faces and names he did not know or did not know well: younger producers such as Alexander Cohen, Kermit Bloomgarden, and David Merrick, playwrights such as William Saroyan and Horton Foote, musical creators such as Lerner and Loewe, and designers such as Oliver Smith. Some of the new generation would loom large in his life and career. One of them, Elia Kazan, had worked on Broadway with the Group Theatre, but he was just coming into his own during the war years.

Even before he had his military discharge in hand, Jo's first order of business was to find an apartment for his family in New York and to set up a new studio; he disliked driving and had no intention of spending two hours each way commuting to and from Connecticut. At a party he and Jean were attending in New York (while he was still in uniform), he had the good fortune to find himself describing his plight to Stephen Clark, the owner of the Dakota apartment house on Central Park West and West 72nd Street. Jo explained that he was looking for a large apartment for his wife and three children but could find nothing within his means. The rent for his last apartment, he told Clark, was under $200 per month, which was about what he would be able to afford once he left the military and resumed work in the theatre. Clark listened sympathetically, then offered him a three-bedroom apartment at the Dakota for about the same rent. Jo accepted the offer on the spot and quickly set about making arrangements to take over Apartment 48 on November 1, 1944. Because of Jean's reluctance to return to Manhattan with three small children, at first Jo used the apartment as a bedroom during the week while he commuted to Newtown on the weekends. When the house underwent major renovations and a pool was added in 1948, Jean was even less inclined to move to the city. But as the children approached school age, the advantages of the private schools in Manhattan could not be easily discounted. For those and other reasons, Jo prevailed and the family moved into the Dakota in the fall of 1951.

The tenancy of the Mielziners at the Dakota occurred during the last gasp of the kind of civilized life envisioned by its creator, Edward Clark, the financial wizard behind the Singer Sewing Machine Company. In the late 1870s, Clark bought land in what was then the upper reaches of Manhattan, so far removed from everything, said his friends, that it might as well be in the Dakota Territory. This whimsical description apparently so appealed to Clark that he decided to call his building the Dakota and had the architect incorporate Wild West symbols into the decoration. He intended to surround himself with his well-to-do friends in forty-two huge apartments and provide them with amenities like a central dining room and reasonably priced housekeeping services while keeping the rents low. When the building was completed in 1884, two years after Clark's death, it actually had sixty-five apartments ranging in size from four to twenty rooms, and space in the upper floors for the staff.

The building remains a masterpiece of eccentricity, with parts of the building not directly communicable to other parts. When Jo moved in, it was equipped with hydraulic elevators that painfully inched up and down. There were also high ceilings, varied and mismatched decorative elements, oversized doors, paneled halls, thick walls, a central court and fountain, and even a private park with tennis and croquet courts in its early days. In 1944, the Mielziner apartment consisted of a living room, master bedroom and bathroom, two small bedrooms, a second bathroom, a kitchen and pantry, and a maid's bedroom and bath. Because there were no dining areas in any of the apartments, Jo and Jean had to set a table and chairs in a section of their living room. When they moved in, the building still functioned on DC electric current and would not be converted to AC for another four years. Housekeeping and repairs could be arranged through the manager's office at fifty cents per hour and meals could be sent up to the apartment at any time of day.

At the time Jo took up residence, the Dakota was not fashionable. Despite having its eastern façade facing Central Park, the building did not appeal to people who wanted to display the "best" East Side address in New York on their engraved stationery. Because of its amenities and low rents, however, tenants were reluctant to move from the Dakota despite its lack of cachet. As time passed, the newer tenants represented an arty, intellectual New York that could and did appreciate the Dakota's oddities, and Jo Mielziner fit in very well there.

Jo established his new studio at 1430 Broadway, in the upper story of the famed Empire Theatre just below 40th Street. Across the street, the Metropolitan Opera was visible from the large front office, whose two windows faced Broadway; this functioned as Jo's own workspace. There were rooms for the secretary and Jo's assistants. Served by malfunctioning elevators (tenants did a lot of weary stair-climbing), drafty in the winter and hot in the summer, the cramped quarters were often difficult to work in. But the office was a few stops downtown on the subway line close to the Dakota, and the rent was affordable—about $100 a month for a lease and sublease for the combined Office no. 50 and the adjoining Office no. 51. And the rent increases were not budget-breaking. More importantly, it was within walking distance of the scene shops and theatres—and the Coffee House Club for lunch.

Now that producers were beginning to pound on his door, Jo moved quickly to hire a secretary and an assistant. He was frantically signing contracts for the spring half of the season with the Theatre Guild, with Max Gordon, and with Eddie Dowling. Three shows were scheduled to open in March and one in April. He called Edward Gilbert, a young designer whom he had met in the Camouflage Society, to help draft the plans for Dowling's upcoming production, and Lisa Jalowetz and Anna Hill Johnstone to work on the other shows. Since the pool of male assistants was severely reduced in wartime, Jalowetz and Johnstone and other young female designers were kept busy during those years working for the reigning Broadway designers who did not join the military. Jalowetz, a refugee from Hitler's Austria, had received her training in scene design from the Max Reinhardt School of the Theatre in Vienna and art schools on both sides of the Atlantic. She had previously worked for Norman Bel Geddes and Oliver Smith and Boris Aronson, whom she married shortly after she left Jo. The southern-born Johnstone received her education at Barnard College in New York. Since there were more opportunities for women in costume design, she had gravitated toward that field but eventually found her niche in Hollywood. Walter Jagemann also came back periodically to take over the drafting and the studio. Since all of them were interested in building their own careers, they could not spare much time

as Jo's assistants. What he needed was a full-time assistant. Eddie Kook came to the rescue and suggested that Jo look over the credentials of a young man he had just met in Philadelphia. His name was John Harvey. Temperamentally and professionally, he proved to be an ideal match and did not leave Jo until 1961.

After a day of Christmas revelry that left him somewhat the worse for wear, Harvey reported for work on December 26, 1944. Whatever plans he may have had to establish a career of his own were set aside during his years with Jo. The only son of a Philadelphian architect and Swedenborgian minister, he had studied on scholarship at the University of Pennsylvania School of Architecture. Although he completed his degree, he was possessed of a rich, full baritone and hoped to break into opera. The Philadelphia Opera Company asked him to become their assistant manager, and he eventually involved himself in designing and building the scenery for their tightly budgeted operation, utilizing the very limited supplies it had accumulated. He gained enough experience as a designer to join United Scenic Artists. After an unprofitable national tour arranged by Sol Hurok, the Philadelphia Opera Company closed down in 1944. John Harvey called the Century Lighting Company in New York to ask whether they might be interested in buying the battered but still usable lighting equipment and salvageable dimmer boards. Kook not only bought the equipment but also returned to New York with news of a potential assistant for Jo.

Although Harvey's drafting technique was superb, he had to learn to quicken his tempo to keep up with Jo's pace. More than drafting, he became Jo's alter ego in setting up the lighting that Jo had designed. Established designers like Jo now had to provide precise plans. It was in this area that Jo gave his assistant more and more responsibility for setting up the light plots and drawing the layouts. It was difficult and painstaking work, particularly in creating the "hanging plots," which were the arrangements of all the elements of scenery and lighting suspended from the gridiron above the stage. Tolerances were so exact that if a drop or a light pipe were just a few inches too close in the plans, it would cause hours of work on stage to reset everything. Because it was sometimes difficult to predict the playhouse in which the shows were to be presented,

John had to predicate all his work on the hypothesis that it would go into the smallest theatres. He also had to function on occasion as the guinea pig to test out props or parts of the scenery to make sure that everything was safe for the actors.

Because Jo expected a high level of achievement, he did not lavish compliments on his assistants, but he paid John Harvey what for him must have been the ultimate compliment. After formally placing John in charge of the studio a year and a half after he arrived, Jo sent him a formal letter on the fifth anniversary of their association saying that he would be paying him a small percentage of his own net income beginning with the following year and increasing slightly thereafter. Since the salary was not munificent

FOR *FOOLISH NOTION* (1945), JO HAD TO CREATE A COMFORTABLE, LIVED-IN-LOOKING LIBRARY IN A MANHATTAN TOWN-HOUSE. THE MOST IMPORTANT ELEMENT WAS A PORTRAIT OF THE ABSENT OWNER OF THE HOUSE, WHICH HUNG ON THE "FOURTH WALL" AND WAS SEEN ONLY IN THE REFLECTION OF A MIRROR ON THE BACK WALL. IN ACTUALITY, THE MIRROR WAS "SCRIM," A TRANSPARENT SCENIC MATERIAL, AND THE PORTRAIT WAS SUSPENDED BEHIND IT. THE PORTRAIT WAS VISIBLE WHEN THE LIGHTS WERE TURNED UP BEHIND IT. (BILLY ROSE THEATRE COLLECTION, NYPL-PA)

to begin with, it may have been small comfort to Harvey, but in those days, assistants were not especially well paid by any established designer.

Secretaries were another matter. Jo expected a great deal of the young men and women he hired to answer the phone, protect him from unwanted callers, take and type his correspondence, correct his atrocious spelling, keep his financial records (personal and business), make his travel arrangements, brew coffee and tea, and relieve him of all the petty details of office management. Occasionally, he had them read scripts, research at the New York Public Library, shop for fabrics or small props, and generally help out when and where he needed them. For all of these duties, he paid them a niggardly salary and expected them to expend a devotion to their job almost equal to his own. From the time he set up his office-studio away from his home in the mid-thirties until 1976, he hired about three dozen secretaries. Jo was a good boss most of the time and became genuinely fond of many of his secretaries, but his tunnel vision about the importance of his work to the exclusion of all other factors occasionally nettled the best of them. Jo sometimes asked too much of everyone, assistants and secretaries alike, but no one who worked for him ever regretted the experience.

Jo retained his studio at 1430 Broadway until May 1949. (The theatre and building were torn down in 1953 and were replaced by an office building.) Seeking to cut his costs, he moved his studio to his big apartment in the Dakota for a few years until he was able to persuade Jean to live in the city with him. After briefly flirting with the idea of buying an entire brownstone for his living and working quarters, he was offered Apartment 1 on the ground floor of the Dakota by the management for his studio. (In Stephen Clark's days, it had been the employees' dining room.) He took it and became the Dakota's only commercial tenant. There he remained for the rest of his working life.

His studio was in full swing simultaneously preparing two shows due to open in March of 1945. The first had all the ingredients of a sure-fire hit. A Theatre Guild production, *Foolish Notion* was written by Philip Barry, the most successful writer of English-style American drawing-room comedies, and starred Tallulah Bankhead, whose presence always kept box offices busy. Tallulah sailed around the stage in Mainbocher gowns ably supported by a talented cast. The comedy, a reworking of the Enoch Arden tale about a husband returning to his wife after a long absence, failed to enchant the critics, most of whom found it talky and repetitive. But the star's loyal fans kept it going for a respectable run.

Max Gordon had summoned Jo for his production of *The Firebrand of Florence*, a musical comedy based on a 1924 play by Edwin Justus Mayer, with music by Kurt Weill and lyrics by Ira Gershwin. The firebrand of the title was Benvenuto Cellini, whose amorous antics provided the plot. Weill (whose sometime wife Lotte Lenya had a principal role) had been the composer of *Knickerbocker Holiday* and of the incidental music for *Two on an Island*, both of which Jo had designed before the war. Weill was a refugee from Hitler's Germany, where his work had been considered too Bolshevist; he was also a Jew. When he reached American shores in 1935 (with his leftist politics intact), he began to absorb American rhythms and musical idioms, incorporating them into his compositions. On Broadway, he believed in collaborating with established writers, sometimes from other fields, frequently persuading them to join forces with him in musical theatre projects.

Weill immersed himself in every phase of the production of his work, writing his own orchestrations, offering suggestions to the production team, helping the performers, doing whatever he could to make the show a success. His devotion to popular theatre was total, and he never felt he had to sacrifice his political beliefs or social concerns on the altar of commercialism. Somehow, he managed to weave a message into his important musicals, which dealt with such topics as the ravages of war, psychoanalysis, the poor, racism, and moral decay. Although Weill has often been been considered more European than American, his musicals influenced American composers more than some of them cared to admit. Despite the ton of money that Max Gordon spent on *Firebrand*, the play was an unfortunate choice for Weill to musicalize and closed after a few weeks.

After the failure of *The Little Dog Laughed*, in 1940, Jo had written to Eddie Dowling of his disappointment "that my first 'Eddie Dowling

FROM MAX GORDON'S 1945 PRODUCTION OF **FIREBRAND OF FLORENCE,** A KURT WEILL AND IRA GERSHWIN COLLABORATION. JO PROVIDED EIGHT DIFFERENT SCENES, EACH CAPTURING THE FLAVOR OF THE PERIOD BY USING SIXTEENTH-CENTURY TRICKS OF PERSPECTIVE. THE CHANDELIERS IN THIS SCENE GET SMALLER IN SIZE AS THEY RECEDE UPSTAGE TO ENHANCE THE ILLUSION OF DEPTH. (MUSEUM OF THE CITY OF NEW YORK, JOHN BENNEWITZ COLLECTION)

Production should have fizzled out in such an unhappy way." His second association with Dowling was to end more happily, and it would introduce him to a playwright with whom he would be associated for the next thirty years. The play was *The Glass Menagerie* and the playwright was Tennessee Williams. Until 1934, Eddie Dowling had made his career in the theatre as a song-and-dance man. He began a second career as a writer of light musical comedies, then launched a third career as an actor, director, and producer of unconventional plays. Because he had directed, produced, and acted in two plays by William Saroyan, the agent Audrey Wood, with her uncanny sixth sense, had sent him Williams's play thinking he could be the right person to produce it.

In November of 1944, Dowling sent the script to Jo, who accepted the assignment enthusiastically. Unfortunately, Dowling was saddled with a co-producer, Louis J. Singer, who had not read the play but controlled the purse strings tightly. With his sweet Irish guile, Dowling had lured Singer into the project with the idea that it might not be a commercial success but would be a worthy artistic failure. Singer proved to be a royal nuisance to Jo. Dowling also sent the script to Laurette Taylor, whose alcoholism and reputation for unreliability had made her *persona non grata* with producers on Broadway for years, despite her stunning performance in *Outward Bound* in 1939. She quickly accepted the offer of the role of Amanda Wingfield. Another copy was sent to the critic George Jean Nathan, who suggested his then-protégée, actress Julie Haydon, for the part of Laura, the shy and crippled daughter. Anthony Ross was an ideal Gentleman Caller, and Dowling, too old for the part, cast himself as Tom. Paul Bowles was commissioned to supply the incidental music.

During Williams's early struggles for recognition, his greatest champion was Margo Jones. Texas-born and bred, Jones wanted to introduce to the world what she saw as Williams's glorious talent. She produced his play *You Touched Me* and encouraged him to continue writing. Because of her single-minded devotion, Williams prevailed upon Dowling to hire her as his directorial assistant.

When Jo and Jones met for the first time, there was an instant rapport, and they developed a friendship that would outlast their first collaboration. While working on *The Glass Menagerie*, Jones was also setting up her Dallas Civic Theatre and was determined to involve Jo in it somehow. She asked him to serve on her board, fully aware that linking a Broadway pro of his stature to her endeavors would not be lost on the Dallas locals. She hired Jo as a consultant, inviting him to Dallas to look over the Globe Theatre, which had been erected in 1936. Jo warned her that the theatre was a fire hazard, but went ahead with the drawing of plans for renovating it. Unfortunately for Jones, his assessment proved correct, and

the fire department would not allow her to open. He continued to help her but kept his involvement at a distance, mainly because, as he candidly informed her, he really did not like theatre in the round such as her Globe.

The working relationship between Jo and Williams became almost mystical. Williams's plays had the kind of lyric spirituality that exactly suited Jo's genius; the plays lent themselves to the subtractions in scenery that Jo felt were needed in contemporary theatre. What Jo most disliked were plays of relentless realism, for which he had to create relentlessly realistic sets. He felt that the stage designer in every case always lost to the movies, in which realism was easily achievable because the camera lens could make the whole world a stage. Jo was happiest with compression and abstraction. He wanted to "design with an eraser" (his favorite aphorism) so that a play's poetry could be released into a theatre space like a genie out of a bottle. In *The Glass Menagerie*, as in *Winterset*, he had not only found such a play but a far better one than he had ever encountered in his career.

Williams indicated in his script outsized images of the Jolly Roger, blue roses, and a huge enlargement of the face of the absent father of Tom and Laura. Jo thought that the visual images were redundant, since they were emphasized sufficiently in the dialogue, and argued successfully for their removal, but he bowed to the playwright's desire for an accent on the father's face by having a photograph, just under life size, printed on linen and rear-lighted to give a slight prominence to it during certain moments of the script. (Many of the revivals of the play have restored the large visual images of the original script to the production.)

To keep the costs at rock bottom, Jo and his assistants scrounged secondhand shops for suitable props. They found a very soiled mulberry-colored sofa, faded dark green velour chairs, and a Grand Rapids "golden oak" dining room table and chairs. He put antimacassars on the backs of the upholstered furniture to establish the small-town status of the Wingfields. When *The Glass Menagerie* was presented in London, Jo went to great lengths to explain to the British compeers just what antimacassars are. Contrary to the press releases of the time, the glass animals were not supplied by Steuben

WHEN JO FIRST READ **THE GLASS MENAGERIE** **(1945)**, HE NOTED THAT TENNESSEE WILLIAMS HAD NOT INDICATED AN EXTERIOR SCENE. TAKING A CUE FROM WILLIAMS'S DESCRIPTION OF THE DRAMA AS A "MEMORY PLAY" THAT SHOULD NOT BE PERFORMED WITHIN REALISTIC SCENERY, JO SUGGESTED THAT THE FIRST LINES OF DIALOGUE, SPOKEN BY TOM, COULD BE DELIVERED OUTSIDE (ABOVE) RATHER THAN INSIDE THE DRAB FLAT (BELOW). JO DESIGNED A TRANSPARENT "FOURTH WALL" ON SCRIM DEPICTING AN ALLEY AND FIRE ESCAPE, WHICH WOULD THEN ALLOW HIM TO LIGHT THE INTERIOR AND EXTERIOR SCENES EITHER SEPARATELY OR SIMULTANEOUSLY, YET GIVE TOM PHYSICAL AND PSYCHIC DETACHMENT FROM HIS MOTHER AND SISTER IN THEIR CRAMPED WORLD. THE PLAYWRIGHT, PRODUCER, AND DIRECTOR UNANIMOUSLY ACCEPTED JO'S IDEAS. (COURTESY OF BUD GIBBS)

Glass but were found in a souvenir shop in New York. Hundreds of them broke and were replaced during the run of the show.

The entire cost of the scenery for the show was $4,200. Because Singer would not hire a costume designer, Jo had to keep a wary eye on the costume selection. The dresses for Taylor and Haydon were bought off the rack in a Chicago department store, then remade and given a worn and faded look. Jo often told a story about Laurette and her costumes. According to a letter he wrote to Hugh "Binkie" Beaumont, the London producer, on the opening night of the Chicago previews, Jo learned that Laurette was not in her dressing room. Since the curtain was due to rise in a half hour, Jo joined in the search for her in the theatre. As he recalled:

> In the basement next to the steam room I found Laurette Taylor, her sleeves of her dressing gown rolled over her elbows and her hands deep in a wash tub filled with dye. As she greeted me she lifted out the party dress, sopping wet and said, "don't worry, Jo, I'll put this over a steam pipe and it will dry during the first act." It did and she wore it.

Jo was never happy with the costumes for the show but could do nothing about it. He suggested to Beaumont that he engage Lucinda Ballard to do the costumes for the London production.

With Louis Singer looking over his shoulder, Jo lighted the show, cue by cue, in one marathon session. Jo had specified a velour backing to prevent light spills, but Singer objected to the expense. The exasperated designer stood his ground and got what he ordered. Since the show was done simply, Jo realized that the only true element of scenery was the lighting, which he wanted to be magical. (Incredibly, Singer later took credit for the lighting of the show.)

Despite advance reports that something unusual was going on at Chicago's decrepit Civic Theatre, no one was quite prepared for the avalanche of praise heaped on every aspect of the show when it opened. The two major Chicago critics, Ashton Stevens and Claudia Cassidy, tripped over themselves with superlatives and kept up an almost daily barrage of praise in their columns. Everything paid off. By the fourth week of the run, the show was selling out. Inevitably, the news reached New York, which was to receive the production in late March.

Margo Jones informed Jo that Williams had added a "drunk scene" for Tom and hoped that he could go to Chicago to light it and fix a few other lighting difficulties before the show reached New York. She and the playwright had been able to resist Singer's attempts to change the ending of the play so that it would conclude with Laura and the Gentleman Caller walking into the sunset together and were anxious to forestall Singer's efforts to alter any part of Jo's contribution. Jo was not able to return to Chicago, but he made all the necessary adjustments when the production moved to New York. Williams wrote Jo to assure him that Dowling's mugging and ad-libs had been cut out and that Taylor knew her lines and gave an astonishing performance. He also thanked Jo for his lighting design.

The Playhouse Theatre had been selected by Singer because it was cheaper to rent than any of the houses Jo might have preferred. Because of the front-to-back depth of his set, he knew that people in the second balcony would have trouble seeing the actors—and they did. (A few people directed their ire at *him*.) His experience fueled his general unhappiness with Broadway theatres and strengthened his resolve to do something about it if and when he ever got the chance.

The reception of *The Glass Menagerie* in New York astonished all of its creators. The production did something for everyone connected with it. For Tennessee Williams it was recognition of his great gifts as a dramatist. Beyond reclaiming her reputation, Laurette Taylor was finally acknowledged as one of the greatest actresses that America had produced. Eddie Dowling enhanced his reputation both as a director, an actor, and a producer with vision. For his co-producer, Louis Singer, it brought reflected glory. For Julie Haydon and Anthony Ross, it forever established a benchmark in the performance of their parts. For Jo, it demonstrated how lighting can do more than illuminate the stage, it can also illuminate the meaning of a play. Without turntables, platform stages, or any other complicated equipment, he designed exactly the kind of scenery and lighting that was necessary for the play. What the play did not receive was the Pulitzer Prize for drama for that year; it went to Mary Chase's play *Harvey*, about an amiable drunk and his chimerical six-foot-tall rabbit friend.

For the road tour—Singer objecting loudly over the cost—the production was redesigned to withstand the rigors of traveling. In late July 1948, it was produced by Binkie Beaumont at the Haymarket Theatre, in London, with Jo's scenery re-created from his plans, the first time one of his sets reached the West End. Helen Hayes was uncomfortable following Taylor in the role of Amanda and did not react well to John Gielgud's direction. Miss Hayes wrote to Jo after the opening:

> Your set was a tremendous hit, but there is a little difference of opin-
> ion about the play, mainly I think because they shy away from
> sad things now in London. I was warned of that before I came
> over—but I think there is a large enough audience for this play to
> make it well worth all the struggle and preparation.

Although she received hosannas for her performance from the English critics, postwar blues, as she suggested, hurt the play's reception. Years later, when Hayes did a revival at the New York City Center, she abandoned her attempt to re-create Laurette Taylor's portrayal of Amanda and played it her way, with better results for the play and satisfaction for herself.

Although *The Glass Menagerie* had a relatively short run at the Haymarket, Jo was grateful for having been introduced to London audiences and to two men, Joe Davis and Ian Dow, who would do their best to steward most of his future productions across the Atlantic. Both worked for H. M. Tennent, a producing organization run by Beaumont that was renowned for the high quality of its presentations. Joe Davis, a hard-working but self-effacing lighting engineer, was the best that London had to offer. Ian Dow, a former actor and stage manager, became Tennent's production manager, roughly equivalent to the American general manager. Jo counted them among his friends as well as his working associates.

The season in New York had a few more months to run. Though his contribution to the flourishing musical comedy stage so far was for the failed *The Firebrand of Florence*, he welcomed the Theatre Guild's summons to work on the new musical in the works by Rodgers and Hammerstein. Lawrence Langner, of the Theatre Guild's producing partnership, had talked a skeptical Ferenc Molnár into allowing

ALTHOUGH HE WAS NOT ON HAND TO DESIGN THE FIRST OF THE RODGERS AND HAMMERSTEIN COLLABORATIONS, JO WAS TAPPED FOR THEIR SECOND JOINT VENTURE, *CAROUSEL* (1945). THE FINAL SCENE OF THE GRADUATION DAY WAS SET BEFORE THE SCHOOLHOUSE BACKDROP WITH ROWS OF CHAIRS IN FRONT. IT WAS A SIMPLE AND MOST EFFECTIVE SOLUTION. (COURTESY OF THE RODGERS AND HAMMERSTEIN ORGANIZATION)

Rodgers and Hammerstein to transform his fantasy *Liliom*, about a Hungarian carnival barker and his simple, trusting wife, into a musical set in New England in a different era. The composer and lyricist themselves were unsure they could pull it off, and like *Oklahoma!* their new venture *Carousel* had a troublesome gestation. The second act, especially, stayed in a state of flux almost to the final tryout performances. Jo never had a completed script to work from and had to design it piecemeal as it developed, a practice that always violated his sense of good design. To compound Jo's unhappiness, he felt that the Guild had mishandled the credits in the program, giving him what he considered minimum billing. To complete the general aura of gloom surrounding the production, President Roosevelt died during its pre-Broadway opening.

FOR *CAROUSEL* RICHARD
RODGERS INSISTED ON
HAVING A REAL CAROUSEL
ONSTAGE—AGAINST THE
OBJECTIONS OF AGNES DE
MILLE, WHO WOULD HAVE
TO CHOREOGRAPH THE
DANCES ON WHAT LITTLE
FLOOR SPACE WAS LEFT.
JO SYMPATHIZED WITH HER
AND WANTED A LESS LITERAL
SOLUTION BUT COULD
NOT FIGHT RODGERS. THE
AMUSEMENT PARK SCENE,
USED ONLY FOR THE PREL-
UDE, MADE FOR A CROWDED
STAGE. (PHOTOFEST)

And yet what the critics saw and heard was a lovely musical with serviceable Mielziner sets, pretty costumes by Miles White, ballets by Agnes de Mille, and wonderful performances by a group of largely unknown actors. Some of them even appreciated the courageous step taken by Rodgers and Hammerstein in eliminating any vestige of comedy from the standard musical on Broadway. *Carousel* played for two solid years on Broadway. After its American run, it opened in London at the Drury Lane Theatre, in June 1950, presented by the British producer Prince Littler, with sets built and painted from Jo's blueprints. Littler would not pay Jo to redesign the scenery to fit into the Drury Lane, and Jo would not predict the end results. In a letter to Rodgers and Hammerstein, he cited

British technicians' tendency to redraw American designs to fit West End theatres with their narrower proscenium arches and different sightlines. The results, he felt, were not up to American standards. He requested that his name not be used as designer in the program credits.

Monetarily, *Carousel* was a high point for Jo. Whenever he had asked for a royalty in the past, he had been turned down, but wonder of wonders, Rodgers agreed to a small percentage of the weekly gross in addition to the usual design fees. Jo and all his design colleagues at the time felt that they never received sufficient compensation for their work as collaborators nor enough recognition for their part in the success of the hits. (Producers were notoriously quick to blame designers if the show failed and slow to credit designers if the show succeeded.) By their contracts, authors and (later) directors were usually the financial winners among the creative collaborators. Furthermore, it would take a few more years before Jo would be allowed to invest in the shows he was commissioned to design. The risks were far greater for investors, but if the shows were successes the rewards could be staggering. Not until *South Pacific* was Jo allowed to invest his money in order to share in the bounty of a box office bonanza.

Many talented people were involved in Jo's next assignment, *Hollywood Pinafore*, produced by Max Gordon. What began as George S. Kaufman's clever idea to rework Gilbert and Sullivan's *H.M.S. Pinafore* into a modern fable about Hollywood and the movie industry disintegrated into an unwieldy and strained muddle. It had the misfortune to follow *Memphis Bound!,* which also used *Pinafore* as the show within a show. Neither version fared well.

In the midst of all of his spring openings, Jo received a call from the office of Secretary of State Edward Stettinius. Would Jo, he asked, please design the stage for the convening of the conference in San Francisco to establish the United Nations? There would be a small travel and daily allowance but no honorarium for the work, just the privilege of being associated with a historic event. Jo accepted, of course, and was put in touch with the office of Alger Hiss, secretary-general pro tem of the conference. Jo recommended that Eddie Kook provide the lighting expertise and the two of them

went off to San Francisco to look over the War Memorial Opera House to see what could be done.

The problems were many. First, since the country was still at war, materials were scarce and San Francisco did not have the craftsmen to do the work. Jo and Eddie decided that everything would have to be assembled in New York and shipped out to the coast. Since blue was officially designated as the color for the United Nations, Jo had to find enough blue velour (1,400 yards) to cover the floor, stairs, and hangings on the stage. When he was unable to get the effect he wanted for the 15-foot swag wreaths that were to hang between four pylons (signifying the Four Freedoms), he found a young model maker in San Francisco named Alexander Anderson, who was able to fabricate them out of balsa wood. Anderson also cut out thousands of paper leaves to staple onto the frames. With

JO RECEIVED THE COMMISSION TO DESIGN THE SETTING FOR THE UNITED NATIONS CONVENTION IN SAN FRANCISCO, IN 1945, ON THE RECOMMENDATION OF HIS OSS MILITARY ASSOCIATE, NAVY LIEUTENANT OLIVER LUNDQUIST. ELEGANT WITHOUT BEING SOLEMN, THE SETTING WAS SIMPLE AND EFFECTIVE. (COURTESY OF OLIVER LUNDQUIST)

the proscenium backed with a blue cyclorama, framing the pylons covered in gold velour and the flags of all forty-six participating nations arranged in a semicircle above the podium, Jo created a dignified setting for this historic event. With Eddie's help, he focused 75,000 watts of brilliant lighting on the stage.

His other problems involved protocol. He had to make sure that no flag pole was raised any higher than another, that the flags were hung correctly, and that changes could be made quickly if the status of any nation changed overnight. The security was tight everywhere so that there would be no mishap to mar the events. Jo and Eddie stayed for the opening session on April 25, 1945, then returned to their own world in New York. It took several months for Secretary Stettinius to send his letter of thanks for Jo's "excellent work." Jo received several photographs of the stage as he had set it—unfortunately, none were in color.

Jo tried to get away to Newtown and his family as often as he could on the weekends, but there was little respite for him during the summer of 1945; he had a full agenda for the upcoming season. His first show, set to open on September 27, was a complete change of pace for him: *Carib Song*, a "sort of calypso gavotte," according to Howard Barnes of the *New York Herald Tribune*. Short on plot, it relied on the dancing of Katherine Dunham and her troupe, which the critics agreed was splendid, though a bit monotonous. It was not a success.

His second show of the new season, *Beggars Are Coming to Town*, opened one month later and closed three weeks after that. The producer was Oscar Serlin, whose overflowing coffers from the still-running *Life with Father* enabled Jo not to have to stint with the designs. Two days after the opening, when Serlin realized that he had a "sure smash flop" on his hands, he asked Jo to do a color sketch of "his magnificent set" as a memento of the occasion. The director was Harold Clurman, whom Jo had known when they both were young hang-abouts at the Theatre Guild's offices but had never worked with. The play had to do with the return of a gangster who had taken the rap for both himself and his partner and had gone to prison for fourteen years. On his return, he discovers that the partner has grown rich as a legitimate night-club operator.

Clurman saw the play as a "parable of success in the modern world" and asked Jo to conceive the set in those terms, giving him metaphorical rather than concrete descriptions of what he wanted:

> *But the set should actually be a dream-world of luxury and success as the modern (machine-age) world conceives it, an "impossible" never-never land of steely power, bathroom ease and New Yorkerish naïveté. There should be as in Hollywood and all places that strive for the ultimate in impressively luxurious taste—something naked and inhuman about it, that is disconnected from ordinary mortality or common people—something beneath the seduction of the mechanical grace that is actually cold and heartless. It is at once a palatial chamber and a koop!* [sic]

The Playwrights Company, which always spoke to Jo in more concrete terms, needed a hit badly after two successive flops and thought it had one in Robert Sherwood's new play, *The Rugged Path*. Its star was Spencer Tracy, then at the height of his fame as a movie star. The production carried hopes of restoring the fortunes of the producing organization, to revive the career of Tracy as a serious stage actor, and to give Sherwood a chance to expound on the war after his years of service as a speechwriter for President Roosevelt. Jo designed seven settings, each of which had to move on and off the stage smoothly: the White House, a Washington bar and grill, offices and homes, a Navy destroyer, the front lines in the Philippines, and the White House again. Tracy played a newspaper editor who becomes involved in the politics of war, then decides it is time for him to get involved in the war itself. He is killed in the Philippines, having not only served his country but also his lofty ideas of human commitment and sacrifice. The production rode a rugged path to Broadway. Full of doubts about himself and the script, Tracy almost left the play in its Boston tryout. Although the critics everywhere liked his performance, they were not enchanted by the play. The Playwrights Company closed it and lost money.

They hoped for better luck with *Dream Girl*, which Elmer Rice had expressly written for the talents of his wife, the actress Betty Field. They sent a copy of the script to Jo. The character to be played by Field, a female Walter Mitty, daydreams herself into many bizarre adventures, while trying to make up her mind to marry a nice young man, all in the course of one day. Like *The Rugged Path*, the play was episodic and required scenes to be changed rapidly and smoothly. A reporter from the *New York Herald Tribune*, observing a rehearsal, was impressed with Jo's solutions for the scenery:

> [Mielziner] has achieved scenery which is almost inaudible. He utilizes a series of quietly moving platforms upon which are mounted scenes that are considerably more than just representational. They are rich, lavish and witty, and are shuttled on tracks so smoothly that Miss Field's transitions from reality to fantasy are accomplished as quickly as the fade-ins and fade-outs of movie technique.

Jo used two complete sets of lights: one for the scenery and one for the actors' faces, and two sets of colors: one for the sets of her actual life and one for the sets of her daydreams. *Dream Girl* was an expensive show to run, requiring twenty-five stagehands, of whom nine were always standing backstage to push and pull the sets on their tracks into and off the playing area. But the Playwrights Company was not dismayed by the costs since they finally had a hit.

In a post-opening letter to Jo, Rice offered many thanks for "a magnificent contribution to the show." Many years later, in a book called *The Living Theatre*, Rice revised his thinking and downplayed the role of designers in production. "At best," he wrote, "scenery, costumes, lights, properties and all the physical paraphernalia of the stage are background material whose purpose it should be to enhance the values of the play and to assist the actors in their task of interpretation." He went on to say that a play, "well written, well cast and well rehearsed" can stand on its own feet and he cited performances of "magical quality" which took place under a single worklight. Coming from Rice, whose long career was enhanced by the brilliance of the designs for his plays, this was a curious comment indeed.

Jo's last production in 1945, *St. Lazare's Pharmacy*, by the Hungarian playwright Miklos Laszlo, opened in Montreal and closed in Chicago and was another lesson in how a good set can be wasted on a poor play. (Later, Laszlo somewhat redeemed himself with a play called *Parfumerie*, which inspired the movie *The Shop Around the Corner*, which

THE RUGGED PATH (1945), STARRING SPENCER TRACY, REQUIRED SEVEN DIFFERENT AND ELABORATE SCENE CHANGES. BECAUSE OF THE COMPLEXITY OF EACH SET, JO WAS FORCED TO LOWER THE CURTAIN BETWEEN CHANGES, WHICH IMPEDED THE ACTION OF A TALKY PLAY. (EILEEN DARBY PHOTOGRAPH)

DREAM GIRL (1945) IS ABOUT A YOUNG WOMAN WHO DRIFTS IN AND OUT OF REALITY. JO'S PROBLEM WAS TO SUGGEST VISUALLY WHERE SHE IS IN THE MIDDLE OF HER DAYDREAMS. PLATFORMS UPON WHICH THE SCENES WERE MOUNTED COULD BE SHUTTLED RIGHT, LEFT, AND CENTER WITHIN TALL GRAY PANELS, AS IN THIS SET, WHERE THERE IS JUST ENOUGH TO SUGGEST AT ONCE A TELEPHONE BOOTH, AN OFFICE, AND THE INTERIOR OF A BOOKSTORE. (BILLY ROSE THEATRE COLLECTION, NYPL-PA)

which inspired the musical *She Loves Me.*) Unfortunately, the producers, Eddie Dowling and the redoubtable Louis J. Singer, were not able to duplicate the success they had had with *The Glass Menagerie*.

In 1945, Jo's studio had worked on eleven shows (one of which, *The Happy Time* by Robert Lorraine, never left the drawing board) and chalked up a bumper year in terms of quantity and quality. When Jo was interviewed in December by a reporter from *Time*, he complained about his one-hundred-hour work weeks and not having enough time to brood. He could solve his problems by hiring fifty men and taking on all the jobs he was offered. He would become a millionaire, he said, but then "I'd simply sicken myself with grouse and good port, and die of shame." The theatre in general, and scene designing in particular, were too unpredictable to allow him to rest on his laurels—as time would tell.

BACKDROP FOR THE MUSICAL *WINDY CITY* (1946), WHICH OPENED AND CLOSED IN CHICAGO. JO USED COLORS FOR THIS THAT HE RARELY CHOSE. (ESTATE OF JO MIELZINER)

In 1946, Jo had six commissions, of which only four reached Broadway. *Sunrise in My Pocket,* by Edwin Justus Mayer, which was to be directed by Margo Jones, never got the backing it needed. *Windy City,* which was produced by another actor-turned-producer, Richard Kollmar (husband of the gossip columnist Dorothy Kilgallen), and choreographed by Katherine Dunham, closed in Chicago. Jo's sets, one critic averred, owed much to the artist Reginald Marsh. While the decision to close was still being mulled over, Jo's scene design made the cover of the June 1946 *Theatre Arts* magazine.

Jo's first show for 1946 was *Jeb,* by Robert Ardrey, produced and directed by Herman Shumlin. What came out of it was not a great play but the making of the career of Ossie Davis, who was appearing for the first time on Broadway fresh out of the Army and with limited acting experience. (Also in the cast was a young actress named Ruby Dee, whom Davis married a few years later.) The play, echoing the tenuous prewar beginnings of the civil rights movement, was laudable in its attempt to deal with racism in its saga of a returning veteran who had lost a leg in combat. The trouble was that it followed two other plays, *Home of the Brave* and *Deep Are the Roots,* which explored similar ground and did it better.

The disappointment over the failure of *Jeb* was submerged by the frantic activity surrounding Irving Berlin's *Annie Get Your Gun,* presented by Rodgers and Hammerstein and starring Ethel Merman as Annie Oakley. The book was by Herbert and Dorothy Fields, Josh Logan directed, Helen Tamiris choreographed the dances, and Lucinda Ballard designed the costumes. When it opened the first week in May, the critics were ecstatic, and the public lined up at the box office to buy tickets to pay off its astounding production costs of more than $300,000! (It took about a dozen weeks for that to happen.)

Jo designed nine different sets, which included a Pullman car, the arena in a circus tent, the deck of a cattle boat, the ballroom of the Hotel Brevoort (a long-gone New York landmark), and the deck of a ferry boat. It was a very complex and heavy set and may have inadvertently given Jo a reputation that was not justified. While the scenery for *Annie Get Your Gun* was being hung in the Imperial Theatre, a steel beam began to buckle far above the stage.

ANNIE GET YOUR GUN (1946) WAS AN ENORMOUS SUCCESS. JO'S CONTRIBUTION WAS IN CREATING JUST THE RIGHT ATMOSPHERE FOR THE ROUGH-AND-TUMBLE ACTION OF THE MUSICAL. THE SCENE SHOWN FOR THE ARENA OF THE GREAT TENT (TOP) WAS HURRIEDLY SKETCHED WITH COLORED PENCILS ON TISSUE PAPER AND GIVEN TO HIS SECRETARY AT THE TIME. THE CATTLE BOAT SCENE (BELOW) WAS SIMILARLY ROUGHED OUT—WITH PLENTY OF THE UBIQUITOUS "MIELZINER BLUE." (COURTESY OF AMY AND MARTHA CURTIS)

Since the gridiron was attached to the beam and the scenery and lights were suspended by counterweights to the gridiron, there ensued frenzied activity to locate the cause of the loud cracking noise that occurred during set-up. When the technicians realized what had happened, their immediate assumption was that the grid was supporting more weight than it could handle. Ultimately, the cause of the buckling was found to be not the heaviness of the scenery and lights but a structural defect, which was, of course, fixed before the show opened. Because of this mishap, however, the belief took root and persisted for many years that Jo's sets were extraordinarily heavy. Although Jo often chose to cover his sets with heavy velour over lighter-weight canvas, the extra weight would not have been that significant, certainly not critical enough to buckle a steel beam.

Annie Get Your Gun, secure as a tenant in the Imperial, engendered a second company to tour the country. Jo redesigned the show for its American tour the following year; it starred Mary Martin as Annie. Rodgers and Hammerstein were unable to get Merman to take her charms to London, so there was no London edition at all.

With the show a sure-fire hit, Jo planned to take off a month to spend with Jean and the children in Newtown before returning to his drawing board for a busy fall and winter season. He had, however, promised to do a series of seminars for Fordham University for the summer of 1946. For the first time in more than twenty years, he was being compelled to sort out what he had been doing for all that time so that he could evolve a coherent set of lectures.

Father Robert Gannon, the president of Fordham University, in the Bronx, was interested in all things theatrical and in prewar days had established at the school a Department of Communication Arts that encompassed theatrical study. In the 1940s, with Broadway's Albert McCleery as director, he had also instituted a series of six-week summer seminars to be taught by "artists and technicians of the highest standing in the professional theatre." Jo agreed to participate and was announced to teach "The Theatre as a Plastic Art." The other courses—on acting, directing, speech, stagecraft, scene painting and model building, and lighting—were intended to culminate in three student productions in the college theatre. One of them, an original play, was to have the settings designed under Jo's supervision.

Although Jo had given speeches and lectures before this, the Fordham seminar was his first experience in laying out a series of talks that would distill from his own experience the essentials of scene designing. He examined his own approach, his guiding esthetic, the sequence and methods of his creation, and the importance of external forces in the process of designing. The timing could not have been more fortuitous. The postwar theatre was changing rapidly. New ideas were taking it in different directions. If he wanted to remain in the forefront of his profession, Jo knew that he would have to advance with them in less traveled grooves. When the course was over, he had a perspective about his work and new insights into the past, present, and future theatre that he had never had time to attain previously. By the end of the summer, to his great satisfaction, he learned that he had succeeded beyond his own expectations in stimulating his students. The Fordham lectures had given him his first platform and the basis for a book that was taking shape in his mind. Finally, because of the lectures, he was awarded his first honorary degree, Doctor of Fine Arts, which Fordham conferred upon him at its commencement the following June. For the high-school dropout, it was the sweetest of graduation days.

Jo's journey through his own subconscious began with his admission that he was born with innate gifts for painting and drawing, which, thanks to his parents, were nurtured and encouraged. When he left the easel for the stage designer's drawing board to make a living, his first efforts were almost direct copies of what he had seen on the stage and were planned with small regard for the play and the players. Later, he designed scenery that pleased the crowds and drew praise from the critics. He painted pretty pictures that detracted from rather than added to the unity of the production. When he had designed *Anatol,* in 1931, he remembered the praise of the critics and the applause of the audience that greeted each one of the scenes he had designed. Too late, he realized that "my settings usurped attention that properly belonged to the script and the actors." He learned to focus attention on the actors and to make sure that his scenery and lighting did all they could to make them seen and heard. Almost by accident he discovered that audibility and visibility were closely related. "I learned the hard lesson that, in lighting, the actors come first, the settings second, and that, to achieve balance, entirely different types of equipment, entirely different colors, entirely different levels of light may be needed for the two elements."

In studying lighting, he soon learned that "good lighting technique is not alone the use of light but the use of the absence of light." Somewhere in his fascination with light lies a key to his art. Jo's life, as well as his art, was an ascent into illumination. He strove for focus and direction as well as for light in the psychic sense. Jo's artistic epiphany occurred almost at the same time that he began his conversion to Catholicism, a period in which he had designed Maxwell Anderson's *Winterset* in 1935, which represented a turning point in his artistic focus.

Jo changed the way he read scripts. He looked between the lines to discover an essence that he could translate into visual terms. Although he was sometimes wrong, he developed—or was born with—an instinct to pull from a script a defining image. For *Winterset*, of course, it was the Brooklyn Bridge towering over the actors of the drama and becoming the symbol of human aspirations. It was often impossible to find the defining image, particularly in the ephemeral dramatic pieces that formed the steady diet on Broadway for several decades, but he did his best to convey what he could of the substance of even the least of plays. What he learned from all of his designing was that the stronger and more complete the play, as in the work of Tennessee Williams, the easier it was for him to locate the central metaphor that could be rendered visually.

In his book *Designing for the Theatre*, Jo wrote, "The designer alone cannot create a style. He may achieve it in the stage picture by itself, but if it is not in harmony with the style of the director or of the actors, it is wrong." Invariably, Jo's most successful achievements resulted from directors who knew what they wanted and threw off sparks. When things went awry—even with skillful directors—it was always a failure in the establishment of a *unified* style. When Jo designed *Jeb* for Herman Shumlin, he felt that the script called for simple scenery with the emphasis on vivid colors and dramatic

lighting. Although Shumlin gave his approval to his approach, when Jo saw the play in its final rehearsals, he realized that he had designed scenery that did not fit the intense realism with which Shumlin had directed the show, and he felt he had contributed to its failure. Conversely, when he presented his views for the designs for *The Glass Menagerie* to Tennessee Williams and Margo Jones, he was gratified that they not only agreed with him but were also willing to accept changes in their own concepts. Rightly, he felt that he had contributed something to the success of the production.

If Jo could find poetry in the ordinary, in plays such as *Ethan Frome* and *Abe Lincoln in Illinois*, if he could show that a ladderback kitchen chair could represent the entire kitchen of a particular family, if a well-aimed light could do the job of a curtain in eliminating an intrusive background, why then pack the stage with unnecessary scenery and props? Jo Mielziner was the designer who persisted the longest and most valiantly in cracking the hold of realistic scenery over productions of American plays of this predominating genre. In *Designing for the Theatre* he expressed what he had passed on to his Fordham classes in 1946—that "literalism has no place in the theatre."

> The good theatre artist is never "actual." He omits the nonessentials, condenses the essentials, accents the details that are most revealing. He depicts only that part of the truth which he deems necessary to the course of the story.

Jo's peers considered him a designer's designer and an artist. From a lifelong immersion in the art of painting, begun at his father Leo's knee, Jo had learned not only how to use color, paint, and line but also how to imbue them with emotion through light and shadow. The work of Robert Edmond Jones and his contemporaries in the years following World War I both stimulated him immensely and gave fresh validity to the idea of a livelihood as a designer in the theatre. A witness to Leo's compromise, painting portraits for his meagre living, Jo found a talent within himself for this legitimate field of design and at the same time was struck by a passion for the theatre.

What he loved most about the theatre were its limitations, which allowed him to exercise his strong sense of discipline by confining his imagination to the physical space of the stage. A scene designer could, if he or she had the talent, transform those limitations into a universe. That became Jo Mielziner's particular genius. He enjoyed the problem-solving that was engendered by the limitations. He reveled in the give-and-take with directors and producers and playwrights. He loved the darkness of the theatre before a play began. Even more, he loved illuminating the darkness as the lights—his lights—began to reveal the contours and colors of the settings—his settings. In communicating his passion to his Fordham students, he also revisited his origins and clearly defined his artistic credo for himself.

Reinvigorated by the seminar and his intensive self-examination, he returned full-time to his drawing board to work on a comedy by Anita Loos called *Happy Birthday*, written for Helen Hayes. The producers, Rodgers and Hammerstein, engaged Rouben Mamoulian to try to repeat the success he had directing *Oklahoma!* Mamoulian's successes in both plays and musicals (on Broadway and in Hollywood) had accustomed him to having his own way. Jo had worked with him as early as 1930 on *The Solid South* and more recently on *Carousel* and was aware that he could occasionally make things difficult. He

told Jo that he wanted to light *Happy Birthday* himself, to which Jo objected politely but firmly. Although a confrontation was brewing, it never happened; Mamoulian withdrew because of film commitments, and Joshua Logan took over.

Happy Birthday is a bit of fluff about a meek librarian from Newark who has a crush on a young bank clerk. She waits for him in a cocktail bar and proceeds to get tipsy. As she sheds her inhibitions the saloon turns topsy-turvy in her head—all of which Jo had to make visible to the audience. Her bar stool starts to jump up and down, a table rises and spreads out, the bottles become iridescent and start to gurgle, and the flowers talk to her. The combination of Jo's tricks (accomplished with the indispensable assist of the prop men) and Miss Hayes's bravura performance turned *Happy Birthday* into a hit.

Another Part of the Forest, which opened a month after *Happy Birthday*, was a sequel in reverse to Lillian Hellman's *tour de force* of 1939, *The Little Foxes*, which had given Tallulah Bankhead the role of her life in Regina Giddens. *The Little Foxes* had been produced by Herman Shumlin, who had employed in his office a young accountant named Kermit Bloomgarden. Having progressed to the post of

A PRELIMINARY SKETCH FOR THE RODGERS AND HAMMERSTEIN PRODUCTION OF *HAPPY BIRTHDAY* (1946). JO SWITCHED THE BAR FROM RIGHT TO LEFT SO THAT HELEN HAYES COULD HAVE A "STRONGER" ENTRANCE IN THE ACTUAL SET. THE ARCHWAY BORE THE LEGEND: "THROUGH THESE PORTALS PASS THE NICEST PEOPLE IN NEWARK." (ESTATE OF JO MIELZINER)

Shumlin's general manager, Bloomgarden opened his own production office in 1945 and became the best representative of the new breed of producer. He became known for taking risks on new playwrights and unusual plays, but being always canny enough to use seasoned people to help the production along. A big cigar usually protruding from his lips, Bloomgarden also had a dark side and was capable of callous acts, particularly when it came to money. Jo, who knew him slightly from his days as general manager, designed ten out of the forty plays that Bloomgarden was to produce over three decades. If there was not a great deal of warmth between them, the two men respected each other, each recognizing in the other a strong drive for perfection.

Despite a carefully wrought production and superior perform-ances, *Another Part of the Forest* was a *succès d'estime*, once defined by George S. Kaufman as a success that ran out of steam. The show had a decent but unspectacular run. In it, Hellman (who also

directed the play) traced the origins of the Hubbard family's for-tune and conflicting ambitions.

In the spring of 1946, Jo received a feeler from actor-playwright Elliott Nugent about doing two plays that he and movie star Robert Montgomery were planning to take to Broadway. Jo responded by saying that he wanted to read the plays first, which somewhat net-tled Nugent. He began his reply to Jo by saying: "I think you're pretty expensive, but I also think you're pretty *good*." In the next flurry of letters, Nugent waxed nostalgic for the days when an entire show came to Broadway for $6,000. (Jo had estimated the sets alone would cost double that.) "My understanding is," Nugent wrote, "that you and I have no deal yet, but that we're having a very interesting flirtation. When you've read the plays, please send me some flowers." Jo's hesitation about doing *The Big Two* probably resulted from reading the script, which was later roundly attacked by the critics, one of whom called it a "shoddy and straggly mixture of comedy, corn, melodrama, romance and political talk." When it opened and closed in January 1947, Jo sent Nugent and Montgomery a consolatory telegram, to which they replied with a parody of "Invictus" by William Earnest Henley:

> Out of the gloom that covers us,
> Black as the pit from pole to pole,
> We thank you for your telegram
> It raised our spirit, soothed our soul.
>
> In the fell clutch of Richard Watts
> We have not winced nor cried aloud;
> Under the bludgeonings of Barnes
> Our heads are bloody but unbowed.

Jo's second show for the new year was a musicalized version of Elmer Rice's 1929 success, *Street Scene*, co-produced by the Playwrights

IN *FINIAN'S RAINBOW* (1947), JO USED FOUR COLUMNS AND A PAINTED TRANSPARENT DROP, THE ESSENCE OF SCENIC ECONOMY, TO SUGGEST THE COLONIAL ESTATE OF SENATOR BILLBOARD RAWKINS OF MISSITUCKY. (COURTESY OF MARY TYLER CHEEK MCCLENAHAN)

Company and Jo's old friend Dwight Deere Wiman. The original play had been an exercise in journalistic realism and for it Jo had designed the exterior of a New York brownstone that everyone mistook for the real thing. Rice, in trying to preserve the spirit of the play, forgot that musicals by their very nature must slip the bounds of realism, dug in his heels, and refused to allow Jo to release the play from its earthbound realism. Consequently, the design, although not an exact duplicate of the original, was similar enough for some of the critics to have recalled the earlier version. The composer, Kurt Weill, persuaded the poet Langston Hughes to write the lyrics. Despite the wealth of talent in the production team (costumes by Lucinda Ballard, choreography by Anna Sokolow) and solid performances by a talented cast, nothing could rescue it from an apathetic public. Like many of Weill's works that did not fare well the first time around, *Street Scene* is periodically revived by opera companies.

Jo's next show, *Finian's Rainbow*, an inspired bit of nonsense about the theft of a pot of gold from leprechauns, was unlike most musicals of the period. Crafted by E. Y. Harburg and Fred Saidy, the plot was an excuse for a veritable Irish stew of social commentary about the American South, the Tennessee Valley Authority, right-wing politics, and a host of other things. Bolstered by a fresh score by Burton Lane, it delighted the critics and the public. The show was sent out on the road by producer Lee Sabinson but with a cut-down set and minimal lighting, which occasioned one of Jo's rare bursts of temper. Because he had redesigned the show for the tour, he was surprised to get negative words from the out-of-town critics. Unbeknownst to him, everything had been further simplified (Jo used the term "vandalized") to ensure a more profitable run on the road, and he asked that his name be removed from the credits. He also redesigned the show for the London production of Prince Littler in 1949.

By this time, Jo found himself collaborating with a new breed of choreographers for whom he had to adapt his designing. Gone were the days of the slap-tap, shuffle-off-to-Buffalo numbers, usually downstage or center stage. In the post-*Oklahoma!* years, the de Mille–style choreographers demanded that their dancers take over

THERE WAS A GREAT DEAL OF ANIMATED DANCING IN *FINIAN'S RAINBOW*, WHICH NECESSITATED LEAVING AS MUCH STAGE SPACE AS POSSIBLE. JO ACCOMPLISHED THIS BY PROVIDING VERY LITTLE SOLID SCENERY AND A LOT OF INSPIRED BACKDROPS, SUCH AS THE ONE SHOWN FOR RAINBOW VALLEY IN MISSITUCKY, THE MYTHICAL SOUTHERN STATE WHERE THE STORY TAKES PLACE. (BILLY ROSE THEATRE COLLECTION, NYPL-PA)

the entire stage, and the designers tried to oblige. For *Finian's Rainbow,* Michael Kidd was choreographing his first Broadway show. Like Balanchine and de Mille, Kidd came from the world of classical ballet and tended to think in abstract terms. When Bretaigne Windust, *Finian's* director, rejected one of his numbers as not being "personal" enough, Kidd reached a turning point in his thinking. He abandoned his initial dances and began devising a scenario for six couples,

with, he noted, "each depicting a different form of love. It was a totally different departure. I made the people characters and realized what Bretaigne meant by 'personal.'" The brilliant results displayed another facet of the kind of dancing that took audiences by surprise in the postwar wave of musicals. Kidd's dancers were recognizable personalities, and after *Finian's Rainbow,* he became one of the most sought-after choreographers on Broadway.

Jo's agenda for the rest of the season included two more musicals, one of which was a revival of an old 1909 warhorse, *The Chocolate Soldier,* one of nineteen revivals that critic Burns Mantle cited in his chronicle of the season. Written by Oscar Straus and based on Bernard Shaw's *Arms and the Man,* it was now in its seventh Broadway reincarnation. Although Guy Bolton took some of the creakiness out of the book and George Balanchine devised the dances, it seemed stale to the critics, with the exception of fresh scenery by Jo and costumes by Lucinda Ballard. The other musical was *Barefoot Boy with Cheek,* by Max Shulman, the script of which George Abbott had sent Jo months earlier. With a college campus as its setting, it was the kind of musical that Abbott loved to direct, filled with youthful performers and bounce. Nancy Walker was cast as Yetta Samovar, a campus revolutionary, at the University of Minnesota (Shulman's alma mater), and Abbott squeezed all the comedy he could out of her shenanigans to radicalize the campus. Designing Abbott's campus musicals was familiar territory for Jo and he created fast-changing sets to match Abbott's fast-paced direction. Most of the critics felt that the collegiate musical (like the sentimental operettas of *Chocolate Soldier* vintage) was passé, and the show lasted only a few months.

The costume designer for *Barefoot Boy* was a towering young designer named Alvin Colt. Jo, who at forty-six was something of a mythic figure to the newer generation of designers, suddenly found himself collaborating with costume designers nearly half his age. When Jo had given up designing costumes in the years before the war, he found that there were a number of ready talents in the field with whom he could function compatibly. They were smart, often ingenious, and passionate about their work. Most were women, who had come to accept that they were to be always at a disadvantage in the male-dominated world of commercial theatre. Costume designers had been taken into United Scenic Artists, Local 829, the stage designers' union, only in 1938. In their struggle for recognition during the thirties, led by Aline Bernstein and Millia Davenport, they received the least amount of compensation among the creative collaborators. Irene Sharaff and Lucinda Ballard, who picked up the cudgels of the pioneers, gradually improved the lot of the costume designers, in terms of recognition and money.

Jo's association with Sharaff began in 1935, when he designed *Jubilee.* Ballard's first show with Jo was *Higher and Higher,* in 1940, and their collaboration went through a dozen productions into 1967. So impressed was he with the talents of both that whenever he was asked by a producer to recommend a designer, he invariably named Irene Sharaff or Lucinda Ballard. When he produced his own show, *Happy Hunting,* in 1956, he hired Sharaff.

Badly paid and overworked, the costume designers were (and still are) generally accorded no more than a line or two in the critics' reviews, if they are lucky. In Lucinda Ballard's words, "I beat my brains out for weeks to have the critics say: 'The costumes were colorful.'" Costume designers feel rightly that the public is not aware of the imagination, preparation, and research that has gone into the costumes, particularly in their design of contemporary clothes, which are accepted so casually by the audience. In her autobiography, Sharaff wrote: "When I began to reflect about the reasons why silhouettes and styles in fashion constantly change, I began to look in the past and the present in a completely different way. They not only represent an important aspect of social history but also deep curious psychological needs of human beings to decorate themselves."

When the costume designing for *Barefoot Boy with Cheek* was assigned to Alvin Colt, Jo did not know that his young collaborator had been an assistant to Ballard. Jo would later work with many other assistants from the Sharaff–Ballard school of costume designing, all of them dedicated professionals. Almost without exception, they found collaborating with Jo an enriching experience.

After *Barefoot Boy,* Jo wanted a rest, and Jean needed a respite from coping with three children. Joshua and Nedda Logan, who had rented a big house in Havana, invited them to take an extra bedroom. In May, leaving the children with the housekeeper, they flew to Cuba to spend two weeks with the Logans, seeing the sights and taking in the nightlife in Havana. Back in his studio, Jo and John began working on a fashion show for the Kaufmann department store, in Pittsburgh, a commercial money-maker. They next turned to two shows scheduled almost back-to-back in October.

The design that Jo did for *Command Decision,* produced by Kermit Bloomgarden, looked deceptively easy. Set during World War II

and centering on the conflicts of military officers whose decisions affect the lives of young airmen, the play takes place in the office headquarters of the commandant of the Fifth American Bombardment Division of the Army Air Force in England, which had to be right without looking stagey. Jo's job included supplying authentic sound effects of the take-offs and landings of planes offstage. The critics were swept away by the power of the play and the performances. Unusual for a war play occurring so soon after the war, *Command Decision* had a comfortable run.

That assignment was a snap compared to Jo's experience with Rodgers and Hammerstein's *Allegro*. Although he had been engaged by the Theatre Guild to do the show eight months before it was scheduled to reach Broadway—he was elated that he would have time to do a first-rate job—he did not count on Hammerstein's slowness in completing the script or the demands placed upon him by everyone. The book, which was original with Hammerstein, is a kind of musical *Our Town*, affirming small-town values over material success and following Dr. Joseph Taylor from birth to middle-age in an exploration of the right and wrong turns of his life. With Lawrence Langner insisting, to save money, that the production be done without platforms or other mechanical means, with the authors countering that the many vignettes had to be provided with changes of scenery, and with Agnes de Mille, who was serving as both director and choreographer, demanding wide open spaces for her dancers,

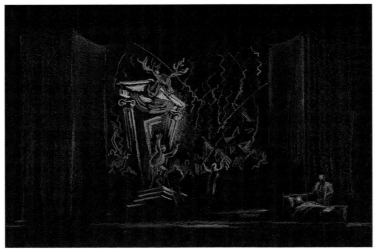

Jo's final effort pleased no one, particularly himself. He had envisioned a stylized setting and had from the very beginning suggested a cinematic technique, using curtains to frame scenes against
a large background cyclorama, but he was not to get his way. The
complexity of the show scenically (which matched Oscar's allegori-
cal script) was overshadowed by the tug of wills between de Mille,
Rodgers, and Hammerstein. Hating both the scenery and the costumes, complaining about the inadequacies of the script, unable to
fuse it into a pure dance-musical, and finding the entire situation
slipping from her grasp, de Mille was the unhappiest of them all.

Allegro's reception in New York was not unqualified disapproval,
as people have consistently believed. Noting its originality, several
critics were reverent; Brooks Atkinson of *The New York Times* was
even rapturous. Rodgers and Hammerstein, however, counted it as
one of their glorious failures even though it ran for nine months
and was sent out on the road. For the touring company, Jo simplified the scenery, which may have better served the earliest concept
than the Broadway version did. The critic for the *Philadelphia Bulletin*,
who saw it both in New York and in his own hometown, found the
cut-down setting better. "The result," he wrote, "is a greater intimacy, less pretension and all more in keeping with the simplicity of
the story."

When Jo signed on for the next play, *A Streetcar Named Desire*, he
was to work with two unknown, but very potent, quantities. One
was named Irene Mayer Selznick, the other Elia Kazan. He had
first met Selznick in Washington, via Spencer Tracy and Katharine
Hepburn, who were seeking advice from friends and professional
associates about doing *The Rugged Path* on Broadway. Sitting in on
some of the discussions, she was impressed by Jo's quiet compe-
tence amid the general turmoil surrounding the tryout performances. Steeped in the movie business as the daughter of Louis B.
Mayer and married to producer David Selznick, Irene Selznick was
searching for a non-Hollywood outlet for her considerable energy
and intelligence as her marriage was slowly eroding. After a good
deal of soul-searching, she got involved in the theatre and stuck to
it for a dozen years. Before her adventure with *Streetcar*, Selznick
had produced one show on Broadway, which was a disaster. But, as
a "quick study," she became a keen student of the Broadway production process.

Tennessee Williams's agent, Audrey Wood, put an enormous
amount of pressure on Selznick to produce his play, which she had
found overwhelming. Guided by her instincts and taste, Selznick
lived up to the challenge. She went after Elia Kazan not only
because the playwright wanted him but also because she felt he was
the right director for the show. Jo was her first and only choice as
designer. She wanted to pack the collaborating committee with the
finest talents she could find.

But her choice of director had left Jo's close friend, Joshua Logan, desolated. It had taken Kazan, known to his colleagues as "Gadg," about ten years to evolve as a director of no mean talent, a man determined to reshape the role of director in the theatre. A graduate of the Group Theatre and the "Method" school of acting and directing, Kazan was not content to be the traffic cop or the rant-and-rave type of director of past generations. He wanted control over every aspect of the production from casting down to the last and most insignificant prop to be used on the set.

Though totally opposite in style and demeanor, coming from different backgrounds and generations, Jo and Kazan liked each other from the start. In his autobiography, Kazan said he was attracted to strong "feminine" qualities in men, such as he found in Tennessee Williams, Marlon Brando, Clifford Odets, William Inge, Robert Anderson, and Jo Mielziner. Jo's internal orderliness combined with his external neatness may have appeared feminine to Kazan, but were to work well with the director's decisiveness and intellect. Jo appreciated Kazan's "strong visual imagination" and went on to say:

> There is nothing more difficult than working with a director who has no convictions. It is even worse when he leans too heavily on my experience and answers my questions with, 'Well, Jo, what do you feel we should do here?' This sort of approach may seem flattering, but a scenic artist can be left in the lurch when an indecisive director finally makes up his mind about what he wants to do long after the designer may have committed himself to quite another style or approach.

Like McClintic and Logan, Kazan was anything but indecisive. The two men not only became close associates but also developed an enduring friendship that included Kazan's wife, Molly, as well. It survived long after Kazan left Broadway for Hollywood. For Kazan, Jo represented everything that was best in the American theatre. A few years before Jo died, Kazan wrote to him:

> Sometimes . . . I think of a book I'm going to write about my life and times and particularly my times in the theatre. And I think of

> the people that brought honor to the theatre and first among them are you and Tennessee. I don't miss much about show business but I do miss seeing you.

When Irene Selznick was faced with finding the right actors for the roles, Williams suggested Jessica Tandy for Blanche DuBois, because he had seen her play a forerunner of Blanche in his one-act play *Portrait of a Madonna*, and thought she was a perfect fit. For the part of Stanley Kowalski, Selznick had chosen the movie star John Garfield, who had cut his acting teeth with the Group Theatre. But Garfield made contractual demands that she could not meet. Kazan suggested Marlon Brando for the role. She thought him talented but, at twenty-four, far too young for the part. Besides, he was known to be unpredictable, moody, and difficult to work with. He also read badly at the audition. However, because he wanted the role so much, she decided to take a chance on him. When Kim Hunter and Karl Malden were chosen for the other important roles, everything seemed to be coming together. From this moment on, everyone relied on Kazan's wizardry with the cast to put it all together.

Streetcar was an enormous challenge for Jo, but one that he relished. Through his scenery and lighting, he had to illuminate the inner and outer lives of the three principal characters, Blanche, Stanley, and Stella. The setting had to operate on two distinct levels, the psychological and the actual. Above all, he had to evoke a feeling of compression. Because Kazan was in Hollywood working on a film during the critical first stages of designing, he and Jo had to exchange ideas by mail, but the collaborative give-and-take flourished. Jo wanted to drop a scrim on the rape scene, but Kazan argued against it, and it was discarded. Jo proposed an expensive iron spiral staircase (rendered rickety and dilapidated by the scene shop) off to the right of the stage, an element not used often in the action, but that, for him, visually represented Stella's tenuous and temporary escape. He got it. Kazan wanted the colors "weather-mellowed, as though the rain grayed them down." Jo accommodated him. Kazan asked him to take Williams's suggestions for lighting literally; the playwright asked that several scenes end with light only on the actors' faces. Jo agreed with this wholeheartedly,

JO TOOK EXTRAORDINARY
PAINS IN THE DESIGNS FOR
A STREETCAR NAMED DESIRE
(1947). HE SENT PRELIMINARY
DRAWINGS TO TENNESSEE
WILLIAMS, WHO SAID THAT
THEY HAD STIMULATED HIM
IN REWRITING THE PLAY. THE
STREET SCENE BEHIND THE
KOWALSKIS' FLAT (TOP) WAS
PAINTED ON A TRANSPARENT
DROP, VISIBLE ONLY WHEN
LIGHTED FROM THE REAR.
ANOTHER LAYER REPRESENTED
THE SIDEWALK, WHICH RAN
THE WIDTH OF THE STAGE.
THE NEXT LAYER, THE
KOWALSKIS' FLAT (BELOW),
WAS STRUNG OUT ACROSS
THE STAGE. BY NARROWING
THE FOCUS OF THE LIGHTING
TO THE ACTORS, JO MADE THE
FLAT EVEN MORE OPPRESSIVE.
BY SUBTLY CHANGING THE
COLORS OF THE GELS, HE
COULD SHOW THE TRANSI-
TION FROM SPRING TO SUM-
MER TO EARLY FALL AND
BLANCHE'S SLIDE FROM
BRIGHT PROMISE TO DARK
DESPAIR. (*TOP*: COURTESY OF
THOMAS LOGAN; *RIGHT*:
COURTESY OF ELIA KAZAN)

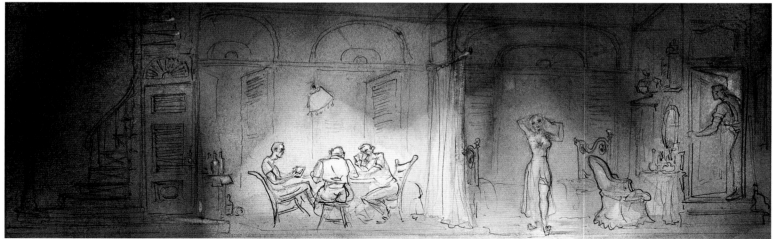

as his renderings for the scene designs attest. Jo wanted a liberal use of scrims behind the strung-out Kowalski flat that formed the main playing area. Kazan wanted what he considered the "too uniform elegance" of the see-through walls counterbalanced by "props and furniture, that are kind of colorfully decaying." Jo complied. And so it went, from inception to completion.

When the play opened in New York, in early December of 1947, the critics were astounded by the play and the production and heaped praise on both. Winning both the Pulitzer Prize and the New York Drama Critics Circle Award, *Streetcar* placed Williams and Kazan at the pinnacle of their careers. Both of them knew how important Jo's contributions were to the play and from this point on, he was sought by both for most of their future productions. Critics, too, could appreciate the depth of Jo's art. Wolcott Gibbs of the *New Yorker* said it for all of them:

> It is possible that some scenic artist somewhere has contrived a more gruesome interior than the decaying horror that Jo Mielziner has executed for the Kowalskis, but I doubt it. It is on the ground floor (outside, a circular iron staircase winds up to another apartment, containing perhaps the least inhibited married couple ever offered on the stage); there is no door between the two rooms, only a curtain; the furnishings are sparse and dreadful; the desolate street outside can be seen through windows, or, rather, through the walls, since Mr. Mielziner's design is by no means literal. It is a wonderful effect and as the evening wears along, oppressive almost beyond words.

Because Jo's scenery was woven into the warp and woof of the play, whenever *Streetcar* is performed within a proscenium arch odds are that the setting will be a variation on Jo's original conception. Shortly after the New York opening, Jo was asked to redesign it for the road company and for the London edition in 1949. The West End version made Jo apprehensive over what was being done to his scenery even though it was being presented by Binkie Beaumont and directed by Laurence Olivier. To accommodate the narrower and smaller stage of the Phoenix Theatre, in London, Olivier (with great apologies to Jo) made changes to the scenery, assuring Jo that he had not violated his "brilliant and beautiful set." But to the

designer's eyes, he had. Olivier and Joe Davis, the technical director, could not fathom Jo's lighting and finally admitted that they did not understand his blueprints. In the midst of the technical rehearsals, Olivier wrote: "Even our most faithful and successful adherence to your plot was pronounced by Irene Selznick to be absolutely nothing like [your lighting]." He circumspectly suggested to Jo that he ask Beaumont to remove Jo's name from the lighting credit on the program and added: "Personally, I would feel more honoured if you left it on." The Beaumont–Olivier production, which starred Vivien Leigh as Blanche, did not receive high praise.

Selznick's concern about the sanctity of Jo's lighting may have come as a slight surprise to him. A few days after *Streetcar* had opened on Broadway, an electrician for the show alerted him to changes the producer had ordered in the lighting, which ignited Jo's temper as few things in life could. He wrote a stinging letter to her, expressing his shock: "I can't believe that you would sanction or approve such dishonesty and sneaky dealings." He reminded her that she had not spared time or money to get the best results for the production. "I can only assume," he continued, "that if there is any truth to this story, this action was the work of subordinates, who were acting without your knowledge."

What particularly galled Jo was that the lighting change took place at a Saturday matinee when the ballet master Antony Tudor was in attendance. He had just contracted with Tudor to design "Shadow of the Wind" for the Ballet Theatre to open in April 1948 and, of course, wanted to impress Tudor with his lighting effects. Jo's original lighting was put back in the show, but after conferences with Selznick and her general manager Irving Schneider, he agreed to simplify the effect so that it became less expensive to run. The modified set and lighting for the "bus and truck" companies were never up to Jo's standards and sometimes were, he felt, a desecration of the original concept.

When Kazan was filming *Streetcar* in 1950, he called Jo to work on the art direction. Although flattered by the offer, Jo demurred, citing his commitments to *Guys and Dolls* and *Mister Roberts* and telling Kazan in a letter that it was "one of the toughest decisions

I have ever had to make. God knows I am human enough to have been tempted by the economic security of a guaranteed picture job, but primarily I have been tempted by the fun of doing a picture with you." (The job fell to Richard Day and George James Hopkins, who represented the dishabille of the Kowalski flat more realistically, but not more effectively.)

On January 1, 1948, there were eight Mielziner-designed shows on the boards, most of them carryovers from the past season. Jo was collecting a weekly royalty from all of them and would begin to receive money from the London transplants in due time. He was forced to add temporary people to his staff to assist John Harvey with the crush of work that was coming into the studio. Despite a healthy income of more than $60,000 for the year, he had to take a

LELAND HAYWARD, LEFT, AND JOSHUA LOGAN, RIGHT, DURING A REHEARSAL OF *MISTER ROBERTS* (1948). (COURTESY OF THE JOHN SWOPE ARCHIVE)

second mortgage and borrow from friends for his renovations to his Newtown house. His income continued to climb year by year. In 1948, although he designed only four shows, one of them, *Mister Roberts*, became a small industry.

Still smarting from losing the director's chair on *A Streetcar Named Desire*, Joshua Logan had thrown himself into the work of adapting a slim war novel by Thomas Heggen called *Mister Roberts*. Leland Hayward, who had moved his major sphere of activities from Hollywood to Broadway, had secured the rights to the book and was hoping that Heggen could make a workable dramatic adaptation of it. When he saw that the author was having difficulties, he implored Logan to help out and Logan and Heggen began to work on it together until they had a good script. Once that was settled, Hayward called Jo to ask him to begin thinking about the sets. Henry Fonda and David Wayne were to be the stars and the advance word from the the pre-Broadway tryouts indicated a slow but certain road to success. It became the hit of the season.

The play takes place during World War II, between VE Day and VJ Day, in the Pacific aboard U.S. Navy Cargo Ship AK601, which sailed, as the script says, from "Tedium to Apathy and back again—with an occasional side trip to Monotony." Again, Jo proved that he could devise the right set for a good script and, again, he was applauded by the critics for doing just that. Hayward was so pleased that he assigned to Jo half of all the shows he would later produce, among them his greatest hits.

Mister Roberts ran and ran (for 1,157 performances on Broadway), was sent on the road with Jo's modified set later in 1948, crossed the Atlantic for a London version in 1950, and was redesigned a second time for a touring company. Of the three variations that Jo designed, the most difficult was for the London production, which starred Tyrone Power and Jackie Cooper. Binkie Beaumont of H. M. Tennent booked the show for the Coliseum Theatre, a huge barn of a house that seated more than two thousand people. It was to be the first straight play performed in the theatre for almost a dozen years. Jo remained in London for six weeks to supervise the construction and lighting and to get the show running. Logan had to redirect the entire play to compensate for the

FOR **MISTER ROBERTS** (1948),
JO TRANSFORMED THE ENTIRE
STAGE INTO THE AMIDSHIPS
SECTION OF THE BOAT (LEFT).
MOST OF THE ACTION TAKES
PLACE CENTER STAGE ON
UPPER AND LOWER LEVELS,
WHICH HE COULD ILLUMI-
NATE FOR THE VARIOUS
SCENES. A TURNTABLE AT CEN-
TER BROUGHT THE BELOW-
DECK STATEROOMS INTO VIEW
AS NEEDED AS THE REST OF
THE STAGE WENT DARK. FOR
THE LONDON PRODUCTION
AT THE COLISEUM THEATRE
(BELOW), WITH ITS FIFTY-FIVE-
FOOT-WIDE PROSCENIUM, JO
SPREAD THE MIDSECTION OF
THE SHIP ACROSS THE STAGE
AND UP TO THE FULL WIDTH
OF THE PROSCENIUM WITH-
OUT LOSING A SENSE OF
CONFINEMENT. BY RELYING
ON LIGHTING TO PICK OUT
SMALL AREAS AND DIMMING
THE FULL EXPANSE OF THE
SHIP, HE WAS ABLE TO GET
THE RIGHT FOCUS ON THE
SCENES THAT JOSH LOGAN
HAD DIRECTED FOR TWO OR
THREE ACTORS AT A TIME.
(*TOP:* COURTESY OF RON
HULL; *LEFT:* COURTESY OF
IAN DOW)

large set. Jo's efforts were rewarded with handsome praise by the London critics, but the play did not have the expected long run on the London boards. It represented a big loss for the English producers, but the ever-gracious Beaumont responded to Jo's concern by saying: "Please believe me this was one of the most exciting experiences I have ever had in the theatre and I look back on it with nothing but great pleasure."

After their mutual success with *Pillar of Fire,* Jo was gratified that Antony Tudor wanted him to design another ballet, and he juggled his work on it with *Mister Roberts* in the winter of 1947–48. Tudor laid out how he wanted the stage to look and sent Jo a lengthy letter filled with tiny drawings and verbal descriptions of the costumes. The music for *Shadow of the Wind* was Gustav Mahler's *Das Lied von der Erde,* and the ballet was set to poems by the Chinese poet Li Po, which expressed an acceptance of the impermanence of life.

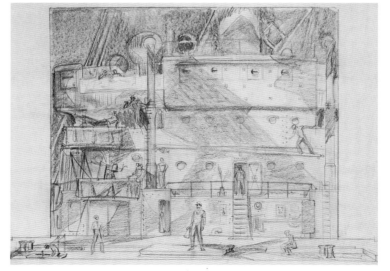

SHADOW OF THE WIND (1948), THE SECOND BALLET JO DESIGNED FOR ANTONY TUDOR. HE CREATED BOTH THE SCENERY AND THE COSTUMES, WITH THE HELP OF ROSE BOGDANOFF. (W. H. CRAIN COLLECTION, UNIVERSITY OF TEXAS THEATRE ARTS COLLECTION)

(The poems were sung by singers in the orchestra pit.) Danced by stalwarts of the Ballet Theatre (now known as American Ballet Theatre) company, the work received six performances during the season but did not become a part of the repertory.

That disappointment was followed by a flop. Howard Barnes, writing in the *New York Herald Tribune* a day after the opening of the musical *Sleepy Hollow*, in early June of 1948, began his review: "To put it bluntly, the settings and costumes are the distinguishing features of 'Sleepy Hollow,' a moribund musical play which has come to the St. James Theatre." These words may have been flattering to Jo and the costume designer David Ffolkes, but the show, based on Washington Irving's story of Ichabod Crane and the Headless Horseman, had been rushed into production in only six weeks, from drawing board to first dress rehearsal. That Jo's design received such high praise is

as much a tribute to the Vail Scenery Construction Company and Robert Bergman's painters as it was to him.

Jo had more than ample time to prepare the designs for *Summer and Smoke*. Before Tennessee Williams left for Europe, in early January of 1948, he asked Jo to come over to see him at his hotel. The playwright was still reeling from the success of *Streetcar*, and Jo reported his chaotic meeting in a letter to Margo Jones, who was to direct *Summer and Smoke*:

> By the time I got to his room, there must have been fourteen people playing a game; one side apparently was determined in getting Tennessee packed, and piles of unopened letters either answered or destroyed; the other team was even more energetically concentrating on finishing three quarts of champagne. What few glasses remained from his cocktail party last Sunday were broken and the champagne was being passed around in a brown crockery bowl. It took me two hours to get what I might have achieved in twelve minutes' earnest conversation. Although Tennessee looked as though he hadn't been to bed or shaved in a week, he was strangely sober and calm in this strange surrounding.

Williams told Jo that he hoped to see a set with the least amount of literal realism. He also asked for a "very moody and romantic sky." They discussed other aspects of the production before Williams asked for some sketches to be sent to him abroad. He reminded Jo that the sketches for *Streetcar* had stimulated his imagination when he was rewriting parts of the play. Jo promised to send them.

Jo's set for *Summer and Smoke* received unqualified praise from almost everyone. The script had its partisans—Brooks Atkinson of *The New York Times*, for one, and Joseph Wood Crutch of *The Nation*, for another—but a few of the other reviewers claimed that Williams was rewriting *A Streetcar Named Desire* with the names changed. Substitute the sexually repressed Alma for emotionally starved Blanche and the young doctor for Stanley, mix in conflicting passions and it seemed like a variation on the same themes. Whatever the playwright's eccentricities, Jo loved working with Williams and had so much faith in the script that he had ventured to buy a share of the production. The run of *Summer and Smoke* did not put it in the category of hits, but when it was revived years later off-Broadway in an almost scenery-less production, with Geraldine Page as Alma Winemiller, it achieved the success that was elusive on Broadway.

Leland Hayward again summoned Jo, this time to design a new play by Maxwell Anderson, *Anne of the Thousand Days*, a retelling of the saga of Henry VIII and his marriage to Anne Boleyn. With even the least sophisticated member of the audience knowing that it did not end happily, its strength depended on how well Anderson could convey the twists and turns of this powerful relationship. Luckily for Jo, it was to be co-produced by his friends at the Playwrights Company. The play was to star the English actors Rex Harrison and Joyce Redman and appeared to contain all the ingredients for a hit.

Anderson and Jo had grown up together in the theatre and were old friends as well as colleagues, but this time Jo was troubled by the script and the scenic effects that the playwright had envisioned and found himself unable to get through to him, as he had in previous experiences. Anderson's script called for nine settings and many "memory" soliloquies that were to be set and lighted separately. As he started to work on it in the new studio in his Newtown house, in the summer of 1948, Jo wrote to Bretaigne Windust about his misgivings:

It has taken me days to try to find a concept for the scenes of memory. I would like to get your reaction to one of the ideas which struck me. Since for technical reasons I am employing a sort of unit for the basic structure, both on the turn tables and in the center, I thought of having it built in a simplified rather abstracted skeleton of the architecture of Henry's period. The various memory scenes, as set up in and around this structure, would be fragmentary, but richly colorful and rather intensified. Segments of each setting, just as in memory, essential details or dramatic details are intensified; non-essentials

JO'S SET FOR *SUMMER AND SMOKE* (1948) WAS STYLIZED TO PLEASE TENNESSEE WILLIAMS BUT WAS EXCESSIVELY CLUTTERED, CONFINING THE ACTORS TO SMALL SPACES ON THE RIGHT AND LEFT OF THE STAGE. THE SYMBOLIC ANGEL OF HUMAN MORTALITY, WHICH DOMINATED THE STAGE, WAS SOMEWHAT OVERSCALED, GIVING THE PLAY A FUNEREAL FEELING. HOWEVER, THE SET WAS PRAISED IF THE PLAY WAS NOT. (COURTESY OF HENRY HEWES)

fade into oblivion. I believe this technique would achieve two essential aims—the first being the dramatization of the memory technique, and the second, a physical and economic lightening of the production.

Anderson did not like Jo's approach and asked for more substantial scenery. As Jo designed and as the more than twenty sets were built, the playwright changed, added, and omitted scenes, all of which caused adjustments in the design and building process. In mid-September, Jo, to cover himself, sent a stern memo to the Playwrights Company, co-producer Leland Hayward, and Bretaigne Windust, warning them about the size and complexity of the production: "I have made every effort to reduce each scene to the simplest terms, particularly in the elimination of built scenery, and substituting painted elements in their place." Despite his efforts, he noted that there would be nine settings and twenty-six scene changes and pleaded for suggestions from the director and playwright to lighten the production further.

If things were not going well in the scenery department, they were out of hand in rehearsals. Windust was replaced by Henry Potter, another old friend of Jo's, and Josh Logan was called in for some doctoring at the end. As the rehearsals progressed, the play appeared to flow beautifully from scene to scene. In Philadelphia, however, when the sets were added, as Jo predicted, all hell broke loose. Rex Harrison was unable to get his bearings when he had to exit and reappear quickly in the next vignette. He had to be grabbed by the stagehands, turned around, and pushed onto the stage with each new scene, causing him to become disoriented. Finally, a war council meeting was convened and producer, director, playwright and designer came to the inevitable decision that the set had to be redesigned and rebuilt—the sooner the better. Not only was it an extra expenditure of many thousands of dollars in reconstruction, but the delay also resulted in a loss of revenue from tickets that had to be refunded.

Jo took the blame for the disaster. He knew that, when all else failed, it was the theatre's unwritten law that the designer was responsible for a show's troubles. (The designer Boris Aronson once remarked, in his Russian-accented English, that every flop had its

"wictim," and the gospel according to Boris was that it was important for the designer not to become the "wictim.") Not only had no one listened to Jo's warning when he began his work during the summer, but he was further punished by receiving next to nothing for redesigning the show. Out of earshot of the producers, Jo referred to the show as "Anne of the Thousand Scenes" and drew a cartoon, which was circulated around his office. It shows Max Anderson (labeled Playwright) dressed as Henry VIII stepping on the train of a pygmy-sized Anne Boleyn (labeled Producer). The caption, a paraphrase of one of the lines in the play, reads:

> HE: I want to fill you up—night after night. I want to fill you
>   up with soliloquies!
> SHE: Bastards! For they would be bastards, you know!

When the production finally arrived on Broadway in early December, a few of the critics, perhaps reacting to what they had read in *Variety* about the show's troubles, were grudging in their praise of the sets but extravagant in their appreciation of the costumes designed by Elizabeth Montgomery of Motley. (The praise was deserved.) The play hung on for a good solid run, largely because of Rex Harrison, making his Broadway debut. His appearance so entranced the Tony Award voters that he beat out Lee J. Cobb, as Willy Loman in *Death of a Salesman*, as the outstanding actor of the season.

The headaches of *Anne of the Thousand Days* behind him, Jo moved on to that now-classic Arthur Miller drama. When Jo wrote *Designing for the Theatre*, he devoted a chapter to the "case history" of *Death of a Salesman* to illustrate his artistic modus operandi. He begins by explaining the aura of "mission" surrounding play production, describing the "intense period of concentration at high emotional level." The (lucky) scenic designer who works all season, he implies, "is compelled to go on month after month at concert pitch. He must also learn how to balance some divided loyalties, because he can almost never work on only one play at any one time." He was referring to the four-month period in late 1948 and early 1949 when he was working on *Salesman* and *South Pacific* simultaneously.

Kermit Bloomgarden, the producer, told Jo that *Death of a Salesman* was a "toughie," a play with forty scenes that moved backward and forward in time. He gave Jo a copy of the script, and Jo indeed found the play a difficult assignment. The playwright gave him little help except for general descriptions. Miller's only thought was that it should be played on three platforms.

In analyzing the script in his own way, Jo looked for the most important visual symbol—"the real background of the story"— which he felt was the salesman's house. He decided that if the house became the main set, all the other scenes not set in the house could be played on a forestage that projected toward the audience. He realized, of course, that he would have to sell this idea to Bloomgarden, since a forestage would mean the loss of the first rows of high-priced orchestra seats. Moreover, the house could not be realistic or solid and would therefore have to be reduced to a skeleton. The fragmentary scenes would have to be played with only the necessary furniture and props to suggest the locale. He could achieve the rest with lighting, projections, and a painted backdrop. He made a quick sketch and floorplan for a meeting with Miller, Bloomgarden, and Kazan, who was to direct the show.

Jo patiently presented his plan and emphasized over and over again that as simple as it was in the telling, it would be a complex and difficult production, one in which timing was the all-important element to ensure that scene would flow into scene without a break in the drama. Miller and Kazan listened intently and at the end of Jo's discourse, they realized that they would have to rethink the production in terms of Jo's plan, but were willing to try it. Miller would get what he really wanted: transitions from flashback to the present without interrupting the action. Kazan quickly recognized the use of cinematic technique in Jo's scheme and saw how the set would dictate his direction. Later, he referred to Jo's skeletonized house as an X-ray—a metaphor that may well have stimulated his imagination. For Bloomgarden, it meant revising his production schedule, postponing the opening—and losing revenues from seats. Yet Jo was told to proceed and meet with Kazan in Boston the following week, when he could present him with a more developed scheme. (At the time, he was deep in his work on *Summer and Smoke* and a proposed theatre for the Pittsburgh Playhouse, both of which he had to set aside.)

On the plane to Boston the following week, Jo made more sketches to show Kazan, relying on his uncanny ability to draw freehand in scale. After an hour's discussion, during which Kazan rejected only a small number of Jo's ideas (some of which he sketched on hotel stationery in Boston), he gave Jo the go-ahead on the formal designs. When Jo reported the results of the discussion to Bloomgarden, the producer pushed him hard to prepare the ground plans and drawings that showed the solution to all the problems—with one exception that was not to be solved until much later. Jo described it in his book:

> The greatest conundrum was in the scene in which the Salesman's two sons, as adults, go to bed in their attic bedroom in full view of the audience and then must appear elsewhere on the set a moment later as they were in their youth, entering downstage dressed in football togs. How were we going to get them out of bed and off-stage without their being seen, when both the beds and their own bodies under the covers were completely visible to the audience, and also provide for an instantaneous costume change?

The scene was so important to Miller and Kazan that there was no question about its being retained. Jo eventually found the solution.

> The heads of the beds in the attic room were to face the audience; the pillows, in full view since there were to be no solid headboards, would be made of papier-mâché. A depression in each pillow would permit the heads of the boys to be concealed from the audience, and they would lie under the blankets that had been stiffened to stay in place. We could then lower them and still retain the illusion of their being in bed.

The trick hinged on lowering the boys to the stage floor, where they would have to make a quick costume change, then immediately reappear on stage. Joe Lynn, who was one of the legendary prop men of his—and any other—time, devised an elevator driven by a hand-operated winch that would lower the platform of the bed once the boys pushed a button under their "pillows." When John Harvey climbed into the bed to try it, the trick bed worked beautifully. When Arthur Kennedy, cast as Biff Loman, asked to try it, something went wrong. Jo, John, and Joe Lynn, who was operating the elevator, were startled by a crunching and grinding sound that turned their blood to ice. The noise came, they gratefully discovered, not from Kennedy's head being caught in the mechanism but from the solid papier-mâché pillow, which had slipped and jammed the elevator. After that, the pillow was made smaller and everything worked smoothly for the entire run. Julia Sze, the costume designer, provided the boys with two layers of clothes: they wore their athletic garb underneath their pajamas, which they quickly stripped off before emerging again on stage. Sze, an inventive young Chinese-American who had collaborated with Jo on *Finian's Rainbow* and *Command Decision*, also appropriately aged or "distressed" the clothes to fit Miller's characters' situation.

While problems can seem to be solved in the scene shops, technical rehearsals have a way of both exposing and creating difficulties. With a set as complex as the one Jo designed for *Salesman* and with 150 light cues (more, incidentally, than were used at the time for musicals), the cast was naturally and noticeably in shock when they had to work in the actual setting. Kazan was unperturbed and made the necessary adjustments to his direction as the actors ran through the performance, and Jo, as a matter of course, made alterations in the lighting when the actors appeared in their costumes and stage makeup. Jo's solution to the ending of the play was handled disingenuously. The last scene takes place on the forestage with Linda Loman kneeling over the grave of her husband, seemingly in a cemetery. In the original plans, the scene called for a

IN *DEATH OF A SALESMAN* (1949), TO MAKE THE SWITCH FROM PAST TO PRESENT, JO HAD TO SHOW WHAT THE HOUSE LOOKED LIKE WHEN IT WAS FIRST BUILT AND LATER WHEN IT WAS HEMMED IN BY OPPRESSIVE APARTMENT BUILDINGS. HE DESIGNED A PAINTED BACKDROP MADE OF LINEN, WHICH COULD BECOME ALMOST TRANSPARENT WHEN STRONG LIGHTS WERE TURNED ON IT FROM BEHIND AND OPAQUE WHEN LIGHTED FROM THE FRONT. WHEN THE LIGHTS WERE OFF, THE INTERIOR OF THE HOUSE WAS REVEALED. (COURTESY OF THE ESTATE OF HILDA AND EDWARD KOOK)

small gravestone, which Jo dutifully designed using a trap door from which it would arise. He showed it to Kazan along with his alternate plan, a drawing of Linda seated on the edge of the stage with her sons bowed low over some funeral flowers on the lower forestage. Again, he planned to use a projection, this time of autumnal leaves, which would bathe the entire set and obliterate the house and background, while he focused light on the huddled group as Linda speaks her final words. Kazan got the message and omitted the gravestone.

Out of a total expenditure of $45,000 for the entire production, the cost of building and painting the scenery was $11,500 and the lighting, $19,000. Jo did things with the lighting and projections and scene painting and construction that he had done before but he

had never blended them together so well. At his elbow throughout the devising of the lighting and projections had been Eddie Kook, whose personal involvement in the production gradually usurped all of his time, to the dismay of his other clients. When Arthur Miller caught up with Eddie, he asked him why all the lights were necessary and received this curious but typically Kookian answer: "The reason is right in front of you—it takes more lights to make it dark." What he meant was that the changes in lighting were so subtle that if fewer lights were used, the dimming would have been quickly noticed by the audience. By using more lights, the changes in the intensities would be practically imperceptible.

The reception of *Death of a Salesman* was all that anyone connected with it could have asked for. It almost brought a wide smile

IN *SALESMAN*, TO SHOW THE LOMANS' HOUSE WHEN IT WAS NEW, THE BACKDROP DISAPPEARED INTO DARKNESS WITH THE LIGHTS OFF AND ANOTHER PAINTED TRANSPARENT CURTAIN WAS DROPPED IN FRONT OF THE STAGE TO SHOW THE TREE-FILLED, SUN-DRENCHED SUBURBAN SURROUNDINGS OF EARLIER YEARS. LEAVES IN VARYING SHADES OF GREEN WERE PROJECTED ON THE CURTAIN. (COURTESY OF ELIA KAZAN)

to the usually dour Bloomgarden face. A short time after the opening, Bloomgarden rushed into an arrangement with Binkie Beaumont in London for a West End production. Jo redesigned the set and lighting and was gratified that Beaumont did not spare expense in duplicating the standards of the New York production. The London *Salesman*, which starred Paul Muni, received an enthusiastic reception from the English press, which was unprecedented for an imported American success.

In time, Jo's set for *Salesman* became its icon. Miller himself stated that no more perfect set has ever been produced for any American play in the twentieth century. Whenever the play is published, it is usually accompanied by a photograph of the actual set or one of Jo's renderings. Indeed, whenever American theatre is discussed in a general way in histories or reference works, more often than not the set will be used to illustrate the text. So identified with the play has it become that—try as they might to come up with something different—designers in every corner of the world will usually try to evoke Jo's set for their proscenium stages.

Jo's design institutionalized the skeletal set and made it, from that moment on, a part of every designer's repertoire of stage arrangements. Moreover, the set became the fullest and finest manifestation of the New Stagecraft and, as such, it has never been surpassed. The movement toward weaving the scenery into the fabric of the play reached its apogee in *Death of a Salesman*. Unlike Robert Edmond Jones's seminal setting for *The Man Who Married a Dumb Wife*, a play that is remembered chiefly for his set, the setting for *Salesman* inextricably became the play and the play became the setting.

Jo's set was not visually beautiful, as were many of his previous efforts, but simplistic beauty was never the aim of the New Stagecraft. Whatever there was of beauty in it arose from the small moments of lyricism in the play itself. During his later years as the dean of designers on Broadway, Jo would modestly disclaim the significant role he played in the success of the play. Good plays, he would say, design themselves.

While solving the multifaceted problems of *Death of a Salesman* with one hand, Jo was with the other hand balancing the design of a musical, which had the smell of success about it from the beginning.

Its genesis was in an almost casual remark dropped to Joshua Logan at the opening-night party for *Mister Roberts*. Jo's guests were his brother and his wife, Kenneth and Mary MacKenna, who had come in from Hollywood not only to visit Ella, Jo, and his family but also to fulfill Kenneth's ongoing mandate as head of the MGM story department to see the Broadway offerings. At the party, Kenneth suggested that Josh look over the advance copy of a book he had been reading: *Tales of the South Pacific*, by James Michener; he thought that somewhere in it was the basis for a musical. Logan read it and immediately grasped its potential. Leland Hayward read it and agreed, and together they began negotiating for the rights and, coincidentally, for the services of Rodgers and Hammerstein. Within a few months, Hammerstein had woven two of the tales into one and Rodgers had started to write the score. Jo signed on to do the sets, but not before a few moments of unpleasant wrangling with Rodgers over his royalty.

For thirty solid days, Jo was lashed to his drawing board pouring out designs for *South Pacific*, while John Harvey and the transitory drafting team translated everything into working plans and blueprints. Jo's usual progress—from quick sketches to defined drawings, to a model to working drawings and elevations, to finished, painted renderings—was telescoped into weeks rather than months in order to get the job done for an April opening on Broadway. (Rodgers was so sure of what he was doing that he went ahead and booked the Majestic Theatre and took ads almost six months in advance of the opening.) Jo was so short of time that he was unable to finish painted renderings of the set. When Richard Halliday, Mary Martin's husband, asked to buy one of Jo's paintings of the full sets to give to his wife as a gift, Jo was embarrassed to tell him that none were ready.

By now, Jo's talent for creating cinematic techniques on the stage was so well known that everyone expected to see new feats of scenic derring-do. *South Pacific* did not disappoint them. Because the action takes place on two Pacific islands during the last phase of World War II, Jo had to move the scenes as the story followed the two interwoven love stories of Nellie Forbush (Mary Martin) and Emile De Becque (Ezio Pinza) and Lt. Joseph Cable (William Tabbert) and Liat (Betta St. John), while also providing the appropriate background of the United States Navy base set on one of the islands. Again, he used a scrim drawn across the stage plus lighting dim-outs to "dissolve" from one set to the next.

The exuberant advance reviews of *South Pacific* in Philadelphia and Boston pushed ticket sales in New York to a new high even for a Rodgers and Hammerstein musical. The day after the musical opened, on April 7, 1949, the eight New York critics ran out of adjectives to express their delight, but one or two of them failed to mention Jo's contribution. Oscar Hammerstein, perhaps sensing the slight, wrote to Jo a week later: "I don't know how to describe your contribution to the success of 'South Pacific.' I only shudder if I try to imagine the play without your ingenuity and rare craftsmanship."

South Pacific ran for almost 2,000 performances on Broadway and was sent to London with Mary Martin sans Pinza thereafter. Jo redesigned both the London and touring productions, which were also sell-outs. Nearly twenty-five years after the opening, Brooks Atkinson tried to explain its immense popularity:

> But in view of the banality and stereotypes of most musical shows, like No, No Nanette, Irene, *and* The Student Prince, *the fundamental humanity of* South Pacific *cannot be ignored. It is interested in the character of its chief men and women. It discusses race prejudice in ethical terms. It belongs to the literature of the human race in music as well as in words.*

FOR THE BALI HA'I SCENE OF **SOUTH PACIFIC (1949)**, THE DROP WAS PAINTED ON BOTH SIDES TO REVEAL TWO ASPECTS OF THE SCENE. ON THE FRONT WAS A NEUTRAL SKY SURROUNDING THE TWIN PEAKS OF THE VOLCANO RISING FROM THE PLACID BLUE SEA. DURING BLOODY MARY'S SINGING OF "BALI HA'I," THE BACK, WHEN LIGHTED, WAS TRANSFORMED INTO A DARK SKY AND DEEP RED SEA. OSCAR HAMMERSTEIN ADDED THE PHRASE "LOW-FLYING CLOUD" TO THE LYRICS OF THE SONG AFTER HE SAW JO'S DRAWING. (ROBERT L. B. TOBIN COLLECTION, THE MCNAY ART MUSEUM)

JO HAD TO KEEP AS MUCH OF THE STAGE AS POSSIBLE FREE OF SOLID SCENERY TO ALLOW FOR THE MOVEMENT OF THE HUGE CAST AND CHORUS IN THE MUSICAL NUMBERS FOR **SOUTH PACIFIC** (1949). MUCH OF THE SCENERY WAS PAINTED ON FLATS, CURTAINS, SHORTER CURTAINS CALLED BORDERS, AND VERTICAL PIECES CALLED LEGS, ALL OF WHICH COULD BE QUICKLY SHIFTED OR LIFTED OFF STAGE. MOST OF WHAT IS SHOWN IN THIS RENDERING IS PAINT ON CANVAS. (COURTESY OF THE RODGERS AND HAMMERSTEIN ORGANIZATION)

Jo's intense schedule during the first half of 1949 left him exhausted. A few weeks after the opening of *South Pacific,* he took Jean to Europe, travelling with Josh and Nedda Logan on the SS *Nieuw Amsterdam.* The four of them spent their first few weeks traveling by car in Spain and France. Jo wrote to Kenneth that the trip "lifted Jean's and my personal weight of burdens," probably referring to their responsibilities at home. (The children were again left in the care of the housekeeper.) In Paris, he found himself short of cash and had to borrow money from the Logans to complete the rest of their trip to Italy and England after they went their separate ways. This was to be the first of Jo's nearly annual visits to Europe, many of them without Jean. He came to regard these trips as health restoratives, both physical and mental.

When he returned to New York, he and his staff moved the studio to his big Dakota apartment and tackled old and new projects on his drawing board. He was not scheduled for any fall openings on Broadway, but he had promised to design the set for a play by John Finch, a fledgling playwright, for Catholic University, in Washington, D.C. The play, originally called *The Downstairs Dragon* but renamed *The Real McCoy,* had been sent to him by the agent Audrey Wood, who thought it had possibilities. Jo thought so, too, and took an option on it for a potential Broadway production. Professing to be a longtime admirer of Father Gilbert Hartke, who had set up and steered the Drama Department at Catholic University into one of the outstanding academic theatrical oases in the country, Jo agreed to design it pro bono as a tribute to the priest's efforts. The director was to be Alan Schneider, a young professor on Hartke's staff. In the fall of 1949, Jo worked in New York with Schneider and the young playwright to whip the play into shape for a winter production in Washington. In his autobiography, Schneider recalled the play and the production:

> Dragon—*I still think of it under its original title—concerned a real dragon living downstairs in a New York museum, and the way in which the people who inhabited the museum dealt with it. Like so many other and later philosophical whimsies with which I have become involved, this one worked better on the page than on the stage. Jo's set was lovely; the reviews were not.*

After a post-reviews' reappraisal of its potential, there was, of course, no thought of taking the production to New York. But Jo and Alan Schneider would meet again in a few years, the next time on Broadway turf.

The Real McCoy closed out the 1940s on a slightly low note for Jo, but the decade had been anything but down for his career. Even when his wartime hiatus was considered, he had designed nearly fifty shows and ballets, of which only two failed to make it into New York. Although the names of younger designers were beginning to appear more frequently among the credits on theatre programs, the forties were dominated by the names of Jo Mielziner and Donald Oenslager. John Mason Brown commented on the friendly rivalry in his column in the *Saturday Review of Literature*, in the fall of 1949, noting that "there have been Oenslager seasons and Mielziner seasons" and continuing: "Incessantly busy as they have been, of the two men it is Mr. Mielziner, who has been more wisely used by Broadway" in permitting him "to turn his back on the drawing rooms and kitchens in which realism delights, and to which by selection and emphasis, he has added a distinction of his own." Brown did hail Oenslager as the theatre's most versatile professional, for in addition to his designing for Broadway the latter taught at Yale's Drama School, designed for the Metropolitan Opera and Colorado's Central City opera house, and found time to write a few books. Inevitably, Brown concluded that the American theatre was indeed fortunate to have both of them plying their trade at the same time.

Jo's decade was filled with honors. The Tony Award committee blanketed almost all of his major productions in 1949 with one award. *Variety* conducted its own poll of critics in those days and named him the "Best Scenic Designer" for the last five years of the forties. The Donaldson Awards presented by *Billboard* were given to Jo for *Dream Girl, A Streetcar Named Desire,* and *Death of a Salesman.* His celebrity was certified by a two-part profile in the *New Yorker* in 1948, in which Alva Johnston collaborated with Jo in painting his early life and background in rather more brilliant colors than reality. Titled "Aider and Abettor," each installment was accompanied by a caricature of Jo by William Auerbach-Levy (an old family friend) for the first part and Irma Selz for the second. The title came from Jo's insistence that the mission of the set designer is "to aid and abet the actors."

But Jo's fame in the forties also brought him other types of recognition. His "silver anniversary" as a designer appeared as a feature article by J. P. Shanley in *The New York Times* in October 1949 and he was invited on radio and television talk shows to discuss his art. He was asked to lecture before the Architectural League of New York in 1946 and received countless other requests for talks and interviews, almost all of which were politely but firmly refused because of the pressures of his work. Among the more piquant manifestations of his celebrity came from his inclusion in a shirt and tie advertisement in Arrow's Theatre Quiz in the June, 1949 *Playbill.* "Question 2: Arrow designs collars that are perfect-setting. Who designed the perfect settings for *Death of a Salesman* and *South Pacific?* Answer: Jo Mielziner." Department stores such as Wallach's and Bergdorf Goodman's in New York wove his name into their advertisements apparently as representative of ultimate perfection and taste. Making sure that everyone would get the pronunciation of Jo's surname correctly, the columnist Walter Winchell referred to him as the "Dezeener Melzeener." Even the nascent television industry paid attention to him. In 1948, CBS commissioned him as a consultant to devise the lighting for their Studio 44, which they paid him for and never used.

Although Jo had been invited to become a member of the Coffee House Club and The Players, no membership did more for his ego than the Century Club. Don Oenslager proposed him and Jo willingly paid the $150 entrance fee to walk through its prestigious portals set within a façade of success. It was to become a refuge for him, particularly in the years when he was alone, and represented his arrival in the world beyond the theatre. His Century Club membership announced to the world that this high-school dropout was a success on a higher level. It gave him new confidence and buoyancy of spirit, which from that day forth never left him.

7

FAME, FORTUNE, AND FAMILY

When Jo returned from his Army service in 1944, he resumed his career on Broadway almost without skipping a beat, but he was coming back to private life that was different from the one he had been accustomed to. Presumably, it was the kind of life that he had craved. After two marriages and divorces, he seemed to have finally found the right mate, someone who was willing to forgo her own ambitions to become solely a wife and a mother to his children. Furthermore, Jean Macintyre was an intelligent and beautiful woman with style and social grace. Unfortunately, her affluent upbringing had given her scant training for her new roles as mother and manager of Jo's household. During the war, she had coped with his absence as best she could. She had learned how to manage on little more than Jo's meager military allotment and had seen two young children through chicken pox, whooping cough, and other childhood illnesses, and awaited the return of her husband, who, she thought, would immediately carry his share of the burdens of family life.

Jean liked living in Connecticut and had enrolled the two boys, Michael and Neil, at the elementary school in nearby Sandy Hook. Unable to tear himself away from his work in New York, Jo became a weekend husband and father and often totally missed going home to Connecticut because he was needed in New Haven, Boston, Philadelphia, or wherever new shows were previewing. Even though his burgeoning income allowed her full-time help, a live-in gardener, membership in the Fairfield County Hunt Club, and other suburban amenities, Jean was alone week after week to cope again with three children and a complex household. She also missed a husband in her bed.

Neither Jean nor Jo had been prepared for the rigors of the "terrible twos" of their first two children. In adopting two boys so close in age, Jo may have been trying to recapture his own early life as one of two male siblings who were born in quick sucession. But there the similarity ended. Since Michael was the more robust of the two, both physically and emotionally, little Neil became the butt of his older brother's taunts. Shy and sensitive, Neil cried easily and sought escape whenever he could. Luckily, with twenty acres surrounding the house, it was easy to lose himself in the woods to avoid the discomforts of home. The arrival of Jennifer brought yet another adjustment, which was not welcomed by the two boys.

Evidence concerning the process of child adoption has shown that the younger the child is placed, the better the chances for assimilation. That way, adoptive parents go through the natural rites of passage of parenthood while the children progress from babyhood to childhood. When Jo and Jean adopted their toddlers, they may have avoided diaper rash, infant formula, and the myriad concerns of infancy, but they had to accept the preconditioning that the children had received at foster homes and the Catholic orphanage. After getting the children on a healthy diet and caring for their physical needs, Jean did not know what to do with them. And Jo, remembering his own father's long absences and generally *laissez faire* attitude, could not or would not understand why Jean did not readily metamorphose into a full-blown mother.

Jean, overwhelmed by her instant motherhood, found release from the family problems in alcohol. Social drinking at luncheons or dinners was always acceptable in their circle of friends. Jo himself liked a martini or a couple of Scotches before dinner to unwind after a hard day at the studio and a nice bottle of wine during dinner, but Jean relied on drink to smooth out the wrinkles and to carry her through her days and nights without Jo. When he was home, she controlled her drinking, but when he was away in New York at work, she would indulge herself. She would become alternately mellow or abusive. The rebellious Michael, unable to measure up to Jean's notion of a good boy, became her particular target. As he resisted her motherly ministrations and suffered her severest abuse, the unwitting observers of the situation, Neil and Jennifer, grew up wary of Jean and unconsciously chose to be more tractable as the easy way out. Consequently, they never suffered the early rejection that Michael did. While it was always difficult for them to

THE MIELZINERS (FOREGROUND) AT THE HOME OF DOROTHY AND RICHARD RODGERS IN 1943. FLORENCE ELDREDGE MARCH IS SEATED ON THE GRASS AND RICHARD RODGERS IS ON THE BENCH. THE OTHER WOMAN ON THE BENCH MAY BE EDNA FERBER'S NIECE. (COURTESY OF JENNIFER MIELZINER)

understand or accept their mother's drinking, as they grew older they became protective of her, making excuses for her behavior when she appeared drunk around other people.

The Mielziners' social life only served to encourage Jean's drinking. In Connecticut, she ran with the hunt club set, whose conviviality was inevitably stimulated by hard drinking. Jo did not participate in or particularly like this society. Once in a while, if he were in Newtown on a Sunday, he would follow the riders over the hills in his Jeep. On weekends, when Jo was home, they socialized with Dick and Dorothy Rodgers, Paul and Millicent Osborn, Edna Ferber, Gadg and Molly Kazan, Josh and Nedda Logan, Fredric and Florence March, Lawrence and Armina Marshall, and other theatre people living nearby. Many of them, slightly older than Jean, were graduates of the Prohibition era, when drinking became not just a social pastime but a political statement.

Eventually, there were occasions when Jean lost control and had to be committed to sanatoriums for drying out. Jo, out of embarrassment, would refer to these bouts as "nervous breakdowns" or a flare-up of her "spastic stomach condition," but his closest friends, the Kooks and the Logans, knew the real causes of Jean's ailments. Unfortunately, her periods of sobriety following her hospitalization never lasted very long, and often her drinking escalated after each "cure."

The relationship between Jean and young Michael developed into a psychological tug of war that appeared to have no resolution. Being Catholics, Jean and Jo took their problem to their religious advisers, usually priests—one of whom was Father Vincent Donovan, the brother of Jo's former military commander, General "Wild Bill" Donovan—and the advice they followed was to separate Michael from Jean. After the fourth grade at home, he was enrolled in a succession of Catholic boarding schools and summer boarding camps. Except for brief periods, Michael spent little time with his family. Inevitably, the rejection took its toll and he grew more and more unruly. In the summer of 1953 while Jean, Neil, and Jennifer were vacationing in Hawaii, a family holiday in which Michael was not allowed to participate, Michael went to pieces; Jo then decided to send him to the George Junior Republic in Freeville, New York, a school that was noted for a mixture of behavioral rehabilitation

with education. It was then popularly known as a private reform school for the incorrigible children of the rich and famous. The school was run very much like a prison with its own solitary confinement known as "the Rock," but Michael appeared to do well within its confinements and strictures. He shed much of his adolescent overweight, grew a few inches, did well in his classes, and was even elected president of the student body just two years after he arrived. Jo was so proud of him that he flew up for his inauguration.

Yet separation from Michael did not appear to ease Jean's problems. As therapy, Jo sent her on a European vacation alone in 1950 and encouraged her periodic "retreats" to the Regina Laudis Priory, in Connecticut, for a few days on her own. In 1952, realizing that he had to keep closer watch over her and to spend more time with Neil and Jennifer, Jo moved them to New York. From that point on, the Newtown house would serve as a weekend and summer retreat. With his family ensconced in the large apartment on the fourth floor and his studio on the first, Jo thought that he would be better able to oversee the activities of the family while pursuing his busy schedule. Neil and Jennifer were enrolled in the best private Catholic schools in New York.

Jo made attempts to be a better father. He built a miniature theatre for them and when he found free moments, he would sit at a table with Jennifer and her friends. They would make squiggles with a pencil on a sheet of paper, and he would convert them into drawings of animals or objects, much to their delight. When Michael and Neil were little and living at Newtown, Jo had begun creating stories of a rabbit named Bitten Ear, which he continued for Jennifer when she was old enough to understand. The stories were engendered by an incident involving the family poodle named Pousey. Whenever Jo was home in Newtown during his leaves from the Army or later on his weekends from New York, the maid customarily served him strips of celery and carrots with his drinks before dinner. One evening, he noticed a rabbit on the lawn. He began to coax it to come closer with carrots until it would come near the family for brief visits. Observing the attention given to the rabbit, Pousey took off after it one night and bit off part of one of the rabbit's ears. Christened "Bitten Ear" by Jo, the rabbit became

the subject of his letters to his little boys when he was away. Bitten Ear took the uniform of his country, fought battles, flew airplanes, became a spy, and had wonderful wartime adventures that Jo related and illustrated with drawings and cartoons. When the war was over, Bitten Ear's adventures in peacetime continued as bedtime stories for Jennifer.

Whatever fathering Jo managed to include in his hectic schedule, it was too little, too late. He justified his failings as a father by reminding himself that he was responsible for the financial upkeep of two households with full-time servants in New York and Connecticut,

the expense of three children in private schools, the maintenance of an office-studio and staff in New York, the partial support of his mother, and what he considered the extravagances of his wife. He bought a horse for Jean so that she could ride in the hunt, and when Jennifer was old enough, she was given riding lessons and her own horse. At home, he surrounded his children with art and fine furnishings, shaped their taste, and expected in return a decent standard of behavior. Because of his own inborn sense of discipline, he could be self-righteous toward Jean and the antics of his children, and in reaction, Jean's alcoholism continued as her resentment grew and became more ominous. In her mind, Jo remained self-absorbed and she and the children held a distant and lesser position in his life.

When the choice was between his duty as a father and his job, Jo invariably chose the latter—but he always felt contrite about his decision. When Jennifer was making her First Communion, Jo felt that he could not tear himself away from the technical rehearsals of a show, missed the ceremony, and suffered for it. Jo's real children were the succession of young assistants, male and female, that he employed during the course of his career. Once, in congratulating one of his friends on the birth of a child, he revealingly referred to himself as a "fake father." If indeed he regarded fatherhood as a role, he was not playing it very well.

Jo's close proximity to Jean now should also have given the household more stability and helped Jean to cope with her roles as homemaker and mother, but, if anything, it contributed to making the environment more mercurial. Jo rebuked Jean for her drinking and spending behind closed doors, but the children were fully aware of the turmoil between them. Feeling that they could never measure up either to Jean's notion of ideal children or Jo's standards of achievement, they stopped trying. Without strong parental supervision, Neil and Jennifer did as they pleased. Despite the good clothes, their own swimming pool, the dancing lessons, and all the other manifestations of material well-being, they expressed their emotional insecurity in different ways. Neil often played truant from school and was sent off to a Connecticut boarding school. Jennifer, who was probably closest to Jean, often had to suffer the embarrassment of being sent from school to the homes of Mildred

Dunnock or George Jenkins or other family friends when Jean was in the middle of one of her binges. She missed many days of school largely because her mother was too hung over to get her ready in the morning. When Neil's rebellion suddenly erupted uncontrollably, he, too, was shipped off to George Junior Republic for a corrective education.

Things inevitably came to a head at home. Despite Jean's enrollment in Alcoholics Anonymous, trips to private sanatoriums, and counseling by family and clergy, her drinking accelerated, and so did her abusiveness. In December of 1956, a week or so before Christmas, her behavior became so violent that Jo had to call the police. She was taken away by the paramedics from Bellevue Hospital to the psychiatric ward, where she remained until Jo had a chance to consult with her doctor in Connecticut and with Dr. Thomas Sheen (Bishop Sheen's brother), the Mielziner family doctor in New York. On their advice she was transferred to Hall-Brooke Sanatorium, in Greens Farms, Connecticut, and placed on tranquilizers. Once stabilized, she returned to the Dakota and Jo held his breath as he hoped for the best. While she was still taking the pills, she started drinking again and the combination proved almost lethal. She was removed to Doctors Hospital, then returned to Hall-Brooke for further treatment. When it became apparent that her hostility toward Jo was unabated and that she would not improve as long as she continued to live with him, Jo turned to Bishop Sheen and Father Donovan for a solution. Reluctantly, Jo agreed to a trial separation in April of 1957. Jennifer remained with Jo until the end of the school year, when she would join her mother in a small cottage Jean had taken in Fairfield for the summer. They agreed that Jennifer should be placed in a boarding school when the new school year began.

Still harboring a lingering hope that their nineteen-year marriage would heal once Jean was cured, Jo faced the fact that he could not live with his wife. The trial separation became a permanent arrangement, but because of their Catholicism Jo and Jean never divorced. Jo agreed to a generous financial maintenance for Jean and Jennifer under the terms of the separation agreement. The Newtown house was sold and the modest profit from the sale was divided between them. Except when Jo and Jean met briefly to sign documents relating to the Newtown house and the separation and spoke on the phone, they never saw each other again after she moved out of New York. She lived in a small East Side apartment just long enough to realize that her friends were really Jo's friends and they soon lost interest in her. Early in 1959, she gave up her apartment and went to California. She eventually returned to her roots in Hawaii, remaining there until her death, at the age of eighty-two, in 1993.

Because they lived from day to day without much guidance from either Jean or Jo, the boys Michael and Neil were unprepared to steward their own futures. When they reached the age of seventeen, without completing their high school diplomas, they went into military service within a year of each other, Michael into the Marines and Neil into the Navy. Remembering his own experience as a Marine during World War I, Jo applauded their decision. It also temporarily relieved him of any further responsibility toward his sons. As for Jennifer, she was sent to the exclusive Orme School, in Mayer, Arizona. Set amid 40,000 acres of ranch country, it was so remote that Jo could rest easy that Jen would not drop out, in her brothers' footsteps. Presumably the school was chosen because of Jennifer's love of horses and riding, which formed a large part of the curriculum, but Jennifer hated the school and fled to the home of Jean's sister Margery, in Los Angeles. Jo allowed her to remain with her Aunt Margie and enrolled her in a school there much more to her liking. In 1959, Jennifer went to Hawaii to join Jean. In few months' time, she had met a young army lieutenant named Robert Errickson, and after the briefest of courtships, they married in December of 1959, a few months shy of her seventeenth birthday. Because she was under the legal age for marriage, Jean had to wire Jo for his permission. He wired back: "Permission granted. What is his name?"

In the years ahead, Jo, the inaccessible *paterfamilias*, gradually slipped into a more comfortable role as friend to his adopted children.

With the arrival of the 1950s, there were signs that things were changing on Broadway. Throughout the Depression and the war years, Broadway had to fight off the onslaught of the movies. Though they had to suffer Hollywood raids on the best talents in New York, which had become a kind of New Haven to try out material for the movie industry, producers had been able to survive, but they were not prepared for the more ominous development of television. Well on its way to becoming the entertainment of choice for Americans, TV was not encroaching only upon the theatres; movie houses suffered, too, and attendance at sports events was dropping.

And there were other body blows dealt to the theatre. One was postwar inflation, which drove up the costs of production at an alarming rate. Mounting a play or a musical cost up to ten times what it had cost during the prewar years. Producing became more of a gamble; so much was riding on a show that only the strong of heart and stomach could attempt it. In the prewar days, a run of a hundred performances could guarantee at least the return of the investment, if not a profit. In the fifties, the break-even point came close to the two-hundredth performance of a play and the three-hundredth for a musical. In the thirties, the producer could also count upon a tour of the show to the major cities to ensure profitability. After the war, audiences in the hinterlands would support only the most successful and highly publicized productions, for which they demanded stars and Broadway-quality scenery and costumes. Higher ticket prices drove away part of the usual audiences for productions both in New York and on the road. Robert Coleman, the critic for the *New York Mirror*, exclaimed in one of his reviews that the public was facing an astounding $7.50 top to see a play on Broadway in 1959!

On top of these woes, during the fifties small theatre groups presenting plays, often by new voices, away from the high-priced precincts of Broadway began to capture attention from the press and, more important, a segment of the regular audiences who were enticed by off-Broadway's ticket prices—and a sense of adventure.

To make things even worse for Broadway, most of the major theatre centers in the country had their own versions of off-Broadway or were in the early stages of establishing today's regional theatre. These anti-Broadway movements generated a new excitement in the theatre and, eventually, propelled the careers of many talented people onto the center stage not only of Broadway but of Hollywood and television.

There were fewer productions on Broadway than ever before in its recent history, fewer by almost half than during the leanest years of the Depression. Now, the marginal play or musical, a work that producers might have gambled on in past decades, was more often than not passed over. It became more and more difficult to pick winners, and from the producers' point of view the critics were making it even harder for their productions to survive. "Theatre," objected J. J. Shubert, "is a business like a department store, and no newspaper sends critics into a department store to disparage the merchandise." With the demise of several newspapers—also victims of the television set and its fast conveyance of news into every home—the power of the press became concentrated, making every printed word weigh in readers' minds as it had never before.

When Jo Mielziner looked around him, he discovered that in addition to the usual competition of his peers, he was watching the slow but steady rise of three of his former assistants, Lemuel Ayers, George Jenkins, and Ben Edwards, as well as other younger and versatile designers. Perhaps, he felt a pinch of satisfaction that most of them were building on his own contributions to stage art in solving the problems posed by the increasingly cinematic approach being taken in playwriting and staging. During the fifties, Jo designed forty-three productions on Broadway, only a scant half-dozen of which were true hits that made a hefty profit, and five of them were musicals, which was symptomatic of the decade's dislocations. Fewer than a dozen of Jo's shows were moderate successes, but the rest were best forgotten—except for, in many cases, his scenery.

Throughout this period, Jo tried hard to become a big-time producer and failed. He also went into business as part-owner of a scene shop, National Scenery Service, which was run by an able young stage technician, Peter Feller, whom Jo had known as the head technician for the wartime show *This Is the Army*. The scene shop was a success productively and financially for three years, but it was not lucrative enough for Jo's partners and it collapsed when Peter Feller pulled out. During the decade, Jo occasionally wore his other hat as commercial designer, always taking it on for the money and then farming it out to his friend Leonard Haber or his assistants. And he found himself becoming pulled more and more into the new field (for him) of theatrical architecture, a field that would later frustrate him, but one in which he believed he could make a difference. It was a varied and interesting decade for Jo, which encompassed the last years of his reign as Broadway's most active and most outstanding designer.

In 1950, Kermit Bloomgarden, who would be at the apex of his producing career during the fifties, asked Jo to design a thriller, *The Man*, by Mel Dinelli, a Hollywood screenwriter. Bloomgarden harbored lingering reservations about the script and, to some extent, was relying on Jo to buttress the play scenically. The action, which takes place in the living room and kitchen of an old Victorian house, built tension as a psychopathic handyman terrorizes an old lady through two long acts. Although there were solid performances by Dorothy Gish and Don Hanmer, the critics saw only the holes in the premise of the play and gave it lukewarm reviews.

The day after *The Man* opened, on January 19, 1950, came *Dance Me a Song*, a revue produced by Jo's old friend and the granddaddy of revues in the past, Dwight Deere Wiman. Although the show was filled with many bright new performers, including Bob Fosse, and some inspired skits, and was one of a spate of revues that year, nothing could save the genre in the fifties. Jo contributed an idea for the first skit, "A Pair for Tonight," and Marya Mannes wrote another, "The Board Meeting." A young playwright named Robert Anderson, who had been recommended to Jo by his secretary Elizabeth Schauffler, contributed one of the most original sketches, "The Lunts Are the Lunts Are the Lunts" and would be heard from again in the future. Tom Prideaux, theatre editor at *Life* magazine, wrote to Jo after seeing the revue: "I thought your sets for *Dance Me a Song* were by far the smartest, most original theatre art that I have beheld in many moons. If the show only measured up to them!"

Jo liked everything and everyone involved in his next show—the script, its author, William Archibald, the director, Peter Glenville, the composer of the incidental music, Alex North, and the star, Beatrice Straight. Peter Cookson, an actor whom Straight had married shortly before the play opened, was also a producer. The play was *The Innocents*, a dramatization of Henry James's "The Turn of the Screw." It is a ghost tale of a governess and her two spooky charges,

OF THE KEY TECHNICAL PEOPLE ON WHOM JO RELIED, NONE WAS MORE IMPORTANT TO HIM THAN PETER FELLER, WHOSE KNOWLEDGE OF STAGECRAFT BECAME LEGENDARY IN THE THEATRE OF HIS DAY. PETE COMBINED ENORMOUS INTELLIGENCE AND DEDICATION TO HIS CRAFT WITH A CONTAGIOUS ENTHUSIASM AND WARMTH OF PERSONALITY THAT FEW COULD RESIST. HE (WITH MUSTACHE) IS SHOWN IN HIS MILIEU AMONG HIS FELLOW WORKERS. (COURTESY OF JOHN SCHWANKE)

JO'S RENDERING FOR THE OPENING SKIT, "A PAIR FOR TONIGHT," WAS BASED ON ONE OF HIS IDEAS AND WRITTEN BY JAMES SHELTON, THE CREATOR OF THE REVUE *DANCE ME A SONG* (1950). (ROBERT L. B. TOBIN COLLECTION, THE MCNAY ART MUSEUM)

a boy and a girl, set in a lonely English country house in the Victorian era. After he read the script, Jo went to Glenville with a novel scenic conception. He asked him: "How would you like the idea of my designing the lighting for this play, complete, and then only using that scenery that was absolutely necessary to cover the lights and serve the actors where things were important, such as a giant staircase?" Glenville readily agreed and Jo went to work creating the lighting first, then the scenery, the exact reverse of his usual technique. Most of the play was performed in a kind of shadowy twilight, broken by aureole spotlighting on the main characters as they played their scenes. For some of them, the lighting cast gigantic shadows on the backdrop, further emphasizing the otherworldliness of the play's action. Only one small incident marred the entire experience for Jo. Before he and Glenville had tackled the

long sessions of lighting, Peter Cookson had walked into the theatre to see the set-up scenery. What he saw was a set under the usual minimal worklights and was appalled by what he considered its cheerlessness. He sent out for an enormous bowl of flowers to make the set appear more hospitable. When Jo saw the flowers on the piano in his set, he threatened to call down the wrath of the unions upon the producer's head if they were not removed. After a few taut moments of discussion, Cookson realized that Jo meant what he said and had the offending flowers taken away. (Trying to keep the theatre off-limits to producers until the lighting is added to the set is sometimes the most difficult task of designers and directors.)

The Innocents represented one of those all too few moments in the theatre when every element coalesces into a seamless theatrical experience to which critics and audience universally respond. John Chapman of the *Daily News* recognized that in Jo's scenery, a "foreboding air of the supernatural" was part of its beauty. Lemuel Ayers was moved to write to Jo: "You have created the finest set I have ever seen in the theatre—a model of perfection. Where can *anyone* go from there? I just threw out all my paints." For his efforts, Jo received his fourth Donaldson Award from *Billboard* magazine and his second Tony Award.

The show was sent out on the road with Sylvia Sidney in the leading role under the banner of the Theatre Guild subscription series, and in 1953, with Peter Glenville's direction and Jo's scenery and lighting, it opened at Her Majesty's Theatre, in London, with Flora Robson as the star. Again, the play and the production received kudos from the press.

Jo had high hopes for the next production he was scheduled to design, in league with Leland Hayward, Josh Logan, Lucinda Ballard, and a cast that included Helen Hayes, but *The Wisteria Trees* did not live up to its promise. According to Logan, the project began with a random remark by Helen Hayes that she had a secret ambition to do Chekhov's *The Cherry Orchard*, but felt she did not think anyone would take her seriously as a great Russian beauty. He began working on an adaptation, placing the action on a plantation in postbellum Louisiana. To get the right feeling for the background, Logan and Jo visited Weeks Hall, a friend from Jo's school

THE DESIGN FOR **THE INNOCENTS** (1950) INCORPORATES ALL OF JO'S FAVORITE ELEMENTS: A HUGE WINDING STAIRCASE LEADING TO THE UNKNOWN, AN OVERSIZED WINDOW, TREES PROJECTED ON A BACKDROP OUTSIDE THE WINDOW, AND A GIANT CHEST DWARFING THE INHABITANTS. ALL OF IT WAS BATHED IN MIELZINER LIGHTING TO SPOTLIGHT ONLY THE ACTORS AND NECESSARY AREAS OF THE STAGE. (COURTESY OF JULES FISHER)

days at the Pennsylvania Academy, who was living in an unchanged antebellum mansion not far from New Orleans. The place, called The Shadows, was a vine-covered prototype for Jo's design, which reeked of Southern decay. After seeing a performance, Florence March wrote to Jo recalling a joke made by a director who said, "Give me a door that acts," saying, "Your walls always act." Despite (or perhaps because of) carrying with her the heavy burden of the recent death of her daughter, Helen Hayes turned in a memorable performance, but the tenor of Chekhov's play was so antithetical to the American character—even the demoralized Southern character—that everything about the production seemed forced or synthetic. Although it was doing well at the box office, Hayes wanted time off during the summer. When it reopened after the hiatus, the show failed, representing one of the few flops in Hayes's career.

With Jean away in Europe, Jo stayed close to his drawing board during the summer of 1950, working on his fall commissions. One of them was for a play by John Steinbeck called *Burning Bright,* to be presented by Rodgers and Hammerstein. *Burning Bright* was an allegory with a message about paternity in the universal sense: Every man must be the spiritual father to every child born, whether or not biological parentage is involved. Guthrie McClintic, Jo's old comrade, was directing the show and charged him to make the scenery as simple as possible. He wanted only the necessary props for a series of locales. The critics loved Jo's sets. Brooks Atkinson of the *Times* called them magical, but found the play pretentious and bombastic, an assessment with which Jo had been in agreement from the moment he had received the script. *Burning Bright* closed quickly, and Rodgers and Hammerstein ended their career as producers of other people's work in New York.

Jo now returned to *Guys and Dolls,* a musical by Frank Loesser, and produced by Cy Feuer and Ernest Martin, all unknown quantities to most of show business. A longtime friend of Feuer's, Loesser was a successful Hollywood songwriter who had been persuaded to write the music and lyrics of the first Feuer and Martin production,

THE BACKDROP FOR THE
OPENING SCENE OF *GUYS
AND DOLLS* (1950). IT
QUICKLY ESTABLISHED THE
TIME, PLACE, AND MOOD OF
THE SHOW. (VIRGINIA
MUSEUM OF FINE ARTS)

Where's Charley?, a musicalization of the old farce *Charley's Aunt,* by Brandon Thomas. Much to everyone's surprise, it turned into a huge success. When *Guys and Dolls* was first announced for production by *The New York Times* in the fall of 1949, Jo was incorrectly listed as the director; George S. Kaufman had that role. Having worked with Kaufman, Jo knew that he would receive only minimal instruction from him regarding the scenery.

When Jo received the preliminary script, he was unimpressed. Loosely based on a Damon Runyon short story, "The Idyll of Miss Sarah Brown," it was actually an amalgam of several stories. Writing to the playwright Emlyn Williams, Jo thought the love affair between the gambler and the Salvation Army lass was implausible and that the show as a whole was trivial, but he conceded that it would probably make a lot of money.

Since there were seventeen scenes in the show and the Kaufman pace was, as usual, rapid, Jo had to manage the quick transitions with scrims and abbreviated sets sliding on and off the stage. The scene that attracted the most attention was the one he designed for the "oldest established floating crap game in New York." When he discussed it with Michael Kidd, the choreographer, Jo asked him whether he could perch some of the dancers on steep ladders running up the walls of the sewer setting for the game. Kidd reacted enthusiastically to the suggestion, styling the number with the dancers climbing, hanging onto the rungs, and leaping from them when they choreographically joined in the gambling. Jo later congratulated himself for contributing to the choreography as well as the scenery.

The critics reacted to the show with uncharacteristic hyperbole. Jo's honky-tonk sets lent the right background to the Runyonesque characters that were re-created by Abe Burrows, all costumed superbly by Alvin Colt. No element was amiss and despite Jo's early misgivings about the plot's implausibility, audiences seemed not to notice or care. Not only did the producers make a lot of money from it, so did Jo. He adapted his original scenery for the touring and London versions and had invested money in the show. *Guys and Dolls* played for nearly 1,200 performances.

The year 1950 had been a good one financially. Jo had made more than $80,000, but half of it was eaten up by office and studio expenses and the other half by his heavy domestic responsibilities. It seemed to him that he was working harder just to stay in place.

Luckily, 1951 started on the right note. Rodgers and Hammerstein had called him as soon as they had decided to go ahead with a musical adaptation of a novel entitled *Anna and the King of Siam* by Margaret Landon, which had already been made into a movie with Irene Dunne and Rex Harrison. Like most Rodgers and Hammerstein works, the gestation period for *The King and I* was protracted and tumultuous. Miraculously, the authors allowed Jo and Irene Sharaff almost complete freedom to come up with designs for scenery and costumes. From the beginning, the star was to be Gertrude Lawrence, but Rodgers and Hammerstein had difficulty finding the right director. Still smarting from what he considered the high-handedness of Rodgers in regard to *South Pacific*, Joshua Logan turned the job down and lived to regret his decision. Their other choice, Lawrence's longtime friend, Noël Coward, was otherwise engaged, and they settled on the playwright-director John Van Druten, who had never directed a musical and was not the wisest choice, as they were to discover. One of the mysteries of this production was why Rodgers and Hammerstein did not entrust the direction as well as the choreography to Jerome Robbins. Robbins had won his spurs as a director-choreographer with two successful shows to his credit, *High Button Shoes* and *Miss Liberty*, and surely could have handled both functions in *The King and I*.

When Rodgers and Hammerstein cast an exotic-featured young performer named Yul Brynner as the titular king, he had been a circus acrobat with a few Broadway credits, the most outstanding of which had been a role in *Lute Song* in 1946. When he took the role he reluctantly left the security of his TV job as the director and host of a variety show on CBS—and the musical proved to be the cornerstone of his career. When the weakness of Van Druten's direction became too obvious to ignore, Brynner stepped in with his own solutions and probably should have been credited as the co-director.

Robbins, meanwhile, had his hands full with the choreography. Although he had appeared in the dancing choruses on Broadway since 1939, his first love was pure dance, without the restrictions and encumbrances of elaborate sets and costumes. On the Broadway musical stage, he frequently had to make dancers out of non-dancers, fit them in a space dictated by the scenery, and work within the confines of a script that his choreography had to serve. Still, for *The King and I*, he was able to try something unique—a blend of story-ballet and Asian-style movement. Robbins worked closely with Jo on the scenery for the ballet, "The Small House of Uncle Thomas," and suggested to Jo that the frozen river that Eliza must cross for her salvation be made of a fine white silk. By projecting a cold blue light on it, Jo would give it the look of ice. Jo, on the other hand, persuaded Robbins to abandon his idea of having Uncle Tom's cabin built realistically in sections and carried in by the dancers. Jo wanted to substitute lightweight translucent cutouts for the cabin to continue an Asian shadow-play motif. Robbins, Jo was to discover, was not easy to work with, not because he was exacting and demanding but because he was not finished with a

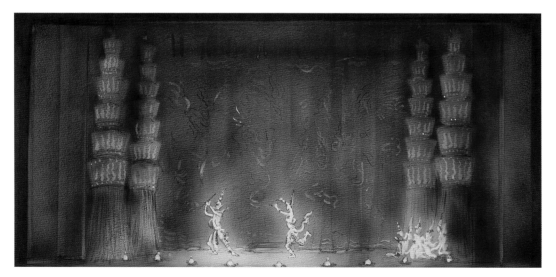

THE DOMINANT SCENIC ELEMENT OF "THE SMALL HOUSE OF UNCLE THOMAS" THAT JO CREATED FOR ***THE KING AND I*** (1951) WAS TWO PAIRS OF GIGANTIC GOLD TASSELS PLACED ON EITHER SIDE OF THE STAGE. (ESTATE OF JO MIELZINER)

ballet until he was finished. Meanwhile, this held the scenery and other elements of the number in limbo. Jo—with producers breathing down his back, with scene studios and prop shops requiring his plans so that they could complete their work, while all the other problems of a complex production swirled about him—had to fall back on his legendary calm to keep everyone on balance.

Jo's designs for *The King and I* supported an important facet of the book: the King's fascination with Western life. During the world tour made by Jo and his second wife Annie Laurie in 1933, they had visited the Royal Palace in Bangkok. Expecting to find beautiful Oriental decor and furniture, Jo had been appalled by the ornate Victorian furniture and chandeliers and the other Western European trappings in the palace. This fact, which he had carefully filed away in his mind, helped him to design the large palace setting, which he filled with Western touches, and the lovely scrim drops used for

the background. His work turned out to be less complicated than his other Rodgers and Hammerstein shows and less costly than Irene Sharaff's costumes, which were made of authentic Thai silks.

The King and I opened on March 29, 1951, at the St. James Theater, and brought laurels to everyone. Despite the premature death of Gertrude Lawrence during the run, it piled up 1,246 performances on Broadway. It enjoyed long tours on the road, was re-created with Jo's sets and lighting and Irene Sharaff's costumes at the Drury Lane in London in 1953, and was transformed into a movie. It was the most costly (to date) of the Rodgers and Hammerstein productions ($360,000), but they profited handsomely from it. One small dividend was Jo's alone. While the show was still in everyone's mind a year or so later, he was approached by a wallpaper company, Murals, Inc., to create a wallpaper mural that captured the flavor of his theatrical design. As usual, he turned

THE LAUNDRY SCENE (SHOWN) FOR *A TREE GROWS IN BROOKLYN* (1951) WAS CUT FROM THE MUSICAL, MUCH TO JO'S REGRET, BUT HE PUBLISHED THE DESIGN IN HIS BOOK ANYWAY. IN ALL OF THE SCENES HE CREATED FOR THE SHOW, HE MADE SURE THAT THE BROOKLYN BRIDGE WAS ALWAYS IN THE BACKGROUND. IT CAN BE SEEN THROUGH THE LINES OF LAUNDRY. (COURTESY OF PAUL STIGA)

the commission over to Leonard Haber, who actually designed the mural and shared in the small profits of the undertaking, Jo receiving 40 percent of the advance and royalties, and Haber, 60 percent. The advertisements pictured a benign Jo seated in a room papered with *The King and I* mural.

Jo had high hopes for the next musical he designed, which opened less than a month after *The King and I*, in April 1951. Based on Betty Smith's bestseller, *A Tree Grows in Brooklyn*, it had an all-star production team: George Abbott was the co-producer, co-author, and director; Arthur Schwartz and Dorothy Fields wrote the music and lyrics; and Irene Sharaff was the costume designer. Shirley Booth starred. The musical's setting gave Jo a chance to revive his love affair with the Brooklyn Bridge, which had begun with his designs for *Winterset*. In the souvenir book for the show, he rhapsodized about how the bridge offered him infinite variety for his designs:

> *In each [scene], the Bridge is in a different mood and therefore has taken on a different shape and a different color. Sometimes the Bridge seems pretty respectable, even conservative and drawn with the respectful attitude towards the vertical and the perpendicular which can cool the ardor of the engineer-draftsman. In other scenes my Brooklyn Bridge flings her steel platform in a rakish curve and in the Halloween Ballet we see a moment when she really loses her temper, bursts her stays and if you can take your eye for a moment off the fascinating dancing, she actually shows her slip!*

The turn-of-the-century tale of two Brooklyn sisters and their troubles with the men in their lives, accompanied by a tuneful and robust score, received glowing reviews from most of the critics but, unaccountably, it was not the long-running hit that everyone expected it to be. Jo's sets of the seamier aspects of Brooklyn life not only caught the spirit of the work but were described as "humorous and a vast help to the proceedings" by the ordinarily reserved Richard Watts of the *New York Post*. Although it was sent out on the road, where it continued to enjoy the good will of the out-of-town critics, *A Tree Grows in Brooklyn*, despite all of its appeal, did not attract the audiences in New York necessary to make it a significant hit.

FOR **TOP BANANA** (1951), JO OPENED UP THE STAGE TO SHOW THE INSIDE OF A TV STUDIO, WHERE MANY OF THE SCENES TOOK PLACE. IT ALSO SERVED THE CHOREOGRAPHER AND THE DANCERS, AFFORDING THEM THE LUXURY OF A LARGE AREA IN WHICH TO PERFORM. (COURTESY OF ROBERT GILROY/JAMES RYAN)

Jo designed only two more productions in 1951. On November 1 *Top Banana* opened to considerable but not record-book success (350 performances). It was the kind of show that appealed to tired businessmen with its gags and fast pace. Phil Silvers played a manic burlesque comedian who gets himself a television show and throws his weight around. Johnny Mercer provided the words and music to accompany the breezy action.

Jo's work on *Point of No Return*, an adaptation by Paul Osborn of the popular novel by J. P. Marquand, became the subject of a case history by Aline Louchheim, which was published in the *New York Times Magazine* on December 9, 1951, about a week before the show opened. The article traced the evolution of the set from Jo's reaction to the typed script to the final dress and technical rehearsals, which required last-minute changes in lighting and manipulation of the sets to accommodate the adjustments made by Henry (Hank) Potter, the director. Since the play reflects the soul-searching of its banker hero, played by Henry Fonda, as he surveys life, Jo had to find the means to go back and forth in time as effortlessly as possible. Jo's first solution was to use a painted transparent scrim depicting a street, which would be the transition from one scene in the past to the next, but as Louchheim would discover, nothing was really set until the very end:

> During the second week of the Boston run and again before the Nov. 27th opening in Philadelphia, Mielziner was on hand. The management had decided that the transitions from the present to the past were not satisfactory. Important changes in the direction and vast alterations in the script were constantly in work, so that actors, story, scenery and lighting could move together in a continuous flow. . . . Only the flexibility of the sets and the possibility of changing them with incredible speed allowed this and other drastic script changes in the last few weeks of out-of-town try-outs. And it was in turn, the very flexibility and ingenuity of the scenery which suggested such changes, all made in the interests of creating a continuous and fast-paced story flow.

Despite Louchheim's paean to his talents as a designer, Jo was less than happy with his experience working with Potter, feeling

JO'S SET FOR *FLIGHT INTO EGYPT* (1952) REPRESENTED THE INTERIOR OF A SEEDY CAIRO HOTEL AND CAUGHT THE HEAT AND DESPERATION CONVEYED IN THE SCRIPT. HE USED LIGHTING EXCLUSIVELY AS THE BRIDGE BETWEEN THE SCENES, WHICH WERE STRETCHED ACROSS THE STAGE. (ESTATE OF JO MIELZINER)

that he was misused by the director. There was a further problem with the production. The star had received letters complaining that a number of people in the audience found him inaudible. To an actor like Fonda, whose dedication to his craft bordered on the fanatical, it was unthinkable that it was his own fault. Jo was called in to survey the acoustics of the theatre as the possible culprit. After he attended a performance, during which he moved to a variety of seats around the theatre, he reported to Leland Hayward, the producer, that he could hear perfectly from every spot in the house despite being "slightly deaf in one ear." Jo suggested that George Izenour be called in to give his evaluation. Izenour pinpointed Jo's use of fabric-covered scenery as the cause of the problem. Because it apparently absorbed the sound of Fonda's voice in certain scenes, Izenour recommended that the scenery be sprayed with a noncombustible plastic coating to provide a harder-surfaced sounding board. John Harvey immediately began a search for the right product, found it, and the problem was solved satisfactorily for Fonda and his public.

In the new year of 1952, Jo started out with a dud. A musical called *A Month of Sundays*, it was produced by Carly Wharton with book and music by Burt Shevelove and Albert Selden. Based on *Excursion*, a play by Victor Wolfson, which was a modest hit of the 1936–37 season, it seemed at first glance seemed to be a natural for musicalization. It tells of a wayward Manhattan to Coney Island excursion boat, which was put out to sea by its retiring sea captain on what was supposed to be its final voyage. Instead of steering it to Coney Island, he headed it toward an island in the Caribbean. Elliot Norton, critic for the *Boston Post*, reviewed it on its tryout run and said, "Clumsily written and dubiously staged [it] never got away from the dock." After more tinkering in Philadelphia, *A Month of Sundays* was adjudged to be hopeless and sank before making it to the isle of Manhattan. Jo's antic set of the SS *Happiness* was, however, deemed the best element in the production.

Jo was to suffer another disappointment with *Flight into Egypt*, which opened in March. Relating the plight of a crippled refugee who is trying to obtain passage to America for himself and his family, a hope that is dashed because of the tight strictures against people with infirmities, the playwright George Tabori built within the space of one day the mounting anxiety of the family in their battle against corrupt and callous officials, who take the last of their money while offering worthless promises. Produced by Irene Selznick and directed by Elia Kazan, it should have been a wrenching experience for the audience, but turned out to be "curiously unmoving," reported Walter Kerr of the *Herald Tribune*. According to Selznick, Kazan and his wife, Molly, "sanitized" Tabori's political message and siphoned off its emotional impact so that it would politically be correct for the era. At that time, the Congressional Sub-Committee on Un-American Activities was in the midst of its anti-Communist witch hunt and was preparing to call Kazan to Washington. In Selznick's version of the events, Molly Kazan changed the play so it carried not a breath of political comment that could be used against her husband and consequently robbed it of its power. Although the critical comments appear to bear this out, it is also likely that certain public figures were looking under the rug for anything that could dirty Kazan's reputation. When he appeared before the Committee in private session, his testimony was considered a betrayal by many in his profession and he was denounced for it for many years.

The short run was another blow for Jo and the creative team. Jo was aware that there were currents undermining the success of *Flight into Egypt*, but he also railed against the Broadway hit/flop mentality. In a letter to Sharaff, he wrote, "That script had as much to say for itself as any that I have read for a number of years but even with that wonderful team, errors in casting, clarification, and editing proved fatal under our cruel and exacting system."

Fortunately, the end of the 1951–52 Broadway season ended on a happier note. Leland Hayward and Joshua Logan took a calculated risk in turning a mid-1930s light comedy, *Having Wonderful Time*, by Arthur Kober, into a musical, *Wish You Were Here.* When Harold Rome was brought into the project to write the words and music and Bob Mackintosh to design the costumes, the creative circle was very much to Jo's liking. The story, about the amatory adventures of a group of young city girls who go for a summer interlude from their dreary jobs as stenographers and telephone

SINCE MOST OF THE ACTION IN **WISH YOU WERE HERE** (1952) TAKES PLACE OUTDOORS, JOSH LOGAN INSISTED ON LOTS OF OUTDOORSY EFFECTS, SUCH AS A BASKETBALL COURT (WHICH EMERGED FROM THE STAGE FLOOR) AND A REAL SWIMMING POOL (WHICH WAS CUT INTO THE STAGE FLOOR). EACH WAS USED FOR ONLY A SCANT FEW MINUTES. IN DUE TIME, THE POOL BECAME THE FOCUS OF ALL THE PREPRODUCTION PUBLICITY. JO WARNED LOGAN AND LELAND HAYWARD THAT, YES, HE COULD DESIGN THE POOL, BUT IT WOULD HAVE TO BE PERMANENT, THUS PRECLUDING OUT-OF-TOWN TRYOUTS AND A TOUR. (LISA LARSEN PHOTOGRAPH, *LIFE* MAGAZINE/TIME WARNER INC.)

operators with hopes of finding husbands, was cast by Logan with young unknowns, a few of whom (Jack Cassidy, Larry Blyden, Florence Henderson, Reid Shelton, Tom Tryon, and Phyllis Newman) were destined not to remain unknown for long.

With out-of-town tryouts impossible, the show opened "cold" on Broadway—on June 25, 1952, one of the hottest days of the year. Although the New York critics were charmed and singled out Jo's tricky sets, which popped up from everywhere onstage, six of the seven reviews did not predict a long and healthy life for the musical. But Logan refused to close it. He returned to the theatre the following evening, sat through a performance, and began to revise the entire production in his head. In the next feverish days, within the framework of Jo's "fantastically lush production" (as he later called it), thus avoiding any expensive remakes of the scenery, he reworked the script and songs. Finally, he began a round of new rehearsals, during which he transmitted his exuberance and optimism to the downcast actors. Within a few weeks, word of mouth began pulling in customers, and after a few more weeks the show was selling out. The "flop" ran for 598 performances.

THE MISTY QUALITY OF THIS RENDERING (AND SUBSEQUENT ACTUAL SCENERY) FOR *THE GAMBLER* (1952) WAS ACHIEVED BY A SCRIM HUNG UPSTAGE (REAR OF SET) WITH THE RAILWAY CLOCK BEHIND IT. NOT SEEN WAS THE ACTOR WHO DELIVERED A LONG MONOLOGUE BEHIND THE SCRIM. JO CHASTENED HIMSELF FOR DESIGNING THE SET THIS WAY BECAUSE THE ACTOR FELT NO SENSE OF THE AUDIENCE AND WAS NOT HAPPY ABOUT IT. "BUT NEITHER IS THE SETTING OR A COSTUME GOOD IF THE ACTOR IS UNCOMFORTABLE," WROTE JO. "PART OF THE DESIGNER'S JOB IS TO GIVE THE PERFORMER EVERY PHYSICAL AND PSYCHOLOGICAL, AS WELL AS VISUAL, ASSISTANCE." (COURTESY OF THE ESTATE OF HILDA AND EDWARD KOOK)

For an October opening in the 1952–53 season, Jo and his staff spent the summer working on *The Gambler* by Ugo Betti, which had been translated and adapted by the actor Alfred Drake and the playwright Edward Eager. The gentlemen on the aisle were somewhat baffled by Betti's morality play on the themes of guilt and justice, love and marriage, good and evil, and a few other sins and virtues added in for good measure. Some of them hid their confusion by calling it Pirandellian, but despite its lofty aspirations and some good acting by Drake in the title role, *The Gambler* was the kind of play from which Broadway audiences traditionally back away.

The critics were split over Jo's contributions. Some thought his scenery, which was set on a revolving stage, was unduly complex for the drama, while others praised his inventiveness. The director of the play, Herman Shumlin, had the last word; in a postmortem letter, he wrote:

> The shooting is over, and we are the [ones who were] shot, but there is still time and space to tell you that you did a magnificent job. I told you before, but I want to say it again, I had to see it all together before I could really tell, and perhaps the best that could be said about the production is exactly that,—that you saw it, and drew it, and made it so that it was all together, a unity.

For Jo, these were sweet words indeed because he never wavered from his position that he always served the directors. Occasionally, when they were unsure of what they wanted, Jo's diplomacy and rare ability to strike to the core of a play, conjuring their best visual image, often persuaded directors to accept his decisions. Most of the time, he was right.

In the fall of 1952, John Harvey supervised the studio's move to the suite on the first floor of the Dakota. It fronted on the inner courtyard and was reached by a short flight of steps and through a dark wainscoted hall. The suite consisted of Jo's office, which he used for his drawing and painting and for meetings with his famous clients. Adjacent to his office was a large closetlike space, where, with Eddie Kook's help, he set up miniature (3-inch) Lekos (ellipsoidal spotlights), each equipped with a frame in which colored gels could be inserted and each controlled by a separate dimmer.

Opposite the lights Jo set up an easel and pin-up board on which he mounted samples of paints made for the scenery to test reactions under color. Not only did he test his colors, he invited the costume designers with whom he was collaborating on a show to use his setup so that they could see how their fabrics would appear against Jo's colors and under his lights. (Lucinda Ballard had access to the darkroom even when she was not working on a Mielziner-designed show.) Jo's secretary and assistants worked in the drafting room. As in most buildings of the Dakota vintage, there was a huge bathroom within the suite, where the staff kept the makings for coffee and tea and where eventually some of the office machines were installed. In the summer, Jo's office was cooled by a window air conditioner. Much later, he provided one for his staff.

Although Jo's secretaries continued to change almost every year and assistants came and went—with the notable exception of John Harvey—each learned the routine of the studio very quickly. Jo was not to be disturbed in the morning, while he drew and painted, and would take calls only from a specified list of people, which always included Bishop Sheen. Meetings were generally arranged in the afternoon, when one or more members of a given collaboration or the production stagehands would appear for consultation. Jo would present the preliminary ground plans and sketches, which could be tiny realizations of his ideas on yellow foolscap or larger drawings to quarter-inch scale on white paper. Once the concept was approved, he would quickly draw and paint a more developed set of plans. After yet more consultation with producers about the construction budget and with the directors on their final thoughts or instructions, Jo's finished designs would be turned over to Harvey, who might do the drafting himself, or more than likely, assign parts to the assistants. He would then build a three-dimensional model out of white construction board to give the idea of scale and location of the scenery and set pieces, which Jo would then present to the director. After Jo's colors had been tested under the lights, he would paint the drawings or elevations his assistants had made from his designs and these, together with the blueprints of the scenery and props, would then be delivered to the scenery house and the prop shop. If Jo had the time between shows or at the end of the season,

he would try to draw and paint finished renderings of the shows either to retain as a record or to give away as gifts. Occasionally, someone like Dorothy Rodgers would buy some of them.

Jo's routine was unvaried. The best word to describe it is controlled. Every step was ordered and reasoned and at every moment he was on top of the total process. Jo loved his work so much that he often resented intrusions, such as the de rigueur socializing that came with his position. He would rather stay in his studio and mix a martini for his staff than go to a cocktail party at the end of the day. Lucinda Ballard remembered that of all of the scene designers she had worked with on Broadway, no one was better prepared for or gave more attention to the productions than Jo Mielziner.

After the quick demise of *The Gambler* in early November of 1952, Jo did not have another show opening until February 19, 1953, when *Picnic*, by William Inge, came to Broadway under the auspices of Joshua Logan in collaboration with the Theatre Guild. Working on the show brought him in contact with Inge as a fresh young playwright from the Midwest who coincidentally happened to be his neighbor at the Dakota. Although they had met casually once or twice, their physical proximity in the building afforded unusual opportunities to discuss the play and Jo's designs inexhaustibly once the production got underway. Since *Picnic* was only Inge's second play (his first, *Come Back, Little Sheba*, had brought him instant recognition in a previous season) and he was a worrier by temperament, Inge was anxious about all aspects of the production.

William Inge worked in the earthy and almost always uncompromising realist tradition of the American stage. Taking from his Kansas background the homey events of life in rural, often suffocating towns along dusty highways, and choosing people of small moment in the family of man, he wrote truthful plays that could touch raw nerves. What might be considered ordinary or petty, he could make serious, even momentous.

When he had begun writing his play about what happens to a society of young, middle-aged, and old women when a muscular and sexually magnetic braggart invades their world, he wanted, with restraint, to expose the women's hopes and fears and the feminine vulnerability under their outward show of strength. His first

JO'S SINGLE SETTING FOR **PICNIC** (1953), THE SHARED BACKYARD CLOSE BY A GRAIN ELEVATOR AND RAILWAY STATIONS, CAPTURED ALL THE NUANCES OF A KANSAS LANDSCAPE WITHOUT UNNECESSARY DETAIL. THE PAINTED SCRIM BEHIND THE TWO HOUSES SAID IT ALL. THE TWO HOUSES, LOOKING WORN AND WEATHERBEATEN WITH THEIR SLIGHTLY SAGGING PORCHES, MIRRORED THE MELANCHOLY OF THE LOVELESS LIVES OF THEIR INHABITANTS. HIS PALE LIGHTING WASHED OVER THE HOUSES, MAKING THE KANSAS HEAT ALMOST PALPABLE. THE CRITICS APPRECIATED HIS EFFECTS, AND TWO ADMIRERS, PRODUCER BILLY ROSE AND PLAYWRIGHT ROBERT E. SHERWOOD, WROTE TO TELL JO THAT THEY FELT THE SET WAS ONE OF THE FINEST HE HAD EVER DESIGNED. (COURTESY OF JO ANN KIRCHMAIER)

against changing the ending, but in time was forced to retreat in the face of the opposition of Logan, the cast, and the out-of-town audiences. (Years later, he reworked the script for a second incarnation known as *Summer Brave*, restoring parts of his earlier script along with its ending. It was not a success.)

Josh Logan took liberties with Inge's script, as did Jo with his less than accurate conception for the side-by-side houses. Inge's boyhood home in Independence Kansas, was a solid, middle-class, two-story house with similar homes next door and in the vicinity. It had a back porch, but it was not nearly as dilapidated as Jo suggested in his setting. The changes were always made with the full acquiescence of or on the advice of the director.

With superb acting by Janice Rule, Ralph Meeker, Betty Field, Susan Strasberg, and Eileen Heckart (with Paul Newman in a small role), *Picnic* swept almost all the honors for the year. For Inge, it won the Pulitzer Prize, and the Drama Critics Circle Award. (Arthur Miller's *The Crucible* edged it out of a Tony.) The play was sent out on the road, made into a movie, and even inspired a musical, which never made it to Broadway.

The production played 477 performances on Broadway. Although Inge wanted Jo to design his next plays, *Dark at the Top of the Stairs* and *A Loss of Roses*, Jo's schedule prevented him from accepting these assignments.

Although Jo was adroit at designing realistic exteriors and interiors as he had done many times in his career, when he had a chance to design musicals, he rejoiced at the opportunity to stretch his art to the limits.

Noting the interest in all things French, particularly since a biography of Henri de Toulouse-Lautrec and the popular movie *Moulin Rouge* had appeared, Cy Feuer and Ernie Martin put together a musical not so much about Toulouse-Lautrec but about the Paris of his day, *Can-Can*. When their former collaborator on *Guys and Dolls*, Frank Loesser, demurred, Martin approached Cole Porter, who was more than receptive to the idea. Since Porter was interested in writing only the songs, the task of writing the book fell to Abe Burrows, who was also directing the show. Michael Kidd was assigned the choreography, Jo the scenery, and Motley, a group of three English designers, the costumes.

version of *Picnic*, entitled *The Front Porch*, had been a rambling and unfocused play. When Lawrence Langner of the Theatre Guild asked Inge to expand it, the script sprawled over six different sets and meandered to an inconclusive ending. With, perhaps, a touch of cunning, Langner suggested that Inge ask Josh Logan to direct the production of the new version, well aware of Logan's knack for shaping a script. The director forced a resistant Inge to cut and trim, to tighten and focus his play, including paring down the number of sets to one and making it the back, not the front, porch. Inge held out

Taking his inspiration from Toulouse-Lautrec and the age of the Impressionists, Jo designed the scenery as a series of poster-art paintings to dazzle the eye. He used bright colors and strong contrasts to create the dozen different scenes and curtains in the show. For one of the curtains, he re-created from memory a map of Paris from an aerial view that he had seen in the Louvre. For another scene, the Quatz' Arts Ball, Jo's staff assembled photographs of actual balls in Paris of the time. Staring at one of them, Jo asked for a magnifying glass and, much to his surprise, recognized a face in the crowd as belonging to his father, Leo! Jo woke up on May 8, 1953, to read the opening paragraphs from the review written by the *Herald Tribune*'s Walter Kerr:

THE MYTH PERSISTS THAT COLE PORTER WAS SO TAKEN BY JO'S RENDERING OF THE PARIS SKYLINE FOR **CAN-CAN** **(1953)** THAT HE WAS MOVED TO WRITE THE SONG "I LOVE PARIS," WHICH HE DID BEFORE THE BOOK AND THE REST OF THE MUSIC WERE WRITTEN—EVEN BEFORE JO HAD BEEN SIGNED TO DESIGN THE SHOW. (ROBERT L. B. TOBIN COLLECTION, THE MCNAY ART MUSEUM)

Let us pause this morning to pay tribute to Jo Mielziner. For the newest Cole Porter carnival, "Can-Can," which whipped flashily into the Shubert last night, Mr. Mielziner has dreamed up three or four of the most engaging and evocative sets of his career.

There is a garret with splintered windows which seems to soar right out over the Paris of 1893. There is an unlikely cabaret built into an underground laundry, with candles alight on every girder, and with the wash flapping fancifully overhead. There is a stunning rooftop on which lazy brick chimneys and drowsily tilting shutters lean toward the Eiffel Tower. And there are, in addition, a half dozen handsomely monochromatic effects—a blue map of Paris used as an act curtain, a reddish-brown Court of Assizes, and a mouldy green Bal de Paradis, which are almost as dazzling as the calculated stunners.

JO EVOKED THE NARROW STREETS AND HILLY STEPS IN THE MONTMARTRE SCENES OF *CAN-CAN*. (W. H. CRAIN COLLECTION, UNIVERSITY OF TEXAS THEATRE ARTS COLLECTION)

Can-Can, with its slender plot about a love affair between a staid judge and the beautiful proprietress of a dance hall was another Cole Porter hit. The show engendered a London edition and eventually a movie with Frank Sinatra.

While Jo was working on *Can-Can*, he was also designing *Me and Juliet*, his fifth Rodgers and Hammerstein musical, which he considered one of the most difficult assignments of his career. As they did for *Allegro*, Rodgers and Hammerstein wholly conceived *Me and Juliet* as a tribute to the theatre without reference to a previous literary source. Trying to avoid all the show-within-a-show clichés, they interwove a musical-in-progress with a strangely unaffecting love story between a singer in the chorus and an assistant stage manager. Because of the complexity of the scenery and what they foresaw as a difficult break-in period for the production, Rodgers and Hammerstein, acting as their own producers, began the pre-Broadway trials not in nearby New Haven but in Cleveland, at the old Hanna Theatre, which had a larger stage for the complicated scenery. Despite the show's sprightly dances by Robert Alton and the usual fast-paced direction by George Abbott, the out-of-town reviews were not raves (except for Jo's scenery). Yet Rodgers and Hammerstein had a ten-month advance in ticket sales and decided to take it into New York in May of 1953 to brave the critics. Predictably, the Broadway critical contingent was disappointed.

Me and Juliet had a physically monumental set. For the first time in his designing career, Jo had to eschew the usual canvas and lumber of scenery and use aluminum and steel as well as specially engineered machinery to effect his wizardry. While it was being installed in the Hanna Theatre, the old gridiron began to sag under the weight of all the heavy scenery. Fearing a repetition of his difficulties at the Imperial Theatre during the installation of *Annie Get Your Gun* in New York, when he was blamed for overloading the stage structure, Jo quickly contacted Jules Hall, the production flyman in New York, and had him flown to Cleveland to inspect the problems and report to him. On the way to the airport, Warren Clymer, Jo's assistant, armed with the plans, briefed Hall about the scenery. After the necessary adjustments were made and calm was restored, the out-of-town performances continued.

The painting of the sets also required special handling. Jo's instructions to the scene shop directed them to execute all the backstage effects in meticulously realistic detail while "free painting" should be employed in the show within the show. Irene Sharaff had to design off- and onstage costumes for the big cast, rounding out the reality-illusion aspect of the production. Calling it a "stunning masquerade," Brooks Atkinson of the *Times* rightly sensed that everyone connected with the creation of the show was unembarrassedly stage-struck. After a healthy, if not outstanding, run *Me and Juliet* was rarely heard of again.

After a summer hiatus in Hawaii, Jo left Jean, Neil, and Jennifer (Michael was at home in summer camp) with her Macintyre relatives in late July of 1953 to return to work on *Tea and Sympathy* by Robert Anderson, a young playwright whom he had befriended and promoted. Audrey Wood, the agent who was handling the script, was not convinced that a serious play about a sensitive prep school boy fighting to assert his sexual identity among his brutish peers and authority figures would attract a producer. But the play caught the eye of Roger L. Stevens, a newcomer in the ranks of Broadway producers. After having made a fortune in real estate, Stevens had indulged himself in his avocation of the theatre and, in 1949, had transferred to Broadway a production of *Twelfth Night* that he had seen at the University of Michigan. Robert Sherwood shared Stevens's enthusiasm for Anderson's play, urging its production on his fellow members of the Playwrights Company.

Anderson's play had also caught the eye of Elia Kazan because his wife, Molly, had taken a personal interest in fostering Anderson's talents. Kazan agreed to direct it. When Anderson sent his play to the movie star Deborah Kerr, he was overjoyed by her enthusiasm, but Kazan was skeptical that Kerr could or would withstand the rigors of the Broadway process. She was so eager to do the play that she astonished everyone by agreeing to audition for Kazan. Kerr, Kazan was to discover, was not a stereotypical Hollywood actress; she had come up through the ranks on the English stage. For Anderson's female lead, she was perfect, evincing, as Kazan described it, an "immaculate delicacy." Without Kerr, the play might have lapsed into mawkishness; with her, everything was believable.

ME AND JULIET (1953), A "BACKSTAGE" SHOW (DESCRIBED BY SOME AS RODGERS AND HAMMERSTEIN'S VALENTINE TO THE THEATRE), REQUIRED TWELVE DIFFERENT SCENES. TO EFFECT THE CHANGES, JO HAD TO USE FIVE GIANT TRACKS WITH SYNCHRONIZED MOTORS HIGH ABOVE THE STAGE IN THE FLY LOFT TO MOVE THE HEAVY SCENERY IN FULL VIEW OF THE AUDIENCE. HE DESIGNED A FAKE BACKSTAGE SCENE PAINTED ON DROP CURTAINS COMPLETE WITH DUMMY LAMPS, LIGHT BRIDGE, AND EQUIPMENT, ALL SEEMINGLY "WORKED" BY ACTORS PLAYING STAGEHANDS FOR THE FAKE MUSICAL PLAYING ONSTAGE. (*TOP:* COURTESY OF THE RODGERS AND HAMMERSTEIN ORGANIZATION; *BOTTOM:* COURTESY OF JULES FISHER)

Anderson was overjoyed to have Jo doing the scenery and promptly invited him to visit Exeter, his own prep school in New England, to imbibe the atmosphere of the place and see one of the dormitories. Because it was a "small" play in terms of its close and often tense interactions among the characters, Kazan explained to Jo that he wanted a setting that would allow "close-ups" in the cinematic sense. He even sketched a ground plan, indicating dimensions and scale. Jo understood. Anderson was eternally grateful to Jo for his scenic contribution to the overall success of the play, which became one of the Playwrights Company's most lucrative productions.

Anderson also got to know Jo's brother Kenneth when he went to Hollywood to write the screen version of *Tea and Sympathy*. As the head of the story department at MGM, Ken had quickly accepted Anderson's screenplay.

Jo's final design for 1953 was for *Kind Sir*, a comedy by Norman Krasna, produced and directed by Joshua Logan, which even the legendary talents of Mary Martin and Charles Boyer could not rescue from the poisoned barbs of the New York critics. When the play opened in early November of 1953, Jo confessed to John Mason Brown that when he was first sent the script, he "begged Josh to let me do a setting made up of spun sugar, selected gossamer wings, and eliminate both a ceiling and a floor." Logan, of course, was not amused. The play—which was about an actress

and her lover (played by Boyer), who pretends that he is married in order to avoid the ensnarement of matrimony—was constantly being rewritten out of town, not only by Logan and the playwright, but apparently by Martin's husband, Richard Halliday. (Even Jo sent his two cents' worth to Logan.) Since playwright Norman Krasna had spent many years of his career as a screenwriter in Hollywood, he later converted *Kind Sir* into a movie vehicle for Ingrid Bergman and Cary Grant, retitled *Indiscreet*.

Jo's thirtieth year as a professional designer had been his best ever; his income topped $85,000, more than half of which had to cover his studio expenses. By the end of 1953, there were nine Mielziner-designed shows on Broadway: *Can-Can, Guys and Dolls, Kind Sir, Me and Juliet, Picnic, South Pacific, Tea and Sympathy, The King and I,* and *Wish You Were Here,* all of them paying him a weekly royalty. Added to this income were his share of the profits of Pete Feller's National Scenery Service and paybacks from his small investments in some of the hits. With the possible exception of Don Oenslager, no stage designer had ever made more money from his profession than Jo up to that time.

For the rest of the 1953–54 season, Jo designed only one more show, *By the Beautiful Sea,* produced by Robert Fryer and Lawrence Carr. Fryer had been the co-producer with George Abbott of *A Tree Grows in Brooklyn*. Since *By the Beautiful Sea* had a turn-of-the-century

Coney Island setting like *A Tree Grows in Brooklyn*, Jo was becoming very expert in designing scenes of that time and place. From the time he had received the outline for the musical, which was written by Herbert and Dorothy Fields with composer Burton Lane, he had doubts about it, which he confided to Lane. But Jo was sufficiently experienced in the ways of musicals en route to Broadway to know that there would be chances to fix the weaknesses. When Lane withdrew as composer, he was replaced by Arthur Schwartz, who had worked on *A Tree Grows in Brooklyn* and on a number of revues that Jo had designed.

By the Beautiful Sea, which opened on April 8, 1954, starred Shirley Booth, and it had Irene Sharaff's costumes, Mielziner's sets, and Helen Tamiris's choreography. But the show lacked a solid book and score and barely lasted the year. Sandwiched between *By the Beautiful Sea* and another musical, *Fanny*, which was on his fall 1954 agenda, Jo was designing a second play by Robert Anderson,

All Summer Long. The play, a mood piece, had first appeared in January 1953 at the Arena Stage in Washington, D.C., which was then emerging as one of the nation's first-rate regional theatres. Since it had been originally presented in the round with only a whisper of scenery, it had to undergo a complete metamorphosis to a Broadway proscenium-stage production. Anderson insisted not only on having Jo but wanted Alan Schneider, who had originally directed the show at the Arena Stage, to stage the New York production, presented by the Playwrights Company. Jo and Alan had worked together at Catholic University in a production, *The Real McCoy*, in 1949.

Adapted from a novel, Donald Wetzel's *A Wreath and a Curse*, Anderson's play about a family in the Midwest living on a house near a steadily rising river was told in eight scenes, which were set both inside and outside the house. The family's eleven-year-old son tries in vain to build a retaining wall all summer long, while the

adults suffer from a case of severe ennui. Inevitably, the river takes the house and the family flees to higher ground. Schneider, who ultimately preferred the Arena Stage setting, admitted that he had made no contribution to design except to comment that Jo had made the kitchen space too small and had the door opening the wrong way for the action he was planning. "With a couple of strokes of his drawing pencil," he wrote, "Jo fixed both the kitchen and the door." Just before the show's Washington tryout, Jo was struck by the idea that his scenery was not serving the play. He took Anderson aside and said, "I'm afraid I've ruined your play for you." But the critics, who liked the evocative setting and lighting, disagreed. Still, noting that *All Summer Long* was awash in symbolism, the critics were unenthusiastic and the show's run trickled out.

When Jo was designing *Jeb* in 1946, he had met David Merrick, who had apprenticed himself to producer Herman Shumlin to learn the art and business of producing. Ambitious, trained as a lawyer in his native St. Louis, Merrick hit upon the idea of turning Marcel Pagnol's 1930s film trilogy *Marius, Fanny*, and *César*, about life and love on the Marseilles waterfront, into a big musical. After beginning negotiations with Pagnol in 1950, he involved Joshua Logan in the project, and while juggling the negotiations, he asked Jo to design the show and help him deal with Logan. (The latter had wanted to take the entire project to Rodgers and Hammerstein, but they insisted that if they were to write it, they would also want to produce it.) Logan came to co-produce the show with Merrick as well as direct it. Harold Rome provided the music and lyrics, and S. N. Behrman collaborated on the book. *Fanny* would star Ezio Pinza and Walter Slezak.

The entire collaboration, although seemingly made in heaven, was explosive, particularly when Logan's cure for the many weaknesses of the book was to expand and expand the production until it seemed like a balloon ready to burst. As a result, *Fanny* was an overlong and overproduced show that complicated the simple tale of the love of an old man for his young wife and the son who was not his. Jo believed that his friend was fundamentally a director and that directing was the thing he did best—whenever Josh heaped producing and writing on his plate, he always came close to nearly choking on the meal. In writing to the beleaguered Behrman after the opening, Jo commented: "I think it is no reflection on his talent to say that like the titans of the Renaissance, they all benefited from the thoughtful and appreciative editing and advice of their very gifted patrons."

Fanny opened on November 5, 1954, and had a run of 888 performances, well served and saved by the box office appeal of Pinza and Slezak. Merrick's own resolve to turn it around cannot be discounted. His brilliant publicist Harvey Sabinson came up with a series of stunts to keep attention focused on the show, and eventually the show began to make money. Never a man to show great loyalty to anyone on his way to the top, Merrick nonetheless harbored some gratitude to Jo and continued to give him assignments when everyone else seemed to have forgotten him.

For many years, Jo's permanent staff consisted of himself, John Harvey, and a secretary. Always needing office help, he enlisted a program at Bennington College, in Vermont, which placed students for ten weeks in a work-study environment. The first students arrived in 1950, and others followed until 1968. Jo used them to file, make up catalogue cards, read scripts, chase down pictures and books at the New York Public Library, paste clippings into his scrapbooks, and do a dozen other tasks around the studio. At the beginning, Jo did not pay them but eventually he gave them $25 per week for carfare and lunch money. At least one of them became genuinely involved in scene design as a career, but the rest moved on to other interests.

To augment his studio staff, Jo hired people who had previous experience in designing or who had received extensive training. With very few exceptions, they had all passed their union exams or were preparing for them while they worked for Jo. When they needed help in perfecting their own techniques, Jo recommended

IN 1956, TWO YEARS AFTER ITS BROADWAY OPENING, **FANNY** WENT TO LONDON. TO ADAPT HIS NEW YORK SETS TO THE DRURY LANE'S PHYSICAL REQUIREMENTS, JO MADE THE THEATRE'S DEEP BACKSTAGE AND HIGH PROSCENIUM THE BACKDROP FOR THE HARBOR SCENE LARGER IN SCALE AND REVERSED THE POSITION OF THE SHIP'S BOOM FROM THE WAY IT HAD BEEN IN NEW YORK. (*TOP:* W. H. CRAIN COLLECTION, UNIVERSITY OF TEXAS THEATRE ARTS COLLECTION; *LEFT:* COURTESY OF IAN DOW)

A SIXTIETH BIRTHDAY PARTY FOR ROBERT EDMOND JONES ORGANIZED BY JO AND EDDIE KOOK, 1947. **1)** JOHN MASON BROWN (CRITIC); **2)** ROBERT BARNHART (SCENE DESIGNER); **3)** RAYMOND SOVEY (SCENE DESIGNER); **4)** WALTER HUSTON (ACTOR AND JONES'S BROTHER-IN-LAW); **5)** HENRY WEISS (MANUFACTURER OF STAGE CURTAINS AND DRAPERIES); **6)** STANLEY MCCANDLESS (LIGHTING EXPERT); **7)** JOHN HARVEY (MIELZINER'S LONG-TIME DESIGN ASSISTANT); **8)** DONALD OENSLAGER (SCENE DESIGNER); **9)** MAC WEISS (MANUFACTURER OF STAGE CURTAINS AND DRAPERIES); **10)** ALBIE MCDONALD AND **11)** BERNIE MCDONALD (BUILDERS OF STAGE SETS); **12)** BRAD ASHWORTH (SCENE PAINTER); **13)** MARC CONNELLY (PLAYWRIGHT); **14)** ROBERT BERGMAN (PAINTER AND HEAD OF SCENE STUDIO); **15)** GEORGE SCHAFF (JONES'S LONG-TIME MASTER STAGE ELECTRICIAN); **16)** NORMAN BEL GEDDES (SCENE DESIGNER); **17)** LEE SIMONSON (SCENE DESIGNER); **18)** ARTHUR SEGAL (HEAD OF SCENE STUDIO); **19)** JO MIELZINER; **20)** EDDIE KOOK; **21)** ROBERT EDMOND JONES; **22)** EUGENE O'NEILL; **23)** ARTHUR HOPKINS (PRODUCER). (COURTESY OF THE ESTATE OF HILDA AND EDWARD KOOK)

Kook had seen Ming's portfolio of student designs and also his paintings in watercolor and gouache. Sensing a talent out of the ordinary, Eddie called Jo on the spot and advised him to take a look at Ming's work. In November, Jo suggested the informal arrangement whereby Ming would do odd jobs around the office in exchange for the privilege of observing Jo's studio operations and picking up practical training. Ming eventually began to lend a hand to John Harvey in drafting ground plans and to Warren Clymer in searching for props. When it became apparent to everyone that Ming had significant contributions to make, John gave him more meaningful work and Jo began to pay him for it. Ming's first real test came in the drafting of the scenery for *Cat on a Hot Tin Roof.* He was assigned the drafting of the bar, which was especially difficult because it had to rest on the tilted stage that Jo had designed. When his drawing was given to Joe Lynn, the master prop man, to build, Joe told him that it could not have been improved upon. To reward him for his diligence, Jo listed Ming as "Assistant to the Designer."

For the next four years, during which Ming passed the union examinations, the young designer worked on more than a dozen Mielziner productions. During several of the studio's busiest periods, he was entrusted not only with the drafting but also with completing the actual painting of some of the elevations, something that Jo had only rarely allowed his assistants to do. After years of total immersion in the Mielziner style, Ming assisted in the studios of several of the leading designers of the time, but he continued to assist Jo sporadically. When, finally, both Jo and Ming knew when it was time for him to strike out on his own, and he left the Dakota studio for good, he did not forget his mentor. In Ming Cho Lee's own work, designs composed of many layers of influence, there remains more than a trace of Jo Mielziner. They remained longtime friends and colleagues.

On November 26, 1954, Jo was notified of the death of Robert Edmond Jones. No one had seen much of Jones in his last years; he had been ill and picked few productions that he wanted to do, wrote a little, and prepared his drawings and designs for an exhibition at Harvard. But the few times that he came out of his retreat in his last decade he showed that he had not lost his touch.

that they sign up for a course given by the Broadway designer Lester Polakov, who had set up a school in 1958 that emphasized practical training. In the fall of 1954, Jo broke his own precedent when he allowed a talented young Chinese student named Ming Cho Lee to become an unofficial and unpaid apprentice. As usual, it was Eddie Kook who was the matchmaker; while giving a graduate seminar at the University of California at Los Angeles, in 1954,

Jo was infuriated by the lack of attention given to Jones's passing and was determined that the theatrical community pay fit tribute to the man who had reinvented scene design for the American theatre. Early in December, with the help of Eddie Kook and a few friends, he organized a memorial service to be held in the Plymouth Theatre, on whose stage so many of Bobby's designs came to life during his peak years. On Sunday afternoon, December 12, 1954, which would have been Jones's sixty-sixth birthday, Jo led the tribute to Bobby and introduced the speakers: Walter Abel, Walter Hampden, Brian Aherne, John Mason Brown, and others.

When Brooks Atkinson of *The New York Times* found out about the memorial tribute, he asked Jo to write a short piece about Jones for the newspaper. In it, Jo told about his personal introduction to the work of Robert Edmond Jones and conveyed the force of Jones's inspiration.

> *His personal fire and enthusiasm were catching. He was violent in his reactions, never neutral, never cold—either utterly rejecting and despising something which he considered below par or being so exalted and burning with the fever of accomplishment that he lifted mediocre talents around him to a high level of craftsmanship.*

Eventually, there was a book written about Jones, which Jo publicly praised but privately condemned for not reflecting more of the man. In the book, published in 1958, the critic John Mason Brown summed up best what ultimately were the contributions of Robert Edmond Jones to the American theatre.

> *His settings were not reproductions of reality. They were extensions of it. They had exaltation in them, too. Although the mood and meaning of a play lived in them, they lived a life of their own. This is why Bobby's sketches have outlasted the productions for which they were made and will continue to do so. The dream that was his walks in them, as summoning as ever, and the more welcome and needed in today's almost dreamless theatre, as reminders of what the theatre can be.*

Jo was one of several of Jones's friends and colleagues who collected the master's designs for personal reasons. Perhaps it was to

remind them that but for his leadership and vision they would all be struggling to find a focus and an acceptance of a new and daring role for the theatrical designer .

Also in November of 1954, Jo wrote to Robert Downing, his friend and favorite stage manager, about anticipated difficulties with the upcoming Cole Porter musical *Silk Stockings*, another Feuer and Martin production. "At this point in the game," Jo confided, "I feel that *Silk Stockings* will be like so many musicals, having the holes darned and the runs patched." But he could not at that time predict the unusual turmoil surrounding its genesis. When the idea of basing a musical on the elegant Ernst Lubitsch movie *Ninotchka*,

JO FELL BACK ON HIS TRIED-AND-TRUE FORMULA OF PROVIDING PARTIAL SETS AGAINST A SERIES OF DROPS AS THE SCENERY FOR **SILK STOCKINGS** (1955). THE RUSSIAN COMMISSAR'S OFFICE (SHOWN) WAS SET WITHIN A RED (WHAT ELSE?) FALSE PROSCENIUM AND WAS DOMINATED BY A HUGE CHANDELIER AND AN OUTSIZED PORTRAIT OF AN ANONYMOUS RUSSIAN OFFICIAL. (COURTESY OF PAUL STIGA)

which had starred Greta Garbo in the late thirties, came to the producers, they began to assemble the group of people who were responsible for most of their past successes: George Kaufman to write the book and direct, Jo to design the show, and Lucinda Ballard and Bob Mackintosh to design the costumes of the enormous cast. The ballet dancemaster Eugene Loring, who had few Broadway credits, was their curious choice for choreographer.

Kaufman, who was sharing the authorship of the book with his wife Leueen McGrath, updated and Americanized the original story, but the basic situation of the movie—Capitalist Boy meets Communist Girl, Capitalist Boy loses Communist Girl, Capitalist Boy gets Communist Girl—remained intact. Jo designed a dozen sets, interiors and exteriors, that ranged from Paris to Moscow. The cast, headed by Don Ameche and Hildegard Neff, could not have been better, but Kaufman did not like the show in its Philadelphia tryout and recommended to Feuer and Martin that they close it forthwith—a judgment they did not want to hear. Instead, they called in Abe Burrows, who reluctantly agreed to help rewrite the script with Kaufman and his wife. What happened next is subject to various interpretations. Either Kaufman was forced from the show or he left voluntarily after a negotiated settlement. To quote Louis Kronenberger, "whoever would have chronicled the road tryout of *Silk Stockings* needed the credentials of a war correspondent." The out-of-town tryout of the show lengthened to thirteen weeks and Cy Feuer took over as director. Determined not to be included among the bad guys or to burn any bridges behind him, Jo wrote to the Kaufmans:

> The situation is embarrassing for me because I am under contract to the management who give me very rigid instructions which I am not at liberty to disregard, and in so many instances, the result is that I appear to be ignoring your personal requests and desires. I hope you will realize that I am not a free agent in this position. I only hope that the final result will be a satisfactory and happy one for us all. Please forgive me if I have been amiss or inconsiderate in the handling of this situation.

Responding to Jo's courteous note, Kaufman wrote to say that he understood. Jo was not at all sanguine about the show's prospects in New York, but much to his surprise, most of the critics liked the show with one or two caveats. *Silk Stockings* was a very profitable assignment for Jo. He had received about $10,000 in fees and a small weekly royalty.

During the turmoil surrounding *Silk Stockings*, in December of 1954 Jo received a call from Elia Kazan, who had just received a new script from Tennessee Williams that he wanted Jo to read. Kazan wanted to set a date when they could discuss designing *Cat on a Hot Tin Roof* in the comfort of their Connecticut retreats. Jo was particularly pleased about the assignment because he had not been offered Williams's *The Rose Tattoo*, which had followed *Summer and Smoke* to Broadway. But Jo had also felt compelled to withdraw from Williams's next play, *Camino Real*. In writing to the playwright to tell him of his intention to bow out, he told him that his schedule simply became too crowded to continue his work on it. The real reason had been that Williams did not like Jo's visual conception for his surrealistic play. (Lemuel Ayers was chosen to replace Jo and he provided "a lugubrious realistic set" in Kazan's words.) In a curiously un-Mielziner gesture, Jo included one of his designs for *Camino Real* in his book *Designing for the Theatre*, as if to prove that *his* was the sounder visual interpretation.

Although Williams eventually accepted Jo's scheme for *Cat on a Hot Tin Roof*, there is some reason to believe that he was not entirely happy with it either. As if to forestall any future contretemps over his ideas for the design, the playwright wrote out a densely typed page-and-a-half description, "Notes for the Designer," which he sent to Kazan and Jo. Not content to describe the room where almost all the action of the play takes place, he discoursed upon the entire house, giving it a history, peopling it with former owners, and evoking its background in the Mississippi Delta. He described it as if it were another character in the play, which indeed it was. He detailed its colors, its textures, the design of its furniture, the windows and doors, even how it looked against the sky above it.

When Jo read Williams's notes as well as the script, he was enthralled. A few months before the play opened, he wrote to the playwright in New York, "You have no idea, Tennessee, how exciting this is to work on. This makes up for months and months of

THE DESIGN FOR THE BED-
SITTING ROOM IN *CAT ON
A HOT TIN ROOF* (1955)
REPRESENTED JO AT HIS BEST.
NOTHING IN THIS RENDER-
ING (FAITHFULLY REPRO-
DUCED IN THE ACTUAL STAGE
SET) WAS SUPERFLUOUS, YET
ITS ECONOMY PERFECTLY
SUITED THE LUSHNESS OF
TENNESSEE WILLIAMS'S PLOT
AND DIALOGUE. (COURTESY
OF ELIA KAZAN)

slaving over trivia." Many years later, when Henry Hewes and Eddie Kook decided to write a book about how scene designers evolve their ideas, Jo gave them a long interview on how his designs for *Cat on a Hot Tin Roof* took shape from the first discussion to the actual production. As was usual in his method, he told them, he looked for the defining moment in the script to give him the visual key to the design. It was, he felt, the vulgar elephant joke that Big Daddy tells to his assembled family. Because he knew that Kazan was not going "to pussyfoot with it," he thought to himself, "if the old man is going to tell this story let him work right down not to the footlights but out beyond," an idea that gave Jo the notion of thrusting the stage out into the audience so that the story would have even greater impact. He devised a raked floor jutting out into the audience beyond the proscenium, which angled the set and freed it from the verticality of the proscenium. To complete the feeling, he floated a ceiling overhead that reversed the angle of the floor and took the eye to the rear of the stage. Kazan approved but warned that Williams might not.

Picking clues from the playwright's notes to him, Jo then decided on a minimum amount of interior decor in what Williams had described as "Victorian with a touch of the Far East." The bed dominated the room and was built to Jo's bentwood design and stained in the style of "spider rococo," for an Oriental look. The Victorian touch was in the carpet, which was actually hand painted and distressed to look "faded and almost mildewed." The only other important piece of furniture on the set was the bar that Ming Cho Lee had to draft so carefully. In keeping with Williams's description of walls that dissolved "mysteriously into the air below the ceiling," Jo designed nonexistent walls that were broken by strips of material hung to look like the columns of a Southern mansion. Behind them he placed a drop onto which he projected jalousies, moonlight, fireworks, and a storm. Although simple in concept, the set was difficult to construct and paint and even more difficult to light, requiring about double the number of instruments that were normally used in a single-set production.

Cat on a Hot Tin Roof was produced by the Playwrights Company, which was not having an easy time of it during the fifties. The company manager, Victor Samrock, agreed only reluctantly to give up the six or eight seats that had to be sacrificed for Jo's thrust stage. The play opened in Philadelphia, with Barbara Bel Geddes, Ben Gazzara, and Burl Ives in the leading roles, and riding upon the encouraging reception by the Philadelphia critics it arrived in New York already surrounded by an aura of success. The New York critics were enthusiastic; Brooks Atkinson of the *Times* called the play Williams's finest. Whatever reservations the playwright may have had about the set, they were largely erased by the reception of his play. It ran for a year on Broadway and another year on the road. Though London producers were not immediately interested in the play, Peter Brook did a production of it in Paris.

Early in 1955, Harry Cohn, the Columbia Studio head, called Joshua Logan to ask him to direct the film version of Inge's *Picnic.* Logan immediately called Jo to ask *him* whether he would be interested in working on the design of the movie. If nothing else, he implied, it would constitute a well-paid vacation from the Broadway hurly-burly. (Possibly the director, recovering from a bout with depression, needed Jo around to give him moral support.) The fee for three weeks' work would be a handsome $13,500. Jo agreed to do it.

On March 27, 1955, a cold, blustery Sunday, Jo flew out of New York into his Hollywood adventure. He decided to keep a diary of his experiences. Met at the airport by a chauffeured limousine in the usual Hollywood manner, he was driven to his brother Kenneth's home, where he was to stay for the next three weeks. At the studio, Jo was given more Hollywood red-carpet treatment by the head of the studio's art department. He was introduced to the official art director of the picture, William Flannery, who professed to be somewhat confused about Jo's duties and the credits on the picture. After Jo reassured him that he was not at all concerned about the credits but only wanted to learn the movie business, Flannery became more relaxed and cooperative. When Jo asked the head of the art department for a drawing board and art supplies, he was taken aback: "Mr. Mielziner, you don't intend to do any drawings, do you?" Jo patiently explained that yes, he planned to do the drawing because that was the way he expressed himself. The art director replied, "Well, of course, we have fine specialists here whose job it is to render. All you have to do is tell them what you want, and they will carry it out." Jo wrote in his journal: "Well, I made it pretty firm and clear that if I had thought it was possible to do good designing by dictation I would have bought a Dictaphone 30 years ago." Eventually, through the intervention of the producer of the picture, Jo was given an office (away from the art department) and all the supplies he needed, but only after everyone agreed that he would show his work only to Logan. Also during his first week, Jo received a visit from the head of the association of art directors, which was Hollywood's equivalent of United Scenic Artists. The official tried to pressure Jo into joining the union and only after Jo explained that his entire tenure in Hollywood would be three weeks and that he was not replacing the nominal art director did he retreat. (In view of later events, not joining the union was a short-sighted decision.)

Jo worked over the script, composing a nontechnical explanation of how color should be handled in the movie. He made sketches of scenes that reflected the discussions he was having with Logan. Finally, he met with James Wong Howe, the celebrated cinematographer whom Jo remembered meeting some twenty-one years before when Ken was an actor-director for Fox and Wong was a fledgling cameraman. They greeted each other warmly and Howe expressed his appreciation for Jo's ideas on lighting, composition, and color, which he had read.

Jo was never able to shake his discomfort in working in a strange room with unfamiliar materials and in a complex medium, but he felt that his ideas would be useful. On April 14, he and Logan and a contingent of technicians left for the film's location in Halstead, Kansas, where they chose the locales for each scene. A few days later, he flew to New York, returning to his familiar drawing board in his comfortable studio the following morning. He also sat down and wrote a letter to Freddie Kohlmar, the producer of *Picnic*, thanking him for his courtesy and encouragement and predicting that the movie would be a big success. And he wrote to Jimmy Wong Howe, continuing to offer advice on colors to use in lighting to enhance skin tones and to create moods and effects. He was gratified that Howe made use of his suggestions in the film. From Hollywood, Logan wrote affirming that Jo was "part of this picture." All in all, it had been an interesting experience for Jo, which he described to Kate Drain Lawson in a letter a few months later:

> As you know, I think I am the only designer who hasn't been [lured into a picture job] after all these years. But one thing frightens me about pictures and that is this terrible passion for decentralization, or rather, departmentalization. I think the only chance for a designer is to come out on a special job and a special salary with special rules and special privileges. I find most of the art directors rather frightened people who sit behind executive desks and look mournfully at the dry brushes and unsharpened pencils. Not for me for any amount of money! If I do it, I will come out and draw, even if it breaks rules.

He admitted to a reporter for the *St. Louis Dispatch* that what he disliked most about his film experience was seeing the lack of control that the designer had over his work. If he had been a young man just starting out, he said, he would have become a cinematographer rather than an art director.

For his three weeks of frustration, Jo and Bill Flannery received Academy Awards for "Best Achievement in Art Direction" in a color film. Jo thought his Oscar was a lousy piece of sculpture and sometimes used it as a doorstop. After his experience with *Picnic*, he decided that he would never make another movie. Much later in his life, when he was no longer getting Broadway assignments, he changed his mind and hoped that someone would ask him to do a film, but no one did.

After his Hollywood sojourn, Jo went to Europe without Jean, who preferred to remain in New York. Instead of his usual restful ocean voyage, he flew to Europe, met the Kazans in Istanbul for a few days, and returned with them to New York on the USS *Constitution*. He was happy to find Jean, "looking beautiful and fresh and rested," waiting for him at the dock. He was eager to return to work on his fall agenda, which included three shows.

Island of Goats, which opened on October 4, 1955, was written by Ugo Betti and closed in less than a week. In general, American audiences have been inhospitable to modern Italian plays, of which Betti's work and the plays of Luigi Pirandello were part of a long succession. According to Peter Glenville, *Island of Goats*, which he directed, contained all the ingredients for disaster. The cast was wrong, he was not the best director for it, and Broadway was not the right place for the production. A drama heavy with symbolism, it tells of three women living on a lonely island in the Mediterranean when a charming tramp (played by the English actor Laurence Harvey in his "unfortunate debut") drops into their midst, seduces each of them, and winds up trapped in their well for his misdeeds. For it, Jo designed a massive and gloomy setting, that swallowed up the play and the actors. He was not the right designer for it either.

If Italian plays are hard nuts to crack on Broadway, audiences seem to have a slightly easier time with adaptations and translations of French plays. During the fifties, for instance, they reacted with kindness and sometimes downright enthusiasm to the plays of Jean Anouilh and Jean Giraudoux, particularly when they were accompanied by big-star casts. Anouilh's play about Joan of Arc, *L'Alouette*, was adapted by Lillian Hellman as *The Lark*. It was to star Julie Harris, who possessed the gift to astound with the honesty of her portrayals. For *The Lark*, Harris did her homework on the life of St. Joan, even reading the transcripts of the original trial records.

The play was directed by Joseph Anthony, one of a number of directors who had also come out of the Actors Studio. With a gentility of nature very similar to Jo's, he worked well with the designer and they collaborated on four more productions in the ensuing years. Incidental music for the production was to be written by Leonard Bernstein, and Alvin Colt was set to do the costumes.

In the play, Joan of Arc's life is told in flashback in brief scenes, and rather than repeat the difficulties that he experienced in

FOR ***THE LARK*** (1955), JO DESIGNED A SERIES OF LOW PLATFORMS THAT WERE PLACED RANDOMLY AGAINST THE CYCLORAMA, A THIN MUSLIN CURTAIN STRETCHED ON A FRAME AT THE REAR OF THE SET. THE FRONT SIDE OF THE CYCLORAMA WAS NEUTRAL AND THE BACK SIDE PAINTED. WHEN LIGHTS WERE TRAINED ON THE LOWER HALF FROM BACKSTAGE, PRISON WINDOWS WERE OUTLINED FOR ONE SCENE; LIGHTS TRAINED ON THE UPPER HALF FOR ANOTHER SCENE REVEALED A ROSE WINDOW. JO PROJECTED THE FLEUR-DE-LIS, FRANCE'S EMBLEM (RIGHT), ON THE FRONT OF THE CYCLORAMA TO CREATE THE THRONE ROOM. THE BRILLIANT "MIELZINER BLUE" OF THE ACTUAL SET HAS FADED CONSIDERABLY IN THIS ORIGINAL PAINTING. (COURTESY OF THE ESTATE OF HILDA AND EDWARD KOOK)

Maxwell Anderson's *Anne of the Thousand Days*, Jo began by eliminating all realistic and solid scenery. Whenever a realistic prop was needed, it could be brought onstage swiftly and just as swiftly removed. The actors moved around the stage, up and down the platforms, to suggest changes of locale, always playing within Jo's lights. All the other changes were effected solely by lights, more than two hundred of them hanging above, around, and in front of the stage. Although relatively simple in concept, the lighting and projections were difficult to accomplish; at that time stage electricians had to make all changes manually.

AT LEFT IS ANOTHER SCENE FROM *THE LARK*. RATHER THAN SHOW AN ACTUAL PRISON CELL, JO PROVIDED A SERIES OF TALL VERTICAL POLES, WITH GUARDS STANDING IN FRONT OF THEM WITH THEIR BACKS TOWARD THEIR CHARGE, JOAN OF ARC. AT THE END OF THE SCENE THE GUARDS PICKED UP THE POLES AND MOVED THEM SWIFTLY OFF THE STAGE. (COURTESY OF ROBERT GILROY/JAMES RYAN)

JO AGAIN RESORTED TO SKELETONIZED SILHOUETTES AND WAGON STAGES TO CONVEY THE HALF-DOZEN SCENES IN **PIPE DREAM** (1955). WITHIN A DOUBLE SET OF PORTALS (FRAMES) HE CREATED THE DISREPUTABLE FLOPHOUSE FOR A DISREPUTABLE SET OF CHARACTERS. (COURTESY OF PAUL STIGA)

Although there were a few quibbles about the play, the critics in New York enthusiastically embraced the production and appreciated the fluidity of Anthony's direction and Jo's scenery, which meshed ingeniously. Julie Harris was hailed by all in the role. Years later, she recalled the setting as a "magical space" full of niches and levels, which were covered in a deep Mielziner blue carpet.

The last of the Mielziner-designed productions for 1955 turned out to be the last Rodgers and Hammerstein show that Jo ever worked on. Everything about *Pipe Dream* represented a change of pace for Rodgers and Hammerstein. Based on the Steinbeck novel *Sweet Thursday,* which was filled with raunchy, down-on-their-luck characters living in southern California's derelict Cannery Row, it recounts a love story between a marine biologist and a prostitute.

However, the gutsy Steinbeck characters and situations came out sanitized. In Hammerstein's book, the prostitute's profession became indeterminate, the biologist less neurotic and consequently less interesting, and the brothel-keeper a Mother Superior figure.

Because there was little dancing in the show, Jo was not required to leave as much free space onstage as he usually did. If anything, his sets for *Pipe Dream* were excessively cluttered and pictorial, forcing him to drop the curtain on scenes and actors while the set was changed behind it. Whether he used this device because he had to cope with the demands of the authors to cover their weak spots in the show or because of the inexperience of the director, Harold Clurman, it was a practice that he loathed.

Pipe Dream came into New York with over a million dollars' worth of tickets sold and a million problems. Rodgers and Hammerstein had miscalculated in casting the operatic soprano Helen Traubel in the role of the Madam, hoping that she would bring zest to the show. Clurman was not at his best in the milieu of a musical. And Rodgers had undergone cancer surgery just before rehearsals began. The New York critics, by and large, liked the score, the songs, and the cast, and agreed with Robert Coleman of the *Mirror* that it was "a pretty good musical," but "pretty good" was the standard for a Rodgers and Hammerstein musical and audiences felt let down.

Financially, Jo did very well in 1955. In addition to his fee for the movie *Picnic,* he had designed five productions, of which four were substantial moneymakers, each bringing him an extra weekly minimum royalty of $125 during their sellout weeks. Since 70 percent of his income that year was eaten up by taxes and the cost of running his studio, he was pinched for money and again had to go to Eddie Kook and the banks for loans. Despite his six-figure income, Jo's most financially distressed period came between 1954 and 1958. With both his wife and his domestic expenses out of control most of the time, Jo was finding it more and more difficult to manage his life. His solution was to try to make money not as a designer but as a theatrical producer.

Although most of 1956 was taken up with establishing himself as a producer, Jo had already made contractual arrangements to complete two productions for the second half of the 1955–56 season. The first, *Middle of the Night*, which marked the Broadway debut of Paddy Chayevsky, starred Edward G. Robinson, who had not been seen on Broadway since 1933, and featured a young actress, Gena Rowlands, who was making her first appearance on Broadway in a leading role.

By 1956, Chayevsky, without having had his work tried out previously off-Broadway or in Hollywood, was one of the most successful of the dramatic writers in television. He had been churning out television scripts for the *Philco Television Playhouse, Goodyear Playhouse, Suspense,* and *Manhunt* for four years. Of the half-dozen or so of the television playwrights who began to move into Broadway, Chayevsky would be the most commercially successful. The return of Edward G. Robinson to Broadway had less to do with a desire to go back to his professional roots than with what was happening in Hollywood in those postwar years. Times were hard for most of the Hollywood regulars but for an aging character actor whose reputation had been recently tarnished by an appearance before the House Un-American Activities Committee and an ugly divorce at the same time, the offer to appear on Broadway must have come as a godsend. And the role of a fiftyish well-to-do cloak-and-suit manufacturer and widower, who falls in love with an attractive but slightly neurotic woman half his age, suited him very nicely. For Gena Rowlands, the role of the young woman turned out to be a springboard to the movies.

At Chayevsky's insistence, the two sets, one a comfortable New York apartment belonging to the widower, the other a drab flat belonging to the girl's family, were earthbound and realistic. Because the action skipped from one apartment to the other throughout the play, to avoid confusion the time of day was indicated by projections on the curtain just before it rose. In vain did Jo try to talk Chayevsky into something more adventurous, more in the style of *Cat on a Hot Tin Roof.* After the show opened early in March, Chayevsky, now experiencing an attack of hindsight, wrote to Jo:

> Now that "Middle of the Night" is all over, let me confess to you
> that your original idea of doing the play with impressionistic sets
> and subsequent mood was absolutely right and would have done

> wonders for the production. This has taught me a lesson I learn in
> everything I do: if you have the best guy there is, listen to him. I
> hope we can work together again soon so that I can take advantage
> of your advice.

Although Chayevsky wrote four more plays for Broadway, they were assigned to other designers. On the strength of Robinson's performance and popular appeal alone, *Middle of the Night* became a hit, much to the satisfaction of Joshua Logan, who both directed and produced the play without benefit of a co-producer for the first time in his career.

Kermit Bloomgarden, teamed with Mrs. Frank Loesser as co-producer, called Jo to ask him to design Frank Loesser's new musical, *The Most Happy Fella,* which was scheduled for a early May 1956 opening. Based on Sidney Howard's *They Knew What They Wanted,* a major hit in the 1924–25 season, it told the story of an aging vintner in love with a young waitress whom he lures into marriage by sending

THIS SCENE FOR ***THE MOST HAPPY FELLA*** (1956), WITH ITS TOUCHES OF PINK ON THE HOUSE AND THE TREE TRUNKS, SUGGESTS THE WARMTH OF A SULTRY CALIFORNIA NIGHT. (COURTESY OF JULES FISHER)

THE SETS IN *THE MOST HAPPY FELLA* WERE PAINTED FOR THE MOST PART IN SUNNY, ALMOST ITALIANATE PASTEL HUES TO EMPHASIZE THE FERTILITY AND HOSPITABLE CHARACTER OF THE LAND. (W. H. CRAIN COLLECTION, UNIVERSITY OF TEXAS THEATRE ARTS COLLECTION)

FOR THE FINAL SCENE OF *THE MOST HAPPY FELLA*, JO STRETCHED A LONG, PAINTED VISTA OF EARTH MEETING SKY IN THE NAPA VALLEY ACROSS THE STAGE. (COURTESY OF DOUGLAS COLBY)

her a photograph of his handsome foreman. Since Loesser's approach was half opera and half Broadway musical in his commingling of a semi-serious tale with comic interludes, Jo's scenery tried to match his conception. Motley's costumes captured the feeling of his sets. Joe Anthony directed the show, which starred the opera singer Robert Weede as the aging vintner and a relative newcomer, Jo Sullivan, as his young bride. It was a hit with both critics and the audiences.

With his design commitments out of the way, Jo concentrated on the musical that he planned to produce later in 1956. Since he had received his first taste of producing in the mid-thirties when he and Kenneth had produced *Co-Respondent Unknown*, Jo had been eager to try it again on his own. He knew it would be difficult for someone who had been accepted exclusively as a designer to be accepted seriously as a producer, but Jones, Simonson, and Geddes had also tried producing. Then there was the additional inducement of the money that a producer of a successful show could make. In a candid note to Leland Hayward in April of 1956, when he was in the middle of producing *Happy Hunting*, Jo poured out his feelings:

> As you well know, Leland, you just don't get scripts, even if you're a good producer; but if you're known as a designer, even as the best designer, the scripts that get to you are not tear-stained but dried out with boredom and refusal. Anyway, with three children and a wife to support, I find that at my age I cannot face doing four or five or six productions a year. And I have to work that hard, because the actual "take-home pay" is too small if I do a sensible two or three productions.

Hayward's reply a few days later went quickly to the point:

> While I certainly understand your position, and the desire and need to get into active production on your part, don't forget that it's possible to produce a play and wind up losing money or not making any, plus the time, and at your age and mine all we've got is time. I hope it works out is all I can say.

Unfortunately for Jo, Leland's words turned out to be prophetic.

A year or two after he returned to civilian life after his military service, word got around of Jo's intention to produce and he was inundated by scripts sent by agents, most of which, as he observed, bore the marks of being passed through many hands. He rejected all of them. In 1948, he decided to test one of his own ideas. Aware of the resurgence of interest in Eugene O'Neill since the production of *The Iceman Cometh* in 1946, he investigated the playwright's oeuvre of plays for possibilities. Although he had designed *Strange Interlude* early in his career, he knew O'Neill only slightly, but he felt emboldened to present him with a proposition to convert *Desire under the Elms* into a play with music. Jo had already approached composer Morton Gould with the idea, and Gould had readily agreed to write the score. O'Neill responded favorably to Jo's idea, telling him that he, too, had thought that *Desire under the Elms* would make a "good opera, or a serious drama with music." He was sure, he said, that Jo and Morton Gould could make a "grand production of this," and he continued: "I know your work and integrity well enough to be willing to put this entirely in your hands." With the playwright's blessing, Jo took an option on the play in October of 1948 and found Edward Eager, a playwright with limited credentials, to write the script. For the next two years, armed with a few songs composed by Gould, Jo pursued the idea, trying to interest investors in the project. He invited his brother Kenneth, Dwight Deere Wiman, Joshua Logan, David Merrick, and William Hammerstein to observe the auditions and offer help and, possibly, money. Disheartened by the lack of interest, Jo gave up. Gould recalled that the project just petered out, but he held himself somewhat responsible for not completing the score.

In 1953, Jo came back to another O'Neill play, *Ah, Wilderness!*, which he felt had possibilities as a musical comedy. He wrote O'Neill and his wife, requesting an interview to discuss his idea. He mentioned that David Merrick in all probability would be his partner in production. Carlotta wrote back in February of 1953 that the idea delighted them, but because of Gene's illness, they would be unable to see him in person. Jo took encouragement from her letter, and he and Merrick began a search for an adapter, lyricist, and composer for the project. Two years later, after O'Neill's death, Jo and Merrick signed an official agreement with the estate giving them the rights to create a musical from the play. After approaching

every known playwright and composer, they were unable to find the right team for the musicalization and Jo withdrew from the agreement, releasing the rights to Merrick in consideration of a percentage of the proceeds if Merrick decided to go it alone with the project. In 1959, Merrick did just that. *Ah, Wilderness!* surfaced as *Take Me Along*, with music and lyrics by Robert Merrill, and book by Joseph Stein and Robert Russell. Largely because of the appearance of TV star Jackie Gleason in a role that was expanded for him (he won a Tony) and because of Merrick's uncanny marketing ability, the show succeeded, but there is no record that Merrick paid Jo his share of the proceeds.

Jo's quest came to an end in 1956, when he became the sole producer of *Happy Hunting*, a patchwork quilt of a musical sewn together by Howard Lindsay and Russel Crouse, who had enticed Ethel Merman to return to Broadway after a six-year absence. A show with Merman in it was a blue-chip investment. Jo knew that it would not only sell tickets but bring him investors. Counting on the sale of a recording, RCA put up $300,000 of the total cost of the production of $400,000 for 20 percent of the profits. The remaining investors were his brother Kenneth; Lindsay and Crouse; Broadway angel Howard Cullman; Jo's attorney, Harold Stern; the show's composer, Harold Karr; the talent agency MCA; Mrs. Abe Burrows; and a consortium of small investors put together by Mary Leech Brady, Jo's secretary at that time. Jo and Merman's husband, Robert Six, each took 25 percent of the profits, with the remainder distributed to the investors. Never undervaluing her presence on Broadway, Merman demanded 6 percent of the weekly gross as her salary until the costs of the musical were recouped, then 10 percent thereafter. Although Jo wanted Alvin Colt to design the costumes, Merman insisted on Irene Sharaff, whose loyalty to the show and the star proved to be less than complete. Jo, of course, was to design and light the set, for which he was to be paid more than $10,000, with a royalty of $125 per week to supplement his one percent of the gross as producer. Everything looked rosy for Jo when the show was announced. The Philadelphia advance performances were sold out and the show posted a $1,250,000 advance in New York while it was still on the road.

Onstage, Merman was a stick of dynamite. Offstage, she was also a stick of dynamite and could explode in temper tantrums. Jo had seen her in action in *Annie Get Your Gun* and knew that Merman acted and belted out her songs in her own way without the by-your-leave of a director, but also that she was the ultimate professional and could be depended upon to please audiences. Salty of language, impatient with what she thought was not up to her standards, she could also drive hard bargains for her services and subdue the management with her demands.

There are different versions of the genesis of *Happy Hunting* and they all involve Merman. In her own autobiography, Merman writes of being approached by Lindsay and Crouse with a thread of the plot for a script that they thought was exactly right for her return to Broadway. In *his* autobiography, Abe Burrows tells of being approached by Lindsay and Crouse to direct the show that Merman asked them to write. He also wrote that she had heard and liked some songs written by "two young fellows named Matt Dubey and Harold Karr," and wanted a script built around their songs. Dubey was a twenty-eight-year-old lyricist who had few credits on his résumé, and Karr, a few years older, was a dentist as well as a composer; their most recent contributions had been songs for *New Faces of 1956* on Broadway and for a Las Vegas nightclub.

The plot was simplicity itself. Capitalizing on the hoopla surrounding the marriage of the movie star Grace Kelly and Prince Rainier of Monaco, Lindsay and Crouse concocted a slightly satirical story of a rich Philadelphia matron who was snubbed by the Kelly family and not invited to the royal wedding. Her revenge is to find a nobleman with better rank than Rainier and marry him off to her daughter. When she finds the suitable match, the Duke of Granada, she falls in love with him herself, much to the relief of her daughter, who wants to wed a Philadelphia lawyer. The choice for the Duke was Fernando Lamas. An Argentinian, he not only looked the part but also had a fine singing voice and seemed an ideal choice. As everyone would discover in time, he also had an ego to match Merman's.

Nothing went well from rehearsals to closing night. Burrows declared at one point that what the show needed was a good play doctor. Since he himself was probably the best play doctor in the business and even *he* did not know what to do with the show, nothing boded well for the entire production. During one of the early rehearsals, Matt Dubey incurred Merman's wrath and was ordered not to communicate with her for the duration of the production. Sharaff and Burrows were also not getting along (she had a predilection for *Candide*, the Lillian Hellman–Leonard Bernstein musical, which she was working on simultaneously). Her young assistant, Patricia Zipprodt, served as her substitute in the costume conferences but felt uncomfortable working with the Who's Who of American theater. Costumes were designed, made, and rejected at great cost. Every time Merman got a change of costume, Lamas demanded an equivalent change in his stage wardrobe. Unfortunately, Jo never knew how to say no. Most of the time, he was in a controlled frenzy trying to design and light a complicated show, which called for fourteen individual scenes and sixteen changes, and to perform competently the functions of producer.

The show grew larger and larger. In addition to the dependable Bob Downing, as stage manager, the show required two assistants to handle the onstage activities of a huge cast. Jo had already augmented his staff to assist in the designing and to cover the paraphernalia of production. Two of his staff, his secretary Word Baker and general assistant Paul Libin, slid into the assistant stage managers' jobs on the show, which launched their own professional careers. To add to his woes, Merman and Lamas may have been cast as lovers on stage, but their hostile relationship offstage began to creep into their performances. Merman accused Lamas of upstaging her and of obstructing her curtain calls. Because she resented any changes in stage "business" once her own performance was locked in, Lamas would take special delight in upsetting her routine. Her complaints flew to Actors Equity and inevitably into the tabloids.

Merman called *Happy Hunting* "a jeep among limousines" and attributed its success entirely to her presence in it. Wolcott Gibbs, in his *New Yorker* review a week after the December 6, 1956, opening, wondered in print about the source for her popularity: "Miss Merman still manages to produce her customary miracle and convulse her admirers continuously. It's a great gift and, as I've said, quite

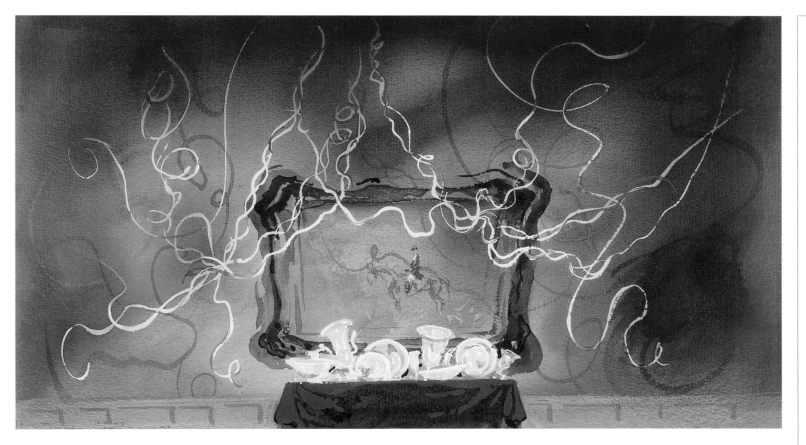

JO NEVER PAINTED FULL SET
RENDERINGS FOR *HAPPY
HUNTING* (1956), A SHOW
FOR WHICH HE SERVED AS
BOTH PRODUCER AND
DESIGNER. THE FINALE WAS
A LAVISH BALL SCENE AT A
HUNT CLUB FOR MAIN LINE
PHILADELPHIANS, SET
AGAINST THE BACKDROP
SHOWN WITH EVERYONE IN
MAGNIFICENT COSTUMES. THE
PRODUCTION COST JO A
SMALL FORTUNE. (ROBERT L.
B. TOBIN COLLECTION, THE
MCNAY ART MUSEUM)

inscrutable to me." Most of his fellow critics considered the show mechanical and old-fashioned in songs, lyrics, book, and spirit, but counting themselves among the legion of Merman admirers, they were happy to see her again in *anything* on Broadway. Although *Happy Hunting* ran for a year and grossed more than $3 million, it was so enormously expensive to run that it was not profitable for anyone except for Merman and her husband and, perhaps, Dubey and Karr, whose song "Mutual Admiration Society" from the show flooded the airwaves for a while. The road tour and a hoped-for NBC special never materialized—both of which might have propelled the show into eventual profitability. There was, however, a record album of it, which is now a collectors' item. Because of his concentration on the show throughout the last half of the year, Jo's

income for 1956 dropped more than $20,000 from the level of the previous year.

In producing *Happy Hunting*, Jo exhibited either an uncharacteristic naïveté or an un-Mielziner-like cynicism about the Broadway process. If he thought that all he had to do was to mix the talents of Merman, Burrows, Lindsay, and Crouse, et al., for a successful concoction, he was acting strangely innocent about a system he knew so well. Time and time again, he had watched projects fall apart when the script or the book of a musical could not support the weight of the other collaborations. Time and time again, the critics had profusely praised *his* work or the efforts of individual actors and (less often) directors or producers but found the whole wanting because of the weakness of the underpinnings. If he was hoping for a miraculous exception in *Happy Hunting*, he did not get it. On very rare occasions in the theatre, a production will become popular with the public despite its obvious warts, which are all dutifully catalogued by the critics. Still, apparently undaunted by his experience, Jo continued his search for other projects.

At about the time Jo started working on *Happy Hunting*, he was approached by Karl Malden and Mildred Dunnock, both of whom he had known for many years, about lighting a staged reading of Eugene O'Neill's masterwork, *Long Day's Journey into Night*. O'Neill's widow Carlotta, who was simultaneously being courted by Orson Welles, Garson Kanin, and José Quintero, all of whom wanted to produce the play after it had made its world premiere in Sweden in February of 1956, was acting like a coy maiden in yielding the rights. Malden and Dunnock, temporarily "between jobs" at the time, decided that if Carlotta would not agree to a full-stage production, she might at least consent to a staged reading—something that could be taken by a group of actors to school and college campuses and cultural centers with the proper reverence. With the help of the *Times* critic Brooks Atkinson, she was persuaded. When they approached Jo, he revealed that he, too, had been trying to reach Carlotta about a possible production. He not only offered to light the staged reading but produce it. Jo called the O'Neill play agent and set up a meeting with Carlotta, who, although not granting him any rights, was not opposed to the concept. They were able to interest Kazan in directing the reading. Roger Stevens, the producer, called Jo to offer financial backing. Jo and Kazan began to draw up lists of possible casts for the reading, but then word of their plans was sniffed out by the *New York Times*, which made premature announcements of the scheme. It drew a sharp letter from Carlotta.

After many wearying months of what Jo described as "endless complicated gyrations" with Carlotta, Jo despaired that the readings would never take place. In July of 1956, he wrote to Malden: "We're dealing with a very sick and unhappy lady who has no firm convictions that last for more than a few hours and then they're disturbed with the latest suggestion from someone else. I frankly am pessimistic about any early production, read, sung or whispered." Very shortly after writing this, it was announced in the *New York Times* that José

Quintero had received the production rights from Carlotta and would be directing the American premiere of *Long Day's Journey into Night* for a November opening on Broadway.

For the next few years, Jo spent a lot of time getting and paying for options on scripts for plays and musicals that never bore fruit. There are a number of necessary attributes for producers. High on the list are an unbounded love for their shows and a fierce determination to make as much money as possible from them. (Occasionally one cancels the other, but many of the most successful producers put the second before the first.) The first of these Jo had in great abundance but he was willing to make some compromises in the second for the sake of the show. He apparently lacked a tough-mindedness and an ability to say no in the interest of saving money. He was too genteel to curb his collaborators' egos when necessary and to deny outrageous requests. Most of all, he disliked the business aspects of production. During one of his aborted producing ventures, Arnold Weissberger, the lawyer for one of Jo's potential co-producers, expressed his client's puzzlement: "[He] is in fact puzzled as to just what Mr. Mielziner believes his function as a co-producer is to be if he has no responsibility for raising any of the money, and no responsibility for expenses or losses. [He] would be paying Mr. Mielziner 25% of the profits simply for the use of Mielziner's name and while we have the highest respect for Mr. Mielziner's name, this seems a bit expensive."

For many years, Jo remained wistful about producing, but ultimately his good sense and past experiences prevailed over his dreams of striking it rich on Broadway.

For 1957, Jo was scheduled to design four shows, only three of which actually reached Broadway. Only one of the three (*Look Homeward, Angel*) achieved more than one hundred performances. The first, *Maiden Voyage*, opened and closed in Philadelphia early in March after only thirteen performances. Written by Paul Osborn, it was a retelling of Greek mythology in a contemporaneous tongue-in-cheek fashion. Kermit Bloomgarden, who was producing the show in association with Anna Deere Wiman, Dwight's daughter, decided that Broadway was not ready for it despite the presence of a cast that included Melvyn Douglas, Valerie Bettis, Tom Poston,

Colleen Dewhurst, Mildred Dunnock, and Walter Matthau, all dressed in Alvin Colt's togas.

Jo's next show, *Miss Lonelyhearts,* opened on Broadway in October. Based on the novel by Nathanael West and adapted by Howard Teichmann, the play recounts the tale of a young journalist who has been given the assignment of answering "Dear Abby"-type letters for a newspaper advice column. Unable to cope with the small tragedies that he reads daily in the letters, he begins a rapid slide from disenchantment to total spiritual disintegration. Because it never caught the corrosive irony of West's novel, the dramatized version never worked satisfactorily. Jo, who used many special projections that Century Lighting produced to his specifications, persuaded Lester Osterman, one of the producers, to give program credit to Century for the projection equipment the company provided.

Although the critics were unkind to the play, they were quick to praise the actors, who included Fritz Weaver and Pat O'Brien, and the director, Alan Schneider. But their most favorable comments were reserved for Jo's scenery. Atkinson of the *Times* wrote: "As a stage designer, Jo Mielziner has caught the tone of the story more concretely than anyone else. His wide, towering surfaces, bizarre planes and torn-off glimpses of particular places capture the mad incantation of the story." Theresa Helburn of the Theatre Guild was so enchanted by Jo's scenery that she wrote him a note of praise. In thanking her, Jo wrote: "I long decided that you can't succeed by yourself in the theatre—you've got to be part of a team . . . and when the rest of the team strikes out, you have to get on, forget it, and go to work on something else."

For Jo, the "something else" was *The Square Root of Wonderful,* which opened at the end of October in 1957. But instead of the success that he needed for his financial and artistic well-being, and despite the presence of Anne Baxter and other actors well known to television audiences, the play, by Carson McCullers, failed. The single-set play was described by one of the critics as a "stack of ugly scenes," in which a divorcée has trouble making up her mind whether to accept her half-mad alcoholic husband back in her life when she has a chance of happiness with a pleasant and solid young architect. The title of the play, *The Square Root of Wonderful*

JO PAINTED TWENTY-ONE DIFFERENT SLIDES, SOME WITH DISTORTED ANGLES, TO BE PROJECTED ON MUSLIN PANELS AS THE BACKDROPS FOR **MISS LONELYHEARTS** (1957): NEWSPAPER OFFICES, BARS, BEDROOMS, AND A VARIETY OF EXTERIORS. WITH A FEW PIECES OF FURNITURE AND PROPS, BROUGHT QUICKLY ON AND OFF THE STAGE, AND CHANGES IN LIGHTING, HE KEPT PACE WITH THE EPISODIC ACTION OF THE SCRIPT. SEVERAL RENDERINGS OF HIS SLIDES (ONE OF WHICH IS SHOWN) WERE PAINTED ON BLACK PAPER TO SIMULATE STAGE CONDITIONS. (BILLY ROSE THEATRE COLLECTION, NYPL-PA)

(which incidentally is "love"), was perhaps the most interesting thing about it.

In July of 1957, Jo's summer holiday in Sun Valley, Idaho, was interrupted by a telegram from John Harvey with the welcome news that Kermit Bloomgarden wanted him to design *Look Homeward, Angel* for a late November opening. Ketti Frings, a screenwriter who had also written for the stage, was in the process of dramatizing Thomas Wolfe's sprawling novel. (Adapting Wolfe's purple-prose work was a feat of playwriting that earned her a Pulitzer Prize.) Bloomgarden found a director in George Roy Hill, a former actor who had written, produced, and directed a number of award-winning television programs in the early 1950s. Elizabeth Montgomery, of Motley, was assigned the job of designing the costumes for a cast that included Anthony Perkins, Jo Van Fleet, and Hugh Griffith. Montgomery recalled that Perkins appeared in New York with a trunkful of costumes designed for him by a Hollywood friend. None of them, of course, was usable.

Since Hill was not planning to arrive in New York from Hollywood until the first rehearsal, he and Jo communicated mostly by letter once he received the first ground plans and sketches. A difficult play to direct because it is broken into many small scenes between two or three characters and other moments that are almost soliloquies, the play was also difficult to design. In his final designs, Jo resorted to a kind of an amalgam of what he did for *Death of a Salesman* and *A Streetcar Named Desire*. The play was dominated by the old Gant boarding house, imbued with an almost palpable spiritual existence, so Jo made it dominate the stage. Since it represents a frustration of the characters' aspirations, toward the end of the play, they try literally to tear it down with their hands.

The play received unconditional raves from all the New York reviewers. It was Jo's only financial windfall for 1957 and its long run helped him through 1958, another bad year for him. As a measure of his financial distress, at the beginning of the 1956–57 school year he had been reduced to asking for partial scholarships at the private schools his children were attending. Because of his and his family's wayward spending of the past ten years, he took on as many design jobs as were offered to him. That meant a more hectic schedule and harder work for him and his staff. Luckily, his phone had not stopped ringing in the fall of 1957, and he anticipated a busy year in 1958.

In the fall of 1957, producers Howard Merrill and Don Coleman had called to ask Jo to design a musical show based on *The Captain's Paradise*, a 1953 movie, which had starred Alec Guinness. (The show had been previously offered to Oliver Smith, but he had apparently bowed out.) The co-author and director of the musicalized version was to be José Ferrer, whom Jo had known for many years. Although Jo had heard some of the music, he had seen only bits and pieces of the script and he was worried that he would be expected to grind out designs scene by scene. He wrote to Ferrer in Hollywood of his concern: "Whenever pressures in the past have forced me to design a production a scene at a time, it has always been regretted by everyone concerned." Swift changes were inherent in the plot, which recounts the escapades of an English sea captain, who plies his small freighter between England and France and sets up two households, one with a proper English wife in a proper English cottage and the other with a Parisian mistress in an attic in Montmartre.

Although the show did not receive universally positive reviews, Jo thought that it would run because of its big advance ticket sales. But the show did not last the season and was followed quickly by another flop, a Maxwell Anderson dramatization of a novel by Brendan Gill called *The Day the Money Stopped*. During his producing days, he had entertained thoughts of presenting it himself, but his brother advised against it. One of Jo's friends, a critic for one of the weekly magazines, asked him why he had gotten involved in such a hopeless project. Jo replied, "When I go a-whoring, I go a-whoring." After four performances, *The Day the Money Stopped* stopped.

A fair number of the plays Jo designed were made into motion pictures during the busiest period in the history of Broadway, when he was too occupied in New York to pursue a tandem career in Hollywood—he had wanted one. In the case of the 1956 film version

LOOK HOMEWARD, ANGEL (1957) REVOLVES AROUND THE GLOOMY VICTORIAN BOARD-INGHOUSE RUN BY THE MATRI-ARCH OF THE GANT FAMILY. JO SKELETONIZED THE STRUC-TURE. AT CENTER, HE PLACED A SMALL TURNTABLE SET WITH TWO DIFFERENT SCENES. ALMOST ALL THE WALLS WERE MADE OF SCRIM, WHICH JO LIGHTED TO RENDER THEM SOLID OR TRANSPARENT AS REQUIRED. (*TOP*: COURTESY OF JULES FISHER; *BOTTOM*: COURTESY OF THE ESTATE OF HILDA AND EDWARD KOOK)

of *The King and I*, Jo had been alerted to it by his many friends: "Someone in Star City," one of them wrote to him, "has certainly profited by close study of your designs for the *King and I*." For years, Jo had watched his designs being pirated for other stage productions and was grateful to people like Jean Dalrymple, who dutifully paid for the use of his designs in her New York City Center revivals of shows he had designed in previous seasons. In 1953, when the producers of *Top Banana* used his sets for a film-for-television version of the show, they dealt with Jo's union rather than himself. (The union took half the fee.) Justifiably upset by this high-handed maneuver, Jo retained a California lawyer to protect his interests. Since the movie of *The King and I* had been produced by Rodgers and Hammerstein, he was unsure about how to react to what he now considered the encroachment upon his designs. The more he thought about it, the more he felt that it involved a matter of principle, and he decided to sue.

When his lawyer informed Jo that he would have to include in his suit not only Twentieth Century-Fox but also Rodgers and Hammerstein, the producers of the film, Jo hesitated long and hard about proceeding, but finally decided to go ahead. Rodgers wrote to Jo to assure him that the studio did not copy or use his designs and expressed regret that the action had to be instituted. He concluded: "Naturally this has no bearing on our personal relationship. I am sure that nothing will ever interfere with that as you and I have known each other for too long and been too fond of each other to allow such a thing to happen."

In May of 1958, Jo gave a deposition to the lawyers, in which he pinpointed those instances in the movie that he felt borrowed heavily from his concepts, particularly noting the scene for "The Little House of Uncle Thomas." He recounted the genesis of the design for that scene, describing the suggestions that the choreographer Jerome Robbins made that he had implemented and augmented, transforming them into tangible scenery. Jo won his suit and received a settlement of $21,000. Of that, $12,500 went to his lawyers and $8,500 to him.

A few years later, in response to a note of congratulations that Jo had sent him after seeing *Flower Drum Song*, Rodgers answered:

I tried to explain to Harold Stern [who had concluded the suit] the other day why you need never have had any concern over our personal relationship in the mix-up a few years back. Some day when you and I sit down for one of those drinks—together that people need occasionally—I'll explain what I mean. Until then my thanks for your thoughtfulness and kindness.

Whether Jo and Rodgers ever sat down and had "one of those drinks" has not been recorded. Jo never again sued anyone over the use of his designs.

Because of the turbulence in his personal life and his professional commitments during the spring and summer of 1958, Jo reluctantly decided to forgo a European vacation. Instead, in flew out to California in April to spend a few restful weeks with Kenneth and Mary. When he returned to his drawing board, he knew he would be facing a full fall season.

With Jennifer out of his orbit and Michael and Neil in military service, Jo tried to keep his connection to his children by sending them rambling, slightly impersonal newsletters about himself in the summer and fall of 1958 and the early months of 1959. In one of them (dated June 22, 1958), he mentioned that he had tried to get permission from the Dakota management to move his studio back into No. 48, which he could use as both living and working quarters, but was denied the request. He had new carpeting and curtains installed, had a television set moved in, and turned it into a living room–bedroom. "It will be many months," he wrote, "before either Jen or Neil or Mike will be here to use the other rooms, but I'm happy to know that they're there for them all." His housekeeper, Olive, made him lunch and dinner and served him his meals in his room, and several times a week he went to the Century Club for dinner, either alone or with a friend like Lewis Galantiere or Father Kusman, who was now periodically flying into New York for visits. To relax he was going more often to movies or watching baseball on television. Weekends were lonely. When he had sold the Newtown house in April of 1957 after the disintegration of his marriage, he had deprived himself of a retreat from the city. Joshua and Nedda Logan often tried to entice him to their Connecticut home on the weekends, but he found their nonstop parties too wearying for him and only occasionally went up just for a Saturday. Once he tried to find some of his father's recipes so that his housekeeper could prepare them on Friday before she left for the weekend so that he could reheat them for himself. His work week left him exhausted a good deal of the time, but this may have been as much a revelation of his emotional well-being as well as physical state. Despite many years of domestic anguish, he missed his family.

Except when he was away for out-of-town tryouts, Jo visited his mother every Sunday. In 1952, when Jean and the children moved into New York from Connecticut, he and Ken had decided to find a place for Ella in the city to be close to the Mielziners. Luckily, Jo found an ideal living situation for her. A woman named Mary James took in elderly female "paying guests" in her large Park Avenue apartment, each of them having her own room, meals, and other amenities as part of the cost. It was expensive, but the brothers agreed to share the costs except for those years when Jo was strapped for money. Ella lived at Miss James's for the rest of her long life.

The first of Jo's four assignments for the 1958 fall season was *Handful of Fire*, written by N. Richard Nash (who had scored a success with *The Rainmaker* in 1954), directed by Robert Lewis, and produced by David Susskind in conjunction with the Playwrights Company. Jo had serious misgivings about the play's chances of success, but, always worried about money, took it on. When he saw the early rehearsals he knew that his first impressions were correct. He wrote in his family newsletter (August 10, 1958) that he was bored to death with it. It opened on October 1, 1958, and closed after five performances.

He was luckier with his second production of that season: *The World of Suzie Wong* would be a commercial success. Jo had been somewhat surprised when Joshua Logan called him in the spring to offer it to him after admitting that he had promised it to one of Jo's younger contemporaries. (Logan probably suspected that Jo was pinched financially.) Paul Osborn's script was based on a novel by Richard Mason; David Merrick was the producer, and Dorothy Jeakins, who was known primarily as a designer for Hollywood films, was set to do the costumes.

Although it was a straight play, *Suzie Wong* had the scenic complexity of a musical. Because Logan was fanatical in his demands for authentic Hong Kong details, they had to fly in a rickshaw from China as well as paper toys in special crates. Unable to use standard equipment for the rain scenes, Jo had to devise special effects for the torrential downpours dictated by the script. He also designed a stunning gauze curtain, which he described for Dorothy Jeakins as "a lyric interpretation of the view of Hong Kong from above: the harbor, mountings, romantic shipping—mixing Chinese junks with European steamships." For it, he proposed to use a palette of turquoises, Cantonese blues, terra-cottas, and sage greens, colors she could reflect in her costumes.

The play deals with a love affair between a Chinese prostitute (heart-of-gold variety) and a young white artist (disillusioned-with-life variety). Jo's scenery, although all that Logan wanted, overpowered the proceedings. The critics loved the colorful and intricate sets and Jeakins's costumes, but were not taken in by the smarmy story. Predicting that it would run and run, Louis Kronenberger described it as "a more slushy than sexy blend of sex and slush, a special treat for matinee ladies munching tear-splashed caramels." Not only did it enjoy a long run on Broadway, it was produced in London by Donald Albery and Clinton Wilder with Jo's sets. The London critics echoed their American counterparts.

In the spring of 1958, Jo had confessed to Eddie Kook that he felt that he was having "a long streak of poor luck" because his telephone had stopped ringing. Yet by the fall of the year, he had almost too much to handle. Jo had already signed with the Playwrights Company to design *The Gazebo*, a comedy murder mystery, which was being co-produced by Frederick Brisson, the husband of Rosalind Russell. Jo, who had met the Brissons in Hollywood, knew them slightly and liked them both. Although Jo considered the play lightweight stuff, he felt that the presence of Walter Slezak and Jayne Meadows and some judicious rewriting might turn the play into a hit. Unfortunately, the play opened in the middle of a newspaper strike in New York and had only one full review, that of Brooks Atkinson in the unstruck *New York Times*. All the other reviews came later in a catch-up edition after the strike was settled and were succinct, to say the least. Although everyone was somewhat amused by the frantic activity of the play, all of which took place in Jo's single set of a handsome Long Island living room, the production closed at the end of the season.

The musical *Whoop-Up*, which opened on December 22, 1958, only ten days after *The Gazebo*, fared worse. Produced by Feuer and Martin, it was also co-authored by them with Dan Cushman, the author of *Stay Away, Joe*, on which the show was based. Feuer, who wore a third hat as director, joined the rest of the creative team consisting of lyricist Norman Gimble, composer Moose Charlap, choreographer Onna White, and costume designer "Johnny" Johnstone. When Jo received a copy of the script, he was so busy working on *Suzie Wong* that his secretary had to read it to him while he was painting at his drawing board. Although Jo thought the play, set on an Indian reservation, was filled with cartoon figures, he felt that its fast and contemporary music might find favor with young audiences.

Because of Cy Feuer's relative inexperience in directing a large musical, Jo tried to help him out by building him a large model and explaining in great detail how the many effects would work. Although the reviews did not catch up with the show until well past the opening because of the newspaper strike, the critics complained about the book, the dancing, the loudness of the music, and almost everything else in the show except Jo's scenery. Most echoed Brooks Atkinson's sentiments that it was "Heap hokum at top speed."

During November, Jo was away from his office eleven days at a stretch, putting the finishing touches on both *Gazebo* and *Whoop-Up* in their out-of-town tryouts. Back in his studio, he was working on three different projects simultaneously. Because of the extraordinarily busy fall season and his own reduced level of energy (he was nearing sixty years of age), he added Will Steven Armstrong to his staff to work alongside John Harvey and Ming Cho Lee. Born and educated in Louisiana, Armstrong had just finished his scene design studies at Yale under Donald Oenslager and had begun an active

THIS SCENE FROM **WHOOP-UP** **(1958)**—ENLARGED MANY TIMES FROM THE ORIGINAL THUMBNAIL SKETCH—OF THE BACK OF A GREYHOUND BUS WAS A PROBLEM NOT ONLY FOR JO BUT ALSO FOR THE STAGE TECHNICIANS, WHO HAD TO SUPPLY THE EXHAUST FUMES AND THE SOUND OF SCREECHING BRAKES. (COURTESY OF DOUGLAS COLBY)

career off-Broadway. Enormously gifted, Armstrong, who designed scenery, costumes, *and* lighting, to Jo's delight, had also assisted Boris Aronson. (Later, in 1961, Armstrong designed the musical *Carnival,* which won him a Tony Award.)

Jo's record for 1958 listed one profitable success (*Suzie Wong*), one moderate success (*Gazebo*), one on the cusp of success (*Oh Captain!*) and three outright flops (*The Day the Money Stopped, Handful of Fire,* and *Whoop-Up*). His design royalties from *Happy Hunting,* his current shows, and one or two holdovers from previous seasons pushed his income to $76,000, without benefit of any commercial or industrial jobs. It was to be the last of his hard times. Although he listed Jennifer as his dependent in 1958, her marriage the following year removed all his children from his direct support. (His sons remained in military service until 1959.) He always professed to be ready to look for ways to simplify his life and to lighten his workload, but his patterns for both had become so entrenched that he found it hard to give up personal comforts or to refuse design jobs. Most of his living economies were insignificant. Although his friends pressed him to take taxicabs to and from the theatre district and the Dakota, he persisted in taking subways and buses. When he did take a taxi, often with friends or assistants, he embarrassed his fellow passengers by giving the driver a nickel tip. And when he was forced to decide about design commissions, he invariably took almost everything that was offered to him, refusing only when it was logistically impossible to shoehorn in another job. Rejecting potential commissions always caused him moments of anguish because as he grew older he dreaded becoming a has-been in a profession that had a tradition of sloughing off the old for the new. He had seen too many of his design colleagues slide into limbo and be replaced by young and fresh talent. For the time being, he was still at the top of his profession.

Jo's compulsions may explain his decision to design the lighting for *Rashomon,* produced by David Susskind and Hardy Smith. Peter Glenville, who was to direct, had originally thought of Jo as the scene designer, but ultimately promised it to Oliver Messel, his fellow Briton and friend. Susskind's office called Jo to ask whether he would "lend" his staff for the lighting. (Jo felt then that "English designers—almost without exception—know nothing about stage lighting and ignore it completely in their designs.") Jo offered his own services as lighting designer, something he had never done before, but he believed that *Rashomon,* based on the classic Kurosawa film, was "a good place to make an exception."

Yet the reception of *Rashomon* by the critics was mixed. Favorable enough to give it a moderate run, the reviews were unanimously positive about Messel's setting and Jo's lighting, which Walter Kerr of the *Herald Tribune* described as "sky-high bamboo reeds . . . against Jo Mielziner's translucent green sky."

In the summer of 1958, Jo had received a call from Elia Kazan, who told him that Tennessee Williams wanted him to design his new play, which had already tried out at a playhouse in Coral Gables, Florida, in April of 1956. Williams had begged Jo and Kazan to fly to Florida to see *Sweet Bird of Youth,* and they obliged by flying down together to see it a few weeks after it opened. Another person who went down to see it was the producer Cheryl Crawford, who immediately contacted Williams's agent, Audrey Wood, to secure the New York production rights. Both Crawford and Kazan believed that it needed a lot more work. The play did not surface for more than two years as a workable Broadway production. When Jo got his copy of the revised script, he immediately began to work to solve its problems with his usual method of turning out quick sketches. Kazan wrote long letters of analysis to the playwright, telling him where he was heading with it, and always sent a copy to Jo, who became immensely excited by the project. "It's so very gratifying," he wrote to his children, "to be working really collaboratively with people of their quality."

In September of 1958 Jo received an eight-page, single-spaced letter from Kazan telling him to *stop* his design process immediately. The reason, he explained, was that he (Kazan) up to that point had "never solved the play from the point of view of the director." Now confident that he was on the right track, Kazan gave Jo a detailed analysis of the play and suggested ways of visualizing the scenery, even providing four little sketches of the ground plan. Jo worked

from Kazan's metaphors: "trap or pit," "past realism," and "from real-ity into the world of dreams." Kazan wrote: "There are only 3 sets but we must have a lot of environments—memory environments, dream environments." He asked Jo not to use a turntable because he wanted a static setting with all the changes made "magically by lights." He also wanted a large upstage screen so that he could proj-ect television images on it.

In November, Jo sent Williams his new sketches. The playwright described his misgivings about some aspects of the design, which was less realistic than the one for *Cat on a Hot Tin Roof*, but resigned himself (as if with an audible sigh): "I must add here, however, that I think a stage-designer always gets his best result when he is least interfered with, that is, after author and director have indicated what the stage-action requires." Kazan concurred that the setting that he and Jo had devised violated the playwright's own concep-tion. In his autobiography, Kazan defended his overriding of Williams's objections:

> *I was again determined, however, to go my own way and produce the play as I saw it, and I was fortunate again that the play was a great hit, because if it hadn't been, Williams and his agent, Audrey Wood, would certainly have blamed the failure on me.*

If the play had not gone well, Jo would also have come in for a fair share of the blame.

The play tells a dark moral tale of a man's search for self-redemption after having lived a sordid life. (Kazan thought it the most thoroughly autobiographical of Williams's plays.) Geraldine Page and Paul Newman played the leading roles. Because of the tight collaboration among all the people working on any of Kazan's productions—director, playwright, actors, designers—there was always a sense of everyone helping everyone else no matter what his or her real function was in the process. Page, who was persuaded to take the role by Kazan even though she felt that she was too young for it, was less than confident when the rehearsals commenced and took a long time to develop into the character. She wrote Jo a note thanking him for bolstering her morale after the opening on March 10, 1959:

> I've admired you always for the great artist that you are and now I know and admire the great human being that you are. Your encouraging words began so early in our trials with this play—they were about all I had to cling to and I clung. I'll never forget your generosity.

Page, a warm person herself, urged on the producer a young costume designer named Theoni Vachloti Aldredge, whom she had known from her days at Chicago's Goodman Theatre. Aldredge, who was Greek-born, had immigrated to the States to study costume design. At the Goodman, she met actor Tom Aldredge (as well as Page), married him, and began designing costumes for the company. When she was signed for *Sweet Bird*, she was unknown to Jo, but he was so impressed with her enthusiasm and talent that he was determined to help her Broadway career. There was a special rapport between them; Jo found her to be bright and sensitive and discovered that they shared a similar sense of taste. As Aldredge summarized the relationship: "We thought alike."

The production was considerably enhanced by the presence of Paul Newman, fresh from Hollywood, in the role of the gigolo Chance Wayne. Jo knew him as the very young actor who acted on Broadway in *Picnic* soon after leaving the Yale Drama School. On the strength of that performance, Newman had won a seven-year contract with Warner Bros. When his career in Hollywood did not live up to his expectations, he bought out his contract after five

years and began looking for a Broadway play. Williams's play was offered and he accepted.

Sweet Bird of Youth—from playwright on down—received such an enthusiastic critical reception from all of the New York critics that it had a successful run in a period when it was becoming increasingly difficult to sell plays without music to audiences.

Jo next turned his undivided attention to a musical about the famous striptease artist Gypsy Rose Lee, which had begun taking shape as early as 1956. There are several versions of its genesis, but it certainly began when David Merrick bought the rights to *Gypsy*, Lee's autobiography. After trying to interest several writers and composers in the project, he cannily decided to add Leland Hayward as his partner, who was coincidentally agent for both Ethel Merman and Jerome Robbins. Signed on as director and choreographer, Robbins suggested Arthur Laurents as the writer of the book. Laurents and Robbins were of one mind about the focus of the musical: Rose Hovick, mother of Gypsy Rose Lee and June Havoc, not the stripper herself. And who better than Ethel Merman to play the role of the brash and obsessive Rose? When Merman agreed to do it, to everyone's surprise, she insisted that Jule Styne compose the music. Stephen Sondheim, who had been promised both the music and lyrics, settled for the role of lyricist.

Possibly because of a difference of opinion among the "money people" on who was the best designer for the job, Jo was not called until December of 1958, which left him only a few months to design what he knew would be a taxing project because of the complexity of the sets and the personalities involved. Having had experience with both Merman and Robbins, who were fanatical in their pursuit of perfection, and knowing Merrick's chicanery, he was prepared for the worst. He confessed to Kenneth and Mary that he would have turned it down, but because of his "bad year [1958] financially," he was going ahead, knowing full well that it "has to be done under great pressure." From his viewpoint, the problems were many. The script was sent piecemeal and with many changes that were required by Robbins. As late as April 27, three weeks before the New York opening, Jo was so concerned by the additional scenery that Robbins was demanding that he telegraphed Merrick to ask him how to proceed. Whenever Jo could, he avoided confrontations with Robbins because, as he told his staff, "If I talk to Jerry, I will not get the show done." (Jo could not forget his experiences with Robbins on *The King and I*, which he had to describe to the lawyers in his suit against Rodgers and Hammerstein. Robbins, he remembered, worked slowly, creating "on his feet" in the sense that he liked to get ideas onstage and work them out as they occurred to him. As both director and choreographer, he could not be pinned down to specifics, making the designing all the more difficult for Jo.)

His contract with Merrick and Hayward was to provide nineteen sets, but Merrick later approved another two for a total of twenty-one. (Jo had to remind Merrick at frequent intervals that extra payment was due him for the increased work.) Because of the immensity of the production, Jo had to augment his staff again. He hired Hugh Hardy, a young Princeton architect, who had been recommended to him by Logan (a fellow Princetonian). Hardy, a Mielziner admirer from his tender years, had attended a lecture Jo gave at Princeton in 1956 and visited him in his studio. Ming Cho

THE ONLY PERSON NOT HAPPY WITH THE SETS FOR *GYPSY* **(1959)** WAS THE DESIGNER HIMSELF. NOT HAVING HAD THE LUXURY OF TIME TO DESIGN IT AS HE WISHED, JO RESORTED TO THE STAGE TRICKS CALLED FOR BY THE QUICK PACE OF THE SHOW: DROPS, TRAVELERS (CURTAINS), SCRIMS, PROPS, WAGON STAGES, PROJECTIONS—THE WHOLE GAMUT. FOR "ROSE'S TURN," HE OPENED UP THE ENTIRE STAGE, PULLED DOWN FAKE DROPS AND BACKSTAGE PARAPHERNALIA FROM THE FLIES, AND PLACED ETHEL MERMAN IN A SPOTLIGHT AGAINST A SPECTACULARLY LIGHTED BACKDROP. (COURTESY OF JULES FISHER)

Lee attested to the frantic activity in Jo's studio as everyone sought to make all the changes that Robbins wanted. He recalled redrafting the dressing room scene ad nauseam.

Whatever its difficulties in gestation, when the show arrived in New York, it was unanimously hailed by all of the New York critics. Walter Kerr, at the *Herald Tribune*, who customarily left before the final curtain to catch a cab to his office to write his review for the morning edition, had to be restrained from departing the theatre before the last note had been sounded, lest he miss much of Merman's final *coup de théâtre* in "Rose's Turn." When his review appeared the following day, he led off with the words: "I'm not sure whether "Gypsy" is new fashioned, or old fashioned, or integrated, or non-integrated. The only thing I'm sure of is that it's the best damn musical I've seen in years." Later on, he praised "Jo Mielziner's vision of a lonely railway track that doesn't even meet in infinity" as "breathtaking."

For the first time in her career, Merman agreed to a road tour, which prolonged Jo's royalties another nine months. What she did not agree to, of course, was a London production, which Binkie Beaumont and other English producers were vying for. When *Gypsy* finally made it to the West End in 1973, Jo's sets had either been plagiarized or simply imitated as the ultimate solution to a musical that was small in scope but sprawling in scenic execution. In 1962, Merrick, ever ready to turn a dollar, tried and failed to sell the original sets to a Dallas State Fair production without Jo's permission. In 1974, it was revived on Broadway with Angela Lansbury playing Rose, as she had done previously in London. Like Jo's scenery for *Death of a Salesman*, wherever and whenever *Gypsy* is played in the professional theatre, it is difficult for designers *not* to imitate it.

Shortly after the opening of *Gypsy*, an exhausted Jo boarded a transatlantic ocean liner for what was to be the first of his yearly sabbaticals as an unencumbered man. Although he varied the routine from time to time, his principal goals were London and Paris. In London, he stayed at the conservative Westbury Hotel, and in Paris he went back to his roots on the Left Bank to discover the Hôtel Lutetia, the very same hotel where his grandmother "Lady Margaret" McKenna had lived shortly after World War I for several weeks while she waited for her apartment to be vacated. A highly

FOR THE RAILROAD STATION SCENE IN **GYPSY (1959),** JO USED A DROP TO PULL THE PERSPECTIVE TO INFINITY, DOUBLING THE EFFECT WITH THE TRACKS BELOW AND THE WIRES ABOVE. CRITIC JOHN CHAPMAN OF THE NEW YORK *DAILY NEWS* WAS SO TAKEN WITH THIS SCENE THAT HE BOUGHT JO'S RENDERING. (COURTESY OF KAREN CHAPMAN BOND)

ornate building, vintage 1910, it was described by an architectural critic as being covered with "decorative pastry" and resembling "an enormous soft cheese with bizarre blisters." It suited Jo, and he and the Hôtel Lutetia's proprietor, M. Bernard, became friends over the decades.

Before he had left for his vacation in early June, he had begun working on the sets for a new play by Jerome Lawrence and Robert E. Lee. It was titled *The Gang's All Here* and was (or was not) about President Warren G. Harding. The authors went to great lengths to explain that their play was not about "*a* President, or *the* President, but about the Presidency itself: the father image, the godhead we send to Washington." (Despite their protestations, most of the critics persisted on reading the Harding presidency into the play.) Jo was again working with director George Roy Hill, with whom he had collaborated so successfully on *Look Homeward, Angel*. The costume designer on the show was Patricia Zipprodt, Irene Sharaff's former assistant, now on her own, with whom he was delighted to be working on an equal footing. Melvyn Douglas played President Griffith Hastings, who cannot measure up to his job and lets the men who have engineered him into office take over the running of the country until his last-minute epiphany, which saves his presidency. The play was a noble failure that ran for about four months.

Jo's final effort for 1959, *Silent Night, Lonely Night*, reunited him with playwright Robert Anderson and director Peter Glenville. Following their initial meeting before Jo's vacation, Glenville wrote assuring him that "you and I seemed to be on the same wave length on every single point that was raised" and that once Anderson saw what Jo was planning, he would readily accept it instead of photographic realism. Glenville added: "Incidentally, with the exception of Tennessee Williams, I have often found that the more brilliant the author the more likely he is, in the early stages, to imagine the sets very realistically and prosaically." To which statement Jo could have added his Amen.

Silent Night, Lonely Night opened on December 5, 1959. Set in a room in a New England country inn, it depicts two unhappy people who find solace with each other on a Christmas Eve and gradually reveal the hidden sources of their pain. They make love for a night, then return to their former lives on the following day. The critics, confronted by a play that felt static—mostly revelation through talk with very little action—invariably labeled it "Chekhovian." Even with the presence of Henry Fonda and Barbara Bel Geddes, the play's lack of success did not bode well for the future of the straight drama on Broadway.

When Jo closed his books on 1959, he found that his income was up more than $7,000 over the previous year, all of it again from his Broadway work. Expenses were up, too, and he was now paying about a third of his income after taxes to his wife, Jean. Again he hoped that he would be able to cut back on his design assignments.

By and large, the fifties had been good to Jo professionally, if not personally. If he had lost some choice assignments, he had still retained his position as the preeminent Broadway designer. He had been able to hold his own amid a field now crowded with a younger generation of designers, some "graduates" of his own studio, born around the time his own career began. Most of his own generation, with perhaps the exception of Donald Oenslager, had all but faded from the scene.

Moreover, assignments were now harder to come by, and it was the rare producer who was willing to take a chance on an untried talent, preferring to stay with Jo or Boris Aronson or Oliver Smith, all proven quantities. The number of plays and musicals introduced on Broadway had slipped below sixty for the decade, and it was now the musical that captured audiences and garnered the long runs. No longer "musical comedy," it was transformed into the "integrated" musical or the "play with music," in which the script dictated the type of songs and lyrics and when and where the dance interludes were placed.

JO WAS PRACTICED IN RE-CREATING WHITE HOUSE INTERIORS (THE FIRST HAVING BEEN FOR *THAT AWFUL MRS. EATON* IN 1924). THE OTHER SETS FOR **THE GANG'S ALL HERE** (1959) INCLUDED A SMOKE-FILLED CHICAGO HOTEL ROOM DURING A PRESIDENTIAL CONVENTION, A BASEMENT ROOM FOR POKER GAMES, AND THE PRESIDENT'S SUITE AT A SAN FRANCISCO HOTEL. ALL WERE EFFECTED IN A WALL-LESS SETTING WITH PROJECTIONS ON A REAR SCREEN AND A FEW PROPS, A FAMILIAR MIELZINER TECHNIQUE. (THE LAWRENCE AND LEE THEATRE COLLECTION, OHIO STATE UNIVERSITY)

Jo was lucky to have designed a great many of the hit musicals of the fifties but was less blessed in the plays that fell to his lot. But there was promise in things to come. For one thing, he was finally to realize his long-cherished wish to design a theatre. After many years of being asked to consult on one project or another, none of which ever led to a completed building, the movers and shakers of the projected Lincoln Center on Manhattan's West Side approached him to participate in the planning of the theatre in the arts complex. Jo wrote in his July 1958 newsletter to his family:

> *Besides needing the fee for the amount of technical work that I have to
> do in the studio to cover it, this will be a way of working out many
> of the ideas that have come to me during these past ten years that
> I've worked on (heretofore unbuilt—but designed—) theatre projects.*

Another ambition was also coming to fruition. Although he never considered himself a writer, he wanted to publish a book about scene design and his method of creating scenery for plays and musicals. He saw it less as a "how-to" book but more than a personal statement of his actual experiences in his long career. The idea was born of his ten lectures in the summer of 1947 at Fordham University. After signing a contract with Harper and Row in the fall of 1958, Jo began to write, sending the first version of the manuscript to Kenneth for review in the spring of 1959. Then, the project bogged down when Simon Michael Bessie, his editor, resigned to form the publishing company Atheneum in partnership with Hiram Hayden and Alfred A. Knopf, Jr. Feeling less confident about his association with Harper, Jo repaid the $1,000 advance and signed with Atheneum. Because of the hectic pace of his next few years, Jo's real work on the book did not start until well into the sixties.

Although Jo knew he would have to reorganize his studio for his new undertakings, he still continued to accept design assignments on Broadway because of his constant uncertainty about the future. What he did not know was that ahead lay the most active years of his professional life, at a time when most men of his age had already passed their peak in performance and productivity.

8

THE SIXTIES: *O TEMPORA! O MORES!*

I n March of 1960, Jo turned fifty-nine. As yet, no gray was showing in his hair, his skin was still smooth, and he continued to look much younger than his age. But for years he had been wearing glasses and having difficulties with his hearing. Always tending toward portliness, Jo fought constant battles with his prodigious appetite for good food and drink. His doctor was worried about his incipient diabetes and gave him pills for his sluggish thyroid gland as well as tranquilizers to help him wind down at the end of the day. Jo's calm and controlled demeanor masked churning emotions, which drained his energies and brought him to a point of exhaustion by mid-afternoon each day. He began to excuse himself from his studio to head upstairs for a brief nap whenever he could, so that he could complete the chores of the day. If he was not on the road during the weekends, he would try to spend as much time as he could resting and reading in his apartment.

JO'S LIFE WAS SIMPLIFIED WHEN HE WAS ABLE TO HAVE HIS LIVING AND WORKING QUARTERS IN THE DAKOTA APARTMENT HOUSE ON CENTRAL PARK WEST AND 72ND STREET. HIS APARTMENT ABOVE THE ENTRANCE REMAINED HIS HOME UNTIL HIS DEATH. HIS STUDIO, ON THE GROUND FLOOR, WAS THE ONLY COMMERCIAL ENTERPRISE ALLOWED IN THE BUILDING. (DUANE MICHALS PHOTOGRAPH)

In 1960, the tenants of the Dakota were notified of the impending sale of the building to William Zeckendorf, then the biggest of the big real-estate tycoons in New York. Alarmed that their domestic tranquility was about to be disturbed, the tenants rallied to save the building from being replaced by what they were convinced would be a characterless steel-and-glass edifice. When the dust settled, the Dakota was bought not by Zeckendorf but by Louis Glickman, another real-estate baron, who turned the residential fortress into a cooperative apartment house. Each apartment was evaluated in terms of shares in the corporation and each was offered to its tenant. Facing a leap in the costs to keep up his studio and apartment, Jo again looked for other quarters in which he

could combine living and working functions, but again could find nothing suitable. He was resigned, however, to giving up his spacious fourth-floor apartment because he knew he could not afford the price nor the maintenance charges. Fortuitously, a three-room apartment on the second floor (formerly the home of playwright William Inge) became available and he placed his bid to buy it. His studio on the first floor was set at 290 shares, with a price of $12,180, and Apartment 20 on the second floor at 340 shares with a price of $14,280, for a total cost of $26,460. By June of 1961, he had to ante up 20 percent of this amount and mortgage the balance. As usual, Jo was short of cash and had to borrow part of the down payment. Later in the year, the purchase was made and Jo moved down to his new apartment, freshly redecorated, at the end of November.

Several of Jo's friends in the building, among them the Worthington Miners, moved out entirely. When the Dakota was first built, it had quickly become an enclave for the upper-middle-class and conservative WASP friends of the Clarks. By the time it turned into a co-op, it housed a diversified assortment of business and arts people, Jews and Gentiles and people of various ethnicities. Jo's neighbors at one time or another included Boris Karloff, Judy Holliday, José Ferrer and his (then) wife Rosemary Clooney, Lauren Bacall and Jason Robards, Leonard Bernstein, Marya Mannes and lesser-known but distinguished representatives of New York's cultural and social world. Many of the old-time employees were let go, which pained Jo. He tried to find jobs for a few of them at Mary James's establishment, where his mother resided. As a measure of his popularity with the rest of the residents, Jo was elected to the Dakota's board of directors almost immediately, serving until 1963, and again in the 1970s. When the old hydraulic elevators had to be replaced, the board asked him to design new cages. (They have been since replaced with reasonable facsimiles of the original cages.)

Jo's new apartment faced West 72nd Street and was directly above the entrance to the building. It was dark, too low to catch much sun during the day. The ceilings were fourteen feet high, the floors were parquet, and the hall that led to it is considered by Paul Segal, a Dakota tenant and architect, the most beautiful in the building.

The door to Jo's apartment had a stained-glass panel, which he fought hard to retain when the fire department ordered it removed. (It remains to this day.) A large arched window dominated the living room wall. Jo covered the walls of his living–dining room with a putty-colored fabric so that he could display his art works against a neutral background. One wall was covered by a large bookcase, which he designed and had constructed to hold his oversized art-book collection. In front of the bookcase, he placed a delphinium-blue sofa, which picked up the blue of the carpet. He used beige linen draperies on the arched window, matching it to a striped fabric covering a French sofa in front of the window. Touches of bright red and blue appeared on cushions, in lamp shades, and on chair seats. On the wall opposite the window he placed the dining table and Italian Directoire chairs. There was no uniformity of wood tones, which ranged from a New England pine table to darker woods. He explained to a visiting reporter: "The things in here are the things I like and are not necessarily matched to each other. I never designed the room. It grew." Scattered throughout the living room was Jo's art collection: Degas drawings and sculptures, Daumier lithographs, a small Picasso, and portraits by Rouault, Vuillard, and Goya, some originals, some prints. On the tables stood an engraved Buddha stone from the Wall of China, a Degas bronze, and a sandstone head of a goddess from one of the temples at Angkor Wat, which he had bought for $23 on his wedding trip with Annie Laurie in 1933. His bedroom contained little more than his bed, his exercise machine, and a secretary-desk, which was the only piece of stage furniture that he had ever acquired. It came from his set for *Abe Lincoln in Illinois*. On the wall above his bed was a watercolor painting by Ming Cho Lee. In the almost fifteen years that Jo lived in the apartment, he changed very little.

The diminution of his living quarters had other effects. When Michael was discharged from the Marines in 1959, he had joined Jo in the larger apartment upstairs. Jo helped him get a job with Masque Sound, which dominated the field in installing sound equipment in theatres, so that he could learn enough to be accepted into the stagehands' union. As Michael became self-supporting, he found his own place. Eventually he was accepted into the union and began

working in the theatre. Neil, discharged from the Navy in 1959, had also returned to Apartment 48 until he sorted out his life. He decided to complete the requirements for a high-school equivalency diploma so that he could go on to college or find a job. Whatever he may have planned for himself was quickly altered by his early marriage to Danielle Freimann, the daughter of the head of the Magnavox Corporation, and subsequent fatherhood. Neil's offspring were not Jo's first grandchildren. Jennifer, a teenaged bride, had become a teenaged mother. Jo professed to be delighted to have grandchildren and, as so often happens, he made a better grandfather than a father.

If things were settling down with his children, Jo had concerns about his brother Kenneth. After twenty years as executive editor of MGM's story department, Ken had abruptly resigned in the spring of 1959 to resume his career as an actor on Broadway in a play by Dore Schary, his boss at the studio. The play, *The Highest Tree*, was a well-intentioned but dull polemic against the testing of atom bombs. The hero, played by MacKenna, is a physicist stricken with leukemia who decides to live out his days speaking against

the horrors of the bomb. Although Ken received good press, the play did not and closed after twenty-one performances. (Donald Oenslager, not Jo, designed the sets.) As events would soon prove, the play was prophetic.

Ken took some television roles and played a judge in the movie *Judgment at Nuremberg* but never returned to Broadway. Few were privy to the confidence that Ken's abrupt resignation from MGM was prompted by his doctor's diagnosis that he was suffering from colon cancer. With his typically reasoned approach to life, he had decided to spend what was left of his good health doing something that he had started out doing and always loved: acting. Unfortunately, there were only limited opportunities for him at his stage in life, but he enjoyed his last experiences. Brooks Atkinson paid him what must have been a gratifying compliment in his review of *The Highest Tree*: "After twenty years of reading books and scripts in Hollywood, Kenneth MacKenna has resumed acting as if he had never stayed home in the evenings." After the failure of painful medical measures to prolong his life in the summer and fall of 1961, Ken died the following January, at the age of sixty-two, in a hospital in Santa Monica.

A handsome and articulate man and an actor of great intelligence, Kenneth MacKenna had found his true métier as an arbiter of what would or would not make a good movie. He had been directly responsible for the making of *Mrs. Miniver* before the war and *Father of the Bride* after the war. On his watch MGM produced *The Asphalt Jungle*, *Quo Vadis?*, *Ivanhoe*, and *The Bad and the Beautiful*, among many others. He had read scripts, novels, stories from newspapers and magazines, original stories, and plays, from which he selected about forty-five for purchase every year. Of his selections, about three dozen or so were actually made into movies.

Ken's death was a devastating blow to his wife, Mary Phillips, and to Jo and Ella. (At the age of eighty-nine, Ella mourned the loss of her elder son, "so young," she said, to die.) Jo lost his oldest and dearest friend, his confidant and counselor. Before his death, Ken had engaged a business manager named Yvonne West to take over his affairs so that Mary would be able to keep the lifestyle that they had enjoyed during their marriage. After Ken's death, Mary, who

never really recovered from the loss, quickly sold their Los Angeles house and moved into a bungalow in Santa Monica. Since Kenneth had been contributing to his mother's upkeep, Mary continued to send Jo checks for the remaining years of Ella's long life.

Amid all of the adjustments to life and death Jo was making during the early 1960s, there was one bright spot. He had fallen in love again and had begun a romance that was probably the happiest of his life. For many years, Jo had been friendly with one of Bishop Sheen's confidential secretaries. Gloria Dickson slipped comfortably into the role of family friend. Because she was privy to Jo's private trials with Jean, there were no secrets between them from the start of their more serious relationship. Although Gloria's feelings about Jo were tempered with sadness about his domestic problems, there was no doubt that she had been attracted to him long before they had begun to see each other on a different footing.

Gloria was a tall and beautiful redhead, full of charm and vivacity. She had a deep contralto voice and a hearty infectious laugh. She was always well dressed and coiffed, exactly the kind of woman Jo liked to have at his side. After his separation from Jean was made official, Jo began to take Gloria to his Broadway show openings and later had her sit at the head of his dining table as hostess of his elegant dinners. When he was invited anywhere, Gloria was sure to be his companion for the day or evening. Finally they began to go to Europe together on Jo's sabbaticals. He adored her and she adored him, but since Jo had already received one church dispensation to erase his first two marriages, he gave no thought to applying a second time, particularly because Jean, too, was a Catholic. Both Jo and Gloria refused to allow this to cloud their relationship. His family and friends not only accepted Gloria, they approved of the relationship and felt it beneficial to Jo. To those who knew of his three disastrous marriages, Gloria was a godsend and no one (not even the good Bishop) could begrudge him the enjoyment of a beautiful companion. Gloria was a particular comfort when, later, events in his professional life appeared to be going awry.

A recurring refrain during Jo's early career as a designer was his dissatisfaction with working in Broadway's theatres. Built during the first thirty years of the century, all of them exemplified architecture

dictated by the high value of the real estate on which they sat and the desire of the owners to cram as many seats as possible into the auditorium, even to the sacrifice of backstage efficiency and front-of-the-house comforts. Consequently, they became "intimate" theatres not by conscious design but by perceived economic necessity. That so many of them succeeded and endured as theatres is more a testament to their presence in a small area of the city and a mystique that grew up around them. In a study of the theatres done in 1983, the authors (the architectural firm of Hardy Holzman Pfeiffer) added to the mystique by concluding: "Their stages are severely limited, their dressing rooms cramped, their support areas inadequate, their technology outmoded, yet they are among the best performance halls known."

In 1946, Jo had written a long article for *The New York Times* in which he set forth not only the commonly shared criticisms of the extant Broadway playhouses but allowed himself to indulge in wishful thinking about what could be accomplished if architects could start from scratch and design theatres for a new age. Beginning at the very doors of the theatre, he pleaded for a better organized box office, which forsook what he called the "speakeasy atmosphere" that suggested "surreptitious manipulations within." Further, he wanted to see large lobbies for playgoers and a lounge not only for refreshments but for the display and sale of the kind of luxury merchandise advertised in the theatre programs. He longed for a truly functional backstage, which could provide space for stacking, storing, and moving scenery. He was prescient about a growing "appetite for repertory" and professed not to understand why a theatre was forced to operate only a few hours a week when the theatre plant could be more efficiently used by presenting more than one attraction at a time at nontraditional hours. He considered the current system wildly inefficient and unbusinesslike and predicted that the time was ripe for new ideas in theatre architecture.

In the years following World War II, the building frenzy that blanketed the nation caught up theatre construction in its net, but not on Broadway, where the oldest playhouses were being systematically knocked over like ten pins. Several hundred new theatres—nobody knows precisely how many hundreds—arose on college campuses, in high schools, in places where an established regional theatre was located, and within cultural enclaves in the larger towns and cities. The Ford Foundation was a significant contributor to the trend, but only to the not-for-profit theatrical groups. Almost none of the new theatres was built for purely commercial purposes. Back in 1948, it had looked as if Jo Mielziner himself would become part of the movement when he was approached by the directors of the Pittsburgh Playhouse to co-design a theatre and school in collaboration with two Pittsburgh architects, Charles and Edward Stotz. Jo at long last hoped to put to use the ideas that had long been brewing in his head. One of the oldest surviving community theatres in the country, the Pittsburgh Playhouse, founded in 1934, had become an established part of the the cultural life of that city.

For more than two years, Jo provided Charlie Stotz with the distillation of his experience in working in inadequate theatres for the past twenty-five years. Stotz, who proved to be an imaginative and cooperative collaborator, was happy to incorporate Jo's ideas into the design. What the two heads envisioned was a flexible proscenium stage sans nineteenth-century ornamentation that would incorporate a forestage (or appended apron) built on an elevator that could be raised or lowered as the production demanded. To increase the speed of changing scenes, they provided six "wagons" or platform stages that could move swiftly into the wings or upstage and a portable turntable to place on top of the permanent stage floor. The backstage was designed to be large enough to store these units

comfortably. Jo specified and designed permanent lighting equipment, including an electronic dimming board recently invented by George Izenour, allowing almost limitless possibilities in changing and combining lighting effects. The theatre, which was to seat 750 people comfortably, also included a lobby that could accommodate all of them.

Unfortunately, the cost of building it was beyond the available financial means of the board of the Pittsburgh Playhouse and the plans were shelved indefinitely. Hopes were kept alive for the next few years, but ultimately, the new scheme was abandoned entirely in favor of renovating the old plant. Charlie Stotz wrote Jo to update him on the status of the project in 1954. Their theatre was never built, and after many years of struggling to survive under a series of artistic directors, the playhouse itself passed out of existence. But Jo's recently nurtured concepts for a different type of proscenium theatre blending traditional and new elements never passed from his mind.

For ten years after that, Jo was much in demand as a consultant and designer of theatres that never got built. In 1951, Huntington Hartford, the heir to the A&P grocery-store fortune, a man renowned for his mercurial enthusiasms, engaged Jo to design the interiors for three theatres that he planned to build on Wilshire Boulevard in Los Angeles, which included a 1,200-seat theatre, a 600-seat movie house, and a 300-seat theatre in the round for television and concert performances. (Lloyd Wright, the architect son of the renowned Frank Lloyd Wright, was Jo's co-designer. Jo found his plans unworkable.) Hartford eventually lost interest in that project and moved on to another, a theatre or a theatre-cum-restaurant on Paradise Island in the British West Indies. For four wearying years, from 1959 to 1963, ideas were bounced back and forth between Hartford and his architects and Jo, but Hartford eventually lost interest in Paradise Island, too, and nothing came of it. While Jo was involved in Hartford's dreams, the producer Roger Stevens, as the head of an investment group, retained Jo's services for a proposed Theatre Square in New York between West 65th and 70th Streets in New York. Approved by Mayor Robert Wagner and Public Works Commissioner Robert Moses, it was an ambitious slum-clearance project that was to cost a minimum of $35 million and to encompass five or six theatres in a complex of apartment buildings and businesses. Stevens and his consortium had depended on money from the federal government; when the money never came, the project died on the drawing boards.

While he was involved in the ambitious New York project, Jo received a call from the Theatre and Arts Foundation of San Diego County in California to join an architectural and design team for a theatre complex for the La Jolla Playhouse, which had been founded in 1947 by a group of movie stars in search of live theatre. After four years of work, plans for a total theatre plant and school were completed by the architects Mosher and Drew and Jo. But the board was forced to abandon the scheme entirely for lack of funds in 1959. Throughout the fifties, Jo was drawn into many other projects that never got beyond the talking stage. He began to wonder whether any of the building projects with which he was involved would ever bear fruit.

In 1955, at the behest of the local New York chapter of the American National Theatre and Academy (ANTA), Jo, Eddie Kook, and Henry Hewes had set up a committee as a kind of "think tank" in the design and building of theatres for the entire country. ANTA had been established in 1935 under President Franklin D. Roosevelt for the purpose of organizing a national theatre, which never came to pass. For ten years, during which the country suffered through a depression and a war, ANTA languished. Then, in 1945, with fresh blood on its board of directors, ANTA was revivified. The solution to promoting its aims was found in authorizing the establishment of local chapters across the country, which could then solicit paying members to subsidize a variety of activities.

The most active of the chapters was the New York local, headed from 1952 on by Virginia Inness-Brown. Under her leadership, the ANTA office in New York became a clearinghouse for information about the theatre, supported a long-lived matinee series of economically produced presentations (run by Lucille Lortel), ran a Broadway theatre (formerly the Guild and renamed the ANTA), set up a job placement service, and published a newsy bulletin named "Chapter One." When Brown asked Jo to set up a subcommittee on theatre

building in 1955, it was in response to a flood of requests that the office had been receiving from people throughout the country who represented groups that were planning theatres.

Jo took the mission of the committee very seriously and gathered around him working members of the New York theatre (producers, fellow designers, directors) as well as architects, engineers, acousticians, and real-estate operators. In the ten years and more of its existence, the Board of Standards and Planning for the Living Theatre (as it was known), with Jo as chairman, Eddie Kook as vice chairman, and Henry Hewes as executive secretary, and on a shoestring budget, prepared recommendations for proscenium and open stages, for the installation of permanent lighting and wiring for extant Broadway playhouses, and for improving backstage facilities. The committee held symposia, inviting such figures as Tyrone Guthrie, George Izenour, Zelda Fichandler, and architects Louis Kahn and Hugh Stubbins to discuss ideas about theatre-building.

Jo became more visible as a theatre consultant or designer *for pay* and gained a window on what was happening around the country. One of the members of the Board of Standards was Max Abramovitz, a partner in the architectural firm of Harrison and Abramovitz, which was heavily involved in planning Lincoln Center.

Another exercise in wishful thinking—and futility—was Jo's work on a project funded by the Ford Foundation. MacNeil Lowry, director of the Program in Humanities and the Arts for the foundation, came to see Jo in the summer of 1959 to ask his opinion of an idea he had been mulling over. Lowry proposed that a group of scene designers and architects be selected to design their "dream theatres" in order to "stimulate architects, designers and theatre people generally to continuing analysis about the stage and its environment." Ford would fund the project up to $100,000. Although the foundation could not undertake the building of any of the theatres, they would support a nationwide tour of three-dimensional models built for exhibition. Jo, of course, jumped at the chance to participate, but only if the foundation would grant sufficient time to complete the designing and model construction. He asked for eighteen months, which in actual time lengthened to two years.

CO-DESIGNED BY JO AND
THE ARCHITECT EDWARD
LARRABEE BARNES, THIS
"IDEAL THEATRE," CREATED
ON PAPER, WAS BASED ON
AN ARCHITECTURAL AND
ACOUSTICAL CEILING EXTEND-
ING DOWN OVER A PROJECT-
ING STAGE. IT WAS CON-
CEIVED AS A VENUE FOR INTI-
MATE MUSICAL DRAMA, BUT
REMAINED A DREAM. (FROM
*THE IDEAL THEATER: EIGHT
CONCEPTS*, PROJECT OF THE
FORD FOUNDATION, 1962)

Jo chose the architect Edward Larrabee Barnes as his collabora-tor for the design of a lyric theatre for "intimate music-drama, which is convertible to proscenium and non-proscenium forms." (Among the other designers with, respectively, collaborating archi-tects in the project were Ralph Alswang with Paul Rudolph; Eldon Elder with Edward Durell Stone; David Hays with Peter Blake; and Donald Oenslager with Ben Schlanger. Each chose a different chal-lenge to address for the exercise, which was exhibited from 1962 to 1964 under the name *The Ideal Theater: Eight Concepts*.) The collabora-tion between Jo and Barnes was not without its problems and even threatened to become bogged down when Jo felt that his co-designer was more interested in form than in function. Eventually,

they mediated their differences to create the model for a "dream theatre" of about a thousand seats for the production of music-dramas or chamber operas such as those written by Gian-Carlo Menotti. The models show an acoustical ceiling extending down over a projecting stage to form a shell that embraces the audience as well as the stage. As a concession to Barnes, the theatre could utilize side stages incorporated into the shell for choruses, to give a wraparound feeling; and as a concession to Jo, the stage could be set in a proscenium or semi-thrust configuration. Outwardly, the theatre looked like a tall truncated cone leaning slightly toward a lower conical section and accurately reflected the interior shape. Although a theatre patterned after the Mielziner–Barnes concept was never built, Hugh Hardy, who worked on the project in Jo's office as an assistant, affirmed years later that his "Minneapolis project" had its origin in the *Ideal Theater* model.

Although he had enjoyed working on the Ford Foundation project, Jo anticipated something more than an architectural exercise or dream in the plans for Lincoln Center. In the mid-fifties, Jo had been invited to become a member of an advisory board strictly on a voluntary basis. Anxious that his contributions become accepted with more seriousness than those of a casual adviser, he resigned from the board and awaited a hoped-for call from the Rockefeller management that would make him part of the team planning the center's only constituent company without roots elsewhere in town, the repertory theatre. For once letting his ambition show through his courtliness, he informed the coordinators that he was frankly not interested in functioning as "adviser" and would accept nothing less than a co-designer's role. Much to his amazement and satisfaction, they accepted his terms and agreed that any architect whom they chose for the building would work with Jo on an equal footing. Through the urging of Robert Whitehead and the recommendation of the architect Max Abramovitz, Jo would become the co-designer of the planned repertory theatre. The overall Lincoln Center board was made up mostly of businessmen and bankers handpicked by John D. Rockefeller III and his close associates. They, in turn, had created a similar board for the proposed "Repertory Theatre of Lincoln Center." That committee's first order of business had been to choose someone to steward the entire project. They had settled on the gentlemanly Robert Whitehead, who before the war had started as out an actor from Canada and had acquired a reputation for producing plays not quite in the mainstream. (His debut as a producer was an astounding 1947 presentation of *Medea* with Judith Anderson and John Gielgud, hardly Broadway's usual fare.) As his artistic partner, Whitehead chose Elia Kazan, then the most admired director on Broadway. Kazan, though, had reservations about how he would function in this new (for him) role of artistic administrator; amid moments of great enthusiasm for the project he would ask himself: Why am I doing this? Although he was among friends with Jo and Whitehead, he remained the reluctant dragon of the trio.

Next, Whitehead and the board of the nascent repertory theatre held a round of interviews with architects and chose Eero Saarinen, with whom Jo had briefly roomed during their days at the OSS in wartime Washington. Shortly after the appointment of Saarinen, John D. Rockefeller III officially announced the designation of Jo as collaborating designer for the "Lincoln Center Drama Repertory Theatre." Not only would Jo help to design that awkwardly named stage, he would serve as a link between the architect and the professional theatre. Soon the announcement followed that Vivian Beaumont Allen, the May department store heiress, would contribute $3 million to the construction of the theatre—which henceforth would be known as the Vivian Beaumont Theatre. (Whitehead fought against naming the theatre for her, hoping to have it named for Eugene O'Neill or another important personage in the American theatre. His efforts did not endear him to the board or Mrs. Allen.) Before her death in 1962, Mrs. Allen immersed herself in the planning of "her" theatre, attending planning sessions and offering suggestions. (Following one of her trips to Europe, she arrived at one meeting with an envelope of tiny swatches of upholstery and drapery fabrics that she had evidently snipped from the Teatro Fenice in Venice.) After her death, her daughter contributed an additional $1.5 million from the Vivian B. Allen Foundation.

Saarinen's presence in the Lincoln Center team of architects guaranteed that the theatre would break conventions in design and engineering. His monumental stainless steel arch for the Jefferson National Expansion Memorial, in St. Louis (completed after his death, it has become the city's trademark); his designs for the buildings comprising the General Motors Technical Center, in Michigan; his concrete dome encasing an auditorium at the Massachusetts Institute of Technology, in Cambridge, Massachusetts—all contributed to his reputation as an architect of bold sculptural forms that owed as much to feats of structural engineering as to pure design. From the beginning, Jo saw that Saarinen would be receptive to any and all ideas about what constitutes a workable theatrical plant. When the architect first visited Jo at the Dakota, he walked around the studio examining everything, stopping every few minutes to ask questions of Jo and his staff out of a profound curiosity. He wanted to know what made things tick in the theatre.

The general progression in beginning a new building is for the clients (in this case, Whitehead and Kazan and the Rockefeller representatives) to meet with the designers to engage in freewheeling discussions about what they want in and from the building. Eventually, what is distilled by these discussions is labeled "the program." Once the clients have agreed upon the program, the

ELIA KAZAN (CENTER) AND ROBERT WHITEHEAD (RIGHT) AS ARTISTIC DIRECTOR AND PRODUCING DIRECTOR, RESPECTIVELY, WERE CHOSEN TO LEAD NEW YORK'S THEATRE INTO A NEW AGE, WITH A REPERTORY THEATRE IN LINCOLN CENTER TO MATCH SUCH ESTABLISHED ENTITIES AS THE METROPOLITAN OPERA AND NEW YORK PHILHARMONIC. IT WAS A GOOD IDEA, BUT ONE IN WHICH MOST PEOPLE PUT LITTLE FAITH AND EVEN LESS MONEY. ARTHUR MILLER (LEFT) WAS TO HAVE BEEN ITS PLAY-WRIGHT-IN-RESIDENCE. (MAGNUM PHOTOS, INC.; INGE MORATH PHOTOGRAPH)

architect (Saarinen and Jo) creates preliminary designs to incorporate its aims. Jo, Whitehead, and Kazan expended Herculean efforts to get as broad a consensus as they could to create the perfect theatre for its purpose. They invited everyone from theatre critics to ticket sellers (and everyone in between) to react to the plans and preliminary designs. All of the experts were entreated to add their two cents to the idea bank.

If Jo had a clear idea of the program, Saarinen (according to his associate Kevin Roche) apparently did not. It was never committed to writing even after six months of meetings, exchanges of sketches and rough models, and copious notes between the designers and the directors. Jo, Whitehead, and Kazan went abroad separately to observe the repertory theatres in Europe, where, unlike America, there had always been a tradition of repertory. For hundreds of years, bands of actors and directors working under one roof and producing plays, both old and new, on a "rotating" schedule (the bill changes from night to night) were almost commonplace institutions in Britain and the Continent. And more frequently than not, they were state supported. With the exception of the established opera companies in a few of the major American cities, the repertory system in the United States had died in the late nineteenth century. Without precedent and in the face of a subliminal hostility toward the notion of a "national theatre," the project was almost doomed from the start philosophically and, as it turned out, architecturally as well. But in the late fall of 1958, when Saarinen and Jo began work, all seemed right with the world.

In early 1959, they met for preliminary discussions with the building committee overseeing the construction of the repertory theatre and urged that the theatre be limited to either a proscenium house or a thrust stage. Should the committee insist on a dual-form theatre, they strongly suggested that it should incorporate two theatres within one structure, one with a proscenium stage, the other with a thrust stage. After weeks of deliberation, the committee decided that, although it did not want an all-purpose theatre, it did want a theatre that would be flexibly equipped to allow the stage to be easily converted from proscenium to thrust. The decision was a disappointment for both Jo, who opted for a proscenium theatre, and for Saarinen, who favored the trendier thrust stage, but compromise being the order of the day, they set to work on the design of a dual-form theatre.

Years later, when producer Joseph Papp was about to move into the Beaumont Theatre, he went to see Jo to ask about the origins of the proscenium–thrust stage conception. Jo told him that the committee had listened to the persuasive arguments presented by Walter Kerr in favor of a thrust stage. Kerr had just written a piece for *Horizon* magazine (July 1959), in which he heralded the "new":

> *The pressures come insistently from all sides: from writers demanding the freedom to tell a new kind of story; from directors reaching desperately for fresh contact with their audiences; from audiences that must be wooed by the promise of an experience unlike that offered by rival and more accessible forms; from real estate men who are realistic about what it takes to keep a playhouse solvent.*

While the committee listened approvingly to Kerr and other proponents of the thrust stage—the formidable Tyrone Guthrie was their standard-bearer—the members were not quite ready to abandon the tried-and-true proscenium stage. Their charge to Saarinen and Jo was to effect a compromise. What resulted was a plan for a theatre with an enormous stage opening of fifty-six feet surrounded by a fan-shaped auditorium of steeply banked seats under a high cathedral ceiling, which combined an imperfect proscenium theatre and a greatly compromised thrust stage. To narrow the stage from side to side for use as a proscenium stage, Jo designed mechanized panels that would close it in. Unfortunately, people sitting on the extreme right and left of the auditorium would be subjected to an incomplete view of the stage when it was in the proscenium mode. To use the stage in its thrust position, a bank of seats immediately in front of it was designed to be lowered by an elevator into the basement to allow for the outward extension of the stage. Two depressed vomitoria for entrances and exits were provided for the actors on either side of the stage. To light the stage when it was in its thrust position, a huge amount of extra lighting equipment had to be added to the ceiling. At Saarinen's insistence, the lighting equipment was to be hidden in the ceiling, in keeping with his idea

THE VIVIAN BEAUMONT THEATRE WAS THE ANTA–WASHINGTON SQUARE PLAYHOUSE DRESSED UP IN FANCY RAIMENT. WHAT WAS LOST IN THE LINCOLN CENTER HOUSE WAS THE SPIRIT OF ADVENTURE, BOTH ARCHITECTURAL AND ARTISTIC, THAT PERVADED THE TIN LIZZIE IN WASHINGTON SQUARE. (EZRA STOLLER PHOTOGRAPH)

of a clean and simple "national theatre," to avoid the look of the light-cluttered commercial playhouse. (He refused to have even the traditional chandelier hanging from the ceiling's high point.)

The result was not only a nightmare for the stagehands when it came time to change the lighting for individual shows but it gave the auditorium a sterile, almost *anti-theatre* look. On the other hand, at Jo's insistence, no seat in the house was to be more than sixty-five to seventy feet from the stage, which led to steep banks of seats surrounding the stage. Although it may have provided better sight lines and a feeling of greater intimacy, the scheme failed to take into consideration the range of ages of all playgoers. Traditional New York audiences, made up then primarily of the middle-aged to the elderly, would not (and did not) take kindly to negotiating steep steps. In his defense of his arrangement, Jo hoped that the theatre would be breaking new ground with a specific aim to attract a wider—and younger—audience. By far the most important perception shared by all parties to the project was that the theatre could not and should not be regarded as competition for Broadway.

Both Whitehead and Jo fought hard for the inclusion of what they called "rehearsal room," a space (originally they wanted two spaces) in the bowels of the building that would serve a couple of functions. With the concept of repertory theatre still uppermost in everyone's mind, it could indeed be a rehearsal room. While one production was playing on the main stage, another could be in

rehearsal on its small, simple stage. It could also serve as a tryout theatre for experimental works that might be considered too risky for a general audience but might attract a special or invited audience interested in avant-garde or developing works. During the panic over escalating costs, the rehearsal space was slated to be eliminated from the plans. While Jo was on vacation, his assistant Hugh Hardy, with Jo's transatlantic approval, hurriedly put together a rough model to show the committee how they could rescue it from the cut. What evolved from ideas put forth originally by Whitehead was a theatre seating 299 people, in a small Greek-style amphitheatre. Designed to have a permanent thrust stage and to keep scenery at an economical minimum, it was also planned to reveal all of its structural and mechanical "guts" to create a space without pretense. It survived the cut and ultimately became the Forum Theatre. (During Papp's tenure it was renamed the Mitzi E. Newhouse Theatre to honor a generous donor.)

Jo was delighted that Saarinen agreed to design the theatre from the inside out; Jo would provide the ideas for the stage and auditorium so that Saarinen could create the enclosure. Because both thought they were creating a theatre for repertory, they provided enormous backstage space for the storage of up to four complete sets on platforms—one set up onstage, one to the right, one to the left, and one behind the stage. On tracks built into the floor, any one of the sets could be moved onstage seemingly at the flick of a switch. Despite the mechanization that was included in the design, the time that it would take to change the scenery from one production to another could not be calculated with any exactness—no two sets would be alike in size or complexity—but Jo guessed that it might take two hours alone just to change the stage from thrust to proscenium. Plays intended for the thrust stage would take more time to set up and change than those intended to be played in sequence within the proscenium. A double turntable built into the stage floor could provide even more changes of scenery. Finally, a cyclorama was designed to be raised high enough in the stagehouse for the set-up platform to pass under it, then lowered again, lending a common background to all the sets. The possibilities for scenic wonders seemed endless.

RIDING THE TIDE TOWARD INTIMATE, CHARACTERLESS, BOXLIKE THEATRES, JO DESIGNED THE FORUM THEATRE BELOW LINCOLN CENTER'S VIVIAN BEAUMONT. KNOWN TODAY AS THE MITZI E. NEWHOUSE, IT FUNCTIONS AS AN OFF-BROADWAY PLAYHOUSE IN THE COMPLEX. (EZRA STOLLER PHOTOGRAPH)

With Eddie Kook at his side, Jo tried to configure all the lighting possibilities. From the fifties onward, great strides were being made in controlling and designing lighting by electronic means. Jo and Eddie wanted the most sophisticated system the budget could bear. Unlike the Broadway playhouses, the Vivian Beaumont would have a permanent installation that could serve not one but many plays. They chose a Century lightboard developed by George Izenour that used computer cards, each of which, when punched during technical rehearsals and then "read" by the machine, could control a cue. In theory, the cards (150 to 200 for an average show) would do the work of the three or four electricians who ordinarily manned a board. With the computer, only one person was required to insert the cards and push the right buttons, thus cutting down on labor costs. Since the lightboard would be located in a booth above the balcony in the auditorium, the electrician would no longer be compelled to work in the blind. Best of all, there was enough room backstage to mount a projector so that it would be possible to achieve rear projections with a clarity unknown to that day in a New York theatre.

For the comfort of the audience, Saarinen designed an inviting yet simple glassed-in lobby, which could accommodate *all* of the audience, if they cared to assemble en masse. In the plaza outside, a reflecting pool for a Henry Moore sculpture would provide a pleasant vista for the intermission crowds. A few steps down from the lobby, he set the box office into a space that could accommodate long lines of ticket buyers. In a like space, on the opposite side of the lobby, were restrooms, though not the lounge that Jo had envisioned in his 1946 musings. To avoid the necessity of a coatroom, Saarinen and Jo put banks of individual lockers in the corridors to the auditorium. They tried to think of everything.

Inevitably, the building costs surpassed their original estimates and more money had to be raised to complete the building. From the first estimate of $3.5 million, the costs doubled to $7 million, then approached $10 million. The original target date for opening had been set for 1963, but several events occurred to upset the apple cart. The first was Saarinen's fatal heart attack in September of 1961, at the age of fifty-one. Although the design of the building had been completed at the time of his death, for all concerned there was a natural psychological letdown in its aftermath. Kevin Roche and John Dinkeloo, the principal associates in his firm, very ably saw the project through. The second event was the announcement of a delay in construction occasioned by the late entry into the arts complex of another constituent. Joining the Metropolitan Opera House, the New York State Theatre, Philharmonic Hall, the Juilliard School, and the Repertory Theatre of Lincoln Center would be a special branch of the New York Public Library to house the combined music, theatre, and dance collections then scattered in its main building on Fifth Avenue. This new Library for the Performing Arts, which would also encompass a museum and a small auditorium, was to be sandwiched between the Met and the Vivian Beaumont. Because of that site's space limitations its architects, Skidmore, Owings and Merrill, submitted a plan to build part of it up and over the Beaumont, which would not affect the theatre but would delay its construction until the engineering problems had been worked out.

Not wanting to delay the formation of the repertory company any longer, Whitehead approached the board with a suggestion: with their approval, he would try to find a space, perhaps an abandoned church or an arena that could be reconstructed as a temporary home for a program of productions during the building hiatus. The board was enthusiastic and he began the search. Unfortunately, in the months to follow, Whitehead could not locate a single structure that would suit the company's needs. He then proposed that a temporary tentlike structure be built on the site of the future Juilliard School. Lincoln Center was willing, but the City of New York, citing building and fire codes, was not. George Woods, the chairman of the repertory board, cooled to the entire idea and considered the matter closed. Whitehead, however, persevered.

Another board member, Dr. George Stoddard, the chancellor of New York University, offered to lend Whitehead, for a period of five years at a rental of $1 a year, a plot of land off Washington Square that the university owned at its Greenwich Village campus. Yet another board member, Robert Dowling, a New York real-estate baron who operated several Broadway theatres under the rubric of

City Playhouses and the president of ANTA's national organization, offered to fund a temporary theatre and lease it to Whitehead and his company at a standard Broadway rental. The only proviso was that the theatre would bear ANTA's name and be built as economically as possible, preferably for around a half-million dollars. With all of the pieces in place, Whitehead again approached the board, submitting a watertight proposal and asking for a grant to begin the operations of the company as soon as the theatre was built. George Woods and the board had no choice but to approve.

Late in 1962, Whitehead asked Jo to begin serious planning of the temporary theatre. Jo offered his services gratis. Although Roche and Dinkeloo, who carried on in Eero Saarinen's name, demurred from heavy involvement, John Dinkeloo helped plan the prefabricated metal enclosure for the building, which would encompass a simplified version of the Saarinen-Mielziner design for the Beaumont sans balcony, flyloft, wings, adequate backstage, and front-of-the-house amenities. Now acquainted with the city's building codes, Jo made all adjustments to the design so that every element would

pass inspection. Since the opening was planned for early 1964, the building had to be built very quickly. Ground was broken in July 1963 after six months of solving the design and engineering problems; another six months was allotted for construction.

The building consisted of a semicircular concrete bowl fifteen feet deep and with wide steps for the seating. The stage, which occupied the center of the semicircle, was backed by a rectangular backstage. Trailers parked behind the building served as the dressing rooms. In an essay for volume one of *Theatre: the Annual of the Repertory Theatre of Lincoln Center* (there was never a volume two), Jo described his theatre:

> The rafters, exposed dark factory trusses of steel hung over the audience's head, are our light pipes on which hang the lighting equipment without masking of any sort. We make no secret of what we need to light our productions. Our thrust stage has a variety of levels and forms. The [scene] designers collaborated and agreed on what was acceptable to the directors of the respective plays. We could not hang scenery; we could draw no curtains; so we created a simple set of screens made of fire-proof woven wood, that hung on tracks and that pushed on- and off-stage. . . . ANTA–Washington Square is reduced to near austerity. There is carpet on stairs up and down the steeply banked aisles. The seats are upholstered. We have air-conditioning, and heating on a cold night. There is enough light in the intermission to read a program. But there is no décor. The scenes and acts are not punctuated by the closing of a curtain. This is done with lights. If we have been bold about it, if we are convinced that it is good, the audience will be convinced as we are.

The funny thing is that Jo was absolutely right about the reactions of audiences to the theatre. They loved it. And amazingly, so did the critics, who called it "a stunning auditorium," "the most attractive playhouse in New York," "a fabulous structure," "a handsome house," "the perfect theatre for the company." Years, many years, after it was finally replaced by an academic building of NYU, people still recalled the theatre with affection, even its eccentricities and discomforts. When it finally opened in January of 1964 (miraculously on schedule), the public walked through a tiny lobby and down steps carpeted in blue-gray and too steep for anyone over a certain age, to their (secondhand) seats in varying shades of blue leatherette, immediately encountering a stage of steps and platforms spread out before them. The metal ceiling above them was cluttered with lighting instruments, all trained on the stage. If perchance it rained or hailed during a performance, the clatter on the roof competed with the actors' voices. To accommodate the 1,100-plus spectators, the rows were spaced too tightly for comfort. From the exterior, the ANTA's corrugated shell made it look like a warehouse or small factory. Despite it all, *Progressive Architecture*, a bible of modern design, declared that the theatre could "stand on its own as one of the finest new playhouse interiors around." The theatre had cost less than $600,000 dollars to build.

The Lincoln Center Repertory Company opened for business on January 23, 1964, with the smell of new construction still hanging in the air. The first production was *After the Fall*, a play contributed by Arthur Miller, the company's premier resident playwright, and directed by Elia Kazan, its artistic director. The play was cast from the company of almost thirty that Whitehead had assembled: Jason Robards, Barbara Loden, Ralph Meeker, David Wayne, Hal Holbrook, and Zohra Lampert, many of whom at that time had not yet achieved stardom. In their reviews, the New York critics had the job of commenting not merely on Miller's new play but the *new* theatre, the *new* company, and *new* approaches to staging (for New York).

The critics saw Miller's play as confessional, particularly in the second act, which deals with the hero's tumultuous marriage with a popular entertainer who has drowned herself in drugs and alcohol. (Miller had been married to Marilyn Monroe.) By and large, they considered the play minor Miller but still approved it as a fascinating character study. They also liked the cast and the directing, but they appeared to be happiest with the theatre itself, its simplicity, its economy, and its effectiveness in pulling the audience, sitting in a half-circle around the stage, into the event. The set, which reflected Kazan's intentions as he outlined them to Jo, was not "decorative." Kazan described it in a letter: "I see figures moving in a kind of limbo which is differently lit from moment to moment with the

mood of each particular memory." Ever conscious of the company's lack of money, Jo tried to design multipurpose units to be reused for other productions to follow. The critics, whose consciousness may have been too indelibly imprinted with Broadway's box sets, somehow missed its point. Walter Kerr's comments seemed to be the most curious: "Very little analysis of the stage shape and its potential value as a psychological force thrusting into the house can be made at the moment, for the simple reason that *After the Fall* does not truly require such a stage." It was a strange reaction from the champion of the thrust stage.

After the Fall was scheduled for a limited engagement to be followed by a revival of Eugene O'Neill's *Marco Millions*, which was designed by David Hays. While the ANTA–Washington Square

THE SCENERY FOR *AFTER THE FALL* (1964) WAS MADE UP OF NON-REPRESENTATIONAL PLATFORMS AND STEPS. JO USED PROJECTIONS AND LIGHTING TO CHANGE MOOD AND SCENE, BUT IT IS DOUBTFUL THAT THE SET SATISFIED ELIA KAZAN. HE TOLD JO THAT HE WANTED IT TO LOOK PRIMORDIAL, FORBIDDING, MYSTERIOUS, AND THREATENING. "IT SHOULD SEEM STAINED WITH OLD HATREDS, OLD BLOODSHEDS. IT SHOULD BE IN FACT INDIGESTIBLE, DIFFICULT, TURGID, OPPRESSIVE." TO THE AUDIENCE IT MAY HAVE APPEARED FUNCTIONAL AND HIGH TECH, BUT JO'S RENDERING CONVEYS MANY OF THE MOODS KAZAN WANTED. (COURTESY OF JULES FISHER)

Theatre was still on the drawing board, Jo and Hays discussed how both of them (and other designers) could utilize the economical system of platforms, levels, and steps that Jo was designing to serve *all* the company's productions. Hays suggested modifications for his *Marco Millions* set during a give-and-take devising of a flexible system that could be personalized by each designer. (While it may have worked in theory, designers are usually far too individualized in their approach to plays to create an all-purpose system.)

After the Fall proved to be the most successful production of the Whitehead–Kazan era. After *Marco Millions*, S. N. Behrman's play *But for Whom Charlie* was installed for an opening on March 12, 1964. The play, a comedy of sorts, was poorly received, and several critics mentioned that it did not appear to be comfortable on the theatre's open stage. It was full of good witty Behrman talk but, as Taubman of the *Times* noted, "the open stage cries out for movement and tension and flaring theatricality." Those were ominous words for the future of the thrust stage. *But for Whom Charlie* ended the first season of the company.

Meanwhile, things uptown were not going smoothly in the building of the Vivian Beaumont. The mechanical contrivances that were included to reduce manpower backstage were not testing out well. One of the contractors, a British company, which had been awarded the contract strictly on the basis of its low bid, was forced by Jo to retain Pete Feller as its American representative to troubleshoot the installation of the turntables. Several of Jo's trusted cohorts left the project in disgust. One of them was George Gebhardt, Jo's favorite electrician, a heavy loss for him. The new switchboard malfunctioned when the computer controls began eating the punched cue cards, not reading them. To add to the problems, the committee was calling for deep cuts in backstage machinery to save money. Being a reasonable man, Jo responded by eliminating and deferring equipment that could be, he hoped, purchased at a more propitious time. He was later infuriated to learn that the money saved from his cuts was added to the architectural budget.

As the Beaumont moved toward completion during 1964, there were increasing difficulties at the ANTA downtown. Whitehead's young company of performers (numbering nearly fifty) had pre-sented their first season of three plays but not in repertory, because of the physical limitations of the stage. With some defections and additions, the company opened the 1964–65 season on October 29 with *The Changeling*, an Elizabethan tragedy directed by Kazan, which was brutally attacked by the critical press and closed early in its projected run.

Rudolph Bing, the general manager of the Metropolitan Opera, announced to the press with his usual bluntness that the composer William Schuman, as president of Lincoln Center, Inc., was trying to induce his assistant manager at the Met, Herman Krawitz, to replace Robert Whitehead. (Krawitz politely refused.) There had been intimations of dissatisfaction with the Whitehead–Kazan régime among a few board members of the repertory company but no open criticism or hostility. In mid-December, after meeting with the board, Whitehead announced that he considered himself dismissed, an action that produced a domino effect. Kazan immediately resigned, Arthur Miller said he would not provide any more new scripts to the company, and Maureen Stapleton withdrew as the lead of the next scheduled production, *The Madwoman of Chaillot*, which effectively shut down the production. The only remaining member of the original quartet of Whitehead-Kazan-Saarinen-Mielziner was Jo, who stayed because he had the most at stake. After waiting so long to build a theatre, he could not pull out when the realization of his dream was so close. It was not in Jo's character to quit. Stanley Gilkey, the general manager of the company, was named acting head and the final productions, Miller's *Incident at Vichy* and Molière's *Tartuffe*, ended the company's career at the ANTA–Washington Square Theatre.

With the company and its organization in shambles, with a growing awareness of the kind of frightening costs necessary to maintain a repertory company finally dawning upon them, with a theatre nearing completion without administrative or artistic leaders, the board of the Repertory Company had to move quickly. Having lived with two Broadway pros for six or seven years, they hired two little-known director-producers of a small, avant-gardist San Francisco theatre named the Actors' Workshop, Herbert Blau and Jules Irving.

The selection of Blau and Irving may have sent a message to Jo. Perhaps the board was beginning to view the Repertory Theatre as New York's own "regional theatre" and accordingly had chosen a pair of managers of a successful regional theatre to steward its fortunes. Indeed, Jo's dream of becoming a resident scene designer of his own perfect theatre died along with the whole idea of a national repertory theatre in New York.

The Lincoln Center planning committee had enjoyed the benefits of Jo's vision, but had not given him an *official* contract as co-designer with Eero Saarinen until November 1960. Not until then did Jo's fee of nearly $40,000 (plus doubling of his studio expenses to cover salaries and overhead) begin to be paid to him in installments. Until the day that Jo could make a living co-designing theatres, he realized his work on Broadway was still his bread and butter. But beginning with the early sixties, there was a palpable feeling that things were not the same on Broadway. For one thing, the statistics were troublesome. Fewer shows were opening each year, fewer straight plays were being produced, and fewer new playwrights were emerging. On the other hand, more people were lining up to buy tickets for the big musicals, more were finding off-Broadway attractions to their liking, and many more were seeking out the fare known by the mischievous name of off-off-Broadway. Part of the problem lay in costs. It was costing more to produce a Broadway show, and more to see one, and the perception persisted that both were out of line with the status of the economy. Although reports were periodically issued to prove this wasn't so, theatregoers became disaffected (the growing feeling was that what was *really* worth seeing was off Broadway) and old and new producers remained wary of the risks (even some of the successful musicals of the period closed without making back their original investments).

For anyone involved with the Broadway theatre, events in the Cold War world of the early 1960s outside the theatre gave no comfort. What, if anything, could take people away from their social and political preoccupations was the parochial and perennial issue for Broadway producers and playwrights. Unfortunately, too many of them guessed wrong and the downhill slide continued.

The season of 1960–61 on Broadway represented a new low: only forty-eight productions, most of them escapist and many originating in movies, television plays, popular novels, and other sources, which critic Louis Kronenberger felt "was essentially hostile to the creative spirit [of the theatre] itself." A pattern was beginning to be set that persisted well past the decade.

When the sixties began, Jo was not as yet feeling the pinch. True, the competition was looming larger. Oliver Smith and Will Steven Armstrong, Jo's former assistant, were picking off the best offerings. The new names among the working designers clearly outnumbered the old. But Jo was still the first choice of Joshua Logan, Roger Stevens, and Leland Hayward and he still felt secure enough to afford to turn down offers that did not interest him or that he may have felt had a slim chance of succeeding.

Jo's first production in 1960 was *There Was a Little Girl*, produced by Robert Fryer and Lawrence Carr, the same team who had hired him for *By the Beautiful Sea* in 1954. It was to be directed by his good friend Joshua Logan. Dramatized from Christopher Davis's novel by Daniel Taradash, the play dealt with the aftereffects of a rape on the victim, her fiancé, and her family. The critics' few positive comments were reserved for Jane Fonda, making her Broadway debut as the young rape victim, and for Jo's scenery. A month later, on March 31, 1960, Jo's luck improved considerably with the opening of *The Best Man*, by Gore Vidal, though its success could not save the Playwrights Company, which faced imminent dissolution. Joe Anthony directed the show, Theoni Aldredge designed the costumes, and Melvyn Douglas starred in it, and with good reviews for everyone, the play had a solid Broadway run and a tour of twenty weeks.

There were several striking coincidences in the first and last of the Playwrights Company's productions. Both were about presidential candidates (*Abe Lincoln in Illinois*, being factual; *The Best Man*, being fictional); both were Broadway hits—among the top half-dozen true successes of the company—followed by tours and movie versions; and both were designed by Jo Mielziner. At the end of his history of the Playwrights Company, John Wharton drew a moral from the comparison: *Abe Lincoln*, he wrote, represented an era (the late thirties) when idealism still existed in the world.

The Best Man, revealing the deep flaws of the presidential candidates of the late fifties, reflected a rampant postwar cynicism. He was dismayed by what he called contemporary playwrights' "insatiable interest in the 'losers' of society," and lamented the lack of "clarity of theme" in their plays. Still, Wharton believed the moral cycle would change and "the 'winners' portrayed in the pre-1950 dramas [would] again attract attention."

Jo's next show, *Christine*, was a lesson for producers who would copy a success in everything but the freshness and imagination of the original. Produced by two relative newcomers to Broadway, Oscar S. Lerman and Martin B. Cohen, the play was adapted by Pearl S. Buck and Charles K. Peck from a novel by Hilda Wernher. It mimicked *The King and I*, but at its core resisted being anything more than an inert musical soap opera. Despite the appearance of Maureen O'Hara in the title role of an American mother in search of her daughter and granddaughter in India (instead she finds love with her widower son-in-law, an Indian doctor) and despite Jo's scenery and Alvin Colt's beautiful costumes, the musical flopped.

TO GET THE PROPER FEEL FOR ***CHRISTINE* (1960)**, A MUSICAL SET IN INDIA, JO CONSULTED EXPERTS ABOUT THE SCENERY. USING ALL THE TRICKS OF HIS TRADE, HE CREATED SETS AND DROPS (RIGHT AND OPPOSITE) OF SURPASSING LOVELINESS, WHICH WERE WASTED ON A SHORT-LIVED PRODUCTION ATTEMPTING TO BE A SECOND *KING AND I*. (BILLY ROSE THEATRE COLLECTION, NYPL-PA)

"How can a show," asked one of the critics, "with Jo Mielziner's costly and colorful settings be so promising and so disappointing?"

Jo missed the opening night of *Christine*, on April 28, 1960, for he and Gloria were already on board the SS *Niew Amsterdam* for Europe. Jo used the trip to visit theatres in East and West Berlin and study the new theatre architecture. He prepared a report in which he expressed surprise with the general lack of adventurousness among the European theatre architects and directors. He was more impressed with their innovative production methods than he was with the buildings, which seemed to him conventional. After making his observations and studying the blueprints of some of the theatres he had seen, he wrote that he was more than ever convinced that architects were on the right track in the American theatre.

While Jo and Gloria were in Paris, they were joined by Bishop Sheen. They spent most of their time together browsing the bookshops, shopping for gifts, and eating at good restaurants. At one point, Sheen asked Jo to serve as his altar boy at the Church of Ste. Marie-Madeleine, where he was officiating at an early Mass.

In spite of his twenty-five years of observing the ceremony, Jo felt unequal to the task and tried to decline, but Sheen insisted. At the beginning of the service, he whispered encouragement: "Don't worry, Jo, I'll give you the signals." During the ritual, as Jo stepped back, he put his right foot into a pan of holy water. Sheen suppressed his mirth as best he could as Jo turned beet-red and tracked water all over the altar steps in full view of the congregation. For the rest of the day, Jo's faux pas was a source of amusement to them all. On the following morning, Jo arrived at the Madeleine to find that the bishop was serving as altar boy to one of the local priests. At the precise moment in the ceremony when Jo had had his mishap, Bishop Sheen repeated Jo's plunge into the pan of water with his own right foot. Jo celebrated that Mass in more ways than one.

His pleasant escape at an end, Jo returned to his studio to face three shows at the beginning of the new Broadway season. The first to open, on November 11, 1960, was *Period of Adjustment*, by Tennessee Williams, without Elia Kazan in the director's chair. As difficult as it was to refuse his old friend, Kazan could no longer cope with the protracted period of gestation that accompanied getting Williams's works ready for the stage. George Roy Hill directed Williams's only true comedy, about the struggle of two

young couples to adjust to the usual gamut of marital problems. As all the approving critics noted, the play revealed an unexplored facet of the playwright's talent.

As a design assignment, the play was not especially taxing for Jo, but Patricia Zipprodt, the costume designer, had a problem. As the young bride in the play, Barbara Baxley had only one costume, a salmon-colored dress and jacket that she was to wear throughout the show. No one seemed to like how it looked in Jo's set and under his lighting. He made no move to change either for the sake of correct costuming. Cheryl Crawford, the producer, Williams and his companion, Frank Merlo, and Pat went off on separate shopping expeditions to find the right dress. Although the costume was changed more than a dozen times during the tryouts, no one could agree on the right color or style. When Jo refused to interject his opinion and no one else stuck to one choice, Pat finally threw up her hands and brought out the original dress again and again. When it was in shreds from the wear and tear of rehearsals, the dress was remade and worn for the run of the show.

Jo's next show, *The Little Moon of Alban*, became almost symptomatic of what was happening more and more on Broadway. Originally written for television by James Costigan, it was a small play that

THE ARCHITECTURE OF THE HOUSE JO DESIGNED FOR **PERIOD OF ADJUSTMENT** (1960) DEFIES LOGIC, PERHAPS MATCHING THE MALADJUSTMENT OF THE YOUNG COUPLE WHO INHABIT IT. (COLUMBIA UNIVERSITY LIBRARY SPECIAL COLLECTIONS)

had to be expanded to fit the conventions of Broadway and to fill a proscenium stage scenically. Television steadfastly remains a medium that deals mainly in close-ups of actors and shallow physical scenes. For Broadway, the playwright had to make external the actions that had been largely defined by the performers' faces on the small screen. Jo's problem was to find a way to shift from episode to episode and yet fill the stage with the appropriate scenery. When the play tried out in Philadelphia, Jo was asked by a writer for the *Philadelphia Inquirer* about his difficulties. He replied:

> I'd rather say that this is the only show I ever did with an eraser. When I saw the script, I knew there just wasn't enough money in the world to pay for all the sets it described. [He went on to cite examples of his designs for The Lark *and* Cat on a Hot Tin Roof.] Using these past examples as a base, I managed a series of confined playing areas which would be walled and signified by light. Herman Shumlin, director for Little Moon of Alban, *wanted some realism like real doors and windows and walls. In the nun's cell, particularly, he wanted certainly one wall. The door wall. I asked him why? Why couldn't an arched, eclesiastic [sic] door frame suggest door and wall and why couldn't a simple, unadorned window frame, hanging in light, suggest the cell window? He agreed, we tried it, it worked.*

Set during the Irish rebellion of 1919, the play, which starred Julie Harris, tells of a struggle between human love and faith in God in both a nurse (Harris) and the English officer (John Justin) who unbeknownst to either had killed her fiancé (Robert Redford) in one of the early uprisings. While she is nursing the wounded Englishman, they fall in love. When the truth comes to light, forcing her to confront this personal irony, she turns away from the young officer and retreats into her faith. The play closed after receiving poor notices from the critics.

Jo's final contribution for 1960 was to have been a play by James Clavell called *White Alice,* to be produced by Roger Stevens and directed by Norman Corwin. Set in a concrete radar tower in an Air Force base on the Bering Strait facing Siberia, the play described the tensions within a claustrophobic room among the men who could, if ordered, rain atomic destruction over a vast area of the

WHEN JO ILLUMINATED JULIE HARRIS'S FACE UNDER A LARGE WHITE NUN'S COIF IN *LITTLE MOON OF ALBAN* (1960), HE DIS-COVERED THAT THE LIGHT FROM THE SPOT TRAINED ON HER FACE ERASED ALL HER SMALL FEATURES. HE CUT DOWN THE SIZE OF THE COIF AND MADE IT BROWNISH WHITE, WHICH REGISTERED AS WHITE UNDER HIS LIGHTING. (COURTESY OF JULES FISHER)

USSR. Timely though its subject was, the production ran into early difficulties and it was abandoned by Stevens, but not before Jo's sets had been designed and built. A few years later, Leah Salisbury, Clavell's agent, asked Jo to consider producing it himself, but he declined and *White Alice* disappeared.

In 1960, while Jo was combining designing for Broadway with his work on the Vivian Beaumont Theatre, he hired a succession of young men to help with the work load. Because John Harvey and Hugh Hardy were trained as architects as well as scene designers, Jo was doubly fortunate to have their services, but even they (with Ming Cho Lee's help) could not handle everything. Architectural draftsmen, model makers, Bennington College interns, a Japanese student-apprentice, and Jo's usual turnover in secretaries crowded the studio. His income from all his projects for the year totaled

FOR ***THE DEVIL'S ADVOCATE***
(1961), A PLAY THAT TAKES
PLACE IN BOTH REAL TIME
AND FLASHBACKS AND IN A
VARIETY OF LOCATIONS, JO
DESIGNED A PLATFORM THAT
WAS DESCRIBED BY STEVE
ARMEN, THEN AN ASSISTANT
STAGE MANAGER FOR THE
SHOW, AS A PENDULUM ON A
TRACK. WHILE ONE SET WAS
ON STAGE, ANOTHER WAITED
IN THE WINGS BEHIND TWO
GIANT WALLS, WHICH FORMED
THE SIDES OF THE PLATFORM,
TO SWING ONTO THE STAGE.
EACH TIME A SCENE SWUNG
OFF STAGE, IT WAS REPLACED
WITH THE NEXT. (COURTESY
OF ELMON WEBB)

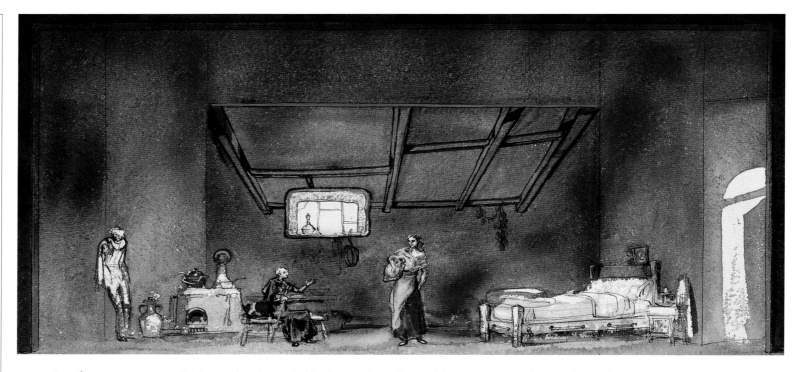

more than $80,000 in 1960, which was deeply eroded by his studio and personnel expenses.

As Jo's right- and left-hand man, John Harvey bore the brunt of managing the studio, dividing the work among the full- and part-time assistants, and providing his own special services to Jo. Early in the new year, Harvey asked for more money and Jo refused, claiming as he did on previous occasions that Harvey's seemingly low salary was more than compensated for by the security of a year-round job, not the usual precarious existence of a freelance assistant. (Jo offered no other benefits except a paid vacation for his full-time staff.) Moreover, Harvey had received a percentage of Jo's net income for many years. Whether it was true that Jo could not afford to pay him more, or that his streak of penury surfaced at this point, the two men agreed upon a parting of the ways after an association of more than sixteen years. Harvey left at the end of March 1961 and was replaced by Richard Casler, a recent graduate of the Yale School of Drama with a few productions to his credit.

Harvey continued to work on the Vivian Beaumont under a special contract. He rekindled his career as a lighting designer and worked on a dozen Broadway shows from 1961 through 1968 and did industrial lighting and work for opera companies. Many expected that his departure from the Mielziner studio would seriously affect Jo's work and creativity; skillful and hardworking as he was, Harvey had contributed the mechanics to make Jo's ideas work. But he did not push Jo's pencil across the drawing board nor think Jo's thoughts, and Jo continued to unfold his special genius.

Both John Harvey's and Richard Casler's names appeared in the credits of the last of the Mielziner contributions to the Broadway season of 1960–61. *The Devil's Advocate*, written, produced, and directed by Dore Schary, was adapted from a popular novel by Morris L. West. For the play's leaps in time and location, Jo resorted to the kind of mechanized scenery that he ordinarily used for musicals. The play told the story of an investigation into the alleged miracles performed by a deserter from the British Army living in a tiny Italian village during the war. Conducting the investigation is a cancer-ridden monsignor, the "Devil's advocate" of the title, played by the English actor Leo Genn. Despite strong performances and Jo's expensive wizardry, the play had a disappointing run.

Leaving his studio in charge of Casler, Jo took a solo trip to Europe, leaving April 18, 1961, aboard the SS *Leonardo DaVinci*. Although he tried to avoid everything that had to do with his work on this trip, he met with a few people who were trying to arrange for him to lecture at an international conference at Royaumont, just outside of Paris. Shortly after arriving home, he had to return to Paris by jet (courtesy of the Ford Foundation and the French government) to deliver the lecture on theatrical architecture and scenography.

His fall design schedule began with *A Short Happy Life*, which he had started to design before he left for Europe. It was a dramatized synthesis of work by Ernest Hemingway, set within the framework of *The Snows of Kilimanjaro*. The creation of A. E. Hotchner, Hemingway's friend and biographer, the play stumbled in its West Coast tryouts and closed in Los Angeles in October of 1961. It gave Jo the opportunity, however, to try something that he had not done before. Because of the episodic nature of the script, Hotchner and director Frank Corsaro wanted to set it Japanese style, with no curtain and just a few props. Jo complied with their wishes. Still, Jo's set and Corsaro's use of it overwhelmed the script. Perhaps because he wanted a chance to do something different, Jo took a drastic cut in his fee in order to design the short-lived production.

Everybody Loves Opal replicated the short unhappy life of *A Short Happy Life*, but it probably should have enjoyed a better fate. Written by John Patrick and produced by Roger Stevens, the play was a comedy that displayed the considerable gifts of Eileen Heckart as an eccentric old woman living in an eccentric old house. The plot revolved around the attempts of her three unsavory guests to murder her for the insurance money. (She proves to be indestructible.) Most of the critics, both out-of-town and in New York, professed to be thoroughly entertained by the play, but Kerr of the *Herald Tribune* and the *Times*'s Howard Taubman (now writing in place of the retired Brooks Atkinson) were not amused and their disapproval

was enough to close it. Jo's set got much more attention than it probably deserved. The *Baltimore Sun* critic used up two paragraphs to describe it:

> It is an immense room with peeling wallpaper, a sagging ceiling (which collapses near the end of the first act) and a general air of decay. A dilapidated stairway runs diagonally across the back two-thirds [of] the way up to the proscenium arch. A track on this stairway enables Opal, with the help of a rope and pulleys, to draw her daily wagonload of junk up to the vast, bat-haunted reaches of the second and third floors.
>
> Festoons of used teabags (she believes in throwing nothing away) dangle over a wash basin (there is no plumbing) and oil stove. Piles of old newspapers, discarded iron and other junk litter the corners, while a buffalo skull, a moose head, a bearskin and a rubber tire (the last framing a faded photograph) decorate the walls.

The year 1961 produced not one solid hit for Jo, and very few for anyone else. Oliver Smith, not Jo, designed Tennessee Williams's new play, *The Night of the Iguana*, and the Howard Dietz–Arthur Schwartz musical, *The Gay Life*; and Will Steven Armstrong, not Jo, designed David Merrick's new musical *Carnival!* Largely on the strength of his commercial and architectural work, Jo's income surpassed $100,000 for the year. So, for the moment at least, Jo did not appear worried about the scarcity of assignments. He completed the 1961–62 season with what he hoped would be its saving grace, a big musical directed by Joshua Logan.

Whether *All American* was doomed from the start by Logan's misguided conceptions and Jo's grandiose scenery can only be surmised. Many years after it had ended its brief life on Broadway, Patton Campbell, the costume designer for the show, reminisced with Logan, who admitted with some sadness that he and Jo had probably scuttled its chances through an overblown production. What should have been a small, charming show had ballooned into a caricature of a big "campus" musical. Based on a story by Robert Lewis Taylor, produced by Edward Padula (fresh from his triumph with *Bye Bye Birdie*), *All American* tells of an immigrant professor (played by Ray Bolger) who gets a job at Southern Baptist Institute of Technology, where football reigns supreme. In trying to interest his students in the subject of engineering, he compares football to mathematical problems. When his theorems are translated to the playing field with unexpected success, he is made the football coach. The rest of the plot traces his rise, fall, and rise. Despite the work of Mel Brooks as writer, Charles Strouse as composer, and Lee Adams as lyricist, the show folded by the end of May.

Before its demise, Jo and Gloria headed for London for a holiday that included both work and play. Jo addressed the Association of British Theatre Technicians, the rough equivalent of United Scenic

JO ADAPTED AN IDEA FOR THE SCENERY OF **MR. PRESIDENT** (1962) THAT CAME TO HIM FROM A MAGNETIC PINBOARD. HE MOUNTED THREE RADIATING WALLS ON A GIANT TURNTABLE AND ATTACHED THE "SET PIECES" TO THE WALLS BY MEANS OF ELECTROMAGNETS THAT WERE BUILT INTO THE THICKNESS OF THE WALLS. ON THE BACK OF THE SET PIECES WERE LARGE METAL PLATES THAT THE STAGEHANDS WOULD POSITION NEXT TO THE ELECTROMAGNETS SO THAT THEY WOULD SNAP INTO PLACE ONCE THEY WERE ACTIVATED BY AN OPERATOR FROM ABOVE THE STAGE. PRESUMABLY, THE MUSIC COVERED THE SOUND OF METAL AGAINST METAL. THE SYSTEM WORKED, BUT JO NEVER USED IT AGAIN. (BILLY ROSE THEATRE COLLECTION, NYPL-PA)

Artists. He was thanked profusely by the members, who a few years later conferred upon him honorary membership—the first American to be so honored—and was told that his talk was "generally agreed to be the best we have ever had." Jo never considered himself a good public speaker, but he was getting so much practice that he was improving steadily. He also discovered that he was enjoying it more and more.

Back home, he was so engulfed in nontheatrical work that he could accept only two productions for the upcoming Broadway season. Richard Casler departed from the studio, putting Jo in dire need of help again. Eddie Kook came to the rescue with Paul Trautvetter, who started working for Jo in June of 1962. Trained and now teaching stage design at Carnegie Institute of Technology, Trautvetter brought with him a wealth of experience, which included lighting shows for ABC television. To work with Jo, Trautvetter gave up a full scholarship to work with Wieland Wagner, who was applying Appia's principles of design to experimental productions at the Bayreuth Opera House in Germany.

His first order of business was to work on Jo's assignment from Leland Hayward: Joshua Logan's production of a new musical by Irving Berlin due to open in October of 1962. The troubles with *Mr. President* began out of town and may really have started at the typewriter belonging to Howard Lindsay and Russel Crouse, the writers of the book. They confronted Jo with a request for thirty-one scene changes to carry a plot that critic Henry Hewes described as "a series of mildly pleasant and disappointingly innocuous jokes about how being President of the United States or First Lady can be a damn nuisance."

In a letter to Elia Kazan, Jo complained about the show and everyone's efforts to save it. "My pleasure in the job," he wrote, "disappeared pretty quickly, particularly when, in trying to bolster the sagging book, rewriting meant throwing in scenic elements that have no style and no relationship to the basic original scheme." On the basis of a large advance, and not on its reviews, *Mr. President* had a moderately healthy run.

What proved to be Jo's first, last, and only Broadway show for 1963 was Tennessee Williams's *The Milk Train Doesn't Stop Here Anymore,* which was presented by Roger Stevens and directed by Herbert Machiz. The world premiere of the play in an early version had occurred at the Festival of Two Worlds at Spoleto, Italy, in the summer of 1962. Machiz and Williams had not gotten along well, but that was one of the lesser problems of the production. It opened in New York on January 16, 1963, during the longest newspaper strike in history (114 days), which accomplished among other things the closing down of the *New York Daily Mirror,* reducing the daily papers to six. Reviews, however, were written, published, and circulated to the theatregoing public in a temporary publication called *FIRSTNITE.* Had the notices been uniformly positive, the play might have had a chance on the strength of the playwright's reputation and the strong performances of the actors. But the play contained already familiar Williams characters and themes—a dissolute woman and her young poet-artist companion—the critics expressed disappointment, and customers didn't stop at the box office anymore.

After *Milk Train,* Jo became so involved with the Repertory Company of Lincoln Center and a host of other projects that there was not another Mielziner set on Broadway for almost two seasons. When it did occur, it came largely as a result of Jo's active solicitation. From the Broadway grapevine, then as now as effective as fiber optics, Jo heard about the projected production of a two-character play called *The Owl and the Pussycat* and wrote a letter to producer Philip Rose asking for the job. He got the assignment. The action takes place in an apartment under the mansard roof of a San Francisco house, presumably a Victorian "Painted Lady." The place is rented to a writer, whose serenity is somewhat shattered by a prostitute, who moves in when she is evicted from her own apartment because of the writer's complaints about the conduct of her trade. What followed was not hard to predict, but the playwright Bill Manhoff carried the comedy off charmingly. The play was a hit and was later moved to London, sans Jo's scenery.

After years of work, not only did Jo see his dream theatre come true at Lincoln Center, but he also published his book *Designing for the Theatre,* made a lot of money creating an AT&T exhibition at the New York World's Fair, and had immense personal satisfaction in designing a setting for Michelangelo's great *Pietà* in the Vatican

FOR ***THE MILK TRAIN DOESN'T STOP HERE ANYMORE* (1963),** JO STRIPPED AWAY ALL FUSSY DETAILS FROM THE HEROINE'S VILLA ON THE DIVINA COSTIERA TO CREATE A BASIC SET, FROM WHICH EVOLVED SEVERAL EXTERIORS AND INTERIORS; HE EMPLOYED LIGHTING TO SHIFT FROM THE BRIGHT ITALIAN LANDSCAPE TO THE HOUSE. TENNESSEE WILLIAMS HAD SPECIFIED AN ORNATE CHANDELIER AS A DOMINANT PROP, WHICH WAS TO METAMORPHOSE INTO A MOBILE SCULPTURE CREATED BY THE YOUNG ARTIST IN THE PLAY. JO ASSIGNED THIS TASK TO THE INGENIOUS PROP MASTER JOE LYNN. (COURTESY OF PAUL STIGA)

Pavilion, also at the World's Fair. Another of his projects was designing the ballroom of the new Hilton Hotel rising on Sixth Avenue. It was a lucrative job that, with automated walls and stages and magical lighting, tried to re-create Las Vegas in New York. These extracurricular activities kept him and his staff busy, for all were coming into bloom at the same time.

Indeed, in 1964 and '65, Jo was taking on too many projects at once. He would submit suggestions and preliminary plans for numerous jobs, most of which he did not get. He did agree to work on two projects that interested him, although they paid less. In 1963, the Department of State had asked Jo to serve on an "Ad Hoc Drama Panel" under the auspices of its Bureau of Educational and Cultural Affairs. The bureau had been charged with spreading the word to the world about the depth and quality of American culture. Lucius Battle, the Assistant Secretary heading the bureau at the time, explained to the panel: "We have a reputation of being a people without a civilization or culture. We need to show more of ourselves to the world. This is easier to do with music and dance, but drama has content."

Jo and Donald Oenslager were asked to co-design a portable theatre to take around the world for the presentation of quintessentially American productions. Needing advice in lighting and acoustics, they invited Eddie Kook and Dr. Cyril Harris, the foremost acoustical expert of the day, to become their collaborators.

THE EAST ROOM STAGE JO DESIGNED FOR THE WHITE HOUSE IN 1965 WAS A CHALLENGE, BECAUSE HE FACED SEVERAL SEVERE LIMITATIONS. HE WAS NOT ALLOWED TO DISTURB THE EXISTING ELEMENTS OF THE ROOM, AND HE HAD TO RETAIN THE CRYSTAL CHANDELIER HANGING LOW OVER THE STAGE. IT CAUSED NO REAL PROBLEM FOR SOLOISTS AND SMALL GROUPS, BUT WAS A CONCERN FOR BALLET AND MUSICAL COMEDY DANCERS, PARTICULARLY WITH REGARD TO LEAPS AND LIFTS. (COURTESY OF NEIL COLLINS/RICHARD STODDARD)

State Department officials told them that the Russians wanted to see the best musical theatre rather than drama, but their own theatres were already too crowded with ballet, opera, and other performances and spectacles to accommodate American productions. So the four men designed their portable theatre to seat about a thousand people. For a year and a half they explored materials, shapes, sizes, engineering difficulties, methods of transportation, and every technical facet of the problem. The Ford Foundation funded the creation of a model and a booklet to explain how the theatre would look and work. By the time they had arrived at a workable design, the State Department regretfully informed them that there were no funds available to carry the project to completion.

The "Porto Theatre," so designated by the four creators, was to be a lightweight fiberglass structure that broke into sections to be transported by three large cargo planes. Weighing only one hundred tons, it was equipped with a theater in the round and every component necessary for a functioning theatre, from box office to public restrooms, plus every technical system necessary for theatrical production. The construction costs at the time (1965) were estimated at $1,200,000. Jo and his collaborators were paid only for engineering, for their drafting and studio costs, and for model-building.

Early in January 1965, a member of President Lyndon Johnson's White House staff called Jo to ask him to design a portable stage for the East Room, where most of the presidential "command performances" took place. When Jo replied that he was interested, he was invited to Washington to meet a White House intermediary, not a staff member, who would explain the project and drive him to the presidential mansion. Jo flew down, looked over the room, and eventually took the job without a fee for his design time, but he requested reimbursement for his staff's time and out-of-pocket expenses. The Rebekah Harkness Foundation agreed to foot the bill, which Pete Feller estimated to be about $75,000. Once the funding was assured, Jo, Paul Trautvetter, and Feller made several trips to Washington to study the problems and find a solution. The old stage, which Jo had remembered from the first time he had visited the White House during President Franklin D. Roosevelt's tenure, was heavy, cumbersome, and difficult to store. It was covered in a dark red velour, which clashed with the gold and white of the room. It was also so low that it was impossible for people in the back rows of the seating to see anything onstage. Exposed spotlights on platforms at a far end of the room provided the only stage illumination. A new stage, which had been talked about during the Kennedy years, was especially close to Mrs. Johnson's heart.

To design a stage that was appropriate, functional, and harmonious with the room, Jo decided to replicate the existing decorative panels, fascias, capitals and pilasters in a lightweight vacu-formed plastic, paint them the off-white of the room, and use them to hide the stanchions that framed the stage and held the curtain and lighting equipment (the latter was controlled by a small dimmer board provided by Century Lighting). Jo raised the stage to thirty-three inches so that the back rows would have better, but still not complete, visibility, and placed steps in a semicircular apron for the president and the first lady to mount to give their speeches. He also designed the stage to be adaptable in depth for different kinds of performances. All the curtains and the maskings were specified to match as closely as possible the gold brocade of the East Room draperies.

When the stage was inaugurated on September 29, 1965, Jo basked in the gasps of approval and applause. In her dedication speech, Lady-Bird Johnson singled him out: "How fortunate we are," she said, "to have this proper platform for the performing arts in the White House . . . a proscenium graced by beauty as well as designed for usefulness by the genius of Mr. Jo Mielziner." Members of Rebekah Harkness's ballet company gave the first performance on its stage, causing more gasps in the audience as ballerinas almost grazed the glistening chandelier during their lifts. Another minor mishap threatened when Secret Service men converged on the stage electrician, who was disappearing into a pillar that disguised the lighting tower so that he could set the lights. Someone failed to alert them that this was all part of the performance. For Jo, the thanks of the Johnsons had to be compensation enough, but he called the assignment "one of the most flattering things that ever happened to me." The next time he saw the stage in use was in 1970 when he was invited to attend a performance of *1776*, which he had designed for Broadway. To this day, Jo's stage continues to be used.

Jo could afford to take the pro bono jobs (as long as his studio expenses were covered) primarily because of what the Hilton Hotel ballroom and the AT&T projects were paying him. From 1961 to 1964, his income climbed steadily, topping $100,000 for each of those years. In 1963, his best year ever, he made $140,000, of which he claimed $68,000 for professional expenses. Even after deducting the high alimony payments to Jean, his mother's upkeep, and his taxes, he was still left with more disposable income than he had ever had before. With the guidance of Eddie Kook, he began making investments in blue chip stocks, rather than Broadway shows. Late in 1965, he transferred power of attorney to Eddie to buy and sell investments for him. Although Jo never had a head for business, his advancing age—he would be sixty-five in 1966—and the increasing scarcity of Broadway assignments prompted him to lay by money for leaner times ahead.

The heavy work schedule took its toll on him. His doctor, Dr. Tom Sheen, warned him about incipient angina and told him to slow down a bit. Now that more and more of the wages of assistants were covered by his clients, he hired extra studio help and gave more responsibility to his assistant designers, even allowing the most talented of them to help with the painting of the elevations, something he had jealously guarded for years. Seeking domestic tranquility, he took on male Japanese housekeeper-cooks after a succession of unsatisfactory female housekeepers, but they proved to be just as unreliable as their predecessors. One of them stormed out of his apartment in the middle of a dinner party, leaving Jo and his guests to fend for themselves in the kitchen. In August of 1963, an agency sent him an Irishwoman named Mary Harkin, who remained with him until October of 1973. After she left, he hired temporary help.

If Jo's professional life was frenetic, his personal life, during the early sixties, calmed him. Gloria Dickson, his perfect companion, was more than willing to join him for late-night dinners with the Kazans and the Whiteheads after long planning sessions for the Vivian Beaumont Theatre. She took her vacations with him, hosted his dinner parties, and was always available when he needed her. (She lived minutes away on Central Park South.) Then, in August of 1964, she came down with a case of shingles so severe that she had to be hospitalized for a time, and it was months before she recovered. Drained, weak, and prey to other ailments, she fell ill with flu, which quickly developed into pneumonia. Her doctors were puzzled and thought she might be suffering from a neurological disease. When it was apparent that she would not be well enough for their annual trip to Paris and London, Jo cancelled their reservations. In April of 1965, Gloria's sister, Marjorie Curtin, took her to St. Joseph's Hospital, in Stamford, Connecticut, for a series of tests to determine the cause of her weight loss and debilitude. After an exploratory operation, her doctors discovered that she was

suffering from a rare congenital liver disease but were hopeful that she would recover with treatment. She remained at the hospital and, despite his busy schedule, Jo took the train almost every day to Stamford to visit her. Sadly, her condition took a turn for the worse, and Gloria died on May 8, 1965, at the age of forty-five.

Jennifer accompanied her grieving father to Gloria's funeral service, which was attended by many of Jo's friends, at St. Paul the Apostle Catholic Church, at the corner of Ninth Avenue and 59th Street in New York. After the Mass, in which Bishop Sheen participated, Gloria was buried in a cemetery on Staten Island. Gloria's absence left a permanent hole in Jo's life. He kept a picture of her at his bedside until the end of his days. Four years after her death, in 1969, in a letter to Margie and Larry Curtin (her sister and brother-in-law) Jo wrote, "I look at Gloria's lovely face, for such a flood of happy memories of her beautiful soul." Although Jo continued to see attractive women from time to time, none was ever to take the place of Gloria. After three failed marriages, his relationship with her had been the most satisfying of his life. Only the obstacle of their mutually shared Catholicism had prevented their marriage. As he grew older, he looked for companionship among his old friends Eddie and Hilda Kook, Lewis Galantiere, Father Stanley Kusman, and among his assistants and theatrical comrades.

Work, as ever, was the constant in Jo's life and had the ability to blunt whatever he was suffering. For the time being, his days were consumed with the opening of the Vivian Beaumont Theatre. Technical problems continued to plague the crew readying it for the opening. An ominous memorandum was sent to Jo, George Izenour, Eddie Kook, and all others concerned stating that an emergency situation existed in making it workable; it was impossible to delay the opening, which had already been postponed once. An assessment of who and what was to blame was postponed until after the opening.

The late Vivian Beaumont Allen, who had favored bedroomy pastel colors, would probably not have approved of the red curtain, red carpeting, red seats, charcoal walls, and bronze ceiling in the theatre that bore her name. The seats, set in steep banks, numbered 1,083 for the theatre in the thrust position and 1,140 in the proscenium position. By raising or lowering an elevator, the change from one position to the other had been cut to about half an hour. Its back-stage area, with its 10,000 square feet of space, could easily contain three backstages of the Martin Beck Theatre, which had the largest area on Broadway. Its four-channel stereo system, cyclorama, and dimmer board for controlling the lights from a rear booth were all touted in the press. What the public and press did not know was that the lighting board never worked and the bulky cyclorama eventually had to be torn down. Some of the other mechanical marvels were simply never finished, others were temperamental and often malfunctioned.

Probably out of deference to Jo's role in the project, Blau and Irving, who now headed the Repertory Company, had asked him to design the opening show, a revival of *Danton's Death*, by Georg Buechner. Not only was an entirely new company in place but many familiar faces backstage had also departed with the end of the Whitehead–Kazan régime. The play, which abounded in political overtones for the mid-sixties, was set in the dark days of the French Revolution and charted how the suspicions among the prime movers of the Terror finally consumed all of them. It opened on October 21, 1965, and whatever the audience and critics thought of the play, they were impressed with the theatre itself. The production, which was presented on the thrust stage in thirty-two scenes, used all of the complex electronic and mechanical equipment that the theatre provided, without regard to the drama's needs. Pieces of scenery rolled out from back to front and side to side, curtains bearing inscriptions noiselessly crossed the stage, lights pierced the dark to reveal yet more scenes changing on a revolving stage, and a guillotine that slowly moved forward for the final sinister image—all contributed to a sense that Buechner's play had been swallowed up by scenic contrivances. This was more the fault of the director, Herbert Blau, than the fault of the designer. Jo always had difficulty with directors who gave their instructions to him in less than concrete terms. And Blau, an academic, could only explain what he wanted in metaphors and verbal nuances. What Jo created reflected his state of confusion and was described by the critic Walter Kerr as a production design "altogether eclectic . . . without stylistic significance."

FOR ***DANTON'S DEATH*** (1965), THE PRODUCTION THAT MARKED THE OPENING OF THE VIVIAN BEAUMONT THEATRE, JO AND HERBERT BLAU, THE DIRECTOR, FELT COMPELLED TO USE ALL THE PRODIGIOUS TECHNICAL FACILITIES OF THE STAGE. (ESTATE OF JO MIELZINER)

After his labors to create scenes of the French Revolution, Jo did his first Broadway assignment after an absence of more than a year. *The Playroom*, billed as "a Contemporary Thriller," took place in an apartment house in New York known as the Montana. The plot revolves around the mischief caused when a teenager hits upon the idea of "kidnapping" her ten-year-old stepsister to break up her father's marriage. One irrational act leads to another and the pot-smoking plotters decide that the best course of action is to do away with little sister. They fail, of course, as did the play. Kermit Bloomgarden, who presented it, proved that even the savviest of producers can come up with a flop.

For Jo, 1965 began and ended on a low note. With fewer Broadway assignments, he could only hope that some of the architectural projects for which his services had been solicited would come to fruition. If the first half of the sixties had been nettlesome professionally and desolating personally for Jo, the second half was destined not to be much better. To begin with, there was a perceptible change in the atmosphere in the theatre. In his forty-year-long career, Jo had become accustomed to change and, for the most part, had adjusted nicely to it. It was not merely the continued slide in the number of productions, not merely the new faces he could not immediately relate to, not merely the escalating costs both to produce and see a show on Broadway, not merely the gradual shift of emphasis from the straight play to the musical, from Broadway to off-Broadway and regional theatre. If anything, there was more theatrical activity in New York and more professional productions across the country than there had been since the twenties. The changes were more subtle and less easily grasped. What Jo was feeling, perhaps, was age, not only his own advancing years but the American theatre's.

One of the most significant manifestations of change was the decline of newspaper publishing. By the end of 1966, New York had lost the *Journal American*, the *World-Telegram and Sun*, and the *Herald Tribune*, which were combined in an act of desperation and survived only for a few months as the *World Journal Tribune*. The remaining dailies were the *New York Times*, the *Daily News*, and the *Post*. The remaining newspapers thus became more and more influential in their treatment of the news and in their commentary. The *Times* gave itself a special mission as the "newspaper of record," and if its drama critic had not held any special importance before, he—always unapologetically male—was now the indisputable leader of the pack. For the first time in anyone's memory, people were paying more attention to theatre critics hired by the *Wall Street Journal* and *Women's Wear Daily*. Another effect of the shrinking press was the rise in importance of the television reviewers; in short time, producers could not afford to dismiss their pithy and frequently pointed remarks.

As the critics of Jo's generation retired and were replaced by younger men, Jo's work was viewed as out of sync with the times, and younger scene designers were proving far more appealing to them. Boris Aronson and Oliver Smith, still in their prime, continued to get the big shows, but new names on Broadway such as Lloyd Burlingame, Robin Wagner, Robert Randolph, and William Ritman—all born *after* Jo's entry on Broadway, all from regional theatre and off-Broadway—were perceived to be closer to the pulse of the new age than Jo Mielziner and his peers.

And just what was the pulse of the new age? Broadway producers, who did not seem to know, continued to churn out the big musical, the trivial comedy, the suspense thriller, the occasional serious drama, many of which had sizable runs and seemed to make a lot of money. (David Merrick was hitting his stride in the last half of the decade, with such commercial hits as *Cactus Flower* and *I Do! I Do!*, and leavening them with such surprising entries as *Rosencrantz and Guildenstern Are Dead* and Peter Brook's production of *Marat/Sade*, which covered him with glory, if not gold.) For the moment, the producing brethren were playing it safe, while off-Broadway was reveling in iconoclasm. Nudity onstage, mimed copulation, homosexuality, obscene language, and corrosive anti-establishment politics were drawing attention to New York's other theatre. The "tribal love rock musical" *Hair* tried to combine all in one fell swoop, and it moved in 1968 from downtown to uptown to settle in for a run of 1,750 performances at the Biltmore Theatre. After that, there was no turning back.

Jo's friend Father Kusman, visiting New York, went with Jo to a performance of *Hair*. As World War II veterans, both took umbrage with the show's draft-card burning scene. Probably on Father Kusman's urging, the two men took out their theatre tickets and burned them on the sidewalk in front of the theatre to register their protest. Whether or not anyone noticed was not important. They had a good time doing it.

When the new year of 1966 rolled in, Jo and Father Kusman were in Rome, having sailed on the SS *Cristoforo Columbo* in December. The two men had an audience with the Pope and visited the great museums and cathedrals of Rome and Florence before returning by air, arriving home in early January. On Jo's drawing board were the preliminary designs for *Venus Is*, a comedy by Chester Erskine that was scheduled to open at the Billy Rose Theatre on April 19. The action of the play occurs on the day of the probe to the planet

Venus and is set on a Pacific Ocean beach. The production was directed by Word Baker, Jo's former assistant, who brought Jo into the production. Unfortunately, only a few hundred people ever got to see the play and Jo's massive set. It opened for low-priced previews on April 9 and closed after the first preview performance. Not until November would there be another Mielziner-designed production on Broadway.

Jo's assignments for the 1966–67 Broadway season trickled in. The first came from David Merrick's office, which was producing a comedy by a young stand-up comic named Woody Allen, who was just beginning to create a stir in the entertainment world. *Don't Drink the Water* concerns a caterer from Newark, on vacation in Europe with his wife and daughter, who has to take refuge in an American Embassy in an unspecified Iron Curtain country because he is suspected of being a spy. Nervous about its chance for success, Merrick buttressed the show by hiring Jo and Robert Sinclair, an experienced director with whom Jo had worked many times before. During the tryout in Philadelphia, Sinclair, who wanted fewer one-line gags and more substance from Allen, left the show in disgust and was replaced by Stanley Prager.

Jo also had doubts about its potential for success, and the play opened to largely negative reviews on November 18, 1966. Jo sent Sinclair the clippings as vindication of his mid-show departure. But Merrick's luck held, and the show found an audience for 588 performances, providing yet another example of the well-worn Broadway adage about word of mouth. Paul Trautvetter, who worked with Jo on the scenery, recalled a typical Merrick trick. One of the scenes in the show involved a cocktail party with a large cast on stage. After the reviews were published, Merrick fired all the actors who were used for that one scene.

Although Jo's assignment for *My Sweet Charlie* also required only one set, it was far more interesting to design than the antiseptic interior for the Woody Allen comedy. The script, adapted by David Westheimer from his novel, was another in a long line of Broadway plays that were trying to explore racism in all of its facets. *My Sweet Charlie* reverses stereotypes by placing a well-educated black man together with a poor, ignorant, and very pregnant white teenager.

Both are refugees—he from an inadvertent commission of a murder during a civil rights demonstration, she from a family who has disowned her because of her pregnancy. Jo's design for their cottage haven was praised to the skies by the critic from the *Boston Herald*, who sensed that he was trying to inject a bit of "poetry and pity" in the otherwise realistic set, but the New York critics hardly noticed Jo's contribution in their generally corrosive remarks about the play. It opened and closed in a month.

Without the buttress of architectural and commercial jobs, Jo's income during the late sixties shrank. Since many of the producers for whom he had been almost the resident designer had either gone out of the business, retired, or died, he could no longer count on assignments coming in like clockwork. And his friend Joshua Logan was spending more and more time in Hollywood making movies. Once when Jo wrote to him out of desperation about how to break into movies, Logan's reply was discouraging. Art direction, he said, was a "closed shop . . . and only a director demanding something special could get someone outside of the art directors' union into this bloody profession." He added that he was almost as discouraged about movies as Jo was about the theatre. "There's a lot of activity," he wrote, "but it is full of politics, jealousy and back-biters."

While his living circumstances had to be reduced to bare minimums (for him), outwardly Jo appeared to be the successful Dean of American Designers. He liked nothing better than a studio humming with activity, which was just as important to him as money. He simply did not like to be out of the swim of things or feel forgotten. He admitted to one of his friends that he was accepting jobs that he would have refused in an earlier time. One of them, *The Paisley Convertible*, was a simple-minded one-set comedy that had been born in a summer theatre, where it should have remained, according to the New York critics. A comedy about a young married couple bent on discovering each other's past sex lives, its startling revelation, which came too late in the play for the long-suffering public to flee, was that neither had one.

It had been Jo's good fortune that he was never fired from a show. There were times when he was "penciled in" but dropped at the last minute before the signing of the contract. More often, it was Jo who had turned down shows, especially during his peak years in the fifties. As the atmosphere became more cutthroat on Broadway during the late sixties, nothing was locked in until contracts were signed and checks were in the mail. In the spring of 1966, Jo thought he would be designing *The Investigation*, Peter Weiss's play about the Holocaust, which was to be directed by Ulu Grosbard for early October. After preliminary discussions between Jo and Grosbard, the director decided that Jo was not right for the show and wrote a polite letter to so inform him. (Grosbard gave the assignment to Kert Lundell.) In the fall of 1966, Grosbard obviously thought that Jo was right for *That Summer—That Fall*, a new play by Frank D. Gilroy, who had won a Pulitzer Prize for *The Subject Was Roses* in the previous year.

In *That Summer—That Fall*, which opened in March of 1967, Gilroy's subject was an updated version of the Phaedra legend, set in the apartment of an Italian-American restaurant owner and his young childless wife. The man's grown "love child" arrives from the West Coast and turns everything topsy-turvy. The young wife falls in love with her stepson, and disaster follows. While commending the playwright's earnest attempt, the critics did not care for the play and it closed quickly. Some of them liked Jo's set, but Martin Gottfried of *Women's Wear Daily* denigrated what he described as Mielziner's "usual naturalistic and heavy symbolic style in dark blood red and fateful shadows."

Another show that Jo should have turned down was David Merrick's production of *The Unemployed Saint*, a new comedy by

MOST OF THE ACTION IN ***THAT SUMMER—THAT FALL*** (1967) TAKES PLACE IN THE FLAT OF THE ITALIAN-AMERICAN FAMILY WHO ARE ITS PRINCIPAL CHARACTERS, BUT FOR THE FIRST AND LAST SCENES, IT MOVES TO A PLAY-GROUND SOMEWHERE IN LOWER MANHATTAN. FOR THE PLAYGROUND, JO REDUCED THE ELEMENTS OF SCENERY TO THREE: A BACK-BOARD, A TALL FENCE, AND A WOODEN BENCH. (COURTESY OF HENRY HEWES)

Bill Manhoff. Because he had grave doubts about the stageworthiness of the play, Merrick booked its tryout at the Royal Poinciana Theatre in Fort Lauderdale, Florida—about as far off Broadway as a producer could get. Jo's designs had contributed to the success of Manhoff's *The Owl and the Pussycat*, so Merrick hired Jo to do the set this time, hoping perhaps for another miracle. The play takes place in the dingy apartment of a young artist, who works on junk sculpture. Although the set was built in New York by the Nolan Scenic Studio and shipped to Florida, Jo never saw it onstage. After reading the script and assessing its potential, he decided that it was not worth a trip to Fort Lauderdale to attend what he was sure would be the show's requiem. The critic for the *Miami Herald* hated the show but loved Jo's set, which he described as "a daffy sort of gem," fun to look at "when the going gets sluggish around it." The going got more than sluggish in Florida and the show went nowhere else.

Jo cleared his desk and departed early in May with Father Kusman for his annual trip to Europe. Aside from his ongoing architectural projects, which tended to drag on for years, Jo had no contracts for Broadway when he returned from his sojourn. Fortunately, two assignments landed on his desk almost simultaneously in the next few months. The first came from fledgling producers Robert Leder and Michael Bregman for *Daphne in Cottage D*, a first play by a twenty-six-year-old former actor named Stephen Levi. All were unknown to Jo and to Broadway. The other came from David Merrick for a musical to be based on the saga of the notorious Mata Hari, which in Merrick's arcane reasoning made an antiwar statement. *Mata Hari* was to be directed by Vincente Minnelli, the creator of many legendary MGM musicals, who had not worked on Broadway since 1939.

Daphne in Cottage D, which lasted a month on Broadway, was another in a long string of two-character plays of self-revelation, a genre (popular at that time) that depended on the gradual stripping away of secrets surrounding the characters. Sandy Dennis and William Daniels played the two lonely people who unravel their psyches in the living room of a cottage in a New England resort. For Jo, a living room was not a difficult set to design, but there were ample forebodings of what loomed ahead with *Mata Hari*. Working on a Merrick

VINCENTE MINNELLI, THE DIRECTOR OF *MATA HARI* (1967), REMEMBERED HIS EXPERIENCE WITH THE SHOW AS LESS THAN A HIGHLIGHT IN HIS CAREER. MOST OF IT, HE THOUGHT, WAS A LOT OF NONSENSE. FOR JO IT WAS A NIGHTMARE, AS MINNELLI CALLED FOR MORE AND MORE SCENERY. HE USED LOTS OF LIGHTING AND SLIDE PROJECTIONS WITHIN A FRAMED STAGE FOR THE PLAY'S MANY VIGNETTES COMBINED WITH ALL-TOO-SOLID SCENERY THAT WAS DIFFICULT TO CHANGE QUICKLY. (COURTESY OF NEIL COLLINS/RICHARD STODDARD)

production was for Jo akin to dancing the carioca in a minefield, but because the producer had his hands full with three or four other shows at the same time, he was not paying his usual hawkeyed attention to *Mata Hari*. Besides, Merrick probably thought he had in his hands the best talent that money could buy: Minnelli as director, Jo as designer, Irene Sharaff as costume designer, Jack Cole as choreographer, and a trio of talented young men—Eddie Thomas, Jerome Coopersmith, and Martin Charnin for the music, book, and words, respectively.

Minnelli, who had become so accustomed to the filmmaking process that he forgot how to direct a show for a live audience, paid excessive attention to the scenery and costumes to the detriment of

JO'S PLATFORMS AND PROJECTIONS ON TRANSPARENT MUSLIN CREATED WHAT ONE CRITIC DESCRIBED AS "AN ADROITLY ANONYMOUS SETTING" FOR **THE PRIME OF MISS JEAN BRODIE** (1968). SHOWN IS THE ARTIST'S STUDIO, WHICH EVOLVED QUICKLY FROM THE SCHOOLROOM SET. (ESTATE OF JO MIELZINER)

the whole. To compensate for the script's deficiencies, he ordered so much scenery that it could not fit in the theatre and had to be stored in the alley outside the loading doors. The show was to open at a special benefit performance for the National Democratic Women's Club at the National Theatre, in Washington, on November 18, 1967, so it could not be postponed. What the spectators actually saw was the *first* technical and dress rehearsal, when everything is expected to go wrong and does. In the usual process, the show is stopped and started while the mechanics are corrected and perfected. There had been no time to whip the show into shape. Jo's nineteen different sets crashed into each other, split apart unexpectedly, and generally behaved uproariously in full view of an audience that by now was having a good time watching the chaos.

Jo took five hundred blows for his part in the disaster and was, in Boris Aronson's phrase, "the wictim" of the evening. As always,

Jo had given the director what he wanted, which turned out to be, as he explained to one of his assistants, "one third Minnelli, one third Mielziner, and one third shit." *Mata Hari* completed its four-week engagement in Washington, Minnelli returned to California's sunny clime, and Merrick, presumably, went back to his office to think of ways to avoid paying the half-million dollars in losses.

The balance of the 1967–68 season was much more to Jo's liking. The Robert Whitehead production of *The Prime of Miss Jean Brodie* gave him an opportunity to collaborate with the English director Michael Langham, to whom he was much more attuned than he was to Minnelli. (Jo always worked well with English directors.) The scenery was to be simple and evocative. Writing to Jo from the Stratford, Ontario, Shakespeare Festival, where he was artistic director, Langham briefly sketched what he wanted: "Don't please concern yourself with the Walk through the old town of Edinburgh; in a zealous spirit of make-believe I think I can cope with that almost unaided. What I need is the stimulus of the floor and props of an old established school, Edinburgh 1880." The only specific requests he made were that the floor should look "worn down by years of stampeding tiny feet" and that the projections should be reflective of the cloistered world of the school. This was all music to Jo's ears. He did not give Langham him exactly what he asked for, but most of the critics approved. (Langham wanted something less mechanized.) Praise came from an unexpected, yet in some ways, predictable source. Martin Gottfried of *Women's Wear Daily*, who with Clive Barnes of the *Times* considered the box set anathema at any and all times, approved of the way Jo handled the scenery. The play, adapted from the novel by Muriel Spark, concerns an eccentric teacher in a conservative Scottish school who fills her charges with romantic notions about themselves without imparting much practical knowledge. When she also praises Hitler and Mussolini as heroic figures, the school principal dismisses her. Zoe Caldwell won the Tony Award for her portrayal.

Jo was not director Alan Schneider's choice for Robert Anderson's new play, *I Never Sang for My Father*, which Jo was working on simultaneously with *Jean Brodie*. (They opened a week apart in January of 1968.) But Anderson had insisted and Jo got the job. Schneider, who distrusted what he considered Mielziner's "assembly-line methods," was described by Jo as a "director who made no preparations, couldn't make up his mind, then felt deserted when like all other designers we find ourselves with a frozen scheme and an unfrozen set of directions." What suffered in the process was Anderson's play. Jo admitted that he was not pleased with his own set. Anderson, who was unhappy that Jo's attention was diverted to other projects, had approved of the scheme but felt that it had been put together too hastily, particularly in the execution of the projected scenery. The play was a series of rapid vignettes portraying the advancing age and inevitable death of a man's parents, which forces him to confront his feelings toward them, particularly the father. Older critics found merit in most aspects of the production but their younger colleagues did not like the play. It was not one of Anderson's major successes.

From the fall of 1967 to the opening of *I Never Sang for My Father*, which he did not attend, there were personal distractions in Jo's life that were demanding his attention. The first was the death of his mother at the age of ninety-four. During the last few years of her life, Ella had been failing steadily. Up to her ninety-second birthday, she had been able to attend all of the shows that her son designed, but after that her eyesight and her mind began to dim. Finally, she suffered a series of small strokes, as a result of which she was admitted to Lenox Hill Hospital in Manhattan in January. She died there late in the evening on February 2. On the night of the opening of *I Never Sang for My Father*, Jo was keeping vigil by the telephone. Since Kenneth had bought four spaces at Forest Lawn Cemetery in Hollywood, Jo had his mother's ashes sent to California for interment.

I NEVER SANG FOR MY FATHER (1968), A KIND OF STAGED MEMOIR OF A FATHER-SON RELATIONSHIP, DEMANDED A CINEMATIC FLOW OF SCENES, WHICH JO ACCOMPLISHED BY USING TWIN TURNTABLES AND PROJECTIONS AGAINST A NEUTRAL BACKDROP TO REPRESENT DIFFERENT LOCALES. THESE RANGED FROM A RAILROAD STATION TO A CEMETERY. BY PAIRING A PROJECTION OF AN ILLUSORY SCHRAFFT'S RESTAURANT WITH A REAL TABLE AND CHAIRS, JO ECONOMICALLY SUGGESTED THE SCENE. (HARVARD THEATRE COLLECTION, HOUGHTON LIBRARY)

Jo's grief at his mother's death was tempered by the realization that she had lived a long, full life and had refused to surrender to the distempers of old age; he recalled only her sweetness and happiness. "Mother was wonderful in that way," he wrote to Mildred Knopf. "She never became bitter, sardonic or complaining. She had much to remember in a rich, creative and happy life. Fortunately her family relationships were almost ideal." Almost to the end of her life, old friends would visit her at Miss James's, where she lived in regal comfort, and she would joyfully reminisce about the old days and talk about the books she was reading and the events of the day—always with her dictionary at her side. When she could no longer read, Jo would tell her the plots of the plays he was designing. When she became confined, Jo would spend his weekly visit quietly talking to her in her room. When she died, Ella left no estate, just her wedding ring and a few odds and ends.

Still another event compounded the dark mood of the late 1960s for Jo. His daughter Jennifer, whose marriage was growing increasingly troubled, decided that she had had enough of her marriage with Bob Errickson and suburban Pennsylvania life and moved to New York with her children. She filed for divorce in 1966 and began seeing Joe Friar, a stagehand whom she had met through her brother Michael. She married Friar a year later. Jo was not sympathetic to any of these happenings in her life.

In New York, Jennifer rooted around trying to find a place for herself in the theatre. Finally, she landed a job in the New York office of ANTA. When ANTA went out of business, she worked for the producer Lester Osterman. When she left Osterman, she found a job as an ambulance driver with an emergency medical service organization in nearby Westchester County. By that time, her marriage to Friar had soured and they had separated. Friar called Jo to tell him that Jennifer was neglecting her two daughters. Taking matters into his own hands and without Jennifer's permission, Friar deposited the children with Jo at the Dakota to await the arrival of their father, Bob Errickson, who was summoned to take them away with him. Jennifer's bitterness toward her father lasted for several years, during which she fought to regain custody of her children. Years later, Krista was returned to her, but Donna Jo preferred to remain with her father.

Jo tended to keep this familial turbulence bottled up, but it took its toll on him. He confessed to Eddie Kook that he was not feeling up to snuff because of "physical and psychological pressures." He had to consult his doctor about the pain he was feeling in his heels, which made it impossible to sit at his drafting stool for more than a few minutes at a time. When the ailment was diagnosed as bursitis, he was told to use wedges in his shoes to relieve the condition. He was also concerned about his lack of work. Although he had one more show to make ready for the spring of 1968 and George Balanchine had asked him to redesign his scenery for "Slaughter on Tenth Avenue" as a free-standing ballet, he had no Broadway assignments for the upcoming 1968–69 season.

Jo was both flattered and gratified by Balanchine's call. Now head of the New York City Ballet, Balanchine entered one of the most creative periods of his career when the company moved to Lincoln Center. Using what he had learned on the Broadway musical stage, creating his own form of Americana, Balanchine returned to Richard Rodgers's music. It was easy for him to re-create "Slaughter on Tenth Avenue" and to add it to his company's repertory. Jo's set, a little shopworn and ragged at the seams, still sees action.

With work on all of Jo's projects at a standstill, Paul Trautvetter, his associate designer for six years, left his staff at the end of April in 1968 to find other avenues for his talent. Rather than replace him, Jo decided to hire assistants as he needed them, a system that most of his fellow designers had followed for years. At this crucial juncture, Tennessee Williams came back into his life with another play. Originally entitled *Kingdom of Earth,* it was renamed *The Seven Descents of Myrtle* for its Broadway opening to make it more marketable. The play, which was not among Williams's strongest scripts, was produced by David Merrick and directed by José Quintero, whose productions of the late O'Neill dramas had lifted his stock to the highest level on Broadway. The combination of Williams, Merrick, Quintero, and Mielziner did not create the right chemical reactions and the production suffered. When Jo received the script from the playwright late in 1967, he immediately wrote to tell him how much he liked it but was concerned about the core of the play.

He asked him questions about the house that was to be the central setting, the background of the characters, and a few other details, which revealed an uncharacteristic vagueness in Williams's writing. When the play opened, Walter Kerr, writing in the Sunday *Times*, said that the play needed Elia Kazan. It also needed a more enthusiastic producer. Williams flourished when he was surrounded by people who bolstered his flagging spirits in times of crisis. Neither Merrick nor Quintero, who either quit or was fired just before the opening, could do so this time. Jo, as usual, remained the most upbeat, but he was swimming against a strong tide of pessimism about the play, which takes place in a Mississippi Delta house. Three main characters battle each other over its ownership. When a developing flood threatens to consume the house, tensions rise to a breaking point. Designing the house as the central focus of the play, Jo saw it as a compression tank.

The critics were disappointed with the play, and their disappointment embraced the entire production. Jo was stung by the criticism of his set, particularly by Clive Barnes's comment that it was "one of those dear Jo Mielziner doll houses with see-through walls." At the studio, Jo managed a wan joke: "Didn't Ibsen become famous because of his doll's house?"

The Williams play behind him, Jo and Father Kusman left for their European sojourn. Jo was denied his annual pilgrimage to the city of his birth because of the student riots in Paris, but he returned to New York reinvigorated by the trip. Yet he faced an empty drawing board.

What kept him busy in the interim was a project that he first embarked on in 1966. His association with the Vivian Beaumont Theatre had brought him both foreseeable and unforeseen benefits. One was a proposal to do a book on theatre architecture in America. Eddie Kook encouraged Jo to submit a proposal to the Ford Foundation, which ordinarily did not give direct grants to individuals but agreed to consider making a grant to the Arts of the Theatre Foundation. Since the founder and chief benefactor of the Arts of the Theatre Foundation was Eddie himself, the foundation could (and did) commission the book, with Jo as author. The Ford Foundation made a grant of $9,200 to the Arts of the Theatre

AFTER DISCUSSING THE SET FOR **THE SEVEN DESCENTS OF MYRTLE** (1968) WITH TENNESSEE WILLIAMS AND JOSÉ QUINTERO, JO CONCLUDED THAT THE PSYCHIC SPINE OF THE PLAY WAS THE HOUSE—THE ENTIRE HOUSE—WHICH EXERCISED ITS SINISTER CONTROL OVER THE CHARACTERS. (IT CALLS TO MIND THE HOUSE IMAGES IN **DEATH OF A SALESMAN** AND **LOOK HOMEWARD, ANGEL**.) BY MAKING IT THE DOMINANT IMAGE, JO HAD TO CHOP UP THE INTERIOR INTO SMALL ACTING AREAS, WHICH TURNED OUT NOT TO BE THE BEST SOLUTION. QUINTERO MAY HAVE BEEN TOO OVERWHELMED TO OBJECT AND MERRICK SAID NOTHING, TAKING SADISTIC PLEASURE IN SEEING THE WHOLE ENTERPRISE SINK. (COURTESY OF MING CHO LEE)

Foundation, which paid Jo $3,200, while the rest went for editorial assistance and illustration. C. Ray Smith, an editor of *Progressive Architecture*, helped Jo write the book, and Jo's assistants provided the illustrations under Jo's guidance. Clarkson N. Potter agreed to publish it under the title *The Shapes of Our Theatre.*

In it, Jo presents a brief historical overview of the evolution of theatrical architecture and the many direct influences that altered its shapes. He even discusses the indirect sociological impact on theatre structures. Rather than including photographs, he filled the book with schematic drawings of various actual theatres pared down to graphs of audience–stage relationships. Included in the text is Jo's spirited defense of his part in the building of the Beaumont. The book leaves no question about Jo's preference in theatrical architecture. After examining recent trends, he simply states: "On the whole, if I were limited to a single stage form, I would choose a flexible Proscenium with an ample forestage." Philosophically, he ended where he had begun, with the thinking that shaped his plans for the Pittsburgh Playhouse in 1949. The book is as much a reflection of Jo's concept of theatre as it is of theatre architecture, particularly in his discussion of 1960s-style "uncommitted spaces," or nontraditional forms. Nonsense, he seems to be saying: theatre by its very nature begs for discipline and definition. That was his constant refrain.

Jo's work on the Vivian Beaumont also resulted in a demand for his services as a consultant on theatrical projects around the country. On a few of them, he was engaged as co-designer with architects

chosen by the client; on others, he served as consultant. Most of the projects died a-borning, but a few were actually built. In early 1964, Robert Schnitzer, the head of the University of Michigan's Professional Theatre Program, asked Jo to meet with university officials to discuss a theatre project in the making. He agreed to fly out to Ann Arbor to meet with the architect Alden Dow, an heir to the Dow Chemical fortune and one of the earliest apprentices of Frank Lloyd Wright in the 1930s. If Jo had any secret misgivings about an association with a Wright disciple, he was willing to bury them for the sake of involvement in the project. Jo had worked with Wright's son Lloyd on the aborted Los Angeles theatre project and had even had an experience with the master himself. Jo had attended a meeting where a model of one of Wright's theatre designs was exhibited. After studying the theatre for several minutes, Jo asked Wright how an actor trapped on the projecting forestage would make a quick exit. Wright replied, "We just won't do that kind of play." Jo also did not like Wright's Kalita Humphreys Theatre, for the Dallas Theatre Center, describing it as an "interesting experiment but a bad theatre."

Jo's past experiences with the Wrightian approach to theatre design did not persuade him that the master or his apprentices were capable of creating a workable playhouse. Predictably, the partnership between him and Dow proved to be unworkable. For a year, Jo and his staff turned out twenty-three versions of the theatre and the accompanying rehearsal rooms, scene shop, costume shop, and so on, while Dow was busily designing a miniature version of Radio City Music Hall. When Jo was convinced that Dow was resisting his contributions, he wrote to Schnitzer and offered to bow out. Because of his nonconfrontational nature, Jo opposed Dow's designs only by implication. When he discovered that the members of the university building committee were also unhappy with the scheme and wanted to jettison Dow, Jo was only too happy to offer the names of Kevin Roche and John Dinkeloo, Eero Saarinen's heirs apparent.

With Roche and Dinkeloo, the project moved forward at a much faster clip, but after another year of work, it stalled for lack of money. In 1969, Eugene Power, a member of the Board of Regents,

THE POWER CENTER AT THE UNIVERSITY OF MICHIGAN REPRESENTED ANOTHER VERSION OF JO'S ORIGINAL CONCEPT OF A "NEW" THEATRE, WHICH BEGAN WITH THE ANTA–WASHINGTON SQUARE PROTOTYPE. FOR A DECADE, HE KEPT DESIGNING THE SAME THEATRE. (COURTESY OF THE POWER CENTER, UNIVERSITY OF MICHIGAN)

made a large contribution from the millions he had made in selling University Microfilms to Xerox. It covered the construction of the theatre but not the building of the service facilities. Eventually the theatre was built, adjacent to Felch Park, on the central campus.

The Power Center is a close cousin of the Vivian Beaumont. Equipped as a dual-purpose theatre, its fan-shaped auditorium is divided into two sections, an orchestra and a balcony with none of its approximately 1,400 seats more than 67 feet from the stage. The thrust stage, 28 feet wide, projects 16 feet beyond the proscenium into the auditorium and is raised and lowered by an elevator. Most of the other costly mechanized equipment had to be cut from the original plans. The exterior of the theatre is built of exposed aggregate concrete with the front of reflecting glass to mirror the trees of Felch Park. The glass, which becomes transparent when lighted from within, forms a wall of the cheerless lobby, which is flanked by two poured-concrete spiral staircases. Even though a scaled-down version of the service facilities was built long after the theatre was finished and in use, the theatre retains an air of incompletion. Jo felt that the structure was too ambitious and large for the university it was to serve. Indeed, the theatre department continued doing productions in the much more intimate Lydia Mendelssohn Theatre.

Other architectural commissions flowed into the Dakota studio during the sixties. For most of them, Jo served as consultant to the architects on the seating arrangement for the auditorium to ensure proper sightlines and on the equipment for lighting and mechanizing the stage. In a few instances, the architects listened politely to his advice, then did what they pleased. In the early sixties, he had been hired by the architects for the Los Angeles Music Center to act as consultant to what became the Ahmanson Theatre and the Mark Taper Forum, but his specifications were largely ignored as he continued to speak against the architecture and the architect. Jo was appalled by a master plan that was dictated by geometric shapes, not by the functions of the building. After he was "retired" from the Ahmanson, he was asked to continue working on the Taper, which is a round theatre. When Jo questioned whether it had been conceived to contain a theatre in the round, the architect replied:

"No, but I want to have a round exterior shape to complement the two other rectangular shapes." Most of his advice for Taper went unheeded. When it opened in 1967, it contained a modified thrust stage with no backstage.

Southern Illinois University at Edwardsville retained Jo as co-designer with the architects for their multipurpose Communications Building, which, like the Vivian Beaumont and the Power Center, utilized a variation of the proscenium–thrust stage arrangement. For several years, Jo also worked on a proposed theatre for the National Life and Insurance Company complex in Nashville, Tennessee. The Chicago office of the architectural firms of Skidmore, Owings and Merrill was retained as architects and Jo was hired as co-designer. At first the space was thought of as a meeting hall for company assemblies, but the company president wanted to branch out into "cultural expression" to accommodate visiting performing companies and high-level entertainment. When that same executive died suddenly, the theatre project was quietly dropped.

Jo's last architectural assignment in the sixties was as consultant to Albert Selden, the leaseholder of the Minskoff Theatre, which was almost totally designed by the time he was brought into the project. Although he told Selden that it was too late for him to have any impact on the building, Jo felt that he could make a significant contribution in having a second balcony omitted from the plans.

Balancing his architectural work with his book authorship, Jo found little time to secure Broadway design assignments. Usually, he never worried about them, but in the fall of 1968 he became aware that for the first time in his forty-four-year career, he had no Broadway shows lined up for the upcoming season. Also for the first time, he agreed to design an off-Broadway production, *Possibilities*. He admitted to everyone that he did not like the play, but he felt it was time to experience New York's other theatrical venue, and he liked the director Jerome Kilty, an actor and playwright with solid professional credentials. Besides, he had nothing else on his drawing board. Jo, who was probably the highest-paid scene designer in Broadway history (to that time), signed a contract that paid him $400 plus $50 per week for six weeks. The producers (there were four of them) leased a little Greenwich Village theatre,

The Players, on MacDougal Street, for presenting the play by Arthur Pitman. The "possibilities" in the title referred to the "four possible outcomes in the life of a young woman having an affair in the 1940s." The main set was a Village apartment, which was augmented by slide projections. It opened on December 4, 1968, and closed after a single performance.

Jo was spared the ignominy of having a Mielziner-less Broadway season by a call from the office of Stuart Ostrow, who was producing *1776*, a new musical. It proved to be one of the happiest experiences in a decade of few high points. Ostrow, a young producer with relatively few Broadway credits, was realizing one of his wildest dreams in working alongside the famous designer. For the show, Jo repeated his use of the jutting stage that he had employed for *Cat on a Hot Tin Roof*, but his original concept was deeply modified by

the changes in the book of the musical. Because the scenery for the Chamber of the Continental Congress was intended to disappear at one point to reveal a battlefield and several other scenes, the main set was designed to fly out of sight. From the beginning, Jo felt that these scenes intruded on the main plot. Ultimately, everyone else agreed and these scenes were cut during the out-of-town tryouts. As a consequence, the scenery became relatively static, except in moments when it was altered slightly to allow the actors to go into the streets of Philadelphia and to Thomas Jefferson's room.

The show, a surprise hit, dramatizes and musicalizes the events immediately preceding the signing of the Declaration of Independence. Jo enjoyed working with the entire creative team: writer Peter Stone, composer and lyricist Sherman Edwards, choreographer Onna White, and costume designer Patricia Zipprodt. Except for Pat and Onna White, it was the first time he had worked with most of them. When Jo was unhappy with Ostrow's choice of a scene shop to build the set, he wrote the young producer a long letter explaining why the low price would be a high price for both of them to pay if the job went to the lowest bidder. Convinced that Jo was right, Ostrow awarded it to Pete Feller.

As usual, critics Martin Gottfried and Clive Barnes dissented amid the show's acclaim, but *1776* engendered a national tour, a bus-and-truck tour, and productions in London and Australia. On Broadway, where it opened on March 16, 1969, it accumulated 1,217 performances. For Jo it was a bonanza at a time when he needed both a lift in morale and income. If he had to have only one Mielziner-designed show for the season, he was lucky that it was *1776*.

Stuart Ostrow had planned to produce another musical, which was being written by Stephen Sondheim and James Goldman. Originally titled *The Girls Upstairs* and conceived as a musical murder mystery, it was offered to Jo, who began preliminary sketches based on a fragmentary scenario. Because Sondheim was heavily involved with *Company*, a musical that was to be produced by Harold Prince, he and Goldman suspended work on *The Girls Upstairs*, and Ostrow dropped his plans to produce it. When Sondheim and Goldman

A SHUTTERED AND ANGLED SET CREATED FOR *1776* (1969) CAME ALIVE WHEN THE SHUTTERS OPENED AND CLOSED TO REVEAL THE CHAMBER OF THE CONTINENTAL CONGRESS IN PHILADELPHIA. WITH THIS ALMOST DANCELESS MUSICAL, JO WAS NOT COMPELLED TO OPEN UP THE STAGE FOR A CHORUS OF DANCERS AND COULD MAKE USE OF PLATFORMS SURROUNDING THE MAIN SET FOR THE SMALL CHANGES OF SCENE. (COURTESY OF JENNIFER MIELZINER)

finally completed it, it was renamed *Follies* under a radically different concept and was produced by Prince and designed by Boris Aronson in 1971.

Jo closed the decade with two productions far from the marquees of Broadway. He was invited to be guest designer at the University of Illinois for a production of *Galileo*, by Bertolt Brecht, to be presented at the inauguration of the Krannert Center for the Performing Arts, for which he had served as consultant. The production was to be mounted in the Playhouse, a 700-seat proscenium–thrust theatre. For Jo, it was a first experience designing a Brecht play, and within an academic environment at that. The director, Clara Behringer, utilized all of the mechanical wonders of the new theatre, which had the effect of making the plant itself the show. Jo's neutral setting was crowded with actors as the story of Galileo's apostasy shifted from one seventeenth-century city to another. Jo designed the scenery in New York and did not attend the opening at the end of October of 1969. He also provided the design for the program cover.

Having read about Jo's designing for off-Broadway, Bob Schnitzer and his wife, Marcella Cisney, who were running the professional theatre program at the University of Michigan, were emboldened to ask Jo to design their production of *The Conjuror*, a new play by Evan Hunter, the author of *The Blackboard Jungle*. The Schnitzers were confident that the play could move to New York, and Jo agreed to design it with a clause that would have given him his standard fee for a Broadway production if, indeed, it did transfer. Perhaps, in the belief that the production was Broadway-bound, it was reviewed by a critic from *Variety* who thought that it was, on the whole, effective. Yet it did not find a berth on the New York stage and ended its life in Michigan.

Although Jo made two visits to Ann Arbor, he did not attend the opening of *The Conjuror*. By the time it opened in early November of 1969, he was already deeply immersed in three productions all with openings in February of 1970. Sherman Edwards, of *1776*, had called Jo "eternally young," and it was true—nothing kept Jo's vital creative juices flowing like work, and he was experiencing a bracing jolt of energy with his new projects.

USING MOSTLY PROJECTIONS AND GRADUATED PLATFORMS, JO HAD TO FOLLOW THE SWIFTLY MOVING VIGNETTES OF THE TWENTY SCENES IN *GALILEO* (1969). WHAT LOOKED DECEPTIVELY SIMPLE WAS IN FACT A COMPLICATED TECHNICAL SHOW WHERE TIMING WAS EVERYTHING. (COURTESY OF NEIL COLLINS/RICHARD STODDARD)

THE CONJUROR (1969) WAS A SELF-CONSCIOUS PIECE ABOUT A PLAYWRIGHT (PLAYED BY JAMES WHITMORE) CONJURING UP A PLAY ABOUT HIMSELF BUT UNABLE TO GET A WORD OF IT ON PAPER. JO DESIGNED A SERIES OF PROJECTIONS TO REPRESENT THE WRITER'S FLASHBACKS, SHOWN ON THREE WINDOWS AT THE BACK OF THE SET. EACH WAS INTRODUCED BY A BLACKOUT. (BILLY ROSE THEATRE COLLECTION, NYPL-PA)

9
DEAN OF DESIGNERS

I n 1970, Local 829 of United Scenic Artists, which Jo had helped to found, made him a life member. It meant that Jo was not required to pay regular dues for the rest of his life, and that was good news. Jo's attitude toward his union was, at best, ambivalent. He realized the necessity for having it represent him and the other designers in the gritty negotiations with producers, but regarding most union policies, he had a litany of complaints: There was no training program for aspirants, the examination process was subject to abuse, the regulations hobbled active designers, union meetings were always at inconvenient times. Finally, he regarded himself as an independent contractor, who should be allowed to make his own rules of conduct. This last objection—shared by most of the older members of the union—was seized upon by the federal government, which instituted an antitrust suit against Local 829 in 1957. The crux of the action centered on whether the scene designers could be considered employees of the producers or independent contractors. Four years and much turmoil later, the union signed a consent decree that cautiously sidestepped settlement of this point but prohibited a "closed shop." In practical terms, nothing was really changed. With the theatre tightly union-organized, producers dared not antagonize the other unions by exercising their right to hire nonunion designers.

In its history, Local 829 was forced to make adjustments whenever it felt threatened. In 1962, when the stagehands flirted with the idea of setting up a special unit for lighting technicians, the union reorganized its categories and henceforth recognized lighting design as a valid specialty. From that moment on, the United Scenic Artists set up nationally the four classifications for designers that are in force today: scenery, costumes, lighting, and "all classifications," which embraced all specialties. Jo was grandfathered into this fourth category, but he never ceased to be vigilant of the union's activities.

In the seventies, Eddie Kook brought about a big change in Jo's life. In 1964, Eddie had sold his Century Lighting Company to Progress Manufacturing Company but remained as its president until 1968, when he finally retired from the company entirely. A man of prodigious energy, Eddie was not about to spend the rest of his life counting his money. He and Jo formed a kind of loose partnership to offer themselves as consultants in theatre design and lighting. Because of his theatre design commissions, Jo had drawn his friend into most of the projects because he always felt more comfortable with Eddie at his side during the discussions of lighting equipment with his clients, so it was an easy step for them to form a professional alliance. Occasionally the contrasting personalities of the two men perplexed potential clients.

Most of the invitations Mielziner and Kook received came from schools and colleges around the country, which involved all-expense-paid trips to the campuses, followed by recommendations made by the partners after they returned to New York. Mielziner and Kook also received an occasional invitation to advise various civic centers building theatres around the country. (Jo's reputation even brought him an occasional inquiry from beyond the borders of the country.) In the early seventies, Jo and Eddie became involved in planning theatres at Wake Forest University in North Carolina and the Denver Center for the Performing Arts. But for the moment, Jo's attention was diverted by an event that threatened the theatre nearest and dearest to his heart, the Vivian Beaumont at Lincoln Center.

During the fund-raising drives for the Vivian Beaumont Theatre during the early sixties, Jo had contributed $1,000 so that a memorial plaque with the name of his brother, Kenneth, could be affixed to one of the seats. At that time, the entire project was suffused with such optimism that everyone connected with it, including Jo, was certain that at last New York would have a *permanent* noncommercial, institutional (dare they say *national?*) theatre. Like the great public theatres in Europe, the Repertory Theatre of Lincoln Center was to be dedicated to the production of the best of American playwriting as well as revivals of the classics.

The first stumble was the replacement of the visionaries Whitehead and Kazan by visionaries of a different cast, Blau and Irving. Another stumble occurred when Blau departed with the blessings of the Lincoln Center brass and Jules Irving became the sole producer. Rather quickly in its history, the whole idea of *repertory* theatre had been abandoned. The boards of directors of the Repertory Theatre and Lincoln Center, Inc. were either woefully naïve or taken by surprise that a system of changing dramatic productions every night might prove to be costly. (Since many of them also sat on the board of the Metropolitan Opera, they certainly *should* have known about the cost of repertory.) Instead of genuine repertory, Irving had to be content with limited engagements of plays in a series. By the 1970 season, Irving and his board realized that the theatre was in deep trouble: Expenses were almost $2.5 million for the season and the box office income (mostly through subscriptions) was only around $1.7 million. Even with foundations, wealthy donors, and government sources kicking in, the deficit remained in the hundreds of thousands of dollars.

The Board of Lincoln Center, Inc., which wholly owned the Vivian Beaumont, turned to the City of New York for help. Early in 1971, Richard Clurman, head of the City Center, offered to take the Beaumont and below-ground Forum over and reconstruct the interior to include two movie theatres and facilities for an American branch of Henri Langlois's *Cinémathèque Français*, complete with museum, film library, screening room, and film lab. The city then moved to buy the theatre from Lincoln Center for $1, and the City Planning Commission approved more than $5 million dollars for the renovation. Hugh Hardy and George Izenour advanced their own separate plans for transforming the Vivian Beaumont into a proscenium theatre without reconstructing the entire auditorium. All options were being studied.

Nothing in New York that involves city planning and public money goes forward until it is thoroughly washed out and hung to dry in public and in the press. Since the universal opinion held unswervingly that the Vivian Beaumont was a white elephant, the problem was what to do with it. (It is architect Kevin Roche's belief that a special "New York syndrome" came into play: After the theatre and its company stumbled in its early trials, both were given up for lost. "They might as well have torn it down," he said.) The city's Board of Estimate was scheduled to meet on September 2, 1971 to decide the fate of the Vivian Beaumont and the Forum. Jo wrote a few weeks in advance of this date to ask whether he would be allowed to speak against the proposed plan. He included an unpublished letter of protest to the *New York Times*. On August 24, the *Daily News* published Jo's opposition to the plan along with his drawings to prove that the Clurman suggestion was architecturally impossible. Confessing that he had remained silent for many months while burning with rage, he explained that he had been inhibited from coming forward sooner by the feeling that he would have been regarded as a "prejudiced party." Silent no longer, he ended his argument with the words: "They say all these wonders will be performed with no violations to the esthetics of the building. There will be complete violation."

Six days later, Clurman countered Jo's charges in the *News* by submitting *his* architects' configuration of the space and citing in great detail how little the Forum Theatre had been used in the six years since it was built and how inefficient the mechanical wonders of the theatre had proved during the same time. The *Times* finally printed Jo's letter on August 29, and on September 2 he got his chance to speak at the Board of Estimate hearing but to no avail. The board approved the plan and sent it to the City Council for its action.

Shortly after Jo's and Clurman's pieces appeared in the *News*, much of of the press jumped in, with support for Jo's stand coming from strange and unpredictable sources. Martin Gottfried of *Women's Wear Daily* and Clive Barnes of the *Times*, not notable Mielziner

admirers, condemned Clurman's action; and Brooks Atkinson, late of the *Times*, wrote to Jo from his country retirement that he was on his side, even though he found the stairs at both the Beaumont and the Forum "alarming" for a "wearer of bifocals." Surprising support came from John Simon of *New York* magazine, who ran a series of articles beginning in early October 1971 in which he challenged the entire rationale of the city's plan. The heading for his first piece was "Is a design by a major architect like child's blocks to be rearranged at will?"

The plan put forth by the city was eventually defeated not by direct legal fiat but by another New York syndrome. If events are allowed to drag on unresolved for too long, eventually everyone loses interest. Henri Langlois gave up, Richard Clurman gave up, and the money that was supposedly earmarked for the renovation simply dried up. The Vivian Beaumont and the Forum were returned intact to Jules Irving and his company, which faltered for another two years until they, too, gave up. The next tenant of the Beaumont was Joseph Papp, who constantly called the theatre "a disaster" and demanded that Lincoln Center provide him with the money to renovate and reinvigorate it.

During Papp's tenure, he got to do some but not all of the modifications that he planned. One of his major changes was to have his designer Santo Loquasto create an exposed lighting grid to hang from Saarinen's ceiling. Papp thought it would serve as an important element to pull together the auditorium and stage, thus creating a closer relationship between actor and viewer. His legendary success at fund-raising sustained him for a while at Lincoln Center. He received several million dollars in operating funds from Mitzi Newhouse, of the publishing empire, for whom he renamed the little Forum Theatre. In the end, Papp found that he was overextending his energies in trying to run the Beaumont, the Newhouse, and the Public Theatre sixty blocks downtown. He gave up in 1977. One of his indirect accomplishments was to save the Vivian Beaumont and the Newhouse from other architectural "improvements."

Although the Beaumont could never shake the onus of being a problematic theatre, Jo's reputation as a theatre designer did not suffer greatly because of it. In 1970, Jo received a letter from a professor of theatre at Wake Forest University asking him whether he might be interested in serving as consultant on a new fine arts center that the university was contemplating building. The young professor, Harold Tedford, and the president of the university, Dr. James R. Scales, met with Jo in New York in January over lunch at the Players Club. Tedford had heard Jo speak at the University of Texas in 1963 and was impressed by Jo's premise that a theatre should be viewed as an instrument of production, not as a monument or as a self-indulgent statement by a particular architect. Although Scales was delighted with Jo's ideas, the building project did not go forward for two years. Then, in 1972, Jo was invited to attend a planning symposium that the university was sponsoring. Jo's presentation there was so persuasive that he was hired by the university as consultant for the new theatre. Eddie Kook served as an adjunct consultant to Jo in lighting.

After four years of planning and construction, two theatres were built: the Main Stage Theatre and the Ring Theatre. The Main Stage was probably Jo's greatest achievement and his finest legacy in theatre design. He scaled the theatre to fit the needs of a 3,000-student university and designed it to be usable by the students. A modern proscenium theatre, it seats fewer than 350 persons in a slightly fan-shaped auditorium that contains not one obstructed view of the stage. The curved orchestra pit is on a hydraulic lift that, when raised to stage level, pushes the apron about fourteen feet into the house to create a modified thrust stage. The grand curtain follows the curve of the thrust, when it is in use. A stage house rises 70 feet above the stage to allow scenery to be flown out of sight. Although there are sophisticated lighting and sound systems built into the theatre, both are not so advanced that students cannot learn the controls. The stage is equipped with an annular ring, which facilitates rapid scene changes and a standard rope counterweight system easily manipulated by student technicians. The proscenium, which is 36 feet across and 20 feet high, is adjustable by means of side panels to close in the opening and a valance above the stage that can be raised to increase the height to 30 feet.

The auditorium ceiling, which contains acoustical "clouds" against inky blue plaster, insures perfect audibility and complements the scheme of wood-paneled walls in gradated shades from darkest to lightest at the back of the house, seats covered in purple fabric, and carpeting of brown and purple tweed. Jo objected to the color of the curtain but was unable to have it changed because it had already been ordered.

Devoted as they were to up-to-the-minute technology, Jo and Eddie accepted President Scales's challenge to make it a workable theatre without undue mechanization. The Main Stage has withstood the test of time and has been universally regarded as a

CLOSE TO HIS HEART AND IDEALS WAS JO'S DESIGN FOR THE LITTLE THEATRE AT WAKE FOREST UNIVERSITY (SHOWN HERE). HE RETURNED TO THE INTIMATE PROSCENIUM THEATRE HE HAD FIRST ENVISIONED FOR THE PITTSBURGH PLAYHOUSE. SIMPLE, UNADORNED EXCEPT BY NATURAL MATERIALS, THE WAKE FOREST THEATRE STANDS TODAY AS HIS MOST SUCCESSFUL MONUMENT IN THEATRE ARCHITECTURE. (COURTESY OF HAROLD TEDFORD AND THE WAKE FOREST UNIVERSITY THEATRE)

near-perfect little theatre. The actress Julie Harris on a visit to the campus considered the students fortunate in being able to learn about production within such an environment. (She would have been interested to know that Jo always used her small-featured face as the litmus test for judging the success of sightlines in an auditorium. If the audience could see Julie Harris's face from every seat, then he felt that the theatre was a success.) The director Michael Bennett was so astonished by it that he wished he could transport it to New York.

Unfortunately, the second theatre designed by Jo and Eddie in the complex has been a failure. Intended as an experimental and adaptable space, its uniqueness has proved to be its rigidity. As its name, "the Ring," implies, it was built as a theatre in the round with seats placed upon risers in self-contained sections or "pods" that were set in tracks around the circular stage so that two, three, or four pods could be used at any given time. Scenery, always a thorny problem in arena stages, was supposed to come from eight slide projectors, which were mounted above the stage in a doughnut-shaped structure. These were supposed to throw scenic images onto a 14-foot screen that encircled the auditorium and was raised about 10 feet off the floor. The scheme never really worked and the doughnut was later removed, which improved both the lighting and acoustics in the little theatre.

Shortly after Jo and Eddie began working on the Wake Forest University fine arts center, Donald Seawell talked to Jo about a theatre center that Seawell and Helen Bonfils, an actress-turned-Broadway producer, wanted to build in Denver. As Seawell put together a design team, Jo was selected as theatre expert, Roche and Dinkeloo were hired as architects, and Gordon Davidson of the Mark Taper Forum was assigned the artistic management of the theatres. Jo exacted a promise from Seawell that he himself would report directly to the client (the Denver Center for the Performing Arts) and not to the architects. He knew that there could occasionally be breakdowns in communication in the link from architect to designer to client, no matter how well the collaboration seemed to be functioning. One of the first steps in the process was a discussion among Jo, Eddie, and Davidson in September of 1973.

HAROLD TEDFORD AND JO MIELZINER WITH A MODEL OF THE RING THEATRE. (COURTESY OF HAROLD TEDFORD)

For the next eighteen months, Jo and Eddie completed their work up to the third phase of their contract: to provide "drawings, models, specifications on the design and technical requirements of the stage and its related facilities and equipment." Jo confided to one of his friends that Davidson had trouble making up his mind about what he wanted. Eventually, Davidson did submit a proposal, which resulted in designs for a three-theatre complex consisting of a 642-seat thrust-stage playhouse; a pentagonal flexible 450-seat theatre for experimental productions; and a 180-seat laboratory theatre. Since there was no lack of money for fulfilling the wishes of Don Seawell and the late Helen Bonfils, the design team had the rare experience of being able to work out their ideas with actual-size models, which were constructed on a Hollywood sound

THE DENVER CENTER THEATRE'S MULTIPLE PLAYHOUSES (OPENED IN 1980) INCORPORATED MOST OF JO'S IDEAS IN ARCHITEC-
TURAL DESIGN FOR STAGE AND AUDITORIUM. THE LARGEST OF THE THREE, THE STAGE (SHOWN), HAD STEEP BANKS OF SEATS
SO THAT PEOPLE SEATED IN THE HIGHEST ROWS COULD STILL FEEL IN INTIMATE CONTACT WITH THE PERFORMERS. (COURTESY
OF DONALD SEAWELL, DENVER CENTER FOR THE PERFORMING ARTS; MELANIE SIMONET PHOTOGRAPH)

A creeping seediness was invading New York's Theatre District along with an onstage permissiveness that followed the rebellious sixties. The area around Times Square began to fill up with sex shops, pornographic movie houses, sleazy massage parlors, and prostitutes parading openly on West 42nd Street. Meanwhile the introduction on stage of formerly taboo subjects and the dropping of objections to nudity, simulated sex and bathroom functions, as well as the loosening of inhibitions about what could be said and how it could be said were symptoms of the times.

While fighting this (to many) unsavory image, producers were staggering under the increased costs of mounting a Broadway show. The half-million-dollar musical was now routine. Plays that once came into New York for just a few thousand dollars now could cost up to $150,000 to produce. To cover their risks and make a sporting attempt to recoup their money, producers began to inch the cost of tickets upwards. (They insisted that theatre ticket prices had fallen behind the inflation rate over the years.) Fifteen dollars for a musical and ten dollars for a play seemed a lot to pay for a night in the theatre on a regular basis and under such conditions. When the public did decide to take a chance and go see a play or a musical, they went to the theatre with such great expectations that only occasionally did they feel satisfied by the returns.

At the cusp of the decade, Walter Kerr had written: "We live, generally speaking, in a time of second-rank theatre, theatre at less than masterpiece heat, and we know it." Several playwrights, discouraged by the firmly entrenched hit-or-else psychology, took their wares elsewhere; former Broadway stalwarts like Jerome Lawrence and Robert E. Lee introduced their new plays in the regional theatre, not on Broadway. (Conversely, plays that began in regional theatres suddenly found it easier to travel to Broadway.) To compound Broadway's difficulties, shows from London were being transferred to New York as complete packages already cast, directed, and designed. Jo's competitors now included the up-and-coming English designers. For Jo, who had weathered five decades by adapting himself to new conditions, it was no longer a question of making necessary adjustments. The kind of play or musical for which the Mielziner touch was always the right one was in short

stage. In February of 1975, the architects took over to draw up the construction plans and Jo's role became minimal. The Denver Center Theatre was completed in 1980.

While architectural consulting could be lucrative in the long run, it was always a tenuous process that dragged on for years. Between the phases of design and building on these projects, Jo had to fill in with whatever scene designing came his way. The early 1970s were not happy years on Broadway, for Jo and for the American theatre.

supply. And when something appeared that he could have designed, someone else often got the job because the producer needed to hold down costs.

The producer Alexander Cohen wrote to Jo saying that he considered him the "Dean of Designers." He was referring not merely to Jo's longevity as a designer on Broadway but to a continuing demand for Jo's talents. Although this was hardly the case, Jo broke almost a year-long drought without a Broadway show with an unforeseeable hit, *Child's Play*. David Merrick hired Jo to design a first play by a teacher named Robert Marasco. Jo's job was to provide a properly sinister set for a Catholic boys' school, where perfectly nice schoolboys are wreaking violence on each other for no apparent cause. The plot centers around the efforts of the school's faculty to find the root of this strange phenomenon. Since the

show was played without intermission on one set, it was a relatively easy assignment for Jo. His design was applauded by almost all of the critics, some of whom had a few reservations about the play itself. With Jo's set design basically intact but the text altered for English audiences, *Child's Play* traveled to Brighton and London. Jo's set was praised wherever it went and it eventually continued on to Rome and South Africa in separate productions.

At the end of the 1969–70 season, *Child's Play* won five Tony Awards—they went to Fritz Weaver for best actor, Ken Howard for best supporting actor, Joseph Hardy for best director, and to Jo for best scenic designer *and* best lighting designer. When he picked up the second Tony as lighting designer, the first time a Tony had ever been awarded in that category, he accepted with thanks to the scene designer who had provided him with such a good set to light.

FOR *CHILD'S PLAY* (1970), JO DESIGNED A FACULTY MEETING ROOM AT A BOYS' SCHOOL, DARKLY PANELED AND ADMITTING LITTLE SUNLIGHT THROUGH LEADED WINDOWS. IT WAS DOMINATED BY ANOTHER MIELZINER TRADEMARK, A HEAVY AND MYSTERIOUS STAIRCASE THAT LED TO QUARTERS WHERE THE SINISTER EVENTS OCCURRED. THE EFFECTIVENESS OF THE PLAY DEPENDED ON THE COLDNESS OF HIS LIGHTING, WHICH HAD TO CONVEY A SENSE OF PERVASIVE EVIL. (COURTESY OF JOHN DOÉPP)

Unfortunately, lightning did not strike twice that February. Jo's second venture, which opened on February 26, was *Georgy*, a musical based on a popular movie, *Georgy Girl*. The producer Fred Coe, who had made his way to Broadway through television, had enjoyed phenomenal success in the fifties and sixties with a string of plays. He, Jo, and the production team worked smoothly, as did Jo's scenery, but the musical didn't. One critic found himself marking time by watching the scenery fold in and out on turntables while the rest of his fraternity simply considered the whole evening listless. It closed mercifully quickly. What Jo got from it as an added bonus was a new refrigerator for his studio. One of the scenes in the show required a vintage refrigerator. When Coe saw the refrigerator in Jo's Dakota studio, he thought it just right for the set and paid for a modern replacement.

Georgy and *Look to the Lilies*, which opened a few days apart, shared several things in common. Both were musical adaptations of successful movies (a now common situation on Broadway), both were designed by Jo Mielziner, and both flopped. The latter, about a German nun who manages to cajole a fugitive from the law to build her a chapel in the New Mexico desert, despite the talents of Jule Styne and Sammy Cahn (music and lyrics), Shirley Booth in the leading role, and Joshua Logan as director, did not transfer neatly into musicalization. Clive Barnes, in a particularly caustic review even for him, made comments about Jo's sets that set off a small furor in the design community on Broadway. Referring to "deplorably frowsy settings provided by the veteran Jo Mielziner," Barnes said:

> *Those, most of them lighted in various shades of orange to suggest the fierce New Mexico sun, clearly have the benefit of being cheap, but also the disadvantage of looking it. See-through houses, see-through cactuses and see-through cafes, especially when so tattily designed and executed, are today somewhat dated. The style of the production and its staging would moreover have gained quite a lot from the delicately suggestive kind of verismo a designer such as Ming Cho Lee might have provided.*

The disparaging remarks brought forth a swift reaction from Ming, who as both protégé and friend of Jo, did not take kindly to Barnes's divisive singling him out as Jo's competitor. Shortly after the show had closed, *The New York Times* printed a letter from Ming and Betsy Lee (April 26, 1970). Chiding Barnes for expounding personal views when his review should have been directed at the "piece at hand," the Lees continued:

> *The world of New York theatre designers is a remarkably cooperative one for all its reputation as being cut-throat and competitive. We see each other's work, criticize it, exchange thoughts and concepts, and learn and grow from being an artistic community. It is vitally necessary to all of us that there be as many different styles of design, as many different points of view, as there are working members of the profession. Only from this can we have a living, growing theatre.*
>
> *In this context, we feel that one passage of the review of* Look to the Lilies *appears to pit designer against designer, and therefore is deeply embarrassing and not constructive, either for the designers, or for the theatre community.*

VERY FEW PEOPLE GOT TO SEE **GEORGY** (1970), A BAD MUSICAL MADE FROM A GOOD MOVIE, WHICH, IF ONE IS TO BELIEVE JO'S RENDERINGS, CONTAINED SOME OF HIS LOVELIEST SCENERY. THE DROP SHOWN HERE CONTAINS A BRIDGE (THIS TIME LONDON, NOT BROOKLYN), AN ALL-TOO-FAMILIAR MIELZINER IMAGE. (COURTESY OF NEIL COLLINS/RICHARD STODDARD)

Like Ming, Jo's assistants far and wide were aghast at Barnes's attack and many wondered whether Barnes was aware that Jo had given Ming his start in the theatre in New York.

After the close of the season, Jo prepared for his annual jaunt to Europe with Father Kusman, sailing on the SS *France* on May 8. Before he left, he and his secretary Phyllis Malinow made notes for a lecture that he was to deliver at the Salzburg Seminar, in Austria, in late June. Throughout the peak years of his career, Jo had turned down many offers to lecture or teach citing a lack of time. Since most of the invitations provided for a modest honorarium at best, he could not afford to accept them. He had hardly lectured at all during the forties and fifties, when he was flooded with requests. But as his schedule eased in the late sixties and early seventies, he began to accept more and more of the offers. For one thing, they were a great boost to his morale. Invariably, in the introductions of

the speakers at the dais was reference to Jo's stature as dean of American designers. By now his accomplishments in the American theatre were the stuff of legend. Students studied his work in their classes, saw his designs reproduced in their textbooks, read his books, and regarded him generally as an icon.

A second inducement was that the honorarium was no longer a token fee. He began to ask for a minimum of $500 for a lecture plus first-class travel expenses and accommodations. Many colleges and universities paid him willingly to stay an extra day or two to teach master classes in design. Jo had developed into an effective speaker, charming audiences with tales of his Parisian background, his studies abroad with the fabled names of continental scene designers, and his work on Broadway with America's greatest directors, writers, and composers. Finally, more and more Jo felt it his mission to impart his knowledge of the theatre and his aesthetics of scene design to new generations.

JO DESIGNED AN IMPRESSIONISTIC MANHATTAN SKYLINE AS A BACKDROP FOR GEORGE BALANCHINE'S BALLET ***WHO CARES?***
(1970), IN FRONT OF WHICH HE HUNG TWO TRANSLUCENT CURTAINS (DROPS) PAINTED ON BOTH SIDES WITH ANILINE DYES.
TO ACCOMPANY THE VARYING MOODS OF THE SEVENTEEN GEORGE GERSHWIN SONGS, THE DROPS WERE BACKLIGHTED TO
REVEAL THE SAME DROP BUT IN DIFFERENT COLORS AND WITH CHANGING DETAILS LIKE STARS AND AUTUMN LEAVES. (BILLY
ROSE THEATRE COLLECTION, NYPL-PA)

To be invited to speak at the Salzburg Seminar in American
Studies was a signal, if unpaid, honor. (Airfare and room and board
were, of course, provided to all the faculty.) Founded in 1947 by a
group of Harvard students as a kind of cultural Marshall Plan to
bridge a gap between America and Europe, the sessions on a variety
of subjects attracted about three hundred people with a record of
achievement in their fields. (Regular university students were not
admitted.) Jo was invited to lead the seminar on American theatre
and delivered a lecture on the development of American musical
theatre. The other American participants that summer were Alan
Schneider, Henry Hewes, and Norris Houghton. Martin Esslin,
then Head of Drama with the BBC, represented the European
point of view. Jo's enjoyment of the experience was particularly
enhanced by staying in an eighteenth-century castle once owned
by Max Reinhardt.

Shortly after Jo returned to New York in July, he signed a
contract with Artie Shaw, the Big Band leader of the thirties and
early forties, to design the scenery for a musicalized version of
F. Scott Fitzgerald's *The Great Gatsby*. In the early stages of developing the show, Shaw may have had second thoughts about becoming a Broadway producer, or perhaps the show itself did not come
together as he envisioned it. Whatever the reasons, it was canceled
in December of 1970. Although Jo received his fee in full, nothing
in his files indicates that he had done anything more than present
preliminary ideas to Shaw. The only other assignment that he
received that fall came from George Balanchine, who asked him to
design scenery for his ballet *Who Cares?* set to the show songs of
George Gershwin. (It had premiered the previous February, but
Balanchine evidently felt the need of sets.) When it was presented
again, dressed in Jo's scenery, on November 21, 1970, at the New
York State Theatre, it was even more warmly received than at first.
Anna Kisselgoff, a dance critic for the *New York Times*, professed to
be surprised by the new look but liked what she saw. (Although
the scenery has been modified and Jo's lighting eliminated, the
scenic drops continue to be used when the New York City Ballet
schedules *Who Cares?* and they still draw gasps of appreciation when
the curtain parts.)

In October, Jo was invited to the Maryland estate of Sargent and Eunice Shriver for a weekend. Long an admirer of the Kennedys, Jo was delighted to be asked to design the setting for a ceremony in which awards given by the Joseph P. Kennedy, Jr., Foundation would be presented. He not only created the setting but designed the awards as well. Later, the foundation reproduced his symbol of the Archangel Raphael on its stationery and small souvenirs.

During the early 1970s, Jo continued to turn down scripts that he felt were without any merit. His instincts usually proved to be correct. Only one of the scripts that he was offered was ever produced, and it opened in an off-off-Broadway house far away from Jo's natural habitat. He should have turned down *Father's Day*, by Oliver Hailey, but took it out of desperation. The production received such a savage review from *The New York Times*

JO DESIGNED THE BALCONY OF A MANHATTAN HIGH-RISE APARTMENT HOUSE AS REALISTICALLY AS HE COULD TO ACCOMPANY *FATHER'S DAY* (1971), A REALISTIC PLAY REPLETE WITH EARTHY DIALOGUE. THE CRITICS FAVORING THE PLAY AND JO'S CONTRIBUTION OUTNUMBERED THE NAYSAYERS, BUT IT WAS SUNK BY A TOTALLY NEGATIVE REVIEW BY CLIVE BARNES OF THE *NEW YORK TIMES*, WHICH WAS FAST EMERGING AS THE FINAL ARBITER OF EVERYTHING THEATRICAL IN NEW YORK. (COURTESY OF BRENDA VACCARO)

that the frightened producers, Joseph Kipness and Lawrence Kasha, closed it immediately.

Jo had no better luck with George Balanchine's *PAMTGG*, which the New York City Ballet premiered at the New York State Theatre in June 1971. Not only did it get universally panned but Jo's set again caught the critical ire of Clive Barnes, who at the time was wearing two hats as the drama and the dance reviewer. (The acronym title came from the jingle then flooding the country: "Pan Am Makes the Going Great" compressed to first letters.) Balanchine choreographed it to the music from the television commercial, which made little sense. Barnes's criticism of Jo's set rankled, and for the first time he spoke out publicly against it to a writer of the *Toronto Globe and Mail*: "Clive Barnes said I'd spent too much money on it. I don't know what business of his it is. But the ballet didn't work. It was incomplete. Balanchine should have postponed it a season." *PAMTGG* is notable as one of the master choreographer's few failures.

While Jo was designing for Balanchine, he received a call from Word Baker, a former assistant who was at the time the artistic director of the Cincinnati Playhouse-in-the-Park, a theatre that had been designed by another Mielziner alumnus, Hugh Hardy. Word had raised $5,000 to entice Jo to design a production there of *Caravaggio*, by Michael Straight, which Word was directing. Since the subject appealed to him and he saw possibilities of using Hardy's thrust stage for something different, Jo accepted the commission. In a rapid cinematic line, the script followed Caravaggio's footsteps from 1594 to 1610 from Rome to Valetta to Naples and finally to the Porto Ercole. Jo decided to use a series of projections combined with set pieces and portable furniture. In an interview with Herbert Whittaker of the *Toronto Globe and Mail*, he explained: "Put the actor on stage with projected scenery only and you are putting him into a dream world. Add some doorways, etc., and a real world is created for him."

What Jo designed came as close to a cinematic dissolve technique as he was ever to achieve on a stage. By using twenty-six projectors (the largest rental order in the history of the Kliegl lighting company to that time) mounted in the ceiling, he could move the "scenery" along with the action. In some scenes, there were fifteen or twenty separate projections happening at the same time.

In order to make the projections work, he suggested that the cinderblock back and side walls in the theatre be painted a deep blue so that the colors of the slides would not be diluted by reflected stage light. Four spotlights subtly followed the actors, enveloping them in a soft halo. In one instance, an image was projected directly onto the back of a cloak worn by one of the characters as he was exiting, which then slid onto the floor. (An effect, no doubt, that would have been called into question by some of the New York critics if they had seen it.) Unfortunately, the exotic theme of the painter's rebellions against prevailing techniques, subjects, and politics—combined with his portrayed homosexuality—did not sit well with the Cincinnati audiences. Although visiting critics from New York and elsewhere went to see the play and several of them liked it, they also thought it was overly long and talky. The show played a limited engagement in July of 1971. Although in recent years Jo had branched out into academic theatre, *Caravaggio* was his first and only experience with regional theatre.

Next, Eddie Kook, in league with Joel Schenker, a real-estate developer turned Broadway producer, imported a modest Canadian free-form musical, *Love Me, Love My Children*, to the tiny Mercer–O'Casey Theatre, in the land of off-Broadway. Jo's contribution was a reconfiguration of the stage and auditorium; he made it into a playhouse with a square playing area, from which rose on facing sides two tiers of seats and on the other two sides a series of steps and platforms that extended the playing area. Aside from a few props, there was no scenery, and none was really necessary. The show, about a girl running away from home, had a modest run.

Several of Jo's shows of the early seventies had reflected subliminally the pervasive messages of the era: the rebellion against the establishment, random violence, and the necessity for universal love. Jo's next two shows were a reversion to Broadway formula and both fared poorly. The first, *Children! Children!* was termed a thriller. Gwen Verdon, formerly of the musical stage, played a babysitter to three horrendous children, who spend the night terrorizing her in various ways. It was produced at the Ritz Theatre, which had been newly refurbished. The critics gave the theatre and Jo's set high marks but declared the play worthless.

The producers of *Voices* may have chosen Jo because of his way with spooky interior scenes. The plot revolved around the misadventures of a young couple who inherit a house only to discover that it is filled with voices of a mother and her children accompanied by ghostly music. Despite Jo's wizardry with the scenery and the presence of Julie Harris and Richard Kiley as the only corporeal bodies onstage, no one took the play very seriously and it closed quickly.

The show that was intended to have Mielziner scenery but did not was a musicalized version of the 1959 movie *Some Like It Hot*. When it finally opened on Broadway, on April 9, 1972, the credit

IN DESIGNING ***CARAVAGGIO*** **(1971)** FOR CINCINNATI'S PLAYHOUSE-IN-THE-PARK, JO USED STARK WHITE AND BLACK PREDOMINANTLY, FLOODING THE STAGE WITH COLOR VIA SLIDE PROJECTIONS OF THE ARTIST'S LUSH PAINTINGS, SOME OF IT SPILLING ONTO THE ACTORS. A FEW SET PIECES ESTABLISHED THE LOCALES: A THRONE, A TABLE, A TRUNK, ETC., BUT SCENES SHIFTED SO RAPIDLY THAT THE ONLY WAY TO KEEP UP THE MOMENTUM WAS THROUGH CHANGING THE PROJECTIONS. (COURTESY OF KATHLEEN DILKES)

for scenery was given to Robin Wagner and for lighting, Martin Aronstein. From the moment that Jo had become involved until curtain time on opening night at the Majestic Theatre in New York, the show represented the classic example of a Broadway musical being put together with baling wire, paper clips, elastic bands, spit, bubble gum, all the king's horses and all the king's men, and anything else to help keep the corpus from falling apart. David Merrick was its producer, and Gower Champion, its (original) director and choreographer. Three book writers—Michael Stewart, George Axelrod, and Peter Stone—were hired at three separate moments in its gestation to provide some kind of coherent basis for the show; Neil Simon was also brought into it during its final tryouts. Jule Styne, the original composer, had to accept contributions from Jerry Herman, while Robert Moore was brought in to take over part of the direction. Even the title changed, beginning with *Doing It for Sugar*, changing to *Nobody's Perfect*, and finally *Sugar*. Out-of-town tryouts began in January in Washington, traveled thence to Toronto, Philadelphia, and Boston, and lasted for twelve weeks (longer than many shows achieved in their entire runs on Broadway that season). The musical was deemed by at least one critic a work of "unswerving mediocrity."

The show's saga began on July 20, 1971, when Jo, then on vacation in Paris, received a phone call from Jack Schlissel, Merrick's general manager, exhorting him to return to New York immediately to begin work on the musical. Jo's explanation that he had booked passage on July 23 and would be back five days later was impatiently overridden by Schlissel, who insisted that Jo fly back immediately. Thus summoned, Jo returned by air to

JO WAS FIRED UNCEREMONI-
OUSLY FROM DAVID MERRICK'S
MUSICAL ***SUGAR*** (1972) AND
REPLACED BY ROBIN WAGNER.
SINCE SO MUCH OF GOWER
CHAMPION'S DIRECTION
EVOLVED AROUND JO'S
DESIGNS, SOME OF HIS ORIGI-
NAL PLANS WERE RETAINED.
THE EXTANT RENDERINGS IN
JO'S FILES ARE CHARMING,
AND ONE WONDERS WHETHER
HE WAS THE "WICTIM" OF A
SHOW DEEP IN TROUBLE IN
ITS OUT-OF-TOWN TRYOUTS.
SHOWN IS MIELZINER'S
UNUSED DESIGN FOR A HOTEL
ROOM. (COURTESY OF NEIL
COLLINS/RICHARD STODDARD)

New York. He met with Gower Champion on the Saturday after his arrival (July 24) and was given the first act of the script only. Even though Jo had not received a contract, Champion told him to begin work at once.

When he did receive the contract, it specified that there would be twelve different sets. (Champion later ordered four more during the Washington tryout.) As is customary with designers, Jo submitted a ground plan and color sketch to Merrick and Champion for their approval. Merrick, whose favorite color was red, did not like the choice of blue velour for the portals (inner proscenium) and asked that it be changed. Jo provided a series of color swatches to Merrick, who finally decided on a russet brown, a neutral enough color, which Jo planned to alter with lighting as the scenes changed.

Previews of the show began at the Kennedy Center in January of 1972. An unrelenting deep red dominated the interior of the theatre, covering the seats, walls, and curtains. When the set was installed, and before Jo had a chance to add the lighting, Champion and Merrick saw only the effect of the red on the brown velour portals and were horrified. Jo flew down to Washington to try to talk them into reverting to blue velour; he knew it was the only color that would work within that theatre and with his scenery. Champion barely spoke to him and Merrick finally told him to "go home."

Back at his studio, Jo called Merrick's office repeatedly to ask when he was to go to Toronto to supervise the lights and sets, but he was always put off by one of Merrick's staff. Finally, Samuel "Biff" Liff, Merrick's production supervisor, told Jo that Champion did not require his presence in Toronto. Jo wrote to Champion to ask for an explanation but did not receive a reply. Finally, it fell to Pete Feller to tell Jo that new sets had been ordered and that they were being designed by Robin Wagner. Next, Wagner himself called Jo to notify him that he was now doing the show.

Wagner, however, had used Jo's approved ground plan for the show, and after the show opened, Jo wrote to Schlissel to remind him that Merrick was still contractually bound to pay him the rest of his fee (for designing the additional scenes) and for the weekly royalties. He added, "In all frankness, I must say that in all my years in the theatre, I have never received the treatment which has been accorded me on this production—this treatment has caused me tremendous damage professionally." Jo attached his bill for the royalties due him plus the extra designing he was obliged to provide for Champion, but there is no record how much of it, if anything, was ever paid. (Merrick's ploy, familiar to everyone on Broadway, was not to pay his obligations but to wait until he could wear down his adversaries and then settle for a far smaller sum.)

Sugar was undoubtedly the hit for tired businessmen in 1972, but the show that "rocked" Broadway was *Jesus Christ Superstar*, by Andrew Lloyd Webber and Tim Rice. It was also designed by Robin Wagner, a brilliant designer who had applied for a job at the Dakota studio in the fifties, when Jo's career was at full tilt. But Jo had a full complement of assistants and turned him down. Wagner later got jobs assisting Ben Edwards and Oliver Smith. Like Jo, Wagner, who got early training at an art school, learned about scenery from his hands-on work in his native San Francisco and in New York. Like Jo, he became known for his prodigious talent for solving difficult problems.

In 1972, Jules Irving was nearing the end his tenure as the head of the Repertory Company at Lincoln Center. It was well known that he had grown weary of keeping a leaking ship afloat and battling with the theatre's board of directors. Perhaps, as a final salute to Jo, Irving asked him to design a revival of Arthur Miller's *The Crucible*. With his budgetary problems at their most critical, Irving presented Jo with a challenge to design the play as economically as possible, and Jo reveled in the task. (At the founding of the Repertory Company, the scene designers' union had given the theatre a special contract that stipulated lower than usual fees.)

Using the thrust stage, Jo designed light changes and projections, rather than realistic scenery. John Berry, the director, agreed with Jo's scheme to keep the focus on the actors. Most of the visual interest in the production came from Carrie Robbins's costumes, which were made of roughly textured fabrics. Whatever furniture and props were necessary were made slightly overscale, as if to dwarf the characters who were being pictured as human pawns in a larger tragic game.

Jo did not then have a union design assistant on his staff and so was not able to present the electricians at the Vivian Beaumont with a completed light plot to show the type and placement of the lights as well as the intensities of the lamps and colors of the gels that he wanted. What happened as a consequence serves to illustrate the evolution of stage lighting as a separate art. Since Jo planned to use simple lighting, when he arrived at the theatre he asked the stagehands to show him the lighting that had been used for the previous production, *Twelfth Night*. Jo picked and chose from what was available in the arrangements already in place, told them

the effects he wanted to achieve, and asked them to assist him. Accustomed to working rigidly, almost by rote, the stage electricians were at first completely nonplussed by Jo's method: He wanted their opinions for certain effects. Eventually, they began to react creatively to his method of making them part of the process of production rather than simply its mechanics.

The Crucible opened to largely favorable reviews, many considering it one of the highest achievements of the Repertory Company under Irving. On May 25, Jo left on his annual European trip with Father Kusman aboard the SS *France*. He made a side trip to Amsterdam because the Toneel Museum had mounted a retrospective exhibition of his scene paintings and drawings. At the end of July, a few weeks after he returned, Jules Irving called Jo from Fire Island, where he was vacationing, to ask him to design a revival of *A Streetcar Named Desire* scheduled for the next season at the Vivian Beaumont. Jo unhesitatingly took the assignment.

Irving told him that Ellis Rabb, the actor-director, would be staging the play. But Rabb put off meeting with Jo until October. Then, after a few meetings with the director, Jo, who did not yet have a firm commitment or a contract, suspected that something was amiss. After months of foot-dragging, Irving called to tell Jo that Ellis Rabb wanted to choose his own designer. Jo felt more than outrage. He felt cheated and abused. When he had started his career in the 1920s, producers had routinely enticed designers "on spec" just to see what kind of scenery they could create on paper. Now, fifty years later, he was being subjected to an updated version of that practice. Jo did not receive a penny for the work he had performed. (*Streetcar* became a hit at the Beaumont and moved to Broadway the following season with Douglas Schmidt's scenery and John Gleason's lighting.)

Before Jo left for Europe, the Pioneer Theatre Company, at the University of Utah in Salt Lake City, had written to Jo to ask whether it would be possible to obtain his plans for the original Broadway production of *A Streetcar Named Desire*. Jo not only lent his plans, for a fee, but he also went to the university to give lectures as a "visiting professor of theatre," also for a fee. He was lionized on campus and was given an honorary doctorate of humane letters, the

IN HIS LATER YEARS, JO WAS SURPRISED TO FIND HIMSELF ENJOYING THE INVITATIONS HE RECEIVED TO LECTURE AT CAMPUSES THROUGHOUT THE COUNTRY. AT THE UNIVERSITY OF UTAH, HE GAVE CLASSES IN ADVANCED SCENE DESIGN AND, AS AN ADDED BOUNTY, WAS ABLE TO PICK FUTURE INTERNS FOR HIS NEW YORK STUDIO; SEVERAL OF THEM APPEAR IN THIS GROUP. (COURTESY OF PIONEER MEMORIAL THEATRE, UNIVERSITY OF UTAH)

first to be awarded by the Department of Theatre, in April of 1972. In accepting the award, Jo wore an uncharacteristic cloak of humility, noting publicly for the first time that he was a first-year high-school dropout and adding that it him took six and a half decades of hard work to achieve the honor he was receiving. (It was actually Jo's fourth honorary doctorate. In addition to his Fordham honor in 1947, Otterbein College had awarded him a degree on the sixtieth anniversary of the founding of its Speech and Theatre Department in 1967, and the University of Michigan had conferred the honor when the Power Center for the Performing Arts was dedicated in 1971.)

Jo was enjoying his renewed vocation as a teacher. Because his experiences at the University of Utah were beneficial both to him and to the students, he and the chairman of the Theatre Department, Dr. Keith Engar, set up an apprentice system for Utah's graduate students in design. Each year, a student of Jo's choice would spend an academic year at Jo's studio and receive credit for the experience. Whatever the first apprentice, Greg Geilman, may have expected from the experience, he was unprepared for what ensued: In his Dakota office Jo handed him three things—a key for the studio door, a coffee cup, and a dictionary. The latter, he explained, was given because "No one in the theatre can spell worth shit." Unfortunately, since these were not the busiest years of Jo's career, there was hardly enough work for a full-time assistant. To fill up the time, they straightened up Jo's files of drawings and performed many make-work projects around the studio.

In the summer of 1972, Jo spent a relaxing weekend at the Connecticut home of Phoebe and Morris Carnovsky, old and dear friends, and an idea for a show was hatched. Present at the creation were Matt Conley, an actor and director, as well as Kathleen Dilkes, the Carnovskys' niece, who was then working as Jo's assistant. To keep himself busy in between roles, Morris had sometimes given concert readings of excerpts from Shakespeare's plays. Someone suggested that Morris could make a full evening of it, with a set and lighting by Mielziner and direction by Matt Conley. What evolved was a one-man show, *Ah, Willy*, which Carnovsky began to tour early in 1973. Done as a favor for his friends, it was never intended to enrich Jo's design coffers.

WITH FEWER PRODUCTIONS ON BROADWAY, MANY VETERAN ACTORS TOOK TO SMALL STAGES TO PERFORM IN ONE-PERSON SHOWS. JO'S FRIEND MORRIS CARNOVSKY PREPARED READINGS FROM SHAKESPEARE FOR ***AH, WILLY*** (1973), PERFORMED SPORADICALLY IN THE EARLY SEVENTIES. JO CREATED A SIMPLE LIBRARY SET AS THE BACKDROP. (COURTESY OF KATHLEEN DILKES)

In the fall of 1972, David Merrick's office called to ask Jo to design Tennessee Williams's new play, *Out Cry*. Technically, it was not Merrick who was producing the play but his foundation, which he had set up with profits from his hits in order to present worthy plays that did not have the potential to be profitable on Broadway. (If one of the plays presented under the foundation's auspices proved to be a runaway hit, Merrick could always transfer it to profit-making status and enjoy the rewards thereof.) *Out Cry* had premiered unsuccessfully first in London, then was restaged later in Chicago, where it had been a modest success. Originally titled *The Two Character Play*, it had been written during one of Willliam's emotional crises and was difficult to understand except as a confessional about the playwright's relationship with his institutionalized sister Rose. There are layers of meaning in its play within a play, some metaphorical, some psychological, with the boundary between truth and reality intentionally blurred. Although the director Peter Glenville remained convinced that Jo was the right designer for the play, he doubted that Jo would have been Williams's choice. If Merrick had chosen him to make amends for the *Sugar* fiasco, it was all right with Jo and he agreed to reduce his fees. With his assistant Katy Dilkes and a Utah apprentice, Jo began to work on the show.

When an important play fails in the theatre, it usually takes everything down with it, actors, director, scenery, costumes, lighting; some, most, or all of the collaborators are judged to be at fault in varying degrees by the critics. When a play by Tennessee Williams failed, it was regarded as a catastrophe, yet it was he who ultimately received the blame. So it was with *Out Cry*. The baffled critics labeled it Pirandellian because it mixed perception with reality, but try as they might, they could not like the play. Peter Glenville believed it would have fared better off-Broadway. Williams was unhappy with the entire production, from the scenery and lighting on up to the actors and the director.

Confronted with a Williams failure, the critics lamented the general decline of the serious play on Broadway. Edwin Wilson, writing in the *Wall Street Journal*, expressed a kind of communal mourning over the lack of success of plays by both Williams and Arthur Miller during the season of 1972–73. He warned of an impoverished theatre:

> *Broadway has always been a stool with three legs: comedy, musicals and drama. At the moment all three legs are a bit shaky, but the third is shakiest of all. If it fails the whole thing is in danger of failing. We need the beauty, the entertainment, and the escape of light fare; but we also need the chance to come face to face with ourselves, to touch the well-springs of our common humanity, which good drama can help us do.*

The out cry in Williams's play, he concluded, took on a special meaning as a cry for help for American drama in general.

Although *Out Cry* was another in a string of disappointments for Jo in these years, he suffered the greatest blow when an opera he was working on for the Metropolitan Opera was canceled in the fall of 1973. When Jo had read of the appointment of Goeran Gentele, the Swedish opera manager, to be head of the Met in the spring of 1972, he immediately wrote to offer his services. In an interview quoted in *The New York Times*, Gentele had mentioned that he was thinking about using the little Forum Theatre at Lincoln Center for intimate operas. Jo wrote an enthusiastic response to this idea of a "Piccolo Met" and enclosed a copy of his book *Designing for*

FOR **OUT CRY** (1973), TENNESSEE WILLIAMS USED AN EMPTY STAGE AS A SYMBOL FOR LIFE ON VARIOUS LEVELS, AND HE RELIED ON JO'S LIGHTING TO CONVEY THE ALTERING MOODS AND STATES OF MIND OF THE TWO CHARACTERS. THE DIRECTOR, PETER GLENVILLE, WANTED A REPRODUCTION OF ONE OF MICHELANGELO'S SLAVE SCULPTURES (E.G., *DYING SLAVE* OR *REBELLING SLAVE*) ON THE STAGE TO SIGNIFY STRUGGLES AGAINST INTERNAL AND EXTERNAL BONDS, BUT JO CHOSE A CONTEMPORARY SCULPTURE BY NANCY GROSSMAN CALLED *UNTITLED*. (COLUMBIA UNIVERSITY LIBRARY SPECIAL COLLECTIONS)

IN ADDITION TO HIS MOOD
LIGHTING FOR **OUT CRY**, JO
USED PROJECTIONS OF
ABSTRACT DESIGNS TO
SUGGEST THE DISJOINTED
PSYCHES OF WILLIAMS'S
PROTAGONISTS. (COLUMBIA
UNIVERSITY LIBRARY SPECIAL
COLLECTIONS)

the Theatre. Gentele's reply, addressed to *Miss* Jo Mielziner, requested more information "on what you have done." Almost by the next post, another letter came quickly on its heels expressing Gentele's profuse apologies; he blamed himself for allowing his office staff to answer his mail. He promised to meet with Jo at a mutually convenient time.

The result of their meeting was not an assignment for the "Piccolo Met" but something unexpected—and much better. He asked Jo to design a production in the opera house of a new *Don*

Giovanni with Leontyne Price and Sherrill Milnes at the top of an all-star cast. It was scheduled to open on March 28, 1974. Jo was enormously excited by the entire project (his young and talented friend Patricia Zipprodt, making her Metropolitan debut as costume designer, was to be his collaborator) and set to work on it with a burst of energy. Despite Jo's eminence in his profession, Met producer Rudolf Bing had never asked him to design an opera, and it rankled. Jo felt that he might now have a door opening at the Met.

Designing for the the vast stage of the Metropolitan, with its huge proscenium opening, challenged Jo's talents. As was his usual custom, he started with the libretto and began to think of the opera in terms of the interrelationships of the characters, whom he did not see as figures set in a huge operatic canvas surrounded by the usual panoply of choruses and dancers. If it was an intimate opera, as he believed it was, he wanted to design an environment that directs the focus on the singers. Although Jo did not like to rely on

IN DESIGNING A METROPOLITAN OPERA PRODUCTION OF **DON GIOVANNI** (1973) (WHICH WAS ULTIMATELY CANCELED), JO DECIDED TO HAVE THE ENTIRE SET COVERED IN BLACK VELOUR. THE SECTIONS IMMEDIATELY SURROUNDING THE SINGERS WOULD BE PAINTED IN VIVID COLORS, WHILE THE REST OF THE SET DISAPPEARED IN BLACKNESS WITHIN THE PROSCENIUM. THE ARCHWAY, DOORWAYS, AND WINDOWS WERE OVERSCALE AND PITCHED SLIGHTLY FORWARD TO EMPHASIZE AN ATMOSPHERE OF ENVELOPING DOOM. RATHER THAN USE THE FULL EXPANSE OF THE STAGE, HE INTENDED TO LIGHT AREAS THAT WOULD CONFINE THE PERFORMERS DURING INTIMATE SCENES, A DEPARTURE FROM THE MET'S USUAL SCENIC STYLE. (COURTESY OF TIM SATERNOW)

models to express his ideas, the Met insisted that he build one to show the director, Dr. Gunther Rennert, the director of the Munich State Opera in Germany. Jo and his small staff, consisting of his assistant Jeff Davis and a Utah intern, Byron Olson, hit one snag. They were working from old specifications of the stage and were using the fifty-foot turntable in the planning. He was unaware that the Met's turntable had been scrapped as unworkable some years before. When he found out, all of the drafting had to be redone.

Jeff Davis dismantled the model and packed it for Jo to take to Germany to meet Dr. Rennert for his approval. Jo left early in February of 1973 for Munich and returned a week later with the opera director's general assent but with modifications, which meant that the serious work on drafting the design could begin. Throughout most of the winter and through the summer of 1973, Jo and his assistants prepared the ground plans, models, drawings, color sketches, and painters' elevations for the opera.

Although Goeran Gentele had tragically been killed in an automobile accident the previous year, Jo had continued to work on *Don Giovanni*, which was indefinitely postponed by Gentele's successor on August 24, 1973. The postponement was attributed to the (everlasting) financial crunch at the Met. (When Jo met with the Met's representative, he was asked to submit a statement of charges for work done. Jo settled for slightly more than half his fee, or about $5,000.) When Jo first got the news, he took the model out to the trash bin outside his studio, an uncharacteristic display of emotion for him. He was devastated on several counts. Above all, he had wanted to design an opera at the Met as a kind of apogee of his long career. Secondly, he knew that the scenery would have been used for many years to come and would have represented a testament to his life's work as a designer, enduring far after his own life span. And he had needed the assignment desperately not only for the necessary income it provided but because he thrived on the art and process of designing.

Although Jo's control of himself was legendary, the events of the past few years had been overwhelming even for someone with his self-discipline. For the first time in his career, he was heard to raise his voice, particularly in his dealings with the architects and planners of theatre projects. He found that he needed more rest, less stress, and frequent catnaps. His health, which had been slipping since he had reached the age of seventy, was affected. His blood pressure shot upward and the poor circulation in his legs sometimes caused him to rely on a walking stick. He could not control his appetite. His doctor, Tom Bellezza, warned him repeatedly not to drink and overindulge in rich food because of his borderline diabetes. He cut himself down to one Scotch a day. He confided to Ming and Betsy that his left arm ached and to his secretary Phyllis Malinow that he sometimes experienced brief blackouts.

Jo's only respite was his yearly trip to Europe accompanied by Father Kusman. For his social life in New York, Jo continued to depend on longtime friends, principally the Kooks and Lewis Galantiere, his Dakota neighbor, and his past and current assistants. He renewed his friendship with Edith Meiser, with whom he shared memories of the Jessie Bonstelle stock company, where both of them had gotten their start. When needed to complete a foursome, Jo's first wife, Marya Mannes, would join in. Since Marya had been a resident of the Dakota for several years, it was inevitable that their paths would cross. They became good friends in their elder years, which bore out Edith Meiser's theory that they had met and married too young.

Jo spent his Thanksgivings and Christmases with David and Leonora Hays or with Phoebe and Morris Carnovsky or with one or another of his associates and their families or friends. When he went to the theatre, he usually was accompanied by Edith or Pat Zipprodt or Susan Bloch. He had met Susan when she was a secretary in the publicity department for the Lincoln Center Repertory Company. As a bright, vivacious twenty-five-year-old, she had come to know Jo in the mid-sixties. She made no secret of her adoration of him and they soon became close friends. (Bloch eventually ascended to the position of the chief publicist for the company at Lincoln Center.) When she discovered Jo's enthusiasm for elephants, they exchanged elephant lore and she sent him postcards of elephants from her travels. In her job as publicist for the American Red Cross, Bloch got Jo a commission to design elephant ear muffs for the antinoise campaign in New York City in the early seventies,

which he did as a lark. Sadly, kidney disease claimed her life at the age of forty-two.

Jo's contact with his three grown children was now minimal. Michael's work as a sound technician in the theatre frequently took him out of town. Neil, who was living in New York after a failed second marriage, would occasionally have dinner with Jo. Jennifer, who had fled New York in 1971, eventually formed a personal and business partnership with a helicopter pilot in Louisiana, where they airlifted hurt and sick men from oil rigs off the coast. On her rare visits to New York, Jo became acquainted with his granddaughter Krista. (Unfortunately, he lost contact with her older sister, Donna Jo, who was living with her father in South Dakota.) During one visit, Jennifer left Krista with Jo at the Dakota, while she went off to a New Year's Eve party. After he thought that the little girl was safely tucked into bed, he discovered her at midnight standing at the big window of his apartment looking down at the street merriment below and listening to the bells and whistles signaling the new year. He quietly went into the kitchen, poured out two glasses of champagne, and returned to the living room. Tapping her gently on the shoulder, he handed her a glass and wished her a happy new year.

Jo always kept in touch with his sister-in-law Mary MacKenna. When his work on his architectural projects drew him sporadically to California, he would stay with her at the Santa Monica bungalow she had bought after Kenneth's death. Never the same without Kenneth, but well fixed financially, Mary's modest, comfortable lifestyle allowed her to continue to send Jo a monthly check from Kenneth's estate. Then, in 1974, after Mary was involved in an automobile accident, doctors examining her X rays found a brain tumor. For the next six months, Mary was in and out of the hospital for treatment. She died of her malady in April of 1975, at the age of seventy-four. Her ashes were interred next to Kenneth's and Ella's at Forest Lawn Cemetery. Her estate continued to send Jo a monthly check.

Although his work on *Don Giovanni* and his consultations on architectural projects kept him busy through most of 1973, there was nothing on the horizon for the 1973–74 season. During this period, his income from his investments represented his principal support and was augmented by fees from his lectures and from leasing his past designs to regional and university theatres. When he looked at the roster of plays planned for Broadway, he found that the big names—Merrick, Shumlin, Bloomgarden—were now attached to designers of the younger generation. The art of producing, if so it can be called, was passing to the hands of managerial types unfamiliar to Jo. Consistently Jo was observing many productions being imported as packages from England—and the trend would never abate. Another trend that did not bode well for established Broadway designers was the increasing number of already mounted shows brought to New York from regional theatre. These, combined with the migrations from off-Broadway and their young crews, meant slim pickings for the likes of Mielziner, Oenslager, Smith, and Aronson during these years.

JOSH LOGAN TRANSPLANTED *THE CORN IS GREEN* FROM WALES TO A LOUISIANA SUGAR CANE PLANTATION IN HIS ADAPTATION OF THE PLAY FOR THE MUSICAL ***MISS MOFFAT*** (1974). JO ABANDONED THE IDEA OF USING BUNDLES OF REAL SUGAR CANE WHEN HE DISCOVERED THAT THEY DETERIORATED RAPIDLY UNDER HOT LIGHTS. (COURTESY OF NEIL COLLINS/RICHARD STODDARD)

In the early spring of 1974, his old friend Joshua Logan called to tell him that he was going to co-produce (with Eugene V. Wolsk and Slade Brown) a musical version of *The Corn Is Green* by Emlyn Williams. Although Logan had wanted Mary Martin for the part of Miss Moffat, the schoolmarm whose faith in the talents of a young Welsh miner leads him to a scholarship at Oxford, the death of Richard Halliday, Martin's husband, had caused her to withdraw and he had shelved his plans. Suddenly, the project was alive again when Bette Davis agreed to repeat the part that she had played in the movie version. (Ethel Barrymore had been the star of the Broadway premiere.) Although Jo did not know all of the creative collaborators, he knew and had worked before with the costume designer Bob Macintosh and was a longtime friend of the playwright Emlyn Williams, who was writing the lyrics and co-authoring the book with Josh. To make things even sweeter, Josh gave Jo a hefty design fee and a $250-per-week royalty, the biggest he had ever had.

Believing that a musical dealing with Wales and coal mining would not strike the right chord with American audiences, Logan relocated the action to a Louisiana plantation. The character of the young man became an African-American who cuts sugar cane under a sweltering sun. The trouble proved to be the casting of Bette Davis in the leading role. Although she had played in Tennessee Williams's *The Night of the Iguana* in 1961 and a revue, *Two's Company*, in 1952, she had never carried a Broadway musical and could neither sing nor dance convincingly. During the rehearsals, she was seized with anxiety. The show, which was designed by Jo to be transported in two trucks, was scheduled to open in Philadelphia in September and tour throughout the country (a new method being tested to recoup the cost of the show) before settling down on Broadway. But Davis's nerves were wreaking havoc on her body. The opening had to be postponed because of Davis's strained back; for a while, she had difficulty in walking and had to be taken back and forth from the theatre in a wheelchair.

The official opening was next set for October 7. Logan's talent to wring performances out of actors was put to the ultimate test with Davis. During the opening preview, Davis dropped a line early

ALTHOUGH JO'S INTERIOR
SETTING FOR *IN PRAISE OF
LOVE* (1974) HARDLY LOOKS
EXTRAORDINARY, IT CON-
TAINS ONE OF HIS SIGNATURE
ELEMENTS, THE CURVED, DIS-
APPEARING STAIRWAY. (ESTATE
OF JO MIELZINER)

in the first act, then stopped the show while she asked the audience directly to allow her to start over. (They were delighted to do so.) During another early preview, she lost her way in the middle of her big number, to everyone's embarrassment. When the show finally opened to the press, the reviews were predictable. Ernest Schier of the *Philadelphia Evening Bulletin*, while noting that "a good part of the show's problems lie with its star," also called the show boring. Among the things he did not like were Jo's sets and Emlyn Williams's lyrics. Rather than continue, Logan and his co-producers decided to close the show in Philadelphia. Although he could have recast the role of Miss Moffat, he was too canny in the ways of show business to attribute the show's failure to Bette Davis's "ailing back." No fat royalty checks would be forthcoming for Jo.

Jo now heard from another old comrade-in-arms, Arthur Cantor, who had known Jo from the days when he was the press agent for *Anne of the Thousand Days*. Cantor lived at the Dakota and often bumped into Jo. Hearing Jo complain that he was not getting any

work on Broadway, Cantor asked him to design *In Praise of Love* by Terence Rattigan. It was to star Julie Harris and Rex Harrison. A sentimental comedy about a terminally ill woman and her self-absorbed writer-husband, who eventually come to terms with her impending death and their abiding love for each other, it was not warmly received by the critics. However, the public liked it well enough to keep it running for six months, which sustained Jo financially until it closed.

On May 23, 1975, Jo and Father Kusman boarded the *Queen Elizabeth II* for their annual trip abroad. Jo disliked the English ship, hated the food, considered the public rooms lavish and overdone, thought the entertainment too loud, complained about his first-class accommodations, and decided thenceforth that he would travel by air. He ended his long travel missive to his children with the words "The good ship 'La France' is dead! Long live the '727'!"

On his return home, Jo heard the unhappy news of Donald Oenslager's death on June 21, 1975. Although the two men had not been close, they were friendly and respectful colleagues who had worked together on a number of projects. Oenslager had a number of Jo's scene paintings in his private collection and made no secret of his admiration for his work. Both men, alumni of Robert Edmond Jones's studio, were among the last of Broadway's true gentlemen. As soon as Jo heard the news, he visited Zorca Oenslager, Don's widow, and offered whatever help he could. He called her frequently and accompanied her occasionally on social engagements. She remained grateful for his friendly ministrations.

In the past, when Jo accepted lecture assignments, arrangements were made directly with him. Now that he had time to spare, he wondered whether it might serve him better to have an agent. The literary agent Audrey Wood tried unsuccessfully to get him under Sol Hurok's wing, but in the fall of 1975 Jo found a proper conduit for his speaking engagements with the United States Institute for Theatre Technology. An organization primarily of and for university-based designers and technicians, USITT set up the National Liaison Committee to arrange for professional designers like Jo to give master classes at campuses across the country. The committee arranged the fees and travel and published the availability of the guest lecturers in their newsletter. Through USITT Jo was engaged by Florida State University and Purdue University for the fall of 1975. Purdue also got Jo to design a production of June Havoc's *Marathon 33* for a February 1976 production.

Jo's lectures had different titles, but almost all were pragmatic discourses and variations on his favorite themes. Usually, he began by relating his own broad cultural background as the son of an artist and journalist, which led him to urge his student audiences to develop a breadth and depth of knowledge about everything they possibly could. He described personal experiences from his early life that time and retellings had rendered more romantic or more colorful in his memory. He warned against narrow specialization

JO'S SET FOR *MARATHON 33* (1976) WAS UNDERSTATED. THE SHOW'S MOST DOMINANT ELEMENT WAS THE LIGHTING, WHICH WAS LEFT TO LEE WATSON, THE LIGHTING DESIGNER FOR PURDUE UNIVERSITY'S EXPERIMENTAL THEATRE. (COURTESY OF BRIDGET BEIER)

and reminded them that they should consider themselves not "jacks of all trades" but "hijackers of all trades"—borrowers of all the best in stage art. His lectures contained strong echoes of Robert Edmond Jones and Lee Simonson, his earliest mentors, when he spoke to them of scene design as an "evocative art, not a descriptive art." He exhorted them to allow audiences to fill in the blanks with their own imaginations. He advised them to study drawing, painting, and drafting so that what they put on paper could be reproduced accurately in three dimensions. Put the actors in the drawings, he advised them, so that they could see the scale of human figure to the scenic environment. Although he approved of mechanical and technical advances in stage technology, he warned them that they represented the means to accomplish a specific end, not an end in themselves. Use mechanics, he told them, to speed the changing of scenes or for other necessary purposes, but do not allow them to dominate the play.

Jo's commentary was usually spiced with stories of his experiences with the fabled designers, producers, directors, and stars with whom he had worked. Sensitive to the traditional prejudices of academics, he told them that "Broadway is not a dirty word"; he maintained that it was still the arena for the best of America's playwrights. He described his collaborations with directors, noting that very few of the men he worked with had an eye for scenery. He repeated his oft-told belief that "good plays design themselves."

Very often, when Jo was asked about the imminent death of the theatre, he would simply say that it still endures despite the onslaught of movies and television because it offers an experience that cannot be duplicated in any other medium. No color, he told them, is so rich as when it is perceived by the human eye in the theatre; no human voice so imbued with emotion as when it is heard in the theatre; and no light so subtle as when it is seen on the stage. He described the theatrical experience as a three-way relationship between actor and audience, audience and actor, and audience and audience. Although beleaguered, he told them, the theatre will not die.

As the dean of designers, Jo was often asked to lend his scene renderings (paintings) for exhibitions around the country. Although he had retained many of his best designs, he had given away a number of his important works to Eddie Kook, Elia Kazan, Joshua

Logan, Leland Hayward, and other friends both in and out of the theatre. Others he had given as gifts to his assistants. Still others he sold directly to interested collectors or through galleries. (He was once appalled to discover that one of the paintings that he had given as a gift to a friend was being auctioned at a New York gallery.) The very first request for his designs to be exhibited had come in 1926, when the Cosmopolitan Club, a women's social organization in New York, asked him to contribute works to a show that included Robert Edmond Jones, Lee Simonson, and Donald Oenslager. A few years later, he had had a one-man show at the Marie Sterner International Galleries in 1932, the first of many in his lifetime. In 1966, when the new Library and Museum for the Performing Arts, a special branch of the New York Public Library, opened its doors, he had the signal honor of having one of its galleries dedicated to a Mielziner exhibition. As late as 1976, he was still sending his designs out for exhibition, the latest to a convention of the Rocky Mountain Theatre Association, in Denver, for which he was keynote speaker. Throughout his long career, his assistants and secretaries were kept busy packing and unpacking his scene paintings.

A schedule for his lectures and exhibitions reached far into 1976, but what he was not getting were commissions to design for Broadway. For all of 1975, no Mielziner-designed show was on the boards in New York. The number of new plays and musicals during the seventies kept dwindling. The few possibilities of assignments that he talked about with producers simply fizzled or he refused them as being meretricious. Then, miracle of miracles, David Merrick called just before Christmas and offered him a new musical, *The Baker's Wife*, based on the 1938 Marcel Pagnol movie. Why Merrick chose Jo to design a big musical after the *Sugar* debacle just a few years before is perhaps best left unanswered. There was always an inscrutability about Merrick's actions.

Jo agreed to design the show for the union minimum fee and took the script with him when he left on December 29 for Prague, where he was to address the Congress of the International Organization of Scenographers and Theatre Technicians in January. When he returned from Europe, he started sketching his ideas and relaying them to Merrick and his general manager, Helen Nickerson. Early in February, he flew to Los Angeles to confer with the director, Joseph Hardy. Merrick had originally offered the book-writing job to Neil Simon, but he had demurred and Joseph Stein had taken over. A young composer named Stephen Schwartz, who had enjoyed triple success with *Pippin, Godspell,* and *The Magic Show* in previous seasons, was writing the score. The star of the show, the Israeli actor Topol, was playing the role that had been immortalized on the screen by the French actor Raimu.

With the departure of his Utah assistant, Jo needed help in his office and interviewed a young designer named Lawrence Miller, who had been recommended to him by Ming Cho Lee and who turned out to be a friend of Stephen Schwartz. Miller began transferring Jo's preliminary sketches and ground plans into a workable presentation for Hardy, Merrick, and the production crew. Reluctantly, Jo had relinquished his role as lighting designer when he and Merrick realized that he could not stand up to the grueling sessions to light the show. (The job went to Jennifer Tipton.)

Although everything was still in the preliminary stage, the design problems had been resolved to Jo's satisfaction and he was ready to present the plans on Monday morning, March 15, 1976. The meeting was over in time for Jo's 1:00 P.M. appointment with Dr. Bellezza, in Greenwich Village. Jo took a taxi for the downtown trip, relieved that the meeting went well. Now he could concentrate on the rest of the planning of the scenes. Painting remained his most joyous occupation, and painting French backgrounds for the show would bring him even greater pleasure. After his examination, Dr. Bellezza told Jo that he wanted him to check into the hospital immediately for tests. He said he would allow Jo to return to his studio to wind up a few matters, but he would be calling the hospital to admit him. Jo hailed a cab near Dr. Bellezza's office for the trip home to the Dakota. Just before the taxi reached the Dakota, the driver noticed that his fare had slumped over in the back seat. He spoke to Jo but received no reply. He drove his car directly into the archway of the building on 72nd Street and summoned the Dakota doorman, who immediately recognized Jo and alerted the Dakota office to summon help. He then sprinted up the few steps to Jo's studio to get Phyllis Malinow, Jo's secretary. (She had been on the telephone making arrangements for Jo's upcoming seventy-fifth birthday party.) When Phyllis climbed into the taxi, she saw that Jo was unconscious, although his eyes were open. She tried blowing air into his mouth but received no sign of life.

It was necessary to get Jo to a hospital immediately. Phyllis returned quickly to the studio to get her handbag so that she could accompany Jo, but by the time she returned to the archway, the taxi had sped off accompanied by a police car to Roosevelt Hospital about a dozen blocks south of the Dakota. She quickly followed in another taxi. On arrival, she called Eddie Kook, Susan Bloch, and Jo's son Neil. Eddie and Susan were in the emergency room in minutes, but by then Jo had died without ever regaining consciousness. It was a little past 2:30 in the afternoon.

Eddie Kook sent Phyllis back to the studio to begin calling friends and associates with the news. He told her that he would notify Michael and Jennifer Mielziner and Jo's closest friends. While she was still making calls, Elia Kazan appeared at the studio, lingered a few minutes and then left. Betsy Lee came down to help out shortly thereafter. In the meantime, Susan Bloch had raced back to her office on West 66th Street to begin putting together an obituary. She called the New York papers and the wire services. She persuaded *The New York Times* to put the notice of his death on the front page and gave the obit writer Albin Krebs the details of his death. A Low Mass would be said at St. Francis of Assisi on West 31st Street on Friday, March 19, on what would have been Jo's seventy-fifth birthday.

The prior of St. Francis was astounded when he faced the standing-room-only crowd at his church the morning of Jo's service. All of show business had congregated to honor Jo—from stagehands to producers. With Jennifer and her brothers still unnerved by Jo's death, Ming and Betsy took over and became the unofficial hosts, greeting all of Jo's friends, associates, and past and current assistants and secretaries. Bishop Sheen was there, but as mourner only, not as a participant in the Mass. Even David Merrick showed up. The prior gave a short eulogy, confessing that he had not known Jo Mielziner but realized that he had been one of the silent congregation that worshipped faithfully at the church. He could only guess at his contributions to the American theatre but noted that Jo, as a convert to Christianity, tried to live by its tenets. Most of those in attendance wished that someone had said something about Jo's humanity, his art, his gentility, his passionate dedication to the theatre. But no one did.

Immediately after the service, Jo's children and about twenty of Jo's close friends and associates were invited to Susan Bloch's apartment for an informal wake. The following Sunday, many of this same group, which included Jo's children, Eddie Kook, Susan Bloch, Ming and Betsy Lee, Patricia Zipprodt, Phyllis Malinow, Lawrence Miller, and a few others assembled at the Staten Island Ferry Terminal to do Jo's final bidding. In his will, he had asked that his sons scatter his ashes into the waters of New York Harbor. Unaware that it was not permissible to drop anything into the harbor from the ferry, they went on board to do their mission. It was gloomy and overcast. The only sailor among them, David Hays, had brought along his pipe so he could determine the direction of the wind. (They wanted to avoid casting Jo's ashes into the wind and having them returned into their faces.) When the wind was right, David signaled and Michael, standing in a tight formation with Jennifer and Neil, opened the canister holding Jo's ashes. At that instant, the sun broke through the clouds as if it had been preset on a celestial dimmer board and shone on the assembled group. If there was that day a special tide that fed into the Atlantic Ocean and east to France, perhaps a bit of Jo went with it. By the time the group reached Staten Island for the return trip, a light rain began to fall. David and Leonora Hays opened their home to Jo's friends and family for a penultimate party of farewell.

If Jo had, in the manner of his death, fulfilled the wish confided to his closest friend and associate, Eddie Kook, that "when I am to go, I hope it will be with my shoes on," he also left unfinished business. Still on his drawing board at the Dakota studio was his almost-finished work on the *The Baker's Wife*. Whatever were David Merrick's feelings about Jo's death, he never lost sight of his job to get the show on. Shortly after Jo's passing, Merrick called Ming Cho Lee and asked him to finish the designs. As a tribute to his former mentor, Ming agreed to do it with two conditions. One was that Jo's estate receive the final one-third payment due under Jo's contract, and the other was that Merrick pay for any assistants who would be required to help him complete it. The producer agreed to both.

To close Jo's studio after the work on *The Baker's Wife* was finally completed, Ming and Betsy Lee gave a final party commemorating Jo at the Dakota. They invited as many of his former assistants as they could locate to assemble for the last time in a place where so many of them had worked and learned and reveled in the glories of Broadway during its peak years along with him. They all realized that there would never be another designer like Jo Mielziner, that he not only opened the greatest era in its history but closed it, too. All of them knew that they had worked for him more as a labor of love than for the money or any other reason. Working for and with him, they, too, were contributors to the great moments in the American theatre as facilitators of his genius. Not one of them ever regretted or forgot their experiences with Jo. Although Jo left his material estate to his children, his assistants were his true heirs and, mostly without the awareness of the next wave of young designers, they continue to pass on his legacy.

AFTERWORD

When Jo was doing double duty at the Theatre Guild in 1923, working onstage as well as backstage by playing the small role of the Dauphin's Page in George Bernard Shaw's *Saint Joan*, he received a penny postcard from the playwright himself; it was addressed merely "the Dauphin's Page." In his tiny script, Shaw instructed Jo to remember, when he was about to make his first entrance, that "you are not preceding a dauphin, you are preceding a worm." Jo never forgot Shaw's admonition or his concern for the proper playing of even the lowliest *dramatis persona*. He used that experience as a metaphor for the position of the scene designer in the theatre. "Lesson Number One," he told the design students at the Yale Drama School in 1972: "the designers never precede the dauphin in the theatre. They are hardworking worms." It was a statement, untinged with bitterness, that advised them that their work would never be fully appreciated, not by their fellow collaborators (except in rare instances and certainly not publicly) and not by audiences. Consider yourself hardworking worms, he warned them, but never use your status as an excuse for not fulfilling your roles fully and well.

OPPOSITE: JO'S FAVORITE PLACE WAS HIS DRAWING BOARD AND HIS FAVORITE OCCUPATION WAS PAINTING HIS SCENE DESIGNS. HE IS SHOWN HERE IN THE EARLY FIFTIES, A PERIOD OF GREAT ACTIVITY IN HIS LIFE. ON HIS BOARD ARE HIS DESIGNS FOR *ME AND JULIET* (1953). (EILEEN DARBY PHOTOGRAPH)

Jo went on to define the role of scene designers, describing them as craftsmen at best. They could never be artists in the real sense, because they were hemmed in by too many practicalities—like the budget and the physical space—and unpredictables—like the people with whom they had to work. Despite these conditions, Jo warned that designers had to be undeterred in their mission. Do what is necessary within the budget, he advised them, but do it beautifully. What designers put on the stage, he told them, has to be "charged, lifted, elevated, illuminated, given a quality beyond life itself." Avoid that responsibility and you do the theatre a disservice.

He described the compensating magic moments in designing. The first was in creating the ground plan, a simple architectural outline of the space to be performed in, broken down into planes and specific focus areas. The second was the creation of the lighting for the scenery he had designed, transforming canvas and paint, sometimes imperfectly wrought, into a world of color, texture, and illusion—all with light, that ineluctable element of all visual art, which onstage he could shape, make move, and most of all imbue with emotion. For him, the theatre was a place of what he called "stunts," which, instead of Truth, were the quintessence of theatre. In a court of law, the witness puts hand on Bible and swears to tell the truth and nothing but the truth, but in the theatre, Jo said, "You put your hand on the book of the Muses and swear to tell only that part of the truth which is exciting."

Although Jo consigned designers to a lesser role as craftsmen in the theatre, once in a while he admitted to having produced some inspired designs. He devoted a lengthy section of his book *Designing in the Theatre* to his work on *Death of a Salesman*, tracing the entire gestation of his creation from initial reaction to opening night. It fairly glows with self-congratulation. As if he knew beforehand that he was working on a landmark production, he preserved every shred of paper on which he had sketched his preliminary ideas for the scenery. What he wrote and drew form the most complete document of his work on any production in his entire canon.

As if to ratify his pride in himself, he loved hearing secondhand stories of how his collaborators felt about his contributions. Elia Kazan once claimed he didn't direct *Death of a Salesman*, Jo did—

with his set. Late in his career, when Jo worked with a younger generation of producers and directors, he always sensed that they were quietly in ecstasy working alongside him. Enjoying his celebrity, Jo always eagerly responded to any request for the use of his drawings in books or exhibitions, sending whatever anyone wanted, so long as they paid the freight. He loved being written about, and he loved to talk about himself.

Someone once posed the question: Can a genius of seventeen still be a genius at seventy? In the arts of the theatre, it depends on the material and the collaborative team. When Jo was at his most successful, the shows were almost all landmark hits, outstanding examples of American theatrical literature and music. If *The Baker's Wife*, when he was in his seventies, was a pallid example of what Jo could design, it was also not *South Pacific*. (David Merrick closed *The Baker's Wife* before it got to New York, for good reasons.) No matter what the set is, if the script or the musical is good or bad to begin with, nothing that the scene designer does will detract from or enhance it to any significant degree. Jo knew this to be an established fact of the profession.

Jo started out as an artist at his easel, but gave up pure art for designing for the theatre with hardly a backward glance. In 1940, the art critic Clement Greenberg wrote that "purity in art consists in the acceptance, willing acceptance, of the limitations of the medium of the specific art," a statement with which Jo would have wholeheartedly concurred. In Greenberg's terms, Jo was probably the purest scene designer of the twentieth-century theatre. Throughout the fifty-odd years of Jo's career, he enjoyed making things happen onstage that no one had ever done before, stretching its limitations to the fullest. If designers can do more today, it is only because they have technologies that were lacking in Jo's era, but they are still doing what Jo did, only more easily and efficiently. He mastered the technique of "cinematic" scenery using the tools that everyone had at hand but using them better. He moved scenery on turntables and on sliding wagons, he flew it up above the stage, he made sections that were double-sided so that they could be turned on pivots, he designed curtains that moved with the scenery, and he challenged scenic artists to paint pictures on drops that could be lighted both from the front and the rear to expose two separate images. He made the movement of the scenery part of its entire effect, often exposing his "stunts" in full view of the audience with self-conscious theatricalism. He broke through the proscenium arch by insisting on lengthening the stage apron to make it a playing area. What he could not change with scenery, he accomplished with projected images and lighting. Jo knew how he wanted the play—not just the scenery—to be illuminated from the moment of his creation at the drawing board. What he visualized was a totality of effect to serve the play and the actors.

Jo left a legacy of scene design techniques to the generations that followed him. His work is still studied and his methods still imitated. Today everything is employed in the same way scenically and for the same purpose that Jo Mielziner used it. Although Robert Edmond Jones gave the impetus for change in scenic art in America, Jo Mielziner transformed the stage and made scenery interact with the script and the actors as no one before him had done it—not Appia, not Craig, not Jones.

And there is a more tangible Mielziner legacy, in the theatre buildings he designed. His ANTA–Washington Square Theatre, heralded in its time and remembered with nostalgia by those who actually knew it before its destruction, was the prototype for the Vivian Beaumont Theatre, a playhouse that everyone loves to hate. Although threatened several times with major reconstruction, it retains its original integrity despite necessary changes. Gone is the "red look" that Jo gave it. Under its present management, the walls have been painted beige, the carpeting has been replaced, and new seats have been installed. Railings have been added to the steep pitch of the upper banks of seats, and the stage has been slightly reconfigured (it's still a long walk for the actors from the stage to the wings in some productions), but the theatre endures much as Jo designed it.

Jo did not live to see the completion of the Wake Forest University theatres that he designed, or the Denver Center Theatre's trio of playhouses. The Power Center of the University of Michigan was unfinished at his death, though the main stage was up and functioning. His Pittsburgh Playhouse was never built. In the postwar period the proscenium theatre was being bashed by critics, and Jo was too timid to defend it, but he felt in his heart of hearts that it was his emotional, spiritual, and artistic home; he knew that his scenic designs looked best behind the proscenium arch. Small wonder that his greatest successes in architectural design were those small gems that rely heavily on traditional forms, despite a modern overlay. They are intimate theatres that succeed because actors and audience are close enough to each other to feel the embrace of the shared experience.

It is doubtful that Jo Mielziner will be remembered as the designer of ideal or great theatres. (No one will.) If Jo is to be remembered at all, it will be in the textbooks of theatre design, in his drawings and paintings preserved in museums and libraries, and, most importantly, in the passage of his tradition from one generation of designers to another. Was he a genius? Sometimes. Was he a hardworking worm? Always.

APPENDICES

CHRONOLOGY OF ALL KNOWN PRODUCTIONS DESIGNED BY JO MIELZINER (1921–1976)

Unless otherwise noted, all shows listed here opened in New York theatres and all scenery and lighting were designed by Mielziner. Costumes by Mielziner as noted. Producers, directors, designers, and notable actors and actresses are included. Names in parentheses denote future stars in small roles.

1921

The Sign on the Door by Channing Pollock*
Opened Garrick Theatre, Detroit, June 27, 1921
Produced by the Jessie Bonstelle Stock Company
Directed by Jessie Bonstelle
With Jessie Bonstelle, Frank Morgan, Sylvia Field, and Kenneth MacKenna
*This is the only play given that summer that seems to fit the set Mielziner designed.

1923

The Earthquake by Theodore Liebler Jr.
Opened Stamford (Conn.) Theatre, June 29, 1923; closed July 12, 1923, Long Branch, N.J.
Produced and directed by William A. Brady Jr.
With Ann Andrews and George Tobias

1924

Nerves by John Farrar and Stephen Vincent Benét
Opened Comedy Theatre, Sept. 1, 1924
16 performances
Produced and directed by William A. Brady Jr.
With Paul Kelly, Winifred Lenihan, Kenneth MacKenna, Humphrey Bogart, and Mary Phillips

That Awful Mrs. Eaton by John Farrar and Stephen Vincent Benét
Opened Morosco Theatre, Sept. 29, 1924
16 performances
Produced by William A. Brady
Directed by Jessie Bonstelle
With Frank McGlynn, Minor Watson, and Katherine Alexander

The Guardsman by Ferenc Molnár (adapted by Philip Moeller)
Opened Garrick Theatre, Oct. 13, 1924
274 performances
Produced by the Theatre Guild
Directed by Philip Moeller
With Alfred Lunt, Lynn Fontanne, Dudley Digges, Helen Westley, and Edith Meiser

1925

Mrs. Partridge Presents by Mary Kennedy and Ruth Hawthorne
Opened Belmont Theatre, Jan. 5, 1925
146 performances
Produced and directed by Guthrie McClintic
With Blanche Bates, Ruth Gordon, and Sylvia Field

The Wild Duck by Henrik Ibsen
Opened Forty-eighth St. Theatre, Feb. 24, 1925
110 performances
Produced by the Actors' Theatre
Directed by Dudley Digges and Clare Eames
With Blanche Yurka and Thomas Chalmers

First Flight by Maxwell Anderson and Laurence Stallings
Opened Plymouth Theatre, Sept. 17, 1925
11 performances
Produced and directed by Arthur Hopkins
With Rudolph Cameron, Helen Chandler, and James P. Houston

Caught by Kate McLaurin
Opened Thirty-ninth St. Theatre, Oct. 5, 1925
32 performances
Produced and directed by Gustav Blum
With Antoinette Perry, Gladys Hurlbut, and Lester Vail

The Call of Life by Arthur Schnitzler (English version by Dorothy Donnelly)
Opened Comedy Theatre, Oct. 9, 1925
19 performances
Produced by the Actors' Theatre
Directed by Dudley Digges
With Egon Brecher, Eva Le Gallienne, Thomas Chalmers, and Douglas R. Dumbrille

The Enemy by Channing Pollock
Opened Times Square Theatre, Oct. 20, 1925
202 performances
Produced by Crosby Gaige
Directed by Robert Milton
With Walter Abel and Fay Bainter

Lucky Sam McCarver by Sidney Howard
Opened Plymouth Theatre, Oct. 21, 1925
30 performances
Produced by William A. Brady Jr., Dwight Deere Wiman, and John Cromwell
Directed by Sidney Howard
With John Cromwell, Clare Eames, and Rose Hobart

Unseen by Lee Wilson Dodd
Opened Hollis Theatre, Boston, Oct. 25, 1925; closed out of town
Produced and directed by Robert Milton
With Lucile Watson

1926

The American Venus (film with color sequences)
Opened Jan. 25, 1926
Produced by Famous Players–Lasky and released by Columbia Pictures
Directed by Frank Tuttle
Scenario by Frederick Stowers
Story by Townsend Martin
Cinematographer: J. Roy Hunt
Art Director: Frederick A. Foord
Designs for theatre scenes by Jo Mielziner
With Esther Ralston, Edna May Oliver, Louise Brooks, Kenneth MacKenna (and Douglas Fairbanks Jr.)

Little Eyolf by Henrik Ibsen
Opened Guild Theatre, Feb. 2, 1926
7 performances
Produced by William Brady Jr. and Dwight Deere Wiman
Costumes for Clare Eames and Margalo Gillmore by Robert Edmond Jones
With Reginald Owen, Clare Eames, Margalo Gillmore, John Cromwell, and Helen Menken

The Masque of Venice by George Dunning Gribble
Opened Mansfield Theatre, Mar. 2, 1926
15 performances
Produced by Brock Pemberton, William A. Brady Jr., and Dwight Deere Wiman
Directed by Brock Pemberton
Women's costumes by Margaret Pemberton
With Selena Royle, Arnold Daly, Osgood Perkins, Kenneth MacKenna, and Antoinette Perry

Seed of the Brute by Knowles Entrikin
Opened Little Theatre, Nov. 1, 1926
72 performances
Produced by William A. Brady Jr. and Dwight Deere Wiman
Directed by Knowles Entrikin
With Walter Abel, Hilda Vaughn, and Jane Seymour

Pygmalion by George Bernard Shaw
Opened Guild Theatre, Nov. 15, 1926
143 performances
Produced by the Theatre Guild
Directed by Dudley Digges
With Lynn Fontanne, Reginald Mason, Henry Travers, and Helen Westley

1927

Saturday's Children by Maxwell Anderson
Opened Booth Theatre, Jan. 1, 1927
310 performances
Produced by the Actors' Theatre
Directed by Guthrie McClintic
With Ruth Gordon and Beulah Bondi

Right You Are, If You Think You Are by Luigi Pirandello
Opened Guild Theatre, Mar. 2, 1927
58 performances
Produced by the Theatre Guild
Directed by Philip Moeller
Costumes by Jo Mielziner
With Edward G. Robinson, Laura Hope Crews, Henry Travers, Morris Carnovsky, and Helen Westley

Mariners by Clemence Dane
Opened Plymouth Theatre, Mar. 28, 1927
16 performances
Produced by the Actors' Theatre
Directed by Guthrie McClintic
Costumes by Fania Mindell
With Pauline Lord, Haidee Wright, and Beulah Bondi

The Second Man by S. N. Behrman
Opened Guild Theatre, Apr. 11, 1927
178 performances
Produced by the Theatre Guild
Directed by Philip Moeller
Gowns by Hattie Carnegie
With Lynn Fontanne, Alfred Lunt, Earle Larimore, and Margalo Gillmore

The Marquise by Noël Coward
Opened Biltmore Theatre, Nov. 14, 1927
82 performances
Produced by Kenneth Macgowan and Sidney Ross
Directed by David Burton
Costumes by Ben Ali Haggin
With Arthur Byron, Madge Evans, Reginald Owen, and Billie Burke

The Doctor's Dilemma by George Bernard Shaw
Opened Guild Theatre, Nov. 21, 1927
115 performances
Produced by the Theatre Guild
Directed by Dudley Digges
Costumes by Aline Bernstein
With Helen Westley, Dudley Digges, Morris Carnovsky, Alfred Lunt, Margalo Gillmore, Henry Travers, and Earle Larimore

Fallen Angels by Noël Coward
Opened Forty-ninth St. Theatre, Dec. 1, 1927
36 performances
Produced by the Actors' Theatre
Directed by Guthrie McClintic
Gowns by Frances Clyne
With Fay Bainter and Estelle Winwood

1928

Cock Robin by Philip Barry and Elmer Rice
Opened Forty-eighth St. Theatre, Jan. 12, 1928
100 performances
Produced and directed by Guthrie McClintic
With Muriel Kirkland and Beulah Bondi

Strange Interlude by Eugene O'Neill
Opened John Golden Theatre, Jan. 30, 1928
426 performances
Produced by the Theatre Guild
Directed by Philip Moeller
With Lynn Fontanne, Glenn Anders, Tom Powers, Earle Larimore, and Helen Westley

The Grey Fox by Lemist Esler
Opened Playhouse Theatre, Oct. 22, 1928
88 performances
Produced by William A. Brady Jr. and Dwight Deere Wiman
Directed by William A. Brady Jr. and Lemist Esler
Costumes by Fania Mindell
With Henry Hull, Chrystal Herne, and George Tobias

The Jealous Moon by Theodore Charles and Jane Cowl
Opened Majestic Theatre, Nov. 20, 1928
72 performances
Produced by William A. Brady Jr. and Dwight Deere Wiman
Directed by Priestley Morrison
Costumes by Raymond Sovey and Mme. Pulliche
With Jane Cowl, Philip Merivale, Guy Standing, and Harry Davenport

The Lady Lies by John Meehan
Opened Little Theatre, Nov. 26, 1928
24 performances
Produced by Joseph Santley, Theodore Barter, and John McGowan
Directed by David Burton
Costumes by Margaret Pemberton
With William Boyd and Shirley Warde

A Most Immoral Lady by Townsend Martin
Opened Cort Theatre, Nov. 26, 1928
160 performances
Produced by William A. Brady Jr. and Dwight Deere Wiman
Directed by Townsend Martin and Dwight Deere Wiman
With Alice Brady and Humphrey Bogart

1929

Street Scene by Elmer Rice
Opened Playhouse Theatre, Jan. 10, 1929
601 performances
Produced by William A. Brady Jr.
Directed by Elmer Rice
With Leo Bulgakov, Mary Servoss, John M. Qualen, and Erin O'Brien-Moore

The Skyrocket by Mark Reed
Opened Lyceum Theatre, Jan. 11, 1929
11 performances
Produced by Gilbert Miller with Guthrie McClintic
Directed by Guthrie McClintic
Costumes by Margaret Pemberton
With Mary Phillips, J. C. Nugent, and Humphrey Bogart

Judas by Walter Ferris and Basil Rathbone
Opened Longacre Theatre, Jan. 24, 1929
12 performances
Produced by William A. Brady Jr. and Dwight Deere Wiman
Directed by Richard Boleslavsky
Costumes by Richard Boleslavsky
With Basil Rathbone, William Courtleigh, and Dorothy Cumming

Meet the Prince by A. A. Milne
Opened Lyceum Theatre, Feb. 25, 1929
96 performances
Produced by Frobisher, Inc.
Directed by Basil Sydney
With Basil Sydney, Mary Ellis, Eric Blore, and J. M. Kerrigan

Young Alexander by Hardwick Nevin
Opened Biltmore Theatre, Mar. 12, 1929
7 performances
Produced by Nevin-Clarke
Directed by Ira Hards
Costumes by Agnes Clarke
With Henry Hull and Jessie Royce Landis

The Little Show with lyrics mostly by Howard Dietz and music mostly by Arthur Schwartz
Opened Music Box Theatre, Apr. 30, 1929
321 performances
Produced by William Brady Jr. and Dwight Deere Wiman with Tom Weatherly
Directed by Dwight Deere Wiman and Alexander Leftwich
Choreographed by Danny Dare
Costumes by Ruth Brenner
With Clifton Webb, Libby Holman, Fred Allen, Portland Hoffa, and Bettina Hall

Karl and Anna by Leonhard Frank (translated by Ruth Langner)
Opened Guild Theatre, Oct. 7, 1929
49 performances
Produced by the Theatre Guild
Directed by Philip Moeller
With Otto Kruger, Frank Conroy, Claude Rains, Gale Sondergaard, and Alice Brady

Jenny by Margaret Ayer Barnes and Edward Sheldon
Opened Booth Theatre, Oct. 8, 1929
111 performances
Produced by William A. Brady Jr. and Dwight Deere Wiman
Directed by Edward Stanhope
With Guy Standing and Jane Cowl

First Mortgage by Louis Weitzenkorn
Opened Royale Theatre, Oct. 10, 1929
4 performances
Produced by W. P. Farnesworth and H. M. Hayman
Directed by José Ruben
With Walter Abel

Dread by Owen Davis
Opened Majestic Theatre, Brooklyn, Oct. 22, 1929; closed out of town
Produced by Sam H. Harris
Directed by Owen Davis
With Spencer Tracy and Madge Evans

The Amorous Antic by Ernest Pascal
Opened Theatre Masque, Dec. 2, 1929
8 performances
Produced by Sam H. Harris
Directed by Ernest Pascal
With Alan Mowbray, Frank Morgan, and Phoebe Foster

Mrs. Cook's Tour by John Floyd and James Kerby Hawkes
Opened Werba's Flatbush Theatre, Nov. 18, 1929; closed in Philadelphia
Produced by William A. Brady Jr. and Dwight Deere Wiman
Directed by Dwight Deere Wiman
With Mary Boland

1930

Uncle Vanya by Anton Chekhov (adapted by Rose Caylor)
Opened Cort Theatre, Apr. 15, 1930
80 performances
Produced and directed by Jed Harris
Costumes for Lillian Gish by Fania Mindell and Tappé
With Lillian Gish, Walter Connoly, Osgood Perkins, and Eduardo Cianelli

Café by Marya Mannes
Opened Ritz Theatre, Aug. 28, 1930
4 performances
Produced by William A. Brady with John Tuerk
Directed by José Ruben
With Rollo Peters and Frances Fuller

The Second Little Show with lyrics mostly by Howard Dietz and music mostly by Arthur Schwartz
Opened Royale Theatre, Sept. 2, 1930
Produced by William A. Brady Jr. and Dwight Deere Wiman with Tom Weatherly

Directed by Monty Woolley and Dwight Woolley
Costumes by Raymond Sovey and Helene Pons
With Al Trahan and J. C. Flippen

Mr. Gilhooley by Frank B. Elser
Opened Broadhurst Theatre, Sept. 30, 1930
31 performances
Produced and directed by Jed Harris
With Helen Hayes, Arthur Sinclair, and Charles Kennedy

Solid South by Lawton Campbell
Opened Lyceum Theatre, Oct. 14, 1930
23 performances
Produced by Alexander McKaig
Directed by Rouben Mamoulian
With Richard Bennett, Jessie Royce Landis, Elizabeth Patterson (and Bette Davis)

Sweet and Low with sketches by David Freedman and songs by Billy Rose and Friends
Opened Chanin's Forty-sixth St. Theatre, Nov. 17, 1930
184 performances
Produced by Billy Rose
Directed by Alexander Leftwich
Choreographed by Danny Dare and Busby Berkeley
Costumes by James Reynolds
With Fannie Brice, James Barton, George Jessel, Arthur Treacher, and Borrah Minevitch

1931

Anatol by Arthur Schnitzler (adapted by Harley Granville-Barker)
Opened Lyceum Theatre, Jan. 16, 1931
43 performances
Produced by Bela Blau, Inc.
Directed by Gabriel Beer-Hofmann
With Joseph Schildkraut, Miriam Hopkins, Patricia Collinge, and Walter Connolly

The Barretts of Wimpole Street by Rudolph Besier
Opened Empire Theatre, Feb. 9, 1931
372 performances
Produced by Katharine Cornell
Directed by Guthrie McClintic
Costumes by Jo Mielziner
With Katharine Cornell, Brenda Forbes, Brian Aherne, Margaret Barker, and Charles Waldron

The House Beautiful by Channing Pollock
Opened Apollo Theatre, Mar. 12, 1931
108 performances
Produced by Crosby Gaige
Directed by Worthington Miner
Costumes by Jo Mielziner
Assts. to Mielziner: Bernice Ladd and Robert Barnhart

Billy Rose's Crazy Quilt with songs by Billy Rose and Friends
Opened Forty-fourth St. Theatre, May 19, 1931
67 performances
Produced and directed by Billy Rose (No credit given to Mielziner for sets.)
With Fannie Brice, Ted Healy, and Phil Baker

The Third Little Show with contributions by Noël Coward, Marc Connelly, and S. J. Perelman
Opened Music Box Theatre, June 1, 1931
136 performances
Produced by Dwight Deere Wiman with Tom Weatherly
Directed by Alexander Leftwich
Choreographed by Dave Gould
Costumes by Raymond Sovey
With Beatrice Lillie and Ernest Truex

I Love an Actress by Laszlo Fodor
Opened Times Square Theatre, Sept. 17, 1931
20 performances
Produced and directed by Chester Erskin
With John Williams, Muriel Kirkland, and Walter Abel

Brief Moment by S. N. Behrman
Opened Belasco Theatre, Nov. 9, 1931
129 performances
Produced and directed by Guthrie McClintic
With Francine Larrimore, Alexander Woollcott, and Louis Calhern

Of Thee I Sing with book by Morrie Ryskind and George S. Kaufman and music and lyrics by George and Ira Gershwin
Opened Music Box Theatre, Dec. 26, 1931 (additional performances at Imperial Theatre)
473 performances
Produced by Sam H. Harris
Directed by George S. Kaufman
Choreographed by Georgie Hale
Costumes by Charles Lemaire et al.
With William Gaxton, Victor Moore, and George Murphy

1932

Never No More by James Knox Miller
Opened Hudson Theatre, Jan. 7, 1932
12 performances
Produced by Robert Sparks
Directed by Chester Erskin
With Rose McClendon

Distant Drums by Dan Totheroh
Opened Belasco Theatre, Jan. 18, 1932
40 performances
Produced and directed by Guthrie McClintic
Costumes by Bernice Ladd

With Pauline Lord and Beulah Bondi

Bloodstream by Frederick Schlick
Opened Times Square Theatre, Mar. 30, 1932
28 performances
Produced by Sidney Harmon
Directed by Sidney Salkow
With Cecil Holm

Bridal Wise by Albert Hackett and Frances Goodrich
Opened Cort Theatre, May 30, 1932
128 performances
Produced by Sigourney Thayer
Directed by Frank Craven
With Madge Kennedy and James Rennie

Hey Nonny Nonny! with music and lyrics mostly by Max and Nathaniel Lief and Michael H. Cleary and sketches by E. B. White, Ogden Nash, and Frank Sullivan
Opened Shubert Theatre, June 6, 1932
38 performances
Produced by Forrest C. Haring and J. H. Del Bondio
Directed by Alexander Leftwich
Choreographed by Dave Gould (Co-designed with Raymond Sovey)
With Frank Morgan, Ann Seymour, and Dorothy McNulty

Gay Divorce with music and lyrics by Cole Porter and book by Dwight Taylor
Opened Shubert Theatre, Nov. 29, 1932
248 performances
Produced by Dwight Deere Wiman and Tom Weatherly
Directed by Howard Lindsay
Choreographed by Carl Randall and Barbara Newberry
Costumes by Raymond Sovey
With Fred Astaire, Claire Luce, Luella Gear, and Eric Blore

Biography by S. N. Behrman
Opened Guild Theatre, Dec. 12, 1932
210 performances
Produced by the Theatre Guild
Directed by Philip Moeller
With Ina Claire and Earl Larimore

1933

The Emperor Jones with music by Louis Gruenberg (based on the play by Eugene O'Neill)
Opened Metropolitan Opera House, Jan. 7, 1933
15 performances
Produced by Giulio Gatti-Casazza
Conducted by Tulio Serafin
Staged by Alexander Sanine
With Laurence Tibbett

Champagne Sec (adapted by Alan Child with lyrics by Robert A. Simon from Johann Strauss's Die Fledermaus)

Opened Forty-fourth St. Theatre, Oct. 14, 1933
113 performances
Produced by Dwight Deere Wiman in association with Westport Country Playhouse
Directed by Monty Woolley
With Peggy Wood, George Meader, Helen Ford, and Kitty Carlisle

A Divine Drudge by Vicki Baum and John Golden
Opened Royale Theatre, Oct. 26, 1933
12 performances
Produced and directed by John Golden
With Josephine Hull, Mady Christians, Walter Abel, and Tamara Geva

I Was Waiting for You by Jacques Natanson (adapted by Melville Baker)
Opened Booth Theatre, Nov. 13, 1933
8 performances
Produced by Edward Choate
Directed by Arthur Beckhard
With Joshua Logan, Myron McCormick, Bretaigne Windust, Vera Allen, and Glenn Anders

The Dark Tower by Alexander Woollcott and George S. Kaufman
Opened Morosco Theatre, Nov. 25, 1933
57 performances
Produced by Sam H. Harris
Directed by Alexander Woollcott and George S. Kaufman
With Margaret Hamilton, William Harrigan, Basil Sydney, and Margalo Gillmore

The Lake by Dorothy Massingham and Murray Macdonald
Opened Martin Beck Theatre, Dec. 26, 1933
55 performances
Produced and directed by Jed Harris
With Katharine Hepburn, Frances Starr, Blanche Bates, and Colin Clive

1934

By Your Leave by Gladys Hurlbut and Emma Wells
Opened Morosco Theatre, Jan. 24, 1934
37 performances
Produced by Richard Aldrich and Alfred de Liagre Jr.
Directed by Alfred de Liagre Jr.
With Dorothy Gish, Howard Lindsay, Kenneth MacKenna, and Josephine Hull

Merry Mount with music by Howard Hanson and book by Richard L. Stokes
Opened Metropolitan Opera House, Feb. 10, 1934
9 performances
Produced by Giulio Gatti-Casazza

Conducted by Tulio Serafin
Staged by Wilhelm Von Wymetal Jr.
Choreographed by Ronna Galli
With Irra Petina, Laurence Tibbett, Gladys Swarthout, and George Cehanovsky

Dodsworth by Sidney Howard from Sinclair Lewis's novel
Opened Shubert Theatre, Feb. 24, 1934
147 performances
Produced by Max Gordon
Directed by Robert Sinclair
Costumes by Margaret Pemberton
With Walter Huston, Fay Bainter, Kent Smith, and Maria Ouspenskaya

Yellow Jack by Sidney Howard with Paul de Kruif
Opened Martin Beck Theatre, Mar. 6, 1934
79 performances
Produced and directed by Guthrie McClintic
With James Stewart, Sam Levene, Myron McCormick, Robert Keith, and Eduardo Cianelli

The Pure in Heart by John Howard Lawson with music by Richard Myers
Opened Longacre Theatre, Mar. 20, 1934
7 performances
Produced by Richard Aldrich and Alfred de Liagre Jr.
Directed by Edward Massey
Choreographed by Albertina Rasch
With Dorothy Hall, James Bell, Tom Powers (and Frances Langford)

Merrily We Roll Along by George S. Kaufman and Moss Hart
Opened Music Box Theatre, Sept. 29, 1934
155 performances
Produced by Sam H. Harris
Directed by George S. Kaufman
Costumes supervised by John Hambleton
Costume asst.: Rose Bogdanoff
Set design asst.: Robert Barnhard
With Mary Phillips, Kenneth MacKenna, Jessie Royce Landis, Walter Abel, and Cecelia Loftus

Spring Song by Sam and Bella Spewack
Opened Morosco Theatre, Oct. 1, 1934
40 performances
Produced by Max Gordon
Directed by Eddie Sobel
With Francine Larrimore and Garson Kanin

Gather Ye Rosebuds by Sidney Howard and Robert Littell
Opened and closed National Theatre, Washington, D.C., Dec. 8, 1934
Produced by Max Gordon

Directed by Robert Sinclair
With Walter Connolly, Ernest Truex, and Eduardo Cianelli

Romeo and Juliet by William Shakespeare
Opened Martin Beck Theatre, Dec. 20, 1934
78 performances
Produced by Katharine Cornell
Directed by Guthrie McClintic
Costumes by Jo Mielziner
Costume asst.: Rose Bogdanoff
With Katharine Cornell, Brian Aherne, Basil Rathbone, Blanche Yurka, Charles Waldron, John Emery, Orson Welles, and Brenda Forbes

Accent on Youth by Samson Raphaelson
Opened Plymouth Theatre, Dec. 25, 1934
229 performances
Produced by Crosby Gaige
Directed by Benn W. Levy
With Constance Cummings and Ernest Cossart

1935
De Luxe by Louis Bromfield and John Gearson
Opened Booth Theatre, Mar. 5, 1935
15 performances
Produced and directed by Chester Erskin
With Melvyn Douglas, Ann Andrews, Blanche Ring, Elsa Maxwell (and Tom Ewell)

Panic by Archibald MacLeish
Opened Imperial Theatre, Mar. 14, 1935
3 performances
Produced by the Phoenix Theatre
Directed by James Light
Choreographed by Martha Graham
With Rose McClendon, Russell Collins, Orson Welles, Wesley Addy, Zita Johann, and Richard Whorf

Flowers of the Forest by John Van Druten
Opened Martin Beck Theatre, Apr. 8, 1935
40 performances
Produced by Katharine Cornell
Directed by Auriol Lee under supervision of Guthrie McClintic
Technical asst.: Rose Bogdanoff
With Katharine Cornell, Brenda Forbes, Margalo Gillmore, Burgess Meredith, and John Emery

Kind Lady by Edward Chodorov
Opened Booth Theatre, Apr. 23, 1935
79 performances
Produced by Potter and Haight
Directed by H. C. Potter
Costumes by Mary Merrill
With Grace George, Henry Daniell, and Alan Bunce

Winterset by Maxwell Anderson
Opened Martin Beck Theatre, Sept. 25, 1935
178 performances
Produced and directed by Guthrie McClintic
With Eduardo Cianelli, Margo, Richard Bennett, and Burgess Meredith

Jubilee with music and lyrics by Cole Porter and book by Moss Hart
Opened Imperial Theatre, Oct. 12, 1935
169 performances
Produced by Sam H. Harris and Max Gordon
Directed and lighted by Hassard Short
Choreographed by Albertina Rasch
Costumes by Irene Sharaff and Connie De Pinna
With Mary Boland, Melville Cooper (and Montgomery Clift)

Pride and Prejudice by Helen Jerome (adapted from Jane Austen's novel)
Opened Music Box Theatre, Nov. 5, 1935
219 performances
Produced by Max Gordon
Directed by Robert Sinclair
Costumes by Jo Mielziner
With Percy Waram, Lucille Watson, Brenda Forbes, Adrianne Allen, and Cole Keith-Johnston

Hell Freezes Over by John Patrick
Opened Ritz Theatre, Dec. 28, 1935
25 performances
Produced by George Kondolf
Directed by Joshua Logan
With Louis Calhern, George Tobias, John Litel, and Myron McCormick

1936
A Room in Red and White by Roy Hargrave
Opened Forty-sixth St. Theatre, Jan. 18, 1936
25 performances
Produced by Dwight Deere Wiman and George Kondolf
Directed by Roy Hargrave
With Chrystal Herne and Joshua Logan

Ethan Frome by Owen and Donald Davis (from a story by Edith Wharton)
Opened National Theatre, Jan. 21, 1936
119 performances
Produced by Max Gordon
Directed by Guthrie McClintic
Costumes by Jo Mielziner
With Pauline Lord, Ruth Gordon, Raymond Massey, and Tom Ewell

Co-Respondent Unknown by Mildred Harris and Howard Goldman
Opened Ritz Theatre, Feb. 11, 1936
121 performances

Produced by Kenneth MacKenna, John Mayer, and Jo Mielziner
Directed by Kenneth MacKenna
With Ilka Chase, James Rennie, Peggy Conklin, and Phyllis Povah

The Postman Always Rings Twice by James M. Cain
Opened Golden Theatre, Feb. 25, 1936
71 performances
Produced by Jack Curtis
Directed by Robert Sinclair
With Richard Barthelmess, Mary Phillips (and Joseph Cotten)

Saint Joan by George Bernard Shaw
Opened Martin Beck Theatre, Mar. 9, 1936
89 performances
Produced by Katharine Cornell
Directed by Guthrie McClintic
Costumes by Jo Mielziner
Costume asst.: Rose Bogdanoff
With Katharine Cornell, Arthur Byron, George Coulouris, Maurice Evans, Eduardo Cianelli, Tyrone Power, and Kent Smith

On Your Toes with music and lyrics by Richard Rodgers and Moss Hart and book by George Abbott
Opened Imperial Theatre, Apr. 11, 1936
318 performances
Produced by Dwight Deere Wiman
Directed by Worthington Miner under supervision of Dwight Deere Wiman
Choreographed by George Balanchine
Costumes by Irene Sharaff
With Ray Bolger, Luella Gear, Tamara Geva, and Monty Woolley

St. Helena by R. C. Sheriff and Jeanne de Casalis
Opened Lyceum Theatre, Oct. 6, 1936
63 performances
Produced by Max Gordon
Directed by Robert Sinclair
Costumes by Jo Mielziner
With Maurice Evans, Barry Sullivan, Percy Waram, and Harry Bellaver

Hamlet by William Shakespeare
Opened Empire Theatre, Oct. 8, 1936
132 performances
Produced and directed by Guthrie McClintic
Costumes by Jo Mielziner
Costume asst.: Rose Bogdanoff
With John Gielgud, Lillian Gish, Judith Anderson, and Arthur Byron

Daughters of Atreus by Robert Turney
Opened Forty-fourth St. Theatre, Oct. 14, 1936
13 performances
Produced by Delos Chappell

Directed by Frederic McConnell
Costumes by James Reynolds
With Maria Ouspenskaya, Eleonora Mendelssohn, Olive Deering, Gale Gordon, Tom Neal (and Cornel Wilde and Edmond O'Brien)

The Wingless Victory by Maxwell Anderson
Opened Empire Theatre, Dec. 23, 1936
108 performances
Produced by Katharine Cornell
Directed by Guthrie McClintic
Costumes by Jo Mielziner
Costume asst.: Rose Bogdanoff
With Kent Smith, Arthur Chatterton, Katharine Cornell, Effie Shannon, Myron McCormick, and Walter Abel

The Women by Clare Booth Luce
Opened Ethel Barrymore Theatre, Dec. 26, 1936
657 performances
Produced by Max Gordon
Directed by Robert Sinclair
Costumes by John Hambleton
With Ilka Chase, Phyllis Povah, Margalo Gillmore, Arlene Francis, and Marjorie Main

1937
High Tor by Maxwell Anderson
Opened Martin Beck Theatre, Jan. 8, 1937
171 performances
Produced and directed by Guthrie McClintic
With Burgess Meredith, Peggy Ashcroft (and Hume Cronyn)

Pan American Casino Revue with music, lyrics, and skits by Sammy Fain, Irving Kahal, Chester Hale, et al.
Opened at the Casino (Dallas), June 12, 1937
142 days of continuous performances in "dinner theatre" format
Produced by George Preston Marshall
Directed by Chester Hale
Costumes by Charles LeMaire and Connie De Pinna
Theatre interior, sets, and lighting by Jo Mielziner
With rotating guest stars Phil Harris, Lanny Ross, Art Jarrett, Borrah Minnevitch, and Chester Hale's Ballet

The Star-Wagon by Maxwell Anderson
Opened Empire Theatre, Sept. 29, 1937
221 performances
Produced and directed by Guthrie McClintic
Costumes by Jo Mielziner
With Lillian Gish, Burgess Meredith, Kent Smith, and Mildred Natwick

Susan and God by Rachel Crothers
Opened Plymouth Theatre, Oct. 7, 1937
287 performances
Produced by John Golden
Directed by Rachel Crothers
With Gertrude Lawrence, Paul McGrath, Nancy Kelly, Vera Allen, and Edith Atwater

Antony and Cleopatra by William Shakespeare
Opened Mansfield Theatre, Nov. 11, 1937
5 performances
Produced by Laurence Rivers, Inc.
Directed by Reginald Bach
Costumes by Jo Mielziner and Cecil Beaton
With Tallulah Bankhead, John Emery, Conway Tearle, Charles Bowden, and Fania Marinoff

Too Many Heroes by Dore Schary
Opened Hudson Theatre, Nov. 15, 1937
16 performances
Produced by Carly Wharton
Directed by Garson Kanin
Set design asst.: Walter Jagemann
With Shirley Booth and James Bell

Father Malachy's Miracle by Brian Doherty (from Bruce Marshall's novel)
Opened St. James Theatre, Nov. 17, 1937
125 performances
Produced by Delos Chappell
Directed by Worthington Miner
Set design asst.: Walter Jagemann
With Al Shean and Mary Wickes

Barchester Towers by Thomas Job (from Anthony Trollope's novel)
Opened Martin Beck Theatre, Nov. 30, 1937
37 performances
Produced and directed by Guthrie McClintic
Set design asst.: Walter Jagemann
With Ina Claire, Effie Shannon, and J. M. Kerrigan

1938
Yr. Obedient Husband by Horace Jackson
Opened Broadhurst Theatre, Jan. 10, 1938
8 performances
Produced and directed by John Cromwell with Fredric March
With Fredric March, Florence Eldridge, Dame May Whitty, Brenda Forbes (and Montgomery Clift)

On Borrowed Time by Paul Osborn (from Lawrence Edward Watkins's novel)
Opened Longacre Theatre, Feb. 3, 1938
321 performances

Produced by Dwight Deere Wiman
Directed by Joshua Logan
Set design asst.: Walter Jagemann
With Dudley Digges, Dorothy Stickney, Frank Conroy, and Dickie Van Patten

Save Me the Waltz by Katharine Dayton
Opened Martin Beck Theatre, Feb. 28, 1938
Produced by Max Gordon with Sam H. Harris
Directed by Robert Sinclair
Costumes by John Hambleton
Set design asst.: Walter Jagemann
With Jane Wyatt, Leo G. Carroll, Mady Christians, Laura Hope Crews, and John Emery

I Married an Angel with music and lyrics by Richard Rodgers and Moss Hart (adapted from a play by John Vaszary)
Opened Shubert Theatre, May 11, 1938
338 performances
Produced by Dwight Deere Wiman
Directed by Joshua Logan
Choreographed by George Balanchine
Costumes by John Hambleton
Set design asst.: Walter Jagemann
With Dennis King, Walter Slezak, Vivienne Segal, Vera Zorina, and Audrey Christie

Sing Out the News by Harold Rome and Charles Friedman
Opened Music Box Theatre, Sept. 24, 1938
105 performances
Directed by Charles Friedman
Choreographed by Ned McGurn and Dave Gould
Costumes by John Hambleton
Costume asst.: Rose Bogdanoff
Set design asst.: George Jenkins
With Joey Faye, Will Geer, Hiram Sherman (and June Allyson and Jimmy Lydon)

Abe Lincoln in Illinois by Robert Sherwood
Opened Plymouth Theatre, Oct. 15, 1938
Produced by the Playwrights Company
Directed by Elmer Rice
Costumes by Rose Bogdanoff
Set design asst.: George Jenkins
With Raymond Massey, Muriel Kirkland, Howard Da Silva (and Kevin McCarthy)

Knickerbocker Holiday by Maxwell Anderson with music by Kurt Weill
Opened Ethel Barrymore Theatre, Oct. 19, 1938
168 performances
Produced by the Playwrights Company
Directed by Joshua Logan

Set design asst.: Walter Jagemann
With Walter Huston, Ray Middleton,
and Richard Kollmar

The Boys from Syracuse with music
and lyrics by Richard Rodgers and
Moss Hart and book by George
Abbott (adapted from William
Shakespeare's *Comedy of Errors*)
Opened Alvin Theatre, Nov. 23, 1938
235 performances
Produced and directed by George
Abbott
Choreographed by George Balanchine
Costumes by Irene Sharaff
Set design asst.: George Jenkins
With Burl Ives, Eddie Albert, and
Jimmy Savo

1939
Mrs. O'Brien Entertains by Harry
Madden
Opened Lyceum Theatre, Feb. 8, 1939
37 performances
Produced and directed by George
Abbott
Costumes by Jo Mielziner
Costume asst.: Rose Bogdanoff
Set design asst.: George Jenkins
With Margaret Mullen, James Lane
(and Gene Tierney)

Stars in Your Eyes with music and
lyrics by Arthur Schwartz and
Dorothy Fields and book by J. P.
McEvoy
Opened Majestic Theatre, Feb. 9, 1939
127 performances
Directed by Joshua Logan
Choreographed by Carl Randall
Costumes by John Hambleton
Costume asst.: Rose Bogdanoff
Set design asst.: George Jenkins
With Ethel Merman, Jimmy Durante,
Tamara Toumanova, Richard
Carlson, Mildred Natwick (and
Jerome Robbins, Alicia Alonzo,
Nora Kaye, and Maria Karnilova)

No Time for Comedy by S. N. Behrman
Opened Ethel Barrymore Theatre,
Apr. 17, 1939
185 performances
Produced by the Playwrights Company
Directed by Guthrie McClintic
Gowns by Valentina
Set design asst.: George Jenkins
With Katharine Cornell, Margalo
Gillmore, Francis Lederer, and
Tom Helmore

Too Many Girls with music and lyrics
by Richard Rodgers and Moss Hart
and book by George Marion Jr.
Opened Imperial Theatre, Oct. 18,
1939
249 performances
Produced and directed by George
Abbott

Choreographed by Robert Alton
Costumes by Raoul Pene Du Bois
Set design asst.: George Jenkins
With Desi Arnaz, Richard Kollmar
(and Eddie Bracken, Van Johnson,
and Diosa Costello)

Key Largo by Maxwell Anderson
Opened Ethel Barrymore Theatre,
Nov. 27, 1939
105 performances
Produced by the Playwrights Company
Directed by Guthrie McClintic
Costumes by Helene Pons
Set design asst.: George Jenkins
With José Ferrer, Paul Muni, Uta
Hagen (and Tom Ewell, Karl
Malden, and James Gregory)

Morning's at Seven by Paul Osborn
Opened Longacre Theatre, Nov. 30,
1939
44 performances
Produced by Dwight Deere Wiman
Directed by Joshua Logan
Set design asst.: George Jenkins
With Dorothy Gish, Thomas
Chalmers, Russell Collins, Jean
Adair, and Enid Markey

Christmas Eve by Gustav Eckstein
Opened Henry Miller's Theatre, Dec.
27, 1939
6 performances
Produced and directed by Guthrie
McClintic
Set design assistant: George Jenkins
With Kent Smith, James Rennie,
Mildred Natwick, Beth Merrill
(and Sidney Lumet)

1940
Two on an Island by Elmer Rice with
music by Kurt Weill
Opened Broadhurst Theatre, Jan. 22,
1940
96 performances
Produced by the Playwrights Company
Directed by Elmer Rice
Costumes by Helene Pons
Set design asst.: George Jenkins
With Betty Field, Martin Ritt, Howard
Da Silva, Luther Adler, and John
Craven

Higher and Higher with music and
lyrics by Richard Rodgers and
Moss Hart and book by Gladys
Hurlbut and Joshua Logan
Opened Shubert Theatre, Apr. 4, 1940
108 performances
Produced by Dwight Deere Wiman
Directed by Joshua Logan
Choreographed by Robert Alton
Costumes by Lucinda Ballard
With Jack Haley, Marta Eggert (and
June Allyson and Vera Ellen)

Journey to Jerusalem by Maxwell Anderson

Opened National Theatre, Nov. 5, 1940
17 performances
Produced by the Playwrights Company
Directed by Elmer Rice
Costumes by Millia Davenport
Set design asst.: George Jenkins
With Arlene Francis, Sidney Lumet,
Joseph Wiseman, Karl Malden,
Arnold Moss, and James Gregory

Pal Joey with music and lyrics by
Richard Rodgers and Moss Hart
and book by John O'Hara
Opened Ethel Barrymore Theatre,
Dec. 25, 1940
270 performances
Produced and directed by George
Abbott
Choreographed by Robert Alton
Costumes by John Koenig
Costume asst.: Frank Spencer
Set design asst.: George Jenkins
With Gene Kelly, June Havoc, Leila
Ernst, Vivienne Segal, and Van
Johnson

Flight to the West by Elmer Rice
Opened Guild Theatre, Dec. 30, 1940
136 performances
Produced by the Playwrights Company
Directed by Elmer Rice
Set design asst.: George Jenkins
With Betty Field, Arnold Moss, Paul
Henried, Karl Malden, Kevin
McCarthy, and Hugh Marlowe

The Little Dog Laughed with music
and lyrics by Harold Rome and
book by Joseph Schrank
Opened Garden Pier Theatre, Atlantic
City, Dec. 30, 1940; closed out of
town
Produced and directed by Eddie
Dowling
Choreographed by Chester Hale
Costumes by Nicholas DeMolas
With Paul Draper, Philip Loeb, and
Arthur Hunnicutt

1941
Mr. and Mrs. North by Owen Davis
from stories by Frances and
Richard Lockridge
Opened Belasco Theatre, Jan. 12, 1941
163 performances
Produced and directed by Alfred de
Liagre Jr.
Costumes by Mildred Manning
With Peggy Conklin and Albert Hackett

The Cream in the Well by Lynn Riggs
Opened Booth Theatre, Jan. 20, 1941
24 performances
Produced by Carly Wharton and
Martin Gabel
Directed by Martin Gabel
Set design asst.: George Jenkins
With Mary Morris, Myron McCormick,
Leif Ericson, and Harry Morgan

The Talley Method by S. N. Behrman
Opened Henry Miller's Theatre, Feb.
24, 1941
56 performances
Produced by the Playwrights Company
Directed by Elmer Rice
Production supervised by Jean Rosenthal
Set design asst.: George Jenkins
With Ina Claire, Philip Merivale, Ernst
Deutsch, and Hiram Sherman

Watch on the Rhine by Lillian Hellman
Opened Martin Beck Theatre, Apr. 1,
1941
378 performances
Produced and directed by Herman
Shumlin
Costumes by Helene Pons
Set design asst.: George Jenkins
With Lucile Watson, Paul Lukas,
Mady Christians, George
Coulouris (and Ann Blyth)

The Wookey by Frederick Hazlitt
Brennan
Opened Plymouth Theatre, Sept. 10,
1941
134 performances
Produced by Edgar Selwyn
Directed by Robert Sinclair
Set design asst.: George Jenkins
With Edmund Gwenn and Heather
Angel

Best Foot Forward with music and
lyrics by Hugh Martin and Ralph
Blane and book by John Cecil Holm
Opened Ethel Barrymore Theatre,
Oct. 1, 1941
326 performances
Produced and directed by George
Abbott
Choreographed by Gene Kelly
Costumes by Miles White
Set design asst.: George Jenkins
With Rosemary Lane, Nancy Walker,
June Allyson, and Robert Griffin

Candle in the Wind by Maxwell
Anderson
Opened Shubert Theatre, Oct. 22, 1941
95 performances
Produced by the Theatre Guild and
the Playwrights Company
Directed by Alfred Lunt
With Helen Hayes, Joseph Wiseman,
and Lotte Lenya

The Land Is Bright by George S.
Kaufman and Edna Ferber
Opened Music Box Theatre, Oct. 28,
1941
79 performances
Produced by Max Gordon
Directed by Kaufman
Costumes by Irene Sharaff
Set design asst.: George Jenkins
With Diana Barrymore, Phyllis Povah,
Arnold Moss, and Hugh Marlowe

The Seventh Trumpet by Charles
Rann Kennedy

Opened Mansfield Theatre, Nov. 21,
1941
11 performances
Produced by Theatre Associates
Directed by Charles Rann Kennedy
Production supervised by Jean Rosenthal
Set design asst.: George Jenkins
With Ian Maclaren and Carmen
Mathews

1942
Solitaire by John Van Druten (from
Edward Corle's novel)
Opened Plymouth Theatre, Jan. 27,
1942
23 performances
Produced by Dwight Deere Wiman
Directed by Dudley Digges
Set design asst.: George Jenkins
With Victor Kilian and Patricia
Hitchcock

Pillar of Fire (ballet)
Opened Metropolitan Opera House,
Apr. 8, 1942
Choreographed by Antony Tudor
Music by Arnold Schoenberg
Costumes by Jo Mielziner
With Lucia Chase, Nora Kaye, Antony
Tudor, Hugh Laing, Jerome
Robbins (and Donald Saddler)

By Jupiter with music and lyrics by
Richard Rodgers and Moss Hart
and book (based on *The Warrior's
Husband* by Julian F. Thompson)
Opened Shubert Theatre, June 5, 1942
421 performances
Produced by Dwight Deere Wiman
and Richard Rodgers
Directed by Joshua Logan
Choreographed by Robert Alton
Costumes by Irene Sharaff
With Ray Bolger, Constance Moore,
Ronald Graham, Benay Venuta
(and Vera-Ellen)

1943, 1944
During these years Jo Mielziner was
in the military.

1945
Foolish Notion by Philip Barry
Opened Martin Beck Theatre, Mar.
13, 1945
103 performances
Produced by the Theatre Guild
Directed by John C. Wilson
Scenery and lighting assts.: John
Harvey and Lisa Jalowetz
With Tallulah Bankhead, Donald Cook,
Mildred Dunnock, and Henry Hull

The Firebrand of Florence with
music by Kurt Weill and book and
lyrics by Edwin Justus Mayer and
Ira Gershwin
Opened Alvin Theatre, Mar. 22, 1945
43 performances

Produced by Max Gordon
Directed by John Murray Anderson
Costumes by Raoul Pene Du Bois
Scenery and lighting assts.: John
Harvey and Lisa Jalowetz
With Melville Cooper, Earl
Wrightson, and Lotte Lenya

The Glass Menagerie by Tennessee
Williams with music by Paul Bowles
Opened Playhouse Theatre, Mar. 31,
1945
561 performances
Produced by Eddie Dowling and
Louis J. Singer
Directed by Eddie Dowling and
Margo Jones
With Laurette Taylor, Eddie Dowling,
Julie Hayden, and Anthony Ross

Carousel with music and lyrics by
Richard Rodgers and Oscar
Hammerstein II and book by
Hammerstein (based on Ferenc
Molnár's *Liliom*)
Opened Majestic Theatre, Apr. 19, 1945
890 performances
Produced by the Theatre Guild
Directed by Rouben Mamoulian
Choreographed by Agnes de Mille
Costumes by Miles White
Scenery and lighting assts.: John
Harvey and Lisa Jalowetz
With John Raitt, Jan Clayton, Jean
Darling, Franklyn Fox, and Bambi
Lynn

Hollywood Pinafore by George S.
Kaufman (adapted from Gilbert
and Sullivan's *H.M.S. Pinafore*)
Opened Alvin Theatre, May 31, 1945
52 performances
Produced by Max Gordon with Meyer
Davis
Directed by George S. Kaufman
Choreographed by Antony Tudor
Costumes by Kathryn Kuhn and Mary
Percy Schenk
Set design asst.: John Harvey
With William Gaxton, Victor Moore,
Shirley Booth, and Annamary Dickey

Carib Song with music by Baldwin
Bergersen and book and lyrics by
William Archibald
Opened Adelphi Theatre, Sept. 27, 1945
36 performances
Produced by George Stanton
Directed by Mary Hunter and
Katherine Dunham
Costumes by Motley
Set design asst.: John Harvey
With Katherine Dunham and Avon
Long

Beggars Are Coming to Town by
Theodore Reeves
Opened Coronet Theatre, Oct. 27, 1945
25 performances

Produced by Oscar Serlin
Directed by Harold Clurman
Costumes by Ralph Alswang and
    Charles James
With Paul Kelly, Luther Adler, Dorothy
    Comingore, Adrienne Ames,
    Herbert Berghof, and E. G. Marshall

The Rugged Path by Robert Sherwood
Opened Plymouth Theatre, Nov. 11,
    1945
81 performances
Produced by the Playwrights Company
Directed by Garson Kanin
Costumes by Rose Bogdanoff and
    Valentina
Set design assts.: Walter Jagemann
    and John Harvey
With Spencer Tracy, Kay Loring, and
    Jan Sterling

Dream Girl by Elmer Rice
Opened Coronet Theatre, Dec. 14, 1945
348 performances
Produced by the Playwrights Company
Directed by Elmer Rice
Scenery: Walter Jagemann and John
    Harvey
With Betty Field, Evelyn Varden,
    Wendell Corey, and James
    Gregory

St. Lazare's Pharmacy by Miklos
    Laszlo (adapted by Eddie Dowling)
Opened His Majesty's Theatre,
    Montreal, Dec. 1945; closed out of
    town
Produced by Eddie Dowling and
    Louis J. Singer
Directed by Eddie Dowling
Set design assts.: Walter Jagemann
    and John Harvey
With Miriam Hopkins

Shango (ballet)
Introduced as independent ballet from
    Carib Song (act 1 finale) in Katherine
    Dunham's company, 1946–49
Choreographed and danced by
    Katherine Dunham
Production designed by Jo Mielziner
    (from *Carib Song*)
Costumes by Motley

1946
Jeb by Robert Ardrey
Opened Martin Beck Theatre, Feb. 21,
    1946
9 performances
Produced and directed by Herman
    Shumlin
Costumes by Patricia Montgomery
Set design assts.: Walter Jagemann
    and John Harvey
With Ossie Davis and Ruby Dee

Windy City with music by Walter
    Jurmann, book by Philip Yordan,
    and lyrics by Paul Francis Webster

Opened Shubert Theatre, New Haven,
    Apr. 18, 1946; closed out of town
Produced by Richard Kollmar
Directed by Edward Reveaux and
    Katherine Dunham
Choreographed by Katherine Dunham
With Al Shean, Loring Smith, and
    Joey Faye

Annie Get Your Gun with music and
    lyrics by Irving Berlin and book by
    Herbert and Dorothy Fields
Opened Imperial Theatre, May 16, 1946
1,147 performances
Produced by Richard Rodgers and
    Oscar Hammerstein II
Directed by Joshua Logan
Choreographed by Helen Tamiris
Costumes by Lucinda Ballard
Set design assts.: Walter Jagemann
    and John Harvey
With Ethel Merman, Ray Middleton,
    Ellen Hanley, and Harry Bellaver

Happy Birthday by Anita Loos
Opened Broadhurst Theatre, Oct. 31,
    1946
564 performances
Produced by Richard Rodgers and
    Oscar Hammerstein II
Directed by Joshua Logan
Costumes by Lucinda Ballard
Set design asst.: John Harvey
With Helen Hayes, Enid Markey, and
    Louis Jean Heydt

Another Part of the Forest by Lillian
    Hellman
Opened Fulton Theatre, Nov. 20, 1946
182 performances
Produced by Kermit Bloomgarden
Directed by Lillian Hellman
Costumes by Lucinda Ballard
Set design asst.: John Harvey
With Patricia Neal, Mildred Dunnock,
    Percy Waram, Leo Genn, Scott
    McCay, Margaret Phillips, and
    Jean Hagen

1947
The Big Two by L. Bush-Fekete and
    Mary Helen Fay
Opened Booth Theatre, Jan. 8, 1937
21 performances
Produced by Elliott Nugent and
    Robert Montgomery
Directed by Robert Montgomery
Costumes by Biana Stroock
Set design asst.: John Harvey
With Claire Trevor, Philip Dorn, Felix
    Bressart, and Eduard Franz

Street Scene with music by Kurt Weill
    and lyrics by Langston Hughes and
    book by Elmer Rice (from his play)
Opened Adelphi Theatre, Jan. 9, 1947
148 performances
Produced by Dwight Deere Wiman
    and the Playwrights Company

Directed by Charles Friedman
Choreographed by Anna Sokolow
Costumes by Lucinda Ballard
Set design asst.: John Harvey
With Norman Cordon, Anne Jeffreys,
    Polyna Stoska, Brian Sullivan, and
    Hope Emerson

Finian's Rainbow with music by Burton
    Lane and lyrics by E. Y. Harburg and
    book by Harburg and Fred Saidy
Opened Forty-sixth St. Theatre, Jan.
    10, 1947
725 performances
Produced by Lee Sabinson and
    William R. Katzell
Directed by Bretaigne Windust
Choreographed by Michael Kidd
Costumes by Eleanor Goldsmith
Set design asst.: John Harvey
With Ella Logan, David Wayne, and
    Anita Alvarez

The Chocolate Soldier with music by
    Oscar Straus and book by Rudolph
    Bernauer and Leopold Jacobson
    (adapted by Stanislaus Stange and
    Guy Bolton)
Opened Century Theatre, Mar. 12,
    1947
70 performances
Produced by J. H. Del Bondio and
    Hans Hartsch
Directed by Felix Brentano
Choreographed by George Balanchine
Costumes by Lucinda Ballard
Set design asst.: John Harvey
With Keith Andes, Billy Gilbert, and
    Frances McCann

Barefoot Boy with Cheek with music by
    Sidney Lippmann, lyrics by Sylvia
    Dee, and book by Max Shulman
Opened Martin Beck Theatre, Apr. 3,
    1947
108 performances
Produced and directed by George
    Abbott
Choreographed by Richard Barstow
Costumes by Alvin Colt
Set design asst.: John Harvey
With Nancy Walker, William Redfield,
    and Ellen Hanley

Command Decision by William
    Wister Haines
Opened Fulton Theatre, Oct. 1, 1947
409 performances
Produced by Kermit Bloomgarden
Directed by John O'Shaughnessy
Costumes by Julie Sze
Set design assts.: John Harvey and
    Arthur H. Ross
With Paul Kelly, Paul McGrath, and
    James Whitmore

Allegro with music and lyrics by Richard
    Rodgers and Oscar Hammerstein
    II and book by Hammerstein
Opened Majestic Theatre, Oct. 10, 1947

315 performances
Directed and choreographed by
    Agnes de Mille
Costumes by Lucinda Ballard
Set design assts.: John Harvey and
    Arthur H. Ross
With Annamary Dickey, John Battles,
    John Conte (and Lisa Kirk)

A Streetcar Named Desire by
    Tennessee Williams
Opened Ethel Barrymore Theatre,
    Dec. 3, 1947
855 performances
Produced by Irene Selznick Mayer
Directed by Elia Kazan
Costumes by Lucinda Ballard
Set design assts.: John Harvey and
    Arthur H. Ross
With Jessica Tandy, Kim Hunter,
    Marlon Brando, and Karl Malden

1948
Mister Roberts by Thomas Heggen
    and Joshua Logan (based on
    Heggen's novel)
Opened Alvin Theatre, Feb. 18, 1948
1,157 performances
Produced by Leland Hayward
Directed by Joshua Logan
With Henry Fonda, David Wayne,
    William Harrigan, Robert Keith,
    Jocelyn Brando, and Murray
    Hamilton

Shadow of the Wind (ballet)
Based on poems by Li Po with music
    "Song of the Earth" by Gustav
    Mahler
Introduced Metropolitan Opera
    House, Apr. 14, 1948
Produced by the American Ballet
    Theatre, Lucia Chase, and Oliver
    Smith, by arrangement of Sol Hurok
Choreographed by Antony Tudor
Production designed by Jo Mielziner
Costume asst.: Rose Bogdanoff
With Hugh Laing, Eric Brown, Igor
    Youskevitch, Alicia Alonzo, John
    Kriza, and Melissa Hayden

Sleepy Hollow with music by George
    Lessner and book and lyrics by
    Russell Maloney and Miriam
    Battista
Opened St. James Theatre, June 3, 1948
12 performances
Produced by Lorraine Lester
Directed by John O'Shaughnessy
Choreographed by Anna Sokolow
Costumes by David Ffolkes
Set design assts.: John Harvey and
    Arthur H. Ross
With Gil Lamb, Betty Jane Watson,
    Mary McCarty, James Starbuck,
    and Jo Sullivan

Summer and Smoke by Tennessee
    Williams with music by Paul Bowles

Opened Music Box Theatre, Oct. 6,
    1948
102 performances
Produced and directed by Margo Jones
Costumes by Rose Bogdanoff
Set design asst.: John Harvey
With Margaret Phillips, Tod Andrews,
    Anne Jackson, and Ray Walston

Anne of the Thousand Days by
    Maxwell Anderson with music by
    Lehman Engel
Opened Shubert Theatre, Dec. 8, 1948
288 performances
Produced by the Playwrights
    Company and Leland Hayward
Directed by H. C. Potter
Costumes by Motley
Set design asst.: John Harvey
With Rex Harrison, Joyce Redman,
    Percy Waram, and John Williams

1949
Death of a Salesman by Arthur Miller
Opened Morosco Theatre, Feb. 10, 1949
742 performances
Produced by Kermit Bloomgarden and
    Walter Fried
Directed by Elia Kazan
Costumes by Julia Sze
Set design asst.: John Harvey
With Lee J. Cobb, Arthur Kennedy,
    Mildred Dunnock, and Cameron
    Mitchell

South Pacific with music and lyrics
    by Richard Rodgers and Oscar
    Hammerstein II with book by
    Hammerstein and Joshua Logan
Opened Majestic Theatre, Apr. 7, 1949
1,925 performances
Directed by Joshua Logan
Costumes by Motley
Set design assts.: John Harvey and
    Furth Ullman
With Mary Martin, Ezio Pinza, Myron
    McCormick, Juanita Hall, William
    Tabbert, and Betta St. John

The Real McCoy by John Finch
Opened University Theatre, Catholic
    University of America, Washington,
    D.C., Dec. 12, 1949
15 performances
Produced by the Theatre Department,
    Catholic University
Directed by Alan Schneider
Scenery from designs by Mielziner
    under supervision of James D.
    Waring
Costumes by Cynthia Ketterer

1950
The Man by Mel Dinelli
Opened Fulton Theatre, Jan. 19, 1950
92 performances
Produced by Kermit Bloomgarden
Directed by Martin Ritt
Costumes by Julie Sze

Set design asst.: John Harvey
With Dorothy Gish, Don Hanmer,
    Peggy Ann Garner, and Richard
    Boone

Dance Me a Song with music by
    James Shelton et al. and sketches
    by Jimmy Kirkwood, Lee
    Goodman, George Oppenheimer,
    Vincente Minnelli, Marya Mannes,
    Robert Anderson, and Wally Cox
Opened Royale Theatre, Jan. 20, 1950
35 performances
Produced by Dwight Deere Wiman
    with Robert Ross
Directed by James Shelton
Choreographed by Robert Sidney
Costumes by Irene Sharaff
With Donald Saddler, Marion Lorne,
    Wally Cox, Jimmy Kirkwood, Bob
    Fosse, and Joan McCracken

The Innocents by William Archibald
    with music by Alex North (based
    on Henry James's *Turn of the Screw*)
Opened Playhouse Theatre, Feb. 1, 1950
141 performances
Produced by Peter Cookson
Directed by Peter Glenville
Costumes by Motley
Set design asst.: John Harvey
With Beatrice Straight, Iris Mann,
    Isobel Elsom, and David Cole

The Wisteria Trees by Joshua Logan
    with music by Lehman Engel
    (based on Anton Chekhov's *The
    Cherry Orchard*)
Opened Martin Beck Theatre, Mar.
    29, 1950
165 performances
Produced by Leland Hayward and
    Joshua Logan
Directed by Joshua Logan
Costumes by Lucinda Ballard
Set design asst.: John Harvey
With Helen Hayes, Kent Smith, Walter
    Abel, Peggy Conklin, and Bethel
    Leslie

Burning Bright by John Steinbeck
Opened Broadhurst Theatre, Oct. 18,
    1950
13 performances
Produced by Richard Rodgers and
    Oscar Hammerstein II
Directed by Guthrie McClintic
Costumes by Aline Bernstein
Set design asst.: John Harvey
With Kent Smith, Barbara Bel Geddes,
    and Howard Da Silva

Guys and Dolls with music and lyrics
    by Frank Loesser and book by Abe
    Burrows with Jo Swerling (based
    on stories by Damon Runyon)
Opened Forty-sixth St. Theatre,
    Nov. 24, 1950
1,194 performances

Directed by George S. Kaufman
Choregraphed by Michael Kidd
Costumes by Alvin Colt
Set design asst.: John Harvey
With Robert Alda, Isabel Bigley, Vivian
Blaine, Sam Levene, Stubby Kaye,
Tom Pedi, and B. S. Pully

1951

The King and I with music by
Richard Rodgers and lyrics and
book by Oscar Hammerstein II
(based on Margaret Landon's novel
Anna and the King of Siam)
Opened St. James Theatre, Mar. 29,
1951
1,246 performances
Produced by Richard Rodgers and
Oscar Hammerstein II
Directed by John Van Druten
Choregraphed by Jerome Robbins
Costumes by Irene Sharaff
Set design asst.: John Harvey
With Gertrude Lawrence, Yul Brynner,
Dorothy Sarnoff, and Doretta
Morrow

A Tree Grows in Brooklyn with
music and lyrics by Arthur
Schwartz and Dorothy Fields and
book by Betty Smith and George
Abbott (based on Smith's novel)
Opened Alvin Theatre, Apr. 19, 1950
267 performances
Produced (with Robert Fryer) and
directed by George Abbott
Choreographed by Herbert Ross
Costumes by Irene Sharaff
With Shirley Booth, Johnny Johnston,
and Nathaniel Frey

Top Banana with music and lyrics by
Johnny Mercer and book by Hy
Kraft
Opened Winter Garden, Nov. 1, 1950
350 performances
Produced by Paul Stone and Mike
Sloane
Directed by Jack Donohue
Costumes by Alvin Colt
Set design asst.: John Harvey
With Phil Silvers, Jack Albertson,
Joey Faye, Rose Marie, and
Herbie Faye

Point of No Return by Paul Osborn
(based on J. P. Marquand's novel)
Opened Alvin Theatre, Dec. 13, 1950
364 performances
Produced by Leland Hayward
Directed by H. C. Potter
Set design asst.: John Harvey
With Henry Fonda, Henry Conroy,
John Cromwell, Leora Dana, and
Colin Keith-Johnston

1952

A Month of Sundays with music by
Albert Selden and book and lyrics

by B. G. Shevelove (and additional
lyrics by Ted Fetter)
Opened Forrest Theatre, Philadelphia,
Jan. 17, 1952; closed out of town
Produced by Carly Wharton
Directed by Burt Shevelove
Choreographed by Anna Sokolow
Costumes by Kenn Barr
With Gene Lockhart, Nancy Walker,
Richard Kiley, and Estelle Loring

Flight into Egypt by George Tabori
Opened Music Box Theatre, Mar. 18,
1952
46 performances
Produced by Irene Mayer Selznick
Directed by Elia Kazan
Costumes by Anna Hill Johnston
Set design asst.: John Harvey
With Paul Lukas, Gusti Huber, Zero
Mostel, Joseph Anthony, and Jo
Van Fleet

Wish You Were Here with music and
lyrics by Harold Rome and book
by Arthur Kober and Joshua Logan
(based on Kober's play *Having a
Wonderful Time*)
Opened Imperial Theatre, June 25, 1952
598 performances
Produced by Joshua Logan and Leland
Hayward
Directed by Joshua Logan
Costumes by Robert Mackintosh
Set design asst.: John Harvey
With Sheila Bond, Jack Cassidy (and
Florence Henderson, Reid Shelton,
and Phyllis Newman)

The Gambler by Ugo Betti (adapted
by Alfred Drake and Edward Eager)
Opened Lyceum Theatre, Oct. 15, 1952
24 performances
Produced by Thomas Hammond and
Wayne Harriss
Directed by Herman Shumlin
Costumes by Robert Mackintosh
Set design asst.: John Harvey
With Alfred Drake, Percy Waram, E.
G. Marshall, Philip Coolidge, and
Ann Burr

1953

Picnic by William Inge
Opened Music Box Theatre, Feb. 19,
1952
477 performances
Produced by the Theatre Guild and
Joshua Logan
Directed by Joshua Logan
Costumes by Mildred Trebor
Set design asst.: John Harvey
With Ralph Meeker, Janice Rule, Eileen
Heckart, Kim Stanley, Arthur
O'Connell (and Paul Newman)

Can-Can with music and lyrics by Cole
Porter and book by Abe Burrows
Opened Shubert Theatre, May 7, 1953

892 performances
Produced by Cy Feuer and Ernest Martin
Directed by Abe Burrows
Choreographed by Michael Kidd
Costumes by Motley
Set design asst.: John Harvey
With Lilo, Peter Cookson, Gwen
Verdon, and Hans Conried

Me and Juliet with music by Richard
Rodgers and book and lyrics by
Oscar Hammerstein II
Opened Majestic Theatre, May 28, 1953
358 performances
Produced by Richard Rodgers and
Oscar Hammerstein II
Directed by George Abbott
Choreographed by Robert Alton
Costumes by Irene Sharaff
Set design asst.: John Harvey
With Isabel Bigley, Bill Hayes, Joan
McCracken, and Ray Walston

Tea and Sympathy by Robert Anderson
Opened Ethel Barrymore Theatre,
Sept. 30, 1953
712 performances
Produced by the Playwrights
Company with Mary K. Frank
Directed by Elia Kazan
Costumes by Anna Hill Johnstone
Set design asst.: John Harvey
With Deborah Kerr, John Kerr, and
Leif Ericson

Kind Sir by Norman Krasna
Opened Alvin Theatre, Nov. 4, 1953
165 performances
Produced and directed by Joshua
Logan
Costumes by Mainbocher
Set design asst.: John Harvey
With Mary Martin, Charles Boyer,
Margalo Gillmore, Dorothy
Stickney, and Frank Conroy

1954

By the Beautiful Sea with music by
Arthur Schwartz and lyrics by
Dorothy Fields with book by
Herbert and Dorothy Fields
Opened Majestic Theatre, Apr. 8,
1954
268 performances
Produced by Robert Fryer
Directed by Marshall Jamison
Choreographed by Helen Tamiris
Costumes by Irene Sharaff
Set design asst.: John Harvey
With Shirley Booth, Wilbur Evans,
and Anne Francine

All Summer Long by Robert Anderson
(from Donald Wetzel's novel)
Opened Coronet Theatre, Sept. 23,
1954
60 performances
Produced by the Playwrights Company
Directed by Alan Schneider

Costumes by Anna Hill Johnstone
Set design asst.: John Harvey
With John Kerr, June Walker, Ed Begley,
Carroll Baker, and John Randolph

Fanny with music and lyrics by
Harold Rome and book by S. N.
Behrman and Joshua Logan (based
on the trilogy by Marcel Pagnol)
Opened Majestic Theatre, Nov. 4, 1954
888 performances
Directed by Joshua Logan
Choreographed by Helen Tamiris
Costumes by Alvin Colt
Set design assts.: John Harvey and
Warren Clymer
With Ezio Pinza, Walter Slezak, Florence
Henderson, and William Tabbert

1955

Silk Stockings with music and lyrics
by Cole Porter and book by
George S. Kaufman, Leueen
McGrath, and Abe Burrows (based
on the film *Ninotchka*)
Opened Imperial Theatre, Feb. 24,
1955
478 performances
Produced by Cy Feuer and Ernest Martin
Directed by Cy Feuer
Choreographed by Eugene Loring
Costumes by Lucinda Ballard and
Robert Mackintosh
Set design assts.: John Harvey and
Warren Clymer
With Hildegard Neff, Don Ameche,
and George Tobias

Cat on a Hot Tin Roof by Tennessee
Williams
Opened Morosco Theatre, Mar. 24,
1955
694 performances
Produced by the Playwrights Company
Directed by Elia Kazan
Costumes by Lucinda Ballard
Set design asst.: John Harvey
With Barbara Bel Geddes, Ben Gazzara,
Burl Ives, Mildred Dunnock, Pat
Hingle, and Madeline Sherwood

Island of Goats by Ugo Betti (trans-
lated by Henry Reed)
Opened Fulton Theatre, Oct. 4, 1955
7 performances
Produced by Roger L. Stevens and
Hardy Smith Ltd.
Directed by Peter Glenville
Costumes by Motley
Set design asst.: John Harvey
With Uta Hagen, Laurence Harvey,
and Ruth Ford

The Lark by Jean Anouilh with music
by Leonard Bernstein (adapted by
Lillian Hellman)
Opened Longacre Theatre, Nov. 17,
1955
229 performances

Produced by Kermit Bloomgarden
Directed by Joseph Anthony
Costumes by Alvin Colt
Set design asst.: John Harvey
With Julie Harris, Sam Jaffe, Boris
Karloff, Joseph Wiseman,
Christopher Plummer, and
Theodore Bikel

Pipe Dream with music by Richard
Rodgers and book and lyrics by
Oscar Hammerstein II (based on
John Steinbeck's novel *Sweet
Thursday*)
Opened Shubert Theatre, Nov. 30, 1955
246 performances
Produced by Richard Rodgers and
Oscar Hammerstein II
Directed by Harold Clurman
Costumes by Alvin Colt
Set design asst.: John Harvey
With Helen Traubel, William
Johnson, and Mike Kellin

Picnic (film) Screenplay by Daniel
Taradash (based on the play by
William Inge)
Opened Warner Beverly Theatre,
Hollywood, Dec. 5, 1955; Radio
City Music Hall, New York,
Feb. 12, 1956
Produced by Fred Kohlmar for
Columbia Pictures
Directed by Joshua Logan
Cinematography by James Wong Howe
Production design by Jo Mielziner
Art direction by William Flannery
Set decoration by Robert Priestly
With Kim Novak, William Holden,
Rosalind Russell, and Susan
Strasberg

1956

Middle of the Night by Paddy
Chayevsky
Opened ANTA Theatre, Feb. 8, 1956
477 performances
Produced and directed by Joshua Logan
Costumes by Motley
Set design asst.: John Harvey
With Edward G. Robinson, June
Walker, Anne Jackson (and Gena
Rowlands)

The Most Happy Fella with music,
lyrics, and book by Frank Loesser
(based on Sidney Howard's play
They Knew What They Wanted)
Opened Imperial Theatre, May 3, 1956
676 performances
Produced by Kermit Bloomgarden and
Lynn Loesser
Directed by Joseph Anthony
Choreographed by Dania Krupska
Costumes by Motley
Set design assts.: John Harvey and
Ming Cho Lee
With Robert Weede, Jo Sullivan, Art
Lund, and Mona Paulee

Happy Hunting with music by Harold
Karr, lyrics by Matt Dubey, and
book by Howard Lindsay and
Russel Crouse
Opened Majestic Theatre, Dec. 6, 1956
412 performances
Produced by Jo Mielziner
Directed by Abe Burrows
Costumes by Irene Sharaff
Set design assts.: John Harvey, Ming
Cho Lee, and Harry Kardeman
With Ethel Merman, Fernando Lamas,
Edith Meiser, and Estelle Parsons

1957

Maiden Voyage by Paul Osborn
Opened Forrest Theatre, Feb. 28,
1957; closed out of town
Produced by Kermit Bloomgarden
with Anna Deere Wiman
Directed by Joseph Anthony
Costumes by Alvin Colt
Set design assts.: John Harvey and
Ming Cho Lee
With Melvyn Douglas, Valerie Bettis,
Tom Poston, Colleen Dewhurst,
Mildred Dunnock, and Walter
Matthau

Miss Lonelyhearts by Howard
Teichmann (from Nathanael West's
novel)
Opened Music Box Theatre, Oct. 3,
1957
12 performances
Produced by Lester Osterman and
Alfred K. Glancy Jr. with Diana
Green
Directed by Alan Schneider
Costumes by Patricia Zipprodt
Set design assts.: John Harvey and
Ming Cho Lee
With Pat O'Brien, Fritz Weaver, Ruth
Warrick, Janet Ward, Henderson
Forsythe, and Anne Meara

The Square Root of Wonderful by
Carson McCullers
Opened National Theatre, Oct. 30,
1957
45 performances
Produced by Saint Subber and Figaro,
Inc.
Directed by George Keathley
Costumes by Noel Taylor
Set design assts.: John Harvey and
Ming Cho Lee
With Anne Baxter, Jean Dixon, Philip
Abbott, and William Smithers

Look Homeward, Angel by Ketti
Frings (based on Thomas Wolfe's
novel)
Opened Ethel Barrymore Theatre,
Nov. 28, 1957
564 performances
Produced by Kermit Bloomgarden and
Theatre 200, Inc.
Directed by George Roy Hill

Costumes by Motley
Assoc. set designer: John Harvey
Asst. set designer: Ming Cho Lee
With Anthony Perkins, Jo Van Fleet,
Hugh Griffith, Arthur Hill, and
Victor Kilia

1958

Oh Captain! with music and lyrics by
Jay Livingston and Ray Evans and
book by Al Morgan and José
Ferrer (based on Alec Coppel's
screenplay *The Captain's Paradise*)
Opened Alvin Theatre, Feb. 4, 1958
192 performances
Produced by Howard Merrill and
Theatre Corporation of America
Directed by José Ferrer
Choreographed by James Starbuck
Costumes by Miles White
Assoc. set designer: John Harvey
Asst. set designer: Will Steven
Armstrong
With Tony Randall, Jacquelyn
McKeever, Abbe Lane, and
Alexandra Danilova

The Day the Money Stopped by
Maxwell Anderson and Brendan
Gill (based on Gill's novel)
Opened Belasco Theatre, Feb. 20, 1958
4 performances
Produced by Stanley Gilkey and
Producers Theatre
Directed by Harold Clurman
Costumes by Betty Coe Armstrong
With Richard Basehart, Mildred
Natwick, Kevin McCarthy, and
Collin Wilcox

Handful of Fire by N. Richard Nash
Opened Martin Beck Theatre, Oct. 1,
1958
5 performances
Produced by David Susskind and the
Playwrights Company
Directed by Robert Lewis
Costumes by Lucinda Ballard
Asst. set designer: John Harvey
With Roddy McDowall, James Daly,
Joan Copeland, and Kay Medford

The World of Suzie Wong by Paul
Osborn (based on Richard Mason's
novel)
Opened Broadhurst Theatre, Oct. 14,
1958
508 performances
Produced by David Merrick, Seven
Arts, and Mansfield Productions
Directed by Joshua Logan
Costumes by Dorothy Jeakins
Assoc. set designer: John Harvey
With France Nuyen and William Shatner

The Gazebo by Alec Coppel (from a
story by Myra and Alex Coppel)
Opened Lyceum Theatre, Dec. 12, 1958
218 performances

Produced by the Playwrights
Company and Frederick Brisson
Directed by Jerome Chodorov
Costumes by Virginia Volland
Assoc. set designer: John Harvey
Asst. set designer: Will Steven
Armstrong
With Walter Slezak, Jayne Meadows,
and Edward Andrews

Whoop-Up with music by Moose
Charlap, lyrics by Norman Gimbel,
and book by Cy Feuer, Ernest
Martin, and Dan Cushman (based
on Cushman's novel *Stay Away, Joe*)
Opened Shubert Theatre, Dec. 22, 1958
56 performances
Produced by Cy Feuer and Ernest Martin
Directed by Cy Feuer
Choreographed by Onna White
Costumes by Anna Hill Johnstone
Assoc. set designer: John Harvey
Asst. set designers: Ming Cho Lee and
Will Steven Armstrong
With Paul Ford

1959

Rashomon by Fay and Michael Kanin
(based on stories by Ryunosuke
Akutagawa)
Opened Music Box Theatre, Jan. 17,
1959
159 performances
Produced by David Susskind and
Hardy Smith
Directed by Peter Glenville
Scenery and costumes by Oliver Messel
Lighting by Jo Mielziner
With Claire Bloom, Rod Steiger,
Oscar Homolka, Akim Tamiroff,
and Noel Willman

Sweet Bird of Youth by Tennessee
Williams
Opened Martin Beck Theatre, Mar.
10, 1959
375 performances
Produced by Cheryl Crawford
Directed by Elia Kazan
Costumes by Anna Hill Johnstone
Assoc. set designer: John Harvey
Asst. set designer: Hugh Hardy
With Geraldine Page, Paul Newman,
Sidney Blackmer, and Madeline
Sherwood

Gypsy with music by Jule Styne,
lyrics by Stephen Sondheim, and
book by Arthur Laurents (based on
Gypsy Rose Lee's autobiography)
Opened Broadway Theatre, May 21,
1959
702 performances
Produced by David Merrick and
Leland Hayward
Directed and choreographed by
Jerome Robbins
Costumes by Raoul Pene Du Bois
Assoc. set designer: John Harvey

Asst. set designers: Ming Cho Lee, Hugh
Hardy, and Will Steven Armstrong
With Ethel Merman, Jack Klugman,
and Sandra Church

The Gang's All Here by Jerome
Lawrence and Robert E. Lee
Opened Ambassador Theatre, Oct. 1,
1959
132 performances
Produced by Kermit Bloomgarden
with Sylvia Drulie
Directed by George Roy Hill
Costumes by Patricia Zipprodt
Assoc. set designer: John Harvey
Asst. set designer: Hugh Hardy
With Melvyn Douglas, E. G. Marshall,
Jean Dixon, Arthur Hill, and Paul
McGrath

Silent Night, Lonely Night by Robert
Anderson
Opened Morosco Theatre, Dec. 5, 1959
124 performances
Produced by the Playwrights Company
Directed by Peter Glenville
Costumes by Theoni V. Aldredge
Assoc. set designer: John Harvey
Asst. set designer: Hugh Hardy
With Henry Fonda, Barbara Bel
Geddes, and Lois Nettleton

1960

There Was a Little Girl by Daniel
Taradash (based on Christopher
Davis's novel)
Opened Cort Theatre, Feb. 29, 1960
16 performances
Produced by Robert Fryer and
Lawrence Carr
Directed by Joshua Logan
Costumes by Patton Campbell
Assoc. set designer: John Harvey
Asst. set designers: Ming Cho Lee and
Hugh Hardy
With Jane Fonda, Whitfield Connor,
Dean Jones, and Joey Heatherton

The Best Man by Gore Vidal
Opened Morosco Theatre, Mar. 31,
1960
520 performances
Produced by Roger L. Stevens
Directed by Joseph Anthony
Costumes by Theoni V. Aldredge
Assoc. set designer: John Harvey
Asst. set designers: Ming Cho Lee and
Hugh Hardy
With Melvyn Douglas, Lee Tracy,
Frank Lovejoy, and Leora Dana

Christine with music by Sammy Fain,
lyrics by Paul Francis Webster, and
book by Pearl S. Buck and Charles
K. Peck Jr. (adapted from Hilda
Wernher's novel *My Indian Family*)
Opened Forty-sixth St. Theatre, Apr.
28, 1960
12 performances

Produced by Oscar S. Lerman and
Martin B. Cohen with Walter Cohen
Uncredited direction by Jerome
Chodorov
Choreographed by Hanya Holm
Costumes by Alvin Colt
Assoc. set designer: John Harvey
Asst. set designers: Ming Cho Lee, Lloyd
Burlingame and Richard Casler
With Maureen O'Hara and Phil Leeds

Period of Adjustment by Tennessee
Williams
Opened Helen Hayes Theatre, Nov.
10, 1960
132 performances
Produced by Cheryl Crawford
Directed by George Roy Hill
Costumes by Patricia Zipprodt
Assoc. set designer: John Harvey
Asst. set designer: Richard Casler
With James Daly, Barbara Baxley, Robert
Webber, and Rosemary Murphy

Little Moon of Alban by James Costigan
Opened Longacre Theatre, Dec. 1, 1960
20 performances
Produced by Mildred Fried Alberg
Directed by Herman Shumlin
Costumes by Noel Taylor
Assoc. set designer: John Harvey
Asst. set designer: Richard Casler
With Julie Harris, Robert Redford,
and Barbara O'Neil

1961

The Devil's Advocate by Dore Schary
(adapted from Morris L. West's
novel)
Opened Billy Rose Theatre, Mar. 9, 1961
116 performances
Produced and directed by Dore Schary
Costumes by Theoni V. Aldredge
Assoc. set designer: John Harvey
Asst. set designer: Richard Casler
With Leo Genn, Sam Levene, Edward
Mulhare, Eduardo Cianelli, and
Olive Deering

A Short Happy Life by A. E. Hotchner
(based on Ernest Hemingway's
works)
Opened Moore Theatre, Seattle, Sept.
12, 1961; closed out of town
Produced by A. E. Hotchner with
Jerome Brody
Directed by Frank Corsaro
Choreographed by Matt Mattox
Asst. set designer: Richard Casler
With Rod Steiger, Nan Martin,
Harvey Lembeck, Keir Dullea, and
Salome Jens

Everybody Loves Opal by John Patrick
Opened Longacre Theatre, Oct. 11,
1961
21 performances
Produced by Roger L. Stevens and
Seven Arts Productions

Directed by Cyril Ritchard
Costumes by Noel Taylor
Asst. set designers: Richard Casler and
Aristides Gazetas
With Eileen Heckart, Stubby Kaye,
Brenda Vaccaro, and Donald Harron

1962

All American with music by Charles
Strouse, lyrics by Lee Adams, and
book by Mel Brooks (based on
Robert Lewis Taylor's novel
Professor Fodorski)
Opened Winter Garden, Mar. 1962
86 performances
Produced by Edward Padula with
Slade Brown
Directed by Joshua Logan
Choreographed by Danny Daniels
Costumes by Patton Campbell
Assoc. set designer: Richard Casler
Asst. set designer: Richard Bianchi
With Ray Bolger, Eileen Herlie, and
Anita Gillette

Mr. President with music and lyrics
by Irving Berlin and book by
Howard Lindsay and Russel Crouse
Opened St. James Theatre, Oct. 20,
1962
265 performances
Produced by Leland Hayward
Directed by Joshua Logan
Choreographed by Peter Gennaro
Assoc. set designer: Richard Casler
Asst. set designer: Paul Trautvetter
With Robert Ryan, Nanette Fabray,
and Anita Gillette

1963

**The Milk Train Doesn't Stop Here
Anymore** by Tennessee Williams
Opened Morosco Theatre, Jan. 16, 1963
69 performances
Produced by Roger L. Stevens
Directed by Herbert Machiz
Costumes by Paul Voelpel
Assoc. set designer: Paul Trautvetter
Asst. set designer: Lloyd Burlingame
With Hermione Baddeley, Mildred
Dunnock, Paul Roebling, and
Maria Tucci

1964

After the Fall by Arthur Miller
Opened ANTA–Washington Square
Theatre, Jan. 23, 1964
208 performances
Produced by the Repertory Company
of Lincoln Center
Directed by Elia Kazan
Costumes by Anna Hill Johnstone
Assoc. set designer: Paul Trautvetter
Asst. set designers: Jack Lindsay and
Robert D. Mitchell
Architectural asst.: Francis Booth
With Jason Robards, Zohra Lampert,
Barbara Loden, Ralph Meeker,
David Wayne, and Hal Holbrook

But for Whom Charlie by S. N. Behrman
Opened ANTA–Washington Square
Theatre, Mar. 12, 1964
47 performances
Produced by the Repertory Company
of Lincoln Center
Directed by Elia Kazan
Costumes by Theoni V. Aldredge
Assoc. set designer: Paul Trautvetter
Asst. set designers: Jack Lindsay and
Robert D. Mitchell
With Jason Robards, Patricia Roe,
David Wayne, Ralph Meeker,
Salome Jens, and Faye Dunaway

The Owl and the Pussycat by Bill
Manhoff
Opened ANTA Theatre, Nov. 18,
1964
421 performances
Produced by Philip Rose, Pat Fowler,
and Seven Arts Productions
Directed by Arthur Storch
Costumes by Florence Klotz
Assoc. set designer: Paul Trautvetter
Asst. set designers: Jack Lindsay and
Chris Thee
With Alan Alda and Diana Sands

1965

Danton's Death by Georg Buechner
(English version adapted by
Herbert Blau)
Opened Vivian Beaumont Theatre,
Oct. 21, 1965
46 performances
Produced by the Repertory Theatre of
Lincoln Center
Directed by Herbert Blau
Costumes by James Hart Stearns
Assoc. set designer: Paul Trautvetter
Asst. set designer: Robert D. Mitchell
With James Earl Jones, Stacy Keach,
and Roscoe Lee Browne

The Playroom by Mary Drayton
Opened Brooks Atkinson Theatre,
Dec. 5, 1965
33 performances
Produced by Kermit Bloomgarden and
Trude Heller
Directed by Joseph Anthony
Costumes by Theoni Aldredge
Assoc. set designer: Paul Trautvetter
With Tom Helmore, Karen Black,
Augusta Dabney, Richard Thomas,
and Peter Kastner

1966

Venus Is by Chester Erskine
Opened Billy Rose Theatre, Apr. 9,
1966
1 performance (closed in previews)
Produced by Martin Lee
Directed by Word Baker
Costumes by Ramse Mostoller
Assoc. set designer: Paul Trautvetter
With Audra Lindley, Avra Petrides,
and Jerry Strickler

Don't Drink the Water by Woody Allen
Opened Morosco Theatre, Nov. 17, 1966
588 performances
Produced by David Merrick with Jack Rollins and Charles Joffe
Directed by Stanley Prager
Costumes by Motley
Assoc. set designer: Paul Trautvetter
Asst. set designer: Leor C. Warner
With Lou Jacobi, Anthony Roberts, Kay Medford, Anita Gillette, and House Jameson

My Sweet Charlie by David Westheimer (from his novel)
Opened Longacre Theatre, Dec. 6, 1966
31 performances
Produced by Bob Banner Associates, supervised by H. R. Poindexter
Directed by Howard Da Silva
Costumes by Jack Martin Lindsay
Assoc. set designer: Paul Trautvetter
Asst. set designer: Leor C. Warner
With Bonnie Bedelia, Louis Gossett, and John Randolph

1967

The Paisley Convertible by Harry Cauley
Opened Henry Miller's Theatre, Feb. 11, 1967
9 performances
Produced by Michael Ellis
Directed by James Hammerstein
Costumes by Alvin Colt
Assoc. set designer: Paul Trautvetter
Asst. set designer: Leor C. Warner
With Marsha Hunt, Betsy Von Furstenberg, and Joyce Bulifant

That Summer—That Fall by Frank D. Gilroy
Opened Helen Hayes Theatre, Mar. 16, 1967
12 performances
Produced by Edgar Lansbury
Directed by Ulu Grosbard
Costumes by Theoni V. Aldredge
Assoc. set designer: Paul Trautvetter
Asst. set designer: Leor C. Warner
With Irene Papas, Jon Voight, Tyne Daly, and Richard Castellano

The Unemployed Saint by Bill Manhoff
Opened and closed Royal Poinciana Playhouse, Palm Beach, Florida, Mar. 20–25, 1967
Produced by David Merrick
Directed by Arthur Storch
Costumes by Jack Lindsay
Lighting by Leo B. Meyer
Assoc. set designer: Paul Trautvetter
Asst. set designer: Leor C. Warner
With Shelley Berman, Dorothy Loudon, and Joseph Bova

Daphne in Cottage D by Stephen Levi
Opened Longacre Theatre, Oct. 15, 1967
4 performances
Produced by Robert Leder and Michael Productions
Directed by Martin Fried
Costumes by Theoni V. Aldredge
Assoc. set designer: Paul Trautvetter
Asst. set designers: John T. Jensen Jr. and Leor C. Warner
With Sandy Dennis and William Daniels

Mata Hari with music by Edward Thomas, lyrics by Martin Charnin, and book by Jerome Coopersmith
Opened and closed National Theatre, Washington, D.C., Nov. 18–Dec. 9, 1967
Produced by David Merrick
Directed by Vincente Minnelli
Choreographed by Jack Cole
Costumes by Irene Sharaff
Assoc. set designer: Paul Trautvetter
Asst. set designers: John T. Jensen Jr. and Leor C. Warner
With Marisa Mell, Pernell Roberts, and Martha Schlamme

1968

The Prime of Miss Jean Brodie by Jay Allen (adapted from Muriel Spark's novel)
Opened Helen Hayes Theatre, Jan. 16, 1968
379 performances
Produced by Robert Whitehead and Robert W. Dowling
Directed by Michael Langham
Costumes by Jane Greenwood
Assoc. set designer: Paul Trautvetter
Asst. set designers: John T. Jensen Jr. and Leor C. Warner
With Zoe Caldwell, Joseph Maher, Douglas Watson, and Catherine Burn

I Never Sang for My Father by Robert Anderson
Opened Longacre Theatre, Jan. 25, 1968
124 performances
Produced by Gilbert Cates with Doris Vidor
Directed by Alan Schneider
Costumes by Theoni V. Aldredge
Assoc. set designer: Paul Trautvetter
Asst. set designers: John T. Jensen Jr. and Leor C. Warner
With Hal Holbrook, Alan Webb, Teresa Wright, and Lillian Gish

Seven Descents of Myrtle by Tennessee Williams
Opened Ethel Barrymore Theatre, Mar. 27, 1968
29 performances
Produced by David Merrick
Directed by José Quintero
Costumes by Joan Greenwood

Assoc. set designer: Paul Trautvetter
Asst. set designers: John T. Jensen Jr. and Leor C. Warner
With Harry Guardino, Estelle Parsons, and Brian Bedford

Slaughter on Tenth Avenue (ballet)
Introduced May 2, 1968, New York State Theatre
Produced by the New York City Ballet
Choreographed by George Balanchine (from ballet in the 1936 Broadway production of *On Your Toes*)
Music by Richard Rodgers
Costumes by Irene Sharaff
With Arthur Mitchell and Suzanne Farrell

Possibilities by Arthur Pittman
Opened The Players Theatre (Off-Broadway), Dec. 4, 1968
1 performance
Produced by Stanley Gordon, Burry Fredrik, Selma Tamber, and Edward A. Wolpin Enterprises
Directed by Jerome Kilty
Costumes by Noel Taylor
Asst. set designers: F. Mitchell Dana and John H. Doëpp

1969

1776 with music and lyrics by Sherman Edwards and book by Peter Stone
Opened Forty-sixth St. Theatre, Mar. 16, 1969
1,217 performances
Directed by Peter Hunt
Choreographed by Onna White
Costumes by Patricia Zipprodt
Asst. set designers: John H. Doëpp and F. Mitchell Dana
With William Daniels, Ken Howard, Howard Da Silva, and Betty Buckley

The Conjuror by Evan Hunter
Opened Lydia Mendelssohn Theatre, University of Michigan, Nov. 5, 1969
Produced by the Professional Theatre Program, Robert C. Schnitzer, Executive Director
Directed by Marcella Cisney

Galileo by Bertolt Brecht (English version adapted by Charles Laughton)
Opened Krannert Center Playhouse, University of Illinois, Oct. 22, 1969
Produced by the Experimental Theatre
Directed by Clara Behringer
Costumes by Fred Voelpel

1970

Child's Play by Robert Marasco
Opened Royale Theatre, Feb. 17, 1970
343 performances
Produced by David Merrick
Directed by Joseph Hardy
Costumes by Sara Brook
Asst. set designers: John H. Doëpp and Stephen Hendrickson

With Pat Hingle, Fritz Weaver, David Rounds, and Ken Howard

Georgy with music by George Fischoff, lyrics by Carole Bayer, and book by Tom Mankiewicz (based on Margaret Forster's novel and Peter Nichols's screenplay for *Georgy Girl*)
Opened Winter Garden, Feb. 26, 1970
4 performances
Directed by Peter Hunt
Choreographed by Howard Jeffrey
Costumes by Patricia Zipprodt
Asst. set designer: John H. Doëpp
With Dilys Watling, Stephen Elliott, and Helena Carroll

Look to the Lilies with music by Jule Styne, lyrics by Sammy Cahn, and book by Leonard Spiegelgass (based on William E. Barrett's novel *The Lilies of the Field*)
Opened Lunt-Fontanne Theatre, Mar. 29, 1970
25 performances
Produced by Edgar Lansbury, Max J. Brown, Richard Lewine, and Ralph Nelson
Directed by Joshua Logan
Choreographed by Joyce Trisler
Costumes by Carrie F. Robbins
Assoc. set designer: John H. Doëpp
Asst. designers: Stephen Hendrickson and Leigh Rand
With Shirley Booth and Al Freeman Jr.

Who Cares? (ballet)
Reintroduced with Mielziner's scenery, New York State Theatre, Nov. 11, 1970; continues in repertory
Produced by the New York City Ballet
Choreographed by George Balanchine
Music by George Gershwin
Costumes by Karinska
With Kay Mazzo, Karin Von Aroldingen, Marnee Morris, and Jacques D'Amboise

1971

Father's Day by Oliver Hailey
Opened John Golden Theatre, Mar. 16, 1971
1 performance
Produced by Joseph Kipness and Lawrence Kasha
Directed by Donald Moffat
Costumes by Ann Roth
Asst. set designers: Dahl Delu and Kathleen Dilkes
With Brenda Vaccaro, Marian Seldes, Biff McGuire, and Donald Moffat

PAMTGG ["Pan Am Makes the Going Great"] (ballet)
Introduced New York State Theatre, June 17, 1971
Produced by the New York City Ballet
Choreographed by George Balanchine

Costumes by Irene Sharaff
With Kay Mazzo and Victor Castelli

Caravaggio by Michael Straight
Produced by the Playhouse-in-the-Park, Cincinnati, July 1, 1971
Directed by Word Baker
Costumes by Caley Summers
Asst. set designers: Stuart Wurtzel and Patrizia van Brandenstein

Love Me, Love My Children with music, lyrics, and book by Robert Swerdlow
Opened Mercer O'Casey Theatre, Nov. 3, 1971
187 performances
Produced by Joel W. Schenker and Edward F. Kook
Directed by Paul Aaron
Stage form designed by Jo Mielziner
Lighting by Dahl Delu
Costumes by Patricia Quinn Stuart

1972

Children! Children! by Jack Horrigan
Opened Ritz Theatre, Mar. 7, 1972
1 performance
Produced by Arthur Whitelaw, Seth Harrison, and Ben Gerard
Directed by Joseph Hardy
Costumes by Ann Roth
Research asst.: Kathleen Dilkes
With Gwen Verdon, Dennis Patrick, and Josef Summer

Voices by Richard Lortz
Opened Ethel Barrymore Theatre, Apr. 3, 1972
8 performances
Produced by Jerry Schlossberg, Jerry Hammer, and Adela Holzer
Directed by Gilbert Cates
Costumes by Theoni V. Aldredge
Research asst.: Kathleen Dilkes
With Julie Harris and Richard Kiley

The Crucible by Arthur Miller
Revived by the Repertory Theatre of Lincoln Center at the Vivian Beaumont Theatre, Apr. 27, 1972
44 performances
Directed by John Berry
Costumes by Carrie F. Robbins
With Aline MacMahon, Philip Bosco, Stephen Elliott, and Pamela Payson-Wright

1973

Out Cry by Tennessee Williams
Opened Lyceum Theatre, Mar. 1, 1973
12 performances
Produced by the David Merrick Foundation and Kennedy Center Productions, Inc.
Directed by Peter Glenville
Costumes by Sandy Cole
Asst. set designers: Kathleen Dilkes and Greg Geilman

With Michael York and Cara Duff-MacCormick

Ah Willy (selections from plays by William Shakespeare)
Opened at the 92d St. YM-YWHA, May 24, 1973
Produced by Matt Conley
Directed by Phoebe Brand
One-person show with Morris Carnovsky

1974

Miss Moffat with book by Emlyn Williams and Joshua Logan (based on Williams's play *The Corn Is Green*) with music by Albert Hague and lyrics by Williams
Opened and closed Shubert Theatre, Philadelphia, Oct. 7–18, 1974
Produced by Eugene Wolsk and Joshua Logan
Directed by Joshua Logan
Choreographed by Donald Saddler
Costumes by Robert Mackintosh
Lighting asst.: Beverly Emmons
Asst. set designer: L. Robin Modereger
With Bette Davis, Dody Goodman, Avon Long, Dorian Harewood, Anne Francine, and Nell Carter

In Praise of Love by Terence Ratigan
Opened Morosco Theatre, Dec. 10, 1974
199 performances
Produced by Arthur Cantor
Directed by Fred Coe
Lighting asst.: Richard Nelson
Asst. set designer: J. Robin Modereger
With Julie Harris, Rex Harrison, and Martin Gabel

1976

Marathon 33 by June Havoc
Revival produced by the Purdue University Experimental Theatre, West Lafayette, Ind., Feb. 20–28, 1976
Directed by Ronald Ross
Lighting by Lee Watson
Costumes by Barbara Medlicott
Asst. set designer: Bridget Beier

The Baker's Wife with music and lyrics by Stephen Schwartz and book by Joseph Stein (based on Marcel Pagnol and Jean Giono's novel *La Femme du Boulanger*)
Opened Dorothy Chandler Pavilion, Los Angeles, May 11, 1976; closed out of town
Produced by David Merrick
Directed by John Berry (replaced by Joseph Hardy)
Lighting by Jennifer Tipton
Costumes by Theoni V. Aldredge
With Chaim Topol (replaced by Paul Sorvino), Portia Nelson, Keene Curtis, David Rounds, and Patti LuPone

Mielziner designed and lighted 267 productions, which includes premieres of Broadway shows, ballets, operas, and two movies. (Two of these designs were repeated later for the ballets *Slaughter on Tenth Avenue* and *Shango*.) Many of the major successes were adapted by Mielziner for road companies; these he counted as "new" designs, lifting his total number to more than 300. Although his concepts for the road and London productions of his Broadway successes remained substantially the same, many times he had to fit them into theatres that were not the size or shape of the standard Broadway houses. London playhouses had narrower proscenium openings (excluding the Coliseum) and deeper stages than conventional American stages. The following are the shows redesigned for London:

The Glass Menagerie, Haymarket, 1948
A Streetcar Named Desire, Aldwych, 1948
Death of a Salesman, Phoenix, 1949
Carousel, Drury Lane, 1950
Mister Roberts, Coliseum, 1950
South Pacific, Drury Lane, 1951
The Innocents, Her Majesty's, 1952
The King and I, Drury Lane, 1953
Guys and Dolls, Coliseum, 1953
Can-Can, Coliseum, 1954
Fanny, Drury Lane, 1956
The World of Suzie Wong, Prince of Wales, 1959
1776, New Theatre, 1970
Child's Play, Queen's, 1971

ARCHITECTURAL AND COMMERCIAL DESIGNS

1930–39
Ceiling of Cape Cinema, Dennis, Mass. (with Rockwell Kent), 1930
Portable stage for Johns-Manville company, 1936
John-David store windows, 1936
Portrait of Katharine Cornell for cover of *Stage* magazine, Jan. 1937
Pan American Theatre, Dallas, dinner theatre, 1937
Esquire Fashion Forum, 1938–40
Decoration for El Morocco nightclub, 1939

1940–49
I. J. Fox store windows, 1940
Schenley Street marketing promotion, 1940
Steuben Glass Christmas window, 1940
Marshall Field millinery department, Chicago, 1941
Fixtures for Century Lighting, 1944
Dais of United Nations convention, 1945

Puppet theatre for Good Teeth Council, 1946
Carl Fischer Hall, refurbishing of auditorium, 1948
Christmas crèche for Mrs. Howell Howard, 1949

1950–59
Catholic World Mission logo, 1950
Murals, Inc., wallpaper (with Leonard Haber), 1952
Oldsmobile 1955 Dealer Announcement show (with Alexander Anderson), 1954
Ziegfeld Theatre curtain and proscenium masks, 1955
Lighting consultant, Berlin Congress Hall, 1957

1960–69
Consultant, Los Angeles Music Center, Mark Taper Forum, 1961
Hilton Hotel grand ballroom and special banquet rooms, lighting and decoration, 1961
ANTA–Washington Square Theatre, 1963
College of Steubenville stage and auditorium (co-designer), 1963
Consultant, Webster College, Loretto Hilton Center, stage and auditorium, 1963
Producer and designer, AT&T Controlled Ride, World's Fair, 1964–65
Setting for Michelangelo's *Pietà*, Vatican Pavilion, World's Fair, 1964–65
Consultant, Univ. of Illinois, Krannert Center, stage and auditorium, 1964
Lincoln Center Repertory Theatre stage and auditorium (co-designer), 1965
Portable stage for East Room of White House, 1965
Univ. of Michigan, Power Center, stage and auditorium (co-designer), 1964
Consultant, Greenwich (Conn.) High School, stage and auditorium, 1966
Consultant, Minskoff Theatre, 1968
Southern Illinois Univ., Edwardsville, stage and auditorium (co-designer), 1968
Decoration for John Wharton's 75th birthday party, 1969
Convent of Sacred Heart, refurbishing of auditorium, 1969
Edison Theatre, Hotel Edison, conversion of ballroom into theatre, 1969
Chapel in residence of Bishop Fulton J. Sheen, 1969

1970–76
Setting and logo for Joseph P. Kennedy Jr. Foundation awards, 1971
"Elephant Ear Muffs" (for a quieter New York) for New York Red Cross, 1972
Jules Fisher, template for light projection, 1972
Lighting consultant, Univ. of Pittsburgh, Stephen Foster Memorial, 1972

Consultant, Wake Forest Univ., Scales Center, two theatres, stage and auditorium, 1972–76
Consultant, Denver Center for the Performing Arts, Denver Theatre Center, three theatres, stage and auditorium, 1973
Consultant, Barbizon Plaza Hotel Conference Center, 1973

NOTES

The following citations refer only to unpublished materials (letters, family documents, office files, etc.) and interviews I conducted with Jo Mielziner's friends, colleagues, assistants, and secretaries. The number next to each note refers to the relevant text page.

INTRODUCTION

13 The accounts of Jo Mielziner's final day and death were given to me by the late Edward F. Kook, the late Leo Herbert, Dr. Thomas Bellezza, and Jo's secretary Phyllis Malinow.

17 Peter Feller Sr. provided many insights into stagecraft practices of the early twentieth century; interview by author, Nov. 16, 1991.

19 Livingston Platt's disappearance remains a mystery. The late Gerald Kahan, the Platt expert, reported to me that in all his years of research he had found nothing to solve it.

23 Information about Bergman's studio was detailed in correspondence between Jo and Kay Coughenour dated Mar. 24, 1972.

24 Information about lighting for the New Stagecraft was provided by the late Edward Kook and by Ron Olson in his Ph.D. dissertation, "Edward F. Kook: Link between the Theatre Artist and Technician," 1978.

25 In a Jan. 9, 1975, letter to the editor of *Theater Design and Technology*, Jo corrected information about the formation of Local 829.

1. THE MISCHLING

27 ff. Genealogical information concerning the Friend family tree came from a variety of sources: Ella Mielziner's genealogical table and notes, discussions and correspondence with Peter Pindar Stearns (another Friend descendant and Ella's grandnephew), and an apr. 23, 1919, letter to Ella from Paris from Margaret Friend.

28 ff. Genealogical information about the Mielziner family tree came from: Ella Mielziner's genealogical table and notes, letters to Ella from various Mielziner family members

abroad and from her nephew Orla Mielziner. Complete information is found in Ella's published biography of Moses Mielziner.

29 Jo to Mary Tyler Cheek, letter about his father, Leo, of July 17, 1967.

30 ff. From Ella's biographical sketch of Jo's childhood. Letters from Ella to Leo provided much information of the years 1908–09.

33 E. G. W. Russell to the Mielziner boys, letter of Dec. 26, 1908.

34 From documents and school records found in the archives of the Ethical Culture School, Riverdale, N.Y.

34 Letters: Felix Warburg to Leo Mielziner, Feb. 27, 1912; Jo to Edward Warburg, Oct. 11, 1965; Arthur Hays Sulzberger to Jo, Jan. 22, 1962.

35 From typed brochure about Camp Saltspray.

35 Letters: James Rorimer to Jo, Sept. 8, 1955; Jo to Joseph T. Fraser Jr., Pennsylvania Academy of the Fine Arts, Mar. 6, 1952; Jo to Robert Stubbs, Pennsylvania Academy, Mar. 4, 1974.

36 ff. School records dated 1917–22, Pennsylvania Academy; Jo to his parents, undated letters of 1917; summer 1918, fall 1918, spring 1919 (from Parris Island); Ella to Jo, undated letter of winter 1917–18; Leo Jr. to his parents, undated letters of 1918; typed résumé in Kenneth MacKenna's file, NYPL-Theatre Collection.

38 Robert Bolton to the author, letters of 1992–95, describing his and Jo's experiences at the National Academy of Design, New York.

39 Pennsylvania Academy of the Fine Arts records.

40 The late Edith Meiser provided information about Jessie Bonstelle's company, of which she was a member; interview by author, Jan. 20, 1992.

42 ff. Jo to his parents and Leo Jr., letters from Paris, Vienna, and Berlin, most undated, between Sept. 1921 and Jan. 1923. Also, undated notes about Craig written late in Jo's life.

2. APPRENTICESHIP

45 (caption) Jo to Nickolas Muray, letter of Feb. 10, 1962.

46 Jo to David Weiss, notes of Dec. 1965 critiquing his dissertation manuscript.

46 ff. Jo to his parents, travel notes of 1923 from Paris describing the Jessner sets and Stanislavski incident. He also sent them thumbnail sketches of sets he had seen.

48 Jo to Edgar Lansbury, letter of July 20, 1967.

49 Jo's brief affair with Winifred Lenihan was mentioned by Edward Kook, interview by author, Apr. 3, 1989.

49 Tribute to Lee Simonson of Jan. 26, 1967.

52 Jo to Theresa Helburn, letter of May 10, 1927.

55 Jo to H. Page Cross, letter about James Rorimer of Jan. 13, 1956.

57 Clara Mannes to Ella Mielziner, letter of Nov. 4, 1930.

57 Marya Mannes to Ella and Leo Mielziner, letter of Oct. 4, 1930.

3. BROADWAY 1925–1935

61 Jo expressed this opinion often in letters and in published and unpublished writings.

62 Jo was not listed in the published credits of *American Venus* but was mentioned in a review of the movie in the *New York Sun*, Jan. 25, 1926.

64 ff. All quoted figures for Jo's incomes now and in succeeding pages are taken directly from his federal tax returns.

64 Jo often repeated this tale of being taken for a messenger to friends and assistants.

71 I am grateful to James Frasher, Lillian Gish's confidential secretary, to whom she told this story about *Uncle Vanya*.

74 Jo's account of Cornell and *The Barretts of Wimpole Street*, Jan. 20, 1973.

76 ff. Jo and Kenneth to their parents, undated correspondence of c. 1932–35, and my interviews with Annie Laurie Witzel's friends and her nephew George Schreiber.

77 Kenneth MacKenna to his parents, undated letters about Jo and Annie Laurie of c. 1934–35.

83 Jo to his parents, letter of Sept. 13, 1933.

83 Kenneth MacKenna to his parents, undated letter of c. fall 1934.

85 Information about Rose Bogdanoff in Jo's studio was given to me by George Jenkins, his assistant at the time.

86 Rose McClendon was a serious (non-singing and dancing) black actress close to achieving stardom on Broadway when she died prematurely at age 51.

87–88 Sidney Howard to Jo, letter of Oct. 24, 1935.

4. FAMILY MATTERS

91 Leo Mielziner to Ella, letter of July 4, 1919.

92 ff. I gleaned much of the information about the Mielziner family life from letters found by Joanna

Caproni in the Truro house owned by Kenneth MacKenna and sold to her parents.

96 I was given much information about Ella's stay at Hawley Manor by Eleanor Mayer, who worked there as a teenager.

96 In a letter of July 29, 1954, Jo asked Milton Lomask, author of the article in *The Sign*, to delete mention of Ella's reaction to his conversion to Catholicism.

96 Jo's feelings about orthodoxy were often expressed to sympathetic ears. The quotation is from his undated letter to Olive Ann Tamborelle, director of the Teaneck, N.J., library.

97 Edward Kook told me he was convinced that Jo was attracted to Catholicism by the church's theatrical panoply. I believe, however, that it was just one of several factors—and an insignificant one— that contributed to Jo's conversion.

5. BROADWAY JO

100 I am indebted to Russell Flinchum, who is writing a biography of Henry Dreyfuss, for information about his career.

101 The contract gives the details of the responsibilities of the collaborators.

102 ff. Much of the information about Mielziner's non-theatrical projects was supplied by George Jenkins, his chief assistant at the time.

102 Although the poster seems to have been lost in the governmental shuffle, it was eventually returned to Jo and was found among his papers.

103 ff. From Olson's unpublished dissertation on Kook, 1978.

106 ff. I am indebted to George Jenkins for information about Jo's studio at 1441 Broadway in the prewar years.

107 I am indebted to Robert McDonald, retired business manager of Local One, IATSE (the stagehands' union), for information about the T. B. McDonald Scenery Construction Company. He is the nephew of Bernie and Albie McDonald and grandson of the founder.

112 Sir John Gielgud to the author, letter of Feb. 12, 1991.

115 This quotation is from the wording of the original caption for the illustration in *Designing for the Theatre*; it was edited and somewhat altered for publication.

117 ff. Jo's idea for the rear-fold traveler curtain was passed to his assistant George Jenkins, whose responsibility was to find a way to do it. He did.

118 Richard Rodgers to Kenneth MacKenna, letter of May 16, 1938.

118 ff. I am indebted to Cornelia Macintyre Foley for information about her sister Jean and the Macintyre family.

119 Ed Poler to Jo, letter of Sept. 27, 1938.

119 I am indebted to the late John Fearnley for information about Jean Macintyre's early years in New York.

120 ff. Jo to Robert E. Sherwood and Elmer Rice, letter of May 14, 1938.

121 Helen Hokinson's *New Yorker* cartoon first appeared in the Jan. 1, 1938, issue.

122 Riding the crest of his success as a designer, Jo set up a fee-plus-royalty schedule for producers in 1939. A few producers balked, but most then paid.

122 (caption) Jo to Irene Sharaff, letter of Aug. 8, 1938.

126 Jo to Eddie Dowling, letter of Aug. 26, 1940.

129 Alfred Lunt to Jo, letter of June 13, 1941.

130 Jo to Max Gordon, letter of Dec. 13, 1941.

131 Charles Rann Kennedy to Carmen Mathews, undated letter in Jo's files.

132 ff. Ronald Naversen's doctoral dissertation, "The Scenographer as Camoufleur" (1989), provided the background for the contributions of scene designers to the war effort.

133 The quotation is from the late Sam Leve's unpublished autobiography (given with his permission before his death).

135 Fulton Sheen to General William Donovan, copy of a letter of Oct. 7, 1943.

135 I am indebted to the late Viggo Rambusch for information about camouflage and his friendship with Jo; telephone interview by author, Feb. 5, 1993.

135 I am indebted to Mary Tyler (Mrs. Leslie) Cheek for information about her husband's friendship with Jo; telephone interview by author, May 5, 1992.

6. BACK TO BROADWAY

138 With no dining room in the apartment, the Mielziners took advantage of the commissary and other services at the Dakota, as evidenced by numerous bills and receipts found among the Mielziner papers.

139 ff. I am indebted to John Harvey for the information converning his

years of tenure at the Mielziner studio; interview by author, May 9, 1991.

140 Jo to John Harvey, letter of Dec. 23, 1949.

141 Jo to Eddie Dowling, letter of Aug. 26, 1940.

142 ff. Jo to Ian Dow, stage manager of the London production of *The Glass Menagerie*, letter of June 2, 1948.

142 Alex Yokel to Jo, undated letter detailing the early travails of the production.

143 Jo to Joe Davis, letter of Sept. 27, 1965.

143 (caption) Jo to Kenneth Macgowan, letter of Mar. 3, 1945.

144 Jo to Hugh Beaumont, letter of Apr. 30, 1948.

144 Margo Jones to Jo, undated letter.

145 Helen Hayes to Jo, letter of Aug. 3, 1948.

145 Lawrence Langner to Jo, letter of Feb. 19, 1947.

146 Jo to Richard Rodgers and Oscar Hammerstein, letter of Feb. 17, 1950.

147 State Department to Jo, memorandum of July 28, 1945.

147 ff. Alexander Anderson to the author, letter of Jan. 30, 1992.

148 Secretary Edward H. Stettinius Jr. to Jo, letter of July 10, 1945.

148 Oscar Serlin to Jo, letter of Oct. 29, 1945.

148 Harold Clurman to Jo, letter of July 29, 1945.

149 Elmer Rice to Jo, letter of Dec. 20, 1945.

152 Office memorandum of Apr. 29, 1946.

152 ff. The book developed from Jo's Fordham lectures was *Designing for the Theatre*. Other undated and unidentified lecture notes were found in his files.

154 Jo to Fred Marshall of United Scenic Artists, letter of June 8, 1946.

155 ff. Elliott Nugent to Jo, letters of May 31, 1946, June 18, 1946, and Jan. 14, 1947.

156 Jo to Lee Sabinson, letter of Oct. 3, 1949.

158 Lucinda Ballard, in conversations with the author over several years before her death in 1993.

159 Office memorandum, undated. Also, notes on *Allegro* of Apr. 4, 1997.

161 Elia Kazan to Jo, letter of Sept. 10, 1974.

161 ff. Letters exchanged between Jo and Kazan during June 1947.

163 Jo to Irene Mayer Selznick, letter of Dec. 9, 1947.

163 Laurence Olivier to Jo, letter of Oct. 14, 1949.

163 Irving Schneider, telephone interview by author, Feb. 11, 1992.

163–64 Jo to Elia Kazan, letter of Apr. 6, 1950.

165 Hugh Beaumont to Jo, letter of Jan. 8, 1951.

166 Jo to Margo Jones, letter of Jan. 7, 1938.

167 Jo to Bretaigne Windust, letter of Aug. 10, 1948.

168 Jo to the Playwrights Company, Leland Hayward, and Bretaigne Windust, memorandum of Sept. 14, 1948.

168 Teddy Van Bemmel, interview by author, May 13, 1992.

169 Elia Kazan to Jo, letter of Nov. 4, 1948.

171 Office memorandum regarding production costs, undated.

172 I am indebted to Arthur Miller for these comments; interview by author, May 16, 1992.

173 Oscar Hammerstein to Jo, letter of Apr. 15, 1949.

174 From notes found in the travel files among Jo's papers.

7. FAME, FORTUNE, AND FAMILY

177 ff. Much of the information about Mielziner family life and Jean Mielziner, in particular, came from a variety of sources: interviews with Michael, Neil, and Jennifer Mielziner; Cornelia Foley, Jean's sister; and correspondence about family matters in Jo's files.

181 George Jenkins, interviews by author, May 15, 1990, and by telephone, Aug. 1, 1993.

184 Peter Glenville, interview by author, Nov. 5, 1991.

184 Unpublished early version of caption for *The Innocents* in *Designing for the Theatre*.

184 Lemuel Ayers to Jo, undated letter received Mar. 8, 1950.

185 Florence Eldridge to Jo, undated letter received Apr. 20, 1950.

185 This was not to be the end of John Steinbeck's play *Burning Bright*. In the fall of 1993, it was transformed into an opera and presented at the Yale School of Music with Elaine Steinbeck in attendance.

186 Views differ about how deeply George S. Kaufman was involved in planning the scenery for his productions. According to Mielziner, he was not especially concerned; according to Donald Oenslager, he was extremely involved.

186 Cy Feuer, interview by author, June 24, 1992.

186 Emlyn Williams to Jo, letter of Sept. 29, 1950.

186 Unpublished early version of caption for *Guys and Dolls* in *Designing for the Theatre*.

187 ff. Jo's deposition of May 20, 1958, for the suit against Rodgers and Hammerstein gives details on the evolution of the scenery for *The King and I*, pp. 86–89.

188 Mary L. Brady (Jo's secretary at the time) to Walter Pietsch, letter of Nov. 7, 1952.

190 Jo to Leland Hayward, memorandum of Apr. 23, 1951.

190 John Harvey to Bob Corrigan of the Union Wadding Company, letter of May 13, 1952.

191 Jo to Irene Sharaff, letter of Apr. 2, 1952.

192 Herman Shumlin to Jo, letter of Oct. 20, 1952.

192 ff. I am indebted to John Harvey, Phyllis Malinow, John Doëpp, and others for the description of the Dakota first-floor studio.

194 Cy Feuer, interview.

196 Warren Clymer, interview by author, Jan. 10, 1992.

196 Notes on painting *Me and Juliet* in Jo's files dated Feb. 2, 1953.

197 Robert Anderson, interview by author, Jan. 28, 1992.

198 Jo to John Mason Brown, letter of Nov. 23, 1953.

198 "Johnny" (otherwise unidentified) to Jo, undated letter recounting the contretemps between Richard Halliday and Joshua Logan.

199 Burton Lane to Jo, letter of Aug. 17, 1953.

200 Robert Anderson, interview.

201 Jo to S. N. Behrman, letter of Nov. 12, 1954.

202 ff. Betsy and Ming Cho Lee, interview by author, Feb. 6, 1992.

203 Jo to Robert Downing, letter of Nov. 15, 1954.

204 Cy Feuer, interview.

204 Jo to Leueen McGrath and George S. Kaufman, letter of Dec. 8, 1954.

204 George S. Kaufman to Jo, undated note.

204 Jo to Tennessee Williams, letter of Nov. 19, 1952.

204 Tennessee Williams to Jo, "Notes for the Designer," undated, regarding *Cat on a Hot Tin Roof*.

204 Jo to Tennessee Williams, letter of Jan. 27, 1955.

205 Jo to Henry Hewes, transcript of interview of July 1968.

206 ff. Jo wrote an account of his experiences in Hollywood during a period from Mar. 27 to Apr. 8, 1955, while he was working on the movie *Picnic*.

207 Jo to Frederick Kohlmar, letter of Apr. 18, 1955.

207 Jo to James Wong Howe, letter of Apr. 18, 1955.

207 Joshua Logan to Jo, letter of Apr. 21, 1955.

207 Jo to Kate Drain Lawson, letter of June 14, 1955.

207 Peter Glenville, interview.

207 ff. Jo to his family, letters of May 6 to 21, 1955.

210 Julie Harris, telephone interview by author, Oct. 20, 1991.

211 Paddy Chayevsky to Jo, letter of Mar. 28, 1956.

212 Jo to Leland Hayward, letter of Apr. 24, 1956.

212 Leland Hayward to Jo, letter of Apr. 30, 1956.

213 Eugene O'Neill to Jo, letter of Sept. 5, 1948.

213 Morton Gould, interview by author, Jan. 7, 1992.

213 Carlotta O'Neill to Jo, letter of Feb. 22, 1953.

213 "Memorandum of Understanding" (between Jo Mielziner and David Merrick) of Nov. 1, 1956.

213 "Agreement to Cancel" (Jo's involvement in a musical version of *Ah, Wilderness*) of Sept. 11, 1956.

214 ff. Patricia Zipprodt, interview by author, Apr. 14, 1992.

216 Karl Malden, telephone interview by author, Nov. 28, 1992.

216 Jo to Karl Malden, letter of July 16, 1956.

216 Arnold Weissberger to Milton Weir, letter of June 10, 1953.

217 Jo to Theresa Helburn, letter of Oct. 11, 1957.

218 Elizabeth Montgomery, interview by author, Feb. 21, 1990.

219 Jo to José Ferrer, letter of Oct. 17, 1957.

219 Kenneth MacKenna to Jo, letter of Oct. 28, 1957.

219 Henry Hewes, interview by author, Jan. 30, 1992.

220 Confidential source to Jo, letter of Aug. 6, 1956.

220 Richard Rodgers to Jo, letter of May 23, 1957.

220 Richard Rodgers to Jo, letter of Aug. 30, 1960.

221 Jo to Dorothy Jeakins, letter of July 10, 1958.

221 Jo to his family, newsletter of July 13, 1958.

221 Jo to his family, newsletter of Oct. 12, 1958.

223 Peter Glenville, interview.

223 Elia Kazan to Jo, letter of Sept. 18, 1958.

223 Tennessee Williams to Jo, letter of Nov. 11, 1958.

225 Geraldine Page to Jo, undated note.

225 Theoni V. Aldredge, telephone interview by author, Dec. 14, 1993.

225 Jo to Kenneth and Mary MacKenna, letter of Jan. 18, 1959.

226 Jack Lindsay, interview by author, Nov. 15, 1991.

227 Betsy and Ming Cho Lee, interview.

228 Peter Glenville to Jo, letter of May 22, 1959.

8. THE SIXTIES: *O TEMPORA! O MORES!*

232 Information from Jo's 1961 financial records in his files.

233 I am indebted to Paul Segal, a resident of the Dakota, for a tour of the building and for showing me the location of Jo's apartment and studio.

233 Michael Mielziner and Neil Collins (Mielziner), interviews by author, Aug. 29, 1992, and Mar. 1, 1992, respectively.

234 Yvonne West, telephone interview by author, Dec. 12, 1992.

239 ff. Interviews by author: Robert Whitehead, June 24, 1992; Hugh Hardy, Mar. 26, 1992; John Harvey; Kevin Roche, Nov. 19, 1993.

242 ff. Correspondence between Jo and Eero Saarinen, 1960 to Saarinen's death (in 1961), relating to the design and construction of the Vivian Beaumont Theatre.

245 Elia Kazan to Jo, letter of Sept. 4, 1963.

246 David Hays, telephone interview by author, Nov. 17, 1993.

246 Jo to Edward Kook, Elia Kazan, Eero Saarinen, and Robert Whitehead, memorandum of May 16, 1960.

250 Patricia Zipprodt, interview.

253 Patton Campbell, interview by author, Mar. 16, 1992.

254–56 Paul Trautvetter, interview by author, Nov. 14 and 15, 1991.

254 Jo to Elia Kazan, letter of Oct. 30, 1962.

258 Jo to Marjorie and Lawrence Curtin, letter of Dec. 23, 1969.

259 ff. Paul Trautvetter, interview.

261 Joshua Logan to Jo, letter of July 13, 1966.

262 Ulu Grosbard to Jo, letter of June 10, 1966.

263 Michael Langham to Jo, letter of Oct. 2, 1967.

264 Jo to Mildred Knopf, letter of Feb. 13, 1968.

266 Jo to Tennessee Williams, letter of Nov. 1, 1967.

268 ff. Alan Billings and members of the Power Center staff, interviews by author, Aug. 26, 1992.

269 Jo to Sam Zolotow, letter of Aug. 17, 1970.

270 Stuart Ostrow, telephone interview by author, Sept. 10, 1993.

9. DEAN OF DESIGNERS

275 Kevin Roche, interview.
275 Brooks Atkinson to Jo, letter of Sept. 3, 1971.
276 ff. Harold Tedford, telephone interview by author, Feb. 8, 1994.
277 ff. Donald Seawell, several telephone interviews by author, Mar. 1994.
277 Samuel Liff, interview by author, Jan. 19, 1992; Peter Feller, interview by author, Nov. 16, 1991; and Robin Wagner, conversations with author over many years.
279 Alexander Cohen to Jo, letter of Jan. 13, 1975.
287 Jo to Jack Schlissel, letter of Apr. 24, 1972.
288 Patrick Horrigan, telephone interview by author, Mar. 7, 1992.
289 Greg Geilman, telephone interview by author, Apr. 5, 1992.
289 Phoebe Brand and Morris Carnovsky, interview by author, Feb. 9, 1992.
290 Peter Glenville, interview.
292 Jeff Davis, interview by author, Jan. 15, 1992, and Byron Olson, telephone interview by author, May 7, 1992.
293 Interviews by author: Dr. Thomas Bellezza, Feb. 24, 1992; Phyllis Malinow, Feb. 3, 1992; and Betsy and Ming Cho Lee.
293 Edith Meiser, interview.
293 Krista Errickson, telephone interview by author, May 24, 1993.
295 Arthur Cantor, interview by author, Apr. 21, 1992.
295 Jo to his family, newsletter of June 30, 1975.
296 Mrs. Donald Oenslager, telephone interview by author, Feb. 2, 1990.
297 Lecture at Purdue University, Nov. 2, 1975.
298 Dr. Thomas Bellezza, interview.
298 Phyllis Malinow, interviews by author, Feb. 3 and 24, 1992, and Mar. 11, 1992.
299 Mrs. Paul Foley, telephone interview, Dec. 29, 1991.
299 Description of the burial of Jo's ashes at sea was given to me by Patricia Zipprodt, David Hays, and Phyllis Malinow, among others.
299 Betsy and Ming Cho Lee, interview.

AFTERWORD

300 ff. This was derived largely from the lecture Jo gave at the Yale Drama School, Apr. 24, 1972.
303 Bernard Gersten, interview by author, Apr. 3, 1990.

BIBLIOGRAPHY

N.B.: Although many biographies of people associated with Mielziner were consulted, only the most notable have been included in this list. Space did not permit inclusion of catalogues for exhibitions of his work. Also not listed are the reviews both from New York and out-of-town newspapers for all of the productions with which Jo Mielziner was involved. I consulted the Mielziner scrapbooks at Boston University for reviews and miscellaneous articles; the *New York Theatre Critics Reviews* from 1940 on; and the bound compilations of reviews prior to 1940 at The New York Public Library for the Performing Arts at Lincoln Center, as well as the files on Mielziner, Jean Macintyre, Kenneth MacKenna, and Mielziner's collaborators. Citations of his obituary in various publications have been omitted as well.

BOOKS AND REFERENCE WORKS

Abbott, George. *Mister Abbott.* New York: Random House, 1963.
The American Theatre: A Sum of Its Parts. New York: Samuel French, 1971.
Anderson, Maxwell. *Off Broadway: Essays about the Theater.* New York: William Sloan Associates, 1947.
——. *Winterset.* Washington, D.C.: Anderson House, 1935.
Appelbaum, Stanley. *The New York Stage: Famous Productions in Photographs.* New York: Dover, 1976.
Appia, Adolphe. *The Work of Living Art.* Translated by H. D. Albright; edited by Barnard Hewitt. Coral Gables, Fla.: Univ. of Miami Press, 1960.
Ashworth, Bradford. *Notes on Scene Painting.* New Haven, Conn.: Whitlock's, 1952.
Atkinson, Brooks. *Broadway.* New York: Macmillan, 1970.
Baral, Robert. *Revue: The Great Broadway Period.* New York: Fleet Press, 1962.
Bay, Howard. *Stage Design.* New York: Drama Book Specialists, 1974.
Behrman, S. N. *People in a Diary.* Boston: Little, Brown, 1972.
Bentham, Frederick. *The Art of Stage Lighting.* London: Pitman House, 1968.
Birmingham, Stephen. *Life at the Dakota.* New York: Random House, 1979.
Boime, Albert. *The Academy and French Painting in the Nineteenth Century.* London: Phaidon, 1971.
Bordman, Gerald. *American Musical Comedy.* New York: Oxford Univ. Press, 1982.
——. *American Musical Theatre.* New York: Oxford Univ. Press, 1978.
Botto, Louis. *At This Theatre.* New York: Dodd Mead & Co., 1984.
Brady, William A. *Showman.* New York: Curtis Publishing, 1936.
Brown, Jared. *The Fabulous Lunts.* New York: Atheneum, 1986.
Brown, John Mason. *Dramatis Personae.* New York: Viking, 1963.
——. *Upstage: The American Theatre in Performance.* New York: W. W. Norton, 1930.
——. *The Worlds of Robert E. Sherwood: Mirror to His Times.* New York: Harper & Row, 1962.
Buckle, Richard. *George Balanchine: Ballet Master.* New York: Random House, 1988.
Burris-Meyer, Harold, and Edward C. Cole. *Theatres and Auditoriums.* New York: Reinhold, 1964.
Burrows, Abe. *Honest Abe.* Boston: Little, Brown, 1980.
Carter, Randolph, and Robert Reed Cole. *Joseph Urban.* New York: Abbeville Press, 1992.
Chapman, John, ed. *The Burns Mantle Best Plays of 1947–48* through *1949–50.* 3 vols. New York: Dodd, Mead, 1948–50.
Chase, Edna Woolman, and Ilka Chase. *Always in Vogue.* New York: Doubleday, 1954.
Cheney, Sheldon. *The New Movement in the Theatre.* New York: Mitchell Kennerley, 1914.
Ciment, Michel. *Kazan on Kazan.* New York: Viking, 1974.
Clurman, Harold. *The Divine Pastime.* New York: Macmillan, 1974.
——. *Lies Like Truth.* New York: Macmillan, 1958.
Cornell, Katharine, with Ruth Woodbury Sedgwick. *I Wanted to Be an Actress.* New York: Random House, 1938.
Courtney, Marguerite. *Laurette.* New York: Atheneum, 1968.
Crawford, Cheryl. *One Naked Individual.* New York: Bobbs-Merrill, 1977.
de Mille, Agnes. *Dance to the Piper.* Boston: Little, Brown, 1952.
DeHart, Jess. *Plantations of Louisiana.* Gretna, La.: Pelican Publishing, 1982.
Eaton, Walter Prichard. *The Theatre Guild: The First Ten Years.* New York: Brentano's, 1929.
Edwards, Anne. *The De Milles: An American Family.* New York: Harry N. Abrams, 1988.
Engel, Lehman. *The American Musical Theater: A Consideration.* New York: CBS Records, 1967.
Fordin, Hugh. *Getting to Know Him: A Biography of Oscar Hammerstein II.* New York: Random House, 1977.
Fuchs, Theodore. *Stage Lighting.* Boston: Little, Brown, 1929.
Fuerst, Walter René, and Samuel J. Hume. *Twentieth-Century Stage Decoration.* 2 vols. 1929. Reprint, New York: Dover, 1967.
Gaige, Crosby. *Footlights and Highlights.* New York: E. P. Dutton, 1948.
Geddes, Norman Bel. *Miracle in the Evening.* Edited by William Kelley. Garden City, N.Y.: Doubleday, 1960.
Gelb, Arthur, and Barbara Gelb. *O'Neill.* New York: Harper & Row, 1973.
Gielgud, John. *Early Stages.* London: Falcon Press, 1939.
Gilder, Rosamond, et. al, eds. *Theatre Arts Anthology.* New York: Theatre Arts, 1950.
Gish, Lillian. *Dorothy and Lillian Gish.* Edited by James Frasher. New York: Charles Scribner's, 1973.
Goldman, William. *The Season.* New York: Harcourt, Brace & World, 1969.
Goldstein, Malcolm. *George S. Kaufman: His Life and His Theater.* New York: Oxford Univ. Press, 1979.
Gordon, Max. *Max Gordon Presents.* New York: Bernard Geis Associates, 1963.
Gordon, Ruth. *My Side.* New York: Harper & Row, 1976.
——. *Myself Among Others.* New York: Atheneum, 1971.
Gorelik, Mordecai. *New Theatres for Old.* New York: Samuel French, 1948.
Gottfried, Martin. *Jed Harris: The Curse of Genius.* Boston: Little, Brown, 1984.
Gottlieb, Polly Rose. *The Nine Lives of Billy Rose.* New York: Crown, 1968.
Green, Stanley. *Broadway Musicals: Show by Show.* Milwaukee: Hal Leonard Books, 1985.
Guernsey, Otis, ed. *The Best Plays of 1964–65* through *1976–77.* 13 vols. New York: Dodd, Mead, 1965–77.
Hansen, Arlen J. *Expatriate Paris.* New York: Little, Brown, 1990.
Harris, Jed. *A Dance on the High Wire.* New York: Crown, 1979.
Hartmann, Louis. *Theatre Lighting.* New York: D. Appleton, 1930.
Helburn, Theresa. *A Wayward Quest.* Boston: Little, Brown, 1960.
Heller, James G. *As Yesterday When It Is Past.* Cincinnati: Isaac M. Wise Temple, 1942.
Hellman, Lillian. *Three: An Unfinished Woman, Pentimento and Scoundrel Time.* Boston: Little, Brown, 1979.
Hewes, Henry, ed. *The Best Plays of 1961–62* through *1963–64.* 3 vols. New York: Dodd, Mead, 1962–64.
Houghton, Norris. *Entrances & Exits.* New York: Limelight, 1991.
Huggett, Richard. *Binkie Beaumont: Eminence Grise of the West End Theatre.* London: Hodder & Stoughton, 1989.
Hyams, Barry, ed. *Theatre: The Annual of the Repertory Theater of Lincoln Center.* Vol. 1. New York: Repertory Theater of Lincoln Center and Playbill, 1964.
Isaacs, Edith J. R., ed. *Architecture for the New Theatre.* New York: Theatre Arts, 1935.
Jones, Robert Edmond. *The Dramatic Imagination.* New York: Theatre Arts, 1941.
Jones, Margo. *Theatre-in-the-Round.* New York: Rinehart, 1951.
Joseph, Stephen. *New Theatre Forms.* New York: Theatre Arts, 1968.
——, ed. *Actor and Architect.* Toronto: Univ. of Toronto Press, 1964.
Kazan, Elia. *A Life.* New York: Alfred A. Knopf, 1988.
Kissel, Howard. *David Merrick: The Abominable Showman.* New York: Applause, 1993.
Kook, Edward F. *Images in Light for the Living Theatre.* Privately printed, 1983.
Kronenberger, Louis, ed. *The Best Plays of 1952–53* through *1960–61.* 8 vols. New York: Dodd, Mead, 1953–61.
Langner, Lawrence. *The Magic Curtain.* New York: E. P. Dutton, 1951.
Larson, Orville K. *Scene Design for Stage and Screen.* East Lansing, Mich.: Michigan State Univ. Press, 1961.
——. *Scene Design in the American Theatre from 1915 to 1960.* Fayetteville, Ark.: Univ. of Arkansas Press, 1989.
Le Gallienne, Eva. *At 33.* New York: Longman, Green, 1934.
——. *With a Quiet Heart.* New York: Viking, 1953.
Leeper, Janet. *Edward Gordon Craig: Designs for the Theatre.* Harmondsworth, England: Penguin, 1948.
Leverich, Lyle. *Tom: The Unknown Tennessee Williams.* New York: Crown, 1995.
Lewis, Emory. *Stages: The Fifty-year Childhood of the American Theatre.* Englewood Cliffs, N.J.: Prentice-Hall, 1969.
Logan, Joshua. *Josh.* New York: Delacorte, 1976.
Longstreet, Stephen. *We All Went to Paris: Americans in the City of Light.* New York: Macmillan, 1972.
Macgowan, Kenneth, and Robert Edmond Jones. *Continental Stagecraft.* London: Benn Brothers, 1923.
MacGregor, Robert M. *Stages of the World.* New York: Theatre Arts, 1941.
Mackintosh, Iain. *Architecture, Actor and Audience.* New York: Routledge, 1993.
Mannes, Marya. *Out of My Time.* New York: Doubleday, 1971.
——, and Norman Sheresky. *Uncoupling: The Art of Coming Apart.* New York: Viking, 1972.
Mantle, Burns, ed. *The Best Plays of 1923–24* and *1924–25.* 2 vols. Boston: Small, Maynard & Co., 1924–25.
——, ed. *The Best Plays of 1925–26* through *1946–47.* 22 vols. New York: Dodd, Mead, 1926–47.
Martin, George. *The Damrosch Dynasty.* Boston: Houghton Mifflin, 1983.
Mason, Francis, ed. *I Remember Balanchine: Recollections of the Ballet Master by Those Who Knew Him.* New York: Doubleday, 1991.
Massey, Raymond. *A Hundred Different Lives.* Boston: Little, Brown, 1979.
McCandless, Stanley. *A Method of Lighting the Stage.* New York: Theatre Arts, 1958.
——. *A Syllabus of Stage Lighting.* Privately printed, 1958.
McClintic, Guthrie. *Me and Kit.* Boston: Little, Brown, 1955.
Mellow, James R. *Charmed Circle: Gertrude Stein & Company.* New York: Praeger, 1974.
Meltzer, Milton. *Mark Twain Himself.* New York: Bonanza Books, 1960.
Meredith, Scott. *George S. Kaufman and His Friends.* Garden City, N.Y.: Doubleday, 1974.
Merman, Ethel, with Pete Martin. *Who Could Ask for Anything More.* New York: Doubleday, 1955.
——, with George Eells. *Merman.* New York: Simon & Schuster, 1978.
Mielziner, Ella McKenna Friend. *Moses Mielziner 1828–1903.* New York: Privately published, 1931.
Miller, Arthur. *Timebends.* New York: Grove Press, 1987.
Miller, Jordan Y. *Eugene O'Neill and the American Critic.* Hamden, Conn.: Archon Books, 1973.
Miller, Tice L. *Bohemians and Critics.* Metuchen, N.J.: Scarecrow Press, 1981.
Minnelli, Vincente. *I Remember It Well.* Garden City, N.Y.: Doubleday, 1994.
Morehouse, Ward. *Matinee Tomorrow.* New York: Whittlesley House, 1949.
Morley, Sheridan. *Gertrude Lawrence.* New York: McGraw-Hill, 1981.
Morrow, Lee Alan. *The Tony Award Book: Four Decades of Great American Theatre.* New York: Abbeville Press, 1987.
Mosel, Tad, with Gertrude Macy. *Leading Lady: The World and Theatre of Katharine Cornell.* Boston: Little, Brown, 1978.
Myerscough-Walker, R. *Stage and Film Décor.* London: Sir Isaac Pitman & Sons, n.d. (circa 1940).
Nathan, George Jean. *The Theatre in the Fifties.* New York: Alfred A. Knopf, 1953.
Oenslager, Donald M. *The Theatre of Donald Oenslager.* Middletown, Conn.: Wesleyan Univ. Press, 1978.

Oppenheimer, George. *The Passionate Playgoer.* New York: Viking, 1958.
Parker, W. Oren, and Harvey K. Smith. *Scene Design and Stage Lighting.* New York: Holt, Rinehart & Winston, 1963.
Payne, Darwin Reid. *The Scenographic Imagination.* Carbondale and Edwardsville, Ill.: Southern Illinois Univ. Press, 1981.
Pecktal, Lynn. *Designing and Painting for the Theatre.* New York: Holt, Rinehart & Winston, 1975.
Pendleton, Ralph, ed. *The Theatre of Robert Edmond Jones.* Middletown, Conn.: Wesleyan Univ. Press, 1958.
Pilbrow, Richard. *Stage Lighting.* New York: Van Nostrand, 1970.
Polakov, Lester. *We Live to Fly/Paint Again.* New York: Logbooks Press, 1993.
Quintero, José. *If You Don't Dance, They Beat You.* Boston: Little, Brown, 1974.
Reit, Seymour. *Masquerade.* New York: Hawthorne Books, 1978.
Rice, Elmer. *The Living Theatre.* New York: Harper & Brothers, 1959.
Rich, Frank, with Lisa Aronson. *The Theatre Art of Boris Aronson.* New York: Alfred A. Knopf, 1987.
Robinson, Edward G., with Leonard Spiegelgass. *All My Yesterdays.* New York: Hawthorne Books, 1973.
Rodgers, Richard. *Musical Stages.* New York: Random House, 1975.
Rollyson, Carl. *Lillian Hellman.* New York: St. Martin's Press, 1988.
Rosenthal, Jean, and Lael Wertenbaker. *The Magic of Light.* Boston: Little, Brown, 1972.
Roust, Park, Jr. *Leslie Cheek and the Arts.* Williamsburg, Va.: College of William and Mary Press, 1985.
Sabinson, Harvey. *Darling, You Were Wonderful.* Chicago: Henry Regnery, 1977.
Sanders, Ronald. *The Days Grow Short: The Life and Music of Kurt Weill.* New York: Holt, Rinehart & Winston, 1980.
Saylor, Oliver. *Max Reinhardt and His Theatre.* New York: Brentano's, 1924.
———. *Our American Theatre.* New York: Brentano's, 1923.
Schneider, Alan. *Entrances.* New York: Viking, 1986.
Schwarz, Charles. *Cole Porter.* New York: Dial, 1977.
Selznick, Irene Mayer. *A Private View.* New York: Alfred A. Knopf, 1983.
Sharaff, Irene. *Broadway & Hollywood.* New York: Van Nostrand Reinhold, 1976.
Sheaffer, Louis. *O'Neill: Son and Artist.* Boston: Little, Brown, 1973.
Sheehy, Helen. *Margo: The Life and Theatre of Margo Jones.* Dallas: Southern Methodist Univ. Press, 1989.
Sheen, Fulton J. *The Electronic Christian: 105 Readings from Fulton J. Sheen.* New York: Macmillan, 1979.
Shivers, Alfred S. *The Life of Maxwell Anderson.* New York: Stein & Day, 1983.
Siegel, Jerrold. *Bohemian Paris.* New York: Viking, 1986.
Silverman, Maxwell. *Contemporary Theatre Architecture.* New York: The New York Public Library, 1965.
Simonson, Lee. *The Art of Scenic Design.* New York: Harper & Brothers, 1950.
———. *Part of a Lifetime.* New York: Duell, Sloan & Pearce, 1943.
———. *The Stage Is Set.* 1932. Reprint, New York: Theatre Arts, 1963.
Skinner, Cornelia Otis. *Life with Lindsay and Crouse.* Boston: Houghton Mifflin, 1976.
Spoto, Donald. *The Kindness of Strangers: The Life of Tennessee Williams.* Boston: Little, Brown, 1985.
Stanley, William T. *Broadway in the West End 1950–1975.* Westport, Conn.: Greenwood Press, 1978.
Stearns, Peter Pindar. *The History and Genealogy of John Friend of Salem, Massachusetts, and His Descendants (c. 1636–c. 1910).* Baltimore: Gateway Press, 1997.
Stoddard, Richard. *Stage Scenery, Machinery and Lighting.* Detroit: Gale Research, 1977.
———. *Theatre and Cinema Architecture.* Detroit: Gale Research, 1978.
Taper, Bernard. *Balanchine.* New York: Times Books, 1984.
Taylor, Theodore. *Jule: The Story of Composer Jule Styne.* New York: Random House, 1979.
Teichmann, Howard. *George S. Kaufman.* New York: Atheneum, 1972.
———. *Smart Aleck: The Wit, World and Life of Alexander Woollcott.* New York: William Morrow, 1976.
Terry, Walter. *The Dance in America.* New York: Harper, 1971.
Theatre Check List. Compiled and published by American Theatre Planning Board, 1969. Reprint, Middletown, Conn.: Wesleyan Univ. Press, 1983.
Voss, Ralph V. *A Life of William Inge.* Lawrence, Kans.: Univ. of Kansas Press, 1989.
Waldau, Roy S. *Vintage Years of the Theatre Guild 1928–1939.* Cleveland: The Press of Case Western Reserve Univ., 1972.
Weales, Gerald. *American Drama Since World War II.* New York: Harcourt, Brace & World, 1962.
Wharton, John. *Life Among the Playwrights.* New York: Quadrangle, 1974.
Williams, Dakin, and Shepherd Mead. *Tennessee Williams.* New York: Arbor House, 1983.
Williams, Tennessee. *Memoirs.* Garden City, N.Y.: Doubleday, 1975.
Zolotow, Maurice. *Stagestruck: The Romance of Alfred Lunt and Lynn Fontanne.* New York: Harcourt, Brace & World, 1964.

UNPUBLISHED THESES AND DISSERTATIONS

Doherty, Lynn. "The Art of Producing: The Life and Work of Kermit Bloomgarden." Ph.D. diss., Graduate Center of the City Univ. of New York, 1989.
Greenhut, Andrew Jay. "Jo Mielziner: His Use of Projected Scenery in the Professional Theatre." Master's thesis, Univ. of Miami, 1961.
Kilgore, David S. "A Study of Jo Mielziner and His Theatre Design." Master's thesis, Univ. of Florida, 1952.
Naverson, Ronald Arthur. "The Scenographer as Camoufleur." Ph.D. diss., Southern Illinois Univ. at Carbondale, 1989.
Olson, Ronald Charles. "Edward F. Kook: Link between the Theatre Artist and Technician." Ph.D. diss., New York Univ., 1978.
Sigler, Mary Gaile. "The Contributions of Jo Mielziner to Modern American Stage Decor." Master's thesis, Univ. of Nebraska, 1957.
Smith, Harry Willard, Jr. "The Emergence of the Designer as a Unifying Force in the Theatre: Edward Gordon Craig, Robert Edmond Jones, and Jo Mielziner." Master's thesis, Tulane Univ., 1960.
———. "Mielziner and Williams: A Concept of Style." Ph.D. diss., Tulane Univ., 1965.
Weiss, David William. "Jo Mielziner's Contribution to the American Theatre." Ph.D. diss., Indiana Univ., 1965.

ARTICLES

Abelman, Lester. "Estimate Board Okays Beaumont Acquisition." *New York News,* Sept. 3, 1971.
"Additional $35,000 Cost for 'Anne' via Scrapping of Heavier Production." *Variety,* Nov. 24, 1948.
Adelman, Louis C. "The Beaumont, a Theater for All Seasons." *The Dramatists Guild Quarterly,* winter 1976.
Alexander, Mary. "Remarkable Ability to Interpret Character." *Cincinnati Times-Star,* Aug. 1923.
"Anent Mr. Mielziner and the Art of Costuming." *Brooklyn Eagle,* Jan. 5, 1936.
Archibald, William. "The Quick and the Dead." *Theatre Arts,* June 1950.
"Art Theatres Union Outlined by Kahn." *New York Times,* May 13, 1926.
"Artist Designs for the Stage." *Art News,* Feb. 27, 1937.
Atkinson, Brooks. "Theater Is Not the Thing." *New York Times Magazine,* Oct. 31, 1954.
Ayres, Anne. "The Cape Cod Experiment." No source, Apr. 3, 1930.
Baldwin, James. "Bette Davis, Miss Moffatt [sic] and Bright Bright Boys." *International Herald Tribune,* Oct. 4, 1974.
Bamberger, Theron. "An Unsuspected 'Brother Act' Is Found." *New York Herald Tribune,* Jan. 21, 1934.
Barnes, Djuna. "His World's a Stage." *Theatre Guild Magazine,* June 1931.
Barnes, Clive. "Somebody Loves an Albatross." *New York Times,* Oct. 10, 1971.
———. "A Special Place in the American Theater." *New York Times,* Mar. 16, 1976.
Barret, Dorothy. "Sets by Mielziner." *Dance Magazine,* Nov. 1946.
Beaufort, John. "'Progress' or 'Outrage' Backstage at Lincoln Center?" *Christian Science Monitor,* Sept. 10, 1971.
Beebe, Lucius. "An Actor to Whom His Own Age Is a Problem." *New York Herald Tribune,* June 6, 1935.
———. "Mielziner and MacKenna Form Partnership Unique in Theatre." *New York Herald Tribune,* Feb. 9, 1936.
———. "Stage Asides: Sets by Jo Mielziner." *New York Herald Tribune,* Oct. 12, 1941.
Bolton, Whitney. "Mielziner's Mood Is Painted in Light." *Philadelphia Inquirer,* Oct. 23, 1960.
Bradford, Barbara. "Designing Woman Visits Bastion of Award Winning Theatrical Designer." *Passaic (New Jersey) Herald-News,* Aug. 14, 1969.
Brady, William A. "A Bow to Dwight Deere Wiman." *New York Herald Tribune,* June 25, 1942.
"Broadway Designer Sets a Stage for the Johnsons." *New York Post,* Sept. 30, 1965.
Brown, John Mason. "Seeing Things." *Saturday Review,* Oct. 22, 1949.
Calta, Louis. "Mielziner to Aid Lincoln Square Plan." *New York Times,* Nov. 12, 1958.
———. "Pittsburgh to Get a Modern Theatre." *New York Times,* Dec. 14, 1948.
———. "Schary Is Seeking to Save Beaumont." *New York Times,* Sept. 18, 1971.
"Cape Cinema in Dennis Opens." No source, July 1, 1930.
Chesley, Gene. "Ten Years of American Scene Design." *Theatre Design and Technology,* Dec. 1974.
"City Takes Over the Beaumont; Plans $5.2 Million Remodeling." *New York Times,* Sept. 3, 1971.
Clurman, Harold. "A Play's Text vs. Its Production." *Nation,* July 11, 1953.
———. "How Production Affects a Play's Content." *Nation,* Mar. 9, 1963.
Clurman, Richard M. "The Beaumont: Who's the Villain of the Piece?" *New York Times,* Sept. 26, 1971.
———. "'Raping the Beaumont Hell! We're Saving It'." *New York Daily News,* Aug. 30, 1971.
"Comments on Jo Mielziner." *New York World-Telegram,* Feb. 29, 1936.
Crowther, Bosley. "Building Upon the Sand." *New York Times,* Feb. 23, 1936.
Davis, Forrest. "Mielziners Plan Joint Stage Career." *Detroit Daily Times,* June 30, 1921.
"Decors of Mielziner." *Art Digest,* Apr. 1, 1932.
"Designers." *Stage,* June 1933.
Douglas, Gilbert. "Broadway Designer, Leaving Army, Tells Advances in Camouflage." *New York World-Telegram,* Nov. 6, 1944.
Downing, Robert. "Mielziner's Great Theatre Influence Only Hinted in Book." *Denver Post,* Sept. 14, 1970.
———. "Streetcar Conductor." *Theatre Annual,* 1950.
Durgin, Cyrus. "Mielziner's 'Mr. President' Settings Use New Device." *Boston Globe,* Aug. 26, 1962.
Esterow, Milton. "Eight Theatres of Tomorrow Shown at Contemporary Museum Here." *New York Times,* Jan. 26, 1962.
———. "Lincoln Center to Utilize an Electronic Lighting Systerm." *New York Times,* Sept. 6, 1963.
"Factories of Illusion: The Scenic Studio." *Stage,* July 1934.
"Feller's Scenic Studio" (Talk of the Town). *New Yorker,* June 2, 1975.
Fields, Sidney. "He Makes the Scene, Man." *New York News,* Nov. 18, 1969.
Gaver, Jack. "Mielziner Designing the Hilton Hotel" (Broadway). *New York Mirror,* Nov. 24, 1961.
———. "Jo Mielziner, Man Behind Sets." *New York Mirror,* Nov. 24, 1961.
Gehman, Richard. "What Makes Merrick Run." *Theatre Arts,* Nov. 1960.
Gelb, Arthur. "Cost-Saving Project: Studio Alliance Cooperative Group Helps Shave Set-Building Budget." *New York Times,* Dec. 3, 1950.
Genauer, Emily. "Mielziner Sets Great in Power." *New York World-Telegram,* Feb. 19, 1937.
———. "Mielziner." *Theatre Arts,* Sept. 1951.
———. "More Than Interior Decoration." *Theatre Arts,* June 1958.
———. "Scene Design's Man of Distinction." *Theatre Arts,* July 1957.
Guernsey, Otis L., Jr. "Jo Mielziner: Stage Designer in Reverse." *New York Herald Tribune,* Oct. 27, 1944.
Gussow, Mel. "Denver Casts a Vote for Theater." *New York Times,* Jan. 27, 1980.
Guthrie, Tyrone. "Growing Influence of the Ballet." *New York Times Magazine,* Apr. 20, 1952.
"Harkness Ballet Opens New White House Stage Designed by Mielziner." *Variety,* Oct. 6, 1965.
Hatch, Robert. "On Being Upstaged by Scenery." *Horizon,* Sept. 1962.
"He Sets the Stage." *Art Digest,* Feb. 15, 1937.
"He Sets the Stage." *Catholic Digest,* July 1962.
Helburn, Theresa. "Notes on 'The Guardsman.'" *New York Times,* Oct. 19, 1924.
Hewes, Henry. "Broadway Postscript: Lighting the Playwright's Way." *Saturday Review,* Sept. 28, 1963.
———. "Practical Dream for Broadway." *Saturday Review,* Dec. 13, 1952.
———. "Scene Designers: Their Art and Their Impact: An SR Survey of Stage Design." *Saturday Review,* Dec. 12, 1964.
Hewitt, Barnard. "Jo Mielziner." *The High School Thespian,* May 1942.
Holmes, Ralph. "Kenneth MacKenna Defends Brother Who Designed 'Street Scene.'" *New York Sun,* Mar. 6, 1929.
Houghton, Norris. "The Designer Sets the Stage: Jo Mielziner." *Theatre Arts Monthly,* Feb. 1937.
Howd, Dean. "Joseph Urban and American Scene Design." *Theatre Survey,* Nov. 1991.
Hunter, Frederick J. "Norman Bel Geddes: The Renaissance Man of the American Theatre." Pamphlet, Theatre Arts Library, Univ. of Texas at Austin, 1969.
"Imagination Is the Best Friend of Broadway's Top Designer." *Milwaukee Journal,* Apr. 3, 1966.
Interview with Mielziner. *Time,* Dec. 24, 1945.
"Interview: Jo Mielziner." *New Yorker,* Mar. 19, 1966.
Isaacs, Hermine R. "Jo Mielziner." *World Theatre,* fall 1952.
Ivins, Molly. "Denver to Open Complex of Repertory Theaters." *New York Times,* Dec. 31, 1979.
Izenour, George C. "Building for the Performing Arts." *Tulane Drama Review* 7, no. 4 (June 1963).
Jamison, Barbara B. "Debate on Aisles: Pros and Cons Flying over Theater Design." *New York Times,* June 28, 1964.
Jerard, Elise. "The Modern Scene: Jo Mielziner, Artist." *Playbill* (for *Joy of Living*), Apr. 1931.
"Jo Mielziner Approaches 50 Years in the Theatre." *Theatre Crafts,* May/June 1970.

"Jo Mielziner Designs for the Theatre." *Theatre Design and Technology*, May 1969.

"Jo Mielziner Finds Youth No Handicap in Stage Designing." *New York Herald Tribune*, Feb. 12, 1933.

"Jo Mielziner Sets Stage for Johnsons." *New York Post*, Sept. 3, 1965.

Johnson, Alva. "Profile: Jo Mielziner." *New Yorker*, Oct. 23 and 30, 1948.

Kazan, Elia. "On Process." *New York Times*, Aug. 9, 1964.

"Kenneth MacKenna Dead at 62; Actor and Former MGM Aide" (obituary). *New York Times*, Jan. 17, 1962.

Kerr, Walter. "Who's at Fault—Films or the Beaumont?" *New York Times*, Sept. 12, 1971.

——. "Building Tomorrow's Stages." *New York Herald Tribune*, Aug. 30, 1964.

——. "The Theater Breaks out of Belasco's Box." *Horizon*, July 1959.

Kisselgoff, Anna. "City Ballet Stages 'Who Cares' with a New Setting by Mielziner." *New York Times*, Nov. 23, 1970.

Kook, Edward F. "The Idea of Living Light." In *The Best Plays of 1956–57*, edited by Louis Kronenberger. New York: Dodd, Mead, 1957.

——. "Jo Mielziner—Artist of the Theatre: Mar. 19, 1901–Mar. 15, 1976." *Theatre Design and Technology*, summer 1976.

Larson, Orville K. "Scrim Curtains: Mielziner and Ingegnieri." *Educational Theatre Journal*, Oct. 1962.

Lee, Ming Cho, and Mrs. Lee. Letter to the Editor, *New York Times*, Apr. 26, 1970.

"Leo Mielziner." *The Universal Jewish Encyclopedia*. Vol. 7. New York: Universal Jewish Encyclopedia, Inc., 1942.

"Lights, Lights, Secret of Casino's Fame." *Dallas News*, July 4, 1937.

Littell, Robert. "When the Scenic Artist Ceases to Be an Interior Decorator and Takes Part in the Play." *New York Post*, circa 1928.

Little, Stuart W. "Design for Drama Theater at Lincoln Center Due Soon." *New York Herald Tribune*, Apr. 26, 1960.

——. "Jo Mielziner Touches Up His Lighting." *New York Herald Tribune*, Apr. 5, 1966.

Lockridge, Richard. "Sets for the Play [*Dodsworth*]." *New York Sun*, Mar. 3, 1934.

Lomask, Milton. "Return to Orthodoxy." *The Sign*, Jan. 1955.

Louchheim, Aline. "Script to Stage: Cast History of a Set." *New York Times Magazine*, Dec. 9, 1951.

Macgowan, Kenneth. "Joseph Urban, Forerunner of the New Stagecraft in America." *Century Magazine*, Jan. 1914.

——. "Leopold Jessner." *Theatre Magazine*, Oct. 1922.

——. "The New Path of the Theatre." *Theatre Arts Magazine*, Apr. 1919.

Mackay, Patricia. "Designers on Designing: Ming Cho Lee." *Theatre Crafts*, Feb. 1984.

"A Man for All Scenes." *Time*, Mar. 19, 1965.

Mayer, Martin. "New York's Monument to the Muses." *Horizon*, July 1962.

McCardle, Dorothy. "White House History Reaches a New Stage." *Washington Post*, Sept. 30, 1965.

McCarthy, John. "Broadway's Artist." *Esquire*, Oct. 1938.

McEwen, Charles. "Proposed Art Center Is Discussed at Wake Forest." *Winston-Salem Twin City Sentinel*, Mar. 24, 1972.

Mielziner, Ella McKenna Friend. "Moses Mielziner: 1828–1928." *The American Israelite*, May 1928.

"Mielziner" (Talk of the Town). *New Yorker*, Mar. 19, 1966.

"Mielziner Joins the Met." *New York Times*, Nov. 2, 1932.

"Mielziner on His Own Theatre Work." *The Stage*, May 17, 1962.

"Mielziner Marks 150th Setting by Scoring One More Success." *New York Herald Tribune*, Mar. 24, 1946.

"Mielziner Our Best Designer." *New York World-Telegram*, Feb. 29, 1936.

"Mielziner Sets 1/3 of B'Way." *Variety*, Nov. 18, 1953.

"Mielziner Setting Reflects No Mood but That of Play." *New York Herald Tribune*, Mar. 27, 1932.

"Mielziner Went from Oils to Stage Settings." *New York Herald Tribune*, July 10, 1932.

"Mielziners Out to Make Money." *New York World-Telegram*, Jan. 24, 1936.

Monahan, Kasper. "Plans Completed for the New Playhouse." *Pittsburgh Press*, Sept. 15, 1949.

Morehouse, Ward. "Broadway after Dark: Dwight Deere Wiman." *New York Sun*, Mar. 10, 1930.

——. "Mielziner Tops as Creative Stage Designer." *Long Island Press*, Jan. 8, 1957.

"Museum Will Show Mielziner Designs." *Richmond (Virginia) Times-Dispatch*, Mar. 5, 1967.

Nadel, Norman. "Jo Mielziner Sets 'Act Their Role.'" *New York World-Telegram & Sun*, Mar. 2, 1966.

Neumann, Pete. "One More Dwelling Place of Wonder." *Cincinnati Enquirer*, July 11, 1971.

"Once Drew Terrible Marks in Art Class." *Cincinnati Times-Star*, Mar. 27, 1928.

"A Pair of Producers Emerge into the Sunlight [Brady and Wiman]." *New York Times*, Feb. 13, 1927.

Pearson, Howard. "B'Way Designer Supervises Sets for U. Musical." (*Salt Lake*) *Desert News*, Apr. 19, 1974.

Raine, George. "Jo Mielziner, Friend and Teacher: He Let Scripts Live." *Salt Lake Tribune*, Mar. 21, 1976.

"Rockwell Kent's Biggest Job." *Literary Digest*, Aug. 23, 1930.

Rolland, Carolyn. "A Show Is Born [*Allegro*]." *Seventeen*, June 1948.

Roosevelt, Eleanor. "My Day." [Includes comments on *Journey to Jerusalem*.] *New York World-Telegram*, Oct. 10, 1940.

Rosenfield, John, Jr. "Dallas Opens $250,000 Show." *Dallas News*, June 12, 1937.

S. C. "Comments on Jo Mielziner." *Coronet*, Aug. 1938.

"Scenic Artist Mielziner Tried His Hand at Acting." *New York World*, Feb. 3, 1926.

"Screen Fade-Outs Rivaled on Stage in 'House Beautiful.'" *New York Herald Tribune*, Apr. 5, 1931.

Segers, Frank. "Fight Beaumont Takeover." *Variety*, Sept. 22, 1971.

Shanley, J. P. "It's Silver for Mielziner." *New York Times*, Oct. 9, 1949.

Shepard, Richard F. "At Lincoln Center, It's Regilding Time." *New York Times*, Apr. 23, 1990.

——. "Lincoln Center Talks Collapse; Whitehead Won't Return to Post." *New York Times*, Dec. 16, 1964.

Shewmaker, Eugene. "A Theatre Portrait: Jo Mielziner." *The Theatre*, Apr. 1961.

Simon, John. "Doublethink at the Forum." *New York*, Oct. 4, 1971.

Skinner, Richard Dana. "The Scenic Art of Jo Mielziner." *Commonweal*, Mar. 30, 1932.

Smith, Harry B. "Tennessee Williams and Jo Mielziner: The Memory Plays." *Theatre Survey*, Nov. 1982.

"Staging of a Play." *West London Observer*, Dec. 19, 1950.

Standish, Miles. "Jo Mielziner: Leading Man of Stage Design." *St. Louis Post-Dispatch*, May 23, 1973.

Stiegler, William, G. "Three in Same Family Achieve Fame in Arts." *Cincinnati Times-Star*, Apr. 4, 1928.

Talese, Gay. "Experts in the Spotlight." *New York Times*, Mar. 30, 1958.

Taubman, Howard. "City Center to Remodel the Beaumont." *New York Times*, Jan. 19, 1971.

Terry, Walter. "Ballet Opens the New White House Stage." *New York Herald Tribune*, Sept. 30, 1965.

"Theater Artist." *Brooklyn Eagle*, Feb. 28, 1937.

"They Stand Out from the Crowd." *Literary Digest*, Apr. 28, 1934.

Thompson, Howard. "MGM Executive Quits to Be Actor." *New York Times*, June 3, 1959.

"A Thrust Forward for the Theater." *P/A Observer*, Nov. 1965.

Tiller, de Teel Patterson, III. "The New Stagecraft." *Arts in Virginia*, spring 1971.

"Unique Stage Set Steals the Show: 'Two on an Island.'" *Life*, Feb. 18, 1940.

Washer, Ben. "Mielziner Modestly Declines High Rating for Scenist's Art." *New York World-Telegram*, Mar. 18, 1931.

"What Jo Mielziner Got from the Army." *PM*, Dec. 10, 1944.

Whittaker, Herbert. "Mielziner's Stage Designs Bear Trademarks of a Master." *Toronto Globe and Mail*, June 29, 1971.

"Youngsters in Stage Designing." *Literary Digest*, July 18, 1925.

PUBLICATIONS BY JO MIELZINER

(listed chronologically)

"From an Art Student in Vienna." *Bookman*, Mar. 1923.

"Concerning Authenticity of Costumes in *Pride and Prejudice*." Letter to the Editor, *New York Times*, Dec. 8, 1935.

"Designing the Display Stage." *Retailing*, June 21, 1939.

"Scenery in This Play?" *New York Times*, Oct. 22, 1939.

"The Theatre Takes Stock." *Theatre Arts*, May 1940.

"So Little Time." *New York Times*, Aug. 12, 1945.

"Make the Theatre Building Pay." *Theatre Arts*, June 1946.

"Making the Dream Theatre Real." *New York Times*, June 14, 1946.

"Notes to Architects." *New York Times*, July 14, 1946.

"Opportunities in Theatre Design." *American Institute of Architects Journal*, Sept. 1946.

"Better Planning." *Theatre Arts*, June 1947.

"State of the Theatre: Report on a Theatre Arts' Roundtable." *Theatre Arts*, June 1947.

"Intimacy Is the Clue to Television Charm." *Variety*, July 28, 1948.

"An Apostle Looks at Video." *Man* (publication of St. Mary's Univ.), Oct. 1948.

"Problems of the American Theatre." *Bulletin of the International Theatre Institute*, Dec. 9, 1948.

"Death of a Painter." *American Artist*, Nov. 1949.

"Pitfalls in New Playhouse Construction." *New York Times*, Mar. 22, 1953.

"4-Ds on the Stage." *Boston Post*, May 3, 1953.

"New Areas Opened by 'Me and Juliet.'" *New York Herald Tribune*, May 18, 1953.

"What Is Beauty in the Home?" *New York Times*, Feb. 13, 1954.

"The Art of Robert Edmond Jones." *New York Times*, Dec. 19, 1954.

"The Lark Sings . . . and Lighting Gives It Wings." *Light*, July–Aug. 1956.

"The Hunting Was Happy." Unpublished manuscript intended for *New York Times*, circa 1957.

"Scene Designing and the Future." In *The Best Plays of 1956–57*, edited by Louis Kronenberger. New York: Dodd, Mead, 1957.

"Practical Dreams." In *The Theatre of Robert Edmond Jones*, edited by Ralph Pendleton. Middletown, Conn.: Wesleyan Univ. Press, 1958.

"A Man's Theater Dream." *The Performing Arts*, Nov. 12, 1959.

"Theatre: Design for Nation-Wide Growth." *University of Chicago Magazine*, Sept. 1961.

"Broadway Designer Describes Set for New York Viewing of 'Pietà.'" *Boston Globe*, Apr. 27, 1963.

"Scene Design." In *Book of Knowledge*. New York: Grolier Society, 1963.

"The Future of Theatre Architecture." In *Futures in American Theatre* (magazine-format compilation of lectures sponsored by theatre dept.). Austin, Tex.: Univ. of Texas, 1963.

Designing for the Theatre. New York: Atheneum, 1965.

"How Do I Work as a Designer?" Unpublished manuscript for book planned by Edward F. Kook and Henry Hewes, Sept. 1968.

The Shapes of Our Theatre. New York: Clarkson N. Potter, 1970.

"Designer Cries 'Rape' at Lincoln Center." *New York News*, Aug. 24, 1971.

"Mielziner Argues Against the 'Butchering' of the Beaumont." *New York Times*, Aug. 29, 1971.

"Art versus Craft." *Theatre Design and Technology*, summer 1976.

"The Arts." Published article found in files of Billy Rose Theatre Collection. Unsourced, n.d.

Review of *Theatre Planning*, edited by Roderick Ham. Unsourced, n.d.

"The Theatre Is Seen." Unpublished manuscript, edited by Robert Downing. Collection of Harry Ransom Humanities Research Center, Univ. of Texas, n.d.

INDEX